TREATING ADDICTED OFFENDERS

A Continuum of Effective Practices

Edited by
Kevin Knight, Ph.D.
David Farabee, Ph.D.

Civic Research Institute
4478 U.S. Route 27 • P.O. Box 585 • Kingston, NJ 08528

Library of Congress Cataloging in Publication Data
Treating Addicted Offenders: A Continuum of Effective Practices
Kevin Knight, Ph.D., and David Farabee, Ph.D.

ISBN 1-887554-47-5
Library of Congress Control Number 2004110497

For our children, Lorelle and Collin Knight and Laura Farabee.

Acknowledgments

We wish to express our sincere appreciation and gratitude for Dr. D. Dwayne Simpson, the Director of the Institute of Behavioral Research and S. B. Sells Professor of Psychology at Texas Christian University. Without his continued guidance, mentoring, and support since our early graduate school years, we would not have been able to achieve the career goals we have achieved. He taught us to look at the big picture, to strive to make a difference in our research, and to always perform at the highest professional level.

Kevin Knight
David Farabee
August 3, 2004

About the Editors

Kevin Knight, Ph.D., is a Research Scientist at the Institute of Behavioral Research at Texas Christian University. His work, reported in several publications, centers on evaluating drug treatment process and outcomes, as well as on developing evaluation systems for correctional settings. Dr. Knight has served as Principal Investigator for three federally funded criminal justice drug treatment projects, and currently is a Co-Principal Investigator on the National Institute on Drug Abuse (NIDA)-funded Criminal Justice Drug Abuse Treatment Studies (CJ-DATS) project. He has been centrally involved in the design and implementation of several longitudinal evaluations of treatment for probation and prison populations. As a result, he works closely with criminal justice agencies and data systems at national, state, and regional levels. He is co-editor of *Offender Substance Abuse Report* and also serves on a number of journal editorial boards and participates in a variety of advisory activities.

David Farabee, Ph.D., is Research Psychologist at the University of California, Los Angeles and Director of the Integrated Substance Abuse Programs (ISAP) Juvenile Justice Research Group. Prior to this he served as lead analyst for criminal justice research at the Texas Commission on Alcohol and Drug Abuse (1992-1995), and as Assistant Professor of Psychiatry and Research Scientist at the University of Kentucky Center on Drug and Alcohol Research (1995-1997). He is currently Principal Investigator of an evaluation of a statewide program to transition mentally ill inmates back into the community (funded by the California Department of Corrections), and Co-Principal Investigator of the Criminal Justice Drug Abuse Treatment Studies (CJ-DATS) (funded by the National Institute on Drug Abuse). He has published in the areas of substance abuse, crime, HIV/AIDS, and offender treatment, was co-editor of the recent book *Treatment of Drug Offenders* (2002, New York: Springer), and is co-editor of *Offender Substance Abuse Report*.

Introduction

Treatment as a Continuum of Opportunities

by Kevin Knight, Ph.D., and David Farabee, Ph.D.

Although addiction tends to be characterized as a chronic, relapsing condition, the treatment of addicted offenders continues to be conceptualized as a discrete event. When questions are asked about treatment effectiveness, "treatment" typically refers to a specific program, such as a nine-month in-prison therapeutic community (TC) program. Questions about "treatment" effectiveness typically overlook the impact of the full continuum of treatment that includes services received prior to and following, as well as ancillary services (e.g., employment services) provided during, the specified treatment program. The reality is that treatment, per se, is not a discrete event but is a continuum of an array of services provided to help the offender overcome a lifestyle of substance use and criminality. It is our hope that this book will be a valuable resource in understanding the variety of components that may potentially contribute to positive changes in an addicted offender's life.

RECOGNIZING THE PROBLEM AND ITS PARAMETERS

As described in the first part of the book, one of the earliest components of the continuum involves drug use testing, screening, and referral to a specific set of treatment services. Identifying who has significant drug-related problems and determining what treatment services they need is contingent on this front-end process being reliable and valid. For example, upon entry into the criminal justice system (CJS), offenders often are faced with having to disclose their history of drug use and crime to correctional officials. Many may choose to "do their time" and deny any drug-related problems and, thus, be likely to return untreated to the community at the same (or perhaps greater) risk level to society as when they entered the CJS. Others may begin recognizing that they have a drug use problem and expressing a desire for help. As conveyed in Chapter 1, the likelihood an offender will disclose prior drug use depends on several factors, including the instrument that is used, the environment in which it is administered, and the way it is delivered. Brief screens, such as the TCU Drug Screen (available at *http://www.ibr.tcu.edu*) are being used effectively in several states, such as Texas, as a way to determine an offender's initial need for treatment. Other problems, such as mental illness, also may need to be assessed when determining the need for treatment services. For example, the PADDI, described in Chapter 2, is a psychometrically sound instrument that is useful in identifying problems in a juvenile population. Likewise, the GAIN-CVI, discussed in Chapter 3, is a tool that can be used to predict violent behavior.

The detection of drug use is invaluable not only at the offender level, but at a systems level as well. By disaggregating arrestee drug test results obtained as part of the ADAM project, Yacoubian and colleagues illustrate in Chapter 4 how intrajurisdictional drug use patterns can be detected and used to help authorities identify high drug-using subsections of a particular geographic region. In Chapter 5, Campos and colleagues describe how the California Department of Corrections has been able to use drug testing as a means for deterring and reducing drug use within California's prison population.

ALTERNATIVES TO INCARCERATION

The second part of the book addresses alternatives to incarceration. Given that correctional agencies are continuing to struggle financially, they simply cannot afford to pursue prison expansion to accommodate the increasing offender population. The search for alternatives has led policymakers to pursue alternative sentencing guidelines that allow low-risk addicted offenders the opportunity to be placed on probation and receive treatment services rather than being incarcerated. For a "first time" offender, an alternative to incarceration may represent his or her entry into the treatment continuum. For those who have been or are currently involved in the CJS, this may represent a continuation in the treatment continuum. Examples of initiatives to provide services for those on probation include the New York City Department of Probation's drug treatment initiative described in Chapter 6 and the Residential Substance Abuse Treatment Programs referred to in Chapter 7. In Chapter 8, Belenko presents the promises and challenges of drug courts, an increasingly popular alternative to incarceration for many addicted offenders. Specific characteristics of drug court programs are presented in Chapter 9, and the dilemmas confronting practitioners in family drug treatment courts are depicted in Chapter 10. This part concludes, in Chapter 11 by Marlowe, with a description of the role of judicial status hearings in drug courts.

IN-PRISON PROGRAMMING

For many addicted offenders, drug use and drug-related crime result in a prison sentence. In most states, and in the federal system, those identified as being drug dependent are given the opportunity (or mandated) to receive treatment services. Two of the early in-prison TC programs that have served as models for other TC programs across the U.S. are the Kyle New Vision Program and the Richard J. Donovan Amity TC programs, described in Chapters 12 and 13. Providing the bigger picture of TC programs in the U.S., Rockholz gives a national update on TC programs for substance abusing offenders in state prisons in Chapter 14. At the federal level, the Federal Bureau of Prisons (BOP) has been involved in providing non-TC treatment for several years, and in Chapter 15, Weinman and colleagues discuss lessons they have learned from their administrative involvement in BOP residential drug treatment programming. As Walters illustrates in Chapter 16, one of the keys to successful treatment in state and federal correctional settings is the focus on changing the offender's criminal as well as drug lifestyle.

ADDRESSING INDIVIDUAL DIFFERENCES AND CO-OCCURRING CONDITIONS

Whether participating in an institutional- or community-based program, offenders present programs with a variety of differences that must be considered when providing treatment services, including differences with respect to admitting offense type, gender, mental illness, and age. As mentioned in Chapter 17, offenders with sex offenses propose special challenges, particularly when treatment services are delivered by untrained or inexperienced staff. Messina and Prendergast point out in Chapter 18 that women represent another specialized population, as exemplified by the fact that the jury is still out on the use of traditional TC treatment for women in prison. Chapters 19 and 20 cover specific legal system (e.g., child support) and employment issues that women may need to have addressed. In addition to type of offense and gender, mental illness is another factor that needs to be considered when providing treatment services to addicted offenders. Chapter 21 discusses new strategies that consider psychiatric comorbidities now available to assist in matching clients to the most appropriate treatment services. Psychopathy and co-occurring intimate partner violence are two additional critical considerations for offender treatment, presented in Chapters 22 and 23 respectively. Finally, youthful offenders are another specialized population. Chapter 24 provides detailed information on a family-oriented intervention that shows some promise for delinquent youth, and Chapter 25 addresses the needs of juvenile inhalant users.

UNDERSTANDING AND FACILITATING THE TREATMENT PROCESS

Understanding the needs of these specialized populations is critical, but the effectiveness of treatment services ultimately depends on the treatment process itself. As Devereux writes in Chapter 26, one of the most critical factors is the length of stay during a specific treatment episode. Simpson and Knight illustrate, in their presentation of the TCU Model of Treatment Process and Outcomes (Chapter 27), that length of stay is but one of several critical components in the "black box" of treatment. As described in Chapters 28 and 29, one of the most critical aspects of the treatment process is getting treatment-mandated offenders ready and motivated for treatment, since the effectiveness of coerced treatment has been mixed (see Chapter 31). And as presented in Chapter 30, an effective treatment process can translate into a positive effect on prisons.

The importance of treatment process, however, extends beyond "primary" treatment into aftercare or re-entry treatment. As pointed out in Chapter 32, recidivism is most likely to be reduced when a seamless system of care is provided from the institution into the community. Gary Field further supports this point in Chapter 33 and illustrates how Oregon has implemented an exemplary continuity-of-care model. Other issues, such as employment and housing, are an important part of this model and become even more important during this later stage of the treatment continuum. As Wexler points out in Chapter 34, favorable outcomes are more likely to be achieved when employment is integrated into aftercare. Overarching all of these re-entry treatment services is the need for increasing supervision's effectiveness using an evidence-based model, such as the one presented in Chapter 35.

THE GOAL: EVIDENCE-BASED, EFFECTIVE PRACTICE

The final part of the book reviews the evidence base that is needed in providing a continuum of treatment opportunities for addicted offenders. As described in Chapter 36, the U.S. government has funded Addiction Technology Transfer Centers (ATTCs) that are serving a vital role in getting science into the field and in bridging the gap between corrections and treatment. As detailed in Chapter 37, getting research findings into practice often entails the use of proven practices to change criminal as well as drug use behavior. Chapter 38 describes another key approach to "technology transfer," through staff training on evidence-based practices. Ongoing collaborative relationships among agencies and research groups, such as those in Pennsylvania described in Chapter 39, also are vital in keeping the field moving forward. And as presented in the final chapter of the book, Chapter 40, strong science for strong practice requires the linking of research to correctional drug treatment through a variety of efforts, including federal initiatives.

Indeed, there are many facets to the continuum of treatment opportunities for addicted offenders. It "ends" only when the offender has been able to enter the community and live a sustained life of recovery, no longer posing a threat to the public. Thus, the title of this book, *Treating Addicted Offenders: A Continuum of Effective Practices*, is intended to help shift our perceptions of treatment as a long-term process rather than a single event.

Table of Contents

About the Editors vii
Introduction ix

PART 1: TESTING, SCREENING, AND REFERRAL

Chapter 1: Self-Report Screens for Identifying Drug-Use Problems

Introduction 1-1
Accuracy 1-2
    Sensitivity 1-2
    Specificity 1-2
    Positive Predictive Value 1-2
    Negative Predictive Value 1-3
Administrative Constraints 1-3
    Screening Time 1-3
    Required Staff Training 1-3
    Cost Considerations 1-3
Window of Detection 1-4
Dependence vs. Abuse 1-4
Interview vs. Self-Administered 1-4
    Obtaining Truthful Responses 1-5
    Screen Administration 1-5
Final Point: Match Screen to Institutional Program Options 1-5

Chapter 2: Problems Identified by the Practical Adolescent Dual Diagnostic Interview (PADDI) in a Juvenile Detention Center Population

High Rates of Co-Occurring Mental Health and Substance Use
  Disorders in Adolescents 2-2
Most Assessment Instruments Developed for Research Settings 2-2
PADDI: Standardizing Clinical Diagnoses 2-3
Administering the Interview; Evaluating the Responses 2-3
    Minimal Training Needed to Conduct the Interview 2-3
    Findings Must Be Interpreted by Professionals 2-3
    Comprehensive Series of Questions 2-4
Study Procedures and Characteristics of Sample 2-4
    Age, Sex, and Ethnicity 2-4
    Educational Achievement 2-4
    Previous or Current Experience With Medication 2-5

Offenses Committed 2-5
Analyzing the Responses 2-5
Findings 2-6
        Many Juvenile Offenders Have Been Victims of Abuse 2-6
        Diagnostic Findings 2-7
                Suicidal Ideation and Self-Harm 2-7
                Little Thought of Harming Others 2-7
                Conduct Disorder and Substance Dependence
                  Most Prevalent Conditions 2-7
                Psychoses 2-7
                Affective Disorders 2-7
                Anxiety Disorders 2-8
        Positive Diagnoses Suggested for 92% of Respondents 2-8
Extent and Patterns of Symptoms Indicate Severity 2-8
Issues for Further Discussion 2-10
Limitations of Our Analysis 2-10

Chapter 3: Predicting Violent Behavior in Adolescent Cannabis Users: The GAIN-CVI

Introduction 3-1
Moffitt's Taxonomy 3-2
                Life-Course Persistent Offenders 3-2
                Adolescence-Limited Offenders 3-2
The Cannabis Youth Treatment Study 3-3
The GAIN Crime and Violence Index 3-3
Testing Moffitt's Theory of Criminal/Violent Behavior 3-3
Changes in Social Environment Related to Changes in Illegal Activity 3-5
Results and Limitations of GAIN-CVI 3-5
        Good Predictive Validity 3-5
        Limited by Self-Report and Failure to Isolate Effects of
          Drug Use Changes 3-5
        Considerable Promise for Predicting Future Crime/Violence 3-6
        Findings Suggest Hope for Maturing Out 3-6
        A Need to Expand the Scope of Treatment Evaluation 3-6
Conclusion: A Dynamic Explanation of Criminal Careers 3-6

Chapter 4: Using ADAM Data to Identify Intrajurisdictional Drug Use Patterns

Introduction 4-1
Major Drug-Use Prevalence Data Collection Efforts 4-2
Drawbacks of Aggregate-Level Surveillance 4-2

Study Spotlights Houston's ADAM Data 4-3
    Sample 4-3
    Self-Report Data 4-3
    Urine Screen 4-4
    Data Limitations 4-4
Data Analysis and Findings 4-4
    Descriptives 4-4
    Drug Prevalence 4-4
    Research Caveats 4-6
Benefits of Disaggregating Drug Data 4-7

Chapter 5: The California Department of Corrections Drug Reduction Strategy Project
Introduction 5-1
DRS Program Design 5-2
    Four Program Sites 5-2
    Two Phases 5-2
DRS Implementation 5-3
    Phase I: Weekly Urinalysis 5-3
    Phase II: Random Urinalysis Plus Other Drug Detection Measures 5-4
Project Results 5-4
    Random Urinalysis Testing 5-4
    Other Drug Detection Measures 5-5
Drug Interdiction Efforts 5-5
    K-9 Teams 5-5
    Drug-Detection Equipment 5-6
Conclusions 5-6

PART 2: ALTERNATIVES TO INCARCERATION

Chapter 6: Matching Drug-Involved Probationers to Appropriate Drug Interventions: A Strategy for Reducing Recidivism
Introduction 6-1
New York City's Anti-Drug Initiative 6-2
    Systematic Approach to Meeting Probationers' Drug
        Treatment Needs an Effective Initiative 6-2
    Client Population Served 6-3
Actual Treatment Participation Lower Than Hoped 6-3
    Most Cases Referred Through CPU Either Were Not
        Admitted or Dropped Out 6-3
    Client Participation in Outpatient Drug Treatment Low 6-4

Despite Low Participation, Treated Clients Less Likely to Recidivate 6-4
Deciding Which Treatment to Offer 6-6
　　　Out-Patient Treatment Not Always Appropriate 6-6
　　　Urine Monitoring of Probationers 6-6
　　　When Out-Patient Treatment Is Indicated 6-7
Policy Implications and Recommendations 6-8

Chapter 7: Measuring Program Quality Over Time—Examples From Three RSAT Programs
Importance of Measuring Program Integrity and Quality Over Time 7-1
Principles of Effective Interventions 7-2
Assessing Program Integrity 7-3
　　　The CPAI Instrument 7-3
　　　Limitations of CPAI 7-3
　　　Advantages of the CPAI 7-4
RSAT Program Assessments 7-4
　　　Community-Based RSAT 7-4
　　　Prison-Based RSAT 7-6
　　　Juvenile RSAT Program 7-7
Lessons for RSAT Administrators 7-8
The Upside 7-9

Chapter 8: The Promises and Challenges of Drug Courts
Introduction 8-1
Illegal Drug Use the Norm for Offender Population 8-2
Drug Court Treatment Initiatives 8-2
　　　Development of Drug Courts 8-2
　　　Drug Court Program Basics 8-2
Initial Research Findings Show Promise 8-3
　　　Drug Court Participants Do Better While in Treatment 8-3
　　　Some Promising Recidivism Outcomes 8-4
　　　Potential for Long-Term Taxpayer Savings 8-4
Research and Policy Challenges 8-5
　　　Improving Retention 8-5
　　　Facilitating Public Health Benefits 8-5
　　　Identifying and Reaching Appropriate Target Population 8-6
　　　Identifying and Improving Effective Treatment Processes and
　　　　　Related Staff Training 8-6
　　　Addressing Knowledge Gaps 8-8
Conclusions 8-8

Chapter 9: The Characteristics of American Drug Court Programs

Florida Model Sparks a Trend 9-2
Drug Court Program Goals 9-3
Locus of Program in Judicial Process 9-4
Targeted Offenses and Offenders 9-4
    Participant Eligibility Criteria 9-4
    Referral, Screening, and Assessment Process 9-4
Program Organization and Operation 9-5
    Program Phases 9-5
    Provision of Treatment Services 9-5
        Services for Special Populations 9-6
        Public Health Services 9-6
        Aftercare 9-6
        Alumni Activities 9-6
    Assignment of Cases to Drug Court Judge(s) 9-6
    Program Policies and Procedures 9-7
        Oversight/Advisory Committee 9-7
        Multi-Disciplinary and Cross-Training 9-7
    Community Relationships 9-7
    Collaboration With Law Enforcement 9-7
Program Resources 9-8
    Judge Time 9-8
    Additional Funds Needed 9-8
    Program Income 9-8
Program Process 9-9
    Time Between Arrest and Program Entry 9-9
    Changes in Existing Criminal Case Process Required to
      Implement Drug Court Program 9-9
    Court Response to Participant Progress, or Rearrest 9-9
    Termination of Unsuccessful Participants 9-10
    Successful Completion and Graduation 9-10
    Program Contacts With Participants 9-11

Chapter 10: Dilemmas Confronting Practitioners in Family Drug Treatment Courts

Introduction 10-1
Risk and Coercion 10-2
Family Drug Treatment Court Incentives and Supports 10-3
Evaluation and Research 10-4
Remaining Challenges for FTCs 10-5

Chapter 11: The Role of Judicial Status Hearings in Drug Court

Drug Courts Are an Alternative to Criminal Prosecution or Incarceration 11-1
Key Components of Drug Courts 11-2
Studying the Effects of Judicial Status Hearings on Drug Court
  Outcomes: Biweekly or As-Needed 11-2
      First Study 11-2
         No Main Effect of Status Hearings 11-2
         Different Effects for High-Risk and Low-Risk Offenders
           in Biweekly vs. As-Needed Hearings 11-3
      Study Limitation Addressed 11-3
         Programs Four to Six Months Long 11-3
         Monthly Meetings With Case Manager 11-4
Follow-Up Study Results 11-4
      Participant Characteristics 11-4
      Distribution Across Study Conditions Confirmed 11-4
      Main Effects Showed No Clear Differences
        Between the Two Conditions 11-5
      Interaction Effects Showed Clear Superiority of Biweekly
        Condition for Participants With Prior Drug Treatment History 11-6
      Study Recruitment Stopped in Response to Possible
        Shift in Risk/Benefit Ratio 11-8
Conclusions 11-8

PART 3: TREATMENT IN CORRECTIONAL SETTINGS

Chapter 12: The Kyle New Vision Program: An Intensive In-Prison Therapeutic Community

Intensive Treatment Pays Off for High-Risk Substance Abusing Offenders 12-2
Therapeutic Community Program Follows Participants to Outside World 12-3
      Orientation Phase 12-3
      Main Treatment Phase 12-3
      Re-Entry Phase 12-3
      Cadre 12-4
The Therapeutic Community Approach 12-4
      Primary Goals 12-4
      Hierarchy 12-5
Critical Program Components 12-5
      Community Enhancement Activities 12-5
      Chemical Dependency Education 12-5
      Counseling Groups 12-5
      Community-Clinical Management 12-6

Incentives and Privileges.....................................12-6
System of Sanctions 12-6
Twelve-Step Fellowships 12-6
Volunteer Programs...12-7
Academic Education 12-7
Family Education Program 12-7
Program Enhancements......................................12-7
Innovative Plans for the Future 12-8
Conclusion 12-8

Chapter 13: California's First Prison Therapeutic Community: A 10-Year Review

Need for New Programs for the Many Substance Abusing
Offenders in Prison 13-1
How It All Began 13-3
Focus on Substance Abuse as a Significant Problem 13-3
Task Force Recommendations 13-3
Recruiting Warden for Program 13-4
How the TC Was Implemented 13-4
Close Coordination Between Program and Correctional Staff 13-4
Working With the Realities—and Help—of the Inmate Population 13-5
Integration of Program Into General Prison Life 13-6
Expanding Eligibility Parameters 13-6
Development of Aftercare Component 13-7
The Amity Model 13-8
Structure and Duration 13-8
Staff and Training 13-8
Curriculum 13-9
Cross Training 13-10
Bottom Line: Program Works to Improve Lives...and Save Money 13-10
Conclusion 13-11

Chapter 14: National Update on Therapeutic Community Programs for Substance Abusing Offenders in State Prisons

Introduction 14-1
National Survey Findings 14-2
Extent of TC Programming...................................14-2
Inmates Served 14-2
Staffing 14-4
TC, or Not TC?...14-4
Some Confusion About What a TC Is...........................14-4

Standards Development 14-5
Field Review Observations 14-5
Critical TC Factors 14-6
Staffing 14-7
Quality Assurance 14-8
Structured Programming 14-8
Monitoring Oversight 14-8
Treatment Model 14-8
Conclusion 14-9

Chapter 15: Lessons Learned From the Federal Bureau of Prisons' Drug Abuse Treatment Programs

Introduction 15-2
Program Development History 15-2
"Narcotics Farms" 15-2
NARA Programs 15-2
Shift in Treatment Approach 15-3
Current Practices 15-3
Biopsychosocial Model 15-3
Nine-Month Residential Program 15-4
Outcome Evaluation Results 15-4
Positive Effect on Recidivism 15-5
Better In-Prison Functioning 15-5
Major Program Issues 15-6
Rapid Program Implementation and Staffing 15-6
Organizational Culture and Climate 15-6
Inmate Recruitment 15-7
Establishing Treatment Milieu 15-8
Dual Disorders 15-8
Future Directions 15-9
Summary 15-9

Chapter 16: Promoting Change in a Drug and Criminal Lifestyle

The Drug-Crime Connection 16-2
The Lifestyle Model 16-2
Lifestyle Concept Defined 16-2
Commonalities of Drug and Crime Lifestyles 16-2
Case Example: Darryl 16-3
How to Address—and Change—Belief Systems That Lead to
Crime/Drug Lifestyles 16-3

Core Element #1: Responsibility 16-4
   Use Life Lessons to Encourage Behavior Modification 16-4
   Discourage Enabling Behaviors 16-4
   Case Example 16-5
Core Element #2: Confidence 16-5
   Enhance Self-Efficacy 16-5
   Promote General Sense of Confidence 16-5
   Case Example 16-6
Core Element #3: Meaning 16-6
   Avoid Labeling 16-6
   Challenge Cognitive Simplicity 16-7
   Case Example 16-7
Core Element #4: Community 16-7
   Ensure Social Support 16-7
   Encourage Client's Sense of Connection 16-8
   Case Example 16-8
Conclusion 16-8

PART 4: SPECIAL POPULATIONS

Chapter 17: Providing Treatment to Substance-Abusing Sex Offenders in Correctional Environments: Lessons From California

Abstract 17-2
Prevalence of Sex Offenders in Prison 17-2
Need for Substance Abuse Treatment in the Inmate Population 17-2
"Legal" vs. "Clinical" Sex Offenders 17-3
Co-Morbidity of Sex Offending With Substance Abuse 17-4
Why Treat the Substance Abuse Disorder of the Sex Offender? 17-5
Barriers to Treating Substance Abusing Sex Offenders 17-5
   Stigmatism 17-6
   Denial 17-6
   Untrained and Inexperienced Staff 17-6
   Institutional Policies Against Disclosure 17-6
   Co-Occurring Antisocial Personality Disorder 17-7
   Lack of a Formal Process for Identifying Clinical Sex Offenders 17-7
Identifying and Treating Substance Abusing Sex Offenders:
Toward a Solution 17-7
   Identifying Those Sex Offenders Suitable for Treatment 17-7
   Identifying the Appropriate Treatment Modality 17-8
   Maximizing Success by Providing Needed Aftercare 17-8
Summary 17-8

Chapter 18: Therapeutic Community Treatment for Women in Prison: Assessing Outcomes and Needs

Growing Number of Incarcerated Women Raises Drug Abuse
Treatment Issues 18-1

Prison-Based Treatment Outcomes for Women 18-3

    Stay'n Out 18-3

    Forever Free 18-4

    Bureau of Prisons 18-5

    California Department of Corrections Treatment Expansion Initiative . . . 18-6

    Selection Bias? 18-6

Women Offenders' Treatment Needs 18-6

    Drug Use and Criminal Involvement Issues 18-6

    Medical Issues 18-7

    Employment/Educational Issues 18-7

    Parenting Issues 18-7

    Relationship Issues 18-8

    Sexual and Physical Abuse Issues 18-8

    Psychological Issues 18-9

Conclusion: More Research Needed 18-9

Chapter 19: Legal System Issues Among Drug-Involved Women Enrolled in a Community-Based HIV Prevention Program

Introduction 19-2

    Drugs-Incarceration Nexus for Women 19-2

    Negative Health Impact of Women's Drug Use 19-2

Study to Assess Need for and Role of Legal System Interventions for
This Population 19-2

    Community Outreach Project on AIDS in Southern Arizona 19-3

    Legal Component and Instrumentation of Study 19-3

Extent of Legal Problems Reported 19-4

    Civil Law Difficulties 19-4

    Criminal Charges 19-4

Drug-Involved Women Victims Believe Legal System Cannot Help Them 19-6

What Surveyed Women Want From the Legal System 19-7

Summary of Findings 19-8

    Women's Legal Problems Tied to Drug Use 19-8

    Drug-Using Women Fear and Avoid Legal System 19-8

    Limitations of the Study 19-9

    Implications for Practice 19-9

Chapter 20: Gender Differences in Employment Among Substance-Abusing Offenders at Drug Court Entry

Introduction 20-1
Missing Link: Employment Services 20-2
The Intervention 20-3
    Three Phases 20-3
    Data Collection Method 20-4
Gender Difference Profiles 20-4
    Employment 20-5
    Substance Use 20-7
    Criminal Involvement 20-7
Conclusions 20-7

Chapter 21: Considering Psychiatric Comorbidities Among Addicted Offenders: A New Strategy for Client-Treatment Matching

Introduction 21-2
    High Rates of Comorbidity 21-2
    Lack of Attention to Mental Health Needs of Drug-Abusing Offenders . . . 21-2
Epidemiological Studies 21-3
    Psychiatric Disorders in Jail Detainees 21-3
    Co-Occurring Substance Abuse and SMI in Probationers 21-4
    BJS Findings 21-4
Assessment Strategies and Instruments 21-5
    Not Enough Screening for Comorbid Mental Illness in
      Substance Abusers 21-5
    Desirable Screening Instrument Attributes 21-5
    Candidate Screening Instruments 21-6
        Diagnostic Approach 21-6
        Symptom Severity Approach 21-7
Treatment 21-8
    Psychiatric Concerns Not Just an "Add On" 21-8
    Strong Argument for Specialized Programming 21-9
    A Treatment-Matching Strategy 21-10
Conclusion 21-10

Chapter 22: How Psychopathic? A Critical Consideration for Offender Treatment

Introduction 22-1
Misconceptions and Myths Abound About Psychopathy 22-2
Distinguishing Between Other Personality Disorders and Psychopathy 22-2

The PCL-R and Substance Abusers 22-3
    Scoring 22-3
    Interpreting PCL Factors in Substance Abusers 22-4
How Psychopaths Differ From Other Offenders 22-5
Age, Gender, and Ethnicity 22-5
Overcoming Obstacles to Integration of Psychopathy Assessment
Into Substance Abuse Treatment 22-6
    Make All Staff Part of Team 22-6
    Integrate Into Social Learning Model 22-6
    Tie Reliable Testing to Day-to-Day Work 22-7
Programming and Individualized Treatment Planning for
Psychopathic Substance Abusers 22-8

**Chapter 23: Treating Substance Abuse Clients with Co-Occurring Intimate
Partner Violence**
High Rate of Co-Occurrence 23-1
Need for Screening and Special Treatment Planning 23-2
IPV Offender Typologies 23-2
Other Clinical Characteristics of IPV Offenders 23-3
    Personality Disorders 23-3
    Depression 23-4
    PTSD 23-4
Screening and Assessment Strategies and Issues for
Substance Abuse Treatment Providers 23-4
    Contextualized Questioning 23-4
    Victim Input 23-5
    Risk Assessment 23-5
Treatment Selection 23-6
    Safety Planning 23-6
    What to Treat First? 23-7
    Structured Treatment for IPV 23-7
    Integrated Treatment or Referral Approaches 23-8
    No Mixed-Gender Groups 23-8
Community Resources and Linkages 23-8
Clinician Training and Supervision 23-9
Future Program Development 23-9

**Chapter 24: Family Empowerment Intervention: An Effective—and Cost-
Effective—Program for Delinquent Youths**
Substance Abuse Programs Needed in Juvenile Justice System 24-1
Theoretical Foundations of the Intervention 24-2

Program Goals 24-3
A Four-Phase Intervention 24-3
Implementing and Evaluating the Clinical Trial 24-4
    Enrollment Process 24-4
    Demographic and Psychosocial Characteristics 24-5
    Follow-Up Process 24-5
Official Record Analyses of Post-Intervention Charges and Arrests 24-5
Self-Reported Delinquency, Post-Intervention 24-6
Alcohol/Other Drug Use 24-6
Emotional/Psychological Functioning 24-6
Cost-Saving Benefits of FEI. 24-7
Conclusions 24-8

Chapter 25: Inhalant Users: A Juvenile Justice Population of Special Risk
Juvenile Inhalant Use and Related Delinquency Patterns 25-1
Damage Caused by Inhalant Abuse 25-2
Findings of the 2000-2001 Texas Youth Commission Study. 25-3
    Purpose and Methodology. 25-3
    Usage Patterns Differ by Gender and Ethnicity 25-3
    Co-Occurring Risk Factors Found in Inhalant Users 25-5
    Relationship of Inhalant Use to Criminality 25-5
Implications for Treatment Planning 25-7

PART 5: FACTORS IMPACTING TREATMENT

Chapter 26: Who Decides Length of Stay in Substance Abuse Treatment?
Introduction 26-1
Research Supports Extended Stays 26-2
Why Not Long-Term Treatment for Everyone?. 26-3
External Factors Impact How Much and What Kind of Treatment Is Provided . . . 26-3
Special Problems of the Dually Diagnosed 26-3
How Political Issues Influence Lengths of Stay in the Criminal Justice Arena . . 26-4
How Economic Issues Dictate Length of Stay. 26-5
    Introduction of Managed Care 26-5
    Interplay of Politics With Economics 26-5
Ethical Issues 26-6
Bottom Line: What Treatment Providers Can Do 26-7

Chapter 27: Correctional Treatment and the TCU Treatment Model
Introduction 27-1
    Scope of Problem 27-1

Positive Impact of Treatment Programs 27-2
Not Enough Treatment Spots 27-2
Delivering and Managing Effective Treatment 27-3
The TCU Treatment Process Model 27-3
Special Interventions and Counseling Manuals 27-5
Process Evaluation Can Lead to Better Outcomes 27-6
Disseminating and Applying Research Findings 27-6

Chapter 28: Implementing a Readiness Program for Mandated Substance Abuse Treatment

Introduction 28-2
Readiness for Treatment a Key to Success 28-2
Methods Not Designed for Criminal Justice 28-2
Special Issues for Corrections 28-3
Brief Description of the Treatment Program 28-3
Intent of the Readiness Series 28-4
Session 1: Activities to Enhance Mood and Self-Esteem 28-4
Tower of Strengths 28-4
Weekly Planner 28-5
Session 2: Activities to Develop a Need for Positive Change 28-5
Downward Spiral 28-5
Change Maps 28-6
Session 3: Activities to Develop a Positive View of the Program and
Identify Important Personal Actions 28-6
Believe It or Not 28-6
Personal Action List 28-6
Top 10 Reasons for "Working the Program" 28-7
Session 4: Activities Providing Strategies for Making the Most of This Time 28-7
Set Effects: Seal Act/Costume Ball 28-7
Set: Sleep/Strength List 28-7
Pegword Memory Technique 28-7
Science of Imagery 28-8
Impact of the Readiness Activities: Research Findings 28-8
Comparisons of During-Treatment Impact: Standard vs. Enhanced 28-8
Reactions to the Series of Activities: A "Consumer
Satisfaction" Questionnaire 28-9
Designing a Readiness for Treatment Program: Conclusions and Caveats 28-10
Motivation to Change or to "Work the Program" 28-10
Implementation Issues 28-11
Final Comments 28-11

Chapter 29: Readiness and Mandated Treatment: Development and Application of a Functional Model

Introduction 29-2
Key Elements of a Treatment Readiness Model 29-2
    Focus on the Consequences of Change ("What if I Change?") 29-2
    Focus on the Treatment Process ("How Do I Change?") 29-4
A Road Map for Readiness 29-4
Practical Applications of the Model 29-6
"What if" Activities 29-7
    Knowledge of Change 29-7
    Acceptance/Attractiveness of Change 29-7
    Resources for Change 29-7
    Confidence in Resources for Dealing With Change 29-8
"How to" Activities 29-8
    Knowledge of Process 29-8
    Resources for Process 29-8
    Confidence in Process 29-9
    Acceptance/Attractiveness of Process 29-9
    Treatment Planning 29-9
Conclusions 29-9

Chapter 30: Corrections-Based Substance Abuse Programs: Good for Inmates, Good for Prisons

Introduction 30-1
Background: TC Philosophy 30-2
The Substance Abuse Treatment Facility at Corcoran State Prison 30-2
Impacts of the SATF TC Programs 30-3
    Substance Use Among SATF Participants 30-3
    Disciplinary Actions 30-3
    Staff Ratings of SATF 30-4
    Staff Absenteeism 30-4
Staff and Inmate Perceptions of SATF 30-5
Implications for Prison Management and Planners 30-6

Chapter 31: The Effectiveness of Coerced Admission to Prison-Based Drug Treatment

Introduction 31-1
The California Substance Abuse Treatment Facility 31-2
Study Design and Methods 31-3
    Sample Population 31-3
    Study Measures 31-4

Substance Use Severity 31-4
Motivation for Treatment 31-4
Recidivism 31-5
Results 31-6
SATF vs. Comparison Group 31-6
Desire for Treatment 31-7
Treatment-Desire Interaction............................ 31-7
Multivariate Models Predicting Six-Month Recidivism 31-8
Discussion 31-9
Matching Treatment to Inmate's Motivation Is Critical 31-9
Study Limitations 31-10
Conclusion 31-10

PART 6: AFTERCARE

Chapter 32: Reducing Recidivism Through a Seamless System of Care: Components of Effective Treatment, Supervision, and Transition Services in the Community

Introduction 32-2
Barriers to—and Bonuses of—Providing Substance
  Abuse Treatment to Offenders 32-2
Treatment Perceived as Opportunity, Not Punishment 32-3
Offenders Often Unwanted in Community Treatment System 32-3
Offenders Have Better Treatment Completion Rates 32-3
Longer Stay in Treatment and Continuum of Care Improve Outcomes 32-4
Recognizing Treatment as a Means of Crime Control Is Good Public Policy ... 32-4
Twelve Principles for Effective Systems of Care Focusing on
  Transitional Policies and Treatment Retention 32-5
#1: Make Recidivism Reduction the Goal 32-5
#2: Treatment and Criminal Justice System
  Features Must Be Policy Driven 32-5
#3: Treatment and Criminal Justice Professionals
  Must Function as a Team 32-5
#4: Use Drug Testing to Manage Offenders 32-6
#5: Target Offenders Whose Treatment Will Have Broad Impact 32-6
#6: Use Treatment Matching Practices 32-7
#7: Create a Treatment Process and Extend
  Length of Time in Treatment 32-7
#8: Use Behavioral Contracts 32-8
#9: Use Special Agents to Supervise Offenders in Treatment 32-8
#10: Sanction Non-Compliant Behavior......................... 32-9
#11: Reward Positive Behavior................................. 32-10

#12: Focus on Quality, Not Quantity 32-10
Summary.. 32-10

Chapter 33: Continuity of Offender Treatment: From the Institution to the Community

Background: Effectiveness of Offender Treatment 33-2
How Continuity of Offender Treatment Improves Ultimate
  Treatment Success Rates 33-2
    Recent Outcome Studies Show Positive Effects..................... 33-2
    The Oregon Demonstration Project 33-3
Theoretical Underpinnings of Programs 33-4
    Justice System Perspective 33-4
    Offender Perspective... 33-5
Obstacles to Continuity of Offender Treatment........................ 33-5
    Segmentation of the Criminal Justice System 33-5
    Lack of Coordination Between Justice System
      and Treatment Programs 33-6
    Loss of Post-Release Structure for Offenders 33-6
    Loss of Incentives and Sanctions at Release 33-6
    Lack of Services in the Community 33-6
    Lack of Treatment Provider Experience With Offenders 33-6
    Community Funding Challenges................................. 33-7
Successful Program Models....................................... 33-7
    Outreach Programs 33-7
    Reach-In Programs 33-7
    Third-Party Continuity Program 33-7
    Mixed Model 33-8

Chapter 34: An Integrated Approach to Aftercare and Employment for Criminal Justice Clients

Offender Employment a Critical Incentive 34-1
Effectiveness of Aftercare in Reducing Recidivism 34-2
Case Management: The TASC Model 34-2
Synergy Between Aftercare Treatment and Employment Services 34-3
    Programmatic Difficulties to Overcome 34-3
    Provider Issues 34-4
Bridging Program-Provider Gaps.................................. 34-4
    Using Distance Learning...................................... 34-4
    Addressing Employers' Legal Concerns 34-4
    Creating a Multi-Value Framework 34-5
    New CREW Model 34-5
Conclusion 34-5

Chapter 35: Increasing Supervision's Effectiveness: An Evidence-Based Model

Introduction 35-1

Questions About the Effectiveness of Supervision 35-2

Traditional Social Control Supervision Framework 35-2

　　　Contact Model 35-2

　　　Supervision Objectives 35-3

　　　Supervision as a Process of Engagement 35-3

Engagement in Pro-Social Values and Behaviors 35-4

Engagement Process 35-5

The Supervision Plan 35-5

　　　Informal Social Controls 35-5

　　　Formal Controls/Services 35-6

Making the Commitment to Change (Early Change) 35-6

　　　Ground Rules 35-8

　　　Agent Deportment 35-8

　　　Communication 35-9

Sustained Change for the Long Term 35-9

Conclusion 35-10

PART 7: RESEARCH TO PRACTICE

Chapter 36: From Research to Practice: How the Addiction Technology Transfer Centers Bridge the Corrections Gap

Responding to the Connection Between Substance Abuse and Crime 36-2

What Technology Transfer Is 36-2

The ATTC Network's Role in Creating Effective Interventions

　That Bridge the Gap 36-3

　　　Federal and State Ties Enhance Effectiveness 36-3

　　　Implementing Change 36-3

Cross-Training Curricula 36-4

　　　Criminal Justice and Substance Abuse Partnerships 36-4

　　　California-Specific Training 36-5

　　　TC Training 36-5

　　　Substance Abuse and Mental Disorders 36-5

　　　Female Offenders 36-6

Creating Meaningful Partnerships in Both Systems 36-6

Applying Change Strategies 36-6

　　　Need to Work With "Big Picture" 36-7

　　　Program Examples 36-7

Summary 36-8

Chapter 37: Moving From Correctional Program to Correctional Strategy: Using Proven Practices to Change Criminal Behavior

Introduction 37-2
Attributes Associated With Criminal Behavior and Recidivism 37-2
Elements of Effective Programs 37-2
Applying Theoretical Principles to Practice 37-3
    The Criminogenic Risk Principle 37-3
    The Criminogenic Need Principle 37-4
    The Responsivity Principle 37-4
    Interplay of Principles 37-4
Cognitive Behavioral Intervention 37-4
    Criminal Thinking—Understanding the Logic and Rewards 37-4
    Targeting Offender Behavior—Social Learning and
    Behavioral Intervention 37-5
Models of Social Learning 37-6
    Community Model of Resocialization for Offenders 37-6
    Types of Community Models 37-6
Elements of Successful Cognitive Programs 37-6
    Basic Program Essentials 37-6
    Cognitive Approaches 37-7
    Incorporating the Principle of Responsivity 37-7
Taking an Integrated Approach 37-8
    Relapse Prevention Strategies 37-8
    Sanctions and Treatment: Accountability and Change 37-8
Evidence-Based Program Structure 37-9
    The Cognitive Community 37-9
    Staff as Community Members and Agents of Change 37-10
Maximizing Results 37-11

Chapter 38: Enhancing Substance Abuse Treatment Skills in Correctional Settings

Preconceptions a Barrier to New Understanding of Addiction 38-1
The Gap Between Science and Clinical Practices 38-2
    Practitioners Want Specific Answers From Science 38-2
    Researchers Need to Consider Under-Studied Treatment Strategies 38-3
    Challenges in Transferring Clinical Success to Treatment Program 38-3
How Bias Affects Treatment and Training 38-3
Continuity of Care 38-4
Training Adult Learners 38-5
Basic Concepts of Training 38-5
Skill Enhancement 38-6

Organizational Skills 38-6
Case Management Skills 38-7
Successful Training Methods 38-8
Conclusion 38-8

**Chapter 39: Assessing Prison-Based Drug and Alcohol Treatment:
Pennsylvania's Ongoing Review Has Improved Programming**
The National Picture 39-2
Need Outpaces Program Services 39-2
Open Question: Which Drug Abuse Programs Work 39-2
Pennsylvania Partnership Purpose and Goals 39-4
Demonstration Project 39-4
DOC Goals 39-4
DOC's Alcohol or Other Drug Programs 39-4
Survey of Drug and Alcohol Programs in Pennsylvania Prisons 39-5
Survey Findings 39-5
Point #1: Considerable Variation in Program
Duration and Intensity 39-5
Point #2: Consistency in Treatment Approach 39-6
Point #3: Consistency in Program Topic Coverage 39-6
Point #4: Great Variation in Program Types 39-6
Point #5: Great Variation in Administrative Criteria 39-6
Practical Implications of Findings 39-7
Program Variability Inhibits Effective Management 39-7
We Need to Know More About Process Effect on Outcome . . . 39-7
Better Tracking Required 39-8
Outcome Evaluation of Pennsylvania's Prison-Based Drug Treatment 39-8
Translating Research to Practice 39-9
The Department as a Learning Organization 39-9
Evaluation Recommendations Implemented or
Under Current Review 39-10
New Screening Tools 39-10
Program Standardization 39-10
Improved Documentation 39-10
Future Projects 39-10
Conclusion 39-11

Chapter 40: Strong Science for Strong Practice: Linking Research to Correctional Drug Treatment

Introduction 40-2
Some Principles of Effective Prison-Based Drug Treatment................. 40-2
Strategies to Encourage Science-Based Drug Treatment in Prisons 40-4
      Create Manual of Correctional Drug Treatment Principles 40-5
      Educate the Public, Policymakers, Legislators, and Prison Officials ... 40-5
      Promote Boundary-Spanning Efforts to Provide Drug
         Treatment in the Criminal Justice System 40-5
      Isolate a Range of Proven, Available, Feasible In-Prison
         Treatment Options 40-6
Research Gaps on Drug Treatment in Corrections 40-6
      Determine Nature and Extent of Current Drug
         Treatment Need and Practice 40-6
      Develop Validated Screening and Assessment Instruments
         for Various Decision Points 40-6
      Determine the Balance of Incentives and Sanctions Available 40-7
      Better Understand Role of Motivation and Coercion in Treatment 40-7
      Examine Treatment Delivery in Context of
         Different Stages of a Prison Term 40-7
      Examine How Effectiveness of Drug Treatment
         Might Be Affected Based on Prison Security Levels 40-7
      Explore How Transitioning Into and Out of Prison Influences
         Effectiveness of Treatment 40-8
      Assess Cost-Effectiveness 40-8
      Learn What Factors Determine Available Treatments—
         and Which Are Appropriate 40-8
      Learn How Correctional Staff and Systems-Level
         Factors Impact Treatment 40-8
Conclusion 40-9

Afterword.. A-1

Appendix: Legal Issues App.-1

Index I-1

Part 1

Testing, Screening, and Referral

Providing an effective continuum of opportunities to treat addicted offenders requires an understanding of treatment need and intensity. Too frequently an offender's need for treatment is based on limited objective information, such as on a brief open-ended interview conducted with an offender shortly after incarceration. When need for treatment is determined, referral to a particular level or intensity of treatment is too often based on treatment availability and not on the most appropriate treatment. Ultimately, the challenge for correctional staff is to determine objectively the best fit between offender substance abuse problems and available correctional substance abuse treatment services.

This section summarizes some of the important testing, screening, and referral components involved in the process of identifying treatment need and determining the most appropriate treatment level or intensity.

In Chapter 1, Kevin Knight addresses the selection and use of self-report screens. Whether used in conjunction with more comprehensive assessments or by themselves, self-report screens can play a vital role in the screening and referral process. Statistical considerations, such as the need for high accuracy, sensitivity, specificity, positive predictive value, and negative predictive value are described. In addition, this chapter addresses practical considerations, such as required staff training, that should be considered when deciding on which self-report screen to select and use.

Chapter 2, by Norman Hoffmann, Ana Abrantes, and Ronald Anton, presents the Practical Adolescent Dual Diagnostic Interview (PADDI), a developmentally appropriate instrument that accurately assesses adolescents for co-occurring conditions. Designed explicitly for use with adolescents, the PADDI can be administered by a variety of individuals, including juvenile justice personnel, trained technicians, and behavioral health professionals. The authors describe the administration of the PADDI to both males and females committed to two juvenile detention centers in Maine and show how their findings support the utility of the PADDI as a screening instrument.

Chapter 3, by Michelle White, Rod Funk, William White, and Michael Dennis, describes another useful screening tool, the crime and violence index (CVI) from the Global Appraisal of Individual Needs (GAIN). Based on CVI scale scores, the authors classified adolescents into three risk groups and tested the Moffitt Theory of Criminal/Violent Behavior, showing that changes in social environment were significantly related to changes in illegal activity. In short, the GAIN's CVI scale is useful in identifying those offenders that pose the highest risk for future criminal violence and, therefore, is useful in determining the most appropriate intensity of services.

In Chapter 4, George Yacoubian, Ronald Peters, and Regina Johnson discuss the utility of examining disaggregated self-report survey and urine specimen data collected as part of the Arrestee Drug Abuse Monitoring (ADAM) program. By extending traditional drug use mapping techniques to include the characteristics of drug users obtained through ADAM, the current study found meaningful differences in drug-positive rates within Houston's 20 police districts, particularly with respect to the use of marijuana, cocaine, benzodiazepines, and opiates. Through a closer look at intrajurisdictional drug use patterns, a better understanding of treatment need at the community as well as national level can be achieved.

Finally, Chapter 5, by Michael Campos, Michael Prendergast, William Evans, and Julian Martinez, takes a close look at the California Department of Corrections drug reduction strategy project. The authors describe how the introduction of systematic random urine testing resulted in reductions in estimated inmate substance use levels. Thus, in addition to being useful in determining offender need for treatment, urine testing also serves a potential means for deterring substance use while the offender is incarcerated.

Chapter 1

Self-Report Screens for Identifying Drug-Use Problems

by Kevin Knight, Ph.D.

Introduction 1-1
Accuracy 1-2
    Sensitivity 1-2
    Specificity 1-2
    Positive Predictive Value 1-2
    Negative Predictive Value 1-3
Administrative Constraints 1-3
    Screening Time 1-3
    Required Staff Training 1-3
    Cost Considerations 1-3
Window of Detection 1-4
Dependence vs. Abuse 1-4
Interview vs. Self-Administered 1-4
    Obtaining Truthful Responses 1-5
    Screen Administration 1-5
Final Point: Match Screen to Institutional Program Options 1-5

INTRODUCTION

Because drug treatment resources within corrections are limited, criminal justice officials often must make a difficult decision as to whether a given offender with drug problems should receive scarce treatment services. Although ideally the provision of services should be based on a comprehensive assessment of an offender's needs, many correctional agencies do not have the necessary financial and staffing resources to con-

This chapter, which orginally appeared in Offender Substance Abuse, *Vol. 2, No. 3, May/June 2002, is a condensation of Knight, K., Simpson, D.D., & Hiller, M.L. (2002). Screening and referral for substance-abuse treatment in the criminal justice system. In C.G. Leukefeld, F.M. Tims, & D. Farabee (Eds.), Treatment of drug offenders: Policies and issues (pp. 259-272). Copyright © 2002 Springer Publishing Company, Inc., New York 10012. Adapted with permission.*

duct comprehensive assessments and therefore often rely on the use of a brief drug-use screening instrument. This article addresses some important factors to consider when deciding on which screening instrument to adopt.

ACCURACY

Perhaps the most critical aspect of a screening instrument is its ability to discriminate accurately between those who do and do not have drug problems. Classification error is inevitable, so it is necessary to decide whether it is better for an agency to select an instrument that is more likely to result in referral to treatment of someone who does not need it, or one that is more likely to lead to denial of treatment to someone who truly does need it.

Five statistical guidelines can help inform the decision process (see Cherpitel, 1997, and Peters et al., 2000). First, a measure of overall accuracy is a good general indicator of the instrument's utility. Based on the entire sample of screened offenders, it represents the overall percentage of those who were classified correctly, with higher values being more desirable. However, because a drug screen's overall accuracy is not likely to be 100%, the four other statistics discussed below also need to be considered.

Sensitivity

Sensitivity focuses only on offenders who actually have drug problems and provides a percentage of those the screen accurately identifies as having problems. For agencies that are mandated to identify and provide services to drug-involved offenders, selecting an instrument with high sensitivity can help improve the chances that those with drug problems are detected. An instrument with a high sensitivity score also tends to identify the largest number of treatment eligible inmates, which may be particularly valuable when treatment slots are empty and need to be filled.

Specificity

As a counterpart to sensitivity, specificity includes only the offenders who actually do *not* have drug problems and is a percentage of those the screen correctly identifies as not having problems. A screen with high specificity decreases the probability that an offender without drug problems will be sent to treatment and may be particularly important for agencies that have few treatment options and a large number of inmates from which to draw.

Positive Predictive Value

Positive predictive value examines only those offenders the screen identifies as having drug problems and provides a proportional measure of how many of those screen-identified individuals actually do have drug problems. For agencies that strive to maximize the number of appropriate referrals, positive predictive value deserves special attention. A high value suggests that those the screen identifies as having drug problems actually do have problems and should receive treatment services. This statistic is particularly helpful for agencies with a limited number of treatment options that want to make sure the distribution of those services is highly efficient.

Negative Predictive Value

Based strictly on inmates the screen classifies as not having drug problems, negative predictive value indicates the proportion of those screen-identified individuals who actually do not have drug problems. In general, a screen with a relatively high positive predictive value will tend to have a relatively low negative predictive value, potentially failing to identify inmates who may be able to benefit from treatment.

Ultimately, the most "accurate" instrument is one that has sensitivity and specificity values, as well as positive and negative predictive values, that correspond with the needs of a specific correctional setting. Under these circumstances, financial and staffing expenditures on inappropriate inmates are minimized.

ADMINISTRATIVE CONSTRAINTS

Screening Time

Correctional systems usually must determine the need for treatment for large numbers of offenders in a short period of time. They have neither the available staff time nor financial resources to administer lengthy individual interviews with each new admission. Although many popular assessments for drug problems are well designed and serve as broad sorting tools that can be used to assist in making recommendations for general treatment or intervention alternatives, they tend to be fairly lengthy and take more time to administer than correctional agencies can afford.

Required Staff Training

Because of high staff turnover, correctional agencies often find that they don't have many staff with the clinical experience and credentials necessary to administer certain diagnostic instruments. Even when qualified staff are available, providing extensive and continued training on form administration may be difficult. Selecting a brief, easily administered screening instrument that requires little staff training can ease this burden greatly. Furthermore, on-going training on some instruments can be provided by existing correctional staff who have experience administering the screen, eliminating the need to hire an outside "expert" whenever new staff are hired.

Cost Considerations

Another concern is whether to choose a screen that is in the "public domain" and thus free, or one that is available commercially for a fee. For example, the Substance Abuse Subtle Screening Inventory (SASSI; Miller, 1985) is a commercially available drug screen used by several correctional agencies. The Texas Department of Criminal Justice-Institutional Division used SASSI until recently; by switching to the Texas Christian University (TCU) Drug Screen (available for download at *http://www.ibr.tcu.edu*)—a "public domain" instrument—the agency was able to save thousands of dollars annually. For smaller correctional agencies, cost may be less of a concern, particularly if the instrument meets diagnostic needs and is already part of the traditional assessment protocol.

WINDOW OF DETECTION

Another consideration is whether an instrument assesses drug-use problems that occurred over the course of several years or during a more recent, restricted time frame. Because there is an increased probability of obtaining valid responses when the diagnostic emphasis is on identifying "current" alcohol or drug problems, a relatively short "window of detection" is usually recommended (Cherpitel, 1997). However, shorter detection windows, such as the past 30 days, may be too restrictive to fill the available treatment services. Furthermore, those who need treatment may be overlooked. For example, a 30-day detection window may fail to detect offenders with drug problems who abstained from recent drug use because of legal pressures or surveillance while waiting for trial. On the other hand, if the instrument assesses the presence of drug-use problems at any point during an offender's life, a long waiting list for treatment may result. In this case, those who may not have had serious drug problems recently could be referred to treatment while those with current drug problems are forced to wait.

DEPENDENCE vs. ABUSE

Diagnostic criteria can vary considerably across instruments, with some focusing on drug dependence and others on abuse. Screens that are based on highly conservative criteria, such as the *Diagnostic and Statistical Manual of Mental Disorders* (DSM; American Psychiatric Association, 1994), are designed to detect individuals with serious drug problems. These types of instruments are the most likely to identify individuals who could benefit from intensive treatment services. An instrument with diagnostic criteria for abuse, rather than dependence, may be more desirable if an agency's goal is to provide offenders who may have any range of drug problem severity with less intensive treatment services, such as drug education classes.

INTERVIEW vs. SELF-ADMINISTERED

The way an instrument is delivered also can play an important role in the selection of a screening instrument. For example, the Addiction Severity Index (ASI; McLellan et al., 1992) is a good comprehensive clinical assessment of drug-use problems, designed to be administered as part of a face-to-face interview. Other instruments, such as TCU Drug Screen, were designed to be brief, self-administered drug screens. Although a lengthy structured clinical interview, such as the ASI, may be the preferred choice of many counselors, time and personnel constraints often make shorter self-administered instruments necessary when the goal is to assess just drug-use problems. When a drug-use screen cannot be given as part of a one-on-one interview, research suggests that results can be obtained reliably when self-administered as part of a small group interview (Broome et al., 1996).

Obtaining Truthful Responses

As important as the screen itself is the administration protocol and whether it encourages respondents to be truthful. Although the accuracy of self-reported drug use with treatment populations can vary considerably across situations, research shows valid drug-use data can be obtained when forms are administered in settings where conditions are favorable for truthful self-disclosure (Wish, 1988).

One of the primary influences on an offender's willingness to self report drug problems is the perceived consequences of disclosure. Inmates fear that correctional decision-making boards will make custody assignments and post-release supervision level decisions based, in part, on what is reported on the drug screen. Unlike community treatment settings where a client is guaranteed confidentiality, correctional staff cannot provide such guarantees. They can, however, make it clear to an inmate that there are positive consequences for responding honestly, such as getting access to drug treatment services. Likewise, dishonest responding can result in negative consequences. For example, parole decisions are based on whether an inmate poses an unacceptable risk to society if released. This risk may be determined, in part, by whether an inmate has been deceptive while incarcerated, such as failing to self admit drug use on a screen when there is a criminal record of drug-related offenses. In short, honest responding is more likely to occur when an offender understands that it is in his or her best interest to be honest when completing the screening instrument.

Screen Administration

Obtaining accurate data also is influenced by the setting in which a screening instrument is administered. For example, when a large number of offenders are confined into a small testing area, the overcrowded conditions can lead to offender management problems that dominate the administrator's time—shifting the focus away from the intent of the screen. In cases where the form can be administered only in a large group setting, proctors can provide invaluable assistance to the interviewer by offering individualized attention to those who may need help, particularly with respect to literacy and behavioral problems. In addition, correctional staff can encourage truthful responding by providing an overview of the instrument, informing inmates why honest responding is important, giving detailed instructions on how to complete the instrument, and encouraging questions. Underreporting is inevitable when the interviewer makes it obvious that the primary goal is to get though the screen as quickly as possible.

FINAL POINT: MATCH SCREEN TO INSTITUTIONAL PROGRAM OPTIONS

Appropriate instrument selection and implementation must be followed by referral to appropriate treatment options. Correctional systems that provide two options (e.g., no treatment or intensive therapeutic community (TC) treatment) do not need elaborate and complex screening and referral protocols that classify inmates into more than two categories of treatment need. Similarly, if multiple treatment options are available, the protocol needs greater precision. For example, those with relatively minor drug problems might be best assigned to receive drug education while incarcerated. Those with moderate problems could be required to participate in weekly counseling sessions and encouraged to attend self-help group meetings. Finally, those with the most severe problems could be referred to the most intensive programs available, such as in-prison TC treatment (see Knight et al., 1999). Although this concept of treatment matching has been around for many years, there still is little science to provide detailed guidance in designing the proper protocol.

Other factors, such as co-occurring psychological problems, the length of an inmate's sentence, and the type of current and prior offenses also play a major role in determining which, if any, treatment options are viable. For drug-involved offenders with severe psychological problems, referral is made ideally to a specialized treatment program that provides both substance abuse treatment and mental health care (Peters & Hills, 1999). When this type of program is not available, correctional officials have to decide whether psychiatric problems are too severe for the offender to be referred to a drug treatment program. In addition, a large percentage of many state correctional populations serve less than a year in confinement, making it impossible for an inmate to complete lengthier residential treatment programs, such as nine- to 12-month in-prison TC programs. For these offenders, a drug screen may serve only to determine if a short-term intensive treatment program or drug education program is warranted. Finally, inmates with certain types of offenses also may be excluded from available treatment options. For example, inmates who have committed certain types of aggravated offense may need to be precluded from participating in an in-prison TC program because of their possible disruptive influence. Although intensive treatment programs may not be an option in each of these specific cases, correctional agencies may want to consider at least offering these inmates access to self-help groups and drug education classes.

About the Author

Kevin Knight, Ph.D., is a Research Scientist at the Institute of Behavioral Research at Texas Christian University, and is co-editor of Offender Substance Abuse Report. *He may be contacted at K.Knight@tcu.edu.*

References

American Psychiatric Association. (1994). *Diagnostic and statistical manual of mental disorders* (4th ed.). Washington, DC: Author.

Broome, K.M., Knight, K., Joe, G.W., & Simpson, D.D. (1996). Evaluating the drug-abusing probationer: Clinical interview versus self-administered assessment. *Criminal Justice and Behavior, 23*(4), 593-606.

Cherpitel, C.J. (1997). Brief screening instruments for alcoholism. *Alcohol Health & Research World, 21*(4), 348-351.

Knight, K., Simpson, D.D., & Hiller, M.L. (1999). Three-year reincarceration outcomes for in-prison therapeutic community treatment in Texas. *The Prison Journal, 79*(3), 337-351.

McLellan, A.T., Kushner, H., Metzger, D., Peters, R.H., Smith, I., Grissom, G., Pettinati, H., & Argeriou, M. (1992). The Fifth Edition of the Addiction Severity Index. *Journal of Substance Abuse Treatment, 9,* 199-213.

Miller, G.A. (1985). *The Substance Abuse Subtle Screening Inventory (SASSI) Manual.* Bloomington, IN: SASSI Institute.

Peters, R.H., Greenbaum, P.E., Steinberg, M.L., Carter, C.R., Ortiz, M.M., Fry, B.C., & Valle, S.K. (2000). Effectiveness of screening instruments in detecting substance use disorders among prisoners. *Journal of Substance Abuse Treatment, 18,* 349-358.

Peters, R.H., & Hills, H.A. (1999). Community treatment and supervision strategies for offenders with co-occurring disorders: What works? In E. Latessa (Ed.), *Strategic solutions: The International Community Corrections Association examines substance abuse* (pp. 81-137). Lanham, MD: American Correctional Association.

Simpson, D.D., & Knight, K. (1997). *TCU/CJ Forms Manual: Drug Dependence Screen and Initial Assessment.* Fort Worth, TX: Texas Christian University, Institute of Behavioral Research.

Wish, E.D. (1988). Identifying drug-abusing criminals. In C.G. Leukefeld & F.M. Tims (Eds.), *Compulsory treatment of drug abuse: Research and clinical practice* (NIDA Research Monograph 86, ADM 94-3713). Rockville, MD.

Chapter 2

Problems Identified by the Practical Adolescent Dual Diagnostic Interview (PADDI) in a Juvenile Detention Center Population

by Norman G. Hoffmann, Ph.D., Ana M. Abrantes, Ph.D., and Ronald Anton, LCPC, LADC, MAC

High Rates of Co-Occurring Mental Health and Substance Use
Disorders in Adolescents 2-2
Most Assessment Instruments Developed for Research Settings 2-2
PADDI: Standardizing Clinical Diagnoses 2-3
Administering the Interview; Evaluating the Responses 2-3
    Minimal Training Needed to Conduct the Interview 2-3
    Findings Must Be Interpreted by Professionals 2-3
    Comprehensive Series of Questions 2-4
Study Procedures and Characteristics of Sample 2-4
    Age, Sex, and Ethnicity 2-4
    Educational Achievement 2-4
    Previous or Current Experience With Medication 2-5
    Offenses Committed 2-5
Analyzing the Responses 2-5
Findings 2-6
    Many Juvenile Offenders Have Been Victims of Abuse 2-6
    Diagnostic Findings 2-7
        Suicidal Ideation and Self-Harm 2-7
        Little Thought of Harming Others 2-7
        Conduct Disorder and Substance Dependence
            Most Prevalent Conditions 2-7

This chapter originally appeared in Offender Substance Abuse Report, *Vol. 3, No. 5, September/October 2003.*

Psychoses 2-7
Affective Disorders 2-7
Anxiety Disorders 2-8
Positive Diagnoses Suggested for 92% of Respondents 2-8
Extent and Patterns of Symptoms Indicate Severity 2-8
Issues for Further Discussion 2-10
Limitations of Our Analysis 2-10

HIGH RATES OF CO-OCCURRING MENTAL HEALTH AND SUBSTANCE USE DISORDERS IN ADOLESCENTS

Observed prevalence rates for co-occurring mental health and substance use disorders in adolescents vary from setting to setting but consistently show levels suggesting the necessity for routine assessment. Estimates tend to range from about 50% in adolescent psychiatric populations (Grilo et al., 1995) to as high as 80% among adolescents receiving services for substance dependence (Stowell & Estroff, 1992). Such differentials may be consistent with observations for adult populations that some co-existing mental health conditions may be substance induced (Lehman et al., 1994).

Concomitant psychopathology among substance-abusing adolescents has been associated with significant negative consequences, including more severe substance involvement, greater suicidal ideation, academic problems, and family difficulties. It has been well established that concomitant psychopathology is associated with poorer treatment outcomes among adult substance-abusing populations, and recent evidence points to similar findings among adolescent substance abusers as well. Findings from the Drug Abuse Treatment Outcome Study for Adolescents (DATOS-A) showed greater rates of substance involvement and illegal acts for adolescents with a concomitant mental health disorder than for those without a co-occurring disorder (Grella et al., 2001). In addition, conduct disorder among substance-abusing adolescents has been associated with greater alcohol and drug involvement and poorer psychosocial functioning in young adulthood (Myers et al., 1998). Given the prevalence and clinical correlates of co-occurring disorders among adolescents, accurate identification and assessment of these disorders is crucial for the development of effective treatment interventions and the reduction of criminal recidivism.

MOST ASSESSMENT INSTRUMENTS DEVELOPED FOR RESEARCH SETTINGS

Although some structured interviews, such as the Diagnostic Interview Schedule for Children (DISC), have been developed for evaluating co-occurring conditions, they were initially developed for research purposes and have limitations for routine clinical applications (Shaffer et al., 1996). Administration of the DISC, for example, is time consuming, averaging over one hour to complete. Extensive assessment instruments such as the Global Appraisal of Individual Needs (GAIN; Dennis et al., 1999) are also too time consuming to be used as an initial screening or assessment instrument in juvenile justice settings. Given the limited resources available in juvenile justice environments, these measures, although well suited for research or treatment applications, are not the optimal choice for juvenile justice use.

A practical instrument to accurately assess adolescents for co-occurring conditions should be adolescent-specific and developmentally appropriate and should obtain a continuous measure of symptomatology to provide indications of severity. The instrument should also demonstrate strong psychometric properties across a wide range of mental health problems, including substance use disorders. In addition, it should be able to provide a foundation for diagnostic documentation in accordance with current diagnostic criteria (APA, 1994; 2000). To date, we are not aware of an assessment instrument that has demonstrated all of these characteristics.

PADDI: STANDARDIZING CLINICAL DIAGNOSES

The Practical Adolescent Dual Diagnostic Interview (PADDI) was developed as a pragmatic clinical assessment tool to standardize diagnostic assessments of adolescents (Estroff & Hoffmann, 2001). Its structured questions are designed to collect information about specific symptoms and behaviors in an objective and value-neutral tone. It attempts neither to cover all possible diagnoses nor to probe every aspect of some of the covered conditions. Rather, it tries to address the more common symptoms and indications of problems in the context of an interview limited to approximately 30 to 45 minutes.

The PADDI has demonstrated its utility in clinical populations (Hoffmann et al., 2001) and in the initial assessment of adolescents in juvenile justice settings (Hoffmann et al., 2003). This chapter considers the presenting problems revealed by the PADDI for both males and females committed to two juvenile detention centers in Maine. These adolescents are expected to be under supervision for some time, so that proper care and case management are likely to be an ongoing concern for juvenile justice officials.

ADMINISTERING THE INTERVIEW; EVALUATING THE RESPONSES

Minimal Training Needed to Conduct Interview

The PADDI is a structured diagnostic interview that covers indications of prevalent mental health conditions and substance use disorders. It is designed explicitly for use with adolescents and is not an adaptation of an adult tool. The PADDI is structured for routine clinical administration and is facilitated by a detailed manual (Hoffmann & Estroff, 2001). Juvenile justice personnel, trained technicians, or behavioral health professionals can administer the interview.

Findings Must Be Interpreted by Professionals

Interpreting findings or making diagnostic determinations, however, requires a professional or team of professionals with appropriate training and expertise covering both mental health and substance use disorders. Professionals who lack expertise in both mental health and substance use disorders can gather pertinent information to aid in determining diagnoses within their areas of competence and in making focused and appropriate referrals to other professionals for those areas in which they might not practice. Juvenile justice staff can use the interview to gather sufficient information to inform referrals to professionals for further evaluation or services.

Comprehensive Series of Questions

The interview includes questions related to depressive and manic episodes, mixed states, psychosis, posttraumatic stress disorder (PTSD), panic attacks, generalized anxiety and phobias, obsessive-compulsive disorder, conduct and oppositional defiant disorders, and possible paranoid and dependent personality disorders in addition to substance use disorders. Questions about dangerousness to self and others, as well as victimization (physical, sexual, and emotional abuse) are also included. As mentioned, the design and branching allow the interview to be administered in a relatively short period of time, in 30 to 45 minutes, depending upon the extent of the problems reported.

STUDY PROCEDURES AND CHARACTERISTICS OF SAMPLE

For this study, we obtained anonymous data consisting of the item responses to the PADDI interviews conducted in routine assessments from the two detention centers in Maine. The organization providing the behavioral health coverage for the detention centers uses the PADDI as part of the standard clinical assessment. The staff removed names and unique identifiers from copies of the protocol for all consecutively admitted committed adolescents so that the data could be processed for statistical analyses of problem prevalences. These data and analyses facilitate administrative oversight of the services as well as comparisons of prevalences between the two facilities. They also provide the information for this report.

Age, Sex, and Ethnicity

Data from a total of 230 adolescents (199 males and 31 females) were analyzed. Ages ranged from 13 to 18, and the average age of the sample was 16.3 (S.D. = 1.10). Approximately 64% of the adolescents were between the ages of 16 and 17. The vast majority were Caucasian (88%), with Native Americans (5%) constituting the only minority ethnic group that numbered more than 10 cases. The remainder of the sample was from other ethnic groups or of mixed ethnicity.

Educational Achievement

Educational achievement appears low for a number of these adolescents. More than 75% were over the age of 15, but 38% had passed no higher than the eighth grade in school. Approximately 30% were at least one year behind the expected grade level for their age group. Although only 13% reported substantial reading difficulties, more than 50% had been in special classes for academic or behavioral problems.

Previous or Current Experience With Medication

A large number of the sample had been prescribed medication for either a medical or mental health condition. Almost two in five (37%) reported being on medications at the time of the interview, and an additional 23% reported receiving medications previously.

Offenses Committed

Nonviolent offenses were cited as the most frequent issue related to the admission (55%), followed by substance related issues (42%). Violent offenses were acknowledged by 27%. There were no significant differences between males and females for the prevalence of either violent or nonviolent offenses. A statistically significant differential for substance related offenses was noted, with males reporting more (44% vs. 23%) than females ($p < .05$).

ANALYZING THE RESPONSES

Item responses from the PADDI forms were entered and verified into Excel spread sheets and converted into SPSS (Statistical Packages for the Social Science) system files for analyses. Diagnostic algorithms were developed on scales related to conditions for which the PADDI captures sufficient information to suggest a specific diagnosis. However, the scales for symptoms of psychosis and generalized anxiety and phobias were not analyzed for placement into diagnostic groups because these scales serve more as screens than for providing diagnostic documentation. The algorithms placed individuals into one of five categories:

- No symptoms;
- Sub-diagnostic;
- Meets minimal criteria;
- Exceeds minimal criteria; and
- Far exceeds minimal criteria.

The "sub-diagnostic" category includes individuals who reported at least one positive response, but not enough other positive responses to meet the minimal indications for a diagnosis. Those in the "exceeds criteria" group report positive indications on at least one additional criterion beyond the minimum, and those in the "far exceeds criteria" group typically endorsed 70% or more of the possible criteria items. For substance use disorders, only substance dependence was considered, because it has been shown to be the most severe (Hoffmann et al., 2003) and chronic condition (Schuckit et al., 2001).

Table 2.1: Problem Prevalences by Gender

Problem Area	Females (N = 31)	Males (N = 199)
Physically abused	36%	30%
Sexually abused **	45%	11%
Emotionally abused *	52%	28%
Any prior suicide attempts	39%	24%
Multiple prior suicide attempts	26%	18%
Considered killing someone	13%	18%
Auditory plus other hallucinations**	23%	4%
Major depressive episodes**	64%	24%
Manic episodes	40%	19%
Panic attacks	13%	8%
PTSD	36%	15%
Conduct disorder	74%	83%
Oppositional defiant disorder	61%	51%
Substance dependence	69%	60%

Note: All prevalences exclude apparent substance-induced indications. * p < .01; ** p < .001.

FINDINGS

Many Juvenile Offenders Have Been Victims of Abuse

Table 2.1 presents general prevalence rates for various problem areas and disorders for male and female adolescents. Although these adolescents have committed offenses resulting in commitment to a juvenile detention center, many have been victims of various forms of abuse. Abuse categories as determined by the PADDI are very conservative and require substantial indications of maltreatment. Physical abuse is defined as being hit so hard as to result in marks or fear of the perpetrator or the need for medical attention in an emergency room. Sexual abuse is identified as unwanted physical contact or coercion to engage in sexual acts. Emotional abuse is defined as being persistently ridiculed or humiliated over a period of time. Given even these conservative definitions, however, almost 75% of the females and 45% of the males reported having been subjected to some form of abuse:

- *Emotional and Physical Abuse:* Emotional and physical abuses are the most common for both genders. The majority of females (52%) report emotional abuse, and 45% report sexual abuse. For males, physical and emotional abuses are reported by about 30% of the adolescents. The overall prevalences for emotional and sexual abuse are greater for females at statistically significant levels.

- *Sexual Abuse:* For both genders, sexual abuse is highly correlated with other forms of abuse. From 36% to 40% of all sexual abuse victims report all three forms of abuse regardless of gender. Fifty percent of females and 67% of males who were sexually abused also report other forms of abuse.

Diagnostic Findings

Suicidal Ideation and Self-Harm. Suicidal ideation and possible suicide risk appear to be of concern with a substantial minority of cases. Overall, 26% of females and 18% of males report a history of more than one suicide attempt or suicidal gesture. A substantial number have considered specific ways in which they might kill themselves, a finding that should increase concerns in this area.

Little Thought of Harming Others. Compared to a history or thoughts of self-harm, serious consideration of harming others appears to be considerably lower. Fewer than 20% of males and 15% of females acknowledged thoughts of serious harm to others. Positive responses to the question of harming others were positively related to confinement for a current violent offense, to acknowledging initiation of fights, or to having used a weapon in a fight.

Conduct Disorder and Substance Dependence Most Prevalent Conditions. Conduct disorder and substance dependence are the most prevalent of the behavioral health conditions found. However, it is probable that some behaviors associated with the substance dependence may account for a portion of the conduct disorder indications. For example, some theft or initiation of fights may be related to getting money for drugs or related to alcohol or other drug use.

Before considering some of the severity indications for these conditions, a discussion of the other mental health areas is appropriate. The indications for psychoses and for affective and anxiety disorders are of significance in that many of these conditions require medications for their proper treatment and management. Although some of these disorders could be substance induced, many are likely to exist as independent conditions that will contribute to relapse to substance misuse if left unaddressed.

Psychoses. Indications of psychosis are problematic to assess from responses to structured questions, because many of the indications of these disorders include observational information. However, acknowledgment of hallucinations does provide an indication that this area warrants further consideration. This is particularly true for auditory hallucinations in the absence of substance use or at times other than when the individual is drifting into or out of sleep. Of the females, 23% reported both auditory and other hallucinations in the absence of obvious associations with substances or sleep. In contrast, only 4% of males report such events.

Affective Disorders. Another area of major concern involves affective disorders, because these, too, may require medications for proper management. When only a constellation of symptoms consistent with major depressive episodes is considered and obvious substance-induced behaviors are excluded, a majority (64%) of females and almost a fourth (24%) of males report such a constellation of symptoms (see Table 2.1). Manic episodes are also relatively common. Of particular concern are those cases in which both manic and major depressive episodes are reported by the same individual.

This would suggest the possibility of an emerging bipolar disorder in which the individual alternated between depressive and manic episodes. Of the entire cohort, 13% reported both depressive and manic episodes at symptom levels that meet the requirements of the *Diagnostic and Statistical Manual of Mental Disorders-IV* (DSM-IV; APA, 1994; 2000) for both types of events. This suggests that as many as one in ten of the adolescents committed to the detention centers may require mood stabilizing medications if the bipolar condition is confirmed by a psychiatrist.

Anxiety Disorders. Anxiety disorders may take many forms. The PADDI conducts only a brief screening for generalized anxiety, phobias, and obsessive-compulsive indications, although it covers panic attacks and PTSD in greater depth. Females are more likely than males to reach levels of symptoms for concern for the various anxiety indicators, but PTSD shows the greatest and most significant differential. This is not surprising in light of the rate of abuse reported by females. That is, given the levels of physical, emotional, and sexual abuse among females, it is expected that a significant number of them would report experiencing indications of PTSD.

Positive Diagnoses Suggested for 92% of Respondents

If only the more prevalent conditions are considered (conduct disorder, major depressive episodes, mania, PTSD, and substance dependence), 92% of the consecutive admissions report positive indications suggesting a possible diagnosis. Even when the thresholds for each disorder are increased so as to exceed the criteria of the DSM-IV and to decrease the likelihood that the findings might include a false-positive indication, 77% of the respondents still emerge as positive for one or more conditions. Using the more stringent requirements, almost 25% of the consecutive admissions are positive for only one condition, but most (52%) are positive for multiple conditions. Not surprisingly, the combination of substance dependence and conduct disorder is one of the most prevalent (10% of the cohort). These estimates do not include possible psychoses or anxiety disorders, which might increase the proportion with diagnosable conditions.

EXTENT AND PATTERNS OF SYMPTOMS INDICATE SEVERITY

For those who meet diagnostic criteria, the extent of symptoms and the pattern formed by the number of diagnostic indications provide an indication of both the severity and validity for several of the diagnostic formulations. The distributions for the number of positive diagnostic indicators are in Table 2.2. The diagnosis and severity of seven conditions presented in the table suggest that for most conditions, the PADDI items make a relatively clear distinction for those who meet diagnostic criteria. The "major depression," "manic episodes," and "substance dependence" categories produce profiles that cause the majority of cases to fall into either the category for no symptoms or the category indicating extensive symptomatology. Conditions such as conduct disorder, however, appear to be dimensional rather than categorical, with more of a normal distribution of problems.

Several points should be made concerning the categorizations in the tables. First, those individuals denying any substance use in the previous 12 months were placed in

Table 2.2: Symptom Profiles for Selected Conditions (N = 230)

Condition (Lifetime)	No Symptoms	Sub-Diagnostic	Minimal Criteria	Exceeds Criteria	Far Exceeds Criteria
Major depressive episode*	62%	8%	9%	10%	11%
Manic episode*	73%	5%	5%	8%	9%
Panic attacks**	81%	10%	3%	5%	1%
Posttraumatic stress disorder	64%	18%	1%	10%	7%
Conduct disorder	3%	15%	35%	27%	20%
Oppositional defiant disorder	12%	35%	14%	7%	32%
Substance dependence†	19%	20%	5%	8%	48%

* Substance-induced conditions are counted as sub-diagnostic.

** Only symptoms for attacks in the previous 12 months are considered.

† Diagnosis considered only if use is reported in the past 12 months; substance abuse cases are counted in the sub-diagnostic category.

the "no symptom" category for substance dependence, and those meeting abuse criteria only were placed in the "sub-diagnostic" category. Second, oppositional defiant disorder is subsumed by conduct disorder in the DSM-IV criteria. That is, if the individual meets both criteria, only the conduct disorder diagnosis is given. This is ignored in the present analyses to illustrate the profile of symptoms for both sets of items. Finally, conditions such as depression and mania that might be substance induced are placed in the "sub-diagnostic" category if the individual reports the symptoms to be associated only with substance use.

As can be seen in Table 2.2, a number of conditions present relatively clear syndromes, whereas others do not. That is, for clear syndromes, those who meet at least the minimum number of diagnostic criteria fall into the moderate to high range of symptoms, whereas those who do not meet criteria usually have no symptoms. This produces a bimodal result in which the majority of individuals fall either into the "no symptom" category or into the moderate or above range of symptoms, and the fewest cases are seen in the "sub-diagnostic" or "minimal criteria" categories. When a clear syndrome is not found, one sees more of a normal distribution, in which most cases are in the "sub-diagnostic" to "minimal criteria" categories.

In the case of substance dependence, the majority of cases (67%) fall into either the no symptom or highest symptom groups. When the abuse-only cases are considered as sub-diagnostic, 20% of the cases are seen in this category, and only 5% of the cases fall into the dependence with minimal criteria met. In contrast, 48% of the entire sample fall into the high symptom category, meaning that they are positive for at least five of the seven dependence criteria. Similarly, major depressive and manic episodes appear to be categorically distributed. Most cases meeting at least minimal diagnostic criteria tend to be in the higher ranges of symptoms, whereas the majority of cases are in the "no symptom" category.

Conduct disorder symptoms appear to be distributed much differently. In this sample, conduct symptoms are approaching a normal distribution, with most cases falling into the "minimal criteria" category and only a few cases into the "no symptom" and highest symptom categories.

These general distributions are similar for both males and females, although the exact percentages vary between the genders. Because the number of females is relatively small, no specific comparisons are made at this time.

ISSUES FOR FURTHER DISCUSSION

The results of this study suggest a number of issues that merit specific discussion. First, the distribution of scores across the five diagnostic categories (no symptoms, sub-diagnostic, meets minimal criteria, exceeds minimal criteria, and far exceeds minimal criteria) is such that, for most problem areas, a clear distinction exists between those individuals meeting DSM-IV diagnostic criteria and those who do not. This finding supports the utility of the PADDI as a screening instrument that can discriminate between adolescents who are likely to meet diagnostic criteria for a given disorder and those who are not.

Second, the prevalence and extent of problems noted in these consecutive admissions to juvenile centers suggest that routine screening and assessment should be conducted for both mental health and substance use disorders. Many of these conditions require professional services and, in some cases, medications for proper care and case management.

LIMITATIONS OF OUR ANALYSIS

Our analysis, as most, has some limitations. First, these data from the PADDI cannot definitively rule out the possibility of substance-induced mental health problems, and the instrument is not intended to make comprehensive diagnostic determinations on all conditions. Thus, although a positive indication on the PADDI may be a clear signal of a need for further evaluation, it is, by itself, not a diagnosis. Additionally, concurrent validity cannot be assumed, because no data exist to corroborate how often the PADDI's impressions are confirmed with a firm clinical diagnosis. Second, the participants in this study may not be representative of all potential users of the instrument. The study is based on consecutive admissions from facilities in a state where the number of minority individuals is small. This precludes generalizing to inner city populations, where minority subcultures might influence reporting

Despite the limitations, this analysis does provide basic statistical information on the PADDI and support for its use. Information on the severity of diagnostic conditions and forms of victimization also support the argument for routine assessment of youths entering juvenile facilities. Further research with other populations and concurrent validity measures will provide more definitive perspectives on this critical area.

About the Authors

Norman G. Hoffmann, Ph.D., is president of Evince Clinical Assessments and clinical associate professor of community health at Brown University. Ana M. Abrantes, Ph.D., is a postdoctoral fellow at Brown University's Center for Alcohol and Addiction Studies. Ronald Anton, LCPC, LADC, MAC, is director of juvenile justice and community programs at Day One for Youth and Families, in Maine. Professor Hoffmann can be reached at by email at evinceassessment@aol.com.

References

American Psychiatric Association (APA, 1994). *Diagnostic and Statistical Manual of Mental Disorders.* 4th ed.. Washington, DC: Author.

American Psychiatric Association. (APA, 2000). *Diagnostic and Statistical Manual of Mental Disorders, Fourth Edition, Text Revision.* Washington, DC: Author.

Dennis, M.L., Titus, J.C., White, M., Unsicker, J., & Hodgkins, D. (2002). *Global Appraisal of Individual Needs (GAIN) Administration Guide for the GAIN and Related Measures.* Bloomington, IL. Retrieved from http//www.chestnut.org/li/gain/gadm1299.pdf.

Estroff, T.W., & Hoffmann, N.G. (2001). *PADDI: Practical Adolescent Dual Diagnosis Interview.* Smithfield, RI: Evince Clinical Assessments.

Grella, C.E., Hser, Y., Joshi, V., & Rounds-Bryant, J. (2001). Drug treatment outcomes for adolescents with comorbid mental and substance use disorders. *Journal of Nervous and Mental Disease, 189,* 384–392.

Grilo, C.M., Becker, D.F., Walker, M.L., Levy, K.N., Edell, W.S., & McGlashan, T.H. (1995). Psychiatric comorbidity in adolescent inpatients with substance use disorder. *Journal of the American Academy of Child and Adolescent Psychiatry, 34,* 1085–1091.

Hoffmann, N. G., Abrantes, A.M., & Anton, R. (2003). Criminals, troubled youth, or a bit of both. *Addiction Professional, 1(4),* 12–16.

Hoffmann, N.G., DeHart, S.S., & Campbell, T.C. (2002). Dependence: Whether a disorder or a disease; it is not a "concept." *Journal of Chemical Dependency Treatment, 8(1),* 45–56.

Hoffmann, N.G., Estroff, T.W., & Wallace, S.D. (2001). Co-occurring disorders among adolescent treatment populations. *The Dual Network, 2(1),* 10–13.

Lehman, A.F., Myers, C.P., Corty, E., & Thompson, J.W. (1994). Prevalence and patterns of "dual diagnosis" among psychiatric inpatients. *Comprehensive Psychiatry, 35,* 106–112.

Myers, M.G., Stewart, D.G., & Brown, S.A. (1998). Progression from conduct disorder to antisocial personality disorder following treatment for adolescent substance abuse. *American Journal of Psychiatry, 155,* 479–485.

Schuckit, M.A., Smith, T.L., Danko, G.P., Bucholz, K.K., Reich, T., & Bierut, L. (2001). Five-year clinical course associated with DSM-IV alcohol abuse or dependence in a large group of men and women. *American Journal of Psychiatry, 158(7),* 1084–1090.

Shaffer, D., Fisher, P., Dulcan, M. K., Davies, M., Piacentini, J., Schwab-Stone, M.E., Lahey, B.B., Bourdon, K., Jensen, P.S., Bird, H.R., Canino, G., & Regier, D.A. (1996). The NIMH Diagnostic Interview Schedule for Children Version 2.3 (DISC-2.3): Description, acceptability, prevalence rates, and performance in the MECA study. *Journal of the American Academy of Child and Adolescent Psychiatry, 35(7),* 867–877.

Stowell, R.J., & Estroff, T.W. (1992). Psychiatric disorders in substance-abusing adolescent inpatients: A pilot study. *Journal of the American Academy of Child and Adolescent Psychiatry, 31,* 1036–1040.

Chapter 3

Predicting Violent Behavior in Adolescent Cannabis Users: The GAIN-CVI

by Michelle White, M.S., Rod Funk, B.S.,
William White, M.A., and Michael Dennis, Ph.D.

Introduction 3-1
Moffitt's Taxonomy 3-2
    Life-Course Persistent Offenders 3-2
    Adolescence-Limited Offenders 3-2
The Cannabis Youth Treatment Study 3-3
The GAIN Crime and Violence Index 3-3
Testing Moffitt's Theory of Criminal/Violent Behavior 3-3
Changes in Social Environment Related to Changes in Illegal Activity 3-5
Results and Limitations of GAIN-CVI 3-5
    Good Predictive Validity 3-5
    Limited by Self-Report and Failure to Isolate Effects of
      Drug Use Changes 3-5
    Considerable Promise for Predicting Future Crime/Violence 3-6
    Findings Suggest Hope for Maturing Out 3-6
    A Need to Expand the Scope of Treatment Evaluation 3-6
Conclusion: A Dynamic Explanation of Criminal Careers 3-6

INTRODUCTION

Substance use and interpersonal violence have exerted a profound impact on American society and the criminal justice system in recent decades. From 1989 to 1998, the number of adolescent drug law violations rose 148%, and the adolescent violent crime index rose 33% (Stahl, 2001; Loeber & Farrington, 1998). In spite of their frequent co-occurrence, considerable controversy exists on the exact relationship between substance use and criminality and interpersonal violence. Simplistic models of causation (substance use causes crime/violence) and intervention (treat the sub-

This chapter originally appeared in Offender Substance Abuse Report, *Vol. 3, No. 5, September/October 2003.*

stance use and the risk of crime/violence will desist or dramatically diminish) have given way to more complex models that posit multiple etiological pathways to criminality and violence, multiple clinical subpopulations of offenders, and integrated models of intervention into substance use, crime, and violence (White et al., 1999). The latter models have the advantage of being able to concentrate criminal justice resources on those substance-involved offenders who are at highest risk for reoffending and for involvement in future violent acts.

This article tests Moffitt's (1993) taxonomy of antisocial behavior by examining the factors that are correlated with criminal activity and violence among adolescents entering substance abuse treatment. Using data from the Center for Substance Abuse Treatment's (CSAT) Cannabis Youth Treatment (CYT) Study, it predicts the way in which changes in social environment affect criminality and violence over time in a population of 600 adolescents treated for cannabis abuse or cannabis dependency.

MOFFITT'S TAXONOMY

Criminologists have long debated the question of whether criminality is a sustained character trait or a behavior mediated by developmental maturity and social and economic circumstances (Sampson & Laub, 1992). In a seminal article published in 1993, Moffitt argued a two-type taxonomy of antisocial behavior.

Life-Course Persistent Offenders

Individuals in Moffitt's first group, the life-course persistent offenders (about 5% to 8% of adolescent offenders), begin offending early in life, commit many crimes, engage in violence, suffer from clear psychopathology (e.g., conduct disorder), continue to commit criminal/violent acts through much of their adulthood, and are less likely to respond to interventions and improvements in their social environment and life circumstances.

Adolescence-Limited Offenders

Individuals in Moffitt's second group, the adolescence-limited offenders, begin offending later in adolescence, engage in crimes of a petty or non-violent nature (e.g., vandalism, property offenses), evidence no underlying psychopathology, and decrease or stop their illegal behaviors as they mature and experience improvements in their environment and life circumstances.

The crime and violence of the life-course persistent offenders are, in Moffitt's model, rooted in deeply embedded personality traits, neuropsychological deficits (e.g., verbal skills), and a poor home environment in childhood, whereas similar behaviors by the adolescence-limited offenders are a developmentally restricted phenomenon often associated with negative peer influences and often resolved through a process of "maturing out." Moffitt's work is part of a larger theoretical field (the life-course perspective) that, when applied to the problem of criminal behavior, seeks to explain why criminality is intractable in some individuals but developmentally transient in others (Thornberry & Krohn, 2003).

THE CANNABIS YOUTH TREATMENT STUDY

The Cannabis Youth Treatment (CYT) study was a multi-site randomized field experiment of 600 adolescents (ages 12 to 18) who met the diagnostic criteria of the *Diagnostic and Statistical Manual-IV* (DSM-IV) for cannabis abuse or dependence and who met the American Society of Addiction Medicine's placement criteria for brief (one to three months) outpatient care. Each of the 600 study participants was randomly assigned to one of five outpatient therapies. Data collected through the course of the study included self-report and collateral reports using the Global Appraisal of Individual Needs (GAIN; Dennis, 1999; Dennis et al., 2002). Quarterly post-treatment follow-up interviews using the GAIN were conducted for 12 months with high (94% to 98%) completion rates, and follow-up was extended to 30 months post-intake (90% completion rate) by way of the CSAT-funded Persistent Effects of Treatment Study of Adolescents (PETS-A; see *www.chestnut.org/li/cyt/* for more information on the CYT study and *http://www.samhsa.gov/pets/* for more information on the PETS-A study).

The ability to administer the GAIN at intake and at sustained follow-up sessions with 600 adolescents provided an opportunity to test Moffitt's taxonomy of antisocial behavior using a population of cannabis-involved adolescents. More specifically, it was possible to test whether the crime and violence index (CVI) subscale scores on the GAIN at intake could be used to predict criminal and violent behavior 30 months later and to examine how changes in social environment altered the risk of future criminality and violence.

THE GAIN CRIME AND VIOLENCE INDEX

The CVI includes subscales that measure propensity for oral violence, physical violence, property crime, interpersonal crime, and drug crime. The number of affirmative responses in the CVI placed each youth in the sample in a low, moderate, or high reoffending risk category. Shifting from low to moderate was associated with increased oral violence, property crime, and drug related crime. Shifting from moderate to high was associated with increased oral violence, property crime, and drug crime, as well as more physical violence and interpersonal crime. There were no significant differences in the demographic (age, ethnicity) characteristics of the three groups. The low CVI group experienced less environmental risk and fewer problems (including substance use and HIV risk behaviors). The rates of childhood victimization, early alcohol and marijuana use, psychopathology (including mental distress, traumatic distress, ADHD, and conduct disorder), sexual activity, and unprotected sex all increased from low to moderate to high. There were no significant differences among the three groups in the number of prior substance abuse treatment episodes.

TESTING MOFFITT'S THEORY OF CRIMINAL/VIOLENT BEHAVIOR

Intake scores on the CVI scale of the GAIN were used to classify an adolescent's risk into three groups. Twenty-nine percent of adolescents were considered low risk (0 to 2 symptoms/types of crime in the past 12 months); 30% were considered moderate

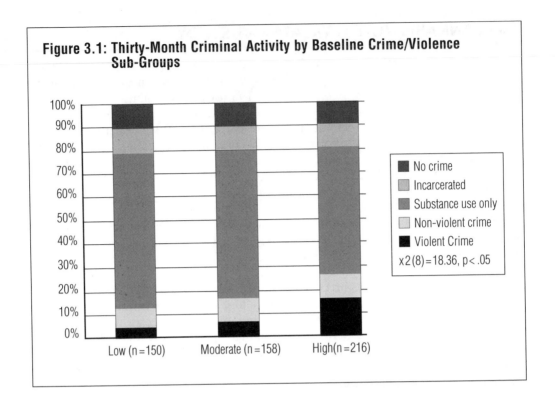

Figure 3.1: Thirty-Month Criminal Activity by Baseline Crime/Violence Sub-Groups

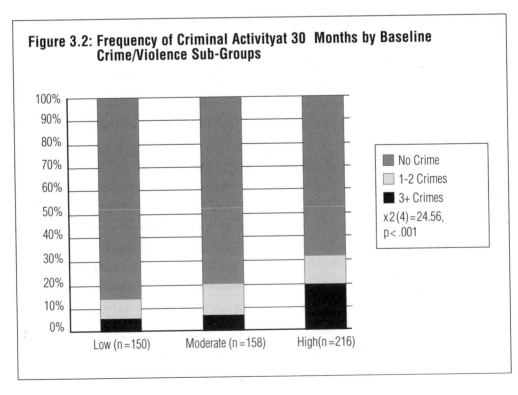

Figure 3.2: Frequency of Criminal Activity at 30 Months by Baseline Crime/Violence Sub-Groups

risk (3 to 6 symptoms/types of crime); and 41% were considered high-risk (7 to 31 symptoms/types of crime). As shown in Figure 3.1, these intake risk groups were associated with higher rates of violent crime 30 months later. Those in the high risk group (16%) were significantly ($p < .05$) more likely to have committed violent crimes than those in the moderate (6%; Odds ratio = 2.8) or low (4%; Odds ratio = 4.5) groups. As shown in Figure 3.2, those in the high-risk group (19%) were also significantly ($p < .05$) more likely to have committed three or more crimes than were those in the moderate (6%; Odds ratio = 3.4) or low (5%; Odds ratio = 4.0) groups.

CHANGES IN SOCIAL ENVIRONMENT RELATED TO CHANGES IN ILLEGAL ACTIVITY

As expected, changes in the social environment were significantly related to changes in illegal activity. Although both the moderate- and high-risk groups significantly reduced their illegal activities between intake and 30 months post-intake, increased social risk (i.e., greater involvement in crime- and violence-related relationships) was associated with continued illegal activity among members of both groups. Reduced social risk over time was associated with reductions in illegal activity. These findings support Moffitt's theory of an adolescence-limited offender population (our moderate CVI group) that matures out of criminal activity as its members experience positive changes in their social environment. As for Moffitt's life-course persistent offender group (our high CVI group), the findings were mixed. The high CVI group was, as expected, at much higher risk than the moderate group for continued involvement, despite changes in social risk, but, unexpectedly in Moffitt's taxonomy, this group's members also reduced their illegal activity when there were positive changes in their social environment (see *http://www.chestnut.org/LI/Posters/index .html* for more information).

RESULTS AND LIMITATIONS OF GAIN-CVI

Good Predictive Validity

The GAIN's CVI scale appears to have good predictive validity. It's subgroup typology is consistent with the two groups hypothesized by Moffitt in terms of types of crime, correlates, and long-term course of behaviors. We found mixed evidence for the sensitivity of the high CVI group to changes in social environment, suggesting that the life course of this group may be more sensitive to changes in social environment than previous models would seem to suggest.

Limited by Self-Report and Failure to Isolate Effects of Drug Use Changes

The most significant limitation of this study is that it is based on self-report data. A second limitation is that the study traces the effects of substance abuse treatment but does not isolate the relationship between post-treatment changes in patterns of drug use and their impact on crime and violence. For example, is the maturing out among the adolescence-limited offender group dependent upon reduction or cessation of substance use, or does it occur independent of the pattern of substance use? Future studies would be strengthened by testing the GAIN-CVI using PATH analysis to examine the extent to which changes in recovery, environment risk, social risk, substance use frequency, and illegal activity predict changes in violent crime using the GAIN's CVI scale and additional scales from the GAIN. It would also be helpful to examine the roles played by traumagenic factors related to the experience of victimization and by the age of onset of antisocial behavior in the developmental trajectory of crime and violence across these various subpopulations (Hawke et al., 2003). Are subjects with high traumatic victimization overrepresented in the high GAIN-CVI group? Another focus for future research is to investigate whether those in the high CVI group who abort their criminal careers are distinguished by later ages of onset of substance use and antisocial behavior than are those who continue such careers.

Considerable Promise for Predicting Future Crime/Violence

These preliminary analyses suggest that the GAIN's CVI scale has considerable promise for identifying those offenders posing the highest risk for future criminal violence. Instruments like the GAIN can help separate offenders who will benefit from brief intervention and minimal monitoring from those requiring treatment and sustained monitoring of much higher intensity. Use of the GAIN-CVI could help steward valuable but overstretched criminal justice resources.

Findings Suggest Hope for Maturing Out

Our findings also offer hope that some members of Moffitt's life-course persistent offender group (our high CVI group) may be able to escape from the career criminal pathway if they receive early treatment, sustained monitoring, and linkage to pro-recovery social networks. The potential impact of enriching the social environment in an effort to prevent the development of criminal careers needs further testing, given estimates that preventing a high-risk youth from a criminal career saves approximately $1.5 million in long-term social costs (Cohen, 1998).

A Need to Expand the Scope of Treatment Evaluation

This study points to the need to evaluate substance abuse treatment on broader dimensions of its impact on crime and violence. Such investigations will likely lead to greater cross-fertilization of the best ideas and intervention technologies of addiction treatment and the criminal justice system. It is important to know how addiction treatment affects post-treatment criminality and violence and, if such effects are positive, what elements within addiction treatment mediate these changes.

CONCLUSION: A DYNAMIC EXPLANATION OF CRIMINAL CAREERS

The life-course perspective that we tested can tell us a great deal about criminal careers. Continuity and change across longitudinal studies of delinquency suggest a dynamic explanation of criminal careers—one revealing multiple risk and protective factors that exert their influence during key developmental windows of vulnerability and opportunity (Thornberry & Krohn, 2003). Preventing and containing criminal careers to protect public safety will benefit from new generations of sophisticated screening and assessment instruments that identify these evolving risk and protective factors. The GAIN-CVI offers one such tool that can help allocate criminal justice resources to maximize intervention effects and protect public safety.

About the Authors

All of the authors are with Chestnut Health Systems in Bloomington, Illinois. Michelle White, M.S., is a research projects manager; Rod Funk, B.S., is a research associate; William White, M.A., is the senior research coordinator; and Michael Dennis, Ph.D., is a senior research psychologist. Michelle White may be contacted by email at mwhite@chestnut.org. Preparation of this article was supported by funding from the Center for Substance Abuse Treatment (CSAT) through the Persistent Effects of Treatment Study (PETS contract no. 270-97-7011, as well as grants no. TI11317, TI11320, TI11321, TI11323, and TI11324, TI11422, TI11433, and TI11432). The content of this article does not necessarily reflect the views or policies of the government.

References

Cohen, M.A. (1998). The monetary value of saving a high-risk youth. *Journal of Quantitative Criminology, 14*, 5–33.

Dennis, M.L. (1999). *Global Appraisal of Individual Needs (GAIN): Administration guide for the GAIN and related measures (Version 1299).* Bloomington, IL: Lighthouse; available at *www.chestnut.org/li/gain.*

Dennis, M.L., Titus, J.C., Diamond, G., Donaldson, J., Godley, S.H., Tims, F., Webb, C., Kaminer, Y., Babor, T., Roebuck, C., Godley, M.D., Hamilton, N., Liddle, H., Scott, C.K., & the CYT Steering Committee. (2002). The Cannabis Youth Treatment (CYT) experiment: Rationale, study design, and analysis plan. *Addiction, 97*, 16–34.

Hawke, J.M., Jainchill, N., & DeLeon, G. (2003). Post-treatment victimization and violence among high risk adolescents following residential drug treatment. *Journal of Child Maltreatment, 8*, 58–72.

Loeber, R., & Farrington, D.P. (Eds). (1998). *Serious & Violent Juvenile Offenders: Risk Factors and Successful Interventions.* Thousand Oaks, CA: Sage.

Moffitt, T.E. (1993). Adolescence-limited and life-course-persistent antisocial behavior: A developmental taxonomy. *Psychological Review, 100(4)*, 674–701.

Sampson, R.J., & Laub, J.H. (1992). Crime and deviance in the life course. *Annual Review of Sociology, 18*, 63–84.

Stahl, A.L. (2001). Delinquency cases in juvenile courts, 1998. *OJJDP Fact Sheet*, August 2001, No. 31. Washington, DC: U.S. Department of Justice, Office of Juvenile Justice and Delinquency Prevention.

Thornberry, T.P. & Krohn, M.D. (Eds.). (2003). *Taking Stock of Delinquency: An Overview of Findings from Contemporary Longitudinal Studies.* New York: Kluwer.

White, H.R., Loeber, R, Stouthamer-Loeber, M., and Farrington, D.P. (1999). Developmental associations between substance use and violence. *Development and Psychopathology, 11*, 785–803.

Chapter 4

Using ADAM Data to Identify Intrajurisdictional Drug Use Patterns

by George S. Yacoubian, Jr., Ph.D., Ronald J. Peters, Jr., Dr.PH, and Regina J. Johnson, Dr.PH

Introduction 4-1
Major Drug-Use Prevalence Data Collection Efforts 4-2
Drawbacks of Aggregate-Level Surveillance 4-2
Study Spotlights Houston's ADAM Data 4-3
    Sample 4-3
    Self-Report Data 4-3
    Urine Screen 4-4
    Data Limitations 4-4
Data Analysis and Findings 4-4
    Descriptives 4-4
    Drug Prevalence 4-4
    Research Caveats 4-6
Benefits of Disaggregating Drug Data 4-7

INTRODUCTION

Computer-generated mapping has been used for more than a decade (Olligschlaeger, 1998). In 1987, for example, the Illinois Criminal Justice Information Authority (ICJIA) developed a crime analysis and mapping program to detect community crime patterns with time and geographic data. Areas ranging from city blocks to entire cities could be analyzed, with spot maps being produced immediately after incident data had been entered into a computer (Webster & Connors, 1987). Similarly, the Microcomputer Assisted Patrol Analysis and Deployment System (MAPADS) was developed by the Chicago Police Department to generate graphs, maps, and reports using crime data from both police and citizens (Casey & Buslik,

This chapter originally appeared in Offender Substance Abuse Report, *Vol. 2, No. 1, January/February 2002.*

1988). In addition to offense-based systems, mapping technology can also identify high drug-using subsections of a particular geographic area.

MAJOR DRUG-USE PREVALENCE DATA COLLECTION EFFORTS

The federal government funds several major data collection efforts to measure the prevalence of drug use within the United States, each of which gathers information on a specific population. The National Household Survey on Drug Abuse (NHSDA), for example, generates self-report drug use estimates for household members ages 12 and older in the contiguous United States (Substance Abuse and Mental Health Services Administration (SAMHSA), 2000a). The Drug Abuse Warning Network (DAWN) includes an annual national probability survey of drug-related problems treated in hospital emergency departments and drug-related death data collected from a nonrandom sample of medical examiners and coroners' offices (SAMHSA, 2000b). Information from more than 500 hospitals and 175 medical examiner/coroner offices in 21 metropolitan areas[1] across the United States is collected annually. The Monitoring the Future (MTF) project began in 1975 as a way to study the drug-using beliefs, attitudes, and behaviors of high school students across the United States. Today, the program surveys approximately 50,000 eighth, tenth, and twelfth grade students annually (Johnston et al., 2000). Finally, the Arrestee Drug Abuse Monitoring (ADAM) Program collects self-report survey data and urine specimens from arrestees in 34 cities across the United States (National Institute of Justice (NIJ), 2000).

DRAWBACKS OF AGGREGATE-LEVEL SURVEILLANCE

Findings from these surveillance systems are reported at the aggregate level. The ADAM annual report, for example, delineates drug positive rates by sex, age, race, and offense category for each of its sites (NIJ, 2000). These findings, while valuable, do not distinguish the various sub-regions that fall within ADAM's county-based framework. Such disaggregation is critical if drug use issues are to be explored *intra*-jurisdictionally.

A number of previous studies have explored drug-related processes at the micro-level (Petronis & Anthony, 2000; Olligschlaeger, 1998; McCoy & McBride, 1979). McCoy and McBride (1979), for example, examined the neighborhood distribution of criminals, drug users, and drug-using criminals in Dade County, Florida. The sample was comprised of 3,446 drug-using criminals, 1,440 non-drug-using criminals, and 3,936 non-criminal drug users. The authors illustrated that drug use and criminal activity were concentrated within a number of sections of Dade County. Most recently, Petronis and Anthony (2000) investigated whether perceived risk of cocaine use and experience with cocaine clustered within neighborhoods and cities in the United States. Six years of data—1979, 1988, and 1990-1993—were utilized from the NHSDA. Logistic regression determined that (1) perceived risk of cocaine use and experience with cocaine clustered within neighborhoods, and (2) neighborhood concentration increased as involvement with cocaine increased (Petronis & Anthony, 2000).

The lack of literature on the disaggregation of drug use data suggests that these patterns may be uniform intrajurisdictionally. Without empirical support, however, this assumption is an unsubstantiated one. If drug-positive rates vary across cities, as the ADAM data reveal (NIJ, 2000), it is reasonable to believe that differences may exist intrajurisdictionally.

STUDY SPOTLIGHTS HOUSTON'S ADAM DATA

The ADAM Program—formerly the Drug Use Forecasting (DUF) Program—was established by NIJ in 1987 (Yacoubian, 2000). The six primary goals of ADAM are: identifying the levels of drug use among arrestees; tracking changing drug-use patterns; determining what drugs are being used in specific jurisdictions; alerting local officials to trends in drug use and the availability of new drugs; providing data to help understand the drug-crime connection; and serving as a research platform upon which a wide variety of drug-related initiatives can be based (Yacoubian, 2000). In the current study, we hypothesized that drug use data from Houston's ADAM Program, once disaggregated, would yield evidence of differences *within* the city of Houston. With this preliminary hypothesis, our project used the methods described below.

Sample

During each day of data collection, trained research interviewers obtained a list of arrestees who had been in custody for no more than 48 hours (Yacoubian, 2000). Following the collection of background information from official records, arrestees were approached by an interviewer and introduced to the protocol. The introduction included the purpose and sponsorship of the study and informed consent provisions. Arrestees were assured that their participation was voluntary, that their responses were confidential, and that they would receive a candy bar as an incentive for participation (Yacoubian, 2000). Subjects were interviewed out of hearing range of police or other arrestees. Interviews lasted approximately 15 minutes, with the length contingent upon the amount and degree of drug use disclosure. During the four quarters of data collection in 1999, 2,683 arrestees were approached for interviewing in Houston. Of these, 71% completed the interview. Of those who completed the interview, 83% provided a urine specimen. The analysis for the current study is based on those 1,572 arrestees who completed the interview *and* provided a urine specimen.

Self-Report Data

Arrestees were first asked several demographic questions, including education level, marital and employment status, and income level. Participants were then asked to report whether they had *ever* used a number of specific drugs. For those drugs the arrestees reported having ever tried, they were asked to indicate age of first use, whether they had used the drug within the past 12 months, the number of times used within the past 30 days, and whether they had used the drug within the past three days. Participants who admitted to drug use were also asked if they considered themselves drug-dependent, and whether they were under the influence or in need of drugs at the time of arrest. Several questions also focused on treatment—whether the person had ever received treatment, was currently in a treatment program, or perceived a need for treatment.

Urine Screen

In addition to the self-report data, a urine specimen was collected to measure recent drug use. The Enzyme Multiplied Immunoassay Test (EMIT) screened for 10 drugs: amphetamines, barbiturates (e.g., Phenobarbital), benzodiazepines (e.g., Valium and Xanax), marijuana, metabolite (crack and powder) cocaine, methadone, methaqualone (Quaaludes), opiates, phencyclidine (PCP), and propoxyphene (Darvon) (NIJ, 2000). All amphetamine-positives were confirmed by gas chromatography/mass spectrometry (GC/MS) to eliminate any look-alike medications.

Data Limitations

It is important to preface the current study with an understanding of the general limitation of the ADAM data. The sample of arrestees was not probability-based. That is, while the data were collected using a systematic protocol (e.g., within 48 hours of arrest), cases were not selected with a known probability. It is difficult to know, therefore, how completely they represent the population of the facility. Interviewers attempted to approach all arrestees who had been in custody for 48 hours or less. Unfortunately, however, losses from early releases, transfers, and limitations of interview time prohibited a census. With this methodological caution, data analysis and findings are presented below.

DATA ANALYSIS AND FINDINGS

Data analysis was completed in three phases. First, descriptive statistics were computed. Second, drug-positive rates were calculated for the entire city of Houston. Third, marijuana-, cocaine-, benzodiazepine-, and opiate-positive rates were disaggregated by Houston's 20 police districts.

Descriptives

The sample is comprised of 1,572 adult arrestees surveyed in Houston in 1999. A majority of the arrestees were male (57%) and black (56%). Sixty percent were between the ages of 21 and 39, and 62% were either high school graduates or had earned their General Equivalency Diplomas (GEDs). Forty-one percent were charged with a miscellaneous offense (e.g., loitering or prostitution), while 24% were charged with a drug- or alcohol-related offense.

Drug Prevalence

The most prevalent drug in Houston was marijuana (31%), followed by cocaine (30%). After marijuana and cocaine, there was a sharp decline in drug-positive rates. Benzodiazepines were third (8%), followed by opiates (7%), phencyclidine (PCP) (5%), and barbiturates (4%). Methadone, propoxyphene, amphetamine, and methamphetamine were all detected in less than 1% of the arrestees. No methaqualone-positives were detected.

Table 4.1: Houston Drug-Positive Data, Disaggregated by Police District[*]

	Marijuana	Cocaine	Benzodiazepines	Opiates
NORTH DIVISION				
District 3	35%	40%	4%	9%
District 6	32%	31%	10%	8%
% Positive of All Districts	15%	16%	12%	18%
NORTHEAST DIVISION				
District 7	36%	42%	15%	7%
District 8	41%	30%	6%	5%
District 9	30%	35%	5%	8%
District 24	25%	0%	0%	0%
% Positive of All Districts	16%	17%	14%	14%
CLEAR LAKE DIVISION				
District 12	17%	23%	7%	0%
% Positive of All Districts	1%	2%	2%	0%
SOUTHEAST DIVISION				
District 13	22%	36%	8%	8%
District 14	39%	28%	8%	9%
% Positive of All Districts	16%	14%	15%	19%
SOUTHWEST DIVISION				
District 15	30%	34%	5%	3%
District 16	40%	20%	5%	5%
District 17	39%	28%	15%	11%
% Positive of All Districts	13%	12%	15%	13%

(continued on next page)

Drug-positive rates for marijuana, cocaine, benzodiazepines, and opiates were then disaggregated by Houston's 20 police districts. As shown in Table 4.1, two findings emerge:

1. Marijuana is the most prevalent drug in 11 of the districts, while cocaine is the most prevalent drug in the other nine districts. This distribution suggests comparable problems with two major drugs of abuse.

2. A majority of drug-positives were concentrated in a small number of police divisions.

Fifty-one percent of the cocaine-positives were found in the North, Northeast, and Central police divisions, 47% of the marijuana-positives were found in the

Table 4.1: (contined)

	Marijuana	Cocaine	Benzodiazepines	Opiates
WESTSIDE DIVISION				
District 18	37%	19%	9%	8%
District 19	38%	21%	10%	10%
District 20	21%	14%	4%	4%
% Positive of All Districts	13%	7%	12%	13%
NORTHWEST DIVISION				
District 4	64%	21%	7%	7%
District 5	19%	15%	6%	2%
% Positive of All Districts	4%	2%	3%	2%
CENTRAL DIVISION				
District 1	24%	30%	9%	4%
District 2	24%	29%	6%	5%
% Positive of All Districts	14%	18%	16%	13%
SOUTH CENTRAL DIVISION				
District 10	26%	44%	8%	5%
% Positive of All Districts	5%	8%	6%	4%

* Excluding Hobby and Bush Intercontinental Airport Police Districts

North, Northeast, and Southeast divisions, 46% of the benzodiazepine-positives were found in the Southeast, Southwest, and Central divisions, and 51% percent of the opiate-positives were found in the North, Northeast, and Southeast divisions. While no one police division was represented in all four of the drug categories, the North, Northeast, and Southeast divisions were identified in three. Taken collectively, these data suggest that, first, different sub-regions within the city of Houston had problems with different types of drugs, and second, the drug problem was heavily concentrated in three police divisions—North, Northeast, and Southeast.

Research Caveats

Three methodological limitations should be noted. First, ADAM collects data solely for arrestees. The findings presented here may not necessarily parallel those from other deviant populations (e.g., probationers) or non-deviant populations. We therefore recommend replicating the current study beyond arrestees to assess the broader implications of these findings. Second, the data utilized in the current study were cross-sectional in nature. That is, one single time frame—calendar year 1999—

was identified for analysis. It is possible, however, that such geographic patterns fluctuate over time. We recommend that longitudinal analyses be conducted to identify any temporal geographic variations. Third, given the differences identified by police division, it is reasonable to suspect that differences would exist had the data been disaggregated further. Police districts are comprised of smaller units of analysis (e.g., neighborhoods and streets). While the ADAM collection system does not collect such micro-level data, future efforts might consider collecting cross-street data to identify more specific drug-using locales.

BENEFITS OF DISAGGREGATING DRUG DATA

In the current study, we examined drug-positive rates from 1,572 arrestees surveyed in 1999 through Houston's ADAM Program. As we hypothesized, the drug use data, once disaggregated, yielded evidence of differences within the city of Houston—notable intrajurisdictional drug-using differences were identified for marijuana, cocaine, benzodiazepines, and opiates.

Extending traditional mapping uses, we have illustrated that the disaggregation of drug use data could be valuable for law enforcement and drug treatment initiatives. The demand for "geographically enabled" data grows as businesses, governments, and organizations begin to appreciate the value of spatial analyses. Mapping by characteristics of suspects, such as drug users, can be useful and easily accomplished. Mapping can help break down jurisdictional law enforcement and access-to-treatment barriers due to its ability to provide visual evidence that criminal groups or individuals move across boundaries at will, perhaps exploiting the lack of communication between agencies.

There are a number of potential uses for such disaggregated data:

- First, the mapping of intrajurisdictional drug use can be used to address specific issues and needs of patrol officers, investigators, and police managers. The geographic drug-using differences identified in the Houston area can be used by the various police districts, precincts, and patrol areas to target specific areas in need of concentrated crime prevention and intervention.

- Second, geographic profiling of drug users could be used as the basis for several investigative strategies, including suspect and tip prioritization, patrol saturation and surveillance, canvasses and searches, and zip code prioritization.

- Third, plotting locations of substance use, employment, and other social services, and relating them to the most recent addresses of probationers or parolees, can be used for improving drug-treatment initiatives.

We hope that drug use mapping continues to grow as a popular tool for law enforcement and other jurisdictional personnel affected by decisionmaking within the criminal justice, public health, and social services systems.

About the Authors

George S. Yacoubian, Jr., Ph.D., is Associate Research Scientist at the Pacific Institute for Research and Evaluation (PIRE), Calverton, M.D. Ronald J. Peters, Jr., Dr.PH, is a research fellow at the University of Texas Health Science Center at Houston, School of Public Health. Regina J. Johnson, Dr. PH, is an assistant professor in the College of Nursing at Texas Austin University. Dr. Yacoubian may be contacted by email at gyacoubiang@pireorg.

Endnotes

[1] Atlanta, Baltimore, Boston, Buffalo, Chicago, Dallas, Denver, Detroit, Los Angeles, Miami, Minneapolis, New Orleans, New York, Newark, Philadelphia, Phoenix, San Diego, San Francisco, Seattle, St. Louis, and Washington, DC.

[2] Albuquerque, Anchorage, Atlanta, Birmingham, Chicago, Cleveland, Dallas, Denver, Des Moines, Detroit, Fort Lauderdale, Houston, Indianapolis, Laredo, Las Vegas, Los Angeles, Manhattan, Miami, Minneapolis, New Orleans, Oklahoma City, Omaha, Philadelphia, Phoenix, Portland, Sacramento, Salt Lake City, San Antonio, San Diego, San Jose, Seattle, Spokane, Tucson, and Washington, DC.

References

Casey, M., & Buslik, M. (1988). *Computerized decision support: Innovative policing in Chicago.* Chicago, IL: Police Department.

Johnston, L.D., O'Malley, P.M., & Bachman, J.G. (2000). *National survey results on drug use from the Monitoring the Future Study, 1975-1999* (Volumes I and II). Rockville, MD: U.S. Department of Health and Human Services.

Latkin, C., Glass, G.E., & Duncan, T. (1998). Using geographic information systems to assess spatial patterns of drug use, selection bias and attrition among a sample of injection drug users. *Drug and Alcohol Dependence, 50,* 167-175.

McCoy, C.B., & McBride, D.C. (1979). *Neighborhood distribution of criminal and drug using behavior.* Miami, FL: University of Miami.

National Institute of Justice. (2000). *1999 Arrestee Drug Abuse Monitoring (ADAM) annual report.* Washington, DC: U.S. Department of Justice.

Olligschlaeger, A.M. (1998). Artificial neural networks and crime mapping. In D. Weisburd & T. McEwen (Eds.), *Crime mapping and crime prevention* (pp. 313-347). Monsey, NY: Criminal Justice Press.

Petronis, K.R., &. Anthony, J.C. (2000). Perceived risk of cocaine use and experience with cocaine: Do they cluster within US neighborhoods and cities? *Drug and Alcohol Dependence, 57,* 183-192.

Substance Abuse and Mental Health Services Administration. (2000b). *Mid-Year 2000 preliminary emergency department data from the Drug Abuse Warning Network.* Rockville, MD: U.S. Department of Health and Human Services.

Substance Abuse and Mental Health Services Administration. (2000a). *Summary of findings from the National Household Survey on Drug Abuse.* Rockville, MD: U.S. Department of Health and Human Services.

Webster, B., & Connors, E.F. (1993). Police methods for identifying community problems. *American Journal of Police, 12(1),* 75-101.

Yacoubian, G. (2000). Assessing ADAM's domain: Past, present, and future. *Contemporary Drug Problems, 27,* 121-135.

Chapter 5

The California Department of Corrections Drug Reduction Strategy Project

by Michael Campos, M.S., Michael L. Prendergast, Ph.D., William Evans, B.A., and Julian Martinez, B.A.

Introduction 5-1
DRS Program Design 5-2
      Four Program Sites 5-2
      Two Phases 5-2
DRS Implementation 5-3
      Phase I: Weekly Urinalysis 5-3
      Phase II: Random Urinalysis Plus Other Drug Detection Measures 5-4
Project Results 5-4
      Random Urinalysis Testing 5-4
      Other Drug Detection Measures 5-5
Drug Interdiction Efforts 5-5
      K-9 Teams 5-5
      Drug-Detection Equipment 5-6
Conclusions 5-6

INTRODUCTION

The Violent Crime Control and Law Enforcement Act of 1994 (Crime Act; Pub.L. 103–322) created the Violent Offender Incarceration and Truth-in-Sentencing (VOI/TIS) Incentive Program, which provided funds for prison bed expansion and stipulated that up to 10% of VOI/TIS funds could be used for inmate drug testing. In January of 1999, the Clinton administration proposed a zero-tolerance policy for drugs in prison in response to the high rates of substance use in state and federal prisons, the link between drugs and crime, and the extensive criminal records of many drug offenders (Office of the Press Secretary, 1999). Further, experts have advocated drug control measures in prisons to help foster abstinence and facilitate substance use

This chapter originally appeared in Offender Substance Abuse Report, *Vol. 3, No. 4, July/August 2003.*

behavior change (e.g., Belenko et al., 1998).

Inmate welfare, staff security, public-health concerns, and the need for recovery-friendly prison environments have been cited as supporting efforts to control in-prison substance use. Rates of violence are elevated among those with alcohol or drug use disorders (Regier et al., 1990), and prison staff report that substance trade strengthens prison-based gangs, leads to inmate-on-inmate violence, and increases inmate-on-staff attacks. In addition, drug-using inmates face an increased risk of HIV and hepatitis-C (HCV) infection (Dolan et al., 1996; Shewan et al., 1994), and infected formerly incarcerated IV drug users may transmit HIV and HCV to the general population through post-release behavior, even if an inmate knows that she/he is HIV- or HCV-positive (O'Mahony & Barry, 1992).

In light of these risks, several state departments of corrections have implemented random urine testing to reduce the use of drugs in prison. Pennsylvania's drug reduction strategy, put in place between 1995 and 1998, and consisting of drug-detecting K-9 teams, drug detection equipment, and random urinalysis and hair testing, led to a 41% reduction in drug finds from cell searches, a 57% decrease in assaults on staff, a 70% decrease in inmate-on-inmate assaults, a 35% decrease in weapons seized during searches, and a reduction in estimates of overall inmate drug use from 10.6% to 2.3% as measured by hair testing (Feucht & Keyser, 1999). In Wisconsin, random urinalysis testing, coupled with progressive sanctioning for positive tests, reduced an initial 26.9% positive drug urinalysis rate to 5% (Vigdal & Stadler, 1989).

Beginning in 1999, the California Department of Corrections (CDOC) conducted a pilot program in four CDOC institutions that included random urinalysis drug testing and systematic drug interdiction practices. This chapter describes the CDOC's Drug Reduction Strategy (DRS) and evaluates the strategy's effectiveness as measured by the rate of drug-positive inmate urinalyses (UAs) and substance interdiction.

DRS PROGRAM DESIGN

Four Program Sites

The four program sites, selected for similar institutional demographics and geographic diversity, were Ironwood State Prison (ISP), California State Prison, Solano (SOL), Pleasant Valley State Prison (PVSP), and Mule Creek State Prison (MCSP). Three sites were designated as intervention sites (ISP, SOL, and PVSP), and one site was designated as a comparison site (MCSP). For the duration of the program, all inmates not in administrative segregation, hospitalized, or in a substance abuse treatment program at the three intervention sites were eligible for random selection for drug testing each week.

Two Phases

The pilot program was divided into two phases (see Table 5.1). During Phase I, weekly urine testing of 150 randomly selected eligible general population inmates augmented existing urine testing procedures (e.g., for cause, after family visits, etc.). Phase II involved systematic use of drug-detecting K-9 teams and drug-detecting equipment and included use of new and preexisting department resources. At all of the sites, stan-

Table 5.1: DRS Design Including Additional Drug Control Interventions for Phase I and Phase II by Institution

	──────────── INTERVENTIONS ────────────				
	Baseline Point Prevalence (Sep-99)	Phase I (Oct-99 to Mar-00)	Phase I Point Prevalence (Apr-00)	Phase II (May-00 to Dec-00)	Phase II Point Prevalence (Jan-01)
ISP	20% random sample	Random UA testing 150 per week	20% random sample	Random UA testing 150 per week + Ion-scanning drug detection equipment	20% random sample
SOL	20% random sample	Random UA testing 150 per week	20% random sample	Random UA testing 150 per week + Drug-detecting canine teams	20% random sample
PVSP	20% random sample	Random UA testing 150 per week	20% random sample	Random UA testing 150 per week	20% random sample
MCSP	20% random sample	Standard procedures(no random testing)	20% random sample	Standard procedures (no random testing)	20% random sample

Note: UA = Urinalysis; ISP = Ironwood State Prison; SOL = California State Prison, Solano; PVSP = Pleasant Valley State Prison; MCSP = Mule Creek State Prison.

dard drug interdiction efforts (e.g., monitoring of phone calls, use of cameras in visiting areas, tracking of inmate trust accounts, for-cause urine testing) continued. Point-prevalence estimates of substance use, derived from a random sample of 20% of the eligible inmate population at each of the four participating institutions, were gathered at Baseline, at the completion of Phase I, and at the completion of Phase II.

DRS IMPLEMENTATION

Phase I: Weekly Urinalysis

Weekly urine testing commenced in October 1999 at ISP, PVSP, and SOL and continued through March 2000. MCSP used its standard drug interdiction procedures, which included camera monitoring of inmate visits, intelligence gathering from inmate phone conversations, inspection of mail and quarterly packages, and for-cause urine testing. At ISP, SOL, and PVSP, approximately 150 inmates were selected weekly from the eligible inmate population and required to provide a urine sample. The UA battery included assays for alcohol, amphetamine, methamphetamine, benzoylecgonine (a metabolite of cocaine), morphine, phencyclidine, barbiturates, and THC metabolites (the psychoactive ingredient in marijuana). Sanctions were enforced for the provision of a drug-positive urine sample and could include:

- Nonrestorable credit forfeiture of up to 150 days;

- Mandatory random drug testing of up to four tests per month for one year;

- Suspension of privileges for up to 90 days;

- Confinement for up to 10 days;

- Endorsement to a substance abuse program such as Alcoholics Anonymous, Narcotics Anonymous, or other substance abuse education.

Graduated penalties were applied for first, second, and third offenses. Similar sanctions were enforced for refusing to provide a sample, and a refusal was considered equivalent to a positive test.

Phase II: Random Urinalysis Plus Other Drug Detection Measures

Implementation of the Phase II interventions began on May 1, 2000, and concluded on December 31, 2000. Phase II involved continued random urinalysis testing at the three intervention sites; however, additional measures were implemented at ISP (drug-detecting equipment) and SOL (drug-detecting K-9 teams). If either the equipment or the K-9 teams detected the presence of drugs in an area linked to specific inmates, for-cause urine tests were required of those inmates. Standard drug interdiction procedures continued at MCSP.

PROJECT RESULTS

Random Urinalysis Testing

Table 5.2 presents the point-prevalence estimates derived from the 20% random samples collected at Baseline, at the completion of Phase I, and at the completion of Phase II. Baseline estimates of inmate substance use ranged from a high of 10.02% at SOL to a low of 4.30% at PVSP. The Baseline point-prevalence estimate for inmate substance use at the comparison site (MCSP) was 7.73%. The composite Baseline point-prevalence estimate for the three intervention sites (7.89%) was comparable to that of the comparison site.

At the completion of Phase I, the point-prevalence estimates ranged from a high of 3.77% at SOL to a low of 1.64% at ISP. The composite Phase I point-prevalence estimate for the three intervention sites (3.04%) was notably lower than the point-prevalence estimate at the comparison site (7.52%). Thus, the introduction of systematic random urine testing appears to have reduced estimated substance use levels at the three Phase I intervention institutions relative to the comparison site.

Table 5.2: A Comparison of Baseline, Phase I, and Phase II Point-Prevalence Estimates at All Four Participating Institutions

	Baseline September 1999	Phase I April 2000	Phase II January 2001
	% Positive + Refusals		
Intervention sites			
ISP	8.90%	1.64%	0.33%
SOL	10.02%	3.77%	2.94%
Phase II intervention site	—	—	1.76%
PVSP	4.30%	3.70%	1.14%
All intervention sites	7.89%	3.04%	—
Comparison site			
MCSP	7.73%	7.52%	4.35%
Overall	7.85%	3.83%	2.11%

Other Drug Detection Measures

Because Phase II involved the addition of drug-detecting K-9 teams at SOL and the use of ion-scanning drug detection devices at ISP, the appropriate comparison for these sites appears to be PVSP. PVSP employed systematic random urine testing during Phase II but did not employ additional drug interdiction measures. The Phase II point-prevalence estimate for ISP was 0.33%, whereas at SOL it was 2.94%. At PVSP, the Phase II point-prevalence estimate was 1.14%. Interpretation of these data is complicated by the fact that SOL is located near an urban center, is a larger institution than ISP and PVSP, and had higher estimated levels of substance use at Baseline and Phase I. In general, the Phase II data do not appear to support an effect for the addition of systematic interdiction measures of the same magnitude as that observed for the introduction of systematic random urine testing during Phase I.

DRUG INTERDICTION EFFORTS

K-9 Teams

In determining the application of the K-9 drug detection teams, CDOC was required to comply with stipulations set forth by the California Court of Appeals in *Estes v. Rowland,* 14 Cal. App. 4th 508 (1993). This decision stemmed from an inmate complaint for relief originally filed in 1986 regarding CDOC use of K-9 teams to search visitors' vehicles for narcotics and other contraband. SOL did not conduct K-9 searches of visitor vehicles; however, the *Estes* decision affected the DRS, because it precluded the use of K-9s to search visitors. In fact, CDOC was required to keep the canines at least 20 feet away from visitors at all times. In order to maintain consistency of application for the two drug interdiction methods employed during Phase II of the project, drug detection equipment was therefore not used on visitors.

K-9 teams proved relatively more successful than the drug detection equipment in making drug discoveries. Over the course of the Phase II intervention, just over one in 10 canine alerts resulted in a drug find (actual substance or remnant materials with trace amounts). In addition, for-cause urine sample collection resulted in a 23% positive-plus-refusal rate. This high rate suggests that the canines were likely alerting to the trace odor of contraband substances, even if no drugs were present at the time of the search. K-9 teams conducted a number of cell searches in conjunction with intelligence reports early in the Phase II intervention and were successful in locating contraband. This suggests the utility of coordinating the application of K-9 units with intelligence gathered from other sources.

Drug-Detection Equipment

A single drug find resulted from the use of the drug detection equipment during the DRS. Drug detection equipment, as employed in the DRS project, was not used to screen visitors, although using the equipment to screen visitors would be more consistent with the implementation of drug detection equipment of this type in other states (e.g., Pennsylvania). Given the decision to limit the use of drug detection equipment to inmates and prison locations, some of the capabilities of the equipment may not have been realized. A second issue related to the application of the drug detection equipment was the relative infrequency with which it was employed to conduct cell searches. This was reportedly due to a preference for standard investigative methods over the use of sophisticated drug detection equipment. The K-9 teams had success locating contraband substances early in Phase II as a result of cell searches. Perhaps drug-detection equipment could have been employed successfully in this manner as well.

CONCLUSIONS

Consistent with the findings from Pennsylvania (Feucht & Keyser, 1999) and Wisconsin (Vigdal & Stadler, 1989), the introduction of systematic random urine testing resulted in reductions in estimated inmate substance use levels. The introduction of drug interdiction measures at two of the program sites did not yield significant increases in drug finds, in contrast to the results obtained for drug interdiction interventions employed in the Pennsylvania program. The results from the CDOC DRS evaluation appear to support the utility of systematic random urine testing as a means of reducing estimated substance use levels. However, one issue raised during the course of the study that bears on its findings was that a significant minority of inmates (13.28%) provided urine samples that may have been adulterated with water. The Pennsylvania and Wisconsin studies did not address the issue of potential urine sample tampering. The CDOC DRS results emphasize the need for careful sample collection oversight as part of any systematic random urine testing program in order to maintain the deterrent power of the intervention.

About the Authors

Michael Campos, M.S., is a staff research associate and Michael L. Prendergast, Ph.D., is a research historian at the UCLA Integrated Substance Abuse Programs. William Evans, B.A., is a correctional counselor at the Office of Substance Abuse Programs in the California Department of Corrections. Julian Martinez, B.A., is a correctional lieutenant at the Institutional Services Unit in the California Department of Corrections. The DRS project was funded by the California Department of Corrections, Contract No: C99.216.

References

Belenko, S., Peugh, J., Califano, J.A., Usdansky, M., & Foster, S.E. (1998, October). Substance abuse and the prison population: A three-year study by Columbia University reveals widespread substance abuse among the offender population. *Corrections Today*, 82–89, 154.

Dolan, K., Wodak, A., Hall, W., Gaughwin, M., & Rae, F. (1996). HIV risk behaviors of IDUs before, during, and after imprisonment in New South Wales. *Addiction Research, 4*, 151–160.

Feucht, T.E., & Keyser, A. (1999). Reducing drug use in prisons: Pennsylvania's approach. *National Institute of Justice Journal (October)*, 10–15.

Office of the Press Secretary. (1999, January 5). President Clinton announces initiatives to break the cycle of crime and drugs. *White House Press Release.*

O'Mahony, P., & Barry, M. (1992). HIV risk of transmission behavior amongst HIV-infected prisoners and its correlates. *British Journal of Addiction, 87*, 1555–1560.

Regier, D.A., Farmer, M.E., Rae, D.S., Locke, B.Z., Keith, S.J., Judd, L.L., & Goodwin, F.K. (1990). Comorbidity of mental disorders with alcohol and other drug abuse: Results from the Epidemiologic Catchment Area (ECA) study. *Journal of the American Medical Association, 264*, 2511–2518.

Shewan, D., Gemmel, M., & Davies, J.B. (1994). Prison as a modifier of drug using behavior. *Addiction Research, 2*, 203–215.

Vigdal, G.L., & Stadler, D.W. (1989, June). Controlling inmate drug use: Cut consumption by reducing demand. *Corrections Today*, 96–97.

Part 2

Alternatives to Incarceration

Psychologists Nathanial Pallone and James Hennessy (2003) identify a number of recent treatment initiatives in the United States, which they refer to collectively as the "Rebellion of 2000." These initiatives include California's Proposition 36, in which adults convicted of nonviolent drug possession offenses are given the option of participating in drug treatment in the community in lieu of incarceration; the governor of New York's plan to reduce the length of prison terms for non-violent drug offenders, replace mandatory imprisonment with treatment, and grant judges greater discretion in handling drug-related charges; and the burgeoning drug court movement, in which drug-abusing offenders who complete a prescribed period of community-based treatment (in addition to satisfying other conditions) can have their conviction records expunged.

Part 2 summarizes recent evaluation research concerning alternatives to incarceration for substance-abusing offenders, including formal diversion and treatment for probationers generally.

In Chapter 6, Gregory Falkin, Sheila Strauss, and Timothy Bohen describe the results of their large-scale evaluation of the New York City Department of Probation's drug treatment initiative. Theirs is one of only a handful of studies in the literature that provides specific points of consideration to assist in client-treatment matching, providing strong support for the need for conducting standardized assessments and expanding the array of community treatment options.

Chapter 7, by Edward Latessa and Jennifer Pealer, addresses the critical issue of program quality and integrity, comparing changes over time in community- and corrections-based residential substance abuse treatment (RSAT) facilities for offenders. Using the Correctional Program Assessment Inventory (CPAI) developed by Gendreau and Andrews (1992), the authors found that 50%-60% of both the community- and prison-based RSAT programs needed improvement at the time of the baseline administration, with the most problematic domains being the lack of client-treatment matching, over-reliance on use of shaming techniques, and insufficient attention to aftercare.

Chapters 8 and 9, by Steven Belenko and Caroline Cooper, respectively, provide overviews of the drug court movement since its inception in Dade County, Florida, more than two decades ago. As drug courts quickly ascended into prominence (their number now well exceeds 1,000), Belenko has documented their progress as well as their common implementation issues. Though his analysis shows some support for drug courts with regard to recidivism outcomes, he offers a number of important caveats and recommendations regarding the need to increase client retention, expand ancillary services, and target higher-risk offenders. Cooper summarizes some of the most current descriptive information available on the drug court movement, using data compiled by the Office for Justice Programs Drug Court Clearinghouse and Technical

Assistance Project at American University, which is arguably the most comprehensive source on drug courts. Her statistics characterizing the drug court process and client supervision compellingly demonstrate the enhanced relationship between the court and treatment systems, relative to standard community treatment referrals, and the impact of this close affiliation on client accountability.

Chapter 10, by Christina Pratt, describes New York's innovative Family Drug Treatment Courts, created to assist in processing the growing number of child abuse and neglect cases involving substance-abusing parents (constituting three-fourths of these cases). The purpose of this approach is to enhance the therapeutic discretion of the presiding judge so that parental substance abuse can be addressed in a manner similar to that of drug courts, reacting to relapses with graduated sanctions rather than incarceration.

Chapter 11, by Douglas Marlowe, David Festinger, and Patricia Lee, moves beyond the issue of drug courts' effectiveness, generally, to explore the impact of the frequency of judicial status hearings for drug court clients (bi-weekly versus as-needed). Although the authors report no overall effect for status hearings, they do report a significant interaction between frequency of status hearings and prior drug treatment, with previously treated offenders providing significantly more drug-free urines in the bi-weekly than in the as-needed judicial status hearing condition.

References

Pallone, N.J., & Hennessy, J.J. (2003). To punish or to treat: Substance abuse within the context of oscillating attitudes toward correctional rehabilitation. *Journal of Offender Rehabilitation*, 37, 1-25.

Chapter 6

Matching Drug-Involved Probationers to Appropriate Drug Interventions: A Strategy for Reducing Recidivism

by Gregory P. Falkin, Ph.D., Sheila Strauss, Ph.D., and Timothy Bohen

Introduction 6-1
New York City's Anti-Drug Initiative 6-2
    Systematic Approach to Meeting Probationers' Drug
      Treatment Needs an Effective Initiative 6-2
    Client Population Served 6-3
Actual Treatment Participation Lower Than Hoped 6-3
    Most Cases Referred Through CPU Either Were Not
      Admitted or Dropped Out 6-3
    Client Participation in Outpatient Drug Treatment Low 6-4
Despite Low Participation, Treated Clients Less Likely to Recidivate 6-4
Deciding Which Treatment to Offer 6-6
    Out-Patient Treatment Not Always Appropriate 6-6
    Urine Monitoring of Probationers 6-6
    When Out-Patient Treatment Is Indicated 6-7
Policy Implications and Recommendations 6-8

INTRODUCTION

In the past decade, probation and parole agencies in New York, California, Arizona, and other jurisdictions have expanded their efforts to divert drug offenders into community-based treatment. While research generally finds that drug treatment is effective in reducing recidivism among clients mandated to treatment (Anglin & Hser,

This chapter originally appeared in Offender Substance Abuse Report, *Vol. 1, No. 6, November/December 2001.*

1990; Hubbard et al., 1997), this chapter provides insight into why it is important to match clients to appropriate forms of treatment and how this might be done. The basic point is that when appropriate interventions (e.g., residential drug treatment, outpatient treatment, urine monitoring) are used with drug-involved clients, scarce treatment resources are utilized more effectively in reducing recidivism and relapse. We demonstrate the value of matching clients to appropriate treatment interventions by presenting findings from an evaluation study of the New York City Department of Probation's (DOP) drug treatment initiative. The main findings follow a brief description of the City's drug treatment initiative as it existed in the early 1990s.

NEW YORK CITY'S ANTI-DRUG INITIATIVE

In 1991, the DOP created a Central Placement Unit (CPU), which contracted with nine outpatient drug-free treatment programs for 965 treatment slots intended primarily for cocaine-abusing probationers. (The contracts are funded 75% by the New York State Office of Alcohol and Substance Abuse Services and 25% by the City of New York.) Probationers who were identified as users of drugs other than cocaine could also be referred to treatment through the CPU. Referrals were made through the CPU, which operated like an 800-number reservation service that probation officers could call to place clients in contracting treatment programs. The recommended course of outpatient treatment was 12 months. The average cost per slot (person-year of treatment) was about $4,000. The contracts paid programs for providing the DOP with intake, treatment services, and information about clients. The treatment programs were to notify probation officers (within 24 hours) whether the probationers showed up for intake, and provide the CPU with a four-page intake report, monthly progress reports, timely communication if the probationer failed to appear for treatment and was at risk of being discharged from the program, and a termination form.

DOP policy required that all high-risk (Levels 1 and 2) probationers receive mandatory drug testing within the first two weeks of entering supervision, regardless of whether they were known to have a history of drug use. Probationers who initially tested negative then received a second urinalysis within another two weeks. Probationers who tested positive on either of these tests were supposed to be referred to drug abuse treatment, as were clients who had a court-ordered drug condition. The contracting drug treatment programs were required to conduct regular urinalysis and report the results to the CPU. The DOP, however, could not require non-contracting treatment programs to test clients regularly or to report the test results to probation officers (though some programs did this voluntarily).

Systematic Approach to Meeting Probationers' Drug Treatment Needs an Effective Initiative

We found, overall, that New York City's drug treatment initiative was effective. Outpatient drug treatment was related to significant reductions in recidivism among clients referred through the CPU, with the greatest reduction in recidivism among those CPU clients who were appropriately matched to outpatient drug treatment on the basis of the severity of their drug use.

The CPU was an important innovation, improving on the past practice that required probation officers to individually identify non-contracting programs that would admit each of their clients who needed treatment. The CPU represented a systematic approach, enabling probation officers to refer clients to a variety of contracting outpatient drug treatment programs with guaranteed slots. The CPU was a significant effort in that the DOP contracted for enough slots to make nearly 2,000 referrals for probationers who needed drug treatment.

Even though the CPU contracts served many drug-involved probationers, however, slots were available for only a portion of the clients who needed drug treatment. Conservatively, we estimate that at least one-quarter of the roughly 20,000 new probationers who entered the system in the year the CPU was established were in need of drug treatment (Falkin et al., 1994). Less than one-tenth ($n=1,860$) of the individuals sentenced to probation during the first year of the CPU's operation (September 1991 to September 1992) were referred to contracting outpatient drug treatment programs one or more times as of December 31, 1993. It is not known how many probationers were referred to non-contracting (residential, drug-free outpatient, or methadone) treatment programs.

Client Population Served

The implementation of the CPU was a success in the final analysis, although it appears that many of the cases referred to treatment may not have been high-risk, cocaine-dependent probationers, as originally intended. More than half of the individuals referred to treatment did not abuse cocaine; about one-third of the CPU referrals were classified as relatively low risk (Levels 3 and 4). Although intended primarily for high-risk, cocaine-dependent probationers, the fact that the CPU actually served many probationers with less serious problems should not be viewed as problematic. As discussed below, referring more cocaine-abusers to outpatient treatment may not have been appropriate and likely would have reduced the effectiveness of the effort.

ACTUAL TREATMENT PARTICIPATION LOWER THAN HOPED

Most Cases Referred Through CPU Either Were Not Admitted or Dropped Out

Over one-third of the cases referred through the CPU failed to appear at treatment intake or were not admitted. Among those who were admitted, the length of time that clients stayed in treatment varied considerably, with retention rates being fairly low overall. Retention in treatment ranged from one day to about two years, with only 5% of probationers remaining for the recommended one year of drug treatment. About one-fifth of the probationers dropped out of treatment in less than two weeks and slightly more than half dropped out within three months. The mean retention rate, which was a little over three months, is comparable with retention rates for other outpatient samples serving mandated clients (Hubbard et al., 1984).

Client Participation in Outpatient Drug Treatment Low

On average clients attended only about half (about 1.5 hours per week) of their scheduled treatment sessions. Although the length of time clients stay in treatment provides one indication of the amount of treatment that clients receive, actual attendance at treatment sessions can vary considerably among outpatient clients. Client participation in treatment, as measured in terms of the number of hours of treatment and the number of sessions that clients attended, was also very low. Probationers participated in only about half of their scheduled treatment activities. On average, all the clients were scheduled for an equivalent of about 10 hours of treatment per month, but they attended an average of only about five hours per month. Clients who stayed in treatment longer were also more actively involved in the treatment process in that they attended more hours/sessions on a weekly basis than those who dropped out earlier. Though clients who stayed in treatment longer (e.g., over three months) actually received substantially larger "doses" of treatment than dropouts, the "dosages" were still fairly low.

DESPITE LOW PARTICIPATION, TREATED CLIENTS LESS LIKELY TO RECIDIVATE

Contracting with outpatient drug treatment programs was nonetheless an effective strategy for reducing recidivism. Three-quarters of the probationers admitted to contracting programs had fewer arrests during the year following discharge from treatment than during the year before they were sentenced to probation. Furthermore, as Figure 6.1 shows, clients who were admitted to treatment had significantly lower rearrest rates than those who were referred but not admitted. Although 44% of all the CPU cases referred to treatment between September 1991 and December 1993 were rearrested by December 31, 1994, 53% of those who were not admitted to treatment were rearrested. In contrast, only 39% percent of those who were actually admitted to treatment were rearrested. (These percentages include all rearrests from the time of sentencing until the cutoff period for the recidivism data.)

Clients who stayed in outpatient drug treatment longer than 90 days were significantly less likely to recidivate than those who dropped out earlier. Figure 6.1 also shows that the percent of probationers who were rearrested declined as the length of stay in treatment increased. Clients who stayed in treatment longer were significantly less likely to recidivate than those who dropped out earlier. Among those who were admitted to treatment, about half of the probationers who stayed in treatment less than three months were rearrested, while only about one quarter of those who stayed longer were rearrested.

Because the time period for measuring rearrest varied among the cases, we standardized rearrest as an annual rearrest rate. We were not able to control for time at risk because we did not have data to determine when probationers were in jail. Figure 6.2 shows the annual rearrest rate for all crimes in relation to the number of days of treatment. (The rearrest rate for clients not admitted to treatment is measured from the date of sentence to probation; the rearrest rate for the other group is measured from the date of admission to drug treatment.) The pattern for the rearrest rate is similar to the one for the percent of clients rearrested. The annual rearrest rate for the

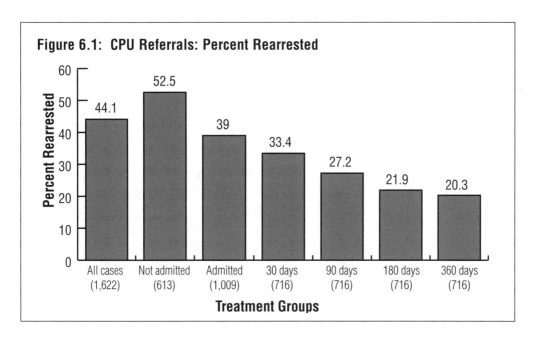

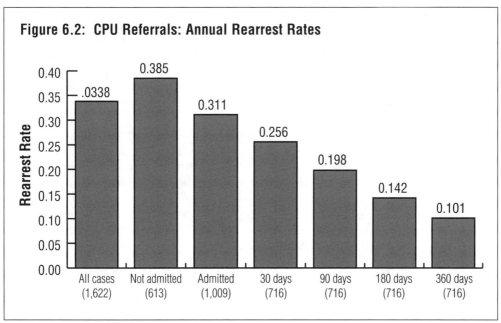

group not admitted to treatment is .385, which is significantly higher than the .311 rearrest rate for the group admitted to treatment. The rearrest rate declines significantly as the length of time clients stay in treatment increases. The clients who stayed in treatment for more than 90 days had a significantly lower rearrest rate (mean = .198) than those who were either not admitted or dropped out earlier. Among those who were arrested, the group that stayed in treatment longer also was significantly less likely to be incarcerated, and the length of time until rearrest was significantly longer. Multiple regression analyses also showed that clients who stayed in drug treatment for more than 90 days had significantly fewer rearrests for drug offenses and violent crimes.

Other factors were also examined for their possible influence on rearrest rates. The number of prior arrests was the strongest predictor of rearrest. Younger probationers and men were found to have higher rearrest rates than older probationers and women. The age at first arrest was positively related to rearrest. Controlling for these variables, time in treatment was still a significant predictor of rearrest. Clients who stayed in treatment 90 days or more had significantly lower rearrest rates than others, including probationers who were referred but not admitted and those who dropped out within 90 days after being admitted to treatment.

DECIDING WHICH TREATMENT TO OFFER

Out-Patient Treatment Not Always Appropriate

Outpatient drug treatment was not appropriate for about one-quarter of the probationers referred through the CPU because the severity of their drug use indicated a need for residential treatment. Using the Offender Profile Index (OPI), a clinical assessment instrument designed for matching criminal justice clients to various drug interventions (Inciardi et al., 1993), we separated the CPU clients into three groups according to their probable need for different interventions: residential drug treatment, outpatient drug treatment, or urine monitoring only. The OPI assigns clients to these various interventions on the basis of the severity of their drug use and a number of aspects of their "stakes in conformity" (which includes criminal involvement, drug treatment histories, job situation, education, and housing).

Data from the pre-sentence investigation drug assessment was mapped retrospectively onto the OPI drug use severity index in order to determine the severity of each probationer's drug use and to provide an appropriate treatment recommendation. About one-quarter of the CPU cases had severe drug problems (i.e., injecting drugs or using cocaine, crack, or amphetamines once a week or more). According to the OPI criteria, these cases required long- or short-term residential treatment.

Urine Monitoring of Probationers

Two-thirds of the sample needed only urine monitoring on the basis of their OPI assessment of drug use and social conformity. This group was comprised of individuals who either used only alcohol or marijuana, or used PCP or barbiturates on a very limited basis (less than once a week). (If PCP or barbiturates are used more frequently, urine monitoring is also indicated, provided that there is an acceptable degree social conformity.) Thus, on the basis of information available in the pre-sentence investigation report, the majority of the sample were not hard-core drug users. Having been referred to outpatient treatment through the CPU, these cases were matched to a more intensive intervention than they may have needed, as indicated by their OPI assessment.

When Out-Patient Treatment Is Indicated

Only about 7% of the sample would have been recommended for outpatient drug treatment on the basis of their OPI drug use severity index. Daily users of alcohol or marijuana, and individuals who use PCP or barbiturates once a week or more, are recommended for outpatient treatment (consisting of a minimum of one counseling session per week lasting at least one hour). Probationers who use PCP and barbiturates once a week or more, and those who used cocaine, crack, or amphetamines less than once a week, are recommended for intensive outpatient treatment (in the OPI scheme this consists of at least three one-hour sessions per week).

Although the OPI categorizes the sample in accordance with the severity of drug use and assigns clients to various treatments depending upon their drug severity, it should be noted that all CPU clients were referred to outpatient treatment. Outpatient drug treatment was adequate (or more than adequate) for about three quarters of the probationers (this includes the cases for which urine monitoring would have been appropriate).

Outpatient drug treatment was most effective for those clients who were appropriately matched to this treatment modality on the basis of the severity of their drug use. Given that many CPU cases had serious criminal records as well as severe drug problems, is it plausible that outpatient drug treatment, usually in modest doses, would reduce recidivism? In order to address this question, separate multiple regression analyses were conducted for the three groups of clients having different treatment needs. At issue was whether outpatient treatment influences rearrest rates after taking into account the client's age, gender, age at first arrest, and number of prior arrests. In each of the three multiple regression analyses conducted for the three OPI groups, the four client characteristics were entered first, and then treatment duration was entered. The analyses focused on determining whether the addition of the treatment variable significantly increased the amount of variance explained in rearrest rates above and beyond that of the other salient client characteristics.

In the model for the group needing residential treatment, most of the variance was explained by the client's age, gender, age at first arrest, and number of prior arrests. The addition of the treatment variable did not significantly increase the amount of variance explained. In other words, outpatient drug treatment did not lower rearrest rates among probationers whose drug use indicated a need for more structured and intensive treatment. Among those who needed urine monitoring only, the client's age, gender, age at first arrest, and number of prior arrests explained about the same amount of variance in rearrest as it did for the group needing residential treatment; however, the addition of the treatment variable increased the overall significance of the model, accounting for about an additional quarter of the total variance explained. This suggests that outpatient treatment was effective in reducing rearrest among probationers who only needed urine monitoring according to the OPI criteria. The model for the group needing outpatient treatment had the greatest predictive power, with the treatment variable adding significantly to the explanatory power of the other predictor variables (client's age, gender, age at first arrest, and number of prior arrests). This model suggests that outpatient treatment was most effective with clients who were appropriately matched to the modality on the basis of the severity of their drug use.

We did not find a significant reduction in rearrest rates among clients whose drug use was serious enough to warrant residential drug treatment. The most significant reductions in recidivism were found among those clients who appear to have needed outpatient drug treatment and actually received these services.

POLICY IMPLICATIONS AND RECOMMENDATIONS

The results from this evaluation study demonstrate that if recidivism rates are to be reduced among substance-abusing probationers, they need to be referred to appropriate drug treatment modalities. This finding is supported by the fact that significant reductions in rearrest rates were associated with increases in the length of outpatient drug treatment, after controlling for other variables that influence recidivism. Outpatient drug treatment was clearly not effective for the group with the most severe drug use. The findings have a number of important implications for probation policy. In general, they suggest that probation departments should refer clients to outpatient drug treatment programs, provided outpatient treatment is an appropriate modality for them. More specifically:

- Contracting with outpatient drug treatment programs is a sound strategy for probationers whose use of drugs is not too severe.

- Since matching clients to appropriate forms of treatment is a key to success, it is necessary to have a variety of drug interventions. These include random urine testing and contracts or agreements with residential as well as outpatient drug treatment programs.

- Probation departments should refer clients to various treatment modalities after assessing clients' needs by utilizing instruments that measure the severity of drug use.

- Since drug treatment can be effective only if clients are actually admitted, probation officers need to ensure that clients appear for their intake appointments—making referrals is not sufficient.

- Because clients do best if they remain in treatment longer, probation departments should find ways to encourage clients to stay in treatment. Various strategies (e.g., providing positive reinforcement and supportive services), should be used to prevent clients from dropping out, especially during the critical, early stage of treatment.

- For clients in outpatient programs, it is essential to monitor attendance and progress in treatment and take to appropriate action to ensure that they attend sessions regularly.

About the Authors

Gregory P. Falkin, Ph.D., has over 20 years of experience in the areas of corrections and substance abuse treatment research and Sheila Strauss, Ph.D. is an expert statistician and survey researcher at National Development and Research Institutes, Inc., New York, NY. Timothy Bohen directs the Central Placement Unit within the New York City Department of Probation. Readers may contact Dr. Falkin by email at greg.falkin@ ndri.org.

This research was supported by the National Institutes on Justice (93-IJ-CX-0056). Opinions expressed in this article do not represent the opinions of the U.S. government, the New York City Department of Probation, or National Development and Research Institutes, Inc. The authors wish to acknowledge Andrew Sutton, Douglas Young, Ph.D., Laura Winterfield, Ph.D., Mangai Natarajan, Ph.D., Akiva Lieberman, Ph.D., and Josephine Hawke, Ph.D. for their help in the research.

References

Anglin, M.D., & Hser, Y. (1990). Treatment of drug abuse. In M. Tonry & J. Wilson (Eds.), *Drugs and crime, Vol. 13* (pp. 393-460). Chicago, IL: University of Chicago Press.

Falkin, G.P., Prendergast, M., & Anglin, M.D. (1994). Drug treatment in the criminal justice system. *Federal Probation, 58* (3): 31-36.

Hubbard, R., Rachael, J., Craddock, S., & Cavanaugh, E. (1984). Treatment outcome prospective study (TOPS): Client characteristics and behaviors before, during, and after treatment [DHHS Publication No. (ADM) 84-1349]. In F. Tims & J. Ludford (Eds.), *Drug abuse treatment evaluation: Strategies, progress and prospects*, NIDA Monograph No. 51. (pp. 29-41). Rockville, MD: National Institute on Drug Abuse.

Hubbard, R.L., Craddock, G.S., Flynn, P.M., Anderson, J., & Etheridge, R. (1997). Overview of 1-year follow-up outcomes in the Drug Abuse Treatment Outcome Study (DATOS). *Psychology of Addictive Behaviors, 11*(4): 261-278.

Inciardi, J.A., McBride, D.C., & Weinman, B.A. (1993). The assessment and referral of criminal justice clients: Examining the focused offender disposition program. In J. A. Inciardi, (Ed.), *Drug treatment and criminal justice*. Newbury Park, CA: Sage Publications.

Chapter 7

Measuring Program Quality Over Time—Examples From Three RSAT Programs

by Edward J. Latessa, Ph.D., and Jennifer A. Pealer, M.A.

Importance of Measuring Program Integrity and Quality Over Time 7-1
Principles of Effective Interventions 7-2
Assessing Program Integrity 7-3
      The CPAI Instrument 7-3
      Limitations of CPAI 7-3
      Advantages of the CPAI 7-4
RSAT Program Assessments 7-4
      Community-Based RSAT 7-4
      Prison-Based RSAT 7-6
      Juvenile RSAT Program 7-7
Lessons for RSAT Administrators 7-8
The Upside 7-9

IMPORTANCE OF MEASURING PROGRAM INTEGRITY AND QUALITY OVER TIME

There is ample evidence that treatment programs can have a substantial effect on recidivism (see Andrews, Zinger et al., 1990; Gendreau & Andrews, 1990; Gendreau et al., 2000). Unfortunately, a closer examination of this research also reveals that not all programs are equally effective. While some of the variation in offender outcome can be attributed to offender characteristics, or even external factors (for example, criminal justice agency policies), we can also assume that the quality and integrity of programs is a contributing factor.

Most research on the effectiveness of substance abuse programs uses recidivism as the primary outcome measure. Indeed, public protection centers around the concept of recidivism; however, research that examines only recidivism may actually be getting just half of the picture. Correctional research should also examine the program quality

---

This chapter originally appeared in Offender Substance Abuse Report, *Vol. 2, No. 5, September/October 2002.*

in order to ascertain how closely a program aligns with what is known to be effective in treating offenders—i.e., the principle of effective interventions (Latessa & Holsinger, 1998). When a program's integrity is measured, the staff are able to pinpoint strengths as well as areas that need improvement. This information can help program administrators and treatment providers determine what components of their treatment should be improved. Furthermore, feedback from measuring program integrity can be used to understand the reasons for program outcomes.

Program integrity is just one critical measure; it is also important for programs to monitor the quality of their interventions over time. Getting a baseline measure of a program's quality can be a starting point for staff to make improvement in the program. By monitoring a program's integrity, the staff can continuously make improvements to the programming. The process of periodically monitoring program integrity and making improvements can serve to improve the program's quality and thus indirectly reduce recidivism.

The study reported on here used a quantifiable instrument to measure the quality of three residential substance abuse treatment programs (RSATs) over a period of three years. We report the study results, which show how program integrity can increase or decrease over time, and discuss the reasons behind the progression or regression of program integrity.

PRINCIPLES OF EFFECTIVE INTERVENTIONS

Several principles of effective interventions have been identified in the work of Gendreau, Andrews, and others:

- Interventions should be behavioral in nature, and reinforce prosocial behavior with modeling.

- The level of service should be matched to the risk level of the offender.

- The level of service should be matched to the offender's criminogenic needs.

- There should be matching of offenders to treatment, staff to the treatment they provide, and offenders to staff based on the responsivity characteristics.

- Offenders should receive intensive services which occupy 40% to 70% of their time for a period of at least six to nine months.

- Programs should be highly structured, with contingencies enforced in a firm but fair manner.

- Staff members should relate to offenders in interpersonally sensitive and constructive ways; staff should be well trained and supervised continuously.

- Offenders' changes on the intermediate targets should be monitored by staff.

- Relapse prevention and aftercare should be integral parts of the treatment process.

- Family members and significant others should be trained how to assist offenders during problem situations.

- High levels of advocacy and brokerage are needed in the community. (Andrews, Bonta, & Hoge, 1990; Gendreau, 1996; Gendreau & Andrews, 1990)

ASSESSING PROGRAM INTEGRITY

The CPAI Instrument

The Correctional Program Assessment Inventory (CPAI; Gendreau & Andrews, 1992) is a tool used to ascertain how closely a correctional treatment program meets known principles of effective correctional treatment. There are six primary sections of the CPAI:

1. Program implementation, i.e., the qualifications, experience, and involvement of the program director;

2. Client pre-service assessment, which examines the assessment practices of the program and the appropriateness of the population;

3. Program characteristics, such as the specific treatment procedures; the intensity of treatment; the matching of staff to treatment, offender to staff, and offender to treatment based on risk, need, and responsivity; the use of rewards and punishments; and the methods used to prepare offenders for return to the community;

4. Characteristics, qualities, stability, training, and involvement of the treatment staff;

5. Quality assurance and evaluation, which assesses the types of feedback, assessments, and evaluations used to monitor how well the program is functioning; and

6. Miscellaneous items such as ethical guidelines, disruptive changes to the program and funding, and levels of community support.

Each section is scored as either "very satisfactory" (70% to 100%); "satisfactory" (60% to 69%); "satisfactory, but needs improvement" (50% to 59%); or "unsatisfactory" (less than 50%). The scores from all six areas are totaled and the same scale is used for the overall assessment score. It should be noted that not all of the six areas are given equal weight, and some items may be considered "not applicable," in which case they are not included in the scoring.

Limitations of CPAI

Several limitations to the CPAI should be noted. First, the instrument is based on an "ideal" type. The criteria have been developed from a large body of research and knowledge that combines the best practices from the empirical literature on "what works" in reducing offender recidivism. Second, as with any research process, objectivity and reliability are always an issue. Although steps are taken to insure that the information gathered is accurate and reliable, given the nature of the process the assessor invariably makes decisions about the information and data gathered. Third, the process is time specific. That is, the assessment is based on the program at the time of the assessment. Changes or modifications may be under development; however, only those activities and processes that are present at the time of the review are scored. Fourth, the process does not take into account all "system" issues that can affect program integrity. Finally, the process does not address "why" a problem exists within a program.

Advantages of the CPAI

Despite these limitations, there are a number of advantages to this process. First, the criteria are based on empirically derived principles of effective programs. Second, the process provides a measure of program integrity and quality; it provides insight into the "black box" of a program, something that an outcome study alone does not provide. Third, the results can be obtained relatively quickly. Fourth, it identifies both the strengths, and weaknesses of a program. It provides the program with an idea of what it is doing that is consistent with the research on effective interventions, as well as those areas that need improvement. Fifth, it provides some recommendations for program improvement. Finally, it allows for benchmarking. Comparisons with other programs that have been assessed using the same criteria are provided, and since program integrity and quality can change over time, it allows a program to reassess its progress over time.

RSAT PROGRAM ASSESSMENTS

The current study used the CPAI to assess program integrity of three RSAT programs—a community-based residential facility for adult males and females, a medium-security prison for males, and a juvenile institution for males. The programs were assessed at two different time periods. The length of time between the first and second assessment varied between two and three years. The two adult sites were operating as modified therapeutic communities (TCs) at the time of both assessments. The juvenile facility operated as a combination 12-step with cognitive components at the first assessment and as a modified therapeutic community at the second assessment.

Community-Based RSAT

Figure 7.1 shows the first and second CPAI scores for the community-based residential substance abuse program. The program improved in all six areas of the CPAI. In addition, the program increased its overall score from 56% (needs improvement) to 74.2% (very satisfactory).

This community-based RSAT program increased its score in the implementation section for two main reasons. First, before the implementation of the RSAT program, the program conducted a literature review of major criminological and psychological journals to determine the effective interventions for offenders and then, based on this research, developed a model that was based on the social learning approach. Second, the program conducted a formal pilot period, which lasted approximately one month. Several changes were made as a result of the pilot experience including

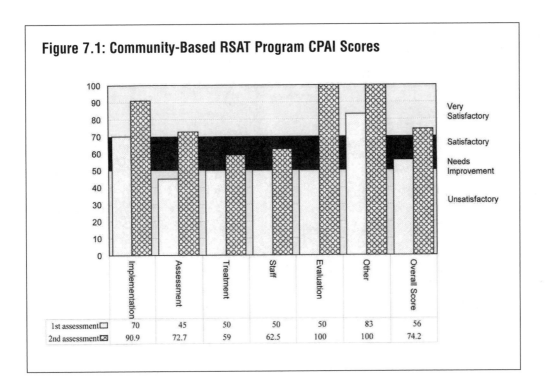

Figure 7.1: Community-Based RSAT Program CPAI Scores

	Implementation	Assessment	Treatment	Staff	Evaluation	Other	Overall Score
1st assessment ☐	70	45	50	50	50	83	56
2nd assessment ☒	90.9	72.7	59	62.5	100	100	74.2

the development of a phase system and privileges and the implementation of treatment staff meetings.

The program improved in the assessment area of the CPAI because it had implemented a standardized and objective risk-and-need instrument to assess the offenders. Furthermore, the program implemented a standardized and objective instrument to assess offenders' substance abuse.

Program quality increased from "unsatisfactory" to "needs improvement" in the treatment area of the CPAI. The program began to target more criminogenic needs than noncriminogenic needs. During the first assessment, the program was targeting areas such as health, hygiene, and self-esteem. While these areas are important, effective programs target offenders' needs that are related to criminal behavior (i.e., criminogenic needs such as antisocial attitudes, antisocial peers, antisocial personality, and substance abuse). In addition, the program assigned staff members to conduct groups based on their knowledge, experience, and ability to model the specific skill being taught.

The program also increased its score in the staff, evaluation, and other sections. All treatment staff have either a certification in chemical dependency counseling or a license in social work. Furthermore, new staff members are hired on personal qualities such as leadership, empathy, firm but fair, confidence, and spontaneity that affect the delivery of treatment. The program reassesses the offenders with the standardized and objective instrument prior to termination. Moreover, the program was involved with a process evaluation in which recidivism data was collected on offenders after they left the facility.

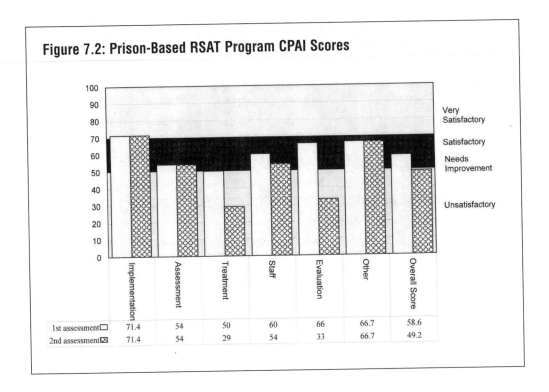

Figure 7.2: Prison-Based RSAT Program CPAI Scores

	Implementation	Assessment	Treatment	Staff	Evaluation	Other	Overall Score
1st assessment□	71.4	54	50	60	66	66.7	58.6
2nd assessment▨	71.4	54	29	54	33	66.7	49.2

Last, the program developed ethical guidelines for all staff to follow when inter-acting with offenders.

Prison-Based RSAT

Figure 7.2 reports the results of the two CPAIs that were conducted on the prison-based RSAT program. The scores decreased in three areas of CPAI—treatment, staff, and evaluation sections—and remained the same in three areas—implementation, assessment, and other. The overall CPAI score for the prison-based RSAT program decreased from 58.6% (needs improvement) to 49.2% (unsatisfactory).

The treatment section decreased from 50% to 29% because even though the program was rooted in a social learning model, the day-to-day operation of the program did not reflect the model. For example, the program was using inappropriate punishment such as shaming and humiliation techniques and the application of the punishments was not consistent and systematic. Furthermore, the program did not have a detailed treatment manual that covered all aspects of the treatment program. Last, offenders were not sys-tematically trained in behavioral rehearsal techniques, in which they are taught to observe and anticipate problem situations, and plan and rehearse alternative prosocial responses in increasingly difficult situations. Furthermore, once released from the pro-gram, the offenders were not given adequate aftercare services that target criminogenic needs.

The staff section also decreased after the second assessment, for two reasons. First, the staff training was inadequate. Staff were not trained on the formal application of

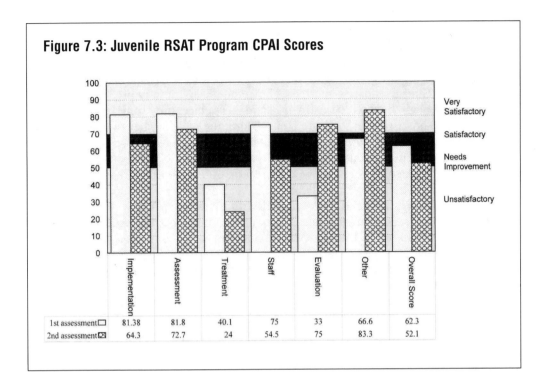

Figure 7.3: Juvenile RSAT Program CPAI Scores

	Implementation	Assessment	Treatment	Staff	Evaluation	Other	Overall Score
1st assessment☐	81.38	81.8	40.1	75	33	66.6	62.3
2nd assessment☒	64.3	72.7	24	54.5	75	83.3	52.1

the material, principles of effective interventions, behavioral strategies, and application of reinforcers. Second, staff morale was very low. Treatment staff reported that they did not have any input into the program.

The last section that changed was the evaluation section. This section decreased from needs improvement to unsatisfactory because the program was no longer assessing the offenders' satisfaction with the program and services.

Juvenile RSAT Program

The juvenile RSAT program also saw a decrease in the overall CPAI score (Figure 7.3)—from 62.3% (satisfactory) to 52.1% (needs improvement). After the second assessment, the program decreased in four areas: implementation, assessment, treatment, and staff, and increased in two areas: evaluation and other. The program decreased in the implementation section because of the hiring of a new program director. The current program director was not instrumental in designing the program. In addition, the program was not systematically conducting comprehensive literature reviews to identify research concerning effective treatment for juvenile offenders.

The juvenile program decreased slightly in the assessment section due partly to the inconsistency of the assessments process. For example, some youth were assessed on responsivity characteristics and some youth were not. Furthermore, the juveniles were assessed at a reception center and the assessments were then given to the program to be placed in the offenders' files. However, some records (such as psychological assessments) were not found in the files.

The program's decrease in the treatment section can be attributed to three main reasons. First, even though the program was based on the social learning model, the program did not consistently utilize cognitive behavioral and social learning techniques. For example, the phase groups were eclectic in terms of a therapeutic model. They were primarily education-based and the TC meetings were largely processing groups. Second, even though there were treatment manuals in place, they were basically worksheets and were not used in a formal manner. Third, the program began using inappropriate methods of punishment, e.g., shaming and humiliation. Additionally, the rewards and punishments were not consistently administered by all staff members. Finally, once released from the RSAT program, there were no structured aftercare components in place for the juvenile offenders to attend.

The score for the staff section decreased with the hiring of new staff members. At the time of the second assessment, the staff did not meet the criteria for previous experience working with the offender population. In addition, the training of staff members appeared to have decreased. Staff members reported that they did not receive any on-going training. In addition, it appeared that staff were not supportive of the treatment goals at the juvenile RSAT program, which may stem from the lack of initial training on the TC model. The lack of staff input resulted in a division between treatment staff and correctional officers.

LESSONS FOR RSAT ADMINISTRATORS

The current study showed how program integrity can be measured over time using the CPAI. The results from the follow-up CPAIs show that there is still some room for improvement for all three programs under review. The lessons learned are relevant to all such programs:

1. *It is not sufficient to label treatment interventions "cognitive behavioral" or to model them after a social learning approach.* It is critical that day-to-day program operation actually reflects these treatment models.

2. *Focus on social behaviors.* There should be consistent and systematic rehearsals of prosocial behaviors throughout all aspects of the programming.

3. *Programs should implement risk, need, and responsivity principles into treatment planning.* Two of the three programs studied received an overall risk/need score from an objective and standardized instrument that can be used to make treatment decisions; however, the majority of offenders in all programs received the same treatment regardless of the risk or need level. Further, the programs were not using effective punishments to eliminate antisocial behavior and encourage prosocial behavior. Instead, these programs used shaming and humiliation techniques, which have not been shown to be effective in reducing offender recidivism.

4. *Sufficient time in the program is critical; early or abrupt termination negatively impacts treatment success.* The RSAT programs studied, like many others, were constrained by the limitations imposed by their funding agencies. Completion of the programs was time-based and offenders were terminated whether or not they

acquired prosocial attitudes and behaviors. Furthermore, the provision of after-care services that the offenders receive once they left the facility was unclear.

THE UPSIDE

This review of three RSAT programs also revealed some promising findings. First, it appears that the foundation for quality programming was in place. Second, the programs were based on a theoretical model (structured social learning), that has been found to be effective in changing offender behavior. Third, the programs had qualified and involved leadership, the staff were qualified, and there was strong external support for the programs. Finally, prior research (Lipsey, 1992) had found that programs that undergo evaluation tend to be more effective in reducing recidivism. By participating in this research process, these three RSATs gained valuable information to improve program effectiveness.

About the Authors

Edward J. Latessa, Ph.D., is Professor of Criminal Justice and Jennifer A. Pealer, M.A., is Research Associate in the Division of Criminal Justice, University of Cincinnati. Dr. Latessa may be reached by email at Edward.Latessa@uc.edu.

References

Andrews, D.A., Bonta, J., & Hoge, R.D. (1990). Classification for effective rehabilitation: Rediscovering psychology. *Criminal Justice and Behavior, 17*, 19-52.

Andrews, D.A., Zinger, I., Hoge, R., Bonta, J., Gendreau, P., & Cullen, F.T. (1990). Does correctional treatment work? A clinically relevant and psychologically informed meta-analysis. *Criminology, 28*, 36-404.

Gendreau, P. (1996). The principles of effective intervention with offenders. In A. T. Hardlan (Ed.), *Choosing correctional options that work* (pp. 117-130). Thousand Oaks, CA: Sage.

Gendreau, P., & Andrews, D. A. (1990). Tertiary prevention: What the meta-analyses of the offender treatment literature tell us about what works. *Canadian Journal of Criminology, 32*, 173-184.

Gendreau, P., & Andrews, D. A. (1992). *Correctional program assessment inventory* (4th ed.). St. John, New Brunswick: University of New Brunswick.

Gendreau, P., Goggin, C., Cullen, F.T., & Andrews, D.A. (2000). The effects of community sanctions and incarceration on recidivism. *Forum, 12*, 10-13.

Latessa, E. J., & Holsinger, A. (1998). The importance of evaluating correctional programs: Assessing outcome and quality. *Corrections Management Quarterly, 2*(4), 22-29.

Lipsey, M. (1992). Juvenile delinquency treatment: A meta-analytical inquiry into the variability of effects. In T. Cook, H. Cooper, D. Cordray, H. Hartmann, L. Hedges, R. Light, T. Louis, & F. Mosteller (Eds.), *Meta-analysis for explanation* (pp. 83-127). New York: Russell Sage Foundation.

Chapter 8

The Promises and Challenges of Drug Courts

by Steven Belenko, Ph.D.

Introduction 8-1
Illegal Drug Use the Norm for Offender Population 8-2
Drug Court Treatment Initiatives 8-2
    Development of Drug Courts 8-2
    Drug Court Program Basics 8-2
Initial Research Findings Show Promise 8-3
    Drug Court Participants Do Better While in Treatment 8-3
    Some Promising Recidivism Outcomes 8-4
    Potential for Long-Term Taxpayer Savings 8-4
Research and Policy Challenges 8-5
    Improving Retention 8-5
    Facilitating Public Health Benefits 8-5
    Identifying and Reaching Appropriate Target Population 8-6
    Identifying and Improving Effective Treatment Processes and
       Related Staff Training 8-6
    Addressing Knowledge Gaps 8-8
Conclusions 8-8

INTRODUCTION

The enforcement of anti-drug laws, the adjudication of drug-involved offenders, and the consequences of drug abuse and addiction have impacted the nation's criminal justice system in profound ways over the past 25 years. Law enforcement agencies have paid increasing attention to drug crimes, state legislatures have ever more punitive anti-drug laws, and criminal courts have sentenced increasing numbers of drug offenders to prison. At the same time, the emphasis on punishment and control, lack of sufficient funding for treatment, and the difficulties of integrating treatment into the criminal justice process (Belenko, 2000) mean that access to treatment has been limited for those subpopulations of drug users who are most likely to enter the criminal justice system. The result has been dramatic increases in probation and parole caseloads, as well as inmate populations.

An earlier version of this chapter appeared in Offender Substance Abuse Report, *Vol. 1, No. 3, May/June 2001.*

ILLEGAL DRUG USE THE NORM FOR OFFENDER POPULATION

In 2002, 11% of all arrests in the United States were for drug offenses (more than 1.5 million arrests). Overall, illegal drug use is the norm among people caught up in the criminal justice system. Nationally, 65% of arrestees test positive for any illegal drug and 79% of arrestees are "drug-involved"—i.e., they tested positive for an illegal drug, had used illegal drugs recently, had histories of drug dependence or treatment, or were in need of treatment at the time of their arrest (National Institute of Justice, 2000; analysis of ADAM data by the author). Nearly half of offenders on probation report histories of regular illegal drug use (mostly cocaine) (Mumola & Bonczar, 1998). Finally, about 80% of jail and prison inmates are substance-involved: They violated drug or alcohol laws, were under the influence at the time of their offense, committed their crime to get money for drugs, have a history of regular illegal drug use, or have been in alcohol treatment (Belenko & Peugh, 1999).

DRUG COURT TREATMENT INITIATIVES

Development of Drug Courts

Over the past several decades, a number of criminal justice treatment initiatives have emerged in response to burgeoning drug-related caseloads. These include Treatment Alternative to Street Crime (TASC) programs (Anglin et al., 1999), diversion, probation-supervised treatment, and intermediate sanctions with treatment components. Although evidence suggests that coerced treatment for offenders can facilitate treatment engagement and improve retention rates (Farabee et al., 1998; Hiller et al., 1998; Knight et al., 2000; Young & Belenko, 2002), many of these earlier treatment initiatives were fragmented, inconsistently or inappropriately used, and had limited monitoring of treatment progress or compliance with court-imposed conditions. In part, drug courts emerged from local concerns about the efficacy of existing models of treatment delivery for offenders.

In this context, drug courts have become a key court-based treatment intervention for drug-involved offenders. Beginning with the Dade County (Miami, Florida) program in 1989 (Finn & Newlyn, 1993), treatment drug courts have established an important presence in America's criminal court system. In many jurisdictions, drug courts have become the preferred mechanism for linking drug- or alcohol-involved offenders to community-based treatment and related clinical interventions (Office of Justice Programs, 1998). Although still serving a relatively small percentage of offenders with substance abuse problems, drug courts have enjoyed considerable positive publicity, government and public encouragement, and special funding. As of November 2003 there were 1,093 operational drug courts, with an additional 414 in the planning stages (American University, 2003). Between 1989 and 2000, an estimated 200,000 drug offenders entered drug court programs, and 55,000 graduated (American University, 2000).

Drug Court Program Basics

Drug courts seek to reduce drug use and associated criminal behavior by engaging and retaining drug-involved offenders in judicially supervised treatment and related services, usually in a special courtroom set aside for the program. Most drug courts provide:

- Timely identification and referral of defendants in need of treatment;

- Regular status hearings before the judicial officer to monitor treatment progress and program compliance;

- A system of sanctions and rewards linked to compliance with program requirements;

- Frequent drug testing; and

- Structured treatment phases (Drug Courts Program Office, 1997).

Upon successful completion, participants have their charges dismissed or sentence reduced, depending upon whether the drug court uses a pre- or post-adjudication model.

Unlike traditional courtrooms, drug court judges are much more proactive, reinforcing positive client behavior and directly monitoring an offender's treatment progress and compliance. Although the judge is central to the drug court model, most drug courts function as a team in which prosecutors, defense attorneys, and counselors work together to help offenders overcome their substance abuse and related problems. A case manager or resource coordinator typically assists participants in getting access to services and monitoring their progress. Sanctions and incentives, often implemented on a "graduated" schedule, are used to hold participants accountable for program noncompliance and to reward them for positive achievements. These are considered by drug court practitioners and researchers as crucial for maintaining compliance, treatment retention, and achieving sobriety (Harrell, 1998; Marlowe & Kirby, 1999; Taxman et al., 1999).

INITIAL RESEARCH FINDINGS SHOW PROMISE

Although drug courts have enjoyed broad public and legislative support, their rapid expansion has occurred in the absence of comprehensive research findings about their efficacy and impact (Marlowe & Festinger, 2000). This probably reflects several factors: the accumulation of years of frustration with the ineffectiveness of standard criminal justice responses to drug abuse and addiction, the intuitive appeal of the drug court concept, a desire to try something new, and the enthusiasm of the first wave of drug court judges, and promising preliminary findings from drug court evaluations.

Drug Court Participants Do Better While in Treatment

In contrast to most other criminal justice innovations, drug courts have undergone considerable scrutiny during their relatively short existence. The Drug Courts Program Office of the U.S. Department of Justice has encouraged drug court research by requiring that all of its grantees undergo an independent process evaluation, and federal research agencies such as the National Institute of Justice and National Institute on Drug Abuse have funded research on various aspects of drug court operations. To date, the primary sources of information about the operations and impacts of drug courts have been process and outcome evaluations of individual drug courts, and the annual survey of operational drug courts conducted by the American University Drug Court Clearinghouse and Technical Assistance Project (DCCTAP). The present author reviewed these surveys, as well as more than 150 drug court evaluations, in three recently published articles (Belenko, 1998; 1999; 2000). This body of research suggests several conclusions:

- Drug courts provide closer and more frequent offender supervision (e.g. number of required court appearances, drug tests, supervision and treatment contacts) than provided under standard probation or pretrial supervision.

- Program retention is substantially longer than typically seen in community-based treatment, whether or not criminal justice-monitored. This is important because research on drug treatment outcomes has consistently found that a longer time in treatment is associated with better outcomes (French et al., 1993; Simpson, Joe & Brown, 1997). On average, an estimated 60% of those who enter drug courts remain in treatment for at least one year, and about 50% graduate. Specific elements of the drug court model (such as graduated sanctions and rewards, judicial supervision, and responses to relapse) that account for increased retention in treatment have not been studied but merit further research.

- Drug use and criminal behavior are reduced relative to baseline levels while drug court participants are under program supervision.

Some Promising Recidivism Outcomes

As criminal justice-based interventions, it is not surprising that most drug courts identify increased public safety as a primary goal. Drug courts hold promise in this area in large part because of their ability to retain drug-abusing offenders in treatment and provide intensive treatment, supervision, and other services. Twenty-three out of 31 evaluations that have reported post-program recidivism (usually after one year) for all drug court participants and a comparison group have found that the drug court reduced recidivism (Belenko, 1998; 1999; 2001).

However, the size of the difference varies across drug courts, and several evaluations have not found an impact. Moreover, few studies have examined post-program recidivism beyond one year, and the available comparison groups are often problematic (Belenko, 1999). There has been little research thus far on the impact of drug courts on other post-program outcomes, such as drug use, employment, family stability, or health. Accordingly it is difficult to draw any conclusions about the effects of drug courts on these domains.

Potential for Long-Term Taxpayer Savings

Finally, several studies of the economic impact of drug courts suggest a potential for taxpayer savings, especially from reduced crime. Other research has concluded that investments in treatment generate net economic benefits (Gerstein et al., 1994; Rajkumar & French, 1996). Although drug courts may have relatively high costs because of increased staffing, frequent court hearings, and treatment costs, they may achieve cost savings through reduced incarceration; lower rates of recidivism, drug use, use of entitlements, and foster care; as well as increases in legitimate employment and improved health. One relatively comprehensive economic analysis of the Multnomah County (Oregon) drug court found a substantial net cost savings due to reduced criminal justice system costs as well as from reduced victimization, public assistance, and medical claims costs (Finigan, 1999). Deschenes et al. (1999) found that the annual operational costs per client in four Los Angeles County drug courts were substantially lower than prison or residential drug treatment costs, but higher than standard probation.

RESEARCH AND POLICY CHALLENGES

The experiences of the first generation of treatment drug courts have illuminated the need for a comprehensive approach to the handling of drug offenders that embodies the goals and needs of both the criminal justice and the treatment/public health communities. Given its popularity, however, more research and knowledge are needed to determine how the drug court model can be used to more effectively intervene with the substance abuse and related health problems of chronic drug offenders through treatment retention and linkages to other health services.

Improving Retention

The importance of treatment retention in improving post-program outcomes suggests that more research is needed on the individual participant, staff, and organizational factors that promote drug court retention. The relatively high rates of successful program completion may reflect the unique structure of the drug court model, the explicit personal involvement of the drug court judge and staff in the offender's treatment outcome and their interactions in court, the enrollment of relatively low-risk offenders (selection bias), or the way in which treatment is integrated into the court process. Although a few drug court studies have begun to examine predictors of retention, there is still little extant knowledge to guide the development of new drug court programs or to modify existing programs to reduce dropout and increase graduation rates. More recent research has suggested that treatment engagement early on in the process is a key component of an effective treatment process (Knight et al., 2000; Sung et al., 2001).

Facilitating Public Health Benefits

Given the multiple health services needs of drug-involved offenders (Hammett et al., 1999; Marquart et al., 1997), there may be important but relatively untapped ancillary public health benefits of drug courts (Belenko, 2002). For example, through their interagency planning, cross-training, drug treatment access, case management, and close client supervision, drug courts may help reduce HIV risk behaviors. The screening, assessment, and referral process provides an opportunity to identify health problems and provide linkages to appropriate clinical interventions. The close supervision and case management typical of drug courts can help to assure better access to health services, follow-through with clinical interventions, and monitor compliance with treatment and medication regimens. But the available research does not yet inform how these linkages are facilitated, or what barriers exist to achieving more effective linkages. Comprehensive health assessments, access to referral networks, appropriate referrals, and follow-up with participants to assure compliance with health care regimens are all important dimensions for improving the effectiveness of drug court-based health services, and keys to better long-term outcomes for drug-involved offenders.

Identifying and Reaching Appropriate Target Population

Other research and operational issues warrant attention if the full potential of drug courts is to be realized. First, targeting, eligibility screening, and assessment processes directly drive the number and type of drug court clients, and thus the types of clinical services needed. Narrow targeting and strict eligibility screening, and program admission procedures that allow higher-risk offenders to drop out prior to "formal" enrollment, may limit the number of participants and produce a "creaming" effect whereby the drug court serves mostly low-risk clients. Such courts may show high levels of compliance and success rates, but may not be cost-effective—clients may have done as well under less intensive adjudication and treatment models. Moreover, the voluntary nature of drug court participation can result in self-selection bias in which highly motivated or lower-risk offenders are more likely to participate.

Identifying and Improving Effective Treatment Processes and Related Staff Training

Drug courts, as do other criminal justice-supervised treatment programs, need to improve staff training in substance abuse and treatment. Although some drug courts offer formal training for judges and staff, others rely more on ad hoc training or the interest and motivation of individual judges. Given the lack of universal training in these areas in standard judicial or probation officer education, such training curricula should be improved and formalized. Given the racial, ethnic, and class disparity between the drug client population and criminal justice program staff, improving cultural competence and sensitivity should also be an important part of any training curriculum. Cultural and gender issues may be closely related to treatment outcomes (Aponte & Barnes, 1995; Fiorentine & Hillhouse, 1999).

There has been little research on the role of treatment process or the organization of service delivery on drug court offenders' compliance, retention, or outcomes (Taxman, 1999). Yet a growing body of research notes the importance of treatment process on improving outcomes for criminal justice-based treatment (Joe et al., 1998; Simpson,

Joe, Rowan-Szal & Greener, 1997), based on clinically appropriate and comprehensive assessment, monitoring, and service delivery (Simpson, 1997). Such systems could be readily implemented within a drug court structure, but few drug courts have implemented either comprehensive and periodic clinical assessments or regular systematic monitoring of therapeutic interactions.

There is evidence that assessment and treatment delivery in drug courts can have shortcomings. In a 1999 survey of 263 drug courts, Peyton and Gossweiler (2001) found a number of service gaps. For example, many drug courts do not appropriately use screening and assessment instruments for placement decisions; many drug courts have difficulty retaining clients because of lack of treatment motivation or poor "treatment attitude"; and relationships with treatment providers are not well structured. Common reasons for early termination in drug courts include failure to engage in treatment, missing too many treatment appointments, poor attitude, and "lack of motivation" (Peyton & Gossweiler, 2001). Many drug courts exclude clients who are deemed to be "not motivated" for treatment, thus limiting the eligibility pool (Taxman & Bouffard, 2002). In a recent study of treatment services in four drug courts, Taxman and Bouffard (2003) found that on average only 22% of observed treatment sessions contained any discussion of cognitive-behavioral issues or strategies, and only 16% of treatment time was spent on cognitive-behavioral components. In addition, information on basic concepts and vocabulary of addiction and treatment were relatively rarely delivered (32% of sessions), and treatment did not seem to adequately reflect the drug use habits of the clients (Taxman, 1999). Overall, Taxman and Bouffard (2003) found that much of the time in clinical sessions was devoted to administrative tasks and support services. Finally, with their focus on intervening with clients' substance abuse and related health and social problems, few drug courts address the important need to restructure their clients' criminal thinking styles, or to build internal motivating strategies to support prosocial behaviors and constructive decision-making.

The drug court model incorporates a nonclinical but authoritative figure (the judge) who makes decisions that directly affect the treatment process. Depending upon the drug court structure, the knowledge and training of the judge and the drug court staff, and the relationship between the judge and treatment provider(s), judicial behaviors, comments, and decisions can support or undermine the treatment process (Marlowe & Kirby, 1999; Marlowe et al, 2003; Satel, 1998). In particular, it may be difficult for court and clinical treatment staff to reach consensus over the appropriate response to relapse. The philosophical or operational tensions surrounding staff's views and attitudes about addiction and recovery can be difficult to resolve yet may have a profound effect on drug court outcomes (Taxman, 1999). An extensive planning process involving key stakeholders, the use of formal Memoranda of Understanding, timely and appropriate information exchange between the court and clinical staff, and regular stakeholder meetings may mitigate some of these difficulties (Belenko & Logan, 2003; Drug Courts Program Office, 1997).

Minimizing tensions between judge and treatment provider can be difficult, but important to resolve. Not only can judicial attitudes or decisions affect the treatment process, but clinical decisions can in turn affect the imposition of sanctions, rewards, or phase advancement. The phased treatment structure of drug courts places an inherent time limit on treatment progress. If a client remains too long in one phase (e.g., due to multiple relapses) then the client might be terminated. Although lack of treatment progress may lead to program termination under other models of criminal justice-based treatment supervision (such as probation or parole), retention time under those models is expected to be shorter than under the drug court model, in which relapse is expected and more acceptable.

Addressing Knowledge Gaps

Although much research on drug courts has emerged over the past few years, there are many gaps in our knowledge about drug court processes and outcomes (Belenko, 1998; 1999; 2001). Despite their popularity, drug courts are still relatively new, and much more information is needed about (1) the operations and impacts of drug courts; (2) the client, program, and system factors that are associated with compliance and successful outcomes; (3) the optimal program structure, and; (4) how drug court participants fare compared with those in other criminal justice-based treatment interventions.

Most important are the need for better-controlled studies of the impacts of various components of drug court interventions; more research on how the components of the drug court model (especially the judicial role) affect program and treatment compliance; studies of the factors affecting in-program relapse and criminal activity as well as post-program relapse and criminal activity; the use of experimental designs, or more appropriate comparison groups, for program impact evaluations; the collection and analysis of long-term outcome data; and the improvement of automated drug court data systems that can support evaluation.

We also lack empirical information on the effectiveness of different drug court treatment and operational models. For example, little is known about the relative efficacy of having a single contracted or court-operated treatment provider compared to referral to multiple community-based programs. The elements of the relationships among drug court staff, treatment and other service providers, and clients that promote or deter successful outcomes have not been well-studied. Data are also lacking on the optimum drug court phase structure, the impacts of different types of sanctions and incentives on client compliance or retention (Taxman et al., 1999), or the styles and behaviors of judges that promote compliance and retention.

Finally, the rapid growth of drug courts and the eventual phasing out of federal funding raise the question of how institutionalization will affect drug court operations in the future. Issues such as transition to state and local funding streams, staff burnout, and the use of drug courts as part of a regular judicial assignment merit further study. The history of policy innovations suggests that early program success is common, but maintaining that success as innovations become institutionalized is much more difficult.

CONCLUSIONS

Drug courts are a relatively new and structurally different approach to engaging offenders in community-based treatment. The encouraging retention rates, relatively low prevalence of drug use and criminal activity during participation, and preliminary evidence for at least a one-year reduction in post-program recidivism suggest that the drug court model can successfully engage many drug offenders in long-term treatment and related services.

Given the dimensions of the offender substance abuse problem, no single program or policy innovation can be expected to be a panacea. However, as drug court programs and policies mature over the next few years, and more research findings become available, there is reason to be hopeful that the growth in the number of offenders with drug or alcohol problems will be slowed. Given the scope of the problem, and the inexorable growth of the offender population under existing laws and policies, the stakes are high. The future success of drug courts and other criminal justice-supervised treatment can have a real impact on reducing the use of incarceration. The staggering social and economic costs of America's high incarceration rate to poor and minority communities increase the urgency to develop, evaluate, and expand effective treatment interventions for offender populations.

About the Author

Steven Belenko, Ph.D., is a Fellow with The National Center on Addiction and Substance Abuse at Columbia University, and is a member of the Offender Substance Abuse Report *editorial board. He may be reached by e-mail: sbelenko@casacolumbia.org*

References

American University (2000, June). *Drug court activity update: Composite summary information.* Washington, DC: U.S. Department of Justice, Office of Justice Programs, Drug Court Clearinghouse and Technical Assistance Project.

American University. (2003). Summary of all drug court activity, November 2003. Retrieved from the World Wide Web, http://www.american.edu/justice/drugcourts.html, February 15, 2004.

Anglin, M.D., Longshore, D., & Turner, S. (1999). Treatment alternatives to street crime. An evaluation of five programs. *Criminal Justice and Behavior, 26:* 168-195.

Aponte, J.F., & Barnes, J.M. (1995). Impact of acculturation and moderator variables on the intervention and treatment of ethnic groups. In J.F. Aponte, R.Y. Rivers, & J.Wohl (Eds.), *Psychological interventions and cultural diversity.* Needam Heights, MA: Allyn & Bacon.

Belenko, S. (1998). Research on drug courts: A critical review. *National Drug Court Institute Review 1(1):* 1-42.

Belenko, S. (1999). Research on drug courts: A critical review. 1999 update. *National Drug Court Institute Review, 2(2):* 1-58.

Belenko, S. (2000). The challenges of integrating drug treatment into the criminal justice process. *Albany Law Review, 63(3):* 833-876.

Belenko, S. (2001). *Research on drug courts: A critical review. 2001 update.* New York: The National Center on Addiction and Substance Abuse at Columbia University.

Belenko, S. (2002). Drug Courts. In C. Leukefeld, F. Tims, & D. Farabee (Eds.), *Treatment of Drug Offenders: Policies and Issues,* (pp. 301-318). New York: Springer.

Belenko, S. & Logan, T.K. (2003). Delivering effective treatment to adolescents: Improving the juvenile drug court model. *Journal of Substance Abuse Treatment, 25,* 189-211.

Belenko, S. & J. Peugh. *Behind bars: Substance abuse and America's prison population. Technical report.* NY: The National Center on Addiction and Substance Abuse at Columbia University, 1999.

Deschenes, E.P., Imam, I., Foster, T., & Ward, D. (1999). *Evaluation of Los Angeles County drug courts.* Long Beach, CA: Center for Applied Local Research, UC Long Beach.

Drug Courts Program Office. (1997). *Defining drug courts: The key components.* Washington, DC: Office of Justice Programs, U.S. Department of Justice.

Farabee, D., Prendergast, M., & Anglin, D. (1998). The effectiveness of coerced treatment for drug-abusing offenders. *Federal Probation, 62*: 3-10.

Finigan, M. (1999). Assessing cost off-sets in a drug court setting. *National Drug Court Institute Review, 2(2):* 59-92.

Finn, P., & Newlyn, A.K. (1993). *Miami's "drug court:" A different approach.* Washington, DC: U.S. Department of Justice, National Institute of Justice.

Fiorentine, R., & Hillhouse, M.P. (1999). Drug treatment effectiveness and client-counselor empathy: Exploring the effects of gender and ethnic congruency. *Journal of Drug Issues, 29(1):* 59-74.

French, M. T., Zarkin, G. A., Hubbard, R. L., & Rachal, J. V. (1993). The effects of time in drug abuse treatment and employment on post-treatment drug use and criminal activity. *American Journal on Drug and Alcohol Abuse, 19:* 19-33.

Gerstein, D.R., Harwood, H., Fountain, D., Suter, N., & Malloy, K. (1994). *Evaluating recovery services: The California Drug and Alcohol Treatment Assessment.* Washington, DC: National Opinion Research Center.

Hammett, T., Harmon, P., & Maraschak, L. (1999). *1996-1997 Update: HIV/AIDS, STDs, and TB in correctional facilities.* Washington, DC: U.S. Department of Justice, National Institute of Justice.

Harrell, A. (1998). *Drug courts and the role of graduated sanctions.* NIJ Research Preview. Washington, DC: National Institute of Justice.

Hiller, M.L., Knight, K., & Broome, K.M. (1998). Legal pressure and treatment retention in a national sample of long-term residential programs. *Criminal Justice and Behavior, 25(4):* 463-481.

Joe G.W., Simpson D.D., & Broome K.M. (1998). Effects of readiness for drug abuse treatment on client retention and assessment of process. *Addiction, 93(8):* 1177-1190.

Knight, K., Hiller, M.L., Broome, K.M., & Simpson, D.D. (2000). Legal pressure, treatment readiness, and engagement in long-term residential programs. *Journal of Offender Rehabilitation, 31(1/2):* 101-115.

Marlowe, D.B., & Festinger, D.S. (2000, December). Research on drug courts: Do the N's justify the means? *Connection,* pp. 4-5.

Marlowe, D. B., Festinger, D. S., Lee, P. A., Schepise, M. M., Hazzard, J. E. R., Merrill, J. C., Mulvaney, F. D., & McLellan, A. T. (2003). Are judicial status hearings a "key component" of drug court? During-treatment data from a randomized trial. *Criminal Justice & Behavior, 30,* 141-162.

Marlowe, D.B., & Kirby, K.C. (1999). Effective use of sanctions in drug courts: Lessons from behavioral research. *National Drug Court Institute Review, 2(1):* 1-32.

Marquart, J., Merianos, D., Hebert, J., & Carroll, L. (1997). Health conditions and prisoners: A review of research and emerging areas of inquiry. *Prison Journal, 77(2):* 184-208.

Mumola, C.J., & Bonczar, T.P. (1998). *Substance abuse and treatment of adults on probation, 1995.* Washington, DC: U.S. Department of Justice, Bureau of Justice Statistics.

National Institute of Justice. (2000). *1999 annual report on drug use among adult and juvenile arrestees.* Washington, DC: U.S. Department of Justice, Author.

Office Justice Programs. (1998). *Looking at a decade of drug courts.* Washington, DC: U.S. Department of Justice, Author.

Peyton, E. A., & Gossweiler, R. (2001). *Treatment Services in Adult Drug Courts: Report on the 1999 National Drug Court Treatment Survey.* Washington, DC: U.S. Department of Justice, Drug Courts Program Office.

Rajkumar, A., & French, M.T. (1996). Drug abuse, crime costs, and economic benefits of treatment. *Journal of Quantitative Criminology, 13(3):* 294-302.

Satel, S. (1998). Observational study of courtroom dynamics in selected drug courts. *National Drug Court Institute Review, 1(1):* 43-72.

Simpson, D. (1997, Fall). Client engagement and duration of treatment. *IBR Research Round-Up.*

Simpson, D.D., Joe, G.W., Rowan-Szal, G.A., & Greener, J.M. (1997). Drug abuse treatment process components that improve retention. *Journal of Substance Abuse Treatment, 14(6):* 565-572.

Simpson, D., Joe, G., & Brown, B. (1997). Treatment retention and follow-up outcomes in the Drug Abuse Treatment Outcome Study (DATOS). *Psychology of Addictive Behaviors, 11(4):* 294-307.

Sung, H., Belenko, S., & Feng, L. (in press). Treatment compliance in the trajectory of treatment progress among offenders. *Journal of Substance Abuse Treatment.*

Taxman, F. (1999). Unraveling "what works" for offenders in substance abuse treatment services. *National Drug Court Institute Review, 2(2):* 93-132.

Taxman, F., & Bouffard, J.A. (2002). Treatment inside the drug court: The who, what, where, and how of treatment services. *Substance Use and Misuse, 37,* 1665-1688.

Taxman, F., & Bouffard, J.A. (2003, September). Drug treatment in the community. *Federal Probation,* 4-14.

Taxman, F.S., Soule, D., & Gelb, A. (1999). Graduated sanctions: Stepping into accountable systems and offenders. *The Prison Journal, 79:*182-204.

Young, D. & S. Belenko. (2002). Program retention and perceived coercion in three models of mandatory drug treatment. *Journal of Drug Issues, 32(1),* 297-328.

Chapter 9

The Characteristics of American Drug Court Programs

by Caroline Cooper, M.A., J.D.

Florida Model Sparks a Trend 9-2
Drug Court Program Goals 9-3
Locus of Program in Judicial Process 9-4
Targeted Offenses and Offenders 9-4
    Participant Eligibility Criteria 9-4
    Referral, Screening, and Assessment Process 9-4
Program Organization and Operation 9-5
    Program Phases 9-5
    Provision of Treatment Services 9-5
        Services for Special Populations 9-6
        Public Health Services 9-6
        Aftercare 9-6
        Alumni Activities 9-6
    Assignment of Cases to Drug Court Judge(s) 9-6
    Program Policies and Procedures 9-7
        Oversight/Advisory Committee 9-7
        Multi-Disciplinary and Cross-Training 9-7
    Community Relationships 9-7
    Collaboration With Law Enforcement 9-7
Program Resources 9-8
    Judge Time 9-8
    Additional Funds Needed 9-8
    Program Income 9-8
Program Process 9-9
    Time Between Arrest and Program Entry 9-9

An earlier version of this chapter appeared in Offender Programs Report, *Vol. 6, No. 1, May/June 2002.*

Changes in Existing Criminal Case Process Required to
Implement Drug Court Program 9-9
Court Response to Participant Progress, or Rearrest 9-9
Termination of Unsuccessful Participants 9-10
Successful Completion and Graduation 9-10
Program Contacts With Participants 9-11

FLORIDA MODEL SPARKS A TREND

When the Dade County (Florida) Circuit Court instituted a special "drug court" docket in August, 1989, its purpose was to provide more effective supervision of defendants with drug possession charges awaiting adjudication. The immediate goals were to reduce the recidivism rate of these defendants while they were awaiting disposition of their cases, reduce the rate of failure appear at trial, and provide at least some level of treatment services. At the time Miami developed its drug court docket—during the height of the "war on crime" era—the volume of drug cases had escalated to a point that left both the judicial and treatment systems unable to handle the caseloads. The primary purpose of the Miami drug court was not therapeutic, although it clearly had therapeutic elements, but rather to promote public safety and more effective judicial supervision of defendants while awaiting trial. The judge assigned to oversee Miami's drug court, Judge Stanley Goldstein, was a former New York City police officer, deemed well equipped to provide stern judicial oversight of this massive and difficult population.

It soon became apparent, however, that many in this large addict population not only complied with—and appeared to welcome—the on-going judicial oversight introduced for the Miami Drug Court docket defendants, but were also very receptive to the treatment services offered. The Miami Drug Court docket was resulting not only in reduced criminal activity on the part of pretrial defendants but in their actual recovery. And with their recovery, many other social and economic benefits for the defendants were evident—education, employment, improved parental and other family relationships, not to mention their improved sense of personal self worth. Within a very short period of time, judges from many other jurisdictions, both within the United States and abroad—many of whom felt discouraged in dealing effectively with their own heightening drug dockets and limited sentencing discretion—came to visit the Miami Drug Court. Invigorated by the interplay of judicial authority, effectiveness, and impact of the Miami Drug Court, many returned to their home jurisdictions to develop a drug court docket, with various permutations to fit their local community needs and justice system "culture."

Drug courts have now been operating in the United States for more than a dozen years. Over 1,100 programs have been implemented and over 500 more are being planned. Drug court activity is underway or being planned in every state, plus the District of Columbia, Puerto Rico, and Guam. Permutations of the adult drug court model are now reflected in drug court programs targeting delinquency (juvenile) and dependency (parents in danger of losing custody) matters as well. In addition, many tribal courts have adopted the drug court concept, with almost 100 "Healing to Wellness Court" programs implemented or being planned.

As the drug court experience matures, researchers and policy makers alike are asking common questions: What impact are drug courts having? What do these programs cost? Will they play a permanent role in the criminal justice system and the way substance involved offenders are handled? Or are they merely a passing fad? What mechanisms and resources will be needed to sustain them when federal funds are no longer available? The range of drug court programs underway, the diversity of populations being served, and the variety of judicial system structures in which these programs operate have both enriched this initial period of drug court activity and made it difficult to conclusively evaluate. Nevertheless, judges involved with drug court programs—many of whom are former prosecutors—continue to unequivocally endorse the drug court approach.

Currently, approximately two-thirds (61%) of the operating drug courts are adult programs, with the remaining drug courts focusing on juveniles (25%); family/abuse and neglect cases (9%) and tribal matters (5%). The states with the most active drug court activity, with at least 50 programs underway or being planned are: California (152 programs); Florida (97 programs); New York (169 programs); Missouri (117 programs); Kentucky (58 programs); and Ohio (68 programs).

In all, the more than 1,600 drug courts either in operation or being planned are four times the number in existence in 1997.

The OJP Drug Court Clearinghouse and Technical Assistance Project at American University (established by the Drug Courts Program Office, Office of Justice Programs, at the U.S. Department of Justice) has been tracking drug court activity and developments since its establishment in 1995. The following are observations that emerge from the Clearinghouse's most recent information gathering activities. Most of the observations cited here are derived from various surveys and other information compiled by the OJP Drug Court Clearinghouse and from its technical assistance activities. (For additional information about American drug courts, including client outcome-related information, see Cooper, 2002.)

DRUG COURT PROGRAM GOALS

Most drug courts state the following primary goals:

- Reduce recidivism;

- Reduce substance abuse; and

- Enhance the likelihood of the participants' recovery over the long term.

Most also note additional goals, including reduce system costs, reduce incarceration rates, and increase public safety. Additional participant outcomes most programs seek, which are designed to promote participant recovery over the long term, include obtaining a high school or GED diploma, obtaining vocational training, obtaining employment, and developing necessary life skills.

LOCUS OF PROGRAM IN JUDICIAL PROCESS

Over 90% of current drug courts are post-plea, post-conviction, and/or for probation violators or use a combination of these approaches. Many programs permit dismissal of the charge or a striking of the plea if the defendant successfully completes
the drug court program and the defendant is eligible for that type of disposition.
Less than 10% of adult drug courts are pre-trial/pre-plea only. This program structure represents a significant shift away from the pre-trial/pre-plea model of the early
drug courts, due, in large part, to the significantly more serious offenders most drug
courts are now targeting.

TARGETED OFFENSES AND OFFENDERS

The range of offenses targeted by drug courts has expanded significantly during
the past several years. While almost all drug courts have been targeting drug possession charges, many more are now also targeting drug-related theft/property offenses,
check/credit card and prescription forgeries, prostitution, and DUI/DWI.

Participant Eligibility Criteria

Most drug courts have expanded the range of permissible criminal histories since
1997. Fewer than than 5% limit participant eligibility to defendants with no prior criminal charges (compared with 13% in 1997), and 76% accept an individual with any number of prior offenses as long as they meet current legal and clinical eligibility criteria.

Almost all drug courts are targeting individuals with at least moderate substance
abuse and 90% indicate they are targeting individuals with severe substance use.
Most programs indicate that they accept participants with alcohol dependency,
although these individuals usually come before the court in connection with offenses involving other drugs. Most programs also report that they will accept participants
involved with any chemical substance, illegal or legal, including prescription drugs
and inhalants. None of the programs, however, are dealing with nicotine addiction.

Referral, Screening, and Assessment Process

Referrals to drug courts are being made from multiple sources. The most frequently cited referral sources are public defenders (90%); prosecutors (88%); privately
retained attorneys (88%); probation staff (66%); pretrial service agency staff (51%);
and law enforcement officials (34%). The initial screening of cases and defendants for
drug court eligibility is generally conducted by the prosecutor and, for pretrial programs, by the pretrial services agency or court staff. In most cases, final determination of program eligibility rests with the drug court judge, often in conjunction with
the prosecutor. Slightly over half of drug court programs indicate that more people are
eligible for the drug court than are accepted.

Screening for substance addiction is a part of the eligibility determination process
once initial criminal justice system eligibility is determined. Over 60% of the programs report that defendants initially identified as eligible for the drug court by jus-

Table 9.1: Frequency of Treatment, Rehabilitation, and Other Services Provided During Drug Court Phases

Services Provided	Phase I	Phase II	Phase III	Phase IV/V
Detox	73%	12%	7%	—
Counseling	87%	87%	80%	2%
Drug Education	84%	73%	62%	1%
Therapy	63%	71%	65%	1%
Medical Screening	60%	45%	38%	1%
Housing Services	44%	48%	45%	1%
Acupuncture	21%	18%	15%	<1%
Job Training	22%	55%	67%	1%
Educational	27%	68%	74%	1%
Development Employment Services Placement	28%	58%	70%	2%
Other Life Skills	36%	74%	74%	1%

tice system officials will be disqualified if their substance abuse screening indicates they are not addicted or exhibit only minimal addiction.

PROGRAM ORGANIZATION AND OPERATION

Program Phases

Most programs are divided into phases, most frequently entailing three or four phases. Those programs that have more than four phases generally include in the additional phase(s) a period of post-program supervision and/or aftercare services. A number of programs are also developing multiple "tracks" for drug court participants to address the diversity of treatment and other rehabilitation needs participants present.

While drug courts are providing a range of treatment and rehabilitation services throughout their period of operation, the most intensive treatment and related services are occurring during the initial phases of the programs, with job training and other life skills being provided as the individual progresses in treatment. Table 9.1 above provides a summary of the services provided.

Provision of Treatment Services

The pattern of treatment provider support for drug court programs has remained fairly constant, with the exception of an increasing number of programs utilizing numerous multiple providers (e.g., more than 10). Approximately one-third of the programs utilize one dedicated provider (which may include in-house court staff) and one-third use six or more providers. The remaining programs utilize two to five providers. Provision of drug court treatment services are increasingly being provided by private treatment organizations, existing local providers and court hired staff. The involvement of county health departments and probation staff has decreased since 1997.

Services for Special Populations. Many programs indicate that they have developed special program components or segments to address the needs of special populations in their drug courts. Among the special components developed include those geared to dually diagnosed participants (53%); female participants (48%); pregnant or postpartum participants (42%); foreign-speaking participants (primarily Spanish) (36%); participants who are parents (35%); victims of domestic violence (35%); participants dealing with childhood trauma (29%); and participants who are HIV positive (28%).

Public Health Services. Almost all of the drug courts report that they are screening participants for possible infectious diseases and other medical conditions, including HIV and tuberculosis, and referring them to local medical service providers for treatment. In a number of instances, relationships are also being developed with local physicians to remove tattoos, and/or with dentists to provide services for persons who have developed dental conditions, particularly those that are a result of their drug use.

Aftercare. Aftercare services for a period following completion of the drug court program are being provided by 60% of the drug courts. Since many of the services traditionally considered as "aftercare" in non-drug court programs are provided as a component of the drug court program before a participant graduates, drug court "aftercare" services generally focus on promoting the continued recovery and stabilization of the participant as well as providing mentoring to new drug court enrollees. These services are generally provided by the drug court treatment provider and consist of relapse prevention, call-in "help" lines, providing peer support/mentoring, and support to new drug court participants.

Alumni Activities. Approximately half of the drug courts currently have an alumni association and an additional 35% indicate that one is being planned. Among the variety of services drug court alumni associations are providing include: mentoring, networking, and representational functions.

Assignment of Cases to Drug Court Judge(s)

Most drug courts assign drug court cases to one judge who hears drug court cases for an average of 10 hours per week in addition to the rest of his/her docket. Approximately 10% of the programs assign drug court cases to a full-time drug court judge whose only assignment is to hear drug court cases. In many instances in which the drug court judge hears drug court cases in addition to his/her full regular docket, the drug court cases are scheduled before or after the regular trial day.

In approximately one-third of the drug courts, the drug court assignment rotates among the judges. Some have a two-year rotation period; a few have a one-year rotation period and one program uses a six-month rotation period. For the remaining programs, the rotation period extends until the drug court judge decides to step down or, in one instance, until the presiding judge appoints a replacement judges.

Program Policies and Procedures

Most programs have developed written Policies and Procedures Manuals. In addition, many have written Memorandum of Understanding (MOU) with at least some of the agencies involved in the drug court program. Most of these MOUs cover the use of information regarding possible admission of drug use by the participant and many also address the participant's possible disclosure of criminal acts that he/she has committed during the course of treatment.

Oversight/Advisory Committee. Slightly over half (53%) of the drug courts in 2002 had established oversight committees (a decrease from the 69% reported in 1997). These oversight/advisory committees provide advisory services and, frequently, guidance in policy and procedural development. In many instances, these committees also assist in gaining community support and resources. The size of these committees varies, with the majority consisting of nine or more members. In addition to justice system representatives, membership on the drug court oversight committees frequently includes representatives from the legal, medical, education, business, faith, and public health sectors of the local community. Many of the committees also have citizen representatives. Since 1997, there has been a marked change in the composition of these committees, with significant decreases in judicial, prosecutorial, and defense representation and an increase in representation from the business community, the local executive branch, and law enforcement.

Multi-Disciplinary and Cross-Training. The multi-disciplinary nature of drug court programs and the collaborative process underlying their operation has highlighted the need for on-going multi-disciplinary and cross training for personnel involved with the program. Among the training topics of particular import have been those relating to the physiologic, cognitive, and emotional aspects of substance addiction and recovery; pharmacology; gender issues; and adolescent development. In terms of cross training, most programs are focusing on providing training on the orientation and provision of treatment services; relevant protocols; confidentiality issues; and the criminal justice process as it applies to drug court-eligible defendants.

Community Relationships

Almost all drug courts are working closely with community groups to provide support services for participants. Through both community networks and involvement with local Alcoholics Anonymous and Narcotics Anonymous groups, participants are often linked with community mentors shortly after entering the drug court. Drug courts are also developing close working relationships with local chambers of commerce, medical service providers, community service organizations, local education systems, faith communities and other local institutions to provide a broad-based network of essential services that can be drawn upon to serve the needs of their participants. As noted above, frequently representatives from these agencies serve on the oversight committees of local drug courts for those programs that have established such committees.

Collaboration With Law Enforcement

Many drug courts are developing working relationships with local law enforcement agencies. Drug court judges are making increasing efforts to explain the drug court process to line officers who are the arresting officers in many drug court cases. The police department in several jurisdictions (New Haven, Connecticut, and San Diego, California, for example) have assigned an officer full-time to the drug court to assist with monitoring and supervision of participants and to immediately execute bench warrants for any participants who fail to appear in court or who are otherwise in noncompliance with drug court orders.

PROGRAM RESOURCES

Judge Time

The percentage of bench time allocated by judges for drug court cases is directly correlated to the number of participants enrolled in the program. For the bulk of programs using one judge to hear the drug court caseload, assigned benchtimes range from 10% to 100% of their available docket time. In addition to benchtime for drug court hearings, drug court judges are contributing significant additional time (generally evenings, lunchtime, and weekends) for drug court functions. These include pre-hearing staffings and a variety of other services related to the management and funding of the program, its integration with other judicial system functions, necessary interagency relationships, and related outreach in the community.

Additional Funds Needed

In addition to the judge time and services of other judicial system staff contributed by the judicial system, almost all programs have needed additional funds for the program, primarily for treatment services and drug testing. Drug courts have continued to use a variety of funding sources to support program operations. Over half of the current drug courts have been recipients of federal funds and 25% have received local funding to support the drug court. A number of state legislatures have appropriated funds for drug court programs. An increasing—though still relatively small—number of programs are also accessing Medicaid and third-party insurance benefits to which their participants are entitled.

Program Income

Many drug courts charge participant fees, ranging from $10 weekly to $4,000 during the period of enrollment. Fees range between $150 and $500 for 60% of the programs. Most programs have set a "cap" on the program fees required, which the weekly payments offset.

Approximately one-third of these programs waived fees for indigent clients, and 25% have instituted a sliding scale for payment, based on the participant's situation. In 2002, 17% of the programs (up from 10% in 1997) waived assessed fees for good performance. The rate of fee collection was reported to be 75% (up from 67% in 1997). The uses for program fees were most frequently reported to be for augmenting treatment services (36%), drug testing (33%), providing local match requirements for grants (17%), and administrative costs (6%).

Drug courts also indicate a significant increase in the frequency in accessing insurance, Medicaid, and other public benefits to which participants are entitled for treatment and related services.

PROGRAM PROCESS

Time Between Arrest and Program Entry

For many programs, entry into the drug court is still occurring very shortly following arrest. An increasing number of drug courts include a re-entry component for persons sentenced to an initial period of incarceration. Sixty percent of these re-entry programs report that less than six months elapse between the offender's original sentencing in court and his/her initial drug court appearance. Most programs report that 10 days or less elapse between the offender's release from incarceration and his/her initial drug court appearance.

Changes in Existing Criminal Case Process Required to Implement Drug Court Program

Most drug courts have made changes in the existing case disposition process to accommodate the drug court program. These changes have included establishing a special calendar for drug court cases, assigning these cases to one or two designated judges rather than criminal judges generally, and establishing a schedule of extra hearings to accommodate the frequent judicial review functions necessary. Most drug courts have also instituted special procedures for screening drug cases at the time of arrest and procedures to immediately execute bench warrants for individuals who fail to appear at the drug court hearing.

Court Response to Participant Progress, or Rearrest

Drug courts are using a variety of strategies to respond to participant relapse, most often in combination and adapted to the specific facts of the situation. The most common judicial responses to participant relapse and/or noncompliance with drug court conditions include increased treatment services, increased urinalysis, increased frequency of hearings, and short-term incarceration. Other responses include imposing house arrest, electronic monitoring, referring participant for acupuncture, referring participant to residential treatment, requiring participant to perform community service, and/or increasing supervision of participant.

All programs recognize that judicial recognition of participant progress in a drug court is as important as judicial response to relapse. Praise from the drug court judge and accolades from peers are characteristic of all programs and, depending upon related factors, promotion of participants to a higher program phase is also common if other program conditions have been met. Eighty-six percent of the programs also reduce the frequency of status hearings as participants progress; however, only 64% of the programs reduce the frequency of urinalysis—a fundamental gauge of substance use—unless the participant is progressing to a higher program phase.

Program responses to new arrests of program participants vary from program to program. Most programs terminate a participant if arrested for a violent offense or a drug trafficking offense. Response to arrests for other offenses, however, generally depends on the nature of the offense and the participant's individual situation. Even if a participant is not terminated, however, the new charge is prosecuted while the participant continues in the drug court.

Bench warrants are issued by all drug courts for participants who fail to appear at court hearings, and 69% of the programs—up from 56% in 1997—have instituted expedited procedures to assure that the participant is picked up immediately and brought before the court. Participants who miss treatment appointments are often contacted by treatment providers who frequently notify the court of any participant's failure to appear as well.

Positive urinalyses usually trigger immediate response from both the treatment provider and the court. Generally treatment contacts are increased and judicial sanctions are imposed. Most programs, however, take into account the circumstances of each participant in determining the appropriate sanctions. Some programs terminate an individual after a specified number of positive urinalyses.

Termination of Unsuccessful Participants

Apart from the commission of new offenses that trigger automatic termination, the most frequently cited reasons for termination of unsuccessful participants include re-occuring drug use, missed court appearances, missed treatment opportunities, alcohol use, and recommendation of treatment provider.

In most instances, program termination results from a number of factors; no one factor is determinative.

Most of the drug courts report that the drug court judge, almost always in consort with the drug court team, makes the final decision regarding termination of an unsuccessful drug court participant. In a small minority of the programs (4%), however, the decision is made by the prosecutor and/or by the treatment provider (5%).

Most (80%) of the participants who have been terminated for non-compliance from the drug court receive sentences of incarceration. Generally, the sentence the defendant receives following termination is the same as he/she would have received if he/she had never entered the drug court.

Successful Completion and Graduation

All drug courts require a minimum period of treatment program participation (generally at least 12 months) and sobriety (usually at least four to six consecutive months) for graduation. In addition, most programs also require a recommendation from the treatment program and evidence that the participant is living in a stable, drug-free living situation. The programs also require participants to comply with other program conditions (e.g., payment of program fees, obtaining employment, earning a GED or high school diploma, or performing a specified amount of community service).

In many drug courts, participants who successfully complete the drug court program have their charges dismissed or guilty plea stricken. If a participant is not eligible for this type of disposition, he/she generally receives some reduction in sentence exposure or applicable probation period, depending upon their criminal history and circumstances of the current charge.

Program Contacts With Participants

Face-to-face contact between the drug court judge and drug court participants generally ranges from weekly or bi-weekly during the first two phases to monthly as participants progress. Participant contacts with other justice system staff (e.g., prosecutors and defense counsel) is frequent and on-going, and generally occurs at each court status hearing, either in person or through reports provided. Most programs also require drug court participants to have at least three contacts per week with the treatment provider and many require four to five, at least during the first phase of program participation. Required contacts with the case managers in most programs are at least weekly initially and decrease during the period of program participation. For most programs, they never decrease to less than bi-weekly, even in the final phases of the program.

In addition to court status hearings and treatment provider and case manager contacts, participants are required to undergo frequent, generally random, urinalysis throughout their period of drug court participation.

Most drug courts impose additional program requirements (e.g., employment or curfew compliance) during the various phases of program operations. The frequency with which these requirements are imposed varies from program to program. Many programs also indicate that periodic field visits are made to participants' homes as part of the drug court supervision process. Twenty-three percent indicate law enforcement officers conduct the visits; 23% indicate case managers make the visits; and 54% indicate that probation staff conduct the visits.

About the Author

Caroline Cooper, M.A., J.D., is Director of the Office of Justice Programs' National Drug Court Clearinghouse and Technical Assistance Project, located at American University, 4400 Massachusetts Ave., N.W., Washington, DC 20016-8159; (202) 885-2875; (e-mail) justice@american.edu; (website) www.american.edu/justice.

Reference

Cooper, C. (2002, July/August). Clients and Current Trends in American Drug Court Programs. *Offender Programs Report, 6(2)*, 19-20; 31-32.

Chapter 10

Dilemmas Confronting Practitioners in Family Drug Treatment Courts

by Christina Pratt, Ph.D., M.S.S.W., C.S.W.

Introduction 10-1
Risk and Coercion 10-2
Family Drug Treatment Court Incentives and Supports 10-3
Evaluation and Research 10-4
Remaining Challenges for FTCs 10-5

INTRODUCTION

Family drug treatment courts (FTCs) are problem-solving experiments, where judges impose accountability not only on substance abusing parents, but also on a social welfare system that is fragmented, uncoordinated, and generally ill prepared for the multiple issues of families with chemical dependency problems.

Three factors play a role in the proliferation of drug courts: the war on drugs; jail overcrowding; and a stream of state and federal funds. New York State offers a particularly vivid example of a court system grappling with the consequences of drugs, crime, and family offenses. Between 1980 and 1999 drug arrests in New York State increased by 430%. In 1998, for example, eight out of 10 defendants arrested in New York City tested positive for drugs at the time of their arrest (New York State Commission on Drugs and the Courts, 2000). Drug interdiction has also taken a toll on the state's Family Courts. From 1984 to 1994, family law cases increased by 65% (Babb & Moran, 1999) and chemical dependency was a problem for nearly 90% of family court respondents, according to a national survey of child welfare and family court professionals (Reid, Macchetto & Foster, 1999).

Welfare reform further exacerbates the problem. With social provisions substantially reduced or eliminated, families are at heightened risk of child removal as rates of unemployment and eviction grow. Moreover, the Adoption and Safe Families Act (ASFA) demands parents clean up their acts within one year or less or irrevocably sever their parental rights and connection to biological offspring.

An earlier version of this chapter appeared in Offender Programs Report, *Vol. 6, No. 1, May/June 2002.*

Since the late 1980s, legislatures across the United States have considered numerous bills concerning pregnant women who use drugs or alcohol. In one year alone, 34 states debated bills relating to prenatal exposure to drugs. An additional eight states attempted, but failed, to pass legislation that would make it a crime to be chemically dependent and give birth. South Carolina has prosecuted the largest number of women for maternal drug use. The policy offers no second chances. Women who test positive for drugs during pregnancy or who deliver babies with positive drug toxicology are arrested and imprisoned. Mothers are charged with drug possession, child neglect, and/or the distribution of drugs to a minor (Paltrow; 2000).

The intersection of chemical dependency, child neglect, and welfare reform constellates in ASFA, a likely accelerant to the termination of parental rights in the absence of FTCs. As welfare limits and a recessed economy impact families, more children will enter an already overburdened child welfare system. More families, chiefly headed by poor women of color, risk child protective involvement, and face routine drug testing and the reality that their parent-child relationship will be terminated (Roberts, 2001).

RISK AND COERCION

In family court, the risk of child endangerment fuels networks of preventive and predictive surveillance. Throughout systems of justice, an insurance model of crime control has developed, indicating a growing reliance on opportunity reduction and loss prevention. Civil libertarian objections to family treatment court monitoring arise, in part, from consideration of broader ideological forces at play. One concern is that "treatment" conditions set by the court work against the rights of both offenders and their families by placing too much power in the hands of non-court professionals. Reminiscent of *Gault*-era rights violations associated with indeterminate rehabilitation, drug courts provide potent incentives to extend the reach of the justice system and deputize far-flung treatment agents to deliver coercive sanctions outside the law, in the interests of harm reduction (Dorf & Sabel, 2000). In an era of privatization and the devolution of public provision, nongovernmental organizations (NGOs) for hire compete with new proprietary vendors for government contracts and court referrals and create a self-propelling market of new stakeholders.

Distinctions are now fuzzy between institutions that are public and those that are private and profit making. Cynics suggest that to save the bureaucracy it has been necessary to hide it by contracting out much of its work (Light, 1999). Disarticulation of the state, high jurisdictional and disciplinary fragmentation, and diminished bureaucratic capacity constitute the environment of public administration within which family treatment courts emerge. Indeed, the most formidable challenge to problem-solving courts, such as family treatment courts, is effective surveillance of the newly deputized court-contracted providers of services, not the individual respondents to the court.

A strategy for minimizing risk thereby transfers the handling of family addiction from the state to private agents with new (and old) technologies and power over the offender, such as routine and random urine screens, surveillance and curfews in sober housing, counseling, Alcohol Anonymous, Narcotics Anonymous, parenting education, and anger management.

When child abuse laws are used to police addiction, the nature of personal liberties shifts significantly. For example, a recent trend in the criminal law finds women who use drugs "presumptively neglectful" resulting in risk of temporary or permanent loss of child custody based on a single drug test (Paltrow, 1999). In New York State, a 1995 ruling noted that a finding of neglect cannot be based solely on a newborn's positive toxicolgy, *In re Nassau County Dept. of Social Services*, 661 N.E. 2d 138 (N.Y. 1995). However, a new family drug court strategy requires all respondents to be subject to violations of orders of protection for their children if weekly court administered drug tests prove positive. As such, offending parents may be incarcerated, or at the very least prohibited from visitation with their children, until subsequent drug tests prove negative.

None of this discussion is intended to discount the dangers of alcohol and drug use. It is indisputable that infants and children harmed by parental addiction cost society valuable and scarce social, educational, and economic resources. Fetal protection and family drug court policies nevertheless remain extraordinarily complicated ideas of law and justice. Scientifically, the magnitude and probability that substance abuse irreversibly harms the child who will be born, and those already born, is inexact (Mathieu, 1996).

In 2002, in suburban New York, despite restraints on the degrees of confinement available to family courts, failure to comply with conditions imposed by family treatment courts meant a jail sentence of one to six months. Prison narratives of confined women attest to the "hard time" and irreconcilable loss associated with termination of parental rights. There is hardly a harsher punishment for a mother than exile from her children (Pratt, 2000).

FAMILY DRUG TREATMENT COURT INCENTIVES AND SUPPORTS

By the mid-1990s, in suburban New York, three-quarters of child abuse and neglect cases appearing as petitions to the family courts involved substance-abusing parents. The rate had quadrupled in less than 15 years fueled by child protective cases implicating a "crack epidemic." Here's how metropolitan suburbs have attempted to grapple with the collision of drug addiction and family life.

Troubled by the destructive cycling of children with positive drug toxicologies into foster care followed by another "positive tox" sibling, family court judges known to incarcerate chemically dependent mothers reversed their practice and strove to create "front end" interventions.

Since January 1999, courts are obliged to implement ASFA to the fullest. In FTCs, family courts must beat the ASFA clock to determine if "deep-end" respondents with long histories in court can be "good enough" nurturing and sober parents within one year. As the analogy goes, family court judges are between a rock and a hard place. The rock represents the standard of drug treatment endorsed by the federal government and supported by research: treatment on demand; comprehensive services; and relapse management. (Addiction, after all, is a chronic relapsing disease.) The hard place is the court itself: litigation delays, poor contact with parents and children, lack of accountability by contract agencies, not enough service or treatment providers, and no assurance of timely access.

Families have one chance, and only one. AFSA recommends "reasonable efforts" to deliver services to reunify families before parental rights are terminated involuntarily. In FTCs, ASFA holds the potential to create a bridge between drug treatment and the courts. On the court side of things, ASFA is the engine of reform. Its system of deadlines forces clearance of delays in resolving cases. Parents carry the burden to be more accountable to the court, they must prove, under an accelerated clock, that they can protect and care for their children.

Remarkable recovery rates and drops in recidivism are evident for graduates of drug courts. Building on that success, family drug courts offer a process by which chemically dependent parents can cross the bridge that ASFA built. FTCs provide the incentive of immediate entry into treatment, the early support of front-loaded services, and the enforcement of frequent (usually weekly) court appearances, urine screens, and supervised visitation.

Respondents are obliged to admit to both substance abuse and child neglect as a requirement of eligibility for the treatment court. The rationale is that this saves urgently needed time. (Typically a hearing to find neglect took a minimum of three months.) With FTCs, the chance of treatment success is improved with immediate participation and access. Clinically, however, psychological and family-based denial systems associated with addiction and child neglect complicate access to FTCs. For some parents, a jail sentence, and even termination of parental rights, is preferable to intensive FTC supervision.

In FTCs, up-front admissions of guilt signal deferred sanctions. Adversarial elements of case processing are instantly eliminated. All attention is focused on the participant's recovery. Initially, assigned counsel was concerned about repercussions when clients fail. The defense bar recognized that it could advise clients facing weak cases to decline participation. In the end, defense attorneys joined the FTC workgroup with the proviso that assessment material be kept confidential and not be used against respondents if they opted out and elected incarceration.

EVALUATION AND RESEARCH

Family systems are complicated. New strategies to monitor the progress of families engaged with many service providers are needed. Unlike criminal cases where the primary players are the prosecution and the defense, child protective cases have three "sides" (the respondent, the child, and the state) and each side has its own attorneys and agendas, in addition to caseworkers, addiction specialists, and foster care agents as players.

Research designs with the family as the unit of analysis and evaluation measures that hold systems accountable for the capacity building of families pose methodological challenges. One of the greatest challenges is the need for court players to adapt to new roles. For the judge, this means operating as a trouble-shooter, team leader, and entrepreneur. Critics tend to degrade this role enlargement to that of a "lowly" case manager (Hoffman, 2000). Law guardians, for example, need to shift from compliance-enforcer to working out reunification visits for children and parents. Inter-organizational relationships are completely reconfigured to reconnect healthier parents and children and resist termination of parental rights.

Preliminary research on FTCs suggests the following:

- Courts can be changed through problem-solving, outcome-driven processes;

- Judges can reposition their roles as community activists;

- Courts benefit from community partners in struggling to solve complex problems;

- The adversarial system can adjust and evolve to promote treatment while protecting rights and protecting rights while restoring community;

- System change, as well as individual change, is possible; and

- Legal, social, and human problems intersect.

Today 750 drug courts exist throughout the nation; about a dozen are family drug treatment courts. No longer "boutique" experiments, real change is evident in how courts do business (Feinblatt, 2001).

FTCs offer a promise of new capacity-building connections for families whose lives are disrupted by addiction and foster care, as well as new incentives for networks of social care to rethink service provision.

REMAINING CHALLENGES FOR FTCS

Several challenges remain for problem-solving courts like FTCs:

- *Leadership.* Given the absence of any curriculum on therapeutic jurisprudence in legal education, where on the horizon is a new generation of entrepreneurial judges willing to build community partnerships?

- *Community/Capacity.* Proposals that offer treatment to increasingly large numbers of substance abusers stress the capacity of treatment resources to meet the demand. Despite evidence that considerable costs are avoided down the line, in an era of managed care and eroding social provision, who pays for up-front expenditures is up for grabs. Strong arguments and advocacy are needed to create new funding arrangements that invest in and reflect the shared interests of collateral systems, e.g., foster care, welfare, and criminal justice.

- *Proliferation.* Will the widespread institutionalization of FTCs dilute the unique character of the problem solving court model? Are the courts threatening due process? Conversely, is the court "soft" on drugs? Family offenses? Will information management systems contribute to a cybernetic panopticon? What are the alternatives?

By placing greater emphasis on achieving meaningful case outcomes, by encouraging players in the courtroom drama to play new roles, and by working to solve problems rather than simply process cases, the FTC seeks to change how the court works and what the public should expect.

All that said, race and class biases in the administration of family drug courts merit fuller critique. In January 2004, over 50% of participants in the Rockland County and Suffolk County FTCs are African-American; and 80% are women. Advocacy for wider social control is problematic when such power manifests disproportionately in poor communities where racism, indifference, and excessive force are all too frequent.

In New York State today, reform manifests itself in experimental courts. Like mental health courts, FTCs advocate outpatient civil commitment of pregnant women and parents who are drug dependent (Mathieu, 1995). This approach relies on the thera-peutic jurisprudence perspective of David Wexler of the University of Arizona Law School (1996).

The drug treatment court model was devised to respond to the problems of court overload and jail overcrowding exacerbated by the war on drugs. The FTC emerges as well to mediate the effects on children of parental substance abuse. It is a recent man-ifestation of a long history in the United States of attempts to manage many societal problems—individual as well as structural—through the relatively limited institution-al apparatus of the criminal justice system. Problems of addiction, crime, social and economic inequality, and the disproportionate targeting of individuals by race, class, and gender are clearly interconnected. These issues pervade the public discourse and open government practices to greater transparency and accountability.

For certain, it is critically important that members of the community who have lost the capacity to refrain from obtaining and using addictive substances have access to therapeutic services. The decision to locate significant treatment resources within the justice system, or to designate the courts as a major point of entry into treatment, is not the only method available for structuring these services. Making drug abuse treatment a part of the public health system, and linking these therapeutic efforts to the full array of structural responses, is another reasonable public policy alternative. At the ambi-tious end of the continuum are policies that target the lack of legitimate opportunity and enterprise capital that make poor communities such fertile sites for the manufac-ture and sale of illegal drugs.

When treatment is built into the courts, the dominant social construct about addic-tion is embedded in notions of individual choice layered with ideas about pathology, desert, and blame. Lost in this web is any clear sense that addiction and its related social harms could be viewed alternatively as public health, public safety, and com-munity justice issues (Clear & Pratt, 2004).

Problem-solving courts, like the FTC model, are changing the justice landscape in fundamental, perhaps enduring ways. Drug courts are sweeping the country in a con-tagion fueled by government grants and well-intentioned, enthusiastic state and local judges frustrated by a perceived lost war on drugs. A new interdependency of function marries the judiciary to community-based services promising to significantly alter the allocation of justice and social service resources. Powerful possibility exists to partner with families and communities and strengthen assets for change.

About the Author

Christina Pratt, Ph.D., M.S.S.W., C.S.W. is Professor of Social Work and Gender Studies, Domincan College, Orangeburg, NY. She may be reached by e-mail at christina. pratt@dc.edu.

References

Babb, B., & Moran, J. (1999). "Substance abuse, families and the courts: Legal and public health challenges." *University of Maryland Journal of Health Care Law and Policy, 3*, 3-43.

Clear, T., & Pratt, C. (2004), Community justice as public safety. *Journal of American Probation and Parole* 28 (1), 42-47.

Dorf, M.C., & Sabel, C.F. (2000). Drug treatment courts and emergent experimentalist government. *Vanderbilt Law Review 53*, 831-883.

Feinblatt, J. (2001). Executive Director, Center for Court Innovation, (personal communication).

Hoffman, M. (2000, June), The drug court scandal. *North Carolina Law Review*, 78, 1437-1527.

Light, P. (1999). *The true size of government.* Washington, DC: The Brookings Institution.

Mathieu, D. (1996). *Preventing prenatal harm: Should the state intervene?*, Washington, DC: Georgetown University Press.

New York State Commission on Drugs and the Courts (2000, June), *Confronting the cycle of addiction and recidivism: A report to Chief Judge Judith S. Kaye.*

Paltrow, L. (2000). Prejudice and punishment: Judging pregnant women who use drugs. Unpublished paper delivered to the American Society of Criminology meeting (San Francisco).

Paltrow, L. (1999). Punishment and prejudice: Judging drug-using pregnant women. In J. Hanigsberg & S. Ruddick, Eds., *Mother troubles: Rethinking contemporary maternal dilemmas* (pp. 59-80). Boston: Beacon Press.

Pratt, C. (2000). *Community justice demonstration grant proposal*, NYS OASAS, Leigh Scheurholz Halfway House for women ex-prisoners.

Reid, J., Macchetto, P., & Foster, S. (1999), *No safe haven: Children of substance abusing parents,* New York: National Center on Addiction and Substance Abuse.

Roberts, D. (2001). *Shattered bonds: The color of child welfare,* New York: Basic Books.

Wexler, D. (1996). "Some therapeutic jurisprudence implications of the outpatient civil commitment of pregnant substance abusers. In D. B. Wexler & B. J. Winick, Eds., *Law in a therapeutic key: Developments in therapeutic jurisprudence,* Durham, NC: Carolina Academic Press.

Chapter 11

The Role of Judicial Status Hearings in Drug Court

by Douglas B. Marlowe, J.D., Ph.D., David S. Festinger, Ph.D., and Patricia A. Lee, M.S.

Drug Courts Are an Alternative to Criminal Prosecution or Incarceration 11-1
Key Components of Drug Courts 11-2
Studying the Effects of Judicial Status Hearings on Drug Court
  Outcomes: Biweekly or As-Needed 11-2
    First Study 11-2
        No Main Effect of Status Hearings 11-2
        Different Effects for High-Risk and Low-Risk Offenders
            in Biweekly vs. As-Needed Hearings .11-3
    Study Limitation Addressed 11-3
        Programs Four to Six Months Long 11-3
        Monthly Meetings With Case Manager 11-4
Follow-Up Study Results 11-4
    Participant Characteristics 11-4
    Distribution Across Study Conditions Confirmed 11-4
    Main Effects Showed No Clear Differences
        Between the Two Conditions 11-5
    Interaction Effects Showed Clear Superiority of Biweekly
        Condition for Participants With Prior Drug Treatment History 11-6
    Study Recruitment Stopped in Response to Possible
        Shift in Risk/Benefit Ratio 11-8
Conclusions 11-8

DRUG COURTS ARE AN ALTERNATIVE TO CRIMINAL PROSECUTION OR INCARCERATION

Drug courts are special criminal court dockets that provide judicially supervised drug abuse treatment and case management services to nonviolent drug offenders in lieu of criminal prosecution or incarceration. Offenders who complete the prescribed

An earlier version of this chapter appeared in Offender Substance Abuse Report, *Vol. 3, No. 3, May/June 2003.*

regimen may have their current criminal charges dropped or may be sentenced to community time served in the drug court program. Defendants are typically required to plead guilty or no contest to the charges or to stipulate to the facts in the arrest report as a condition of entry into drug court. Therefore, termination from the program for noncompliance or unremitting drug use ordinarily results in a criminal drug conviction and sentencing to supervised probation or incarceration.

KEY COMPONENTS OF DRUG COURTS

The National Association of Drug Court Professionals (NADCP, 1997) defines the key components of drug court as including:

- Access to a range of drug abuse treatment and rehabilitative services;

- Ongoing status hearings in court;

- Random weekly urinalyses; and

- Graduated sanctions for infractions and rewards for achievements.

Although substantial evidence suggests that drug courts can increase treatment retention and reduce drug use and criminal recidivism among offenders (Belenko, 1998, 1999, 2001; Guydish et al., 2001), few studies have attempted to isolate the effects of any one of these "key components" to confirm its contributions to outcomes or to determine its optimum dosage (e.g., Marlowe, 2002; Marlowe & Kirby, 1999).

STUDYING THE EFFECTS OF JUDICIAL STATUS HEARINGS ON DRUG COURT OUTCOMES: BIWEEKLY OR AS-NEEDED

First Study

In prior work, we conducted the first study designed to isolate the effects of judicial status hearings on drug court outcomes (Festinger et al., 2002; Marlowe et al., 2003). We randomly assigned consenting misdemeanor drug court clients either to attend status hearings in court on a biweekly basis throughout their enrollment in the drug court program ("biweekly" condition) or to be monitored by their treatment case managers, who petitioned the judge for status hearings only in response to serious infractions or noncompliance ("as-needed" condition). Apart from the assigned schedule of status hearings, all participants were eligible for the same drug abuse treatment, case management, urinalyses, and sanctions and rewards.

No Main Effect of Status Hearings. Results revealed no main effect of status hearings on counseling attendance, urinalysis results, self-reported drug use, self-reported alcohol intoxication, or self-reported criminal activity during the scheduled 14-week course of the drug court program (Marlowe et al., 2003). Further, there was no difference in participants' graduation rates from the program (Festinger et al., 2002) or in urinalysis results, self-reported drug problems, self-reported alcohol problems, or self-reported criminal activity at six months or 12 months post-admission (Marlowe et al., 2002).

Different Effects for High-Risk and Low-Risk Offenders in Biweekly vs. As-Needed Hearings. Importantly, however, certain "high-risk" offenders performed significantly better when assigned to biweekly hearings, whereas "low-risk" offenders performed better when assigned to as-needed hearings. Specifically, participants who (1) met the *Diagnostic and Statistical Manual of Mental Disorders* (DSM-IV; APA 1994) criteria for antisocial personality disorder (APD) or (2) had a prior unsuccessful history in drug abuse treatment achieved more drug abstinence and were more likely to graduate from the program when assigned to biweekly hearings, whereas subjects without these risk factors performed more favorably when assigned to as-needed hearings (Festinger et al., 2002). The differential effects for the high-risk vs. low-risk offenders apparently "canceled each other out" in the main-effects analyses for the sample as a whole. This finding is consistent with the criminal justice concepts of Responsivity Theory and the Risk Principle, in which intensive interventions are theorized to exert their optimal effects for high-risk offenders but to be possibly ineffective or contraindicated for low-risk offenders (e.g., Andrews & Bonta, 1998). In fact, previous failed experiences in treatment and a diagnosis of APD or psychopathy are among the most commonly identified risk factors for criminal re-offending (e.g., Gendreau et al., 1996).

Study Limitation Addressed

An important limitation of the original study was that it was conducted in a single jurisdiction with a single drug court program and a single judge, a constraint that raised questions about the generalizability of the results. We therefore replicated the design in two new jurisdictions located in rural and urban settings.

Consecutive admissions to misdemeanor drug courts in the state capital of Dover, Delaware, and the rural farming community of Georgetown, Delaware, were approached for participation in this study from March 5, 2001, through July 1, 2002. Eligible defendants were at least 18 years old, were residents of or attended court hearings in Kent County or Sussex County, Delaware, were charged with a misdemeanor drug offense, and had no history of a violent offense or of drug-dealing or manufacturing. Participants were randomly assigned at intake either to attend biweekly status hearings (n = 37) or to attend as-needed status hearings in response to infractions or noncompliance (n = 37). As is explained later, we were required to stop recruitment prematurely because certain subjects were performing exceptionally poorly in the as-needed condition.

Programs Four to Six Months Long. The drug court programs were scheduled to be four to six months in length, although many clients required additional time to satisfy the conditions for graduation. To graduate, a client must have, at a minimum, completed a standard regimen of eight weekly drug-education counseling groups, provided 14 consecutive drug-free urine specimens, and paid court fees and costs. Approximately one-quarter of the participants attended status hearings before one of two judges, and the remainder attended hearings before one of two judicial officers called "commissioners." The commissioners generally had the same authority and responsibilities as the judges, except that they could not officially terminate a client from the program. When termination from drug court was indicated, a supervising judge convened an official termination hearing and generally acted upon the findings and conclusions of the commissioner.

Monthly Meetings With Case Manager. Clients were also assigned to a case manager with whom they met on an individual basis at least monthly during the initial phases of treatment. The case manager coordinated treatment referrals and submitted monthly progress reports to the court, and the case manager or a court liaison appeared at status hearings. Finally, clients provided weekly urine samples on a randomly selected day under direct observation of a treatment staff person. The urinalysis testing was performed using the enzyme multiplied immunoassay technique (EMIT) with confirmation by gas chromatography mass spectrometry (GCMS) of positive results for delta-9 tetrahydrocannabinol (THC), opiates, cocaine, amphetamines, and phencyclidine (PCP), plus any additional substances detected from a baseline 10-panel screen or otherwise believed to be used by the client.

Preliminary outcome analyses were conducted during the first 14 weeks of drug court, which is the minimum time at which subjects could graduate from the program. When data on a continuous dependent measure were skewed, we calculated the natural logarithm and conducted between-group comparisons on the transformed scores. In all instances, the results were the same regardless of whether we used the raw scores or transformed scores in the analyses.

FOLLOW-UP STUDY RESULTS

Participant Characteristics

Fifty-eight percent of eligible misdemeanor drug court clients consented to participate in the study. The participants were mostly young adults (mean ± SD=26.99 ± 9.43 years), male (75%), Caucasian (68%) or African American (25%), single (90%), high school educated (11.81 ± 1.60 years), and employed (83%). Their most serious current criminal charges were possession of drug paraphernalia (49%), possession or use of cannabis (29%), possession or use of narcotics (13%), conspiracy to possess narcotics (5%), or other misdemeanor charges (5%). Thirty-one percent had a prior criminal conviction, 19% had been previously incarcerated, and 32% met DSM-IV criteria for APD. They were represented by public defenders (35%), private defense counsel (30%), or were pro se (35%).

Participants reported currently abusing cannabis (56%), alcohol (52%), opiates (18%), cocaine/stimulants (10%), sedatives (6%), or hallucinogens (5%). Roughly one-fifth (19%) had a prior history of drug abuse treatment. Using recommended cut-off scores on the Addiction Severity Index (ASI) for classifying the treatment needs of offenders (Lee et al., 2001), 44% of participants produced "sub-threshold" drug composite scores similar to a non-substance-using population (drug composite score 0.04); 51% produced "moderate" drug composite scores similar to a national sample of substance abuse clients in outpatient treatment (> 0.04 and 0.24); and 5% produced "severe" drug composite scores similar to a national sample of substance abuse clients in residential drug treatment (> 0.24).

Distribution Across Study Conditions Confirmed

A check on randomization confirmed that all but one of these demographic, drug-use, and criminal-history variables were equally distributed across the two study conditions. An exception was that as-needed participants were more likely to be charged with a drug-possession offense, whereas biweekly participants were more likely to be charged with possession of drug paraphernalia. Because outcomes were related to current criminal charges, we controlled for this covariate in the outcome analyses. Equivalent proportions of individuals from the two counties were represented in the two study conditions, and outcomes did not differ between counties or between courts (i.e., between judges and commissioners); therefore, we did not nest the data by county or by court.

We obtained aggregate anonymous admissions data (i.e., Treatment Episode Data Set [TEDS] items) on all drug court clients in Delaware in order to evaluate the representativeness of our sample. Study participants were younger (27.17 ± 8.91 yrs. vs. 31.20 ± 10.47 yrs., $p < 0.001$), more likely to be primarily abusing opiates (11% vs. 3%, $p < 0.001$), less likely to be primarily abusing alcohol (9% vs. 26%, $p < 0.001$), and less likely to be employed (6% vs. 23%, $p < 0.001$) than individuals who refused to participate in the study.

Ninety-five percent (35 out of 37) of participants in the as-needed condition and 81% of participants (30 out of 37) in the biweekly condition continuously remained in their assigned condition following random assignment, leaving a final cohort of 65 subjects. More participants dropped out of the biweekly condition because of the onerous time demands. The small number of dropouts limited our power for detecting attrition bias; however, there appeared to be no differences at baseline between dropouts and those who remained in the study. It is possible, however, that participants who were performing more poorly in the program may have dropped out of the biweekly condition at a relatively higher rate to reduce the likelihood that the judges or commissioners would detect their infractions. Our results might therefore have overestimated positive outcomes for biweekly participants.

Main Effects Showed No Clear Differences Between the Two Conditions

We maintained excellent integrity of the experimental conditions. As can be seen in Table 11.1, participants in the biweekly condition were scheduled to attend significantly more status hearings than were participants in the as-needed condition, and they actually did attend many more status hearings. There were, however, no differences in counseling sessions attended, urinalysis results, self-reported drug use, self-reported alcohol intoxication, self-reported criminal activity, or graduation rates.

We used a general estimating equation (GEE) to compare the longitudinal distributions of urinalysis results over the 14 weeks, counting missed samples as drug-positive. GEE analyses can accommodate a binary outcome measure and are robust to nonindependent longitudinal measurements. Results revealed a significant main effect for time, $x^2 (1, N = 65) = 23.18$, $p < 0.05$, indicating that increasing numbers of participants in both conditions tested negative for drugs over successive weeks. There was, however, no main effect for condition or for the condition-by-time interaction. Repeated-measures analyses similarly revealed no longitudinal effects on participants' self-reported drug use, alcohol intoxication, or criminal activity during the first three months of the program.

Table 11.1: Performance During the First 14 Weeks of Drug Court and Program Completion Status

	As-Needed (n = 35)			Biweekly (n = 30)		
	M	SD	%	M	SD	%
Status hearings scheduled	0.91	1.04	57	5.00	1.30 *	100 *
Status hearings attended	0.82	1.01	51	4.52	1.45 *	100 *
Counseling sessions attended	6.70	2.70	91	7.63	1.94	100
Total drug-free urines provided	7.76	5.36	83	10.00	4.56	97
Consecutive drug-free urines provided	6.33	5.19		7.41	4.70	
Self-reported days of illicit drug use	4.22	8.85	31	2.61	5.99	23
Self-reported days of alcohol intoxication[†]	4.30	9.82	28	1.70	4.09	27
Self-reported days of illegal activity	0.41	1.93	7	0.09	0.42	4
Graduated			63			80
Terminated/absconded			29			17
Still enrolled in program			9			3

Note: % = proportion of participants meeting any criterion on each variable; between-group comparisons on continuous measures controlled for participants' most serious current criminal charge.
*p < 0.0001.
[†]Felt the effects of alcohol or had 5 drinks in one day

Interaction Effects Showed Clear Superiority of Biweekly Condition for Participants With Prior Drug Treatment History

We replicated the interaction effect from our previous study concerning participants' prior history of drug abuse treatment. As depicted in Figure 11.1, participants with a prior history of drug treatment provided substantially more drug-free urine samples during the first 14 weeks of drug court when assigned to biweekly hearings than when assigned to as-needed hearings (11.50 vs. 2.67), and this difference was marginally significant after controlling for current criminal charge, $F (1, 52) = 3.84$, $p = 0.055$. The specific cell-comparison for subjects with a prior drug treatment history was highly significant, $F(1, 11) = 12.95$, $p = .005$, and accounted predominantly for the significant interaction effect we detected. Similarly, after controlling for current criminal charge, participants with prior drug treatment histories provided more consecutive drug-free urine samples when assigned to biweekly hearings than when assigned to as-needed hearings ([9.33 vs. 1.50], $F [1, 52] = 3.87$, $p = 0.055$).

Because these effects were large—Hedges bias-corrected effect size (ES) = 1.92 standard-deviation (SD) units for total clean urines, and 1.77 SD units for consecutive clean urines—they approached statistical significance with small cell sizes for participants with prior drug treatment histories (as-needed, n = 6; biweekly, n = 6). Although the large differences were not influenced by data outliers or by other (detectable) unusual sample characteristics, small cell sizes always raise concerns about whether the data are skewed or whether the sample is representative of the target population. We therefore dichotomized the urinalysis results using a median split and performed nonparametric analyses that do not assume normality in the distributions and that per-

Figure 11.1: Interaction of Drug Treatment History and Schedule of Judicial Status Hearings on Urinalysis Results During the First 14 Weeks of Drug Court, Controlling for Current Criminal Charge (Hedges bias-corrected effect size = 1.92 SD units; p = 0.055)

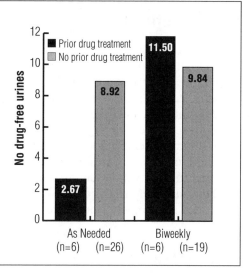

Table 11.2: Program Completion Status for Participants With Prior Drug Treatment Histories

	As-Needed		Biweekly		p
	n	%	n	%	
Graduated	1	17	5	83	0.05
Terminated	4	67	1	17	0.08
Absconded	1	16	0	0	0.30

mit exact p-values to be calculated for small samples. The results of a Cochran-Mantel-Haenszel contingency-table analysis yielded a nonsignificant trend, x^2 (1, N = 62) = 2.20, p = 0.14, despite the fact that such an approach greatly reduces statistical power.

There were also significant differences in graduation rates and termination rates for participants with a prior history of drug treatment. Over 80% of participants with a prior drug treatment history graduated from the program when assigned to biweekly hearings, compared with fewer than 20% of those assigned to as-needed hearings, x^2 (1, N = 12) = 5.33, Fisher's exact p = 0.04 (see Table 11.2).

It is possible that participants' prior drug treatment histories may have simply reflected the magnitude of their drug abuse problems. That is, participants with more severe or longer-term drug problems may have been more likely to be previously referred to treatment. In fact, participants with prior drug treatment histories did have higher baseline ASI drug composite scores, F (1, 60) = 3.60, p = 0.06, and higher baseline ASI drug clinical factor scores, F (1, 62) = 3.39, p = 0.07. Although this suggests that subjects with prior drug treatment histories did have more severe drug problems, these ASI indices of drug severity did not interact with group assignment to predict outcomes.

Study Recruitment Stopped in Response to Possible Shift in Risk/Benefit Ratio

Because the legal repercussions of failing in drug court are serious, we reported these early findings to the Institutional Review Boards (IRBs) and Research Steering Committees overseeing the study, and it was ultimately determined that the risk/benefit ratio had shifted, at least for a subset of participants. This would require us to alter the consent form and to inform current and future participants about the possible risks of being scheduled for as-needed hearings. The drug court program staff also became understandably reluctant to continue randomly assigning clients to as-needed hearings. We therefore suspended recruitment for the study. Unfortunately, because we were required to stop recruitment after attaining only about 75% of our targeted N, we did not have sufficient statistical power to follow up on some of our other previous findings, such as whether or not there was an interaction effect for subjects with APD.

CONCLUSIONS

This randomized, controlled study replicated the results from our previous experimental work indicating that certain types of high-risk drug court clients required a higher "dosage" of judicial status hearings to achieve improved outcomes (Festinger et al., 2002). Misdemeanor drug offenders who had prior drug abuse treatment histories attained substantially greater abstinence and were more likely to graduate from the drug court program when assigned to high-dose, biweekly status hearings.

It remains an open question whether this effect of prior treatment history reflects the severity of subjects' drug problems, past negative experiences with drug treatment, or some unidentified mediating variable. Arguably, individuals with a prior drug abuse treatment history who wind up in drug court may have already failed at one or more experiences with standard treatment. Such individuals may require a more intensive and structured intervention in order to show improvement. It is also possible that prior negative experiences with treatment might have made these clients less likely to make use of standard treatment interventions. Enhanced supervision by the judge or commissioner may have been required to get them to give treatment a "second chance." Regardless of the explanation for the effect, prior drug treatment appears to be a robust index for matching clients to particular schedules of status hearings. This finding lends practical guidance to drug courts. Judicial status hearings are expensive and time consuming and should be targeted to clients who will benefit most from them.

As noted, the small cell sizes for the interaction analyses do raise questions about the representativeness of the sample. Because the effects were detected in sequential randomized studies in different jurisdictions, greater confidence can be placed in the reliability of the findings. Nevertheless, the replication results remain open to some dispute until they are confirmed in an adequately powered trial.

Another important limitation is that the interaction effects were not under experimental control. Although the analyses were stimulated by a priori hypotheses, the interaction effects were the result of post hoc examinations and thus could reflect unstable or chance findings. Consequently, we are evaluating the effects of prospectively matching drug court clients to the appropriate schedule of judicial status hearings based upon whether they have a past drug abuse treatment history or meet criteria for APD. Results from this matching study will indicate the stability of our findings and will permit us to estimate the size of the effect and the cost-effectiveness of using risk status to assign drug court clients to appropriate "service tracks" from the outset of treatment.

About the Authors

Douglas B. Marlowe, J.D., Ph.D., is the Director of Law & Ethics Research at the Treatment Research Institute at the University of Pennsylvania, and an Adjunct Associate Professor of Psychiatry at the University of Pennsylvania School of Medicine. David S. Festinger, Ph.D., is a Behavioral Scientist in the Section on Law & Ethics Research at the Treatment Research Institute at the University of Pennsylvania. Patricia A. Lee, M.S., is the Research Coordinator of the Section on Law & Ethics Research at the Treatment Research Institute at the University of Pennsylvania. Dr. Marlowe may be reached by email at Marlowe@Tresearch.org or through the Treatment Research Institute, 600 Public Ledger Bldg., 150 S. Independence Mall West, Philadelphia, PA 19106-3475; phone: (215) 399-0980; fax: (215) 399-0987.

The research for this study was supported by Grant #R01-DA-13096 from the National Institute on Drug Abuse with supplemental funding from the Center for Substance Abuse Treatment. Portions of the data were presented at the 64th Annual Scientific Meeting of the College on Problems of Drug Dependence, Quebec City, Canada. The authors gratefully acknowledge the ongoing collaboration of the Kent County Superior Court, Sussex County Superior Court, Attorneys General Offices of Kent and Sussex Counties, Public Defenders Offices of Kent and Sussex Counties, Delaware Association of Criminal Defense Lawyers, Delaware State Division of Substance Abuse and Mental Health, Kent County Counseling, Sussex County Counseling, and Thresholds, Inc. Carol Foltz, Ph.D., and Karen Dugosh, Ph.D., helped with the statistical analyses; Rhonda Graybeal, J.D., and Meghan Johle assisted with project management; and Michelle Drummond and Jessica DeFelice helped with data collection.

References

American Psychiatric Association (APA). (1994). *Diagnostic and statistical manual of mental disorders* (4th ed.). Washington, DC: American Psychiatric Press.

Andrews, D.A., & Bonta, J. (1998). *The psychology of criminal conduct*, 2nd ed. Cincinnati: Anderson.

Belenko, S. (1998). Research on drug courts: A critical review. *National Drug Court Institute Review, 1*, 1–42.

Belenko, S. (1999). Research on drug courts: A critical review: 1999 update. *National Drug Court Institute Review, 2(2)*, 1–58.

Belenko, S. (2001). *Research on drug courts: A critical review: 2001 update.* New York: National Center on Addiction and Substance Abuse at Columbia University.

Festinger, D.S., Marlowe, D.B., Lee, P.A., Kirby, K.C., Bovasso, G., & McLellan, A.T. (2002). Status hearings in drug court: When more is less and less is more. *Drug and Alcohol Dependence, 68*, 151–157.

Gendreau, P., Little, T., & Goggin, C. (1996). A meta-analysis of the predictors of adult offender recidivism: What works! *Criminology, 34*, 575–596.

Guydish, J., Wolfe, E., Tajima, B., & Woods, W.J. (2001). Drug court effectiveness: A review of California evaluation reports, 1995–1999. *Journal of Psychoactive Drugs, 33*, 369–378.

Lee, P.A., Marlowe, D.B., Festinger, D.S., Cacciola, J.S., McNellis, J., Schepise, M.M., Merrill, J.C., Harrell, A.V., & McLellan, A.T. (2001). Did "breaking the cycle" (BTC) clients receive appropriate services? [abstract]. *Drug and Alcohol Dependence, 63 (Suppl. 1)*, S89. Presentation at the 63rd Annual Scientific Meeting, College on Problems of Drug Dependence, Scottsdale, AZ.

Marlowe, D.B. (2002). Effective strategies for intervening with drug abusing offenders. *Villanova Law Review, 47*, 989–1025.

Marlowe, D.B., Festinger, D.S., Lee, P.A., Benasutti, K., Croft, J., & McLellan, A.T. (2002). A randomized, controlled evaluation of judicial status hearings in drug court: 6-month outcomes and client-program matching effects [abstract]. *Drug and Alcohol Dependence, 66*, S111–S112. Presentation at the 64th Annual Scientific Meeting of the College on Problems of Drug Dependence, Quebec City, Canada.

Marlowe, D.B., Festinger, D.S., Lee, P.A., Schepise, M.M., Hazzard, J.E.R., Merrill, J.C., Mulvaney, F.D., & McLellan, A.T. (2003). Are judicial status hearings a key component of drug court? During-treatment data from a randomized trial. *Criminal Justice & Behavior, 30*, 141–162.

Marlowe, D.B., & Kirby, K.C. (1999). Effective use of sanctions in drug courts: Lessons from behavioral research. *National Drug Court Institute Review, 2*, 1–31.

National Association of Drug Court Professionals (1997). *Defining drug courts: The key components*. Washington, DC: Office of Justice Programs, U.S. Department of Justice.

Part 3

Treatment in Correctional Settings

A vital part of the treatment continuum for addicted offenders is the provision of drug treatment services to incarcerated offenders. Indeed, correctional settings provide a unique opportunity to deliver treatment services to substance abusing offenders who might otherwise not seek or have access to treatment services. By providing appropriate evidence-based treatment during incarceration, correctional systems can help offenders not only overcome their drug addiction, but their criminal lifestyle as well.

This section describes some of the key ingredients to effective correctional treatment programming, including depictions of specific in-prison treatment programs.

In Chapter 12, Dorothy Seaton discusses how providing intensive treatment at the Kyle Correctional Center has paid off for high-risk offenders. The six- to eight-month in-prison therapeutic community (TC) is a three-phase intensive treatment program that has been in operation since 1992. Outcomes have been favorable when the in-prison treatment program is coupled with community-based aftercare. When compared with offenders who were eligible for but did not participate in the treatment program, offenders who completed both the in-prison and mandatory post-release aftercare programs have been found to have significantly lower relapse and recidivism rates.

Chapter 13, by Rod Mullen, James Rowland, Naya Arbiter, Lew Yablonsky, and Bette Fleishman, is a review of the 10-year history of California's first prison TC at the Richard J. Donovan Correctional Facility (RJDCF). Noting that close coordination between program and correctional staff was imperative in the implementation of the program, the authors also point to the realities of working with inmate populations and how the inmates played a helpful role in the process.

Peter Rockholz, in Chapter 14, presents results from a national survey designed to inventory and obtain basic information about prison TCs in North America. Given the apparent confusion over what constitutes a "real" TC versus a residential program with some "TC-like" components, the author points to the need for a current initiative designed to develop national prison TC standards. The article goes on to address critical TC factors, such as the primary approach to treatment being "community-as-method."

In Chapter 15, Beth Weinman, John Dignam, and Ben Wheat summarize lessons they have learned from their administrative and clinical experiences with the Federal Bureau of Prisons' (BOP) drug abuse treatment programs. In particular, the authors point to how correctional settings pose significant opportunities as well as challenges when providing drug abuse treatment. They indicate that effective treatment in correctional settings requires careful planning and implementation and must include strong support from top management, a specific treatment orthodoxy, a systematic treatment documentation, a clearly defined system of incentives and sanctions, a qualified, well-trained staff, a community re-entry component, and a commitment to outcome and process evaluation.

This section on treatment in correctional settings concludes with Chapter 16, "Promoting Change in a Drug and Criminal Lifestyle," by Glenn Walters. Pointing to the commonalities of drug and crime lifestyles, the author makes the argument for the need to consider the core elements of change: responsibility, confidence, meaning, and community. Correctional treatment staff need to emphasize these four core elements if change is to be lasting and meaningful.

Chapter 12

The Kyle New Vision Program: An Intensive In-Prison Therapeutic Community

by Dorothy M. Seaton, MHR, LCDC

Intensive Treatment Pays Off for High-Risk Substance Abusing Offenders 12-2
Therapeutic Community Program Follows Participants to Outside World 12-3
    Orientation Phase 12-3
    Main Treatment Phase 12-3
    Re-Entry Phase 12-3
    Cadre 12-4
The Therapeutic Community Approach 12-4
    Primary Goals 12-4
    Hierarchy 12-5
Critical Program Components 12-5
    Community Enhancement Activities 12-5
    Chemical Dependency Education 12-5
    Counseling Groups 12-5
    Community-Clinical Management 12-6
    Incentives and Privileges 12-6
    System of Sanctions 12-6
    Twelve-Step Fellowships 12-6
    Volunteer Programs 12-7
    Academic Education 12-7
    Family Education Program 12-7
    Program Enhancements 12-7
Innovative Plans for the Future 12-8
Conclusion 12-8

An earlier version of this chapter appeared in Offender Substance Abuse Report, *Vol. 1, No. 1, January/February 2001.*

INTENSIVE TREATMENT PAYS OFF FOR HIGH-RISK SUBSTANCE ABUSING OFFENDERS

The Kyle Correctional Center located 25 miles south of Austin, Texas, in the small Hill Country community of Kyle, houses the New Vision In-Prison Therapeutic Community (IPTC) and Substance Abuse Felony Punishment (SAFP) Drug Treatment Program. Operated by the GEO Group, Inc., the New Vision Program is a six- to eight-month program that has been in operation since May 1992.

When the Texas Criminal Justice Treatment initiative—viewed as a farsighted and progressive attempt to break the crime and drug connection and the high recidivism rates for criminal drug and alcohol abusers—was signed into law in 1991, New Vision was the first IPTC in Texas and, at that time, it was the largest in the U.S. All 520 beds were, and still are, dedicated to chemical dependency treatment residents. In March, 2003, the program was modified to accept Substance Abuse Felony Punishment (SAFP) residents from the Texas Department of Criminal Justice (TDCJ) Parole Division. Currently up to 170 of the 520 treatment beds may be occupied by SAFP men who were/are on parole and were sent to the Kyle Program because of a parole violation, such as a dirty urinalysis or failure to report to the parole officer.

All residents admitted into the New Vision program are received from TDCJ—IPTC residents from Institutional Division and SAFP residents from Parole Division. They must meet the appropriate admission requirements to ensure they are physically and mentally able to handle the stressors involved in the intensive treatment program. Various screening and assessment tools are used to ensure each resident is appropriate for the program and all information is available to formulate an effective individual treatment plan.

Research has shown that intensive prison treatment programs such as the one at Kyle are most effective with higher-risk offenders, those with more severe crime and drug or alcohol-related problems. Repeat offenders with a long history of drug or alcohol abuse and often with no prior chemical dependency treatment also respond well to the more intensive, long-term intervention provided by the Texas Treatment Initiative.

Kyle IPTC graduates, particularly those who completed the aftercare program, have a much lower relapse and recidivism rate than offenders who did not receive IPTC treatment. A Texas Christian University study (Knight, Hiller & Simpson, 1999) reported that 75% of Kyle graduates who also completed the residential aftercare program were *not* returned to prison within three years; this was significantly better than the untreated comparison group with 58% who remained out of prison. Clearly, completing IPTC, Transitional Treatment Center (TTC) programs, and aftercare was a strong foundation for breaking the prison/addiction cycle and building a life of freedom and sobriety for the Kyle graduates. The positive effects of treatment often "trickle down" to the graduates' families, co-workers, and neighbors after their release from prison and completion of the aftercare program, providing lasting benefits to Texas communities in terms of reducing the need for ongoing social services and law enforcement costs to the taxpayers.

Of interest, the TCU study also reports that, "To optimize and demonstrate its effectiveness, the referral process (including judges, prisons, and parole boards) must become systematic and disciplined, and evaluations should improve by focusing on issues that translate into policy decisions" (p.350). When screening and selection of program participants is done to provide these services to the appropriate clients, the results can be dramatic, and inspiring.

THERAPEUTIC COMMUNITY PROGRAM FOLLOWS PARTICIPANTS TO OUTSIDE WORLD

Drug treatment at Kyle New Vision is followed by mandatory participation in community-based TTCs providing up to three months of residential treatment and 12 months of non-residential aftercare treatment.

The New Vision program is a three-phase intensive treatment program. Progression from one phase to another is based upon an individual demonstrating effective functioning in treatment. Residents enter the therapeutic community (TC) in the Orientation Phase and proceed through each phase of treatment by successful completion of treatment assignments, active participation, and staff recommendation. The phase system is a developmental system in which each of the phases represents improvements in the resident's assumption of personal responsibilities and his accomplishment of constructive behavior and attitude changes.

Orientation Phase

The Orientation Phase is designed to acquaint the resident with the basic concept and philosophies utilized within the TC, including rules, tools, regulations, policies, and structure of the hierarchy. The resident assimilates into the community through full participation and involvement in all activities. The resident is introduced to the concepts of substance abuse and the addiction process, relapse, relapse prevention, denial, and development of the individual treatment plan. A participant's understanding of the basic concept of the TC is demonstrated by the resident successfully passing the Orientation Mastery Test.

Main Treatment Phase

The Main Treatment Phase is focused on exploration of the problems faced by the resident in recovery and options for their solution. The resident continues to learn the process of addiction and recovery. He also begins to identify the deficiencies in his life skills which have made it difficult to deal with stress-producing life situations. The resident begins to learn to accept responsibility for his behavior and begins to recognize new self-management strategies with less reliance on authority figures. Socialization, personal growth, and psychological awareness are pursued through all of the therapeutic and community activities.

Re-Entry Phase

The Re-Entry Phase provides a period for the resident to solidify changes from earlier work into lasting habits, which help build and maintain a recovery lifestyle free of chemical dependency and criminal behavior. While preparing for discharge and parole, careful attention is placed on the development of a comprehensive relapse prevention plan and continuum of care plan that includes follow-up aftercare, employment, housing, recovery group sponsors, peer support groups, and other community resources. Family issues, relationships, and the transition process are areas of focus during the Re-Entry Phase. Continuous emphasis is placed on increasing self-esteem and family values, and the development of social and personal growth skills that aid in the resident's readiness for transition.

Cadre

A very effective and unique fourth part of treatment in the New Vision program is the Cadre Program. The Cadre is a small, hand-picked group of up to 20 residents who have successfully completed the basic requirements of all three phases of primary treatment. Cadre service is voluntary, and only those who do well in the program are selected. They have demonstrated through positive, constructive, and responsible behavior their motivation and knowledge of the therapeutic community. Cadre members are peer facilitators who serve as role models and assist in the facilitation of group activities under the direct supervision of counseling staff.

THE THERAPEUTIC COMMUNITY APPROACH

The New Vision Program provides all the basic elements of a TC: a structured daily schedule of activities, a hierarchal community government structure, community enhancement activities, educational seminars and lectures, therapeutic groups, individual and group counseling, Twelve-Step Fellowships, work, and academic education. The program takes a holistic approach to chemical dependency treatment with an emphasis on cognitive intervention work. Chemical dependency is viewed as a problem of the whole person. Problems may include thinking processes, value identification, occupational and/or educational functioning, and interpersonal skills as well as spiritual and moral issues.

The disease model of addiction, which includes physiological, psychological, and social factors, states that substance abuse has a cause, a course, a predictable outcome, and is progressive. Recovery is viewed in the same manner with a cause, a course, a progression, and a predictable outcome. It is important to recognize that recovery involves more than abstinence. It means learning how to live joyfully as a responsible and productive member of the community. Effective role modeling, full-time program continuity, and maintenance are facilitated by the use of experienced residents in key positions of responsibility. The New Vision Program is a comprehensive program of recovery within the highly structured regimen of the TC.

Primary Goals

The primary goal of the New Vision program is to provide residents an opportunity through their active participation in all aspects of community to develop the attitudes, skills, and behaviors necessary to lead a responsible, drug-free lifestyle. The program provides a system in which such changes, leading to effective drug-free functioning by the resident, may best be facilitated. Effective functioning is defined as:

- Assumption of personal responsibility for one's own feelings and behaviors;

- Demonstration of the ability to initiate and continue satisfactory interpersonal relationships; and

- Acquisition of the skills necessary to secure and maintain productive employment.

The program is resident-driven with staff support and guidance. The TC is composed of resident peer groups and counseling staff which constitute the community or family, with the staff being the ultimate rational authority figure in each community.

Hierarchy

The resident hierarchy structure is similar to a community government. Residents, led by staff, are all members of the community. Position assignments represent job functions of positions of responsibility within the structure board and are arranged in a hierarchical structure denoting lines of communication and responsibility. Jobs higher on the structure board represent more responsibility and are awarded according to individual progress in treatment and productivity. The structure board is composed of hierarchical job functions with upward or downward mobility determined by the resident's attitude, behavior, and productivity within the community. Positions on the structure board are filled through the application process and staff review and assignment. New residents enter the structure with opportunities for upward mobility. Job assignments begin with the most menial task (service crew) and move to higher levels of coordination and management (Team Leaders, coordinators, TOPS members, Senior Coordinator). The social organization depicts the basic aspect of the TC's rehabilitative approach to mutual self-help, work as therapy, peers as role models, and staff as the ultimate authority.

CRITICAL PROGRAM COMPONENTS

Community Enhancement Activities

Community enhancement activities assist the resident with assimilation into the community. These include the morning meeting, evening meeting, and community/family meetings, which include the entire treatment family group. The meetings provide an important opportunity to motivate the group, share information, build unity, and reinforce the sense of community and its structure.

Chemical Dependency Education

Didactic educational programs on a wide variety of recovery topics are considered an integral part of the intensive treatment provided in the TC. Tutorial as well as small and large group instruction are utilized to provide a variety of methods to accommodate learning styles. Training or teaching sessions are conducted in an informational format on the various aspects of substance abuse treatment and self-improvement. The major focus is on personal growth concepts, job skills training, clinical skills training, and substance abuse education. Treatment groups and lectures are held daily.

Counseling Groups

The counseling groups are face-to-face interactions between residents and counselors that help residents identify, understand, and resolve the issues and problems of substance abuse and life. These groups include encounter groups, confrontation groups, agenda groups, process groups, skills training, peer support groups, affirmation groups, and peer review sessions. Individual counseling is provided to each resident on a regular basis, although the primary focus of the TC is group counseling and client-driven group/community interaction.

Community-Clinical Management

Community-clinical management provides for a treatment environment that is physically and emotionally safe. Security staff play an integral role in ensuring that acting-out behaviors from a "prison mentality" are not allowed to threaten the physical or emotional safety of the community. The objective is to protect the community as a whole and to strengthen it as a safe, productive, and wholesome environment for social learning.

Incentives and Privileges

Incentives and privileges are earned rewards that reflect and reinforce the value of earned achievement. Privileges are earned based on positive and productive involvement in the treatment process. As the resident progresses through each phase of treatment, privileges are earned along with added responsibilities.

System of Sanctions

There is also a system of sanctions awaiting those who choose to stray outside the boundaries of acceptable behavior. Consequences for inappropriate behavior are designed to reinforce prosocial attitudes and behaviors. To address behavior on a routine basis, residents utilize the pull-up system. The pull-up system allows staff and residents to formally or informally address another resident's negative behavior within the family structure. Pull-ups are a method by which a resident is made aware of negative behaviors or attitudes. They are designed to increase his awareness of the behavior, help him become accountable for actions, reinforce positive attitudes, and promote the benefits of mutual self-help. There are two types of pull-ups, verbal and written. The type of pull-up depends on the inappropriate behavior to be addressed. A pull-up is a personal therapeutic tool used to assist residents in developing responsibility for personal actions. Negative behaviors are also addressed by the treatment group/family in encounter groups, and in treatment team staffings that include staff from security, education, treatment, and sometimes medical, along with the treatment resident himself.

Twelve-Step Fellowships

Twelve-Step Fellowships are used as a voluntary reinforcement of the principles presented in mandatory treatment groups and lectures. The various Twelve-Step self-help groups (Alcoholics Anonymous (AA), AA Big Book Study, Narcotics Anonymous (NA), Secular Organizations for Sobriety, Adult Children of Alcoholics, Winners Circle, and Milliti Islami) assist in strengthening the resident's commitment to recovery and help build a bridge to the "free world" in terms of seeking and receiving healthy peer support resources. Volunteers from the recovery fellowships in the local outside community provide weekly speakers and meeting facilitators for the various Twelve-Step meetings held in the unit and attended on a voluntary basis by the residents.

Volunteer Programs

The Kyle unit has the finest volunteer program in any TDCJ unit in the state. We received recognition from TDCJ for the Best Utilization of Volunteers in 1998 and again every year since that time. Our volunteer pool is over 200 strong, and includes many graduates of the New Vision Program, who are allowed to return as volunteers after one year. There are two speaker meetings each week at the Kyle unit, Thursday night NA and Saturday night AA. Each week there are Spanish-speaking AA volunteers at the Sunday night Spanish AA meeting. Monday night Big Book Study has a volunteer facilitator at each meeting. Kyle has no shortage of volunteers. People call asking if they can please come out to one of the fellowship meetings because they have heard from friends what a wonderful experience it is to meet the residents and share their recovery stories and experiences with them. Volunteers usually leave with one question, "When can I come back?" The residents of the new Vision Program get a lot from their volunteers, but the volunteers also get inspiration from the residents. The meetings are as close to free-world meetings as possible in the institutional setting. Meetings and volunteers are coordinated by staff and a unit steering committee comprised of resident volunteers from each cell block.

Academic Education

The Kyle Correctional Center also provides academic education with a primary purpose of helping residents develop skills in reading, written communication, mathematics, science, and social studies. This helps to prepare them for a positive transition into society with adequate skills and confidence to be productive, working members of their community. Academic classes include Adult Basic Education (ABE), Pre-GED, GED, English as a Second Language (ESL), and Life Skills. Any resident without a GED or high school diploma is evaluated and placed in school when he is admitted to the treatment program. The value of education instilled in prison can be the key to future education and personal growth beyond a resident's wildest dreams.

Family Education Program

Another important component within the New Vision Program is the Family Education Program. Family education services are provided to each program participant and his family, whenever possible. Family education is offered on weekends for residents and family members on the resident's approved visitors list. The family education counselor presents education services weekly as an integral part of the holistic approach to recovery at New Vision.

Program Enhancements

The New Vision Program provides a number of activities, which enhance the treatment process. Special activities, holiday programs, organized recreational sports, community service projects, contests, and talent shows are scheduled to promote creativity, team building, and community pride, and to improve communication and social skills. Also, New Vision routinely recognizes the achievements, talents, and accomplishments of the TC participants. Upon successful completion of the New Vision Treatment

Program, residents participate in a monthly transition celebration. The term "transition celebration" is used to more appropriately indicate the completion of one stage of recovery and transition to the next phase. A Certificate of Completion and New Vision "Sobriety Ribbon," inscribed with the New Vision logo and 12-Step fellowship groups, are awarded to each resident completing the program. During the transition celebration, residents who have completed educational or vocational courses are also recognized. Just as the name denotes, the New Vision Program provides each resident with an opportunity to rebuild and restructure his life with a new outlook, a new destiny, and on a new path to a lifetime of recovery. (See Exhibit 12.1 at page 12-9 for reports on several people who have completed the Kyle program.)

INNOVATIVE PLANS FOR THE FUTURE

The New Vision Program and its staff are not content to rest on past accomplishments. In 2004 they will become nationally accredited by the American Correctional Association as an ACA Therapeutic Community following their audit of 117 required standards by the nationally recognized correctional accreditation organization. Preparations for this milestone accreditation have been in the making for nearly a year.

A new Relapse Prevention Group was initiated in February, 2004, that meets weekly (for a six-week cycle) to examine healthy recovery lifestyle changes and plan for dealing with risky situations and triggers. The Relapse Prevention Group is voluntary, and nearly 50 men responded to the invitation to sign up for the first cycle.

Also in February, 2004, the GEO Group, Inc., Kyle New Vision Treatment Program, began a community service project in partnership with the local PAWS Animal Shelter in Kyle. The immediate goal is to have the offender community service squad perform duties at the shelter, such as maintenance of the grounds, cleaning the kennels, and walking or bathing dogs that need exercise and attention. The long-term goal is to build a small kennel at New Vision and admit six to eight canine "offenders" for socialization and obedience training. Upon graduation from New Vision, the dogs would be prepared for adoption or transfer to other training programs for working dogs (drug dogs or service dogs for the handicapped).

And as always, New Vision enthusiastically cooperates with colleges and universities in research studies on any aspect of prison treatment or addiction.

CONCLUSION

The New Vision Program is making a real difference in the lives of the hundreds of men in the New Vision treatment family. While they are in treatment and afterward on parole, and after completing parole, they continue to enrich the lives of their families and their communities throughout the state of Texas because of the things they learned at New Vision. Through the New Vision Treatment Program, men are overcoming their drug and alcohol abuse problems and successfully reentering society—free from addiction and criminal behaviors.

About the Author

Dorothy M. Seaton, M.H.R., L.C.D.C., is the New Vision Training Coordinator.

Reference

Knight, K., Simpson, D. D., & Hiller, M. L. (1999), 3-Year reincarceration outcomes for in-prison therapeutic community treatment in Texas. *The Prison Journal, 79*(3), 337-351.

Exhibit 12.1: Personal Studies Show Kyle's Success a Proven Possibility

In 1994 two Texas prison offenders graduated from the Kyle New Vision drug treatment program. Both men went on to complete the required post-release inpatient and outpatient aftercare components. However, finding a job was weighing heavily on their minds. They went on job search after job search, finally finding employment washing cars at a local car wash. This was not the perfect job for either man; one had almost completed the credits needed to graduate from college. But both men were dedicated to staying clean and sober and free, and they realized that they needed to establish a positive employment record as ex-offenders. Both men worked hard at their jobs and their recovery. Each man found a sponsor in the local Narcotics Anonymous (NA) group, and began establishing a sober support system in the community. When they completed the residential aftercare program, they remained at the car wash. Eventually they received promotions and now the two men who started out washing cars run the car wash. One is manager of the car wash, and the other is manager of the detail shop. Both men eventually married. One married a recovering addict; she owns her own catering business, and they bought a very nice home four years ago. He got custody of his two daughters, and has put them both through college. He also gained guardianship of his nephew when the boy was a troubled 14-year-old. The couple is very active in NA and their home group. The other man married, and he and his wife have adopted four "unwanted, at-risk" children. He started an NA group in the small town where he lives with his wife and children. Both men freely return to Kyle New Vision on a volunteer basis any time they are asked. They are happy to share their experiences in living a free and sober life with the current residents to show that treatment can be the start of a whole new life.

In 1998, a graduate of the Kyle program stated, as he was walking out the back door, "I'll be back every year to share with the guys." We have heard this before, but most program graduates lack the commitment to follow up a year later. Approximately 10 months later the man called and said that he had been accepted in the Texas Department of Criminal Justice (TDCJ) Approved Partner's Program, a program that allows ex-offenders to return to TDCJ units only six months after they are released to volunteer in Twelve-Step meetings. He let us know that his one-year anniversary was near, and that he wanted to return to speak at the Saturday night Alcoholics Anonymous (AA) meeting. One year from his release he came to speak at AA, and he brought his grown son, whom he had not raised because of his addiction. He shared his story with more than 120 residents that night who were currently in treatment on this unit. He talked about his goal to go to college; he had received his GED while in treatment on the same unit in 1998. In August 2000, he called again, asking to come back on his second anniversary. This time he had to ride the bus halfway across the state of Texas because he did not have dependable transportation. He asked if he could bring his brother, from who he had been separated for nearly 10 years. Again, he shared his experience, strength, and hope with more than 120 men. This time he informed his Kyle "family" that he had enrolled in college studying psychology. This 50-year-old man who could barely read and write prior to completing the New Vision Program had become a college student. He has returned every year since his release. In 2003 he received a certificate in Business Administration from a community college; he graduated with honors and received a Rudy Tomjanovitch Scholarship to continue his education. When he spoke on his anniversary in 2003, more than 200 current residents attended. He is now a regular TDCJ-Approved Volunteer (having graduated from the Partners Program). He brought his brother—the brother who turned him in to his parole officer over 15 years ago. They are now best friends. This Kyle graduate called recently to let us know he will soon receive his associate's degree in business administration—with honors—and he has been asked to join an honor society. This was a man who was never able to stay out of prison for more than one year from the age of 17 until the age of 50.

In August, 2000, a man was paroled from New Vision after serving many years of his adult life in prison. He had been a Cadre member at New Vision for seven years; he was one of the original residents in the Program in 1992, but had such a long sentence he was not granted parole until 2000. He steadily worked on his alcoholism problems and other life problems, such as family relationships, while in treatment. At the same time, he worked as a peer facilitator, helping the New Vision staff teach the program to newcomers. He was already a college graduate in business, and after his parole, he returned to college to obtain his required credits to become a chemical dependency counselor. He graduated with honors from the Licensed Chemical Dependency Counselor (LCDC) training program, and accepted an invitation to join Phi Theta Kappa, an honors fraternity. He returns to New Vision regularly as a speaker at the AA meeting to share his experience, strength, and hope with current residents, and has brought his sponsor and other friends to share as well. He received his Counselor Intern certification from the Texas Commission on Alcohol and Drug Abuse (TCADA) and hopes to return to New Vision as a member of the counseling staff soon. He has reunited with his family, and is very active in the AA groups in his community.

Chapter 13

California's First Prison Therapeutic Community: A 10-Year Review

by Rod Mullen, A.B., James Rowland, A.B., Naya Arbiter, Lew Yablonsky, Ph.D., and Bette Fleishman

Need for New Programs for the Many Substance Abusing
  Offenders in Prison 13-1
How It All Began 13-3
    Focus on Substance Abuse as a Significant Problem 13-3
    Task Force Recommendations 13-3
    Recruiting Warden for Program 13-4
How the TC Was Implemented 13-4
    Close Coordination Between Program and Correctional Staff 13-4
    Working With the Realities—and Help—of the Inmate Population 13-5
    Integration of Program Into General Prison Life 13-6
    Expanding Eligibility Parameters 13-6
    Development of Aftercare Component 13-7
The Amity Model 13-8
    Structure and Duration 13-8
    Staff and Training 13-8
    Curriculum 13-9
    Cross Training 13-10
Bottom Line: Program Works to Improve Lives...and Save Money 13-10
Conclusion 13-11

NEED FOR NEW PROGRAMS FOR THE MANY SUBSTANCE ABUSING OFFENDERS IN PRISONS

The California Department of Corrections (CDC) has the second largest number of prison inmates in the United States, and has experienced dramatic growth in inmate population in recent years; and while growth has leveled in the past two years, estimates are that the inmate population will increase to 218,000 by 2006 (Arax, 1999). Substance

---

This chapter originally appeared in Offender Substance Abuse Report, *Vol. 1, No. 2, March/April 2001.*

abuse has been identified as a "major contributing factor to the criminal lifestyle of a large portion of the offenders committed to the California Department of Corrections" (California Dept. of Corrections RFP C99.120, p. 12), since over 75% of CDC's inmates have histories of substance abuse, and drug offenders represent the largest offense category of new felon admissions (33.8%). Further, a third of all parole violators who were returned to custody for new terms were returned for drug offences (Id.).

For many years California engaged in a massive expansion of prisons as the bulwark of its approach to crime. However, that approach is under scrutiny. In January, 1998, the Little Hoover Commission (an independent government agency) completed a comprehensive and highly publicized report to the governor and the state legislature stating "there is increasing evidence that the growing inmate population reflects a correctional system that is not using the most cost-effective strategies available" (Terzian, 1998).

The Little Hoover Commission cited California's recidivism rate, one of the highest in the U.S., as evidence that it was time for the state to develop alternative strategies to cope with the increasing number of men and women incarcerated. In its report, the Commission repeatedly cited the success of the Amity Therapeutic Community (TC) at the Richard J. Donovan Correctional Facility (RJDCF) near San Diego. Following the

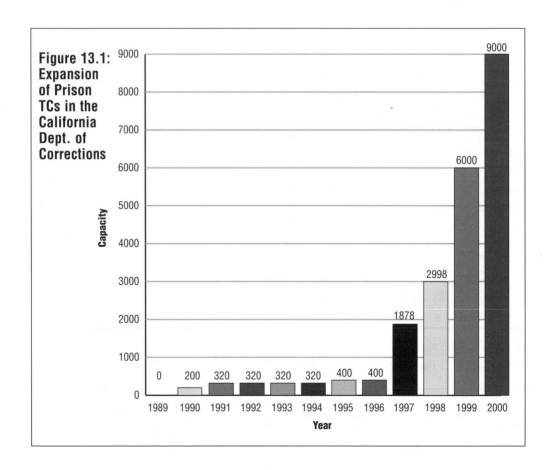

Figure 13.1: Expansion of Prison TCs in the California Dept. of Corrections

Commission's recommendations, legislation passed at the end of the 1997-1998 fiscal year that authorized a major expansion of Amity-style therapeutic community programs. Subsequent legislation has brought the number of TC beds authorized for the CDC to 9,000, with funded aftercare for all participants (see Figure 13.1). "This," in the words of Youth and Adult Correctional Secretary Robert Presley, "is the largest single state initiative in United States history targeting criminal drug offenders" (Mullen, 2000, p.12).

HOW IT ALL BEGAN

Focus on Substance Abuse as a Significant Problem

In 1987, CDC Director James Rowland contacted Amity's CEO, Rod Mullen, with whom he had collaborated before to provide treatment programs for juvenile offenders. Rowland explained that CDC's rapid prison expansion was not addressing the fact that 70% or more of CDC inmates had serious and chronic substance abuse problems. He surmised that these inmates' substance abuse was the key factor in their violating parole more quickly than other parolees, so that many were "doing life on the installment plan." Rowland requested that Mullen tour several CDC institutions and parole regions, and then make a presentation to Rowland's executive staff and wardens regarding both the potential effectiveness and immediate feasibility of implementing substance abuse treatment for CDC inmates and parolees.

Mullen's report to the CDC Administrative Planning Session helped CDC focus on substance abuse as a significant problem, which led to the formation of an ongoing task force reporting to Director Rowland.

Task Force Recommendations

The task force decided that CDC should participate in "Project Recovery," a national technical assistance project sponsored by the Center for Substance Abuse Treatment (CSAT), U.S. Department of Health and Human Services. (Note: Projects Reform and Recovery also spawned the Texas Criminal Justice Initiative and Key-Crest in Delaware. Positive outcomes from these programs and the Amity California TC, and federal Residential Substance Abuse Treatment (RSAT) funding, have driven a greater investment nationwide in treatment for incarcerated offenders.) That involvement led to:

- Formation of the CDC Office of Substance Abuse Programs (OSAP);

- Establishment of a department-wide CDC Substance Abuse Advisory Panel; and

- A 1989 report to the California Legislature which included plans for a model in-prison TC and establishment of two parolee networks to provide assistance to identified substance abusers paroling from prisons.

CDC followed Amity's recommendations that the prison TC be established at a new institution, one that had no history of previous substance abuse programs and where the warden was willing to give the program an opportunity to prove itself.

Recruiting Warden for Program

Director Rowland turned to a seasoned veteran of over 30 years who had worked his way through the ranks, Warden John Ratelle, who had just activated the RJDCF. He asked if Ratelle would be willing to house the proposed model program.

Warden Ratelle agreed, conditioned upon Rowland's consent that the program could be terminated immediately if Ratelle believed it was not working. Ratelle then visited the Amity/Pima County Jail Program, funded by the Bureau of Justice Assistance as a "national demonstration program" at the Pima County Adult Detention Facility in Tucson, Arizona. He viewed a jail pod where 50 sentenced drug offenders engaged in a therapeutic community using former-addict counselors, a curriculum specifically developed by Amity, and an Amity-developed program of cross training between correctional officers and treatment staff. Male and female offenders attended TC activities together (but were housed separately). Participants averaged two prior convictions and four years of heavy drug use. An evaluation revealed that, 30 months post-release, only 35% of the 362 program completers had been re-arrested (Glider, 1997). Although fewer women were able to access treatment, their outcomes were better than their male counterparts' (e.g., 86% of the women were employed six months post-release vs. 60% of the men, and no women who went on to community-based treatment were re-incarcerated within 30 months).

Warden Ratelle, who as a young officer had worked at the California Rehabilitation Center, admitted that he came to look at the Pima County program with a great deal of skepticism. "I've seen a lot of programs come and go, and a lot of them were 'games' where inmates lay around all day, continued to use drugs, went to meetings occasionally, manipulated untrained correctional counselors, got their day-for-day credit—and then got out and immediately went back to drugs and crime." When he talked to inmates at Amity's jail project, he met some "old cons" who had been incarcerated in CDC. They talked about how the Amity program was different from other programs they had participated in. He observed the demanding work schedule, saw that the program curriculum was dealing with "real issues," and that the encounter groups did not allow inmates to shift the blame for their mistakes to others.

He decided that he was willing to take the risk of starting the TC, since, he reasoned, if recidivism to re-incarceration were reduced even by 10%, it would save millions of dollars. He also knew that the section of RJDCF where Amity was to be located had more violence than the rest of the prison. He hoped that the program would reduce violent incidents, which at an estimated cost of $85,000 per occurrence could *alone* justify the expense of the program.

A CDC Request for Proposal was issued, and Amity was the successful bidder. The project began in the fall of 1990 at the Richard J. Donovan Correctional Facility (RJDCF) near San Diego, a 4,600-inmate Level III security institution.

HOW THE TC WAS IMPLEMENTED

Close Coordination Between Program and Correctional Staff

From the time the contract was awarded Amity worked closely with Warden Ratelle's staff, OSAP, and security officers on Facility Three of the RJDCF, where the program was to be located. Amity fielded a team of senior counselors and program administrators, all recovering addicts, all ex-offenders, and representing all ethnic groups, with between 10 and 25 years of experience working with criminal addicts. This group "walked the yard," talked to inmates, learned the specific inmate culture of RJDCF, conducted interviews, met the men who formed the MAC (Men's Advisory Council) for Facility Three, and passed information back to Amity's management about what was needed to mount a successful TC.

As part of the start up, Amity pointed out that the 200-bed, double-celled housing units had no space for program activities. CDC responded by purchasing two doublewide trailers, placing them in close proximity to the housing unit, and modifying them for program activities.

Warden Ratelle worked closely with the Amity Program Director, and instructed his staff, "We are going to give [Amity] our full support; we are not going to allow the program to be subverted." His attitude toward Amity's staff was always supportive and respectful, though almost all of them were "experienced-trained" professionals who had been drug users, criminals, and had been previously incarcerated. Ratelle's only requirement was that anyone with a record be out of an institution for five years and off parole. He accepted Amity management's verification that they had at least three years of sobriety. He said, "You are the experts at changing these guys, you have proven that. We know how to run a prison. You work with us and we'll support you." All Amity staff participated in the standard CDC weeklong security training to learn institutional security procedures and to receive their RJDCF security clearances. Initially, Amity fielded a small permanent staff and rotated other staff between its Tucson programs and RJDCF until those that seemed most capable had been permanently selected as staff. Most of the entry-level staff previously had been participants in the Amity/Pima County Jail Project. Amity realized from its experience in the Pima County Jail that many counselors who are effective in community-based programs cannot be so in the much more restrictive correctional environment.

Working With the Realities—and Help—of the Inmate Population

CDC initially had difficulties screening inmates into the Amity program; the educational requirements for entrance proved too exclusive, and RJDCF classification staff was not experienced with this type of inmate selection. A visit by a committee of the state legislature to view the program in November 1990 precipitated extensive and immediate changes in inmate classification when they discovered that the program had only 13 participants five months after funding had been provided legislatively. The next 187 inmates were quickly installed in Building 15, Facility Three of RJDCF by February of 1991. There were frequent disputes, and some scuffles occurred, as the "Amity inmates" displaced general population inmates from their cells but, despite the tension, no serious incidents occurred.

The design of the prison precluded Amity participants from being isolated from the general population. So it was necessary to target many of the "shot callers" on Facility Three for support. This included inmates serving life sentences, and other long-term inmates who had reputations and the respect of the inmate population. Many of these men joined Amity. Those who did not join spread the word that Amity was different, that it was not the equivalent of protective custody, that the participants were not "snitches," and should not be harassed on the yard.

Integration of Program Into General Prison Life

Initially, the plan was for all Amity participants to work together in a new textile mill, which was to be opened by the Prison Industry Authority at RJDCF in 1991. For a variety of reasons the mill did not open until several years later, so Warden Ratelle insisted that the men mix with the general population for their minimum 36-hour weekly work assignment, eat with general population, and share the recreational facilities on the yard. Ratelle felt that this model was more realistic. "If they were on the outside and had a problem," said Ratelle, "they would have to maintain a job and deal with it after work. I don't see why we should make it easier for these guys." So Amity participants performed their institutional work assignments with non-program inmates (many of whom used drugs), and then most participated in a minimum of 20 hours a week of intensive Amity TC activities, often at night and on weekends in order to accommodate the institutional work schedule. The exception was 40 men who were selected as "cadres" for Amity—these men worked on a one week on/one week off schedule. During their work-week, they cleaned and maintained program areas, landscaped the grounds, copied materials, and did other support tasks. During their week "off" they participated full time in program activities. Amity, out of its CDC contract, developed duty statements for the "cadre" group and paid them the prevailing institutional wage.

The Amity program was shaped both by Warden Ratelle's hard-nosed attitude and his unstinting support. While he made many demands, he also respected the genuine efforts made by the program staff and inmates to establish a very different culture and identity in the middle of one of the most unruly areas in the prison. He insisted that there be absolutely no incentives for men participating in the program. In fact, men who volunteered for the program were not eligible for work furlough, since it would interfere with their completing the required time in program. Because of this, and the program's intensity, Amity developed a reputation as being tough. Despite that, the program received in excess of 100 inmate applications for the 10 to 20 program slots that became available monthly.

Expanding Eligibility Parameters

Warden Ratelle initially refused Amity's request to recruit several inmates serving life sentences as peer mentors, but then allowed two lifers to move into the Amity housing unit and become part of the program on a trial basis. These men, one Caucasian, the other African-American, both with convictions for extremely violent crimes, became role models for the remainder of the men. The friendships they formed sent a powerful message not only to Amity inmate participants, but also to the entire 1,100-man facility that Amity was different, that the deeply ingrained racial prejudice that was part of prison life was not accepted. One of the lifers, a former street and prison gang leader, said:

> I've been in here for 17 years and I am respected by other men in any institution where I've done time. I've taken a lot of first-termers deeper into the convict life. Now I'm using the respect I have to speak out against gangs, violence, and all that stupidity. At Amity young guys look up to me and they listen when I tell them to stop gang banging, to get out of prison, stay out, and to get a real job and take care of their kids.

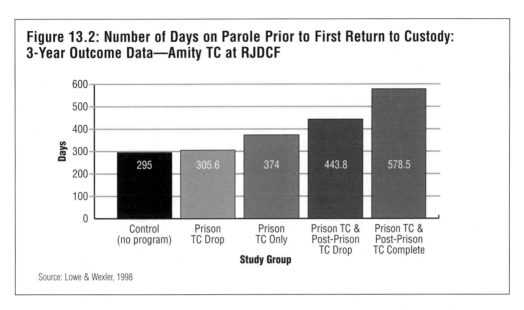

Figure 13.2: Number of Days on Parole Prior to First Return to Custody: 3-Year Outcome Data—Amity TC at RJDCF

Source: Lowe & Wexler, 1998

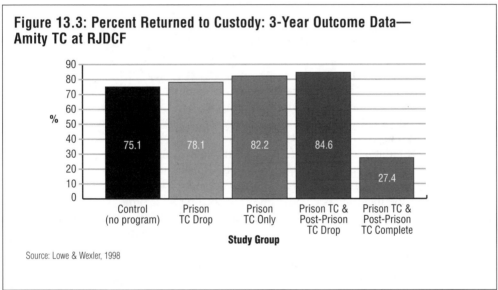

Figure 13.3: Percent Returned to Custody: 3-Year Outcome Data—Amity TC at RJDCF

Source: Lowe & Wexler, 1998

Amity has six lifers in the program today; since the program's inception there has never been a negative incident with any of the lifers housed in the Amity unit.

Development of Aftercare Component

Critical to the success of Amity was the development of a residential facility for men who paroled from the program. The initial contract did not fund aftercare, so Amity leased a large house to use as an office, and also housed six to 10 parolees who had completed the RJDCF program there. Initially OSAP wanted Amity to send RJDCF completers to other community-based providers in San Diego. But inmate participants said, "we've already been to those places, and we've failed there." They told Amity staff that they needed an Amity facility in the community that was a real continuance of what they had started in the prison in order to succeed. Additional funding was secured and, in 1993, Amity opened a 40-bed facility in Vista, north of San Diego, which allowed about one-third of Amity in-prison completers to enter an Amity residential program, which built upon the curriculum used at RJDCF. The outcomes (see Figures 13.2 and 13.3) show the importance of this very closely linked aftercare in helping the men maintain sobriety, get jobs, and keep from returning to drugs and criminality.

THE AMITY MODEL

Structure and Duration

The population in prison TCs typically began their drug abuse, criminality, and incarceration as teens; have dysfunctional, abusive, and criminogenic families; have little formal education; have inadequate work skills and experience; do not "buy in" to mainstream morality; have little sense of personal responsibility; have antisocial personality disorders; have neither the attitudes nor the skills necessary to take responsibility for their offspring; have almost exclusively negative social and personal relationships; have poor interpersonal and decision making skills; and have never achieved a high degree of functioning in any non-criminal realm of life. In short, they need habilitative, rather than rehabilitative, services. Habilitation entails complete cognitive, emotional, and behavioral restructuring. This means that the TC must be highly structured, very intensive, and relatively long term. Amity's model is delivered for as close to 24 hours per day, seven days a week, 365 days per year as prison security regulations and budgeted staffing permit.

For example, Amity has successfully used intensive curriculum-based retreats and workshops for many years in its community-based programs as a key element of emotional and cognitive restructuring. These often occur in 24-, 48-, or 72-hour segments and, with sleep and meal breaks, sometimes last as long as seven days. However, security and institutional work constraints resulted in an adaptation: 26-hour workshops at RJDCF, held over two days. These intensive workshops form the backbone for delivery of the Amity curriculum.

While throughout the treatment field there is constant pressure to reduce time in program, many of Amity's best successes spent as long as 18 months in the prison TC, followed by a year in Amity's community-based TC at Vista. For the type of participant in the Amity TC at RJDCF, it became clear that treatment should last a minimum of nine months, followed by a minimum of six months in community-based aftercare, for a total of no less than 15 months. It was also evident that residential aftercare was much more effective in reducing recidivism than non-residential services.

Staffing and Training

Commitment, competence, credibility, and congruence are key factors in this area. Staff must be highly committed to work in an environment where the "convict code" and institutional security are the two established cultures. They must be seen as credible to both security staff and inmates alike. They must be trained in a manner relevant to the unique environment in which they work. Last, they must be absolutely congruent in their expectations of program participants, each other, and correctional security and parole personnel.

In early days of TCs, there was no formal staff. Those who led the TC communities were recovering addicts who were highly motivated, experienced, and had more "clean time" than those they led. All leadership, however, was done from the position of personal demonstration; this made TCs both powerful and extremely credible to participants, as all staff shared the same assumptions and agreed upon the same protocols. As TCs matured and became more dependent upon mental health funding, staffing characteristics changed, becoming more akin to other health service organizations. The emphasis was placed more heavily on "individual treatment plans" than on building a recovering community in which all, including "counselors," were members first.

While an emphasis on professionalism has many benefits, particularly in terms of experience and stability, it can result in a loss of vitality and credibility. Over the past decade this has been addressed at Amity/RJDCF by having an internship training program at the Vista facility—eventually resulting in men who were once inmate participants coming back to RJDCF and to other prison TCs operated by Amity as very credible counselors.

Throughout the decade, Amity staff training has included weeklong immersion trainings annually. These are much more in depth than typical in-service trainings, and require staff to learn to do themselves what they are going to ask those they lead to do:

- Self-disclose;

- Deal with difficult personal issues;

- Learn about each other;

- Learn to respect different cultures;

- Become skilled and enthusiastic teachers; and

- Work cooperatively with each other from a common set of shared beliefs about "what works."

Staff also participate in staff encounter groups. These groups help in resolving issues between staff, keeping morale high, maintaining a sense of staff "community," and demonstrating that the methodology used in the treatment program is part of a life-long recovery process.

Curriculum

Most TCs have a set of practices that are passed on from generation to generation, mostly orally. What written curriculum is available is often drawn from other treatment programs, most of which work with a better-educated and less criminal population. Amity has developed an extensive written and videotaped curriculum—developed through subcontract with Extensions, an organization that specializes in developing TC curricula—that aims to provide guidance for counselors and participants alike in tackling issues relevant to the convicted drug abuser. The intensive cognitive, emotional, and behavioral restructuring occurs through the delivery of a curriculum designed to accommodate a wide variety of abilities, cultural backgrounds, and learning styles. It has to be interesting, relevant, and interactive—making every student a "teacher."

Cross Training

Amity developed and refined cross training at the Amity/Pima County Jail project. At Amity/RJDCF all Amity staff attend regular security trainings. Throughout the decade, moreover, two- and three-day trainings are provided quarterly for institutional, parole, and administrative correctional staff. This ensures that the Amity treatment model is understood by all the correctional professionals who work with it.

BOTTOM LINE: PROGRAM WORKS TO IMPROVE LIVES … AND SAVE MONEY

Dr. Harry Wexler, who had conducted the NIDA-funded outcome study of the Stay'N Out prison TC in New York, worked with Amity management and CDC to write a proposal to the National Institute on Drug Abuse to evaluate the Amity/RJDCF TC. He proposed a random assignment study to insure that the outcome results were credible. Results of the study indicate that the program is effective in reducing recidivism. The overall results of this study can be seen in Figures 13.2 and 13.3, presented earlier in this chapter. They demonstrate the effectiveness of the combined Amity in-prison and post-prison programs to reduce recidivism to reincarceration.

In terms of the "bottom line," the 1997 LAO report on prison population growth determined that if the Amity results could be replicated through an expansion of substance abuse treatment to 10,000 beds over seven years, the state would not have to build an additional 4,700 beds (Nichol, 1997). That scenario would also result in a one-time capital outlay savings of $210 million with annual savings of $80 million a year.

But these substantial savings to CDC reflect only part of the cost benefit of Amity at the RJDCF. Most of these men were third-strike candidates, with a mean expected cost to the California Department of Corrections of their next conviction in excess of $500,000 each.

Regarding violence reduction, in 1995 Warden Ratelle stated, "The Amity unit is a safer environment for correctional officers to work in. It gives them an opportunity to be more involved, and there are less disciplinary write-ups, resulting in cost savings for management." He noted that there had been no serious incidents of violence at Amity, even though "the inmates in the Amity program are some of the most incorrigible inmates in the correctional system, and one of the hardest groups to work with, with an average of at least eight years of prison time, strong gang affiliations, a long history of substance abuse, and violent backgrounds."

Warden Ratelle's observations were corroborated by Dr. David Deitch (1998) of the Pacific Southwest Addiction Technology Transfer Center at the University of California at San Diego, who stated,

> A careful and detailed study of adverse behavior incidents among inmates in the therapeutic community environment contrasted to inmates not in treatment [at the RJDCF] shows all types of disciplinary infractions, a

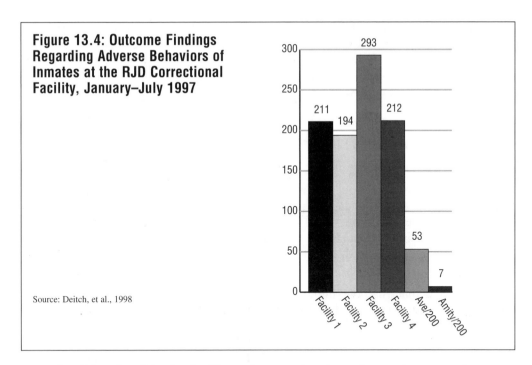

Figure 13.4: Outcome Findings Regarding Adverse Behaviors of Inmates at the RJD Correctional Facility, January–July 1997

Source: Deitch, et al., 1998

lawful and strikingly significant less number in such reports among the "Amity" treatment population.

The average number of write-ups per 200 inmates (the size of each housing unit) is 53 throughout the correctional facility (though higher on Facility III where the Amity unit is located.) As can be seen in Figure 13.4 and Exhibit 13.1, the number of incidents was significantly less in the Amity unit.

Dr. Deitch said further, "There is a similarly positive striking reduction of work injury, sick leave and other personal quality of life/cost impact among custody assigned to the treatment unit [Amity] versus officers in all other yards and housing units." This is significant, as it speaks to the ability of an effective TC to make the treatment environment safe for inmate participants, and also to make it a better working environment for CDC custody personnel. Given that both male and female correctional officers have major health problems at a rate of more than two times the general population matched for age, reducing stress among officers is a very significant issue. From an institutional management perspective an effective TC is a "win-win" when it can significantly reduce operating costs in the institution, and improve employee morale and health.

CONCLUSION

A statement by James Gomez on the celebration of Amity's tenth year at the RJDCF is a fitting conclusion to this program review:

> It was a pleasure as the Director of Corrections to be involved in the groundbreaking program between CDC and Amity. This collaboration has been used as a national model which has provided the expansion of prison

drug treatment programs not only in California, but also in may other states throughout the nation. As a member of the National Institute of Corrections, I have the opportunity to travel throughout the nation to look at programs as well as to try to set policy on some national issues. The Amity program demonstrated that some things do work.

Exhibit 13.1: A Warden's Pleasant Surprise

In 1992, Warden Ratelle decided to do a surprise urine drop of the entire Amity in-prison program. He told no one of his decision—neither his staff nor the Amity program staff—so that the results would reflect what was really occurring in the unit. After weekend visitation, the time when most drugs come into the institution, he simultaneously locked down each cell in the entire unit where the Amity inmates are housed, and had every inmate give a urine specimen under security officer supervision.

> I knew that I had two hundred guys with serious drug problems living together, and not isolated from the main yard. We were busting guys on the yard for drugs regularly, so I knew that if the guys in Amity wanted to get drugs, they could. I assumed that 25% of the people in the Amity program would turn up "dirty." But the results were that only one Amity participant was positive for drugs—marijuana. I was shocked, but I was very impressed. That was the single most important event for me in convincing me that the program was really working.

About the Authors

Rod Mullen, A.B., is President and CEO, Amity Foundation. James Rowland, A.B., now retired, was Director, California Department of Corrections, from 1987 to 1991. Naya Arbiter is a principal of Extensions, LLC. Lew Yablonsky, Ph.D., is Emeritus Professor, California State University, Northridge. Bette Fleishman is Chair of the Amity Foundation Board of Directors.

References

Arax, M. (1999, June 1). A return to the goal of reforming inmates. *Los Angeles Times*.

California Department of Corrections (1999). *Request for proposal C99.120*. Sacramento, CA: State Publications Office

Deitch, D., Koutsenok, M., McGrath, P., Ratelle, J., & Carleton, R. (1998). *Outcome findings regarding in-custody adverse behavior between therapeutic community treatment and non-treatment populations and its impact on custody personnel quality of life*. San Diego, CA: University of California-San Diego, Department of Psychiatry, Addiction Technology Transfer Center.

Glider, P., Herbst, D., & Mullen, R. (1997). Substance abuse treatment in a jail setting. In G. DeLeon (Ed.), *Community as method: Modified therapeutic communities for special populations*. New York, NY: The Greenwood Publishing Group.

Lipton, D.S. (1998, February 24). *Incorporating therapeutic communities that work into the correctional armamentarium.* Testimony before the California State Senate Committee on Public Safety.

Lowe, L., & Wexler, H. (1998) *The R.J. Donovan in-prison and community substance abuse program: Three year return to custody data.* New York, NY: National Develolpment and Research Institutes.

Mullen, R. (2000). *Amity Foundation—Amity at R.J. Donovan 10 year anniversary.* Porterville, CA: Amity Foundation.

Mullen, R., (1996). Therapeutic communities in prisons: Dealing with toxic waste. In Kevin Early (Ed.), *Prison based treatment programs in America.* New York, NY: Praeger.

Mullen, R., & Arbiter, N. (1992). Against the odds: Therapeutic community approaches to underclass drug abuse. In Peter H. Smith (Ed.) *Drug policy in the Americas.* Boulder, CO: Westview Press.

Mullen, R., Ratelle, J., Abraham, E., & Boyle, J. (1996, August). California program reduces recidivism and saves tax dollars. *Corrections Today, 58*(5), 118-123.

Mullen, R., Schuettinger, M., Arbiter, N., & Conn, D. (1998). Reducing recidivism: Amity Foundation of California and the Department of Corrections demonstrate how to do it. In T. Miller, *Frontiers of justice: Volume II. Programs in the adult correctional system.* Brunswick, ME: Biddle Publishing Company.

Nichol, C. (1997). *Addressing the state's long-term inmate population growth.* Legislative Analyst's Office, Policy Brief. Sacramento, CA: State of California Publications.

Terzian, R. (1998). *Beyond bars: Correctional reforms to lower prison costs and reduce crime.* Little Hoover Commission, Milton Marks Commission on California State Government Organization and Economy. Sacramento, CA: State Publications Office.

Weikel, D. (1997, April 25). In prison, a drug rehab that pays off. *Los Angeles Times,* pp. 1&18.

Winett, D., Lowe, L., Mullen R., & Missakian, E. (1992). Amity right turn: A demonstration drug abuse treatment program for inmates and parolees. In C. G. Leukefeld & F. M. Tims (Eds.), *Drug abuse treatment in prisons and jails.* National Institute on Drug Abuse Research Monograph Series 118: Alcohol, Drug Abuse, and Mental Health Administration. DHHS Publication No. (ADM) 92-1884, 84-98, 1992.

Yablonsky, L. (1994) *The therapeutic community.* Gardner Press.

Yablonsky, L. (1997). *Gangsters: Fifty years of madness, drugs, and death on the streets of America.* New York, NY: New York University Press

Chapter 14

National Update on Therapeutic Community Programs for Substance Abusing Offenders in State Prisons

by Peter B. Rockholz, M.S.S.W.

Introduction 14-1
National Survey Findings 14-2
    Extent of TC Programming 14-2
    Inmates Served 14-2
    Staffing 14-4
TC, or Not TC? 14-4
    Some Confusion About What a TC Is 14-4
    Standards Development 14-5
    Field Review Observations 14-5
Critical TC Factors 14-6
    Staffing 14-7
    Quality Assurance 14-8
    Structured Programming 14-8
    Monitoring Oversight 14-8
    Treatment Model 14-8
Conclusion 14-9

INTRODUCTION

During the past decade, the therapeutic community (TC) has re-emerged as a preferred, effective methodology for reducing both relapse to drug abuse and recidivism to the criminal justice system among substance abusing offenders. The "community as method" concept—a hallmark of the TC process—is identified as the key defining dis-

This chapter originally appeared in Offender Substance Abuse Report, *Vol. 2, No. 4, July/August 2002.*

tinction between TC programs and other types of prison-based residential substance abuse treatment programs. Encouraged by several national evaluative research studies of in-prison TC programs, and supported through funding under the federal Residential Substance Abuse Treatment (RSAT) program, the majority of state correctional agencies have chosen to implement TC programs in their prisons. This chapter reports the results of a national survey of TC programs in state prisons conducted by the Association of State Correctional Administrators (ASCA), and findings of field testing of national prison TC standards conducted by the Criminal Justice Institute, Inc. (CJI), and then identifies critical issues related to implementing TC programs and other types of residential treatment in prisons and poses challenges faced by emerging national prison TC standards in distinguishing TCs from other prison-based programs.

NATIONAL SURVEY FINDINGS

During July, 2000, ASCA conducted a survey to inventory and obtain basic information about prison TCs in North America. Completed surveys were received from all 50 states, the Federal Bureau of Prisons (BOP), New York City, the City of Philadelphia, Puerto Rico, and Canada. Preliminary results are presented below, along with a discussion of implementation and process issues.

Extent of TC Programming

As illustrated in Table 14.1, the survey identified 252 prison TC programs in 40 states and three non-state jurisdictions (Canada, New York City, and Philadelphia). Four additional states indicated they planned to implement TCs by the end of 2002; the resultant total of 44 states anticipated adding 38 more TCs, bringing the total to 289 by the end of year 2002. Only Arizona, Montana, North Dakota, and the BOP reported having neither TCs nor plans to develop TCs in the next year. Four states (California, 37; New York, 25; Texas, 25; Florida, 15) account for over one-third (37%) of the existing TCs.

As illustrated in Figure 14.1, the greatest period of new program start-ups has been during the years 1997–2000; 41.8% of existing programs opened since 1997, with a peak of 51 programs starting in 1999. Newer programs tend to be relatively smaller than those already in operation. For example, the planned, new programs are 38% smaller on average compared to existing programs (i.e., mean capacity of 95 versus 154).

Inmates Served

Individual institutions report their TC programs ranging in capacity from 15 to 1,000 participants, with a mean of 154 (median = 100). Three-fourths (73.9%) of the TC programs serve only men, 22.5% serve only women, and 3.6% report serving both. About half (48.4%) of the programs had an inmate capacity below 100; 20% were over 200. The total reported inmate capacity of existing prison TC programs in the United States was 40,362 (four facilities not reporting). With planned expansion, this figure was projected to exceed 44,000 by the end of 2002. Actual one-day census reports suggested an average TC bed utilization of 95.2% (41 facilities not reporting). Program census figures ranged from 13 to 1,000 with a mean of 142 (median = 85). During 1999, it was reported that 31,493 inmates successfully completed TC programs.

Table 14.1: Prison TC Programs in the United States, 2000

State/Juris.	# TCs	% Private	Male Cap.	Female Cap.	Total Cap.
AL	2	0%	224	0	224
AK	1	100%	0	48	48
AZ	0				
CA	27	100%	4,562	1,952	6,514
CAN	3	34%	90	0	88
CO	6	83%	372	72	444
CT	4	0%	220	60	280
DE	10	100%	1,016	126	1,142
BOP	0				
FL	15	100%	3,175	172	3,347
GA	4	100%	68	48	116
HI	4	0%	272	15	293
ID	2	100%	86	0	86
IN	2	100%	194	72	266
KS	4	100%	284	30	314
LA	5	0%	316	50	366
ME	1	100%	40	0	40
MD	1	0%	550	0	550
MA	10	100%	418	75	493
MI	3	100%	408	60	468
MN	2	0%	96	0	96
MS	1	0%	396	0	396
MO	4	75%	1,331	90	1,421
MT	0				
NE	3	0%	162	19	181
NV	1	100%	106	0	106
NJ	7	100%	1,211	60	1,271
NM	6	34%	482	80	562
NY	26	4%	4,546	629	5,175
NYC	2	100%	702	200	902
NC	0				
ND	0				
OH	5	60%	480	81	561
OK	9	78%	573	102	875
OR	3	100%	150	60	210
PA	8	25%	552	102	657
PHL	5	100%	322	100	422
RI	4	100%	122	28	150
SC	4	75%	656	132	788
TN	8	38%	263	128	391
TX	25	40%	6,636	1,612	8,248
UT	5	0%	287	126	413
VT	2	100%	109	0	109
VA	9	0%	1,364	461	1,825
WA	2	100%	100	100	200
WV	4	0%	187	36	223
WI	1	0%	45	0	45
WY	2	100%	28	28	56
Totals	**252**	**59.2%**	**33,201**	**6,954**	**40,362**

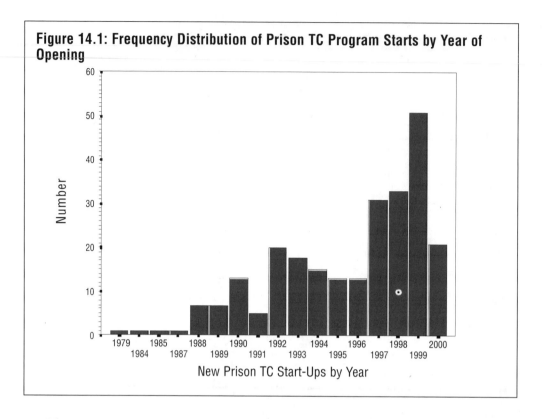

Figure 14.1: Frequency Distribution of Prison TC Program Starts by Year of Opening

All programs specified substance abuse as a primary participant characteristic. All custody levels were represented. Six programs were exclusively for youthful offenders, five for sex offenders, and four for those with co-occurring psychiatric disorders. Other special population programs include those specifically designed for pre-release, chronic relapsers, parole violators, chronic DUI offenders, batterers, and violent and aggressive inmates.

Staffing

A majority (58.7%) of TC programs are operated by private providers under contract, with the remainder run by public employees of either the state correctional agency or the Single State Agency (SSA) for alcohol and drug abuse services. The existing programs (19 facilities not reporting) employed 2,701 staff, with an average (mean) per program of 11.5 (median = 7). The mean number of participants per staff member was 15.4.

TC, OR NOT TC?

Some Confusion About What a TC Is

While state officials were asked in the survey to respond only about prison programs that they identified as TCs, the responses raise questions—and will likely rekindle debate—about what constitutes a "real" TC versus a residential program with some TC-like components. Certainly, many of the programs reflected in the results of the survey only vaguely resemble what is understood by TC experts to constitute a "real" TC. In fact, many programs operate with a traditional medical model approach, utilizing combinations of the 12-step programs and various curriculum-driven, cognitive-behavioral, psycho-educational training and other therapies. While many of these programs borrow some of the identifiable structures of TCs (e.g., morning meeting, structure board, written philosophy), they often lack those core processes that are at the essence of what De Leon (1997) describes as the "community as method" approach of the traditional, including what are known as "modified," TC programs. It was that approach, along with practical experience and De Leon's theoretical framework, that shaped the author's original draft of prison TC standards that were initially field tested in the Ohio prison system in 1993, and formed the basis for the first version of the Therapeutic Communities of America (TCA) draft standards.

Standards Development

The current initiative to develop national prison TC standards—now a joint project between TCA and the American Correctional Association (ACA)—is, in part, an attempt to identify essential elements of TCs (necessarily modified for prison settings) toward offering accreditation for these programs. The TCA/ACA accreditation process must reliably distinguish between nominal TCs and "real" TCs. Unless the TCA/ACA initiative requires compliance with a small number of essential standards that truly reflect the "heart and soul" of the TC, it is unlikely that the accreditation process will accomplish this distinction. In an effort to identify essential, defining TC standards, and to propose modifications to the TCA/ACA accreditation process in development, CJI has identified 10 critical standards (nine of which are directly excerpted from the TCA draft), and developed observable indicators for each of them for consideration of the authors of the accreditation standards (see Table 14.2, next page).

Field Review Observations

CJI has conducted formal and informal reviews of prison TC programs in six states using the TCA-developed draft standards along with CJI's critical standards instrument. In three of those states, all existing TC programs across the state were reviewed. In general, a clear concern was raised about the probability that several programs, purported by state officials and program operators to be TCs, would likely pass the national prison TC standards (assuming a minimum compliance rate in the range of 80%-85%) without meeting the core standards that distinguish TCs from other types of residential programming. In some cases, program operators could argue convincingly that they complied with several standards, and might potentially "pass" others depending upon the background and philosophy of the individual reviewer(s). Unless the accreditation process requires compliance with those standards that most clearly differentiate TC programs from others, programs with little resemblance to the traditional TC "community as method" approach might be able to achieve accreditation as TC programs.

Table 14.2: Criminal Justice Institute Critical Standards and Observable Key Indicators for Prison TC Programs

Critical Standard*	Key Indicators
1. The primary approach to treatment is "community-as-method." [CP1]	• Observers sense that there is a pervasive attitude of "we are all in this together" rather than a traditional "patient-therapist" or individual focus and approach. • Observers feel that there is a meaningful involvement and relationship between program participants rather than a collection of individuals primarily focused on their own personal issues.
2. Treatment activities emphasize experiential learning (direct and vicarious)—"doing" rather than "getting" therapy. [CP5]	• Clinical interventions and learning experiences place participants in roles and situations that achieve social learning—rather than focusing on individual, cognitive solutions. • Group dynamics are utilized to give participants direct feedback on the effects of their behavior and attitudes on other participants and the community as a whole.
3. Negative behaviors and attitudes are confronted immediately and directly by peers, and this practice is seen as acceptable by the community, is reinforced by it, and acts residents within the area.	• "Pull-ups" (i.e., verbal, awareness raising comments) between program participants occur "on the floor" frequently, and with a feeling of genuine commitment. • Obvious inappropriate behaviors and attitudes are not let go by to neutralize prison culture attitudes. [CM6]
4. There are clearly defined privileges—e.g., status advancement, more desirable living space—that are earned based upon clinical progress. [CM4]	• Promotion is based upon achievement of personal growth rather than on time or completion of prescribed activities or curriculum. • There is a sense that participants are genuinely motivated to strive for advancement and that the privileges are meaningful and reinforcing of positive actions.
5. A major focus of participant learning is on the development of affective skills, including the ability to identify and express feelings in a pro-social manner. [CP8]	• Participants strive to keep each other focused on their feelings, on the "here and now" "gut level", and on connecting current behavior with feeling states, rather than supporting intellectualization and other ego defenses. • There is evidence that painful emotions are openly shared and freely expressed (e.g., tears, etc.) and that the environment provides safety and sanctuary for this to occur.

(continues on next page)

CRITICAL TC FACTORS

Several process factors, set out below, must be considered when determining whether prison TC programs meet the definition and intent of "real" TC programs.

Table 14.2: Criminal Justice Institute Critical Standards and Observable Key Indicators for Prison TC Programs, cont'd.

Critical Standard[*]	Key Indicators
6. There is a clear sense of cooperation between clinical and security staff and residents, rather than an authority-based, oppositional relationship ("we-they dichotomy").	• Participants assume responsibility for unit compliance with expectations of security, resulting in minimal need for correctional officers to give directions. • Staff/participant interactions demonstrate respect in both directions.
7. Participants perform all possible house chores, e.g., cleaning, maintenance, clerical, expediting, etc. [TC2]	• To the greatest extent possible, participants exhibit both "pride and quality" and ownership in their community and its environment. • The apparent attitude of participants is that their job functions are meaningful and support the positive functioning of the community, rather than simply being busy work.
8. Participants are encouraged to "act as if" as a means of developing a positive attitude. [TP9]	• Senior participants actively seek to help junior participants become fully engaged in the TC process. • Senior participants demonstrate positive qualities of "right living" as a way to encourage others to strive toward their role modeling.
9. Peer feedback occurs more frequently than staff counseling. [TP6]	• There is continuous evidence that participants actively seek to provide positive counsel and support to each other. • Group sessions are dominated by peer interactions rather than by staff providing individual counsel and information.
10. The program uses groups as a primary clinical intervention, including encounters, probes, marathons, tutorials, etc. [TC5]	• Interactive groups are utilized several times per week to address current behavioral and attitudinal issues between participants. • The primary mode of group therapy is encounter, rather than discussion or psycho-educational sessions.

[*] Selected from *Revised TCA Standards for TCs in Correctional Settings*, prepared for the Office of National Drug Control Policy (ONDCP) by the Criminal Justice Committee of Therapeutic Communities of America (TCA), November 1, 1999.

Staffing

The substantial expansion of prison TCs across the nation resulted in a rapid depletion of experienced TC practitioners, particularly those who have participated in a TC themselves, available to manage and staff the new prison TCs. While it is desirable, as noted in the national standards, to have a reasonable mixture of "professionally trained" clinicians and "TC naturalists" (i.e., those who have graduated from TC programs), low supply and high demand have prevented this in several states. There are not enough ex-addict, ex-offender staff (e.g., TC graduates) to meet the national demand.

Compounding this are policies in several states that prohibit ex-offenders from working in prisons in any capacity. Additionally, in an effort to ensure staff competency, many states require TC staff to have college degrees and/or chemical dependency counselor certification or licensing. While this has the effect of improving the professionalism of treatment planning and other functions, it does not necessarily enhance TC processes and further reduces the pool of eligible TC naturalists. In fact, in the author's experience, greater reliance on academic degrees and professional certification than on TC experience results in lessened potency of the core clinical TC processes.

Quality Assurance

In an effort to ensure high quality of services and cost-effectiveness (particularly where TC program services are contracted for with private providers) several states require that prison TCs be licensed as substance abuse treatment programs by a state agency. As with the paradoxical impact of counselor credential requirements, this has been observed in several cases, unfortunately, to lead to decreased quality and potency of the TC process. It is hoped that the greatly anticipated availability of national standards for prison TCs will enable states to resolve this dilemma by accepting the TCA/ACA standards in lieu of licensing.

Structured Programming

A similar situation has been observed in states where standardization of programming is deemed an important goal and thus required in provider contracts. Program standardization has been observed to result in over-reliance on formal curriculum delivery and an over-reliance on the use of discussion groups, as opposed to an interactive and less predictable group encounter approach. The latter, of course, requires highly trained staff who are intuitively knowledgeable about such attributes of substance-dependent offenders as self-deception and manipulative behavior—especially among those with antisocial personality disorder. Structured programs tend to place greater emphasis on process over outcomes—e.g., participants can complete a curriculum involving written and oral assignments and yet change little of their behavior. Traditional TCs instead emphasize personal growth as judged by peers and staff through behavioral and attitudinal change demonstrated within intensive interpersonal relationships and interactive social learning practices.

Monitoring Oversight

It has been observed that when state agencies attempt to develop monitoring instruments to measure basic performance of prison TCs they tend to emphasize "low bar" standards (e.g., beds made, shirts tucked in, completion of written assignments). This can result in minimal compliance with the "low bar," while the programs miss the more critical achievement of effective clinical depth.

Treatment Model

While there are many similarities between the medical model and TC approaches, the few differences are monumental in creating the community treatment effect (see

Table 14.3: Comparison of Basic TC and Medical Model

TC Model	Medical Model
Views addiction as one of many secondary problems, and views the whole person as the problem	Views addiction as a primary disease, and as the central problem to be addressed in treatment
Treatment utilizes a behavioral approach	Treatment utilizes disease management approach
Program participants viewed as community or family "members"	Program participants viewed as "clients" or "patients"
Community process is primary therapeutic agent and occurs 24 hours/7 days a week	Treatment is therapist-directed (i.e., doctor-patient) and often manual-driven, occurring during sessions
Psycho-educational and didactic groups are seen as tools to support the TC process	Psycho-educational and didactic group and individual methods are the clinical approach—the sessions are the treatment
Effective TCs utilize a mixture of TC graduates, other recovering persons, and trained clinicians as staff and traditionally trained	Programs encouraged and/or required to utilize only clinical staff that are certified, degreed, or otherwise credentialed
Personal issues are public—confidentiality is maintained within the TC group	Personal issues are private—confidentiality is maintained within the client-counselor relationship
Staff role defined as facilitating a mutual self-help, positive peer process	Staff role defined as providing treatment services
Greater emphasis on affective skills development	Greater emphasis on cognitive skills development
Group encounter is primary clinical intervention	Individual counseling is primary clinical intervention
Staff share personal information and are engaged in the community process	Staff maintain professional distance and function outside the milieu process

Table 14.3). It is important for programs to examine and carefully integrate these approaches and to help staff resolve their philosophical differences. In some cases, TC methods create both ethical and personal conflicts for traditionally trained chemical dependency counselors.

CONCLUSION

The TC benefits that are realized by inmates and their families, by society (the reduction of direct and indirect costs to the public), and by correctional agencies (improvement in institutional management) will continue to provide an impetus for the further growth and proliferation of prison TC programs both nationally and internationally. At

the same time, it is incumbent upon state agencies to recognize the challenges presented during this rapid period of expansion. For example, the importance of dedicated residential TC aftercare programming for released inmates has been well established
through evaluative research (Martin et al., 1999). It is equally important that TC-spe-
cific staff competencies be developed and enhanced through qualified, ongoing staff
training activities, and that the inclusion on staff of ex-offender/ ex-addict TC naturalists be supported.

National standards hold great promise in assisting prison TC programs. However,
standards-writers face the challenge of distinguishing TCs from other residential treatment approaches and therefore supporting the clinical depth necessary to achieve the
effectiveness of the first-generation, model prison TCs. The potential danger is that,
without continued support and enhancement, these programs may lose their effectiveness and the result will be the incorrect proclamation that "TCs don't work." Finally,
especially in those states with few experienced TC practitioners, it is important to
engage the assistance of national experts in the design, implementation planning, and
development of TC programs in order to ensure their efficacy and longevity. This is an
exciting time, as the field of corrections is experiencing an opportunity to significantly reduce recidivism by effectively addressing the problem of substance abuse among
offenders.

Editors' Note

*Since this chapter was originally written, ACA has revised and field tested the new
standards, and has begun to accredit programs based on them.*

About the Author

*Peter B. Rockholz, M.S.S.W., is a Senior Associate with the Criminal Justice Institute,
Inc., a member of the editorial board of the* Offender Substance Abuse Report, *and a
faculty member at the Yale University School of Medicine. He may be contacted by
email at PRockholz@cji-inc.com.*

References

De Leon, G. (Ed.). (1997). *Community as method: Therapeutic communities for special populations and special settings.* Westport, CT: Praeger Publishers.

Martin, S. S., Butzin, C. A., Saum, C. A., & Inciardi, J. A. (1999). Three-year outcomes of therapeutic community
treatment for drug-involved offenders in Delaware: From prison to work release to aftercare. *The Prison Journal,
79*(3), 294-320.

Chapter 15

Lessons Learned From the Federal Bureau of Prisons' Drug Abuse Treatment Programs

by Beth A. Weinman, M.A., John T. Dignam, Ph.D., and Ben Wheat, Ph.D.

Introduction 15-2
Program Development History 15-2
    "Narcotics Farms" 15-2
    NARA Programs 15-2
    Shift in Treatment Approach 15-3
Current Practices 15-3
    Biopsychosocial Model 15-3
    Nine-Month Residential Program 15-4
Outcome Evaluation Results 15-4
    Positive Effect on Recidivism 15-5
    Better In-Prison Functioning 15-5
Major Program Issues 15-6
    Rapid Program Implementation and Staffing 15-6
    Organizational Culture and Climate 15-6
    Inmate Recruitment 15-7
    Establishing Treatment Milieu 15-8
    Dual Disorders 15-8
Future Directions 15-9
Summary 15-9

An earlier version of this chapter appeared in Offender Substance Abuse Report, *Vol. 1, No. 5, September/October 2001.*

INTRODUCTION

The Federal Bureau of Prisons (BOP) is continuing the unprecedented period of expansion which began a decade or so ago. This rapid growth is largely due to an aggressive federalization of many drug crimes, one component of the so-called "war on drugs" initiated by the Nixon administration, and the subsequent incarceration of offenders who previously would have been sentenced to state and local systems, if at all. The actual numbers are staggering: between April 1991 and January 2004 the population of incarcerated federal offenders has more than doubled, from 61,691 to 174,642. Of the many BOP missions, one which has become of significantly greater import as a result, is the provision of high quality, empirically based drug abuse treatment services to all inmates with a demonstrated need for and interest in treatment.

This chapter provides a brief history and current status of drug treatment programs in federal prisons; reviews existing research on the outcomes and effectiveness of programs; discusses a variety of organizational and clinical issues faced in developing and managing a drug treatment operation of such large scale; and points to future directions in assessment and treatment in corrections and elsewhere.

PROGRAM DEVELOPMENT HISTORY

"Narcotics Farms"

The BOP's long history of providing drug abuse treatment to its inmates began in 1919, when the Narcotics Unit of the Treasury Department urged Congress to set up a chain of federal "narcotics farms" to incarcerate and treat heroin users. The first of these "farms" did not open until 1936, at the United States Public Health Service (PHS) Hospital in Lexington, Kentucky; a second opened in Fort Worth, Texas, in 1938. The Lexington/Fort Worth approach was to treat drug users in an institutional setting different from the urban communities thought to be fostering their drug addiction, to address their basic "immaturities" and personality disorders, and to return them to their communities to resume their lives free from their psychological dependence on drugs (Inciardi, 1988).

NARA Programs

The next formal BOP effort to treat drug abusers began with the passage of the Narcotic Addict Rehabilitation Act (NARA; P.L. 89-793) in 1966. NARA consisted of four separate Titles, each designed to manage treatment for drug addicts. NARA Title II authorized treatment of certain addicts convicted of specific federal crimes and was administered by the BOP. NARA addicts could be sentenced for up to 10 years of institutional treatment, but were eligible for earlier release to community supervision and aftercare if judged to have completed treatment. The NARA experience demonstrated that civil commitment could be used successfully as a way to treat addicts who might not otherwise be treated. Compulsorily treated drug dependent inmates seemed to do as well as or better than inmates who received care in non-compulsory programs (Kitchener & Teitelbaum, 1986).

Shift in Treatment Approach

NARA mandates inspired a major shift in the way convicted addicts and others were managed in the Bureau of Prisons. In 1970, an experimental treatment program emerged at the Lexington facility. It was a therapeutic community (TC) where all but the most severe security infractions were managed by the inmates themselves (Conrad, 1972). Programs and services were later extended to addicted offenders not eligible for NARA. "Drug Abusers Program" (DAP) units were implemented in federal prisons in 1971. These DAP units, generally staffed the same as the NARA units, used similar TC processes, and followed NARA policy and procedures. The success of these early programs, particularly in promoting more positive adjustment while incarcerated, led to the "functional unit management" approach to housing all BOP offenders, an innovation which remains the standard today.

In 1978 there were 33 DAP units in BOP institutions, but the programs varied widely in terms of quality and focus. In response to these program inconsistencies, then-Director Norman Carlson appointed a Task Force, which published *The Drug Abuse Program Incare Manual,* a set of core standards for BOP drug abuse programs, which led to program improvements. But in the early 1980s drug abuse treatment efforts regressed in response to new pressures of a burgeoning inmate population, diminishing resources, an absence of effective leadership and support for drug programs, and inadequately trained staff. The residential, unit-based treatment model that had emerged over time gave way to a reliance on less expensive, non-residential treatment approaches across institutions (cf., Murray, 1992).

CURRENT PRACTICES

The Anti-Drug Abuse Acts of 1986 and 1988 led to renewed interest and resources for in-prison drug treatment programs. In 1989 the BOP convened a group of drug treatment and corrections professionals to develop a comprehensive drug treatment strategy for the agency. The group's recommendations, which constitute the basic structure of the program to this day, included:

1. Creation of new treatment and administrative positions dedicated solely to implementing drug abuse treatment initiatives across all agency sites;

2. Thorough screening and assessment procedures to identify inmates in need of drug abuse treatment upon entry and throughout their incarceration; and

3. A multi-pronged treatment delivery strategy to accommodate the entire spectrum of inmate need and motivation, including: drug abuse education, non-residential and residential (unit-based) treatment, and transitional drug abuse treatment upon inmates' return to general population and/or to the community.

Biopsychosocial Model

The core philosophy underlying all of the agency's drug abuse programs is that individuals must assume personal responsibility for their behavior. Despite the influence of environmental conditions and circumstances, the primary target for change is the individual's conscious decision to engage in drug-taking and criminal behavior. Therefore, the principal goal of treatment is to equip the individual with the cognitive, emotional, and behavioral skills necessary to choose and maintain a drug-free and crime-free lifestyle.

The Bureau subscribes to a biopsychosocial model of treatment which guides interventions in all of its drug abuse programs. This cognitive-behavioral approach emphasizes comprehensive lifestyle change as the key to treatment success. Issues such as, family relationships, criminality, and health promotion are targeted for change in addition to traditional treatment goals of relapse prevention and abstinence. The acquisition of positive life skills is the means through which drug abuse treatment program participants can change the negative thinking and behavior patterns which led to their drug use and criminality in the past. Through individual and group counseling, participants can gain awareness of the negative consequences of their previous thinking/behavior patterns and can learn and develop alternative and pro-social skills.

Nine-Month Residential Program

The agency's residential drug abuse treatment program is the flagship of its drug abuse treatment strategy. Currently, 53 BOP institutions operate residential drug abuse treatment programs, with a combined annual capacity of over 18,000 inmates. The program lasts nine months and participants receive a minimum of 500 treatment hours; a basic treatment protocol, one for men and one for women, exists to maintain some level of consistency throughout all residential treatment programs. The current treatment protocol has three phases of treatment:

- Orientation/ induction into treatment;

- An intensive treatment phase; and

- A transitional treatment phase.

Typically, inmates are involved in treatment four to five hours a day, five days a week. The remainder of the day is spent in pro-social activities such as work, school, religious services, and/or recreation activities. Each residential drug abuse treatment program is staffed by a psychologist who supervises the drug abuse treatment staff, each of whom carries a caseload of no more than 24 inmates. Treatment is voluntary. All inmates who complete a residential program are required to continue treatment upon transfer to half-way houses, called Community Corrections Centers (CCCs), typically for the last six months of their custody. During this CCC placement, inmates are treated by community-based providers, who are asked to follow the Bureau's treatment philosophy to enhance the continuity of care. Coordination with United States Probation also occurs to ensure a seamless transfer of information between the agencies as inmates leave BOP custody and fall under their supervision.

OUTCOME EVALUATION RESULTS

The hallmark of any good drug treatment program is the parallel application of a strong evaluation component to assess treatment effectiveness. Given the scale of the

BOP's most recent drug abuse treatment initiative, and the cost involved in launching and maintaining it, a quality outcome evaluation process was considered essential to preserving the integrity and long-term success of the program. With funding and assistance from the National Institute of Drug Abuse (NIDA), the BOP embarked on an ambitious outcome evaluation program from the outset. Given the comprehensive nature and complexity of this longitudinal evaluation project, outcome results in their entirety are not yet available. Promising preliminary and long-term results on the residential drug abuse program component have been published in an interim report (Pelissier et al., 1998, 2000).

Original research plans presumed that random assignment of inmates into the residential drug abuse treatment programs would occur. However, it was determined early in the process that inmates were not readily volunteering for treatment. New federal sentencing guidelines, implemented in November 1987, effectively eliminated federal parole and inmates did not believe they received any "tangible" benefits for participating in residential drug treatment. This prevented true random assignment to treatment groups, so evaluators identified matched comparison subjects for whom treatment was not readily available.

Positive Effect on Recidivism

Early outcome results (Pelissier et al., 1998) suggest early post-release success on the part of residential drug abuse program graduates. Eighty percent of the male inmates and 70% of the female inmates who entered the drug abuse treatment program completed the entire program. Evaluators tracked these inmates six months following re-entry into the community and found that inmates who completed the residential drug abuse treatment program were 73% less likely to be arrested for a new offense than those who did not participate in a residential drug abuse program. Moreover, inmates who completed the residential drug abuse treatment programs were 44% less likely to use drugs or alcohol than those who did not participate in a residential drug abuse treatment program. These findings are particularly impressive given the rigorous design and methodology of the evaluation project, the large sample size (1,866 inmates), and the uniqueness of this multi-site sample (20 programs at various institutions).

Data based on a three-year follow-up study (Pelissier et al., 2000) support these earlier findings and further suggest that the BOP's residential drug abuse treatment programs made a significant difference in the lives of inmates following their release from custody and return to the community.

Better In-Prison Functioning

In a separate study (Innes, 1997) researchers looked at in-prison functioning of inmates housed in high security institutions who had completed a BOP residential drug abuse program. Results indicated that in the two years following treatment, rates of institutional misconduct by inmates who completed the residential drug abuse treatment dropped by nearly 50%. This finding was replicated for minimum, low, and medium security male inmates who completed residential drug abuse treatment (25% average reduction in misconduct rates) and for minimum and low security female inmates who completed residential drug abuse treatment (70% reduction in misconduct rates). These findings suggested that drug abuse treatment in corrections-based settings, in addition to reducing the likelihood of post-release relapse, also assists in the general management of inmates and may play a vital role in increasing safety and security within correctional institutions.

MAJOR PROGRAM ISSUES

The Bureau of Prisons has faced a number of challenges in developing, implementing, and managing effective drug abuse treatment programs for inmates. Many of those challenges continue today, but much has been learned since this large-scale treatment initiative began. The following discussion sets out some of the more significant issues encountered in attempting to strike a necessary but delicate balance among administrative, political, research, and treatment concerns.

Rapid Program Implementation and Staffing

Key to sound program development is careful program implementation. In the early days of the BOP's latest drug treatment initiative there was significant pressure for a speedy start-up of new drug abuse programs. In just the first three years, the agency activated 3,100 residential treatment beds at 31 different correctional institutions across the country. The most daunting task during this rapid implementation process was hiring a large treatment staff complement. Funding was not an issue; Congress had appropriated sufficient resources for the program and the agency subsequently created new positions. The problem was finding sufficient numbers of professional staff with the skills, experience, and motivation to work with drug-addicted offenders. Most new staff had good clinical experience generally, but many did not have much experience working specifically in drug abuse treatment. Others had correctional experience and brought with them the knowledge and savvy essential to working with offenders, but had very little clinical experience, let alone drug abuse treatment experience. Still others had stellar drug counseling credentials, but had no experience working with incarcerated offenders and had some difficulty adjusting to a correctional work environment.

Thus, the need for a comprehensive and intensive training effort was evident. This was quite challenging, given that it had to occur concomitantly with an aggressive agenda of new program development. But in 1993 a multi-tiered training strategy was implemented which addressed basic, advanced, specialty, and remedial training needs for all drug abuse treatment staff. This system remains in place today and, along with annual continuing education funding, insures quality professional training for the more than 400 treatment staff. Targets of training include not only the requisite evidence-based treatment practices, but inmate management and inter-departmental coordination skills as well.

Organizational Culture and Climate

The latter is pertinent to another matter regarding rapid implementation. Although the BOP had managed drug addicted offenders for years, the creation of many intensive residential drug treatment units in a relatively short span of time at institutions with little experience managing such programs did raise certain organizational culture and climate issues. Due to funding and political imperatives, drug program staff needed to focus exclusively on assessment and treatment as the residential units developed, and at times this clashed with the agency's long and successful tradition of expecting all staff, regardless of specialty, to "be correctional workers first." In contrast to many state and local prison systems, there is no firm distinction made between "custodial" and "professional" staff in the BOP. When it comes to inmate management and maintaining the security of work areas throughout a correctional facility, all employees are responsible and may need to fulfill multiple roles when practical or necessary. It took time at some facilities for new drug treatment staff to be perceived (and to perceive themselves) as "part of the team" and for other staff to recognize that effective drug treatment contributed to institution safety and security. Significant inroads have been made; more than a decade later there is wide acceptance of drug treatment staff/programs and acknowledgment of the special expertise required to treat addicted offenders.

Inmate Recruitment

Recruiting inmates for residential treatment was more difficult than originally anticipated. With no paroling authority to consider treatment participation as a means to earn an early release, motivation for inmates to volunteer for treatment was low. Other incentives to engage in treatment were tested—e.g., small financial incentive awards for each quarter an inmate successfully participated in treatment; tangible goods such as tee shirts with the drug program logo; and maximum consideration for half-way house placement. However, such incentives did little to motivate inmates to fill up the 3,100 treatment beds that came on-line between 1989 and 1991.

In September 1991, a General Accounting Office report, "Despite New Strategy, Few Federal Inmates Receive Treatment" (General Accounting Office, 1991), outlined some of the challenges in implementing such a large-scale program and emphasized the lack of incentives (i.e., early parole dates) as most responsible for difficulties recruiting inmates. In part as a result of this report, in 1994 the Violent Crime Control and Law Enforcement Act (VCCLEA) was passed and had a significant impact on BOP drug abuse treatment programs. This legislation required the agency to provide residential drug abuse treatment, the most intensive and comprehensive component of the program, to 100% of inmates needing and wanting treatment by the end of fiscal year 1997 and every year thereafter. In addition, the VCCLEA provided the Director of the Bureau of Prisons the discretion to provide up to one year off of a non-violent inmate's incarceration upon his or her successful completion of the residential drug abuse treatment program.

Not surprisingly, the number of inmates volunteering for the residential treatment program increased dramatically. The residential treatment units were filled, but a new administrative burden threatened to distract treatment staff from providing quality services. Significant paperwork was necessary to verify that inmates did, indeed, have a legitimate substance abuse problem (many inmates attempted to malinger in an effort to obtain early release), that inmates could meet the "nonviolent" eligibility criterion, and that inmates generally met all other stipulations in the VCCLEA. In addition, inmates became increasingly litigious, filing lawsuits because they believed they were unjustly refused treatment or expelled from a residential drug abuse treatment program, or they believed that their offenses, determined by the Bureau to constitute a violent crime, was actually "nonviolent."

In response to the VCCLEA and its sequelae, the agency embarked on an ambitious expansion plan, which would become the largest drug abuse program expansion in the history of corrections. Among the many components of this plan were a redoubling of efforts to recruit and develop new drug abuse treatment staff; to redesign and test the most efficacious staff training approaches; to refine and implement a standardized drug treatment protocol; to expand the transitional services component so that offenders stayed engaged in treatment as they returned to their home communities. By the close of fiscal year 1997, the BOP satisfied the requirement of providing treatment to all eligible inmates and has continued to meet that requirement each subsequent year. To date, over 111,000 inmates have received residential drug abuse treatment in the BOP, and nearly 19,000 of them have obtained early release from BOP custody as a result of their participation.

Establishing Treatment Milieu

Much time and effort have been expended from the start of this initiative in developing clear policy statements and comprehensive treatment curricula to insure that drug abuse treatment staff have the tools to provide quality drug abuse treatment in a prison setting. However, it was soon learned that policy guidance and established treatment protocols were not enough. While some residential program staff expanded on that base by cultivating a strong sense of community on their units where the lessons of treatment permeate every aspect of inmates' lives, other programs merely "taught" the required curriculum content. At the latter programs, opportunities for communicating consistent therapeutic messages about the need for complete and congruent lifestyle and behavioral changes are often lost. Administrators and supervisors note this disconnect is easily perceived by inmates who exploit it and may "complete" treatment without truly engaging in meaningful attempts to change.

Creating a sense of and responsibility to a community in which inmates are held accountable for all behavior, in and out of treatment sessions, is an important but sometimes overlooked goal of all the residential programs. There can be many reasons for the absence of a community in some programs. One reason may be the prior training and orientation of many DAP Coordinators who lead and supervise treatment operations. They are psychologists who, more often than not, have had good clinical training but in areas other than traditional drug abuse treatment. Developing a sense of community is generally not within their realm of experience or expertise. To remedy this, and to insure that more residential units build a community milieu, an aggressive training plan in this area for all treatment staff is in development.

Dual Disorders

Comorbidity is an unavoidable issue when planning treatment services for large numbers of incarcerated offenders, as some inmates present with co-existing psychiatric disorders as well as substance abuse or dependence (U.S. Department of Health and Human Services, 1994). The BOP has established two residential drug abuse units (one each for males and females) to address the needs of this special population. The programs integrate the existing residential DAP format with targeted interventions unique to inmates' mental illness. For example, recovery maintenance discussions might focus heavily on medication noncompliance as a significant relapse trigger and emphasize preventive strategies for avoiding mental health decompensations. Given the arguably greater risk for relapse, comprehensive aftercare and release planning is also a key component of the programs. Treatment staff consult extensively with halfway house providers, probation officers, BOP community corrections staff, and others to educate them about inmates' dual diagnosis status and to recommend appropriate treatment, including psychiatric support.

FUTURE DIRECTIONS

Data to support the success of the BOP's residential drug abuse treatment programs are encouraging and suggest that the current model is effective. An important follow-up research question is: What specific program elements facilitate the most change among inmates participating in prison-based treatment? Disentangling the effects of different program elements is crucial to improving the efficiency and effectiveness of the agency's drug treatment effort. Toward this end, a federally funded joint research project, in collaboration with the Institute of Behavioral Research at Texas Christian University, commenced in 2001. Project objectives include assessment of inmate engagement indicators and change during treatment; monitoring of key inmate reactions to treatment that represent barriers to recovery; identification of program attributes and intervention strategies associated with treatment effectiveness; and dissemination of effective assessment systems and treatment models for correctional populations.

SUMMARY

Providing drug abuse treatment in correctional settings poses significant challenges and opportunities. The BOP and other correctional agencies must respond to shifting public priorities, new legislative mandates, institution mission changes, staff turnover, and other factors as they face the formidable task of administering high quality and effective programs. Given this reality, correctional drug abuse treatment programs must be carefully planned and implemented in accordance with the following principles:

- *Strong support from top management* communicates the importance of the program within the agency and encourages strict adherence to established parameters and rules of program development.

- A *specific treatment orthodoxy* (i.e., admission criteria, treatment dosage, treatment philosophy) that is supported by scientific evidence must be established.

- *Systematic treatment documentation* must occur to foster replicability of functions (i.e., assessment, psychological testing, curricula, treatment for special populations, treatment plans, treatment summaries, and program policies) across institutions. Specific program documentation insures program consistency throughout the system.

- *A clearly defined system of incentives and sanctions* must be in place to motivate inmates toward treatment, to reward positive behaviors, and to deter undesirable behaviors.

- *A qualified, well-trained staff* is essential. Clinical training for drug abuse treatment staff should be conducted regularly as should cross-training between treatment and correctional staff. This ensures that all staff understand their vital contribution to participants treatment goals in the correctional environment.

- *A community re-entry component* must continue the established treatment regimen in the offender's home community and treatment must be combined with appropriate supervision.

- *A commitment to outcome and process evaluation* is vital to maintaining treatment effectiveness. Administrators, funding sources, and staff require constant feedback on the successes and deficiencies of the program to allow program adjustments in response to measured results.

The Bureau of Prisons' most recent drug abuse treatment initiative has been exhaustively reviewed and examined since its inception by Congress, federal regulators, independent evaluators, and the Department of Justice leadership. While it continues as a work in progress, it has been consistently judged thus far as effective in positively changing inmate behavior both in the institution and upon release to the community.

Editor's Note

Bureau of Prisons drug abuse program documents are available upon request through the National Institute of Corrections Information Center.

About the Authors

Beth A. Weinman, M.A., is the National Drug Abuse Programs Coordinator within the Psychology Services Branch, Correctional Programs Division, for the Federal Bureau of Prisons. John T. Dignam, Ph.D., is the Mid-Atlantic Psychology Administrator for the Federal Bureau of Prisons. Ben Wheat, Ph.D., is the Chief of Behavioral Sciences, in the Psychology Services Branch, Correctional Programs Division, for the Federal Bureau of Prisons. Information about drug abuse programs in the Bureau of Prisons should be directed to Beth Weinman at the Federal Bureau of Prisons, 320 First Street, N.W., HOLC Building, Washington, D.C., 20534.

Opinions expressed in this article are those of the authors and do not necessarily represent the opinions of the Federal Bureau of Prisons or the Department of Justice.

References

Conrad, H.T. (1972). NIMH Clinical Research Center Lexington, Kentucky: Current status. In L. Brill & L. Lieberman (Eds.), *Major modalities in the treatment of drug abuse.* New York: Behavioral Publications.

Inciardi, J.A. (1988). Compulsory treatment in New York: A brief narrative history of misjudgment, mismanagement, and misrepresentation. *Journal of Drug Issues, 18,* 547-560.

Innes, C, (1997). Patterns of misconduct in the federal prisons system. *Criminal Justice Review, 22,*157-174.

Kitchener, H.L. & Teitelbaum, H. (1986). *A review of research on implementation of NARA Title II in the Bureau of Prisons.* Washington, DC: Federal Bureau of Prisons.

Murray, D. W. (1992). Drug abuse treatment programs in the federal Bureau of Prisons: Initiatives for the 1990's. In C.G. Leukefeld & F.M. Tims (Eds.), *Drug abuse treatment in prisons and jails.* (National Institute of Drug Abuse Research Monograph 118, DHHS Publication No. 92-1884). Washington, DC: Supt. of Docs., U.S. Government Printing Office.

Pelissier, B., Gaes, G., Rhodes, W., Camp, S., O'Neil, J., Wallace, S., & Saylor, W. (1998). *TRIAD drug treatment evaluation project: Six-month report.* Washington, DC: Federal Bureau of Prisons, Office of Research and Evaluation.

Pelissier, B., Rhodes, W., Saylor, W., Gaes, G., Camp, S.D., Vanyur, S.D., & Wallace, S. (2000) *TRIAD drug treatment evaluation project: Final report of three-year outcomes: Part I.* Washington, DC: Federal Bureau of Prisons, Office of Research and Evaluation.

United States General Accounting Office. (1991). *Drug treatment: Despite new strategy, few federal inmates receive treatment. Report to the Committee on Government Operations, House of Representatives.* Washington, DC: Author.

United States Department of Health and Human Services. (1994). *Assessment and treatment of patients with coexisting mental illness and alcohol and other drug abuse. Center for Substance Abuse Treatment: Treatment Improvement Protocol.* Rockville, MD: Author.

Chapter 16

Promoting Change in a Drug and Criminal Lifestyle

by Glenn D. Walters, Ph.D.

The Drug-Crime Connection 16-2
The Lifestyle Model 16-2
    Lifestyle Concept Defined 16-2
    Commonalities of Drug and Crime Lifestyles 16-2
    Case Example: Darryl 16-3
How to Address—and Change—Belief Systems That Lead to
  Crime/Drug Lifestyles 16-3
Core Element #1: Responsibility 16-4
    Use Life Lessons to Encourage Behavior Modification 16-4
    Discourage Enabling Behaviors 16-4
    Case Example 16-5
Core Element #2: Confidence 16-5
    Enhance Self-Efficacy 16-5
    Promote General Sense of Confidence 16-5
    Case Example 16-6
Core Element #3: Meaning 16-6
    Avoid Labeling 16-6
    Challenge Cognitive Simplicity 16-7
    Case Example 16-7
Core Element #4: Community 16-7
    Ensure Social Support 16-7
    Encourage Client's Sense of Connection 16-8
    Case Example 16-8
Conclusion 16-8

An earlier version of this chapter appeared in Offender Substance Abuse Report, *Vol. 2, No. 1, January/ February 2002.*

THE DRUG-CRIME CONNECTION

There is no doubt that drug use and crime are highly correlated. More at issue is the reason for this correlation. While 57% of state prisoners and 45% of federal prisoners report using an illegal substance in the month leading up to the confining offense and 52% and 34% of state and federal inmates, respectively, report being under the influence of alcohol and/or illegal drugs at the time of the offense (Mumola, 1999), we are at a loss to explain the nature of this relationship. Some investigators speculate that drug and alcohol use cause crime (Newcomb & McGee, 1989), while others assert that crime causes drug use (Pettiway et al., 1994), and still others espouse an epiphenomenal interpretation in which the drug-crime connection is attributed to some third variable, such as age or general deviance, known to correlate with both drug use and crime (Fagan et al., 1990). Another possibility is that drug use and crime are overlapping lifestyles that interact with one another reciprocally and possess many of the same underlying attributes, characteristics, and belief systems (Walters, 1998).

THE LIFESTYLE MODEL

Lifestyle Concept Defined

Before discussing how the lifestyle model conceives of the drug-crime relationship and how this knowledge can be used to promote change in substance abusing offenders, the lifestyle concept must first be defined. Lifestyles, according to the perspective adopted in this chapter, are rigid interactive patterns that a person enlists to cope with the problems of everyday living. These patterns are considered maladaptive to the extent that they are broadly applied to dissimilar situations. The drug and criminal lifestyles consist of rigid interactive patterns that overlap to some degree. A criminal lifestyle is defined by the interactive patterns of irresponsibility, self-indulgence, interpersonal intrusiveness, and social rule breaking, while a drug lifestyle is characterized by irresponsibility/pseudoresponsibility, stress-coping imbalance, interpersonal triviality, and social rule breaking/bending (Walters, 1998). Interactive styles may demarcate a lifestyle but the actual impetus for the pattern is a person's belief systems—particularly how he or she perceives him- or herself (self-view) and the surrounding environment (world-view).

Commonalities of Drug and Crime Lifestyles

The belief systems that support a drug or criminal lifestyle share a number of features in common:

1. A strong sense of non-accountability runs through both the drug and criminal lifestyles; this is most clearly evident in situations where the individual is confronted by the negative consequences of his or her drug use and criminal behavior. Whether it is the government, the police, or the "snitch" who testified against them, those who enact a drug or criminal lifestyle seek to externalize responsibility for the self- and other-destructive choices they have made in life.

2. Those who adopt a drug or criminal lifestyle lack confidence in their ability to get their wants and desires met without drugs or crime; they seem more confident in the lifestyle than they are in themselves.

3. Belief systems congruent with crime and drug abuse are habitually rigid and simplistic, with dichotomous "black-and-white" thinking predominating.

4. Both the drug and criminal lifestyles presume weak social cohesion or community.

These four patterns of belief were aptly expressed by an inmate I had the opportunity to speak with; let's call him Darryl.

Case Example: Darryl

Darryl is a 44-year-old, married, black male inmate serving a 27-month sentence for conspiracy to possess with intent to distribute cocaine. He owns an extensive criminal record and has spent nearly two decades of his adult life in jail and prison. Arrested 13 times before the age of 18, Darryl lived in group homes from age 11 until he was sent to a training school at age 14. He ran away from the training school after only a few days and was placed in a juvenile detention facility until age 16. Darryl's criminality showed no signs of abating once he turned 18. To the contrary, it seemed to accelerate. The record reflects that Darryl has been arrested 18 times as an adult for such varied offenses as drug possession, forgery, petit larceny, burglary, robbery, and possession of a deadly weapon.

The Lifestyle Criminality Screening Form (LCSF; Walters et al., 1991) is a brief chart audit form designed to assess a person's level of engagement in a criminal lifestyle. Darryl's score on this measure (14) is well above the cutoff traditionally associated with significant involvement in a lifestyle of crime (10).

Darryl's drug history is as extensive as his criminal background. He states that he began drinking alcohol at age 7 and was drinking heavily by the time he was 9 years old. In his life Darryl has used a wide variety of chemical substances but seems to prefer alcohol, cocaine, heroin, marijuana, PCP, and amphetamines. Just prior to his current incarceration his drug of choice was crack cocaine. Darryl reports that he has participated in drug programs both in and out of prison and found them helpful, though they have apparently done little to curb his appetite for mood-altering substances.

The Drug Lifestyle Screening Interview (DLSI; Walters, 1994) is to the drug lifestyle what the LCSF is to the criminal lifestyle, except that the DLSI is administered as an interview while the LCSF is based on chart information. Darryl's total score on the DLSI (15) exceeds the normal cutoff used to assess significant involvement in a drug lifestyle (10). These results suggest that Darryl has strong allegiance to the drug and criminal lifestyles.

HOW TO ADDRESS—AND CHANGE—BELIEF SYSTEMS THAT LEAD TO CRIME/DRUG LIFESTYLES

To address the belief systems that underpin commitment to a drug or crime lifestyle, such as Darryl's, we must consider the core elements of change. There are four core elements of change according to the lifestyle perspective: responsibility, confidence, meaning, and community. These elements are believed to be the necessary and sufficient conditions for change in persons previously dependent on a drug and/or criminal lifestyle. The manner in which these core elements are realized, however, may vary widely from person to person. As such, the four elements, unlike the 12 steps of Alcoholics Anonymous or Narcotics Anonymous, are guideposts for change rather than blueprints that must be followed religiously. In fact, most people abandon drugs and crime without formal assistance or participation in self-help groups (Walters, 2000). It is speculated that these individuals accomplish self-desistance through the four core elements.

CORE ELEMENT #1: RESPONSIBILITY

Use Life Lessons to Encourage Behavior Modification

There is no better teacher than experience and it is the natural consequences of our actions that hold the greatest promise of stimulating change. By heeding these consequences we learn to modify our behavior in order to achieve more satisfying results. These natural learning experiences are referred to as life lessons. Such lessons are more potent initiators of change than anything a counselor or therapist might mimic in a therapy session. By helping clients understand, appraise, and predict the natural consequences of their actions we are providing them with a skill they can use to alter their behavior and circumstances. The short-term effects of crime and drug use are often highly reinforcing and central to lifestyle initiation and maintenance. The negative long-term ramifications of drug use and crime, on the other hand, are more important in facilitating desistance from a drug and criminal lifestyle. With the aid of naturally occurring life lessons we can teach clients to pay closer attention to the long-term negative consequences of their lifestyle toward an eventual goal of achieving greater balance in their anticipation of the possible short- and long-term outcomes of their actions.

Discourage Enabling Behaviors

Besides enlarging client awareness of the negative repercussions of crime and drug use it is also critical that we identify the forces that prevent clients from fully realizing the natural consequences of their behavior. One of the more powerful forces in this regard is enabling. To enable is to prevent people from experiencing the natural negative consequences of their actions. Enabling inhibits the corrective experiences and life lessons that foster change. Family members, friends, and mental health professionals are frequent enablers; their enabling stems from concern for the client, but has results that serve to constrict the client's opportunities for change. Educating friends and family members about the pitfalls of enabling is one way of neutralizing its debilitating effect. When working with clients, I stress their personal responsibility for the choices they have made in life. Outside circumstances, whether poverty or enabling, and internal processes, whether genetics or intelligence, may limit a person's options but they do not determine a person's choices. Just knowing that they have a choice can be highly empowering to clients who for the most part accept on faith the premise that their actions are compelled by influences outside their control.

Case Example

Darryl was physically and sexually abused as a young child and attributes much of his subsequent criminality and substance abuse to these experiences. While these assaults undoubtedly had an impact on Darryl, it was not until he came to realize that his drug and criminal activities stemmed from the choices and decisions he made in response to these experiences rather than being a direct extension of these experiences that he embarked on his present course of change. At an early age he decided that he was no longer going to be victimized but would instead assume the role of victimizer. Victimizing others both physically and psychologically, he became a bully and a master manipulator. This attitude manifested itself in nearly all of his relationships. Believing that he had been betrayed by a psychologist he met as a child, Darryl swore that he would never trust another mental health professional again. As a consequence, he learned to simulate whichever psychiatric symptoms fit his purposes, which in many cases had as its goal gaining access to minor tranquilizers. It was not until he was confronted by the negative natural consequences of his behavior without the enabling influence of psychotropic medication that he truly appreciated his own role in the evolution of his drug and criminal lifestyles.

CORE ELEMENT #2: CONFIDENCE

Enhance Self-Efficacy

As was mentioned earlier, those committed to a lifestyle are often more confident in the lifestyle than they are in themselves. How, then, can we encourage confidence in people lacking this particular self-attribute? Bandura (1997) discusses four primary pathways to enhanced self-efficacy, a more situationally specific form of confidence. The least effective of Bandura's four methods of self-efficacy enhancement is verbal encouragement and reassurance, in which the helper tries to persuade the client that he or she possess the ability to overcome the problematic situation. A second method of self-efficacy enhancement involves manipulating the client's arousal level as exemplified by systematic desensitization. Self-efficacy can also be facilitated by offering clients the opportunity to vicariously observe other people successfully performing the targeted task. The most effective means of self-efficacy enhancement, according to Bandura, is performance accomplishments, whereby the client is instructed in the skills required to master the problematic situation and then given the opportunity to implement these skills in simulated and real-life situations. The lifestyle perspective seeks to promote both self-efficacy and general confidence in clients. Self-efficacy is important in preparing clients for the high-risk situations they will likely encounter upon release from jail, prison, or supervision, while a general sense of confidence is crucial in preparing clients for situations for which they received no formal training.

Promote General Sense of Confidence

Some attributional styles are more effective in promoting confidence than others. There are three primary dimensions of attribution relevant to change: internal-external, stable-unstable, and global-specific (Weiner, 1990). People in a drug lifestyle often make internal, stable, and global attributions for negative events and external, unstable, and specific attributions for positive events. In that responsibility is considered a cornerstone of change, attributions should be internal whether the event is positive or negative. Differences will occur, however, on the other two dimensions. With respect to negative events like relapse, the client should be encouraged to form internal, unstable, and specific attributions because internal attributions promote accountability, unstable attributions instill hope, and specific attributions establish goals for change. This might entail attributing a return to drug use to a lapse in judgment or failure to use previously learned skills. Positive events, conversely, might be more properly ascribed to internal, moderately stable, and moderately global attributions as a means of reinforcing the individual's self-confidence.

Case Example

One of the first conversations I held with Darryl centered on the topic of psychotropic medication. Although psychologists in the Bureau of Prisons do not prescribe psychotropic medication they screen inmates to determine whether an inmate should be referred to the consulting psychiatrist for evaluation. The psychiatrist then decides whether psychotropic medication is indicated. I shared with Darryl my belief that his problems were behavioral rather than psychopathological in nature and so did not require consultation with the psychiatrist. Later Darryl confided that he saw this as a challenge and thought of various ways to circumvent the system in an effort to gain access to psychotropic medication. This is something he had done in the past with great success. For whatever reason, he resisted the impulse to manipulate and dealt with his problems in ways other than sedating himself with chemicals. In addition, I directed Darryl to resources in the institution where he could cultivate skills capable of bolstering his self-confidence. By learning to cope with his problems in ways other than through drugs, Darryl was beginning to change the belief systems upon which his drug and criminal lifestyles are based.

CORE ELEMENT #3: MEANING

Avoid Labeling

Categorization is a skill we acquire early in life which helps make sense of a highly complex and potentially confusing environment. However, we lose vital information when we categorize people. No label can adequately capture the complexity of a human being, yet we continue to refine our human categorizing systems, a process that may well dehumanize our clients. Moreover, a label runs the risk of becoming a self-fulfilling prophecy, particularly for someone in search of an identity. The terms we affix to those who engage in a drug or criminal lifestyle—alcoholic, junkie, criminal, convict—are nearly always derogatory and unlikely to inspire either confidence or self-worth in those so labeled. Instead of labeling the individual, I would recommend that we consider labeling the lifestyle. The negative effects of labeling can best be avoided by limiting our categorization efforts to the lifestyle and gauging where the individual stands relative to that lifestyle. This frees the individual from the restrictions imposed by a label while providing some guidance and direction for identifying actions and patterns requiring alteration.

Challenge Cognitive Simplicity

Labeling individuals reflects a wider tendency to oversimplify the world and the people in it. Reductionism has a role in science and life but when we start believing that the product of our reductionistic efforts fully captures the human phenomenon under investigation we are doing a disservice to ourselves and our clients. Reductionism is a tool that is as flawed as it is useful. Accordingly, it is essential that we remind ourselves of its limitations in order to take full advantage of its strengths. People involved in a drug or criminal lifestyle also engage in extensive reductionism, reducing objects and events to dichotomized categories while trying to construe the world through "black-and-white" spectacles. Three potentially effective means by which these rigid, oversimplified belief systems can be changed are to challenge a client's most cherished assumptions by adopting a contrary position (devil's advocate), forming a collaborative relationship with the client (Socratic dialogue), and contrasting an idea with its opposite to achieve a new idea or synthesis (dialectic method).

Case Example

There is little doubt that Darryl has entertained oversimplified thinking, reinforced, in part, by a series of substance abuse programs that have encouraged him to view himself as an addict and junkie. The concept of addiction, in fact, may be one of the most nefarious influences unleashed on an unsuspecting clientele. By reducing everything to this hypothetical construct we block off legitimate avenues of understanding and change (Walters, 1999). Darryl thinks nothing of calling himself an addict or junkie. This type of thinking or belief system has been modeled and reinforced by practically every substance abuse program Darryl has ever attended. In working with Darryl it has been my intent to challenge these labels and have him develop a more inclusive and complex self-definition. With assistance from the dialectic method and cognitive restructuring Darryl has commenced to create a different view of himself and the surrounding environment. Only time will tell whether he will be able to maintain these changes once he is released from prison.

CORE ELEMENT #4: COMMUNITY

Ensure Social Support

"Community" encompasses a person's social commitments, obligations, and involvements. Without social support the odds that changes made in prison or in a drug program will take root once the individual is released to the community are substantially reduced. Social support, unlike enabling, infers acceptance of the individual rather than acceptance of the individual's behavior. Criminal and drug use activities are rejected, although belief in the individual and the individual's capacity for change are steadfast. This is a difficult attitude to maintain, particularly for those who have been hurt repeatedly by the individual's criminal and drug-use behavior. However, it can be instrumental in nurturing a sense of community in substance abusing offenders. Moreover, social support can act as a buffer against stress and social alienation while providing clients with the opportunity to construct a new identity.

Encourage Client's Sense of Connection

Community means perceiving one's connection with the surrounding environment. The significance of this particular core element of change is that it promotes spirituality and opens the door to transcendence. I have found the analogy of throwing a pebble into a pond useful in explaining this concept. Upon striking the surface of the pond a pebble generates many ripples, some of which are a great distance from the point where the pebble entered the water. My intent in sharing this analogy with clients is to illustrate the fact that our actions impinge on people with whom we have no direct contact. Whether the effects, or ripples, are positive or negative depends on the choices we make. The ability to move beyond our current situation and life status, something known as transcendence, is a key feature of the spirituality that gives birth to community and supplies the person with a sense of connection to something outside him- or herself. By creating a shaman effect, the relationship corollary of the pharmacological placebo effect, the therapist can help bridge the gap that often separates a client from his or her culture and community (Walters, 2001). Community, in speaking to the social nature of the human organism, can serve as a linchpin for change in those previously committed to a drug or criminal lifestyle.

Case Example

When he was in the community using drugs and committing crime Darryl had no sense of community. He thought only of himself and believed that if he were arrested or killed he would be the only one affected. Through an accumulation of life experience and involvement in programs like Parenting and Victim Impact he has learned that he influenced a great many people over the course of his drug and criminal lifestyle. There is every indication that he now understands that just as his impact in the past had been largely negative he is capable of making a positive impact in the future should he choose to do so. Darryl not only wants to serve as a positive role model for his children and a reliable partner for his wife, he also wants to help others who have gone through many of the same problems he has encountered in life. He states that he speaks with other prisoners about this from time to time and would like to work with youth upon his release, if not as an occupation than as a volunteer.

CONCLUSION

There is no presumption within the lifestyle model that formal intervention is necessary for change. More to the point, professional treatment may actually impede personal growth to the extent that it encourages external attributions for change, destroys client confidence, simplifies life through imposition of labels and diagnoses, or makes the client feel like an outsider. In the past I have made the distinction between assisted and unassisted change. I now see this distinction as arbitrary and artificial. Most change is assisted to one degree or another, and so whether the principal helpers are professionals or a person's family, friends, neighbors, and coworkers may be moot. The magnitude to which a person and those who assist him or her emphasize the four core elements described here can serve as a barometer of how lasting and meaningful the change is likely to be.

About the Author

Glenn D. Walters, Ph.D., is a clinical psychologist and coordinator of the drug abuse program at the Federal Correctional Institution-Schuylkill, Minersville, Pennsylvania. Opinions expressed in this article are those of the author and do not necessarily reflect the views of the Federal Bureau of Prisons or U.S. Department of Justice. Correspondence concerning this article should be directed to the author, whose email address is gwalters@bop.gov.

References

Bandura, A. (1997). *Self-efficacy.* New York: Freeman.

Fagan, J., Weis, J. G., & Cheng, Y.-T. (1990). Delinquency and substance abuse among inner-city students. *Journal of Drug Issues, 20,* 351-402.

Mumola, C. J. (1999). Substance abuse and treatment, state and federal prisoners, 1997. *Bureau of Justice Statistics Special Report* (NCJ 172871). Washington, DC: U.S. Department of Justice.

Newcomb, M. D., & McGee, L. (1989). Adolescent alcohol use and other delinquent behaviors: A one-year longitudinal analysis controlling for sensation seeking. *Criminal Justice and Behavior, 16,* 345-369.

Pettiway, L. E. Dolinsky, S., & Grigoryan, A. (1994). The drug and criminal activity patterns of urban offenders: A Markov chain analysis. *Journal of Quantitative Criminology, 10,* 79-107.

Walters, G. D. (1994). Discriminating between high and low volume substance abusers by means of the Drug Lifestyle Screening Interview. *American Journal of Drug and Alcohol Abuse, 20,* 19-33.

Walters, G. D. (1998). *Changing lives of crime and drugs: Intervening with substance-abusing offenders.* Chichester, England: Wiley.

Walters, G. D. (1999). *The addiction concept: Working hypothesis or self-fulfilling prophecy?* Boston: Allyn & Bacon.

Walters, G. D. (2001). The shaman effect in counseling clients with alcohol problems. *Alcoholism Treatment Quarterly, 19,* 31-43.

Walters, G. D. (2000). Spontaneous remission from alcohol, tobacco, and other drug abuse: Seeking quantitative answers to qualitative questions. *American Journal of Drug and Alcohol Abuse, 26,* 443-460.

Walters, G. D., White, T. W., & Denney, D. (1991). The Lifestyle Criminality Screening Form: Preliminary data. *Criminal Justice and Behavior, 18,* 406-151.

Weiner, B. (1990). Attribution in personality psychology. In L. A. Pervin (Ed.), *Handbook of personality: Theory and research* (pp. 465-485). New York: Guilford.

Part 4

Special Populations

The ability to identify and treat substance abusers who otherwise may not have sought help is a commonly touted advantage of the criminal justice system. But a consequence of this approach is that the wide criminal justice "net" can increase the proportions of drug treatment clients for whom traditional treatment models are inappropriate, including sex offenders, those with co-occurring psychiatric disorders, and youth. Conversely, substance abuse is perhaps the most important single factor accounting for the increase in the number of women involved in the criminal justice system. Therefore, the overlap of the substance abuse treatment and criminal justice systems has resulted in changing clientele for both. This section examines some of the clinical and correctional implications of these "special populations."

Chapter 17, by William Burdon, Trudy Kilian, Igor Koustenok, and Michael Prendergast, raises some common issues surrounding the treatment of substance-abusing sex offenders in prison and describes how they are being addressed by the California Department of Corrections. The authors establish the importance of accurate classification (i.e., legal versus clinical sex offenders), describe the role of substance abuse among sex offenders, and point out important barriers to treating this population in prison, such as stigma, denial, institutional policies regarding disclosure, and aftercare considerations.

Chapter 18, by Nena Messina and Michael Prendergast, focuses on treating female prison inmates using the therapeutic community (TC) model. The authors begin by questioning whether TC methods are appropriate for substance-abusing female inmates, and synthesize the results of four evaluation studies to draw their conclusions. The inconsistent results are attributed to variations in study quality, but also to the lack of attention to a panoply of factors that disproportionately affect women, such as medical, employment, prior sexual and physical abuse, and parenting issues.

Chapter 19, by John Bogart and Sally Stevens, describes a study of legal issues and legal assistance for a sample of 214 out-of-treatment injecting drug- and/or crack-using women enrolled in an HIV prevention study based in Arizona. The study reveals high rates of past and current legal problems, with the women reporting legal needs ranging from assistance with homelessness to child custody. The authors conclude with qualitative findings regarding the effectiveness of a combined counselor/attorney intervention.

Chapter 20, by Carl Leukefeld, Michele Staton, Allison Mateyoke-Scrivner, Hope Smiley, J. Matthew Webster, and Matthew Hiller, draws from a sample of drug court participants in Kentucky. The authors report a variety of gender differences in drug use and treatment needs, but particularly stress the importance of providing vocational assistance for women.

In Chapter 21, James Swartz highlights the need to consider psychiatric co-morbidity when matching clients to treatment. After reviewing current prevalence data, Swartz argues for the need to develop brief screening measures that can be used to place co-morbid offenders into integrated programs that address addiction and other psychiatric conditions concurrently, but with a warning to limit the co-occurring diagnoses to the most serious disorders.

Chapter 22, by Henry Richards, provides an overview of the meaning and measurement of psychopathy (emphasizing its distinction from antisocial personality disorder) and lays out why it should be included as a screening criterion for treating substance-abusing offenders. Richards provides evidence that certain types of therapeutic interventions actually result in increased levels of violence and other crimes among psychopaths, and concludes the chapter with a set of clinical recommendations to intervene with psychopathic substance abusers more effectively.

Chapter 23, by Robert Walker and TK Logan, centers on the treatment of substance abusers who have also committed intimate partner violence—a group constituting half of all men receiving substance abuse treatment. The authors refute the notion that intimate partner violence is a consequence of substance abuse; in fact, they caution that such explanations help clients rationalize their behavior. The chapter identifies typologies of intimate partner violent offenders, discusses assessment issues, and offers specific therapeutic approaches to be employed with this population.

Chapter 24, by Richard Dembo and James Schmeidler, describes the results of the Family Empowerment Intervention (FEI) for delinquent youths. This 10-week intervention treats young offenders in conjunction with their families to, among other things, restore the family hierarchy, restructure boundaries, improve communication, and connect the family to other community systems such as the school or church. Although the outcomes for these youths were similar to those of youths randomly assigned to an extended services intervention (ESI) group overall, significant performance was found for FEI program completers.

In Chapter 25, Jane Maxwell and Richard Spence report findings from a survey of juvenile offenders entering Texas Youth Commission (TYC) reform schools. The results reveal that inhalant-using youth have an array of co-occurring problems—even relative to TYC youth who abuse other substances, including more extensive histories of childhood abuse, more severe mental health problems, and increased risk of HIV/STDs. The authors also stress the need to assess cognitive impairment among inhalant users prior to determining type and level of care.

Chapter 17

Providing Treatment to Substance-Abusing Sex Offenders in Correctional Environments: Lessons From California

by William M. Burdon, Ph.D., Trudy Carol Kilian M.S., Igor Koutsenok, M.D., and Michael L. Prendergast, Ph.D.

Abstract 17-2
Prevalence of Sex Offenders in Prison 17-2
Need for Substance Abuse Treatment in the Inmate Population 17-2
"Legal" vs. "Clinical" Sex Offenders 17-3
Co-Morbidity of Sex Offending With Substance Abuse 17-4
Why Treat the Substance Abuse Disorder of the Sex Offender? 17-5
Barriers to Treating Substance Abusing Sex Offenders 17-5
       Stigmatism 17-6
       Denial 17-6
       Untrained and Inexperienced Staff 17-6
       Institutional Policies Against Disclosure 17-6
       Co-Occurring Antisocial Personality Disorder 17-7
       Lack of a Formal Process for Identifying Clinical Sex Offenders 17-7
Identifying and Treating Substance Abusing Sex Offenders: Toward a Solution 17-7
       Identifying Those Sex Offenders Suitable for Treatment 17-7
       Identifying the Appropriate Treatment Modality 17-8
       Maximizing Success by Providing Needed Aftercare. 17-8
Summary 17-8

An earlier version of this chapter appeared in Offender Substance Abuse Report, *Vol. 1, No. 1, January/February 2001.*

ABSTRACT

The rapid expansion of mandatory prison-based substance abuse treatment programs in California has brought with it some interesting challenges. Among these has been the realization that a larger than expected number of sex offenders with documented histories of substance abuse has been mandated into these programs to receive substance abuse treatment. This trend has raised some serious questions regarding whether and how effective substance abuse treatment can be delivered to these individuals. This chapter begins by making an important distinction relating to the definition of sex offenders. This is followed by a brief discussion of the relationship between substance abuse and sex offending behavior and some of the obstacles to treating substance-abusing sex offenders. The chapter concludes with the presentation of a proposed framework for addressing some of the obstacles to providing effective treatment to this population of offenders.

PREVALENCE OF SEX OFFENDERS IN PRISON

Of the almost 1.2 million individuals incarcerated in state prisons at year end 2002, approximately 9.8% (118,500) were incarcerated for sex-related offenses: 2.6% (30,900) for rape and 7.2% (87,600) for other sexual assault (BJS, 2003). In California, there were approximately 157,000 individuals incarcerated in the state's prison system as of the end of 2001 (California Department of Corrections [CDC], 2002). Of these, approximately 8.1% (12,700) were incarcerated for sex-related offenses: 1.4% (2,200) for rape, 4.5% (7,100) for lewd acts with a child, and 2.2% (3,400) for other sex-related offenses (CDC, 2002). More importantly, the CDC has reported that approximately 11.8% (18,500) of the state's prison population is required to register as a sex offender (CDC, 1999). Thus, while there are 12,700 individuals incarcerated for sex-related offenses in the California state prison system, there are an additional 5,800 sex offenders incarcerated in the state's prison system for non sex-related offenses.

NEED FOR SUBSTANCE ABUSE TREATMENT IN THE INMATE POPULATION

California has approximately 23,000 inmates involved in some form of substance abuse treatment, more than any other state in the nation. Of this total, approximately 15,000 inmates receive treatment by attending various addiction and counseling groups (Camp & Camp, 1998). The remaining 8,000 inmates receive intensive substance abuse treatment in one of 32 prison-based therapeutic community (TC) programs operating in 18 of the state's prisons. Most of these programs came into existence in the latter half of the 1990s, when the California State Legislature enacted numerous pieces of legislation mandating the expansion of prison-based substance abuse treatment programs based on the TC model of treatment. This series of legislative mandates was based largely on evidence accumulated in evaluation studies, which found that prison-based TC treatment was successful at reducing relapse to drug use and criminal recidivism (Field, 1985; 1992; Inciardi et al., 1997; Wexler,

1996; Wexler et al., 1992). In 1998, the legislature directed CDC to develop a strategic plan to eventually provide treatment to all state prison inmates with substance abuse/dependence problems.

This ongoing initiative represents perhaps the largest expansion of prison-based substance abuse treatment in the nation (and perhaps the world). However, the programs currently being implemented within the California state prison system have one very important distinction. Whereas previous prison-based TC programs have relied on treating inmates who volunteered for treatment, the prison-based TC programs in California (with few exceptions) are mandatory for inmates who have a documented history of substance abuse, and who fail to meet certain established exclusionary criteria (e.g., documented prison gang affiliations, time spent in administrative segregation for violence, inmates with Immigration and Naturalization Service holds). The decision to make these programs mandatory was based on research which has shown that coerced or mandated treatment can be just as effective as voluntary treatment (Anglin et al. 1989; Brecht & Anglin, 1993).

The rapid expansion of mandatory prison-based substance abuse treatment programs in California has brought with it some interesting challenges. Among these has been the realization that a larger than expected number of sex offenders with documented histories of substance abuse has been mandated into these programs to receive substance abuse treatment. This trend, combined with the difficulties associated with providing effective prison-based and community-based aftercare to this unique population of individuals, has raised some questions within CDC and among the agencies contracted to provide treatment services in these prison-based TCs. Most importantly, can effective substance abuse treatment be delivered to these individuals? And how?

This chapter will begin by making an important distinction relating to the definition of sex offenders, followed by a brief discussion of the relationship between substance abuse and sex offending behavior and some of the obstacles to treating substance-abusing sex offenders. The chapter concludes with the presentation of a recently proposed framework for addressing some of the obstacles to providing effective treatment to this unique population of offenders.

"LEGAL" VS. "CLINICAL" SEX OFFENDERS

The term "sex offender," as it is used within the criminal justice system, refers only to an individual who has been convicted of a sex-related offense. The term "paraphiliac," however, refers to an individual who has been clinically diagnosed as having a sex-related disorder according to criteria laid out in the *Diagnostic and Statistical Manual*, 4th ed. (DSM-IV). These two terms, therefore, describe two different, although not mutually exclusive, types of individuals: "legal" sex offenders (i.e., individuals convicted and imprisoned for committing illegal sex acts) and "clinical" sex offenders (i.e., individuals who are clinically diagnosable as having a paraphilic disorder and who may or may not be incarcerated for committing an illegal sex act). This distinction is important for two reasons:

- First, not all individuals who are incarcerated for a sex-related offense (i.e., sex offenders) are diagnosable as having a paraphilic disorder (e.g., most rapists).

Conversely, not all paraphiliacs who are incarcerated have been convicted of a sex-related offense.

- Second, when discussing treatment options for this population, there is only "problem-specific" treatment, not "crime-specific" treatment. That is, treatment, in common discourse, is designed to address a particular problem that the individual may possess—e.g., substance abuse/dependence, sex-related personality disorder—as opposed to a behavior that the individual has engaged in—that is, a criminal act. Thus, just as treatment for substance abusers focuses on their substance abuse/dependence and not the crime they committed that resulted in their imprisonment, so too must treatment for paraphiliacs focus on the personality disorder of these individuals and not the particular crimes (sex-related or not) that resulted in their imprisonment.

CO-MORBIDITY OF SEX OFFENDING WITH SUBSTANCE ABUSE

Research on sex offenders has not adequately addressed the degree to which sexual deviancy coexists with substance abuse involving different types of drugs. However, there is empirical support for a relationship between sexual deviancy and alcohol abuse (Allnut, Bradford, Greenberg, & Curry, 1995; APA, 1999; Firestone et al., 1998; 1999; 2000; Langevin & Lang, 1990).

Langevin and Lang (1990) administered an alcohol and drug use survey, the Michigan Alcoholism Screening Test (MAST; Selzer, 1971), and the Drug Abuse Screening Test (DAST; Skinner, 1982) to 461 male sex offenders. The use survey revealed that 89.7% of the sex offenders reported some lifetime alcohol use and that 61.2% had some lifetime drug use. However, self-reported alcohol use on at least a weekly basis at the time of offense was more prevalent than drug use. In addition, with respect to having an alcohol or drug problem, 52.1% scored above the threshold for alcoholism on the MAST, while only 19.9% scored above the threshold for drug abuse on the DAST.

In a study that looked specifically at the co-morbidity of alcoholism and certain types of paraphilia, Allnut et al. (1995) administered the MAST to 728 male subjects at a university psychiatric hospital sexual behaviors clinic, who were classified into seven categories of paraphilia, and found that 30.6% of them also had co-morbid alcoholism—a rate that is more than twice the 14% rate found in the general population of the United States. The researchers also found that the rate at which alcoholism was co-morbid with paraphilic disorders was greatest among violent sexual sadists and fetishists. These two paraphilias have also been shown to be among those that are most likely to be accompanied by secondary paraphilic disorders (Abel & Osborn, 1992; APA, 1999).

In a series of studies on criminal recidivism among sex offenders conducted at the Royal Ottawa Hospital Sexual Behaviors Clinic, Firestone et al. (1998; 1999; 2000) collected a series of substance abuse-related measures on samples of child molesters, incest offenders, and rapists. Among these measures, the MAST was the only measure of a current substance abuse-related disorder. For all three types of offenders, MAST scores significantly discriminated between recidivists and non-recidivists; recidivists consistently scored higher on the MAST than did non-recidivists. These results pertained to general criminal recidivism (i.e., any criminal act), which included sexual recidivism and violent recidivism. Among child molesters, MAST scores also discriminated between recidivists and non-recidivists for sexual recidivism, but not for violent recidivism. Conversely, for rapists, MAST scores discriminated between recidivists and non-recidivists for violent recidivism, but not for sexual recidivism. For incest offenders, MAST scores discriminated between recidivists and non-recidivists for both sexual and violent recidivism.

Finally, a 1997 survey of inmates in state and federal correctional facilities asked inmates if they were under the influence of alcohol or drugs at the time they committed their offense (BJS, 1999). Among those charged with sexual assault (i.e., rape and sexual assault), 40% reported that they were under the influence of alcohol at the time of their offense, 22% reported that they were under the influence of drugs, and 45% reported that they were under the influence of alcohol or drugs. The interesting point to note about these findings is the degree to which reported alcohol use overlaps reported alcohol or drug use at the time of offense. Thus, it appears that even when offenders were using drugs at the time they committed their offense, they were also using alcohol.

WHY TREAT THE SUBSTANCE ABUSE DISORDER OF THE SEX OFFENDER?

If and when individuals with sex-related personality disorders also suffer from substance abuse/dependence, treating the substance abuse/dependence disorder is perhaps as important as is treating the paraphilic disorder. This is true for a number of reasons.

To begin with, it is widely agreed among experts in the field that substance abuse is a primary trigger of sex offending behavior (Pacific Southwest Addiction Technology Transfer Center [PSATTC], 1999). As such, substance abuse, if not treated, runs a substantial risk of rendering even the most effective treatment for the sex-related disorder useless. In addition, where substance abuse programs for offenders exist, responsible public policy dictates that sex offenders who request treatment for their substance abuse problem receive it. Refusing to treat substance-abusing sex offenders in prison (especially those who request it), is likely to bring up due process issues when they become subjected to high supervision for drug behavior upon release to parole (PSATTC, 1999). Furthermore, treating substance-abusing sex offenders in prison (for both the sex disorder and the substance abuse problem) will better prepare them for post-prison life and, to the extent that it is effective and complete, will increase the chances that they will enter and remain in community-based aftercare following their release to parole. Finally, an uninterrupted continuum of substance abuse treatment is perhaps the best means of ensuring relapse prevention, which in turn will lead to higher rates of successful outcomes (i.e., lower rates of recidivism).

BARRIERS TO TREATING SUBSTANCE ABUSING SEX OFFENDERS

Although the importance of treating substance-abusing sex offenders in prison for both their sex disorders and substance abuse problems can be easily established, there exist a number of obstacles that make the delivery of treatment to this population of offenders difficult in a correctional environment.

Stigmatism

Within the prison subculture, sex offenders are stigmatized to the point where they sit alone at the bottom of the social hierarchy. Indeed, sex offenders in prison are stigmatized not only among other inmates, but also among custody staff, and even among treatment staff who are charged with delivering substance abuse treatment to them. As a result, sex offenders often spend their entire incarceration trying to hide their offending behavior out of a legitimate fear for their safety and are unlikely to disclose their status, even in an otherwise supportive environment (i.e., a substance abuse treatment program).

Denial

Denial is a defining characteristic of both substance abusers and paraphiliacs, and is almost certain to be exhibited in the substance abuse treatment setting. Paraphiliacs who deny that they have any paraphilic interests or have committed any inappropriate sex acts are among the most difficult to treat (APA, 1999). Compounding this is the likelihood that, in a substance abuse treatment setting, some sex offenders, in an attempt to hide their identity, may readily admit to having a substance abuse problem as a means of misdirecting therapeutic interventions that are aimed at breaking through denial and run the risk of exposing their status as sex offenders.

Untrained and Inexperienced Treatment Staff

Treatment staff who are not properly trained and experienced in working with sex offenders almost certainly inhibit the delivery of effective substance abuse treatment services to these individuals. Yet, most treatment staff in prison-based substance abuse treatment programs are untrained and inexperienced in working with sex offenders. Overcoming this obstacle will require recruiting and hiring individuals with some form of advanced clinical training, including, perhaps, an advanced degree or special certification. In turn, this will result in increased treatment costs associated with compensation as a means of ensuring that these qualified and experienced individuals are part of the treatment staff.

Institutional Policies Against Disclosure

Relating to the obstacle of stigmatization and consistent with their primary responsibility for maximizing security and minimizing disruptive behavior, prisons often have strict policies regarding the disclosure of inmate offense and conviction information. This is especially true of individuals incarcerated for sex-related offenses. As a result, even if treatment providers have staff who are trained and experienced in working with sex offenders, they are often unable to identify which offenders among their client population are sex offenders.

Co-Occurring Antisocial Personality Disorder

The delivery of effective treatment is also inhibited when the client, in addition to having a sex-related personality disorder, is also clinically diagnosable with an antisocial personality disorder (ASPD) or some other type of personality disorder, which makes the client less amenable to treatment for the sex-related or substance abuse disorder. Indeed there is evidence that supports the contention that the risk of reoffending among individuals with ASPD actually increases as a result of receiving treatment designed to confront their offending behavior and substance abuse (Seto & Barbaree, 1999). It is important, therefore, that there exist some means of identifying these individuals and either excluding them from treatment or directing them into some other form of treatment that is capable of at least monitoring them closely for an extended period of time.

Lack of a Formal Process for Identifying Clinical Sex Offenders

Finally, as mentioned earlier, there is a difference between individuals who have committed a sex-related offense and those who are diagnosable as having a sex-related disorder (although the two are not mutually exclusive). Currently, however, the only means of identifying sex offenders in need of specialized substance abuse treatment is their criminal record. In a substance abuse treatment modality designed to also treat sex-related disorders, continued use of this sole criteria for identifying sex offenders is likely to result in an inefficient use of resources, since it is certain to result in individuals being classified into a highly specialized treatment modality who do not need it.

IDENTIFYING AND TREATING SUBSTANCE ABUSING SEX OFFENDERS: TOWARD A SOLUTION

One proposed model attempts to overcome many of these obstacles to providing effective treatment to substance-abusing sex offenders by differentiating between *legal* sex offenders and *clinical* sex offenders and then offering specialized substance abuse treatment for those who are considered to be *clinical* sex offenders (PSATTC, 1999).

Identifying Those Sex Offenders Suitable for Treatment

The process begins with a clinical assessment of "legal" sex offenders; one that can effectively differentiate between legal and clinical sex offenders, as well as assess offenders for substance abuse disorders and psychopathy (i.e., ASPD). The objective of this clinical assessment process would be to place legal sex offenders into one of four categories, which distinguish not only between paraphiliacs and non-paraphiliacs, but also between those offenders considered appropriate for substance abuse treatment and those considered not appropriate. This latter distinction (between appropriate and not appropriate for treatment) would be based on whether the offenders have a substance abuse problem and whether or not they also suffer from some degree of psychopathy. This process addresses two critical issues:

1. *The clinical consideration of to whom treatment should be provided*—i.e., who can be treated and who cannot; and

2. *The fiscal considerations of providing treatment to those who can and will benefit the most*—i.e., determining the best use of available resources.

Once these distinctions have been made, it is important to have an alternative treatment modality that specializes in treating both the substance abuse and sex-related disorders of those clinical sex offenders considered appropriate for treatment.

Identifying the Appropriate Treatment Modality

Because of the unique needs of substance-abusing sex offenders, a TC modality of treatment may not be the most appropriate. A more appropriate treatment modality may be one that is more cognitively oriented, with similar curricula for dealing with the sex and substance abuse disorders—e.g., overcoming denial, acceptance of responsibility, relapse prevention. Alternatively, it might be feasible to have a "hybrid" program that has separate treatment components within the same program. In such a program, the provider might use cognitive behavioral therapy to treat the sex disorder and a modified TC method to treat the substance abuse disorder.

Maximizing Success by Providing Needed Aftercare

Finally, as has been demonstrated in more recent research (Knight et al., 1999; Martin et al., 1999; Wexler et al., 1999), continuing care and supervision in the community following release to parole maximizes successful treatment outcomes. The modality and intensity of aftercare, however, is dependent on the particular circumstances of each case and should be determined through a pre-release assessment process. This process should be designed to assess clients' progress in prison-based treatment as well as to identify their post-release treatment and ancillary service needs (e.g., housing, general assistance, education) as well as the level of supervision that will be required upon release to parole.

It is likely that community-based treatment for sex offenders will have to last substantially longer, perhaps indefinitely in some cases, than what is considered sufficient for non-sex offending substance abusers. Furthermore, due to current laws that require the public identification of sex offenders in the communities to which they are released, it is often difficult for these individuals to access basic ancillary services, which, when available, contribute to decreasing their risk of re-offending. Finally, due to the unique nature of the sex offender, these individuals are likely to require a higher level of parole supervision, both during their time in community-based treatment and perhaps even for a longer period of time after they have completed their treatment.

SUMMARY

Clearly, not all substance-abusing "legal" sex offenders will be amenable to substance abuse treatment. As discussed above, individuals diagnosed with paraphilic disorders are not likely to have successful outcomes in standard substance abuse treatment programs that do not address their unique needs and circumstances. Similarly, some of these individuals may be psychopaths, which may make them unsuitable for most types of substance abuse treatment, even modalities specifically designed for sex offenders. In addition, there exist a number of obstacles to providing effective treatment to substance abusing sex offenders in a correctional setting.

This model does not address all of these obstacles (e.g., untrained and inexperienced staff, denial, institutional policies against disclosure). Indeed, it presents additional issues that have to be addressed in order to make it function effectively (e.g., developing an efficacious screening and assessment process). However, it does provide an overall framework within which correctional and treatment professionals can begin to work together at addressing some of the remaining obstacles and toward providing effective substance abuse treatment to this unique population of offenders.

About the Authors

William M. Burdon, Ph.D., is Assistant Research Psychologist and Project Director for two state funded evaluation studies of prison-based substance abuse treatment programs, UCLA Integrated Substance Abuse Programs, Los Angeles, California. Trudy Carol Kilian, M.S., is a social services consultant and information specialist located in Placerville, California. Igor Koutsenok, M.D., is Associate Clinical Professor of Psychiatry, UCSD Department of Psychiatry, and Associate Director of the UCSD Pacific Southwest Addiction Technology Transfer Center, La Jolla, California. Michael L. Prendergast, Ph.D., is Associate Research Historian and Principal Investigator of several federal and state funded projects examining the effectiveness of treatment programs for substance-abusing offenders, Integrated Substance Abuse Programs, Los Angeles, California.

For more information on the authors' work, contact William M. Burdon, Ph.D. at wburdon@ucla. edu.

References

Abel, G. G., & Osborn, C. A. (1992). Stopping sexual violence. *Psychiatric Annals, 22,* 301-306.

Allnut, S. H., Bradford, J. M. W., Greenberg, D. M., & Curry, S. (1995). Co-morbidity of alcoholism and the paraphilias. *Journal of Forensic Sciences, 41(2),* 234-239.

American Psychiatric Association (1999). *Dangerous Sex Offenders: A Task Force Report of the American Psychiatric Association.* Washington, DC: American Psychiatric Association.

Anglin, M. D., Brecht, M., & Maddahian, E. (1989). Pretreatment characteristics and treatment performance of legally coerced versus voluntary methadone maintenance admissions. *Criminology, 27(3),* 537-557.

Brecht, M., & Anglin, M. D. (1993). Treatment effectiveness for legally coerced versus voluntary methadone maintenance clients. *American Journal of Drug and Alcohol Abuse, 19(1),* 89-106.

Bureau of Justice Statistics (1999). *Substance abuse and treatment, state and federal prisoners, 1997* (NCJ-172871). Washington, DC: Bureau of Justice Statistics, U.S. Department of Justice.

Bureau of Justice Statistics (2003). *Prisoners in 2002* (NCJ-200248). Washington, DC: Bureau of Justice Statistics, U.S. Department of Justice.

California Department of Corrections (1999). *Number of inmates in the institutional population on August 31, 1999 who are required to register as a sex offender.* Sacramento, CA: Data Analysis Unit, California Department of Corrections.

California Department of Corrections (2002). *California prisoners and parolees 2002.* Sacramento, CA: Offender Information Branch, California Department of Corrections.

Camp, C. G., & Camp, G. M. (1998). *The Corrections Yearbook (1998).* Middletown, CT: Criminal Justice Institute, Inc.

Field, G. (1985). The Cornerstone program: A client outcome study. *Federal Probation, 49,* 50-55.

Field, G. (1992). Oregon prison drug treatment programs. In C. G. Leukefeld & F. M. Tims (Eds.), *Drug abuse treatment in prisons and jails* (NIDA Research Monograph 118, DHHS Publication No. ADM 92-1884). Rockville, MD: National Institute on Drug Abuse.

Firestone, P., Bradford, J. M., McCoy, M., Greenberg, D. M., Larose, M. R., & Curry, S. (1998). Recidivism factors in convicted rapists. *Journal of American Academy Psychiatry and Law, 26(2),* 185-200.

Firestone, P., Bradford, J. M., Greenberg, D. M., McCoy, M., Larose, M. R., & Curry, S. (1999). Prediction of recidivism in incest offenders. *Journal of Interpersonal Violence, 14(15),* 511-531.

Firestone, P., Bradford, J. M., McCoy, M., Greenberg, D. M., Larose, M. R., & Curry, S. (2000). Prediction of recidivism in court referred child molesters. *Sexual Abuse: A Journal of Research and Treatment, 12(3),* 203-222

Inciardi, J. A., Martin, S. S., Butzin, C. A., Hooper, R. M., & Harrison, L. D. (1997). An effective model of prison-based treatment for drug-involved offenders. *Journal of Drug Issues, 27(2),* 261-278.

Knight, K., Simpson, D. D., & Hiller, M. (1999). Three-year reincarceration outcomes for in-prison therapeutic community treatment in Texas. *The Prison Journal, 79(3),* 337-351.

Langevin, R., & Lang, R. A. (1990). Substance abuse among sex offenders. *Annals of Sex Research, 3,* 397-424.

Martin, S. S., Butzin, C. A., Saum, C. A., & Inciardi, J. A. (1999). Three-year outcomes of therapeutic community treatment for drug-involved offenders in Delaware: From prison to work release aftercare. *The Prison Journal, 79(3),* 294-320.

Pacific Southwest Addiction Technology Transfer Center (1999). *Mixing of sex offenders in custodial drug treatment therapeutic community units: Problems and potential solutions.* Proceedings of the Research to Practice Symposium, La Jolla, CA: UCSD Pacific Southwest Addiction Technology Transfer Center.

Selzer, M. L. (1971). The Michigan alcoholism screening test: The quest for a new diagnostic instrument. *American Journal of Psychiatry, 127(12),* 1653-1658.

Seto, M. C., & Barbaree, H. E. (1999). Psychopathy, treatment behavior, and sex offender recidivism. *Journal of Interpersonal Violence, 14(12),* 1235-1248.

Skinner, H. A. (1982). The drug abuse screening test. *Addictive Behaviors, 7,* 363-371.

Wexler, H. K., Falkin, G. P., Lipton, D. S., & Rosenblum, A. B. (1992). Outcome evaluation of a prison therapeutic community for substance abuse treatment. In C. G. Leukefeld & F. M. Tims (Eds.), *Drug abuse treatment in prisons and jails* (NIDA Research Monograph 118, DHHS Publication No. ADM 92-1884). Rockville, MD: National Institute on Drug Abuse.

Wexler, H. K. (1996). The Amity prison TC evaluation: *Inmate profiles and reincarceration outcomes.* Presentation at the California Department of Corrections, Youth and Adult Correctional Agency, Sacramento, CA, November 5, 1996.

Wexler, H. K., Melnick, G., Lowe, L & Peters, J. (1999). Three-year reincarceration outcomes for Amity in-prison therapeutic community and aftercare in California. *The Prison Journal, 79(3),* 321-336.

Chapter 18

Therapeutic Community Treatment for Women in Prison: Assessing Outcomes and Needs

Nena P. Messina, Ph.D., and Michael L. Prendergast, Ph.D.

Growing Number of Incarcerated Women Raises Drug Abuse
  Treatment Issues 18-1
Prison-Based Treatment Outcomes for Women 18-3
  Stay'n Out 18-3
  Forever Free 18-4
  Bureau of Prisons 18-5
  California Department of Corrections Treatment Expansion Initiative ... 18-6
  Selection Bias? 18-6
Women Offenders' Treatment Needs 18-6
  Drug Use and Criminal Involvement Issues 18-6
  Medical Issues 18-7
  Employment/Educational Issues 18-7
  Parenting Issues 18-7
  Relationship Issues 18-8
  Sexual and Physical Abuse Issues 18-8
  Psychological Issues 18-9
Conclusion: More Research Needed 18-9

GROWING NUMBER OF INCARCERATED WOMEN RAISES DRUG ABUSE TREATMENT ISSUES

From 1995 to 2002 the nation's state prison population increased by 27%, and the nation's federal prison population increased by 71% (Harrison & Beck, 2003). Typically, men are about 15 times more likely than women to be in a state or federal

---

An earlier version of this chapter appeared in Offender Substance Abuse Report, *Vol. 1, No. 4, July/August 2001.*

prison, relative to their number in the U.S. population. However, this gap has been steadily decreasing over the past two decades, as increases in the number of incarcerated women have been consistently larger than the increases in the number of incarcerated men (Beck, 2000; 2001). For example, recent reports indicate that the number of incarcerated women increased 42% between 1995 and 2002, a much higher rate than the increase in the number of incarcerated men (27%) during that same time period (Harrison & Beck, 2003). The growth in the female prison population has largely been due to the increased use of incarceration for drug-related offenses, which also created an increased demand for appropriate drug treatment programs for women within prison settings.

The therapeutic community (TC) treatment model has become the preferred method of substance-abuse treatment in American prisons over the past two decades (DeLeon, 2000). Rehabilitation in the TC environment focuses on a global change in lifestyle involving abstinence from drugs, elimination of antisocial activities, and the development of employable skills and prosocial attitudes and values (DeLeon, 2000). Despite the growing number of drug-dependent women entering the criminal justice system, programs, policies, and services continue to focus predominately on men, as traditional TC programs were male-oriented, initially tailored to treat substance-abusing men. Yet studies have shown that men and women have different pathways to crime and addiction (Wasilow-Mueller & Erickson, 2001), continue to use drugs for different reasons (Covington & Surrey, 1997), and enter treatment for different reasons (Grella & Joshi, 1999). Women's patterns of drug abuse have been shown to be more socially embedded than men's and primarily revolve around interpersonal relationships (Bloom, Owen, & Covington, 2003; Blume, 1992). Among women, histories of sexual and physical abuse in childhood are major pre-existing conditions in subsequent delinquency, addiction, and criminality (Grella, Stein, & Greenwell, in press; Pollock, 1998). Women are frequently initiated to drug use by their male partners, and often continue to use drugs to cope with abusive relationships (Covington & Surrey, 1997; Owen, 1998). The different pathways and patterns of drug abuse for women and men are considered to be directly related to the likelihood of treatment entry and recovery (Bloom, 1999; Grella & Joshi, 1999).

The extent to which traditional TC methods meet the specialized treatment needs of drug-dependent women in prison is largely unknown. No research studies have directly examined this issue. To date, much of the existing research has focused on the differences between men and women *entering* prison TC treatment (Langan & Pelissier, 2001; Peters et al., 1997; Messina, Burdon, & Prendergast, 2003a; Straussner & Zelvin, 1997). However, the rising number of drug-dependent women entering prisons poses a variety of treatment issues for prison-based treatment providers and the criminal justice system overall.

This chapter pieces together the available research on the effectiveness of prison-based TCs for women. A small body of literature has evaluated post-treatment outcomes for women in prison-based TCs and is summarized in the next section. The final section discusses the treatment needs of women offenders, with recommendations for addressing these needs.

PRISON-BASED TREATMENT OUTCOMES FOR WOMEN

Only eight studies could be found that reported post-treatment outcomes for women who participated in prison-based TCs. The earliest post-treatment outcome study was conducted at the Stay'n Out program in New York, three others were conducted at the Forever Free program at the California Institution for Women, three are from the federal Bureau of Prisons, and one from the California Department of Corrections Treatment Initiative Evaluation. These evaluations are summarized in chronological order in Table 18.1.

Stay'n Out

Findings from 247 incarcerated women who participated in Stay'n Out, a prison-based TC program in New York, demonstrated effectiveness for reducing recidivism (Wexler et al., 1990). Women in the TC had significantly lower rearrest rates (18%)

Table 18.1: Prison-Based TC Outcomes for Women (W)

Study	Year	Sample Size	Prison-TC Program	Comparison Group(s)	Findings
Wexler et al.	1990	N = 398	Stay'n Out	1) W in other trt. 2) W with no trt.	TC W had reduced recidivism, compared with (1). TC W had higher with % positive parole discharge, compared with (2). Longer time in trt. associated with positive parole discharge.
Jarman	1993	N = 413	Forever Free	1) W in 2 other prisons 2) W with no trt.	No differences in outcome were found between TC W and comparison groups. TC W who completed trt. had increased success on parole, compared to TC drop-outs.
Prendergast et al.	1996	N = 96	Forever Free (graduates)	1) W with no trt.	TC graduates had more success on parole than (1). Post-trt. drug use patterns are less clear.
Prendergast	2001	N = 215	Forever Free	1) W with no trt.	TC W had increased employment rates, decreased rates of incarceration, drug use, and arrest, compared with (1).

Note: "treatment" is abbreviated "trt." in this table.

(Continued on next page)

Table 18.1: Prison-Based TC Outcomes for Women (W) *(cont'd.)*

Study	Year	Sample Size	Prison-TC Program	Comparison Group(s)	Findings
Pelissier et al.	2001	N=281	Federal Bureau of Prisons	1) W with no trt.	Preliminary 6-month outcome: W in trt. had substantial reductions in drug use and rearrest, compared with (1). Short-term positive impact for women.
Rhodes et al.	2001	N=547	Federal Bureau of Prisons	1) W with no trt.	No differences between trt. W and (1) at 3-year evaluation. No evidence of long-term trt. effectiveness for W in program.
Pelissier et al.	2003	N=2,315	Federal Bureau of Prisons	1) W with no trt. 2) M with trt.	Prior commitments and disciplinary actions during incarceration increased the drug use and recidivism for men and W. Mental health trt. decreased drug use for W only.
Messina et al.	2003	N=8,550	CDC	1) Men with trt.	Men were more likely to participate in aftercare than W, but W who participated stayed longer. Men were more likely to be reincarcerated than W.

Note: "treatment" is abbreviated "trt." in this table.

compared with 29% of the 113 women who participated in other types of prison-based programs (e.g., counseling and milieu therapy). The women's TC group also had a significantly higher percentage who were positively discharged from parole (77%) compared with 53% of the 38 women in the no-treatment control group (i.e., those who volunteered for the program but did not participate). In addition, longer time in the TC program was associated with positive discharge from parole.

Forever Free

Another study compared 196 women who participated in the Forever Free program in the early 1990s at the California Institution for Women (CIW) with 107 women from two other California prisons (i.e., the matched subjects group) and with 110 women at CIW who did not apply for the Forever Free program. Forever Free participants could volunteer to enter continuing residential treatment following release to parole for up to six months. In terms of background characteristics, the women who volunteered for

Forever Free had more severe problems than women in the comparison groups initially. No significant differences in success on parole were found between the TC participants and the comparison groups. However, 62% of those who graduated from treatment had increased success on parole compared with 38% of the program dropouts (Jarman, 1993). It should be noted that at the time this study was conducted, the Forever Free program used a treatment model that was closer to a psychoeducational 12-Step approach than to a traditional TC.

A subsequent evaluation of the Forever Free program reported the post-treatment outcomes of 47 program graduates compared with a group of 49 women who applied to Forever Free but were not able to enter (Prendergast, Wellisch, & Wong, 1996). Those who completed the prison-based treatment had statistically significant higher levels of successful discharge from parole than did women in the comparison group (52% vs. 27%). Results for post-treatment drug use are not as clear. Compared with women in the no treatment group, women who completed the prison-based treatment self-reported less use of heroin and amphetamines at follow-up, but larger percentages reported use of marijuana and cocaine.

Findings from the most recent evaluation of the Forever Free program are positive. The study involved a follow-up of 119 women who received treatment in Forever Free and a comparison group of 96 similar women from the general CIW population who did not receive treatment (Prendergast, Hall, & Wellisch, 2001). At follow-up, Forever Free participants had a significantly longer time to reincarceration (312 days vs. 261 days for the comparison group) and were significantly less likely to have used drugs or alcohol at any time since release (51% vs. 76%) (Prendergast et al., 2001). Forever Free participants were also significantly more likely to be employed (65% vs. 45 %).

Bureau of Prisons

This study reported six-month outcome data from an evaluation of the federal Bureau of Prisons (BOP) residential programs serving both men (n = 2,099) and women (n = 547). These programs, while consisting of long-term (9-12 months) residential treatment, adhere closer to a cognitive model than to a traditional TC model. Preliminary analyses compared 150 women who entered residential prison treatment to 131 women who did not enter the treatment program (98 comparison inmates had prison treatment available but did not enter and 33 had no treatment available). Although preliminary analyses were not conducted separately for men and women, results indicated that individuals who entered and completed the prison-based treatment had substantial reductions in drug use and rearrest during the first six months following release (Pelissier et al., 2001).

However, the long-term (three-year) evaluation results were not as promising. Findings from the full sample of women (n = 547) indicated that treatment was not effective for reducing recidivism or relapse to drug use for women over time (Rhodes et al., 2001). The most recent BOP study compared and contrasted the correlates of success for 1,842 men and 473 women who participated in prison-based treatment (Pelissier et al., 2003). Findings showed that a history of prior commitments and disciplinary actions during incarceration increased the likelihood of post-treatment drug use and recidivism for both men and women. However, participation in mental health treatment decreased post-treatment drug use for women only.

California Department of Corrections Treatment Expansion Initiative

Based on previous research in California testifying to the effectiveness of prison-based TCs, the California Department of Corrections (CDC) designed an initiative to expand treatment opportunities for inmates. As part of this initiative, the CDC established TC treatment programs in designated housing units within many of its prisons, including all of the institutions that house women. Preliminary findings from the CDC Initiative focus on the treatment group only (men = 4,164 and women = 4,386), who entered the 16 participating programs between July, 1998, and March, 2001, who paroled prior to February 1, 2002 (i.e., in order to be at risk for one year prior to obtaining 12-month return to custody data), and for whom intake data were available (Messina, Burdon, Hagopian, & Prendergast, 2003b). Men were significantly more likely to participate in aftercare than women (46% vs. 41%); yet, men who participated in aftercare did not stay as long as women (4.6 months for men vs. 5.1 months for women). In addition, men were significantly more likely than women to be reincarcerated within 12 months from parole (40% vs. 31%), and were returned sooner than women (8.4 months for men vs. 9.2 months for women). Separate regressions analyses showed that length of prison TC treatment and motivation for treatment significantly increased the likelihood of aftercare participation and decreased the likelihood of reincarceration for both men and women. The presence of a co-occurring psychiatric disorder was the strongest predictor of recidivism for both men and women (Messina et al., 2003b).

Selection Bias?

All of the above evaluations used quasi-experimental designs in which selection bias is a possible explanation for the findings. That is, in the absence of random assignment, the background characteristics of women who volunteer for treatment differ from those of the comparison group in ways that would bias the outcomes (although not necessarily in favor of the treatment group). Only the Bureau of Prisons evaluation explicitly controlled for selection bias in its analysis, so greater confidence can be placed in its findings.

WOMEN OFFENDERS' TREATMENT NEEDS

Some success in using the TC model to treat women in prison has been reported, but the ability of these programs to fully meet the specialized treatment needs of drug-dependent women offenders remains to be seen and many gaps continue to exist in the overall knowledge base regarding appropriate treatment services for women generally and for women offenders specifically. The following discussion describes various life factors relevant to women offenders' patterns of drug abuse and criminal behavior, with recommendations for addressing their specific needs in prison-treatment programs.

Drug Use and Criminal Involvement Issues

Compared with men, women offenders more often report poly-drug use, earlier use of cocaine and heroin and use by injection, and more frequent drug use prior to arrest or incarceration (Langan & Pelissier, 2001; Messina et al., 2003a). Women offenders are also more likely to report illegal activities as their primary source of income prior to incarceration; although criminal histories for women are predominantly drug-related, including their involvement in prostitution (Bloom, Chesney-Lind, & Owen 1994; Messina et al., 2003a). Women offenders' severe patterns of drug abuse and crime indicate a need for more comprehensive treatment plans that address women's pathways to drug abuse and crime.

Medical Issues

Women are also at greater risk than men of venereal disease and HIV infection due to their increased participation in prostitution for money or drugs (Maruschak, 1999; Stevens & Glider, 1994). In addition, some women may be pregnant and in need of pre-natal and postpartum care, as well as proper nutritional training (Grella, 1999). Drug-dependent women often suffer from a variety of chronic health problems including anemia, hepatitis, toxemia, hypertension, and diabetes (Stevens & Glider, 1994). The medical issues that drug-dependent women offenders experience require knowledgeable treatment staff and suitable referral services for medical care. Program services should also provide health-education and promote proper hygiene and nutritional practices.

Employment/Educational Issues

Drug-dependent women offenders are more likely than their male counterparts to be financially dependent on family members and to be in need of public assistance (Hser, Anglin, & Booth, 1987; Messina et al., 2003a). Most of these women have not completed high school and have inadequate vocational skills (Langan & Pelissier, 2001; Prendergast, Wellisch, & Falkin, 1995). Those who do report employment prior to their arrest typically worked at low-paying jobs (Peters et al., 1997; Prendergast et al., 1995). Incarcerated women in general have more difficult economic circumstances than incarcerated men prior to entering prison. Women in prison are nearly two times less likely to have been employed full-time prior to their arrest and almost four times more likely to have been receiving welfare assistance than men (Beck, 2000). Basic education, literary skills, and *marketable* vocational training are particularly important components of treatment programs for women.

Parenting Issues

Exacerbating the need for appropriate education and vocational training is the fact that most women offenders have children and are typically the primary childcare providers (Henderson, 1998; Stevens & Glider, 1994). An important factor in terms of continuing societal impact is that the children of drug-dependent women offenders are at high risk to continue intergenerational patterns of drug abuse, criminal behaviors, and neglectful parenting (Sheridan, 1995). Greene and associates (2000) found that a number of criminogenic influences experienced by women offenders were replicated in the lives of their children, including sexual/physical abuse, poverty, and violence. The nature of the relationship that women offenders in drug abuse treatment have, or develop, with their children is an important factor in their rehabilitation. In fact, many of these women are faced with the loss of, or the threat of the loss of, custody of their children and are in need of legal advice (Grella, Joshi, & Hser, 2000; Prendergast et al., 1995). Incarcerated women often experience feelings of guilt regarding their ability to provide for their children, which increases existing beliefs of low self-worth (Grella, 1999). The greater incidence of mothers' involvement in their children's lives makes parenting programs a critical part of treatment for women. Incarcerated mothers are in need of activities that increase contact with their children and that strengthen the mother-child relationship.

Relationship Issues

Women's patterns of drug abuse are more closely linked to relationships with their sexual partners than they are for men (Covington & Surrey, 1997; Henderson, 1998; Langan & Pelissier, 2001). Women tend to define themselves and their self-worth in terms of their relationships, and relapse to drug use is often related to ongoing and/or failed relationships (Covington & Surrey, 1997). In addition, partner opposition to recovery can include elements of intimidation, threats, and violence (Amaro & Hardy-Fanta, 1995). Women offenders also tend to form intimate relationships with other inmates that mirror their relationships prior to incarceration (Owen, 1998). These relationships could interrupt the treatment process if they become predatory or co-dependent. Drug-dependent women need to develop strong interpersonal skills to help them assess their past and present relationships with their partners in the context of their addiction, while also learning appropriate skills for maturely coping with future relationship issues.

Sexual and Physical Abuse Issues

Many drug-dependent women offenders report incest and molestation as children (19% to 55%) prior to their drug abuse (Langan & Pelissier, 2001; Messina et al., 2003a; Peters et al., 1997). Many have reported that the trauma that results from such abuse is a key contributor to chronic drug abuse among these women (Greene, Haney, & Hurtado, 2000; Henderson, 1998; Stevens & Glider, 1994; Wolf-Harlow, 1999), and that early victimization and the severity of drug abuse are stronger predictors of criminal activity for women than for men (McClellan, Farabee, & Couch, 1997). Childhood victimization further increases the risk of interpersonal violence in women's adolescent and adult relationships (Bloom, Chesney-Lind, & Owen, 1994; Messina et al., 2003a). A high percentage of drug-dependent women report physical or sexual abuse by husbands or boyfriends (Brown, Sanchez, Zweben, & Aly, 1996; Travis, 1998). Sensitivity to these types of issues is necessary for women to form trusting relationships with treatment staff. Treatment staff training should include information about how to avoid inappropriate relationships and sexual misconduct. The association between sexual/physical abuse, drug abuse, and crime among women suggests a need for treatment components that address past abuse and the mental health issues that often result from such trauma. Some theorists and clinicians believe that an all-female counseling staff is the best practice for women participating in prison TCs (Bloom, Owen, & Covington, 2003). Gender-specific staff can promote a strong therapeutic alliance and provide strong female role models, supportive peer networks, and attention to women's patterns of abuse from childhood to adulthood (Bloom et al., 2003; Covington, 1999; 2000; 2002a; 2002b).

Psychological Issues

Women offenders are more often diagnosed with co-occurring psychiatric and drug abuse disorders than men, specifically depression, post-traumatic stress disorder (PTSD), panic disorders, and eating disorders (Bloom, 1999; Henderson, 1998). Co-occurring psychiatric disorders are a major factor in post-treatment recidivism and relapse to drug use (Messina et al., 2003b). Women offenders are also more likely than men to be taking and/or abusing prescribed medications for psychological disorders (Messina et al., 2003a). Women's severe drug-abusing histories, combined with their increased likelihood of psychological impairment and use of prescription drugs for psychological disorders, indicates the need for a comprehensive assessment of participants at intake as a means of informing treatment staff of their diverse psychological needs.

CONCLUSION: MORE RESEARCH NEEDED

Definite conclusions as to the TC model's ability to provide appropriate care to drug-dependent women offenders are difficult due to the limited amount of empirical research in this area. An additional limitation of the existing research is that most of the analyses are bivariate comparisons, which do not allow for the control of pre-existing differences that might mask treatment effects. A few studies of prison-based TC treatment for women have found some success, as indicated by reduced recidivism and increased positive discharge from parole. However, other findings are less clear, and the evaluation of federal BOP programs found no evidence of treatment effectiveness for women offenders at the three-year follow-up.

A larger question concerns the extent to which the TC approach itself is appropriate to women inmates—or at least whether the TC model should be modified significantly to address the specific needs and learning styles of women offenders. Studies have consistently shown that women in the criminal justice system are typically women with complex histories of abuse, trauma, and addiction (Bloom et al., 2003; Messina et al., 2003a). Moreover, abuse and addiction are the most common pathways to criminal behavior for women (Grella et al., in press). Both men and women offenders have similar categories of needs with regard to addiction, physical or mental health issues, and vocational/educational training. However, research on the differences between drug-dependent women and men offenders suggests that the degree of intensity of these needs and the ways in which they should be addressed by treatment programs to reduce the risk of relapse and recidivism are quite different (Covington, 1998). For example, many theorists and clinicians are opting for women-only groups with gender-specific staff and nonhierarchical and nonconfrontational treatment environments (Bloom et al., 2003). Women studies have shown that women in women-only groups discuss issues that they will not discuss in mixed-gender groups, such as histories of prostitution and sexual abuse (Covington, 2002a; Grella, Polinsky, Hser, & Perry, 1999). Issues left unaddressed in treatment may magnify feelings of guilt, shame, and failure, adversely affecting outcome (Grella et al., 1999). However, even programs that provide services responsive to women's needs may not be able to address all of these needs due to funding constraints.

The rapidly increasing numbers of incarcerated women, the findings from the above outcome studies, and the previous discussion of the treatment needs of women offenders clearly indicate that future research is needed to evaluate the provision of traditional and modified-TC services for incarcerated women. These types of studies could begin to address the gap in knowledge regarding drug abuse treatment for women offenders in general and by providing specific information on the types of services and approaches that should be emphasized when treating women in prison.

About the Authors

Nena P. Messina, Ph.D., is an Associate Research Criminologist at the UCLA Integrated Substance Abuse Programs (ISAP). Michael L. Prendergast, Ph.D., is a Research Historian at the UCLA ISAP and is a member of the OSA Editorial Advisory Board. The authors may be contacted by phone at (310) 445-0874.

This research was supported by California DOC Contract C98.346.

References

Amaro, H., & Hardy-Fanta, C. (1995). Gender relations in addiction and recovery. *Journal of Psychoactive Drugs, 27,* 325-337.

Beck, A. (2000). *Prisoners in 1999.* Bureau of Justice Statistics Bulletin, Washington, DC: U.S. Department of Justice, Bureau of Justice Statistics.

Beck, A. (2001). *Prison and jail inmates at midyear 2000.* Bureau of Justice Statistics Bulletin, Washington, DC: U.S. Department of Justice, Bureau of Justice Statistics.

Bloom, B. (1999). Gender-responsive programming for women offenders: Guiding principles and practices. *Forum on Corrections, 11(3),* 22-27.

Bloom, B., Chesney-Lind, M., & Owen, B. (1994). *Women in California prisons: Hidden victims of the war on drugs.* San Francisco: Center on Juvenile and Criminal Justice.

Bloom, B., Owen, B., & Covington, S. (2003). *Gender-responsive strategies: Research, practice, and guiding principles for women offenders.* Retrieved from http://nicic.org/pubs/2003/018017.pdf.

Blume, S. (1992). Women, alcohol and drugs. In J. Lowinson, J., P. Ruiz, R. Millman, & J. Langrod (Eds.), *Substance abuse. A comprehensive textbook* (pp. 794-807). Baltimore, MD: Williams & Wilkins.

Brown, V., Sanchez, S., Zweben, J., & Aly, T. (1996). Challenges in moving from a traditional therapeutic community to a women and children's TC model. *Journal of Psychoactive Drugs, 28(1),* 39-46.

Covington, S. (1998). Women in prison: *Approaches in the treatment of our most invisible population.* Binghampton, NY: Haworth Press.

Covington, S. (1999). *Helping women recover: A program for treating substance abuse. Facilitator's guide—special addition for use in the criminal justice system.* San Francisco, CA: Jossey-Bass Publishers.

Covington, S. (2000). Helping women recover: Creating gender-specific treatment for substance-abusing women and girls in community correctional settings. In M. McMahon (Ed.), *Assessment to assistance: Programs for women in community corrections* (pp. 171-233). Latham, MD: American Correctional Association.

Covington, S. (2002a). Helping women recover: Creating gender-responsive treatment. In S.L.A. Straussner & S. Brown (Eds.), *The handbook of addiction and treatment for women: Theory and practice* (pp. 21-25). San Francisco, CA: Jossey-Bass Publishers.

Covington, S. (2002b). A women's journey home: Challenges for female offenders and their children. Paper presented at the annual meeting of the Western Society of Criminology, February 22, 2002.

Covington, S., & Surrey, J. (1997). The relational theory of women's psychological development: Implications for substance abuse. In S. Wilsnak & R. Wilsnak (Eds.), *Gender and alcohol: Individual and social perspectives* (pp. 335-351). Piscataway, NJ: Rutgers University Press.

DeLeon, G. (2000). *The Therapeutic Community: Theory, Model, and Method.* New York, NY Springer Publishing Company.

Greene, S., Haney, C., & Hurtado, A. (2000). Cycles of pain: Risk factors in the lives of incarcerated mothers and their children. *The Prison Journal, 80*(1), 3-23.

Grella, C. (1999). Women in residential drug treatment: Differences by program type and pregnancy. *Journal of Health Care for the Poor and Underserved, 10(2)*, 216-229.

Grella, C., & Joshi, V. (1999). Gender differences in drug treatment careers among clients in the National Drug Abuse Treatment Outcome Study. *American Journal of Drug and Alcohol Abuse, 25(3)*, 385-406.

Grella, C., Joshi, V. & Hser, Y. (2000). Program variation in treatment outcomes among women in residential drug treatment. *Evaluation Review, 24(4)*, 364-383.

Grella, C., Polinsky, M., Hser, Y. & Perry, S. (1999). Characteristics of women-only and mixed-gender drug abuse treatment programs. *Journal of Substance Abuse Treatment, 17(1-2)*, 37-44.

Grella, C.E., Stein, J.A., & Greenwell, L. (in press). Associations among childhood trauma, adolescent problem behaviors, and adverse adult outcomes in substance-abusing women offenders. *Psychology of Addicted Behavior.*

Harrison, P., & Beck, A. (2003). *Prisoners in 2002.* Bureau of Justice Statistics Bulletin, Washington, D.C: U.S. Department of Justice, Bureau of Justice Statistics.

Henderson, D. (1998). Drug abuse and incarcerated women. *Journal of Substance Abuse Treatment, 15(6)*, 579-587.

Hser, Y., Anglin, M., & Booth, M. (1987). Sex differences in addict careers. 3. Addiction. *American Journal of Drug and Alcohol Abuse, 13*, 33-57.

Jarman, E. (1993). *An evaluation of program effectiveness for the Forever Free Substance Abuse Program at the California Institute for Women, Frontera, California.* Sacramento: California Department of Correction, Office of Substance Abuse Programs.

Langan, N., & Pelissier, B. (2001). Gender differences among prisoners in drug treatment. *Journal of Substance Abuse, 13*(3), 291-301.

Maruschak, L. M. (1999). *HIV in prisons 1997.* Bureau of Justice Statistics Bulletin, Washington, DC: U.S. Department of Justice, Bureau of Justice Statistics.

McClellan, D., Farabee, D., & Couch, B. (1997). Early victimization, drug use, and criminality: A comparison of male and female prisoners. *Criminal Justice and Behavior, 24(4)*, 455-476.

Messina, N., Burdon, W., & Prendergast, M. (2003a). Assessing the needs of women in institutional therapeutic communities. *Journal of Offender Rehabilitation, 37(2)*, 89-106.

Messina, N., Burdon, W., Hagopian, G., & Prendergast, M. (2003b). Predictors of prison TC treatment outcomes: A comparison of men and women participants. Paper presented at the American Society of Criminology Conference, Denver, CO. November 21, 2003.

Messina, N., Wish, E., & Nemes, S. (2000). Predictors of treatment outcomes in men and women admitted to a therapeutic community. *American Journal of Drug and Alcohol Abuse, 26*(2), 207-227.

Owen, B. (1998). *"In the mix": Struggle and survival in a women's prison.* Albany, NY: State University Press of New York

Pelissier, B., Camp, S., Gaes, G., Saylor, W., & Rhodes, W. (2003). Gender differences in outcomes from prison-based residential treatment. *Journal of Substance Abuse Treatment, 24*, 149-160.

Pelissier, B., Wallace, S., O'Neil, J., Gaes, G., Camp, S., Rhodes, W., & Saylor, W. (2001). Federal prison residential drug treatment reduces substance use and arrests after release. *American Journal of Drug and Alcohol Abuse, 42*, 315-337.

Peters, R., Strozier, A., Murrin, M., & Kearns, W. (1997). Treatment of substance-abusing jail inmates: Examination of gender differences. *Journal of Substance Abuse Treatment, 14*, 339-349.

Pollock, J. (1998). *Counseling women offenders.* Thousand Oaks, CA: Sage Publications.

Prendergast, M. L., Hall, E. A., & Wellisch, J. (2001). *An outcome evaluation of the Forever Free Substance Abuse Treatment Program: One-year post-release outcomes* (Final Report submitted to the National Institute of Justice, Grant 99-RT-VX-K003). Los Angeles: UCLA Integrated Substance Abuse Programs.

Prendergast, M., Wellisch, J., & Falkin, G. (1995). Assessments of and services for substance-abusing women offenders in community and correctional settings. *Prison Journal, 75*, 240-256.

Prendergast, M., Wellisch, J., & Wong, M. (1996). Residential treatment for women parolees following prison-based drug treatment: Treatment experiences, needs, and services, outcomes. *Prison Journal, 76(3)*, 253-274.

Rhodes, W., Pelissier, B., Gaes, G., Saylor, W., Camp, S., & Wallace, S. (in press). Alternative solutions to the problem of selection bias in an analysis of federal residential drug treatment programs. *Evaluation Review.*

Sheridan, M. J. (1995). Proposed intergenerational model of substance abuse, family functioning, and abuse/neglect. *Child Abuse and Neglect, 19(5)*, 519-530.

Straussner, S. L. A., & Zelvin, E. (1997). *Gender and addictions: Men and women in treatment.* London: Jason

Aronson Inc.

Stevens, S. J., & Glider, P. J. (1994). Therapeutic communities: Substance abuse treatment for women. In F. M. Tims, G. DeLeon & N. Jainchill (Eds.), *Therapeutic Community: Advances in Research and Application*. NIDA Research Monograph, 144, 162-180. Washington, DC: U. S. Department of Health and Human Services.

Travis, J. (1998). *Women offenders: Programming needs and promising approaches*. Washington, DC: National Institute of Justice. U.S. Department of Justice, Office of Justice Programs.

Wasilow-Mueller, S., & Erickson, C. (2001). Drug abuse and dependency: Understanding gender differences in etiology and management. *Journal of American Pharmacological Association, 42(1),* 78-90.

Wexler, H., Falkin, G., Lipton, D., & Rosenblum, A. (1990). Outcome evaluation of a prison therapeutic community for substance abuse treatment. In *Drug Abuse Treatment and Jails* (pp. 156-175). National Institute on Drug Abuse Research Monograph Series 118. U.S. Department of Health and Human Services. Alcohol, Drug Abuse, and Mental Health Administration. Rockville, MD: U.S. Government Printing Office.

Wolf-Harlow, C. (1999). *Prior abuse reported by inmates and probationers*. Bureau of Justice Statistics Bulletin, Washington, DC: Bureau of Justice Statistics, U.S. Department of Justice.

Chapter 19

Legal System Issues Among Drug-Involved Women Enrolled in a Community-Based HIV Prevention Program

by John G. Bogart, J.D., and Sally J. Stevens, Ph.D.

Introduction 19-2
    Drugs-Incarceration Nexus for Women 19-2
    Negative Health Impact of Women's Drug Use 19-2
Study to Assess Need for and Role of Legal System Interventions for
  This Population 19-2
    Community Outreach Project on AIDS in Southern Arizona 19-3
    Legal Component and Instrumentation of Study 19-3
Extent of Legal Problems Reported 19-4
    Civil Law Difficulties 19-4
    Criminal Charges 19-4
Drug-Involved Women Victims Believe Legal System Cannot Help Them 19-6
What Surveyed Women Want From the Legal System 19-7
Summary of Findings 19-8
    Women's Legal Problems Tied to Drug Use 19-8
    Drug-Using Women Fear and Avoid Legal System 19-8
    Limitations of the Study 19-9
    Implications for Practice 19-9

This chapter originally appeared in Offender Substance Abuse Report, *Vol. 2, No. 5, September/ October 2002.*

INTRODUCTION

Drugs-Incarceration Nexus for Women

During the past two decades the number of women incarcerated in this country has increased at an alarming rate. Two major reasons for this increase are (1) the increase in the abuse of illegal drugs, and (2) the enforcement of increasingly punitive anti-drug laws (Peugh & Belenko, 1999). With the emergence of crack cocaine use in the 1980s, women's drug use shifted to this highly addictive, relatively inexpensive-per-dose drug and many of these women have flooded the criminal justice system (Lockwood et al., 1998). To support their crack use, many women engage in non-violent criminal behavior such as prostitution and the selling of crack cocaine (Stevens & Bogart, 1999). Punitive changes in arrest and sentencing policies of street-level drug violators has affected women drug users more than men, as women are more likely to be arrested for drug crimes than they are for violent crimes (Proband, 1997).

Negative Health Impact of Women's Drug Use

Health-related consequences of women's drug use are many, including infection with Hepatitis B (HBV) and C (HCV), human immunodeficiency virus (HIV), and other sexually transmitted diseases (STDs). Women who inject drugs are at increased risk for HIV and HCV as they often inject *after* the man has done so, using the same needle (Su et al., 1996). Further, both injecting and non-injecting substance users often engage in dangerous sexual activity as a consequence of or incident to drug use. Numerous studies indicate the relative efficiency of male to female sexual transmission of HIV (Haverkos & Quinn, 1995). Efficiency of vaginal HIV transmission is increased by the presence of an STD, which may itself be undetected or asymptotic, thus going unrecognized and untreated (Eng & Butler, 1996), leading to serious health complications such as autoimmune deficiency syndrome (AIDS), pelvic inflammatory disease, cervical cancer, and infertility.

Programs designed to prevent such health conditions among drug-using women have advocated for interventions to go beyond simply providing HIV education and testing. To increase effectiveness, interventions need take into consideration the context of the women's lives including community characteristics; economic status; family, peer, and partner relations; and legal issues (Miller & Neaigus, 2001, Stevens & Bogart, 1999).

STUDY TO ASSESS NEED FOR AND ROLE OF LEGAL SYSTEM INTERVENTIONS FOR THIS POPULATION

In response to the increase in HIV infection among drug-using women, the National Institute on Drug Abuse (NIDA) funded several research studies to examine the effectiveness of promising interventions to reduce HIV risk behavior among drug-involved women. As one might expect, these studies found that the vast majority of these women were involved with the criminal justice system (Villareal-Perez et al., 2001). While a small percentage of women reported lengthy prison sentences, the majority reported numerous episodes of arrests and subsequent incarceration at local jails resulting in relatively short sentences. In an attempt to better understand the legal issues of drug-involved women enrolled in "street outreach" HIV prevention programs, this chapter describes the civil and criminal legal issues of 214 women, their reasons for not using the legal system when becoming a victim of physical or sexual assault, and the types of issues for which they would like legal assistance.

Community Outreach Project on AIDS in Southern Arizona

The Community Outreach Project on AIDS in Southern Arizona (COPASA for Women) was funded by NIDA from 1997-2002. An HIV prevention research study, COPASA for Women enrolled out-of-treatment active injection drug- and crack cocaine-using women as well as sexual partners of injection drug-using men. The goals of the study were to (1) assess HIV sex and drug risk behaviors; (2) assess related socio-contextual variables including legal issues, social support, and economic status; and (3) compare the differential effectiveness of two interventions on the decrease of HIV risk and problematic legal issues, as well as on the increase in social support and economic status. To be eligible for the study, women had to self-report recent drug use, have a positive urinalysis screen for an illegal substance, show evidence of recent drug injection track marks, and/or report being the sexual partner of a male user of injection drugs. Once enrolled in the study, a baseline assessment was administered which was followed by a two-session basic intervention. After completion of the basic intervention, half of the women were randomly assigned to a six-session (two basic plus four additional sessions) women-centered intervention. Those assigned to the women-centered intervention worked with a counselor/attorney team who assisted the women in addressing their substance use and HIV risk behaviors, as well as their social, economic, and legal issues.

Legal Component and Instrumentation of Study

The legal component was one of six women-centered sessions conducted by the project staff. In a 60- to 90-minute legal session the project attorney and a program counselor met with each woman in a private setting to ensure confidentiality.

During the first five to 10 minutes of the session the project attorney discussed with the client the purpose and value of the session; explained the structure of the questionnaire used to compile the personal and legal information and data; defined and explained the language used and the legal system in general; and tried to make each client comfortable and willing to discuss her personal history within the legal system. The next 30 to 45 minutes were used to conduct the interview and complete the legal questionnaire. Upon completion each client was given approximately 30 minutes to discuss with the project attorney any specific legal problems or questions she might have. Each legal problem and issue was individually evaluated and discussed, and an "action plan" was developed to provide the client with legal and practical advice on how to deal with each legal issue. Every client was advised that if any legal issues or problems arose in the future while in the project, she should contact her project counselor and request a "special session" with the project attorney, at which time additional advice, information, assistance, and/or an action plan would be (and was) provided.

After the initial legal session was completed, the project counselors followed up with each client to determine whether the client found the legal session and action plan helpful, as well as to find out whether the client implemented the suggested action plan or legal advice, and the results if she did.

Women who did not have, or were disinclined to discuss or reveal, legal issues or problems were given advice and information by the project attorney on how the legal system worked as well as given practical advice on how to prevent and avoid legal problems in the future.

The legal questionnaire consisted of nine broad categories, most with sub-categories for more specific detail. The broad categories included (1) general questions pertaining to past use of attorneys, along with past and present civil and/or criminal problems; (2) specific civil and criminal problems; (3) past and present criminal history including recent illegal activity; (4) physical and sexual assaults within the past 12 months and client use of the legal system with respect to reported assaults; (5) personal history regarding domestic violence issues; (6) historical sexual abuse and inappropriate sexual conduct; (7) use of drugs, alcohol, and/or tobacco during pregnancies; (8) use of condoms; and (9) present legal problems.

EXTENT OF LEGAL PROBLEMS REPORTED

Of the 214 women, 37% were Caucasian, 31% Mexican-origin Hispanic, 15% American-Indian, 10% African American, and 7% bi-racial. The average age was 36 years and the average number of children in their care was one. At the time of the interview, approximately 40% were single; 40% separated, divorced, or widowed; and 20% married. Of the 88% who reported having legal problems in the last three years, 62% reported civil problems and 81% reported criminal problems. Of the 93% who reported fewer than 50 arrests, the average number of arrests was 10.3 (s.d. 11.9). For some, criminal involvement started as a minor; almost one-third (29%) had a juvenile conviction. The women reported continued concerns about legal problems, with over half (59%) reporting being worried about future legal problems.

Civil Law Difficulties

A majority of the women (155) reported having civil problems, usually more than one type of current civil legal problem. Domestic legal problems included child-related problems (22% child custody; 17% child support; 13% child visitation) and partner-related problems (13% divorce; 2% separation). Civil lawsuits included domestic problems (30% restraining order; 25% domestic relations), landlord-tenant evictions (18%), and damage-related problems (8% general; 6% auto accident). Other civil legal problems included immigration concerns (7%) and forfeitures (4%).

Criminal Charges

Criminal charges are presented in Table 19.1. Of the 214 women, almost all (189 or 88%) had been charged with a crime sometime during their lifetime, with the vast majority having been charged with more than one type of crime. Criminal charges reported by 20% or more of the women included drug charges (48%), shoplifting (38%), paraphernalia (27%), theft (23%), domestic violence (22%), prostitution (21%), driving while intoxicated (20%), and parole/probation violation (20%). Of those who were charged with a crime, the average number of times charged was 19.7. However, given the wide range of one to 196, more useful descriptions of average lifetime charges

Table 19.1: Type of Criminal Charges

Criminal Charge	Charged in Lifetime N (%)	Number of Times Charged Mean/Range	Juvenile Conviction/ Offenses N (%)
Drug charges	103 (48%)	4.3 (1-75)	13 (6%)
Shoplifting	81 (38%)	4.2 (1-50)	20 (9%)
Paraphernalia	58 (27%)	3.7 (1-25)	3 (1%)
Theft	50 (23%)	2.3 (1-15)	11 (5%)
Domestic violence	48 (22%)	3.5	4 (2%)
Prostitution	45 (21%)	11.6 (1-99)	3 (1%)
Driving while intoxicated (DWI)	43 (20%)	1.7	1 (.05%)
Parole/probation violation	43 (20%)	2.9	5 (2%)
Assault	41 (19%)	4.3	3 (1%)
Contempt of court	38 (18%)	6.1	3 (1%)
Criminal trespass	37 (17%)	3.1	5 (2%)
Major driving violation	35 (16%)	4.3	2 (1%)
Disorderly conduct	28 (13%)	6.5	2 (1%)
Burglary/Breaking & Entering	27 (13%)	2.1	4 (2%)
Forgery	27 (12%)	3.2	2 (1%)
Robbery	19 (9%)	2.6	2 (1%)
Criminal damage	15 (7%)	2.3	2 (1%)
Weapons offenses	12 (6%)	1.4 (1-5)	2 (1%)
Fraudulent schemes	10 (5%)	1.0	1 (.05%)
Contributing to delinquency of a minor	9 (4%)	1.4	1 (.05%)
Kidnapping	9 (4%)	1.0	2 (1%)
Homicide/manslaughter	8 (4%)	1.5	0
Child abuse/neglect	6 (3%)	1.2	0
Credit card fraud	4 (2%)	1.0	1 (.05%)
Arson	2 (1%)	1.0	0
Rape	2 (1%) (1 & 6 times)	3.5	0
Sexual offenses	2 (1%) (both claimed 50)	50	0
Runaway	N/A	N/A	12 (9%)
Curfew	N/A	N/A	6 (3%)

Other charges were reported by 59 (26%) of the women. The majority of other offenses included Alcohol Related Offenses (n=15; 7%; average times charged = 5.6) and Failure to Appear (n=5; 2%; average times charged = 1.3). Other types of offenses (i.e. extortion, hindering prosecution, loitering, trespassing, vandalism) each were reported by less than 1% of the women.

Table 19.2: Reasons for Not Using Legal System

Reasons	Why did not prosecute physical assailant (N=71)	Why did not get RO against physical assailant (N=84)	Why did not prosecute sexual assailant (N=26)	Why did not get RO against sexual assailant (N=31)
No point, nothing will be done	30%	27%	31%	29%
Street code	28%	16%	12%	3%
Did not want to	27%	37%	19%	23%
Didn't want to get abuser in trouble	21%	11%	0%	0%
Afraid of getting into more trouble myself	20%	7%	4%	10%
Afraid of abuser	18%	12%	19%	13%
His arrest would negatively impact my life	18%	6%	4%	3%
Afraid of legal system	16%	2%	15%	7%
Did not know assailant	10%	12%	15%	23%
Childcare/child custody	4%	1%	0%	0%
Arrest warrant	3%	1%	4%	3%
Immigration problems	3%	1%	0%	0%
Didn't know I could	0%	0%	4%	3%

Note: RO = Restraining Order

include the mode, the median, and quartile breakdowns (75% of the women had fewer than 23 lifetime arrests; 50% had fewer than eight lifetime arrests). Juvenile convictions were reported by 29% of the women, with the most frequent convictions/status offenses being shoplifting (9%), runaway (9%), drug charges (6%), and theft (5%).

DRUG-INVOLVED WOMEN VICTIMS BELIEVE LEGAL SYSTEM CANNOT HELP THEM

Of the 214 women, 102 (48%) indicated that they had been physically assaulted in the previous 12 months. Of these, 71 (70%) reported that they did not pursue prosecution of their physical assailant. The reasons these women gave for not using the legal system when crimes of physical and sexual assault were committed against them are presented in Table 19.2. The most frequent reasons for not pursuing prosecution included:

- Their belief that nothing would be done by the legal system (30%);

- Use of the "street code," under which women stated they, family, or friends would deal with the situation privately (28%); and

- That they simply did not want to (27%).

Other frequently cited reasons for not seeking prosecution included being afraid of getting into trouble themselves (21%), afraid the assailant's arrest might negatively impact their life (18%), afraid of the abuser (18%), and afraid of the legal system (16%). Eighty-two (82%) of the women did not pursue a restraining order against their physical assailant.

The most frequently cited reasons for not obtaining a restraining order were their not wanting to (37%), the belief that nothing would be done by the legal system (27%), and street code (16%).

With regard to sexual assault, 39 (18%) of the women reported having been sexually assaulted in the previous 12 months. Of those, 26 (67%) did not pursue prosecution of their sexual assailant. Again, the most frequently cited reason for not pursuing prosecution was their belief that nothing would be done by the legal system (31%), followed by that they did not want to prosecute (19%), fear of abuser (19%), fear of legal system (15%) and that they did not know assailant (15%). Of those reporting sexual assault, 31 (79%) did not pursue a restraining order against their sexual assailant. Frequently given reasons for this included their belief that nothing would get done by the legal system (29%), did not want to (23%), and did not know assailant (23%).

WHAT SURVEYED WOMEN WANT FROM THE LEGAL SYSTEM

Table 19.3 describes the type of legal issues with which the women reported wanting help. The five most frequently reported issues with which the women wanted—or

Table 19.3: Legal Issues Participants Would Like Help With

Legal Issues	Yes (%)	Possible (%)	No (%)
Homelessness	23%	10%	67%
Old warrant on a matter that you didn't show up for	21%	16%	63%
Current civil matter that you don't have legal representation for	16%	17%	67%
Child custody	12%	4%	84%
Current criminal charges that you don't have legal representation for	10%	20%	70%
Child Protective Services (CPS)	8%	5%	87%
Child support	7%	9%	84%
Pressing charges against someone who has assaulted or raped you	2%	4%	94%
Restraining order against partner who is hurting/threatening you	1%	5%	93%
Immigration	1%	5%	94%

Note: N = 209 ; rows may not add up to 100% due to rounding

possibly wanted—legal help were homelessness (23%, 10%), warrant for a matter for which they did not appear in court (21%, 16%), current civil matter (16%, 17%), child custody (12%, 4%), and for a current criminal charge (10%, 20%).

SUMMARY OF FINDINGS

Women's Legal Problems Tied to Drug Use

The majority of the women involved in the out-of-treatment COPASA for Women project reported past and present involvement in the legal system, with 88% reporting legal problems in the past three years and 85% reporting having used the services of an attorney. For the most part, these women remained criminally involved (69% reporting legal problems in the previous six months and 52% reporting being involved in illegal activity for gain or drugs). Given that 90% of the women were either injection drug and/or crack cocaine users, it is not surprising their criminal involvement was associated with their drug use. These charges can be grouped into three categories:

- Drug-related charges (i.e. drug charges, paraphernalia, DWI);

- Charges related to supporting their drug use (i.e. shoplifting, prostitution, forgery); and

- Charges resulting from the consequences of drug use (i.e. domestic violence, child custody, landlord-tenant/evictions).

Clients who completed COPASA and who participated in focus groups to assist with interpretation of the data noted that even those crimes not always thought to be associated with drug use—i.e., major driving violation, weapons offense, child support, damages—were related to their drug use and often to the drug use of their partners, family members, and peers as well.

Drug-Using Women Fear and Avoid Legal System

Women participating in the COPASA for Women project often avoided dealing with the legal system until arrested, and then often lived "underground" when released. Forty percent had pending criminal charges, with 42% of those with pending charges having children in their care. While only 2% reported being charged with "failure to appear for a criminal violation," almost half (49%) had a current warrant for their arrest. Women who had children in their care were not only more likely to have pending charges, but were also more likely to have a warrant for their arrest, suggesting that those with children are particularly fearful of the legal system. This fear may be propelled by the possibility of losing custody of their children and/or feeling anxious about not having a safe place for their children to live if incarcerated.

The majority of the study sample avoided utilizing the legal system when a victim of physical or sexual assault. Seventy percent of those physically assaulted and 67% of the sexually assaulted did not pursue prosecution of their assailant. While the reasons for not pursuing prosecution differed for those physically versus sexually assaulted, the data suggest not only a fear of the legal system but a general lack of faith in its ability to benefit them. Particularly for those who reported physical assault, a counter-establishment "street code" method for dealing with the assault was preferable. This typically involved dealing with their assailant themselves, or along with family and friends, sometimes confrontationally, to obtain justice.

Notwithstanding the lack of faith in the legal system, when offered legal assistance by the project attorney, many of the women indicated a desire for legal assistance. The women also disclosed that they were not certain if they needed assistance for various issues because they did not understand the issue or if the issue needed or could use legal resolution. For example, while 23% wanted legal assistance for homelessness, an additional 10% reported that they might possibly want help. Those possibly wanting help were not sure if their homelessness issues could be improved by utilizing the legal system. Also, women reported "possibly wanting legal help" or "not wanting legal help" if they thought that legal help might lead to more legal problems. For example 20% reported possibly wanting help and 70% report not wanting legal help for a criminal charge for which they did not have legal representation. This data again shows that the drug and criminally involved women are fearful of approaching the legal system to resolve legal issues and move on with their lives.

The helpfulness of the legal component was assessed through facilitation of focus groups during the final year of the study. The women reiterated their fear and lack of faith in the legal system along with their doubt and mistrust of legal public defenders. The women reported that the legal component at COPASA was particularly helpful for a number of reasons including (1) their perception that the project attorney was "removed" from the legal system, (2) the attorney traveled to the COPASA site to see them (comfortable and convenient environment), (3) the client's counselor was included in the session(s), and (4) the attorney took time to explain the legal system and how it interfaced with their specific legal issues. Because of the scope of the legal component the project attorney could not typically provide legal representation; a limitation that was perceived by the women as negative.

Limitations of the Study

Two study limitations need mentioning. First, while the study sample was recruited through a combination of targeted and snowball sampling (word of mouth from study participants to others who were eligible for the study), caution should be used when generalizing to other drug and criminally involved female populations, as well as to other legal jurisdictions. Second, legal data was obtained through self report from the clients. Collateral data (i.e. court records, significant others) was not collected.

Implications for Practice

Despite the limitations, the study findings have several important implications for professionals in this field:

- Women who access out-of-treatment HIV prevention projects such as COPASA for Women are extensively criminally involved, making criminal justice settings an ideal place to begin interventions to address HIV risk, drug use, and criminal involvement. While many women report short jail stays and jail personnel report lack of time and space to provide services, identification of women who need these services along with active—and possibly mandated—referrals into services is called for.

- The extent of criminal involvement is a barrier to these women's empowerment (gainful employment, child custody) and must be addressed in out-of-treatment HIV risk-reduction programs if we are to increase women's empowerment, independence, and pro-social behaviors. Embedding legal assistance within outreach projects may result in women addressing their legal issues, thereby allowing them to move on with their lives.

- Women who have children in their care are a particularly hidden population and often live "underground" because of their fear of losing custody of their children or that the children will not have a safe place to live if the mother is incarcerated. Policy makers and funders should consider funding in-jail drug detoxification and treatment programs in which women can simultaneously detox from drugs while receiving credit for time served. This should be coupled with a Safe House. a living arrangement where the children can stay while the mother completes her jail sentence. Visitation between the mother and her child should be ongoing along with family counseling.

- Given the potential for relapse, drug treatment initiated within the institution should be continued after release from incarceration.

Proactive and innovative approaches such as these may, with time, curb the increases in new HIV infection cases, drug addiction rates, and incarceration rates among disenfranchised women living in the United States.

About the Authors

John G. Bogart, J.D., is an attorney in private practice in Tucson, Arizona. Sally J. Stevens, Ph.D., is a Research Professor, Southwest Institute for Research on Women, University of Arizona, Tucson, Arizona. Correspondence should be directed to John G. Bogart, Esq., email: bogartjohn@aol.com.

This project was funded by the National Institute of Health, National Institute on Drug Abuse, grant no. 1 ROI DA 10651. The opinions expressed are the views of the authors, which do not necessarily reflect the views of the funding agency.

References

Eng, T., & Butler, W. (Eds.) (1996). *The hidden epidemic: Confronting sexually transmitted diseases.* Washington, DC: National Academy Press.

Haverkos, H.W., & Quinn, T.C. (1995). The third wave: HIV infection among heterosexuals in the United States and Europe. *International Journal of STD and AIDS, 6,* 1-6.

Lockwood, D., McCorkel, J., & Inciardi, J.A. (1998). Developing comprehensive prison-based therapeutic community treatment for women. In S.J. Stevens & H.K. Wexler (Eds.), *Women and substance abuse: Gender transparency,* Binghampton, NY: Haworth Press.

Miller, M., & Neaigus, A. (2001). Networks, resources and risk among women who use drugs. *Social Science and Medicine, 52* (6), 967-978.

Peugh, J., & Belenko, S. (1999). Substance-involved women inmates: Challenges to providing effective treatment. *The Prison Journal, 79*, 1, 23-44.

Proband, S.C. (1997). Increase in women prisoners. *Overcrowded Times, 8*, 2; 4-5.

Stevens, S.J., & Bogart, J.G. (1999). Reducing HIV risk behaviors of drug involved women: Medical, social, economic, and legal constraints. In W.N. Elwood (Ed.), *Power in the blood: AIDS, politics and communication*, pp. 107-120. Mahwah, NJ: Lawrence Erlbaum Associates.

Su, S.S., Pach, A., Hoffman, A., Pierce, T.G., Ingels, J.S., Unfred, C., & Gray, F. (1996). *Drug injector risk networks and HIV transmission: A prospective study*. Unpublished report to the National Institute on Drug Abuse.

Villareal-Perez, V., Bogart, J. G., Cameron, M., & Stevens, S. J. (2001, August 3). Legal interventions to reduce substance use and related consequences of use among criminally involved women. Presented at the Center for Substance Abuse Treatment-sponsored Bridging the Gap Summer Institute, Pinetop, AZ.

Chapter 20

Gender Differences in Employment Among Substance-Abusing Offenders at Drug Court Entry

by Carl Leukefeld, D.S.W., Michele Staton, M.S.W.,
Allison Mateyoke-Scrivner, B.A., Hope Smiley, B.A.,
J. Matthew Webster, Ph.D., and Matthew L. Hiller, Ph.D.

Introduction 20-1
Missing Link: Employment Services 20-2
The Intervention 20-3
    Three Phases 20-3
    Data Collection Method 20-4
Gender Difference Profiles 20-4
    Employment 20-5
    Substance Use 20-7
    Criminal Involvement 20-7
Conclusions 20-7

INTRODUCTION

The linkages between drug abuse and crime have been well documented (see Greenberg & Adler, 1974; Leukefeld et al., 2002; Nurco et al., 1985). A 1997 survey of inmates in state and federal correctional prisons indicated that 83% of state prisoners reported past drug use and 57% reported using a drug in the month before their offense (BJS, 1998). In addition, Innes (1988) reported that 50% of federal inmates and 80% of state inmates had been drug-involved before incarceration. The Drug Use Forecasting (DUF) system, renamed ADAM (Arrestee Drug Abuse Monitoring), has

---

An earlier version of this chapter appeared in Offender Substance Abuse Report, *Vol. 2, No. 6, November/ December 2002.*

consistently indicated that over half (51% to 83%) of male arrestees in major urban cities test positive for drugs (DUF Annual Report, 1996).

Drug treatment for drug offenders has had successes (Leukefeld et al., 2002). The interest in examining effective intervention approaches arises from data collected on programs that have shown promise including the Stay'n Out Program in New York (Wexler & Williams, 1986), the Cornerstone Program in Oregon (Field, 1985), the Amity Program in California (Wexler, 1995) and the Key/Crest Program in Delaware (Martin, et al., 1999). One alternative approach to offender treatment is drug court (Belenko, 1998). Drug courts provide court-mandated, comprehensive interventions designed to control criminal activity and drug use among offenders who are living in the community (CASA, 1998). Over 300 drug courts have been developed in 48 states and Washington, D.C. (Office of Justice Programs, 1997). Approximately 100,000 offenders with drug problems have participated in drug court programs nationwide since their inception in 1989 (American University, 1998). Since 1989, nearly 71% of participants in drug court programs have either successfully completed drug court or are currently involved in the program (U.S. Government Accounting Office, 1997).

MISSING LINK: EMPLOYMENT SERVICES

Among offender programs including drug court, one of the most neglected areas of treatment is employment. Although employment services are needed and often wanted by drug abusers, employment assistance is generally not part of drug treatment (Platt, 1995; Schottenfeld et al., 1992).

Employment has been associated with moderating relapse and increasing treatment retention (Wolkstein & Spiller, 1998) and treatment outcomes have been related to pre-treatment employment (Wickizer et al., 1994). However, there are unrealistic expectations among drug abusers when actual employment skills are compared with employment expectations (French et al., 1992), especially since poorly paid, entry-level service employment is widely available in the U.S. (Burtless, 1997) and is the usual type of employment for drug users. In addition to difficulties finding a job, a drug abuser may encounter difficulties related to poor work habits, failure to report to work, and frequent lateness or absence without an appropriate excuse (Schottenfeld, et al., 1992).

The research literature has also identified gender differences in employment and employment-related issues. For example, women in substance abuse treatment are often less likely to be employed than men, more often reporting a homemaker role (Wallen, 1992; Westermeyer & Boedicker, 2000). There are several barriers to obtaining employment for women such as childcare, limited transportation, and limited education and/or job skills, which are difficult to obtain without adequate resources (Bride, 2001; Knight et al., 2001, Ross & Lawrence, 1998; Suffet, 1999; Sterling et al., 2001).

Given the gender differences in employment, the research literature has not closely examined factors that potentially impact employment among substance-abusing offenders. The study reported here profiles employment histories, drug use, and criminal involvement among a sample of male and female substance abusers in two Kentucky drug court programs. These participants are involved in a National Institute on Drug Abuse-funded research project that is examining the effect of implementing an employment intervention in two existing drug court programs. The intervention, grounded in established job readiness and life skill training approaches, focuses on obtaining, maintaining, and upgrading employment. This chapter describes the employment intervention used in the Kentucky Drug Court programs, and profiles differences in employment, drug use, and criminal involvement by male and female offenders.

THE INTERVENTION

The employment intervention, which is grounded in established job readiness and life skill training approaches, was developed by the project team. Three established interventions were modified and are incorporated into the employment intervention and manual: the Ex-Inmates Guide to Successful Employment (Sull, 1998), Job Readiness Activity (State of Kentucky, 1995), and Offender Employment Specialist Manual (NIC, 1997). In addition, existing clinical approaches used with substance abuse clients are incorporated, which include job skill training, social skills training (Leukefeld, et al., 2000), strengths based case management (Siegal et al., 1996), and motivational interviewing (Miller & Rollnick, 1991).

Focus groups were used in the developmental phases of the employment intervention. The focus groups included drug court participants who identified critical factors related to obtaining, maintaining, and upgrading employment skills (Staton et al., 2002). As expected, focus group findings indicated that drug court participants encountered a variety of employment issues which included difficulty in balancing work and treatment involvement. Focus group participants also expressed a desire for job readiness training/job placement opportunities and indicated that a major employment issue is finding employers who would hire ex-offenders and drug abusers.

Three Phases

Grounded in the focus group findings, employment manuals, and established clinical approaches, the enhanced drug court employment intervention was implemented. The intervention includes three phases designed to coincide with the three phases of drug court—obtaining employment, maintaining employment, and upgrading employment (See Table 20.1).

Motivational interviewing, structured story telling, and thought-mapping are used in weekly group sessions (see Leukefeld, et al. 2000). Individual sessions incorporated motivational interviewing, thought-mapping, behavioral contracting, and strengths based case management to focus on problem-solving, job searches, filling out job applications, resume writing, and job interviewing. Individual sessions also help participants who are struggling with particular issues that impede their employment success. Examples of these issues include continued use of drugs and alcohol, co-workers who use drugs on the job, conflict with co-workers, and criminal thinking.

By June, 2002, 232 participants were randomly assigned to the employment intervention across the two Kentucky drug court sites. Participants anecdotally reported an increased self-confidence after preparing their resume and practicing identifying their personal employment strengths and talents. Participants also expressed a change in how they view work and employers in general. Some participants, who initially described work as a waste of time due to low entry-level wages, viewed themselves later as "investments for employers" and someone employers can trust. Other feedback includes an appreciation among participants who believe they are capable of finding

Table 20.1: Drug Court and Employment Intervention Phases

Phase	Length of time	No. of individual sessions	No. of group sessions	Content
I. Obtaining Employment	4-5 weeks	5	10	Getting immediate employment, employment behavioral contracting, and job readiness assessment
II. Maintaining Employment	32 weeks	5	24	Resolving conflicts at work, setting goals and problem solving, and life skills development
III. Upgrading Employment	16 weeks	5	13	Identifying possible employers, job development, and job placement

successful employment and academic pursuits. Even for participants who are not ready to upgrade their employment status, progress was noted as self-discovery about the importance of their employment.

Data Collection Method

The overall project focuses on enhancing employment opportunities for substance-using offenders. The study design includes the recruitment, intervention, and follow-up of 500 drug court participants using a pre-test/post-test experimental design with random assignment and follow-ups to examine the drug court employment intervention. The two sites selected for the project are Fayette County Drug Court (Lexington, KY) and Warren County Drug Court (Bowling Green, KY). Drug court clients are recruited into the study within 30 days after entering drug court. After a client consents, a face-to-face baseline interview is administered. The baseline interview includes measures of employment, drug and alcohol use, and criminal justice involvement. During the informed consent process, potential participants are told that study participation includes random assignment to the enhanced employment intervention or to "treatment as usual." Participants are paid for completing baseline interviews and follow-up interviews. After completing a baseline interview, participants are randomized into the intervention group or the control group (drug court as usual). Those selected for the enhanced intervention group received the employment intervention in addition to standard drug court treatment. Data are collected from participants in the intervention group and the comparison group again at follow-ups.

GENDER DIFFERENCE PROFILES

The second objective of this chapter is to examine whether male and female substance abusers report different employment problems, different drug use (using

Table 20.2: Employment History by Gender

	Males (N = 327)	Females (N = 173)
Percent working full time prior to DC ***	54.5%	31.0%
Percent lost a job in the past year	26.9%	19.1%
Mean # of different jobs in the past 5 years*	3.9	3.2
Mean length of longest full-time job (years) **	4.8	3.4
Mean income from employment 6 months before DC ***	$4899	$2058
Mean # of days worked legitimate job in 6 months before DC***	92.6	57.3
Mean # of days worked illegal job in 6 months before DC†	52.4	40.1
Percent extremely bothered by employment problems 6 months before DC	15.0%	22.7%
Mean # days experienced employment problems in 6 months before DC	42.3	44.4
Percent who considered employment counseling extremely important *	23.5%	32.6%

† $p \leq .10$, * $p \leq .05$, ** $p \leq .01$, *** $p \leq .001$

Addiction Severity Inventory measures), and different criminal histories. The present study includes 500 drug court clients; 65% are male, 35% female. When demographics were examined, there were no significant differences by gender. A majority of participants identify themselves as Caucasian (62%). The mean age is 31; the mean number of years of education is 11.8. About 18% are married and 53% characterize their home as in an urban place.

Employment

As noted in Table 20.2, more males than females reported working full time prior to drug court entry (54.5% vs. 31.0%, $p \leq .001$) as well as an increased number of different jobs in the previous five years when compared to females (3.9 vs. 3.2, $p \leq .05$), and increased length of time in a stable job (4.8 years vs. 3.4 years, $p \leq .01$). Males also reported an increased number of days working a legitimate job during the six months before entering drug court (92.6 vs. 57.3, $p \leq .001$) and increased income during the six months before drug court ($4,899 vs. $2,058, $p \leq .001$) when compared to females. In addition, males reported increased involvement with illegal jobs during the six months before treatment entry (52.4 days vs. 40.1 days, $p \leq .10$) compared to females. More females than males considered employment counseling extremely important (32.6% vs. 23.5%, $p < .05$).

Table 20.3: Substance Use by Gender

	Percent ever used	Mean age of first use	Percentused in 30 days before DC	Meanyears of regular use
Alcohol				
Males	99.1%	14.4*	56.3%*	8.0**
Females	97.1%	15.3*	46.2%*	5.1**
Marijuana				
Males	97.9%	15.2	53.8%**	7.4**
Females	96.0%	15.8	39.3%**	5.6**
Cocaine				
Males	82.3%	20.9	36.4%	3.7
Females	86.7%	21.4	42.2%	4.5
Sedatives				
Males	48.0%	19.3*	22.3%	1.3
Females	48.0%	20.9*	18.5%	1.9
Amphetamines				
Males	27.2%	18.5**	4.3%	.4
Females	27.7%	20.6**	2.3%	.6
Methamphetamines				
Males	32.7%	22.0*	9.2%	.3**
Females	31.2%	24.4*	11.0%	1.4**
Opiates				
Males	34.3%	21.7	16.5%	1.2
Females	32.9%	22.8	13.9%	1.9
Multiple substance use				
Males	85.6%*	18.8**	52.9%*	5.2
Females	78.6%*	20.3**	41.6%*	4.7

* $p \leq .05$, ** $p \leq .01$

Table 20.4: Criminal Involvement By Gender

	Males (N = 327)	Females (N = 173)
Percent arrested as juveniles***	37.0%	22.0%
Mean age of first adult incarceration***	22.6	25.1
Mean # of times incarcerated as an adult	5.3	4.7
Mean # of mos. incarcerated in lifetime	13.3	11.6

***p≤ .001

Substance Use

Table 20.3 shows gender differences in substance abuse for lifetime use of a specific drug, mean age of first use, percent used in the 30 days before drug court, and the mean number of years of regular lifetime use. More males reported ever using more than one substance when compared to females (85.6% vs. 78.6%, p ≤ .05). More males than females also reported using alcohol (56.3% vs. 46.2%, p≤.05), marijuana (53.8% vs. 39.3%, p≤.01), and more than one substance per day (52.9% vs. 41.6%, p< .05) in the 30 days prior to entering drug court.

Consistent with other studies (i.e., Staton, et al., 1999a), males were significantly younger than females when they first used alcohol (14.4 vs. 15.3, p≤.05), sedatives (19.3 vs. 20.9, p≤.05), amphetamines (18.5 vs. 20.6, p<.01), methamphetamines (22.0 vs. 24.4, p≤.05), and more than one substance in the same day (18.8 vs. 20.3, p≤.01). As expected with an earlier age of initiation, males also reported an increased number of years of regular use of alcohol (8.0 years vs. 5.1 years, p≤.01), and marijuana (7.4 years vs. 5.6 years, p<.01). However, it was interesting that females reported more years of regular use of opiates (1.9 years vs. 1.2 years, p≤ .10), and methamphetamines (1.4 years vs. 0.3 year, p<.01).

Criminal Involvement

As shown in Table 20.4, when compared with females, males reported being significantly younger at age of first incarceration (22.6 vs. 25.1, p≤.001). In addition, a significantly higher percentage of males (37.0% vs. 22.0%, p≤.001) reported being arrested as a juvenile when compared to females.

CONCLUSIONS

Employment is considered by many treatment providers to be an important part of substance abuse treatment, but employment and vocational activities generally receive limited attention. This chapter focused on gender differences in employment history, substance abuse, and criminal involvement among a sample of drug court offenders. Consistent with other literature (i.e., Westermeyer & Boedicker, 2000), findings showed that males reported a more involved employment history than females including more jobs in the past five years, increased length of time in a stable job, increased number of work days (legal and illegal) prior to treatment entry, and increased income. These findings have implications for substance abuse treatment providers because employment may be an important enhancement to treatment. In addition, employment needs may be very different for males and females. Assessments should be used to examine employment history, skills, and job goals as part of the treatment planning process.

These findings indicate that a higher percentage of males reported lifetime substance use, as well as more substance use during the 30 days prior to entering the drug court program when compared to females. In addition, findings from this study indicate that males reported earlier ages of substance use initiation than females, and subsequent increased years of use. This finding is consistent with literature suggesting that earlier initiation of substance use is related to earlier initiation of other problem behaviors (Staton et al., 1999a; 1999b). Males in this study also reported earlier ages of first arrest than females, and were more likely to be arrested as a juvenile. Engaging in problem behaviors at younger ages should also be considered in treatment planning assessments—particularly among offenders. The extent of involvement in these problem behaviors (including drug use and criminal involvement) at younger ages may be predictive of severity of later involvement and should be considered in treatment.

There are limitations associated with this study. Drug court program eligibility determined study eligibility; therefore, participants were not randomly selected. Only two drug courts from one state are included in the study. In addition, behaviors reported were self-reported, which can have limitations for recall. Although participants volunteered and consented to participate in the study, it is not known how truthful they were about their self-reported behaviors. In spite of these limitations, these findings can help us to better understand gender differences in employment among substance abusing offenders, particularly factors which may impact obtaining, maintaining, and upgrading employment.

Finally, the overall project expands the limited research on employment and enhancing employment for male and female substance abusing offenders. Clearly, employment interventions should be examined to determine their utility for enhancing and keeping drug abusers in treatment and for changes in treatment outcomes for both males and females. Additional project studies are planned to examine the extent to which participants in the enhanced employment intervention will have increased successes with finding and keeping stable employment, as well as meeting and overcoming employment barriers and on-the-job problems. It is expected that the enhanced employment participants will remain in the drug court program longer with decreased drug use and criminality after treatment. Project findings should provide important insights for developing employment interventions, as well as for further drug-abuse offender employment research. The enhanced employment intervention manual also could be useful for practitioners and case managers in criminal justice and substance abuse settings.

About the Authors

Carl Leukefeld, D.S.W., is a Professor at the University of Kentucky and Director of the UK Center on Drug and Alcohol Research. Michele Staton, M.S.W., is Study Director at UKCDAR. Allison Mateyoke-Scrivner, B.A., is Data Analyst at UKCDAR. Hope Smiley, B.A., is Research Assistant at UKCDAR. J. Matthew Webster, Ph.D., is an Assistant Professor at UKCDAR. Matthew L. Hiller, Ph.D., is an Assistant Professor at UKCDAR. For more information, contact Dr. Leukefeld by email at: cleukef@uky.edu.

This study is supported by Grant No. RO1-DA13076 from the National Institute on Drug Abuse.

References

American University (1998). *Looking at decade of drug courts.* Washington, DC: U.S. Department of Justice Drug Court Clearinghouse and Technical Assistance Project.

Belenko, S. (1998). Research on Drug Courts: A critical review. *National Drug Court Institute Review, I*(1), 1-30.

Bride, B.E. (2001). Single-gender treatment of substance abuse: Effect on treatment retention and completion. *Social Work Research, 25,* 223-232.

Bureau of Justice Statistics (1998). Sourcebook of Criminal Justice Statistics. Washington, D.C.: U.S. Department of Justice.

Burtless, G.T. (1997). Welfare recipients' job skills and employment prospects. *The Future of Children: Welfare to Work, 7*(1), 39-51.

CASA—Center on Addiction and Substance Abuse. (1998, January). *Behind bars: Substance abuse and America's prison population.* New York: Columbia University.

DUF (1996). *Drug Use Forecasting annual report on adult and juvenile arrestees.* NIJ, Research Report. Washington, DC: U.S. Department of Justice.

Field, G. (1985). The cornerstone program: A client outcome study. *Federal Probation, 49,* 50-55.

French, M.T., Dennis, M.L., McDougal, G.L., Karuntzos, G.T., & Hubbard, R.L. (1992). Training and employment programs in methadone treatment: Client needs and desires. *Journal of Substance Abuse Treatment, 9*(4), 293-304.

Greenberg, S. W., & Adler, F. (1974). Crime and addiction: An empirical analysis of the literature 1920-1973. *Contemporary Drug Problems, 3,* 221-270.

Innes, C.A. (1988). *Special report: Profiles of state prison inmates,* 1986. Washington, DC, Department of Justice, Bureau of Justice Statistics.

Knight, D.K., Logan, S.M., & Simpson, D.D. (2001). Predictors of program completion for women in residential substance abuse treatment. *American Journal of Drug and Alcohol Abuse, 27,* 1-18.

Leukefeld, C, Godlaski, T, Clark, J., Brown, C., & Hays, L. (2000) *Behavioral therapy for rural substance abusers.* Lexington, KY: University Press of Kentucky.

Leukefeld, C. Tims, F., & Farabee, D. (2002). *Treatment of drug offenders: Policies and issues.* New York: Springer Publishing.

Martin, S.S., Butzin, C.A., Saum, C.A., & Inciardi, J.A. (1999). Three-year outcomes of therapeutic community treatment for drug-involved offenders in Delaware: From prison to work release to aftercare. *The Prison Journal, 79*(3), 294-320.

Miller, W. R., & Rollnick, S. (1991). *Motivational interviewing: Preparing people to change addictive behavior.* New York: Guilford Press.

National Institute of Corrections (1997). *Offender Employment Specialist Training.* Longmont, CO: U.S. Department of Justice, National Institute of Corrections.

Nurco, D.N., Ball, J.C., Shaffer, J.W., & Hanlon, T.F. (1985). The criminality of narcotic addicts. *Journal of Nervous and Mental Disease, 173,* 94-102.

Office of Justice Programs. (1997). *Defining drug courts: The key components.* Washington, DC: U.S. Department of Justice.

Platt, J.J. (1995). Vocational rehabilitation of drug abusers. *Psychological Bulletin, 117*(3), 416-433.

Ross, P.H. & Lawrence, J.E. (1998). Health care for women offenders. *Corrections Today, 60*(7), 122-127.

Schottenfeld, R.S., Pascale, R., & Sokolowski. S., (1992). Matching devices to needs: Vocational services for substance abusers. *Journal of Substance Abuse Treatment, 9*(1), 3-8.

Siegal, H.A., Rapp, R.C., Kelliher, C.W., Wagner, J.H., O'Brien, W.F., & Cole, P.A. (1996). The role of case management in retaining clients in substance abuse treatment: An exploratory analysis. *Journal of Drug Issues, 27*(4), 821-831.

State of Kentucky (1995). *Job readiness activity manual.* Frankfort, KY: Department of Employment Services.

Staton, M., Leukefeld, C., Logan, TK, Zimmerman, R., Lynam, D., Milich, R., Martin, C., McClanahan, K., & Clayton, R. . (1999a). Risky sex behavior and substance use among young adults. *Health and Social Work, 24*(2), 147-154.

Staton, M., Leukefeld, C., Logan, TK, Zimmerman, R., Lynam, D., Milich, R., Martin, C., McClanahan, K., & Clayton, R. (1999b). Gender differences in substance use during adolescence and initiation of sexual activity. *Population Research and Policy Review, 18*(1/2), 89-100.

Staton, M., Mateyoke, A., Leukefeld, C., Cole, J., Hopper, H., & Logan, TK (2002). Employment issues among drug court participants, *Journal of Offender Rehabilitation, 33*(4), 73-85.

Sterling, R.C., Gottheil, E., Glassman, S.D., Weinstein, S.P., Serota, R.D., & Lundy, A. (2001). Correlates of employment: a cohort study. *American Journal of Drug and Alcohol Abuse, 27,* 137-147.

Suffet, F. (1999). Some sex-neutral and sex-specific factors related to employment among substance abuse clients. *American Journal of Drug and Alcohol Abuse, 25,* 517.

Sull, E.C. (1998). *The ex-inmate's complete guide to successful employment (2nd ed.).* Buffalo, NY: Aardvark Publishing.

U.S. General Accounting Office. (1997, July). *Drug courts: Overview of growth, characteristics, and results* [GAO/GGD-97-106]. Washington, DC: Author.

Wallen, J. (1992). A comparison of male and female clients in substance abuse treatment. *Journal of Substance Abuse Treatment, 9,* 243-248.

Westermeyer, J. & Boedicker, A.E. (2000). Course, severity, and treatment of substance abuse among women versus men. *American Journal of Drug and Alcohol Abuse, 26,* 523.

Wexler, H.K., & Williams, R. (1986). Stay'n Out therapeutic community: Prison treatment for substance abusers. *Journal of Psychoactive Drugs, 18*(3), 221-230.

Wexler, H.K. (1995). Amity prison TC: One year outcome results. Unpublished report to NDRI.

Wickizer, T., Maynard, C., Atherly, A., Frederick, M., Koepsell, T., Krupski, A., & Stark, K. (1994). Completion of clients discharged from drug and alcohol treatment programs in Washington State. *The American Journal of Public Health, 84*(2), 215-221.

Wolkstein, E. & Spiller, H. (1998). Providing vocational services to clients in substance abuse rehabilitation. *Directions in Rehabilitation Counseling, 9,* 65-78.

Chapter 21

Considering Psychiatric Comorbidities Among Addicted Offenders: A New Strategy for Client-Treatment Matching

by James A. Swartz, Ph.D.

Introduction 21-2
    High Rates of Comorbidity 21-2
    Lack of Attention to Mental Health Needs of Drug-Abusing Offenders . . . 21-2
Epidemiological Studies 21-3
    Psychiatric Disorders in Jail Detainees 21-3
    Co-Occurring Substance Abuse and SMI in Probationers 21-4
    BJS Findings 21-4
Assessment Strategies and Instruments 21-5
    Not Enough Screening for Comorbid Mental Illness in
        Substance Abusers 21-5
    Desirable Screening Instrument Attributes 21-5
    Candidate Screening Instruments 21-6
        Diagnostic Approach 21-6
        Symptom Severity Approach 21-7
Treatment 21-8
    Psychiatric Concerns Not Just an "Add On" 21-8
    Strong Argument for Specialized Programming 21-9
    A Treatment-Matching Strategy 21-10
Conclusion 21-10

An earlier version of this chapter appeared in Offender Substance Abuse Report, *Vol. 1, No. 5, September/ October 2001.*

INTRODUCTION

High Rates of Comorbidity

Studies of the general population and of clinical and incarcerated populations have shown that drug abusing and drug dependent individuals have very high rates of comorbid psychiatric disorders (Kessler et al., 1994; Regier et al., 1990). Although there is variation depending on methodological differences, estimates are that between 25% to 50% of drug dependent individuals have a lifetime comorbid psychiatric disorder (Regier et al., 1990). The converse is also true: individuals with major psychiatric disorders have comparably high rates of drug use and dependence (Buckley, 1998; Mueser et al., 1992; Regier et al., 1990). While the comorbidity rates for major psychiatric disorders are significant for non-institutionalized drug-dependent individuals, they are even higher for individuals in treatment programs and higher still for prison inmates. For example, a national epidemiological study that included a sample of prison inmates found a comorbidity rate of 90% for antisocial personality disorder, schizophrenia, and bipolar disorder among inmates dependent on alcohol or other drugs (Regier et al., 1990).

Lack of Attention to Mental Health Needs of Drug-Abusing Offenders

Despite the high rate of psychiatric comorbidities among addicted offenders, drug treatment programs in the criminal justice system, like community-based programs in general, have tended to focus on treating drug dependence and have not addressed the issue of psychiatric comorbidities commensurate with the extent of the problem (Edens et al., 1997; as an exception, see Sacks et al., 1997). For example, a fairly recent national survey of adults on probation conducted by the Bureau of Justice Statistics (BJS) indicated that while 41% of all adult probationers had substance abuse treatment as a condition of probation, only 7% were required to have psychiatric or psychological counseling (BJS, 1997).

The lack of attention to assessing and treating psychiatric comorbidities among chemically dependent offenders is unfortunate as the costs of such neglect are likely high. Past research has indicated that addicted individuals with one or more comorbid psychiatric disorders are among the most difficult to treat in traditional single-focused contexts and consequently are the most in need of specialized treatment programming (Buckley, 1998, Mueser et al., 1997; Woody et al., 1997). Placed in a drug treatment program not equipped to handle psychiatric comorbidities, such individuals—to the extent they remain in treatment at all—may prove to be disruptive, draining a disproportionate amount of staff time and resources away from individuals more suitable for treatment focused on drug abuse. Worse, because of their inability to comply with the strict treatment regimens required by drug programs, comorbid individuals may be released by the program or never admitted in the first place. Thus, psychiatrically comorbid individuals with some of the most severe drug abuse and ancillary problems (e.g., risk for HIV infection; Woody et al., 1997) end up in treatment that is not appropriate or in no treatment at all.

This chapter argues that drug treatment for offenders would have improved outcomes if psychiatric comorbidities were assessed *before* treatment placement: Addicted offenders meeting the diagnostic criteria for a severe mental illness would be referred to specialized integrated services programs while those not meeting the criteria would be referred to standard drug treatment programming. Three areas are discussed: the epidemiology of psychiatric comorbidities among addicted offenders, assessing psychiatric comorbidities, and developing model treatment programs for addicted offenders with comorbid psychiatric conditions.

Potentially, any of a wide range of psychiatric disorders could be eligible for consideration when screening for and treating individuals with a comorbid drug use problem. For example, attention deficit hyperactivity disorder (ADHD) and antisocial personality disorder (ASP) have been identified as prevalent and clinically significant among various offender populations (e.g., Wexler, 1995). However, since there are relatively scarce treatment resources in the criminal justice system, it would likely be better to focus on the most severe psychiatric disorders, which require the greatest clinical attention. Researchers have identified three psychiatric disorders, collectively referred to as severe mental illnesses (SMI), as among the most serious disorders in terms of their long-term consequences to the individual and society and their treatment difficulty: schizophrenia, bipolar disorder (i.e., manic-depression), and major depression (Johnson, 1997).

EPIDEMIOLOGICAL STUDIES

Coincident with the emphasis on identifying and treating drug use among offenders, there have been many epidemiological studies of the extent of substance use, abuse, and dependence among offenders. For example, the Arrestee Drug Abuse Monitoring (ADAM) program has assessed the level of drug use among arrestees on a quarterly basis for over a decade now (cf., National Institute of Justice, 2000) and questions on drug use are routinely included in national surveys of state and federal prison inmates (BJS, 1993, 1998a, 1998b) and probationers (BJS, 1997). No comparable ongoing efforts exist to assess the extent of mental illness among offenders let alone the rates of psychiatric comorbidities. A number of smaller scale studies provide data on the prevalence of psychiatric illnesses among addicted offenders. While inconclusive, these studies suggest that the problem of psychiatric comorbidities is prevalent and warrants more attention and resources than have been expended to date.

Psychiatric Disorders in Jail Detainees

An early study of psychiatric illness in an offender population found that there were significantly elevated rates of almost all psychiatric disorders among jail detainees as compared to general population rates. For example, schizophrenia was about three times more prevalent in arrestees compared to general population rates at the time (Teplin, 1990). Similarly, manic-depression or bipolar disorder and major depression were also much more prevalent among the assessed detainees than among members of the general population. In a related study that utilized the same data to assess the rates of comorbid disorders, 85% of the jail detainees with a severe mental disorder (schizophrenia or a major affective disorder) met the criteria for lifetime alcohol abuse or dependence while 58% met the criteria for lifetime drug abuse or dependence (Abram & Teplin, 1991).

Co-Occurring Substance Abuse and SMI in Probationers

A recent study included a statewide survey of Illinois adult male and female probationers. The survey assessed lifetime and current rates of substance dependence and SMI (Lurigio et al., 2000). Relative to recently published rates for the general population (Kessler, et al., 1994), the prevalence rates for psychiatric disorders for the probationers were elevated, especially for lifetime (11.2%) and current (18.8%) psychotic disorders. This study also found elevated rates of SMI among probationers and found that those who were dependent on substances were also more likely to have an SMI and vice versa (see Table 21.1). For example, among those with a past-year substance use disorder, about 17% also had a past-year major depressive episode compared to about 11% of those without a substance use disorder.

BJS Findings

In another study, the BJS published the combined findings of national surveys of state and federal inmates and of probationers that included a number of questions designed to assess the rates of psychiatric illnesses (BJS, 1999). Among the major findings were that 16% of state prison inmates, 7% of federal inmates, and 16% of those

Table 21.1: Percentage of Illinois Adult Probationers Reporting Psychiatric Conditions: Current (Last Year) Substance Abusers vs. Non-Abusers

Current Psychiatric Disorders (period)	Non-Substance Abuser	Substance Abuser	p	Total Sample
Major Depressive Episode (past 2 weeks)	10.6	16.9	*	13.2
Manic Episode (at interview)	1.9	4.5		3.0
Hypomanic Episode (at interview)	3.3	9.4	**	
Suicide Risk (past month)	13.6	24.1	**	18.1
Post-Traumatic Stress Disorder (past month)	1.9	4.9	*	3.2
Psychotic Disorder (at interview)	10.3	12.4		11.2
Mood Disorder with Psychotic Features (at interview)	6.9	12.7	*	9.4

* p<0.05; ** p<0.01; *** p<0.001 (Chi-Square Test).
Reproduced from Lurigio, A. J., Swartz, J. A, Cho, Y. I., Johnson, T., Graf, I., & Pickup, L. (2000) with permission from the Illinois Office of Alcoholism and Substance Abuse.

in jails or on probation had some kind of lifetime mental or emotional condition. One important issue limiting the findings of the BJS results is that rather broad, non-diagnostic questions and information were used to assess rates of non-specific mental illnesses. For example, the criteria for assessing an individual as having a psychiatric illness was whether or not the person self-reported an overnight stay in a "mental hospital" or had a "mental or emotional condition" in his or her lifetime.

Although none of these studies provides a solid national estimate of the rate of comorbid SMI among addicted offenders, they do provide evidence that between 10% to 25% or more of addicted offenders may also have a severe lifetime psychiatric comorbidity. Thus, it is quite likely that a similar percentage of offenders currently in drug treatment under the supervision of the criminal justice system also have an SMI. A limited study of participants receiving drug treatment in a day reporting center supports this thesis. That study found that 12% of the drug treatment participants reported symptoms consistent with a lifetime diagnosis of a major depressive episode, 8% with a manic episode, and 3.4% for schizophrenia/schizophreniform disorder (Swartz & Lurigio, 1999). In total, 19% of the treatment participants met the criteria for a lifetime diagnosis of an SMI. However, none of these participants had been diagnosed as having a psychiatric comorbidity and, consequently, none were receiving specialized services.

ASSESSMENT STRATEGIES AND INSTRUMENTS

Not Enough Screening for Comorbid Mental Illness in Substance Abusers

Coincident with targeting drug abuse and the relative inattention to mental illness and psychiatric comorbidities, there has been much more emphasis on developing screening and assessment tools for drug use as opposed to developing comparable instrumentation for comorbid mental illnesses. As a result, there are many offenders currently in drug treatment programs with undiagnosed and untreated comorbid psychiatric conditions. Unless psychiatric symptoms are especially flagrant, they may go undetected throughout the offender's tenure in the criminal justice system and never be clinically addressed.

The consequences of having such conditions undetected and untreated are manifold: a greater chance of relapse to drug use, a greater chance of rearrest and reincarceration, and continued cycling through the criminal justice system. Additionally, addicted offenders with SMI comorbidities may have a more difficult time than other participants in drug treatment programming with following the often stringent requirements of such programs and hence may have high drop-out rates or be more disruptive of the program milieu, lessening the effectiveness of the treatment program for all participants. For these reasons, it is vitally important that we adjust our screening and assessment strategies away from the single-minded focus on substance abuse and toward a more comprehensive diagnostic psychiatric profile calibrated to a comprehensive and integrated treatment strategy.

Desirable Screening Instrument Attributes

Considering the high volume of screenings and assessments that must be conducted by personnel without specialized training in criminal justice settings, Hepburn (1994;

see also Swartz, 1998) has described the ideal characteristics of a screening instrument for substance abuse among offenders. Briefly, these characteristics include: standardized and replicable scoring criteria, brevity, and ease of administration and scoring. To these we might add that the instrument should have criteria and diagnostic categories consistent with a recognized diagnostic system such as the DSM-IV (American Psychiatric Association, 2000), should be available in several languages including English and Spanish, and should include disorders of drug use as well as the SMI diagnoses.

Unlike the case with substance use disorders, however, there is no parallel for defining the optimal content of a screening instrument for psychiatric disorders. First, there are many more DSM-IV (American Psychiatric Association, 2000) Axis I non-substance use disorders than substance use disorders. Thus, while it is possible to briefly screen for all drugs of abuse or simply for any drug abuse or dependence, it is not possible to concisely screen for every Axis I psychiatric diagnosis. Second, even if it were possible to screen for every DSM-IV Axis I disorder, not everyone with a disorder needs treatment. There appears to be a gradient of clinical severity and treatment need; even among those with seemingly severe psychiatric disorders, some are able to function adequately without clinical intervention (Regier et al., 1998). The challenge, then, is to determine which psychiatric disorders should be screened for and to define when a disorder is severe enough to warrant clinical intervention or at least further assessment.

Candidate Screening Instruments

Diagnostic Approach. Two different approaches have been taken to make screening for psychiatric disorders more manageable. One approach is to determine if an individual meets the diagnostic criteria for a limited number of diagnoses by focusing on those more likely to be clinically severe and to require treatment intervention. At a minimum, the restricted subset of all DSM-IV diagnoses includes those previously enumerated as constituting SMI: non-affective psychotic disorders or (equivalently) disorders of the schizophrenic spectrum, bipolar disorder, and major depressive disorder. Among the available tools that take the diagnostic approach to screening are the Composite International Diagnostic Interview—Short Form (CIDI-SF; Kessler et al., 1998), the Mini-Neuropsychiatric Interview (MINI; Sheehan et al., 1998) and the Referral Decision Scale (RDS; Teplin & Swartz, 1989). Like the longer assessment instruments for psychiatric diagnosis such as the Diagnostic Interview Schedule (DIS; Robins et al., 1981) and the Composite International Diagnostic Interview (CIDI; Robins et al., 1988), from which they were derived, the MINI, the CIDI-SF, and to a lesser extent the RDS are modular, with each module consisting of a self-contained sequence of questions for diagnosing a specific disorder or class of disorders. For example, one module of the MINI screens for psychotic disorders while a second module screens for bipolar disorders. Administration time can be shortened by omitting modules that screen for disorders that are not of interest. Despite this administrative flexibility, however, there are problems with all of these instruments individually and with this class of instruments generally that limit their usefulness in criminal justice settings.

Essentially, the diagnostic approach to screening equates illness severity and need for clinical intervention with diagnosis. Those who have one or more of the screened-for diagnoses are referred for further assessment and possibly treatment. Those who do not have one of the screened-for diagnoses are not referred for a fuller assessment. The potential drawback is that individuals who have a severe manifestation of a disorder that is not screened for (e.g., post-traumatic stress disorder, generalized anxiety disorder), but which nevertheless requires clinical intervention, are missed (i.e., false negatives). Moreover, despite the administrative flexibility of selecting which diagnoses can be included in the screening, the necessity of obtaining valid DSM-IV diagnoses adds a level of complexity to the instruments manifest as skip patterns and probes. Given the lack of clinical interviewing skills of many individuals administering screens in criminal justice settings, the inclusion of even a small number of skip patterns and probes can reduce the validity of the instrument. Although the RDS addresses some of these issues by being brief (15 items) and having no skip patterns, validation studies have shown that the RDS has an unacceptably high false positive rate (i.e., low positive predictive value; Hart et al., 1993; Rogers et al., 1995; Veysey et al., 1998). In addition, the RDS uses DSM-III-R (American Psychiatric Association, 1987) diagnostic criteria and was never normed or validated for use with women (Teplin & Swartz, 1989).

Symptom Severity Approach. The problems related to screening for the need for psychiatric treatment using a diagnostic approach has recently led to a second approach that de-emphasizes diagnosis and focuses on symptom severity and level of impairment (Kessler et al., 2002). Although not a new idea (see Murphy, 2002), this approach has gained more currency of late because large-scale epidemiological surveys such as the Epidemiological Catchment Area (ECA) study and the more recent National Comorbidity Survey (NCS) have found surprisingly high prevalence rates of psychiatric disorders. In both studies, between 20% to 30% of the general population met the DSM criteria for at least one past-year Axis 1 disorder (Regier et al., 1990; Kessler et al., 1994; Kessler & Walters, 2002). As it seemed unlikely this large a proportion of the general population required mental health treatment services, the findings of these surveys were of limited use for guiding federal and state treatment resource allocation. This conclusion focused attention on screening for the symptom severity and level of functional impairment given the presence of a DSM-IV Axis I diagnosis as a better way of discriminating the need for psychiatric treatment (see Regier et al., 1998; Slade & Andrews, 2002). Examples of screening tools that take a symptom severity approach to screening are the psychological problems section of the Addiction Severity Index (ASI; McLellan et al., 1992), the Brief Psychiatric Rating Scale (BPRS; Overall & Gorham, 1962), the Symptom Checklist 90 (SCL-90; Derogatis et al., 1973), and the recently developed K6/K10 scales (Kessler et al., 2002).

Among this class of scales the K6/K10 scales appear to be the best candidate instrument(s) for use with criminal justice populations. Beginning with a pool of 612 items derived from 18 existing psychological screening scales (e.g., the Beck Depression Inventory (Beck et al., 1961), Symptom Checklist-90), Kessler and his colleagues (Kessler et al., 2002) used analytic procedures derived from item response theory to distill a subset of 10 questions (the K10) and a completely overlapping subset of 6 questions (the K6) that identified, with maximum sensitivity, individuals meeting the following two criteria: a past-year diagnosis of any DSM-IV Axis I psychiatric disorder and a Global Assessment of Functioning (GAF) score below 60 (i.e., moderate to severe impairment in functioning; see APA, 2000). These particular criteria were selected because they comported with the criteria used by the U.S. Substance Abuse and Mental Health Services Administration (SAMHSA) in their block grant formula for funding public mental health services to the states (see Kessler et al., 2003). The intent was to include one of these scales in general population surveys such as the National Survey on Drug Use and Health (NSDUH; formerly the National Household Survey on Drug Abuse [NHSDA]) to help states comply with the provisions of Public Law 102-321, which establishes the federal requirements for states to provide estimates of serious mental illness to qualify for and set the amounts of block grant funding (Kessler et al., 2003).

Calibration of the K6/K10 scales cut-scores was done to identify those individuals above the ninetieth percentile in symptom severity, consistent with estimates that 6% to 10% of the general population are in need of psychiatric treatment services at any one time (Kessler et al., 2002). In further validation testing, the K6/K10 scales were found to perform as well as longer screening instruments such as the WHO-DAS (Rehm, et al., 1999) and the CIDI-SF in identifying individuals with serious mental illness, with the two scales performing about equally well in the U.S. and Australian general populations (Furukawa, Kessler et al., 2002; Kessler et al., 2003). Because of the near equivalent performance of the K6 and the K10, the shorter K6 was added to the NHSDUH and the U.S. National Health Interview Survey (NHIS) questionnaires to provide estimates of the need for psychiatric treatment in the general population. Kessler et al. (2003) note, however, that the K10 might be more sensitive than the K6 in populations where a larger proportion of those assessed has clinically significant emotional distress (e.g., criminal offenders). We have recently administered the K6/K10 scales to a sample of Chicago arrestees and found that 16% screened positive for an SMI (Hahn & Swartz, 2004).

Presently, the main barrier to using the K6 or the K10 with criminal justice populations is that they have not been validated and normed for these populations. For example, given the higher prevalence of serious mental illness in criminal offenders, the general-population derived cut-points for the K6/K10 might not correctly identify the proportion of cases with the most severe disorders (Peirce & Cornell, 1993). Moreover, the item weights for scoring the K6/K10 instruments for use with general population samples might not be optimum for criminal justice populations though using the unweighted items seems to provide reasonably accurate diagnoses.

TREATMENT

Psychiatric Concerns Not Just an "Add On"

Although descriptions of drug treatment programming in criminal justice settings discuss the issue of comorbid psychiatric disorders, they are often presented in the context of a range of "ancillary" problems that include a variety of other treatment needs such as vocational training, GED classes, medical problems, and family counseling (e.g., Peters, 1993; Wexler, 1994). In other words, comorbid psychiatric disorders are treated as additional problems to be addressed while going about the main clinical task of dealing with addiction. It is rare in the clinical literature to see reports of psychiatric comorbidity treated as a unique clinical entity (or, arguably, entities, depending on the specific configuration of comorbid disorders) that warrants a significantly altered treatment philosophy and approach and not merely the addition of psychiatric services to the standard drug treatment regimen (El-Mallakh, 1998; Mueser et al., 1997). Programs that have provided psychiatric services in an adjunctive or sequential fashion to drug treatment services have not been as successful as programs that have developed a truly integrated treatment model with consistent philosophies and treatment plans (El-Mallakh, 1998; Mueser et al., 1997).

The lack of specific and qualitatively different programming for addicted criminal offenders with comorbid psychiatric disorders is unfortunate because research suggests that such individuals require a treatment approach and follow a clinical course that are distinct from single-disorder populations. Generalizing across all configurations of comorbidity and drug addiction, those with comorbid disorders tend to be more difficult to treat, to require more intensive treatment services, and to have poorer outcomes (El-Mallakh, 1998; Ries & Comtois, 1997). The need for specialized treatment programs for this population is underscored by the fact that individuals with comorbid psychiatric disorders and drug dependence are at increased risk relative to the general population for infection with HIV and for contracting AIDS (Cournos & McKinnon, 1997; Woody, et al., 1997).

Strong Argument for Specialized Programming

The paucity of research in the area of psychiatric comorbidities and integrated treatment programming for offenders may be due, in part, to the lack of specialized programming and, in part, to the common use of assessment and screening tools (e.g., the Addiction Severity Index) that do not generate psychiatric diagnoses. However, using psychiatric comorbidity as a treatment-matching variable may lead to higher retention rates and to treatment that is more effective. In one study, for instance, improvement in psychological functioning had the strongest association with overall improvement in functioning across multiple domains, including reduced alcohol and other drug abuse (McLellan et al., 1981). This finding led the authors to the consideration that: "It may be that therapy directed toward the psychological problems of addicted individuals has more pervasive and powerful effects on overall outcome than therapy centered upon their substance abuse problems alone" (p. 237). For the most part though, their exhortation for modified treatment to address psychological problems and drug addiction conjointly has been unheeded.

A strong argument can be made that specialized programming for offenders with psychiatric comorbidities would enhance client-treatment matching within the drug treatment system and enhance drug treatment programming generally. A considerable amount of research generated over the past 15 to 20 years has attempted to improve treatment retention and outcomes by determining what patient characteristics and (less often) what programmatic factors can be used to better match drug dependent individuals to a specific type or intensity of treatment programming (e.g., see Condelli, 1994 for a discussion of the closely related issue of factors related to treatment retention). For the most part, drug treatment-matching studies have focused on a rather simplistic strategy of matching participants by their drug use severity with a particular treatment intensity (cf., McLellan & Alterman, 1991). Despite the failure to show any substantial gains in treatment effectiveness using this approach, there have been few other proposed treatment-matching strategies. Consequently, as noted by Farabee et al. (2001):

Unfortunately, the literature regarding the criteria for patient-treatment matching has yet to provide much guidance beyond the need to place those with more severe substance abuse problems in more intensive structured programs (p. 35).

A Treatment-Matching Strategy

Perhaps then, a more productive treatment-matching strategy would be to sort offenders for treatment according to the presence or absence of a comorbid SMI. Those with comorbid mental illnesses would be referred to integrated services treatment programs while those without a comorbid condition would be referred to traditional drug treatment programming, with or without further matching on the basis of the severity of drug use. If this strategy is correct, there should be improved retention and outcomes for standard drug treatment programs as inappropriate treatment candidates will have been removed creating a more cohesive and presumably more productive therapeutic environment. Additionally, under such a scenario, there would no longer be a need to hunt for a treatment program willing to take a person with an SMI (many programs currently refuse treatment to such individuals when their symptoms are flagrant or their psychiatric history is known) as there would be programs specifically geared towards treating such individuals. Arguably then, there is a clear need to design, implement, and study programs configured to provide integrated treatment services to addicted criminal offenders with comorbid psychiatric disorders.

CONCLUSION

There is growing evidence from a variety of sources that we can no longer focus on single diagnostic entities when designing optimum treatment programs within the criminal justice system. A more sophisticated and potentially productive approach is to consider multiple, concurrent psychological disorders that by current estimates are relatively common among addicted offenders. Much work in this regard needs to be done:

1. Epidemiological studies of at least the same scope and precision as currently apply to large-scale studies of drug abuse are needed. We must determine what percentages of arrestees, detainees, inmates, and probationers have comorbid substance use and psychiatric illnesses and in which combinations.

2. Quick, valid, reliable, and easy to administer and score screening instruments need to be developed that allow for assessment of comorbid conditions and support clinical decision-making.

3. Offenders with comorbid conditions should be treated within integrated services programs with specially trained clinicians and personnel with the acumen and skills to work with an especially difficult patient population.

In implementing a treatment matching strategy for addicted offenders with comorbid psychiatric illnesses, there is an important caveat: Although there are many candidate diagnoses for inclusion as comorbid conditions, caution should be used in extending the diagnostic net too wide until almost any psychiatric condition qualifies.

If ASP is included in the mix, for example, then over half of addicted offenders would be considered comorbid. (For this reason, we would again emphasize our view that a *first step* in implementing integrated services programs more broadly should focus on schizophrenia, bipolar disorder, and major depression because of their relative severity among psychiatric disorders.) Conversely, use of a strategy that emphasizes clinical severity regardless of the specific diagnosis, such as is implemented in the K6/K10 scales, might provide an equally focused treatment matching strategy.

Clearly, this prescription for reconfiguring the current treatment system is a tall order for a criminal justice system that, in aggregate, has difficulty providing even adequate levels of effective substance abuse treatment. Nevertheless, we can not afford to ignore the accumulating evidence that such a redesigned system would likely yield better outcomes than the current one and that any steps we make in the direction of addressing psychiatric comorbidities would make drug treatment that much more effective.

About the Author

James A. Swartz, Ph.D., is an associate professor at the Jane Addams College of Social Work of the University of Illinois at Chicago. He may be contacted by email at jaswartz@uic.edu.

References

Abram, K. M., & Teplin, L. A. (1991). Co-occurring disorders among mentally ill jail detainees. *American Psychologist, 46(10)*, 1036-1045.

American Psychiatric Association [APA]. (2000). Diagnostic and Statistical Manual of Mental Disorders, Revised Third Edition. Washington, DC: Author.

American Psychiatric Association [APA]. (1987). Diagnostic and Statistical Manual of Mental Disorders (4th ed.), Text-Revision. Washington, DC: Author.

Beck, A T., Ward, C. H., Mendelsohn, M., Mock, J. & Erbaugh, J. (1961). An inventory for measuring depression. *Archives of General Psychiatry*, 4, 561-571.

Buckley, P. F. (1998). Substance abuse in schizophrenia: A review. *Journal of Clinical Psychiatry, 59(3)*, 26-30.

Bureau of Justice Statistics [BJS]. (1993). *Survey of state prison inmates, 1991* (U.S. DOJ Publication No. NCJ 136949). Washington, DC: U.S. Government Printing Office.

Bureau of Justice Statistics [BJS]. (1997). *Characteristics of adults on probation, 1995* (U.S. DOJ Publication No. NCJ 164267). Washington, DC: U.S. Government Printing Office.

Bureau of Justice Statistics [BJS]. (1998a). *Substance abuse and treatment of adults on probation, 1995* (U.S. DOJ Publication No. NCJ 166611). Washington, DC: U.S. Government Printing Office.

Bureau of Justice Statistics [BJS]. (1998b). *Profile of jail inmates 1996* (U.S. DOJ Publication No. NCJ 174463). Washington, DC: U.S. Government Printing Office.

Bureau of Justice Statistics [BJS]. (1999). *Mental health and treatment of inmates and probationers* (U.S. DOJ Publication No. NCJ 164620). Washington, DC: U.S. Government Printing Office.

Condelli, W. S. (1994). Domains of variables for understanding and improving retention in therapeutic communities. *The International Journal of the Addictions, 29(5)*, 593-607.

Cournos, F., & McKinnon, K. (1997). HIV seroprevalence among people with severe mental illness in the United States: A critical review. *Clinical Psychology Review, 17(3)*, 259-269.

Derogatis, L.R., Lipman, R. S., & Covi, L. (1973). SCL-90: An outpatient psychiatric rating scale, preliminary report. *Psychopharmacology Bulletin*, 9, 13-28.

Edens, J. F., Peters, R. H., & Hills, H. A. (1997). Treating prison inmates with co-occurring disorders: An integrative review of existing programs. *Behavioral Science and Law, 15(4),* 439-457.

El-Mallakh, P. (1998) Treatment models for clients with co-occurring addictive and mental disorders. *Archives of Psychiatric Nursing, XII(2),* 71-80.

Farabee, D., Prendergast, M., Cartier, J., Wexler, H., Knight, K., & Anglin, M. D. (May/June 2001). Overcoming barriers to implementation of effective correctional drug treatment programs. *Offender Substance Abuse Report, 1(3),* 35-37, 46-47.

Furukawa, T. A., Kessler, R. C., Slade, T., & Andrews, G. (2002). The performance of the K6 and K10 screening scales for psychological distress in the Australian national survey of mental health and well-being. *Psychological Medicine, 33,* 357-362.

Hahn, A., & Swartz, J. A. (2004). *Use of the K6/K10 screening scales for serious psychological distress among arrestees.* Manuscript in preparation.

Hart, S. D., Roesch, R., Corrado, R. R., & Cox, D. N. (1993). The Referral Decision Scale: A validation study. *Law and Human Behavior,* 17, 611-623.

Hepburn, J. R. (1994). Classifying drug offenders for treatment. In D. L. MacKenzie & C. D. Uchida (Eds.), *Drugs and Crime: Evaluating Public Policy Initiatives* (pp. 172-187). Newbury Park, CA: Sage.

Johnson, D. L. (1997). Overview of severe mental illness. *Clinical Psychology Review, 17(3),* 247-257.

Kessler, R. C., Andrews, G., Colpe, L. J., Hiripi, E., Mroczek, D. K., Normand, S. L., et al. (2002). Short screening scales to monitor population prevalences and trends in non-specific psychological distress. *Psychological Medicine, 32,* 959-976.

Kessler, R. C., Andrews, G., Mroczek, D., Ustun, T. B., & Wittchen, H. U. (1998). The World Health Organization Composite International Diagnostic Interview Short-Form (CIDI-SF). *International Journal of Methods in Psychiatric Research,* 7, 171-185.

Kessler, R. C., Barker, P. R., Colpe, L. J., Epstein, J. F., Gfroerer, J. C., Hirpi, E. et al. (2003). Screening for serious mental illness in the general population. *Archives of General Psychiatry, 60(2),* 184-189.

Kessler, R. C., McGonagle, K. A., Zhao, S., Nelson, C. B., Hughes, M., Eshleman, S., Wittchen, H. U., & Kendler, K. S. (1994). Lifetime and 12-month prevalence of DSM-III-R psychiatric disorders in the United States: Results from the national comorbidity study. *Archives of General Psychiatry, 51,* 8-19.

Kessler, R. C., & Walters, E. (2002). The national comorbidity survey. In M. T. Tsuan & M. Tohen (Eds.), *Textbook in psychiatric epidemiology* (2nd. ed., pp. 343-362). New York: John Wiley & Sons.

Lurigio, A. J., Swartz, J. A, Cho, Y. I., Johnson, T., Graf, I., & Pickup, L. (2000). *Alcohol, tobacco, and other drug use among adult probationers in Illinois: Prevalence and treatment need, 2000.* Chicago: Illinois Department of Human Services, Office of Alcoholism and Substance Abuse.

McLellan, A. T., & Alterman, A. I. (1991). Patient treatment matching: A conceptual and methodological review with suggestions for future research. In *Improving drug abuse treatment* (DHHS Publication No. ADM 91-17544, pp. 114-135). Washington, DC: U.S. Department of Health and Human Services.

McLellan, A. T., Kushner, H., Metzger, D., Peters, R., Smith, I., Grissom, G., Pettinati, H., & Argeriou, M. (1992). The fifth edition of the Addiction Severity Index, *Journal of Substance Abuse Treatment, 9,* 199-213.

McLellan, A. T., Luborsky, L., Woody, G. E., O'Brien, C. P., & Kron, R. (1981). Are the "addiction-related" problems of substance abusers really related? *The Journal of Nervous and Mental Disease, 169(4),* 232-239.

Mueser, K. T., Bellack, A. S., & Blanchard, J. J. (1992). Comorbidity of schizophrenia and substance abuse: Implications for treatment. *Journal of Consulting and Clinical Psychology, 60,* 845-856.

Mueser, K. T., Drake, R. E., & Miles, K. M. (1997). The course and treatment of substance use disorders in persons with severe mental illness. In L. S. Onken, J. D. Blaine, S. Genser & A. M. Horton (Eds.), *Treatment of drug-dependent individuals with comorbid mental disorders* (NIH Publication No. 97-4172, pp. 86-109). Washington, DC: U. S. Department of Health and Human Services.

Murphy, J. M.. (2002). Symptom scales and diagnostic schedules in adult psychiatry. In M. T. Tsuang & M. Tohen (Eds.), *Textbook in psychiatric epidemiology* (2nd ed. pp. 273-332), New York: John Wiley & Sons.

National Institute of Justice. (2000). *ADAM 1999 annual report on adult and juvenile arrestees.* Washington, DC: U.S. Government Printing Office.

Overall, J. E., & Gorham, D. R. (1962). The Brief Psychiatric Rating Scale. *Psychological Report, 10,* 799-812.

Peirce, J. C., & Cornell, R. G. (1993). Integrating stratum-specific likelihood ratios with the analysis of ROC curves. *Medical Decision Making, 13(2),* 141-151.

Peters, R. (1993). Drug treatment in jails and detention settings. In J. A. Inciardi (Ed.), *Drug treatment and criminal justice* (pp. 44-80). Beverly Hills, CA: Sage.

Regier, D. A., Farmer, M. E., Rae, D. A., Locke, B. Z., Keith, S. J., Judd, L. L., & Goodwin, F. K. (1990). Comorbidity of mental disorders with alcohol and other drug abuse: Results from the Epidemiological Catchment Area (ECA) Study. *Journal of the American Medical Association, 264(19),* 2511-2518.

Regier, D. A., Kaelber, C. T., Rae, D. S., Farmer, M. E., Knauper, B., Kessler, R. C., & Norquist, G. S. (1998). Limitations of diagnostic criteria and assessment instruments for mental disorders. *Archives of General Psychiatry*, 55(2), 109-115.

Rehm, J., Üstün, T. B., Saxena, S., Nelson, C. B., Chatterji, S., Ivis, F. & Adlaf, E. (1999). On the development and psychometric testing of the WHO screening instrument to assess disablement in the general population. *International Journal of Methods in Psychiatric Research, 8,* 110-123.

Ries, R. K., & Comtois, K. A. (1997). Illness severity and treatment services for dually diagnosed severely mentally ill outpatients. *Schizophrenia Bulletin, 23(2),* 239-246.

Robins, L.N., Helzer, J.E., Croughan J., & Ratcliff, K.S. (1981). National Institute of Mental Health Diagnostic Interview Schedule: Its history, characteristics, and validity. *Archives of General Psychiatry, 38,* 381-389.

Robins, L. N., Wing, J., Wittchen, H. U., Helzer, J. E., Babor, T. F., Burke, J., Farmer, A., Jablenski, A., Pickens, R., Regier, D. A., Sartorius, N., & Towle, L. H. (1988). The Composite International Diagnostic Interview. *Archives of General Psychiatry, 45,* 1069-1077.

Rogers, R., Sewell, K. W., Ulstad, K., Reinhardt, V., & Edwards, W. (1995). The Referral Decision Scale with mentally disordered inmates: A preliminary study of convergent and discriminant validity. *Law and Human Behavior, 19,* 481-492.

Sacks, S., Sacks, J., DeLeon, G., Bernhardt, A. I., & Graham, G. L. (1997). Modified therapeutic community for mentally ill chemical "abusers": Background; influences; program description; preliminary findings. *Journal of Substance Use & Misuse, 32(9),* 1217-1259.

Sheehan, D. V., Lecrubier, Y., Sheehan, K. H., Amorim, P., Janavs, J., Weiller, E., et al. (1998). The Mini-International Neuropsychiatric Interview (MINI): The development and validation of a structured diagnostic psychiatric interview for the DSM-IV and ICD-10. *Journal of Clinical Psychiatry, 59,* 22-33.

Slade, T. B., & Andrews, G. (2002). Empirical impact of DSM-IV diagnostic criterion for clinical significance. The *Journal of Nervous and Mental Disease. 190(5),* 334-337.

Swartz, J. A., & Lurigio, A. J. (1999). Psychiatric illness and comorbidity among adult male detainees in drug treatment. *Psychiatric Services, 50(12),* 1628-1630.

Teplin, L. A. (1990). The prevalence of severe mental disorder among male urban jail detainees: Comparison with the epidemiological catchment area program. *American Journal of Public Health, 80(6),* 663-669.

Teplin, L., & Swartz, J. (1989). Screening for severe mental disorder in jails: The development of the referral decision scale. *Law and Human Behavior, 13(1),* 1 - 18.

Veysey, B. M., Steadman, H. J., Morrisey, J. P., Johnson, M., & Beckstead, J. W. (1998). Using the Referral Decision Scale to screen mentally ill jail detainees: Validity and implementation issues. *Law and Human Behavior, 22(2),* 205-215.

Wexler, H. K. (1994). Progress in prison substance abuse treatment: A five year report. *The Journal of Drug Issues, 24(2),* 349-360.

Wexler, H. K. (1995). The success of therapeutic communities for substance abusers in American prisons. *Journal of Psychoactive Drugs, 27(1),* 57-66.

Woody, G. E., Metzger, D., Navaline, H., McLellan, T., & O'Brien, C. P. (1997). Psychiatric symptoms, risky behavior, and HIV infection. In L. S. Onken, J. D. Blaine, S. Genser, & A. M. Horton (Eds.), *Treatment of drug-dependent individuals with comorbid mental disorders* (NIH Publication No. 97-4172, pp. 156-170). Washington, DC: U. S. Department of Health and Human Services.

Chapter 22

How Psychopathic?
A Critical Consideration
for Offender Treatment

by Henry J. Richards, Ph.D.

Introduction 22-1
Misconceptions and Myths Abound About Psychopathy 22-2
Distinguishing Between Other Personality Disorders and Psychopathy 22-2
The PCL-R and Substance Abusers 22-3
      Scoring. 22-3
      Interpreting PCL Factors in Substance Abusers 22-4
How Psychopaths Differ From Other Offenders 22-5
Age, Gender, and Ethnicity 22-5
Overcoming Obstacles to Integration of Psychopathy Assessment
  Into Substance Abuse Treatment 22-6
      Make All Staff Part of Team 22-6
      Integrate Into Social Learning Model 22-6
      Tie Reliable Testing to Day-to-Day Work. 22-7
Programming and Individualized Treatment Planning for
  Psychopathic Substance Abusers 22-8

INTRODUCTION

Meaningful behaviors, including those comprising substance abuse and criminality, always occur as person-environment interactions. Various approaches to understanding and changing behavior tend to emphasize one side or the other of this interactive equation. Psychopathy is a clinical personality construct with a strong emphasis on the person side of the behavioral equation. By virtue of its empirical predictive power, psychopathy has become a critical variable in building models of criminal offending for use in theory-building, research, the assessment of risk for future offense, and, increasingly, for the planning of treatment interventions (Bodholdt et al., 2000). A decade after

---

An earlier version of this chapter appeared in Offender Substance Abuse Report, *Vol. 3, No. 2, March/April 2003.*

Richards and Montalbano (1993) proposed that routine psychopathy screening and assessment be adopted as part of the emerging consensus on standards of care for substance-involved offenders, the evidence for doing so is stronger than ever.

Psychopathy as a research and clinical construct has become virtually identified with the instrument most commonly used to measure it in clinical settings: the Hare Psychopathy Checklist-Revised (PCL-R; Hare, 1991, 2003). The PCL-R has been developed and validated over two decades through a comprehensive, interdisciplinary, international research program spearheaded by Robert D. Hare of the University of British Columbia. There is also a shorter screening version, the Psychopathy Checklist-Screening Version (PCL:SV) (Hart et al. 1995). Building on a list of clinical criteria and case observations of the psychoanalytic psychiatrist Hervey Cleckley (Cleckley, 1976), Hare and colleagues have created a reliable and valid clinical instrument for identifying psychopathic offenders. Psychopaths differ in important ways from both members of the general public and from other offenders by being at higher risk for general and violent recidivism and by presenting unique supervision and treatment needs.

MISCONCEPTIONS AND MYTHS ABOUND ABOUT PSYCHOPATHY

Anyone who commits an especially egregious crime may be referred to as a "psychopath" in the mass media, which also mistakenly uses "psychopath" as a synonym for any persistent violent offender. The association of psychopathy with violence is merited, but not across the board and without distinctions. Most serial killers are psychopaths, most individuals who kill a police officer fit the psychopath prototype, and among violent offenders, psychopaths are most likely to reoffend with a crime of violence (Hare et al., 2000). On the other hand many violent offenders are not psychopaths and many psychopathic offenders have no violent offenses in their criminal history. While psychopathy is an important variable indicating greater risk for future violence among violent offenders, nonpsychopathic individuals with a history of violence are more at risk for future violence than psychopaths who have not been violent in the past. Another part of the "psychopathy mystique" involves the perception of the psychopath as having higher than average intelligence. Psychopaths may frequently be cunning, grandiose, and deceptive, and these behaviors may serve to convince others that they are bright, but research shows that psychopathy is not strongly related to intelligence.

This chapter discusses the assessment of offenders for psychopathy, and addresses programmatic issues in the treatment of psychopathic substance abuse offenders.

DISTINGUISHING BETWEEN OTHER PERSONALITY DISORDERS AND PSYCHOPATHY

Unfortunately, confusions about psychopathy are perpetuated by a frequently encountered lack of rigor in the use of the terms antisocial personality and sociopath, which are related to, but not synonymous with, psychopathy. These terms can be differentiated by their connections to general theoretical approaches and specific assessment methods. Antisocial personality disorder (APD) is a specific DSM-IV (American Psychiatric Association, 1994) diagnosis that, in keeping with the DSM atheoretical approach, is defined primarily in terms of the early onset of specific, overt criminal or harmful acts and the persistence of this behavior in adulthood. Sociopathy, on the other hand, has its origins in theoretical understandings that emphasize the contribution of social and cultural factors—such as lower-class status, poverty, and subcultural mores—to persistent criminality. As a primarily explanatory, socio-cultural concept, sociopathy lacks the specific criteria for identifying specific individuals as diagnostic cases.

APD as specified in DSM-IV is diagnosed primarily from the combination of early childhood onset of conduct disorder and the continuation of criminal and destructive acts in adulthood. In contrast, the assessment of psychopathy utilizing the PCL-R involves the use of a set of affective, interpersonal, cognitive, and life-style traits. These traits are clinical constructs, rather than concrete criminal or socially egregious acts. The distinction between APD and psychopathy can appear to be hairsplitting until one realizes that large proportions of offenders (from 40% to 70% depending on the setting) meet the criteria for APD, whereas only 10% to 30% meet the more clinical trait criteria for psychopathy. The rate of APD is so high in most settings that it is considered by some to be a "garbage category" of little practical value.

THE PCL-R AND SUBSTANCE ABUSERS

Scoring

The PCL-R is a set of 20 clinical rating items (see Table 22.1) used by appropriately trained clinicians to assess the life-long presence of a trait. Each item is scored 0, 1, or 2, corresponding to whether the trait is not applicable, has limited applicability, or is clearly applicable to the individual. Evidence is gathered from all available records (school, correctional, hospital, arrest, and conviction records, etc.) and, when feasible, a clinical interview. Scores range from 0 to 40, and scores of 30 and higher indicate severe psychopathy. When insufficient data is available, an item is not rated and the scale scores are prorated based on the average of rated items (for valid assessment, only a limited number of such omissions is allowed).

The items of the PCL-R can be grouped into categories, or factors, representing sub-components or aspects of psychopathy. Currently, the PCL-R is scored to produce two highly correlated factor scores in addition to a total score:

- *Factor 1* reflects the core emotional, cognitive, and affective personality aspects of psychopathy, and correlates highly with measures of narcissistic personality disorder. This factor has two sub-scales: Interpersonal and Affective facets of psychopathy.

- *Factor 2* overlaps conceptually with APD, and reflects an impulsive, irresponsible, criminal lifestyle that often involves substance abuse or dependency. Factor 2 is also moderately associated with lower IQ scores. This factor's subscales are Lifestyle and Antisocial facets of psychopathy.

Mathematical techniques for identifying factors and exploration of assessments with different populations (women, racial and ethnic groups) are contributing to both refinements to this model and the development of alternative models.

Interpreting PCL Factors in Substance Abusers

Some special considerations emerge in evaluating the construct validity of psychopathy and interpreting its factors in a substance abusing population. Some psychopathy-like characteristics (particularly those related to Factor 2) could be the result of substance use, acting through either neurological changes or learned interpersonal and affective patterns that make up a drug-using lifestyle, or both. However proper rating of the PCL-R stresses evidence for lifelong patterns of behavior. Doing this makes it possible to draw a distinction between ingrained personality characteristics and more temporary behaviors related to a drug-oriented lifestyle. For example, grandiosity, shallow affect, and lack of empathy that occur only during or immediately after periods of drug abuse, and in the absence of childhood or adolescent precursors (such as unemotional, cold, and callous traits), would not be positively scored on the PCL-R or PCL: SV.

Table 22.1: Clinical Rating Items in the PCL-R

Item	Factor
1. Glibness/superficial charm	1
2. Grandiose sense of self-worth	1
3. Need for stimulation/proneness to boredom	2
4. Pathological lying	1
5. Conning/manipulative	1
6. Lack of remorse or guilt	1
7. Shallow affect	1
8. Callous/lack of empathy	1
9. Parasitic lifestyle	2
10. Poor behavioral controls	2
11. Promiscuous sexual behavior	—
12. Early behavioral problems	2
13. Lack of realistic long-term goals	2
14. Impulsivity	2
15. Irresponsibility	2
16. Failure to accept responsibility for own actions	1
17. Many short-term marital relationships	—
18. Juvenile delinquency	2
19. Revocation of conditional release	2
20. Criminal versatility	—

HOW PSYCHOPATHS DIFFER FROM OTHER OFFENDERS

Psychopaths differ from both the general population and from non-psychopathic offenders on a wide range of behaviors (Hare, 1991). For example, psychopaths are less responsive to distress cries of children and adults (Blair et al., 1997), and to the recognition and attribution of emotion in others (Herpertz & Sass, 2000). Medical imaging (fMRI) of the brains of psychopaths performing a verbal task with emotionally charged words shows dramatic differences from the functioning of the normal brain (Kiehl et al., 2001). The psychopathic brains demonstrate processing primarily in fairly primitive areas involving recognition and categorization of stimuli as either threats or rewards. The brains of non-psychopaths, including offenders low on the PCL-R, tend to involve many more areas of the brain, engaging areas dedicated to memory, abstraction, and complex emotions. Interestingly, the brains of individuals with histories of social deprivation and substance abuse show functioning that is intermediate between that of psychopaths and normals. Psychopaths also differ in the way they relate to themselves, being highly narcissistic (Richards & McCamant, 1996) and more likely to engage in self-deceptive enhancement, i.e., the denial of faults or weaknesses (Paulhus, 1998). The latter point has implications for substance abuse treatment in regard to the denial of substance abuse-related problems. Incarcerated psychopaths are also more likely to be involved in institutional misbehavior (Edens et al., 2001). After release, psychopaths are more likely to recidivate, to recidivate violently, and to commit premeditated, instrumental violent crimes, as opposed to engaging in expressive, emotion-driven, or impulsive violence (Hare et al., 2000).

Psychopaths treated during incarceration adjust poorly to the therapeutic environment whether in prison therapeutic communities (TCs; Hobson et al., 2000) or forensic hospitals (Reiss et al., 1999). At least some forms of treatment of psychopaths may be counterproductive—e.g., one study found that psychopaths treated in a TC recidivated more rapidly and more violently than psychopaths that had not received treatment (Ogloff et al., 1990). Although the program examined in this study used extreme methods that are no longer typical of TCs, the finding of negative to poor treatment response has been replicated in other programs, utilizing other treatment approaches, including education, vocational training, cognitive behavioral therapy, and substance abuse specific treatments. For example, psychopathy scores have been found to predict higher rates of positive urinalysis findings for cocaine and benzodiazepine use among clients in methadone maintenance programs (Alterman et al., 1998).

AGE, GENDER, AND ETHNICITY

Psychopathy appears to be valid across the lifespan. Although personality disorders are not diagnosable in individuals younger than age 18, some children with conduct disorder and delinquency demonstrate callous-unemotional traits that may be precursors to adult psychopathy (Frick et al., 2001). For older youth, a version of the psychopathy checklist has been in the pilot phase for the last several years, and soon should be generally available. The post-release performance of psychopathic offenders, in contrast to other offenders, does not improve with age and psychopathic offenders are more likely to be violent later in their careers (Hare et al., 1988; Porter et al., 2001).

Although numerous studies support the reliability and validity of the PCL-R with white North American adult offenders there are fewer studies of its generalizability to African Americans and women. African-American male psychopaths do not demonstrate the same pattern of cognitive deficits found in their white counterparts (Newman & Schmitt, 1998). Nonetheless, PCL-R scores predict recidivism among African-American offenders (Hare, 1991).

A recent review concluded that PCL-R assessments with institutionalized and non-institutionalized women are reliable and internally consistent, and that severe psychopathy is less frequent among female offenders (11% to 16%) than male offenders (15% to 30%) (Vitale & Newman, 2001). In a large substance abuse treatment efficacy study of women treated in a prison (over 400 participants), psychopathy scores were significantly associated with poor treatment response in regard to program retention, removal for serious noncompliance, violent and disruptive rule violations, avoidance of urinalysis testing, treatment module attendance, and therapist ratings (Richards et al., 2003). Survival analysis of community outcome data revealed that psychopathy scores (particularly Factor 1 scores) predicted new charges in the community better than a combination of other variables, including time in treatment and type of treatment (TC versus assessment-driven treatment). Since over 60% of the participants of this study were African American, its findings lend support for the ethnic and gender generalizability of the psychopathy as a valid treatment-relevant variable.

OVERCOMING OBSTACLES TO INTEGRATION OF PSYCHOPATHY ASSESSMENT INTO SUBSTANCE ABUSE TREATMENT

Make All Staff Part of Team

Resistance to acknowledging the legitimacy and importance of psychopathy as a risk and treatment factor stems, in part, from the fear that overemphasis of psychopathy could result in marginalizing social, environmental, and cognitive factors. Also, there may be cultural barriers to incorporating the "diagnosis" of psychopathy into offender treatment. Some addictions and corrections professionals may view the psychopathy concept as an overextension of the medical model. Faith-based thinkers might protest that psychopathy implies a limit to the God-given freedom and responsibilities of the person. Psychopathy can be used to justify therapeutic nihilism (Meloy, 1988), the belief that there is no hope for some offenders.

Power and status issues are also evoked by implementation of psychopathy assessment. Staff may also feel that use of the PCL-R will result in the abdication of authority to make key decisions to a few psychologists or other professionals with training in narrow "clinical" disciplines that have historically remained distant from direct intervention and recovery activities. Staff members do not feel left out or professionally invalidated when they are appropriately trained to recognize psychopathic traits and when their behavioral observations are treated as important assessment data (Hare, 1996).

Integrate Into Social Learning Model

The clinical focus of psychopathy can be integrated within the dominant institutional and community corrections paradigm, which, with the exception of co-occurring programs, is usually not clinical, but often follows a social learning model. This model explains persistent criminal offending as resulting primarily from the "Big Four"— antisocial cognitions, antisocial associates, antisocial personality complex, and history of criminal behavior (Andrews & Bonta, 1994). Three of the four can be targets of intervention. This model's emphasis on "stinking thinking," and the power of people, places, and things (disinhibitors such as drugs) resonates well with addictions professionals and people in recovery. Psychopathy can be viewed as a further refinement of the personality component of this model. Psychopathic offenders will, on average, be high on the other risk factors as well, but this does not reduce the importance of assessment. For example, moderate to highly psychopathic offenders with active criminal associates are reasonably at greater risk than offenders with similar levels of psychopathy who are surrounded by pro-recovery, pro-social peers. Psychopaths whose resentment and distrust of authority may stem more from a basic self-centeredness and desire for dominance, rather than from negative experiences with negligent or abusive authority figures, may not be able or willing to jettison this basic automatic attitude. Nevertheless, they may be helped to accept that substance use has been more punishing and depriving than rewarding, and to respect a specific program or counselor enough to profit from their guidance and treatment.

Tie Reliable Testing to Day-to-Day Work

Practical obstacles also arise in implementing psychopathy assessment in offender substance abuse programs. Due to competing demands on staff time and the ongoing training investment required to create and maintain program capacity to perform reliable ratings, there is often a temptation to find shortcuts to even the brief screening version of the PCL-R. Although a few self-report measures designed to measure psychopathy do correlate moderately with PCL-R scores, to date none of these methods are adequate replacements for the PCL-R. The fact that psychopathic individuals are likely to be deceptive in their test-taking style and to minimize and deny problems suggests that self-report inventories are unlikely to be very effective in accurately measuring psychopathy in other than pure research conditions, where offenders have little reason to manipulate test results.

The PCL-R should be rated and interpreted under the direction of a psychologist with appropriate training. Even with this kind of oversight, reliable PCL-R ratings are more the result of intensive standardized training in doing the ratings than a function of years of education or degrees earned. Nonetheless, many jurisdictions and programs will opt to reserve this task for licensed or certified clinicians, which will limit the availability of the assessments. Record review for the PCL-R can average an hour and a half, which when combined with a clinical interview increases the time needed to over two hours. The PCL:SV or Screening Version can be used to screen cases in about half an hour, with individuals scoring over a cut-off receiving a PCL-R assessment. Also, PCL-R assessments can be limited to individuals requesting admission to programs involving alternatives to incarceration. In these cases the ratings help to insure that the offender is likely to profit from the treatment without sabotaging or undermining therapeutic opportunities for others, and that he or she will not present undue risk to the community related to psychopathy. For example, for several years,

Maryland's DOC used an assessment unit of counselors to administer the PCL-R and the ASI as a two-pronged criminal risk and addiction need assessment combination, for entry to its Correctional Options Program (COP) and other alternatives to incarceration. Addiction counselors and community corrections supervisors consistently reported that these assessments were extremely valuable in conducting their day-to-day work with offenders.

PROGRAMMING AND INDIVIDUALIZED TREATMENT PLANNING FOR PSYCHOPATHIC SUBSTANCE ABUSERS

In addition to demonstrating the ability to reliably rate the PCL-R based on the synthesis of record review and clinical interview data, appropriate training of raters includes an in-depth understanding of the relevant theory, contemporary research, and implications of these for practice. Once this is accomplished, psychopathy scores can be integrated into program decision-making and treatment planning. As a minimum, I recommend the following:

- *Provide Individualized Feedback to Participants.* Explain the implications of their psychopathy assessment for substance abuse treatment and recovery. Don't give feedback in isolation, but in the context of the participant's other characteristics, including strengths. Focus feedback on change and relapse prevention for specific psychopathy-related behaviors such as entitlement, impulsivity, proneness to boredom, and deception.

- *Be Consistent.* Consistent structure is critical for offenders with even moderate psychopathy. The treatment approach should be compatible with the responsivity principle (Bonta, 1995). Offenders who score high on the PCL-R (total score of 30 or higher, or over 10 on Factor 1) have attachment deficits. Their treatment should not rely extensively on bonding, interpersonal trust, and identification with a group, or with an altruistic value system.

- *Avoid Using Emotionally Charged Verbal Confrontation to Motivate and Engage Psychopaths.* Confrontation is highly stimulating and rewards the psychopath's tendency to view interactions as power-oriented. Instead, identify practical, rewarding consequences of treatment progress and use self-relevant information and activities. Structure program participation to minimize activities that compete with treatment. Honestly assess whether the treatment activities are inherently interesting and engaging.

- *Provide Frank Indoctrination in Goals of Skill Building.* Social skills training, e.g., must be explained as intended to help the offender to attain goals through engaging in mutuality, rather than as a means to manipulate others. Discussions of empathy are optimally directed at helping offenders to objectively understand the natural consequences of their crimes—their becoming the object of retribution, suspicion, and distrust—rather than on inducing guilt, remorse, or otherwise helping them to subjectively "appreciate" the significance of the harms they have inflicted on others or on society as a whole.

- *Don't Use Process-Oriented Group Therapy for Psychopaths Unless Consciously Undertaken as Adjunct to More Structured, Directive Interventions.* A process-group with psychopaths that emphasizes therapist and participant feedback regarding interpersonal behavior is particularly useful for refining treatment goals and ongoing assessment of progress.

- *Staff Must Protect the Program.* Staff should be trained to recognize psychopathic subversion of treatment goals and values and must be alert for signs of physical or emotional intimidation such as divulging (or threatening to divulge) the therapeutic self-disclosures of others, or otherwise exploiting the therapy situation, such as using it as a place to sell drugs or recruit for sexual partners.

- *Organize Staff for Team Decision-Making and Open Sharing of Multiple Perspectives on Offender Progress.* Residential or custodial staff may have unique access to behavior that is masked during formal treatment sessions. Foster mutual support, professional feedback, and cohesiveness among staff to prevent splitting, isolation, and manipulation of staff members. (Staff members are recurrently vulnerable to falling into romantic, sexual, advocate, "rescuer," or other inappropriate special roles with psychopaths. Psychopaths gradually compromise staff members by encouraging subtle, at first apparently harmless, changes in role definitions and professional/personal boundaries. Discussing *Without Conscience: The Disturbing World Of the Psychopaths Amongst Us* (Hare, 1993) is an ideal staff-building exercise that will set the stage for detecting these shifts.)

- *Don't Let Psychopaths Subvert Leadership Roles.* Psychopathic offenders will often manipulate to gain unofficial or formal mentoring and leadership roles in treatment programs and self-help organizations. These individuals are rarely able to manage these roles responsibly. At best, they will use such roles to avoid addressing their own problems while focusing on the liabilities or weakness of others.

- *Consider Day Treatment.* Depending upon the precipitating events, the psychopathic participant who is disruptive to a residential program environment but not to therapist-led treatment sessions might profit from conditional participation as a day-treatment therapy "commuter" while housed in the general population.

- *Avoid Stigma.* Stigmatizing the psychopathic offender is a negative and counterproductive form of stereotyping. Staff should be "data-based" in their descriptions of offender behavior and not simply blanket the participant as "a psychopath." Analysis of the PCL-R item scores for the individual with a manual in hand (a revision will soon be available) is invaluable for adding specificity to observations. The frequency and severity of conning, lying, impulsive angry responding, callous acts, and self-aggrandizing can be decreased though an ongoing cycle of consistent identification and intervention.

- *If Program Is Large Enough, Consider Separate Treatment Track for Highly Psychopathic Individuals.* Offenders who are not highly psychopathic gain little from being in groups with those who are. In these mixed settings, psychopaths are more likely to attempt to simulate normal behavior and to be seen as leaders. In the process, they undermine the treatment of others—sometimes unwittingly— due to their limited buy-in and their cold, callous approach to emotional issues. In homogeneous groups of psychopaths, these offenders can more legitimately take on leadership roles.

- *Stay Up to Date.* Organize a committee that will keep your staff informed of the latest developments in the assessment and treatment of psychopathy by routinely checking key journals and websites and providing a summary at staff meetings.

About the Author

Henry J. Richards, Ph.D., is Assistant Research Professor, Department of Psychiatry and Behavioral Sciences, University of Washington School of Medicine. He may be reached by email at: hrichard@u.washington.edu

References

Alterman, A. I., Rutherford, M. J., Cacciola, J. S., McKay, J. R., & Boardman, C. R. (1998). Prediction of 7-month methadone maintenance treatment response by four measures of antisociality. *Drug & Alcohol Dependence, 49* (3), 217-223.

Andrews, D.A., & Bonta, J. (1994). *The Psychology of Criminal Conduct.* Cincinnati, OH: Anderson Publishing.

American Psychiatric Association. (1994). *Diagnostic and statistical manual of mental disorders* (4th ed.). Washington, DC: Author.

Blair, R. J. R., Jones, L., Clark, F., & Smith, M. (1997). The psychopathic individual: A lack of responsiveness to distress cues? *Psychophysiology, 34,* 192-198.

Bonta, J. (1995). The responsivity principle and offender rehabilitation. *Forum on Correctional Research, 7,* 34-37.

Bodholdt, R. H., Richards, H. J., & Gacono, C. B. (2000). Assessing psychopathy in adults: The Psychopathy Checklist—Revised and Screening Version. In C. B. Gacono (Ed.), *The clinical and forensic assessment of psychopathy: A practitioner's guide* (pp.55-86). Mahwah, NJ: Lawrence Erlbaum Associates.

Cleckley, H. (1976). *The Mask of Sanity.* 5th edition. St. Louis, MO: Mosby.

Edens, J. F., Poythress, N. G., & Lilienfeld, S. O. (1999). Identifying inmates at risk for disciplinary infractions: A comparison of two measures of psychopathy. *Behavioral Sciences and the Law, 17,* 435-443.

Frick, P. J., Barry, C. T., & Bodin, S. D. (2001). Applying the concept of psychopathy to children: Implications for the assessment of antisocial youth. In C. B. Gacono (Ed.), *The clinical and forensic assessment of psychopathy: A practitioner's guide.* (pp.3-24). Mahwah, NJ: Lawrence Erlbaum Associates.

Hare, R. D. (1991). *The Hare Psychopathy Checklist — Revised.* Toronto, Ontario: MultiHealth Systems.

Hare, R. D. (1993). *Without conscience: The disturbing world of the psychopaths among us.* New York: Simon & Schuster.

Hare, R. D. (1996). Psychopathy: A clinical construct whose time has come. *Criminal Justice and Behavior, 23,* 25-54.

Hare, R. D. (2003) *Hare Psychopathy Checklist-Revised* (PCL-R) (2nd Ed.) North Tonawanda, NY: MultiHealth Systems.

Hare, R. D., Clark, D., Grann, M., & Thornton, D. (2000). Psychopathy and the predictive validity of the PCL-R: An international perspective. *Behavioral Sciences & the Law, 18*(5), 623-645.

Hare, R., McPherson, L., & Forth, A. (1988). Male psychopaths and their criminal careers. *Journal of Consulting & Clinical Psychology, 56,* 741-747.

Hart, S. D., Cox, D. N., & Hare, R. D. (1995). *Manual for the Psychopathy Checklist: Screening Version (PCL:SV).* Toronto: Multi-Health Systems.

Herpertz, S. C., & Sass, H. (2000). Emotional deficiency and psychopathy. *Behavioral Sciences & the Law, 18*(5), 567-580.

Hobson, J., Shine, J., & Roberts, R. (2000). How do psychopaths behave in a prison therapeutic community. *Psychology, Crime & Law, 6*(2), 139-154.

Kiehl, K.A., Smith, A.M., Hare, R.D., Forster, B.B., & Liddle, P.F. (2001). Limbic abnormalities in affective processing in criminal psychopaths as revealed by functional magnetic resonance imaging. *Biological Psychiatry, 50*, 677-684.

Kroner, D. G., & Mills, J. (2001). The accuracy of five risk appraisal instruments in predicting institutional misconduct and new convictions. *Criminal Justice & Behavior, 28*(4), 471-489.

Meloy, J. R. (1988). *The psychopathic mind: Origins, dynamics, and treatments.* Northvale, NJ: Jason Aronson.

Newman, J. P., & Schmitt, W. (1998). Passive avoidance learning in psychopathic offenders: A replication and extension. *Journal of Abnormal Psychology, 107*, 527-532.

Ogloff, J., Wong, S., & Greenwood, A. (1990). Treating criminal psychopaths in a therapeutic community program. *Behavioral Sciences & the Law, 8*, 81-90.

Paulhus, D. L. (1998). *Paulhus Deception Scales: BIDR 7 User's Manual.* North Tonawanda, NY: MultiHealth Systems.

Porter, S. Birt, A. R., & Boer, D. P. (2001). Report on the criminal and conditional release profiles of Canadian federal offenders as a function of psychopathy and age. *Law and Human Behavior, 25*, 647-662.

Reiss, D., Grubin D., & Meux, C. (1999). Institutional performance of male "psychopaths" in a high-security hospital. *Journal of Forensic Psychiatry, 10*(2), 290-299.

Richards, H. J., & Montalbano, P. (1993). Psychopathy, criminality, and substance abuse. In H. J. Richards (Ed.), *Therapy of the substance abuse syndromes.* (pp.287-345). Northvale, NJ: Jason Aronson Publishers.

Richards, H. J., Casey, J. O., & Lucente, S. W. (2003). Psychopathy and treatment response in incarcerated female substance abusers. *Criminal Justice & Behavior, 30*(2), 251-276.

Richards, H. J., & McCamant, K. (1996). Narcissism and psychopathy: Concurrent validity of the PCL-R, the Rorschach and the MCMI. *Issues in Criminological & Legal Psychology, 24*, 131-135.

Vitale, J. E., & Newman, J. P. (2001). Using the Psychopathy Checklist-Revised with female samples: Reliability, validity, and implications for clinical utility. *Clinical Psychology: Science & Practice, 8*(1), 117-132.

Chapter 23

Treating Substance Abuse Clients with Co-Occurring Intimate Partner Violence

by Robert Walker, M.S.W., L.C.S.W., and TK Logan, Ph.D.

High Rate of Co-Occurrence 23-1
Need for Screening and Special Treatment Planning 23-2
IPV Offender Typologies 23-2
Other Clinical Characteristics of IPV Offenders 23-3
      Personality Disorders 23-3
      Depression 23-4
      PTSD 23-4
Screening and Assessment Strategies and Issues for
  Substance Abuse Treatment Providers 23-4
      Contextualized Questioning 23-4
      Victim Input 23-5
      Risk Assessment 23-5
Treatment Selection 23-6
      Safety Planning 23-6
      What to Treat First? 23-7
      Structured Treatment for IPV 23-7
      Integrated Treatment or Referral Approaches 23-8
      No Mixed-Gender Groups 23-8
Community Resources and Linkages 23-8
Clinician Training and Supervision 23-9
Future Program Development 23-9

HIGH RATE OF CO-OCCURRENCE

Estimates suggest that 50% or more of men in treatment for alcohol abuse or dependence have also perpetrated intimate partner violence (IPV) within the past 12 months (Chermack et al., Fuller & Blow, 2000; O'Farrell & Murphy, 1995). The high preva-

This chapter originally appeared in Offender Substance Abuse Report, *Vol. 4, No. 3, May/June 2004.*

lence rate of IPV among males in substance abuse treatment suggests that substance abuse programs may be an important setting for identifying and treating or referring offenders. Recent research (Schumaker et al., 2003) has confirmed that screening and assessing male substance abuse clients for intimate partner violence will identify substantial percentages of men with these problems. In fact, the prevalence of intimate partner violence among male substance abusers is probably high enough to warrant a presumption of the problem, just as women in substance abuse treatment can be presumed to have victimization histories. In spite of the high prevalence of these problems in treatment populations, however, substance abuse treatment programs rarely address perpetration patterns or consider them in addition to substance use disorders.

Studies suggest that between 25% and 80% of intimate partner violence offenders are alcohol abusing or dependent (Collins et al, 1997); however, there are complex relationships between substance abuse and partner violence. Some studies have examined alcohol abuse and intimate partner violence but there is no definitive picture of cause/effect relationships between the two. Even less information is available on the role of specific drugs with partner violence. In the absence of research findings, many clinicians may rely on practice experience or program guidelines to direct practice when clients disclose partner violence perpetration.

NEED FOR SCREENING AND SPECIAL TREATMENT PLANNING

In substance abuse treatment settings there is a tendency to understand violence as secondary to substance use—along with a concomitant belief that if the substance abuse problem is reduced, then violence will likewise disappear. This belief is unsupported by research. In fact, this belief may even make matters worse because, when communicated to clients, it provides a handy rationalization for their violent conduct. Furthermore, the idea that substance abuse treatment alone can reduce violence may create a false expectation of increased safety among victims who place exaggerated hopes on substance abuse recovery. Likewise, this belief can lead courts to refer violent men to substance abuse treatment under the false notion that a short residential or outpatient episode will address long-term patterns of IPV. It is critical for substance abuse treatment programs to develop greater expertise at identifying and either treating or referring clients who present with partner violence victimization.

The identification of clients with co-occurring violence perpetration and substance abuse or dependence can result in program and treatment goals that may be more complex than traditional treatment goals. Overall treatment planning will have to address both violence risk reduction and reduction of substance use and other related problems. This chapter reviews steps a program can take to better screen for, assess, and treat substance abusers with co-occurring domestic violence perpetration.

IPV OFFENDER TYPOLOGIES

Intimate partner violence offenders have been studied to learn more about general types or categories of behavior based primarily on overall aggression patterns. The broadest classifications identify antisocial offenders who are "generally" violent and perpetrate violence against family members as well as others. Holtzworth-Munroe and

Stuart (1994) developed a basic offender typology consisting of three main types from the literature on offenders: (1) family-only offenders; (2) dysphoric-borderline offenders; and (3) generally violent antisocial offenders.

This classification of offender types has been widely shared in clinical training, but the science on it is still limited. Holtzworth-Munroe et al. (2003) studied the typologies after 1.5 and three years to observe the stability of these three types over time. One of the questions was whether the types might represent different phases on a temporal continuum rather than stable character types. This study showed that the three major types remained relatively stable over time, suggesting that those with higher levels of violence (borderlines and generally violent males) at baseline remain more violent over time than the family-only type (Holtzworth-Munroe, et al., 2003). Findings relating to the persistence of antisocial traits are consistent with the extensive research on childhood conduct disorder and its development into adult aggression and substance abuse (Magdol et al., 1998).

The types of targeted victims also can be important in distinguishing different offender types. This criterion differentiates between offenders whose violence is directed generally toward others, including strangers and acquaintances, or toward family members (Holtzworth-Munroe & Stuart, 1994; Saunders, 1992). Researchers note that offenders who are more generally violent have been found to engage in more severe violence than family-only men (Holtzworth-Munroe & Stuart, 1994). Hence, clients who appear to be more generally violent should be assessed for severity and frequency of violent acts. Also the 2003 study suggested that there was a fourth type—a "low-level" antisocial type (Holtzworth-Munroe, et al., 2003). All four of these "types" are likely to be found in substance abuse treatment programs.

OTHER CLINICAL CHARACTERISTICS OF IPV OFFENDERS

There are several mental disorders in addition to substance abuse that are commonly found among intimate partner violence offenders, including personality disorders, depression, and posttraumatic stress disorder (PTSD). These three disorders have considerable co-occurrence and share a general likelihood of emotional instability. With many substance abuse treatment programs addressing dual diagnosis concerns, there is increasing likelihood of encountering clients with multiple co-occurring problems including mental health and violence issues. Awareness of the association of mental health problems with violence and substance abuse may sensitize assessment and treatment professionals about the extent and degree of violence among clinical populations.

Personality Disorders

Male IPV perpetrators may have personality disorders, including borderline personality disorder (BPD) and antisocial personality disorder (ASPD) (Hamberger & Hastings, 1988; Hamberger & Hastings, 1991). This is not surprising since criteria for both of these disorders include social and relationship disturbances (APA, 2000). Men with IPV are more likely to have BPD than men who are in conflictual but non-violent relationships (Murphy, Meyer & O'Leary, 1993). However, other research has found a low percentage of batterers with BPD, but a high percentage of batterers with narcissistic and antisocial traits (Gondolf, 1999). ASPD may be present in only a portion of intimate partner violence offenders, but these men may also represent a particularly dangerous type of offender. An important study of violent couples (excluding those with only pushing or shoving incidents) identified a group of males with far greater stealth in their perpetration; the researchers called this group "cobras" for their cold and calculating approach to violence (Gottman et al., 1995; Jacobson & Gottman, 1998).

Depression

IPV offenders have high levels of depression, with greater depression linked to higher levels of aggression (Maiuro et al., 1988; Pan et al., 1994). When depression is accompanied by hostility, the risk of aggression is even greater. This would suggest that clinicians might need to re-think how depression is assessed and treated in substance abuse programs. The stereotypical idea of a sad or withdrawn depression may be very different from the mood disorder of IPV offenders. Most importantly, the presence of depression in IPV offenders may predict violence toward others in the family including children (Flett & Hewlitt, 2002).

PTSD

Dutton Saunders, Starzomsky, and Bartholomew (1994) have also examined attachment disorders and trauma related symptoms among batterers. They identified disrupted attachment and excessive fear of rejection or abandonment in batterers, and the idea of attachment disorder may help explain offenders' dependency and jealousy regarding their partners. Men with IPV often tend to be more dependent on their partners than men with disturbed relationships who are non-violent (Murphy et al., 1993). Dutton and colleagues (1994) reported that attachment problems may be related to trauma symptoms and borderline personality organization. Trauma symptoms among IPV offenders raise an additional clinical problem for most mental health professionals. PTSD and trauma suggest a treatment approach using empathy and support whereas treatment for offender behavior generally suggests a more confrontive and focused approach.

SCREENING AND ASSESSMENT STRATEGIES AND ISSUES FOR SUBSTANCE ABUSE TREATMENT PROVIDERS

Contextualized Questioning

Within the substance abuse assessment process, substance abuse clinicians should include questions about clients' criminal conduct (generally in the context of substance use) and about general violence as well as intimate partner violence. The Conflict Tactics Scale (CTS; Straus et al. 1996) provides an introductory script that clinicians will find useful as an entrée to domestic violence screening questions. It contextualizes these questions by describing couples having conflict and experiencing specific aggressive acts either as a perpetrator or victim. This framework can be adapted in screening by having clinicians state, "When you have been in conflict with your partner (either in the past or now), have you ever found yourself losing control of your temper?" "Have you ever found yourself being more physical about your anger with your partner?" "Have you ever engaged in sex that others might describe as rough or forced?" When these questions are contextualized within the substance use questions, and prefaced with a "couples conflict" theme, clients may endorse these behaviors. Clients who endorse these items should be assessed thoroughly for violence perpetration.

Clinicians may question the validity of self-reports of substance use and violent behavior. However, research has long supported the validity of this approach for substance use (Del Boca & Noll, 2000; Rutherford et al., 2000). Clearly, the context of interviews can influence reliability (Babor et al., 1987) but even at the beginning of treatment self-reports have been shown to be reliable (Rutherford et al., 2000). Concern about deception in self-reports is most likely when the clinician is viewed as closely affiliated with the courts, probation, or parole systems. In domestic violence offender treatment, these associations may further affect the validity of client self-reports. Research on self-report information about partner violence perpetration is limited (Heckert & Gondolf, 2000). Current research suggests that men underreport based on situational factors such as their beliefs or desire to keep the relationship, rather than because of psychopathology or impression management (Heckert & Gondolf, 2000). However, self-report remains the most accessible means of data collection—particularly among clinical populations.

Assessment for intimate partner violence is two-fold; it focuses on information about the specific kinds of abuse committed and risk assessment information about the likelihood of future violence toward a partner. For collecting basic information about IPV perpetration, clinicians can use the perpetration items from the Conflict Tactics Scale (Straus et al., 1996). These questions will address physical, sexual, and emotional abuse, but do not cover stalking, which has been shown to be a variant of IPV (Logan et al., 2001). Questions about IPV should be presented to substance abuse clients in a matter-of-fact manner, and with benign persistence, because denial can be even more entrenched for violence than for drug use. The CTS, if used as directed gives frequency information within the past year. Clinicians can use similar questions to the CTS for lifetime information to get a better understanding of how long clients have been violent with partners.

Victim Input

While difficult on clinical and legal grounds, clinicians who have talked with victims will have far more complete information for assessing degree of lethality and overall risk for violence among IPV perpetrators. Confidentiality can be very difficult to manage when integrating victim information into an assessment or into treatment. However, due to IPV client denial and rationalization, clinicians rarely have a valid picture of IPV without victim information.

Risk Assessment

The second part of the assessment is a risk assessment to estimate how violent clients are and how likely they are to re-offend. As with other risk assessment approaches, a history of violence can be used to estimate future likelihood of violence. However, there are other factors that should be considered including:

- *Childhood conduct disorder*—clients with early conduct disorder are far more likely to be aggressive and antisocial in adulthood and these traits appear to be largely unaffected by interventions in childhood or later;

- *Overall history of aggression*—either in general or specifically with partners;

- *Exposure to violence as a child*—clients may be "socialized" into IPV during formative years;

- *Specific drug use pattern*—while most clients are polydrug users, use of alcohol and stimulants (including cocaine) has the greatest likelihood for adding to the lethality risk; while alcohol and others drugs do not cause violence, they can greatly increase the physical harm during violent acts;

- *Extreme jealousy or paranoia*—jealousy can be a motivating factor for greater attempted control over the victim and can also motivate stalking behavior;

- *Co-occurring mental disorders*—depression, personality disorders, PTSD; and

- *Relationship status*—when women separate from their partners, the risk for violence is greatest. In addition, if the offender believes his partner is having an affair, risk is heightened.

TREATMENT SELECTION

After clients have been screened and assessed for IPV, clinicians can document their findings in the clinical record. However, they should remember that as substance abuse treatment progresses, clients may disclose violence later in treatment, thus calling for re-assessment of the IPV problem. If clients are assessed as having a serious IPV problem, the program should have alternative service plans available. Programs should not consider using traditional substance abuse treatment as a "catch-all" that will solve IPV problems along with other substance abuse problems.

Safety Planning

When clients have been assessed for IPV, safety planning should begin immediately. In addition, safety planning needs to be a continuing focus throughout treatment. Safety planning is very different for offenders than for victims. With victims, safety planning is devoted to avoiding the offender or establishing contingencies such as law enforcement or other criminal justice interventions for managing crises. With offenders, safety planning is a method for reducing the likelihood of committing violent acts and of reducing the harm caused by aggressive behavioral styles. In essence, safety planning is a contingency strategy (Gondolf, 2000a). Safety planning, as used in substance abuse programs can be compared to relapse prevention and these approaches (trigger awareness, alternative strategies, etc.) can be modified to focus on safety issues. Safety planning also teaches social skills for inhibiting impulses. A commonly used safety skill is the "time-out"—an approach for showing clients how to walk away from potentially violent situations. Timeouts and related methods are not treatment for the causes of violence but they can contain it and make the situation safer as treatment progresses (Wexler, 2000). In fact, 53% of men who actually avoid re-assaulting their partners after treatment have used methods like time-outs (Gondolf, 2000a).

What to Treat First?

The classic dilemma for programs with clients who have co-occurring disorders is "what should be treated first?" Current literature suggests that integrated treatment is optimal—that is, one clinician treating both conditions simultaneously or at least two clinicians in close consultation at every step in the treatment process (Minkoff, 2001; Minkoff & Regner, 1999). In substance abuse treatment, IPV presents a more difficult challenge, however, because the typical treatment plan for IPV is as time-consuming and as lengthy as substance abuse treatment. As a general rule, when clients have been assessed with substance abuse and IPV, programs should treat substance abuse first without focusing on IPV only if clients are clearly substance dependent and cannot detoxify for long enough to begin more complex treatment. In these cases, clients should be placed in inpatient or residential treatment until they are stable enough to utilize outpatient treatment. Treatment for IPV problems should not be initiated until clients are cognitively clear enough to process interpersonal information.

Clients who are assessed with substance abuse, but not dependence, can begin receiving treatment that simultaneously addresses IPV and substance abuse. However, the focus should be primarily on substance abuse until clients demonstrate sufficient cognitive clarity to make the associations between violence and substance use and other triggers. Once substance abuse treatment has begun making progress, clients should be offered either a referral to a structured IPV treatment program or be included in IPV treatment within the substance abuse program.

Structured Treatment for IPV

Structured intervention programs for domestic violence offenders were started over two decades ago because of a lack of appropriate interventions for IPV. Structured group psychoeducational approaches are focused on IPV and related behaviors and thinking errors. Most use a standardized content or "curriculum." These structured programs also work closely with the court systems that refer men into treatment. The most widely discussed model of IPV treatment is the "Duluth model." Like many substance abuse programs, the Duluth program, the Domestic Abuse Intervention Project (DAIP), focuses on the legal system as a key component to effective reduction of violence and programs for offenders (Pence, 2002; see also Aldarondo & Mederos, 2002). The Duluth approach uses education and video scenarios to start client discussion on how situations could be handled without violence. In addition, structured group approaches for IPV use client self-report logs to track control issues and actions. Structured programs confront beliefs that support violence, such as negative or demeaning views of women; however, the specific efficacy of this kind of treatment for IPV has not yet been studied.

Group treatment for IPV, like that for substance abuse, has become the most common form of intervention for many of the same reasons that it has been used in substance abuse treatment. Group approaches expand the social networks of IPV offenders in order to support nonviolence (much like self-help), as well as providing offenders the opportunity to learn as well at teach others (Edleson & Tolman, 1992). While research has not been able to show the efficacy of any specific group treatment, it does provide limited support for overall program effectiveness (Gondolf, 2000b).

Integrated Treatment or Referral Approaches

Ideally, substance abuse programs would incorporate IPV issues into their overall treatment approach. However, few substance abuse programs can afford to provide a full course of IPV, given that most IPV programs last for six months. Programs can refer clients to IPV programs during and after substance abuse treatment, based on client progress and need. At a minimum, substance abuse treatment programs should screen and assess for IPV and offer a brief course of safety planning interventions. This limited treatment strategy would include the following interventions:

- Helping clients identify their trigger situations for violence and abuse (including threats);

- Teaching clients about the use of time-outs and other self management techniques, which may include using chemical dependency self-help sponsors to withdraw from situations and think about consequences;

- Challenge clients' need for control of others and relate this issue in IPV to control issues with substances;

- Confront clients' rigid role definitions for men and women and explore how these views can encourage violence as well as interfere with recovery; and

- Confront clients' explanation of their violence as merely a function of "being drunk" or "getting high."

No Mixed-Gender Groups

Programs that treat substance abusers who are IPV offenders should under no circumstances conduct groups with mixed-gender participants. Given the high prevalence of abuse victimization of women in substance abuse treatment (Logan et al., 2002), the combination of offenders and victims in the same treatment setting is completely unsupportable and could be shown to be far more harmful than any intended treatment benefit.

COMMUNITY RESOURCES AND LINKAGES

Substance abuse treatment programs that lack the resources to integrate more than minimal IPV content into their services should develop collaborations with community providers of IPV treatment. This means establishing linkages not only to IPV offender programs, but to shelter centers for victims, as well. Having a range of referral options is critical as programs begin exploring IPV among their clients. Even during treatment of IPV offenders, clinicians may learn of risk to victims and may need to make referrals to victims' services for their safety and to reduce the risk of clients' future violence. The linkages should include social services, because extended services may be needed for clients and their families upon discharge from substance abuse treatment. Since depression, PTSD, and personality disorders are likely among IPV offenders, referral paths should be established with mental health centers for follow-up care after substance abuse treatment discharge.

Programs should have clear understandings with local court staff, judges, and probation/parole officers about the services that are and are not provided by the substance abuse program. The criminal justice system may make referrals with expectations of a "one-stop" treatment center where all the clients' problems—IPV and substance abuse—are treated. As mentioned above, courts may see substance abuse treatment as the intervention for IPV, a mistaken belief that programs should try to correct. Clinicians who work with IPV offenders will need to have secure liaisons with the court system in order to be effective as service providers. While this is true of substance abuse treatment of offenders, it is all the more critical with IPV offenders in treatment.

CLINICIAN TRAINING AND SUPERVISION

Clients with IPV present complex challenges to clinicians. Programs should enlist training that addresses approaches for assessment, including risk assessment, and treatment of IPV offenders including clinical factors as well as legal considerations such as when and how to carry out duties to warn and protect (Jordan et al., in press). Clinical training should include information about offender characteristics, the associations of substance abuse with violence, overall dynamics of IPV, and the effects of IPV on victims including child witnesses to violence. Ideally, programs would have clinical staff who are cross trained in IPV and substance abuse so that these intersecting problems can receive an integrated treatment approach.

FUTURE PROGRAM DEVELOPMENT

The successful treatment of IPV offenders may depend on the development of more comprehensive services such as the use of a drug court model for the combined problems. The use of a this model would mean far better court supervision of offenders and much better monitoring of treatment compliance which should mean increased safety benefits for victims. While science has yet to clearly identify all the interactions of IPV and substance use, it is clear that the two problems intersect for a significant percentage of clients in substance abuse treatment. Identifying clients with IPV problems in substance abuse treatment populations could contribute to increased treatment appropriateness and to better understanding by the courts of the needs of these offenders. Funding sources should also consider blended funding to bridge the service gap between these two clinical problems areas.

About the Authors

Robert Walker, M.S.W., L.C.S.W., and TK Logan, Ph.D., are professors and researchers at the University of Kentucky Center on Drug and Alcohol Research. Mr. Walker may be contacted by email at Robert.Walker@uky.edu.

References

Aldarondo, E., & Mederos, F. (Eds.) (2002). *Programs for men who batter: Intervention and prevention strategies in a diverse society.* Kingston, NJ: Civic Research Institute.

American Psychiatric Association. (2000). *Diagnostic and Statistical Manual of Mental Disorders,* 4th Edition, Text Revision. Washington, DC: American Psychiatric Press.

Babor, T.F., Stephens, R.S., & Marlatt, A. (1987). Verbal report methods in clinical research on alcoholism: Response bias and its minimization. *Journal of Studies on Alcoholism, 48,* 410-424.

Chermack, S.T., Fuller, B.E., & Blow, F.C. (2000). Predictors of expressed partner and non-partner violence among patients in substance abuse treatment. *Drug and Alcohol Dependence, 58,* 43-54.

Collins, J.J., Kroutil, L.A., Roland, E.J., & Moore-Gurrera, M. (1997). Issues in the linkage of alcohol and domestic violence services. In M. Galanter (Ed) *Recent developments in alcoholism, vol 13: Alcohol and violence: epidemiology, neurobiology, psychology and family issues* (pp. 387-405). New York: Plenum Press.

Del Boca, F.K, & Noll, J.A. (2000). Truth or consequences: The validity of self-report data in health services research on addictions. *Addiction. 95,* 347-360.

Dutton, D.G. Saunders, K., Starzomsky, A., & Bartholomew, K. (1994). Intimacy-anger and insecure attachment as precursors of abuse in intimate relationships. *Journal of applied Social Psychology, 24,* 1367-1387.

Edleson, J.L, & Tolman, R.M. (1992). *Intervention for men who batter: An ecological approach.* Newbury Park, CA.: Sage Publications.

Flett, G.L., & Hewlitt, P.L. (2002). In C. Wekerle & A. Wall, (Eds), *The violence and addiction equation: Theoretical and clinical issues in substance abuse and relationship violence* (pp. 64-97). New York: Taylor & Francis Group.

Gondolf, E.W. (1999). MCMI-III results for batter program participants in four cities: Less "pathological" than expected. *Journal of Family Violence, 14(1),* 1-17.

Gondolf, E.W. (2000a). How batterer program participants avoid reassault. *Violence Against Women, 6(11),* 1204-1222.

Gondolf, E.W. (2000b). A 30-month follow-up of court-referred batterers in four cities. *International Journal of Offender Therapy and Comparative Criminology, 44(1),* 111-128.

Gottman, J.M, Jacobson, N.S. Rushe, R.H., Shortt, J.W., Babcock, J., La Taillade, J.J., & Waltz, J. (1995). The relationship between heart rate reactivity, emotionally aggressive behavior, and general violence in batterers. *Journal of Family Psychology, 9,* 227-248.

Hamberger, L., & Hastings, J. (1988). Personality characteristics of spouse abusers: A controlled comparison. *Violence and Victims, 3,* 31-48.

Hamberger, L.K., & Hastings, J.E. (1991). Personality correlates of men who batter and nonviolent men: Some continuities and discontinuities. *Journal of Family Violence. 6,* 131-147.

Heckert, D.A., & Gondolf, E.W. (2000). Assessing assault self-reports by batterer program participants and their partners. *Journal of Family violence, 15(2),* 181-197.

Holtzworth-Munroe, A., & Stuart, G.L. (1994). Typologies of male batterers: Three subtypes and the differences among them. *Psychological Bulletin. 116,* 476-497.

Holtzworth-Munroe, A., Meehan, J.C., Herron, K. Rehman, U., & Stuart, G.L. (2003). Do subtypes of maritally violent men continue to differ over time? *Journal of Consulting and Clinical Psychology, 71,* 728-740.

Jacobson, N., & Gottman, J. (1998). *When men batter women.* New York: Simon & Schuster.

Jordan, C.E., Nietzel, M., Walker, R., & Logan, TK (In press). *Intimate partner violence: clinical and practice issues for mental health professionals.* New York: Springer Publications.

Logan, TK., Walker, R., Cole, J., & Leukefeld, C. (2002). Victimization and substance use among women: Contributing factors, interventions, & implications. *Review of General Psychology, 6(4),* 325-397.

Logan, TK, Leukefeld, C.G., & Walker, R. (2001). Stalking as a variant of intimate violence. In K Davis, I Hanson & R. Maiuro (Eds). *Stalking and obsessive behaviors* (pp. 265-291). New York: Springer Publishing Co.

Magdol, L. Moffitt, T.E., Caspi, A., & Silva, P.A. (1998). Developmental antecedents of partner abuse: A prospective-longitudinal study. *Journal of Abnormal Psychology, 107,* 375-389.

Maiuro, R., Cahn, T., Vitaliano, P.P., Wagner, B.C., & Zegree, J.B. (1988). Anger, hostility and depression in domestically violent and nonviolent control subjects. *Journal of Consulting and Clinical Psychology, 56,* 17-23.

Minkoff, K. (2001). Developing standards of care for individuals with co-occurring psychiatric and substance use disorders. *Psychiatric Services, 52,* 597-599.

Minkoff, K. & Regner, J. (1999). Innovations in integrated dual diagnosis treatment in public managed care: The Choate dual diagnosis case rate program. *Journal of Psychoactive Drugs. 31*(1), 3-12.

Murphy, C., Meyer, S., & O'Leary, K. (1993). Family of origin violence and MCMI-II psychopathology among partner assaultive men. *Violence and Victims, 8,* 165-176.

O'Farrell, T.J., & Murphy, C.M. (1995). Marital violence before and after alcoholism treatment. *Journal of Consulting and Clinical Psychology, 63,* 256-262.

Pan, H., Neidig, P., & O'Leary, D. (1994). Predicting mild and severe husband-to-wife physical aggression. *Journal of Consulting and Clinical Psychology, 62,* 975-981.

Pence, E. (2002). The Duluth domestic abuse intervention project. In E. Aldarondo & F. Mederos (Eds), *Programs for men who batter: Intervention and prevention strategies in a diverse society* (pp. 6-1–6-46). Kingston, NJ: Civic Research Institute.

Rutherford, M.J., Cacciola, J.S., Alterman, A.I., McKay, J.R., & Cook, T.G. (2000). Contrasts between admitters and deniers of drug use. *Journal of Substance Abuse Treatment. 18,* 343-348.

Saunders, D.G. (1992). A typology of men who batter: Three types derived from cluster analysis. *American Journal of Orthopsychiatry, 62,* 264–275.

Schmaker, J.A., Fals-Stewart, W., & Leonard, K.E., (2003). Domestic violence treatment referrals for men seeking alcohol treatment. *Journal of Substance Abuse Treatment, 24,* 279-283.

Straus, M., Hamby, S., Boney-McCoy, S., & Sugarman, D. (1996). The revised conflict tactics scales (CTS2): Development and preliminary psychometric data. *Journal of Family Issues, 17,* 3, 283-316.

Wexler, D. B. (2000). *Domestic violence 2000: An integrated skills program for men.* New York: W.W. Norton & Company.

Chapter 24

Family Empowerment Intervention: An Effective— and Cost-Effective— Program for Delinquent Youths

by Richard Dembo, Ph.D., and James Schmeidler, Ph.D.

Substance Abuse Programs Needed in Juvenile Justice System 24-1
Theoretical Foundations of the Intervention 24-2
Program Goals 24-3
A Four-Phase Intervention 24-3
Implementing and Evaluating the Clinical Trial 24-4
    Enrollment Process 24-4
    Demographic and Psychosocial Characteristics 24-5
    Follow-Up Process 24-5
Official Record Analyses of Post-Intervention Charges and Arrests 24-5
Self-Reported Delinquency, Post-Intervention 24-6
Alcohol/Other Drug Use 24-6
Emotional/Psychological Functioning 24-6
Cost-Saving Benefits of FEI. 24-7
Conclusions. 24-8

SUBSTANCE ABUSE PROGRAMS NEEDED IN JUVENILE JUSTICE SYSTEM

Intervening with adolescents experiencing substance abuse problems remains a critical need for the juvenile justice system. Evidence from national surveys (Office of National Drug Control Policy, 1998) and the National Institute of Justice Arrestee Drug

An earlier version of this chapter appeared in Offender Substance Abuse Report, *Vol. 2, No. 3, May/June 2002.*

Abuse Monitoring Program (1999) indicate continued, high levels of drug use among young people. It has become well established that youths' participation in crime is closely related to their substance use. Although juvenile violent crime has declined in recent years, overall juvenile crime continues to grow (Butts & Harrell, 1998); and juvenile arrests for drug use are escalating (Snyder & Sickmund, 2000). There was a 132% increase in the number of drug violation arrests per 100,000 juveniles between 1990 and 1999. These increases, with the rate of drug cases being handled formally in juvenile court up 121% between 1989 and 1998, have resulted in an increasingly clogged and backlogged juvenile court system. Evidence indicates an increased co-occurrence of substance use and mental health problems among juvenile offenders (Winters, 1998; Dembo & Schmeidler, 2003). Demographic projections indicate a substantial increase in U.S. youth population in the next 10 years—which threatens to place enormous pressure on an already overburdened juvenile justice system (Snyder & Sickmund, 2000). Hence, juvenile drug use, together with the often multiple problems arrested youths experience, present formidable challenges to juvenile justice agencies (Dembo et al., 1996; Dembo, Williams & Schmeidler, 1998).

We recently completed a National Institute on Drug Abuse (NIDA) funded clinical trial called the Youth Support Project (YSP), which implemented and evaluated the impact of a family empowerment intervention (FEI) involving arrested youths processed at the Hillsborough County, Juvenile Assessment Center (JAC) and their families. This brief report summarizes the theoretical foundation and practices of the FEI, and presents information relating to the impact of this innovative, cost-effective service that shows promise as an intervention for youth with substance abuse problems. For a detailed discussion of the methods and results of the clinical trial, see Dembo & Schmeidler (2002).

THEORETICAL FOUNDATIONS OF THE INTERVENTION

The FEI was a 10-week systems-oriented and structural approach to family preservation. The manualized intervention offered highly interactive, experiential activities that facilitated a positive emotional climate within the family, helped revitalize the family's natural strengths, and improved the interpersonal skills of family members. In addition, many of the FEI activities facilitated development of a more effective, adaptive, and workable family structure. The FEI was informed by four theoretical approaches:

- *Systemic.* Family members are viewed as interconnected, interdependent units of a larger system. Their thoughts, beliefs, and behaviors are seen as part of an interactive pattern in which each member influences, evokes responses from, and/or responds to someone else (Bateson et al., 1956; Bateson, 1979). The systemic perspective does not view one family member as having "the problem." Instead, it shows something about the larger picture in the family, and directs a focus on the interactive patterns in the family, rather than the individual, thus enabling families to move away from blaming, scapegoating, or looking for a simple cause.

- *Structural.* The structural approach emphasizes family organization and interactive processes as key concepts in understanding a family (Minuchin, 1974, 1981, 1984). Family dysfunction is understood as a reflection of difficulties in these areas. The central elements of the structural perspective are hierarchy, subsystems, boundaries, alignments, and triangulation.

- **Transgenerational.** The transgenerational perspective views the family as comprising an entire kinship network of at least three generations. The current family system is seen as being profoundly influenced by its history and family legacy. Families can be viewed as repeating themselves over time. What happens in one generation will often get played out in another one. The genogram, a diagram of the family's interrelationships, was used to learn about the family's generational context.

- **Psychoeducational.** Providing the family with successful life management and interpersonal skills is a core FEI objective. Emphasizing skill building and behavioral change, the FEI uses a wide range of primarily cognitive-behavioral and instructional approaches to improve communication, conflict-resolution, anger-management, and problem-solving skills within the family; and to help both the juvenile and the family as a whole develop better social skills at school and in the community.

PROGRAM GOALS

FEI has nine specific goals, derived from the intervention's theoretical foundations. The goals are separate, yet interrelated, objectives that strengthen family structure and functioning (Cervenka et al., 1996): (1) restore the family hierarchy (parents above children); (2) restructure boundaries between parents and children; (3) encourage parents to take greater responsibility for family functioning; (4) strengthen family structure through implementation of rules and consequences; (5) enhance parenting skills; (6) have parents set limits, expectations, and rules that increase the likelihood the client youth's behavior will improve; (7) improve communication skills among all family members and the ability to have fun together; (8) improve problem-solving skills, particularly in the client youth; and (9) when needed, connect the family to other systems such as school, church, and community activities.

A FOUR-PHASE INTERVENTION

Ideally, the intervention worker, called a field consultant (FC), met with the family three times a week for 10 weeks, in four phases:

1. **Introduction** (session 1 or 1-2): The FC and all family members involved were introduced and the family given a description of the intervention and supervision design, a review of the intervention procedures (including videotaping or audiotaping family meetings), and timing. Responses were given to any questions the family may have had about the program.

2. **Consultation** (sessions 2-3 through 9-12): The FC took the lead in conducting these sessions, which involved demonstration of methods used for sharing, asking, and inquiring among family members.

3. ***Family Work*** (sessions 10-13 through 27): The family members took the lead in reorganizing ways of communicating, relating, and thinking about family functioning.

4. ***Graduation*** (sessions 28 through 30): In these sessions, there was a review of the intervention and preparation for separation from the FEI. Graduation took place after the FC and clinical supervisor agreed that the family had met the goals of the intervention.

IMPLEMENTING AND EVALUATING THE CLINICAL TRIAL

Enrollment Process

Youths processed at the JAC who were arrested on misdemeanor or felony charges were sampled for inclusion in the project. Information on youths processed at the JAC has consistently indicated high rates of involvement in alcohol and other drug use. For example, a study of nearly 4,000 youths processed at the JAC found 13% of the youths claimed they used alcohol, and 13% indicated they used marijuana/hashish, 100 or more times in their lifetimes (Dembo et al., 1998). Further, urine test data on 222 diversion-eligible youth, and 310 arrested youths entering the juvenile justice system, processed at the JAC during December 2001, indicated drug positive rates of 33% and 51%, respectively. The drug positives were for marijuana primarily, followed, at a much lower level, by amphetamines and cocaine.

When openings occurred on the FCs' caseloads, a listing of recently arrested youths was classified by gender and race/ethnicity (African-American, Latino, and Anglo). An equal number of youths in each of these six categories was randomly selected to process for enrollment in the YSP—a sampling procedure designed to over-sample Hispanics and females. After consenting to participate and completion of baseline interviews, families were randomly assigned to one of two intervention groups: Extended Services Intervention (ESI) or FEI. Youths in both groups received services routinely provided by the juvenile justice system, but the ESI group did not receive any intervention services. Families in both groups had 24-hour-a-day, seven-day-a-week access to YSP staff, who provided information about different community agencies and assisted them in obtaining appropriate referrals.

Initial interviews were completed with 315 youths processed at the JAC from September 1, 1994, through January 31, 1998. Each youth was paid $10 for completing the 1.5- to two-hour initial interview. Depending on when youths entered the project, up to three annual follow-up interviews were sought. Completion rates were high: in Year 2, 88% of 315 interviews; Year 3, 85% of 200 interviews; and Year 4, 76% of 120 interviews. The follow-up interviews averaged 1.5 hours. Each youth was paid $20 for a completed follow-up interview. Excluding youths who moved out of state (who were not routinely followed) and youths who could not be located, net re-interview rates were 96%, 93%, and 91%, respectively. There were no significant differences in the re-interview rates for FEI and ESI youths. In each re-interview wave, over 90% of the interviews were completed within 120 days following the anniversary of the preceding interview. A discriminant analysis comparing the 278 Year 2 re-interviewees with the other 37 youths on 32 baseline demographic, offense history, and psychosocial characteristics found no overall differences between the two groups.

Demographic and Psychosocial Characteristics

Most youths were male (56%), and averaged 14.5 years of age; 56% were Anglo, 41% African-American, 26% Latino. Seventeen percent of the youths indicated they lived with both their biological parents; an additional 64% indicated they resided with either their mother only (51%), mother and another adult (5%), or mother and stepfather (8%). Information on the occupational status of the household chief wage earner or other sources of household income, our measure of socio-economic status, highlighted the low- to moderate-income status of the youths' families.

The youths reported high rates of getting very high/drunk on alcohol: 19% reported being drunk 12 or more days in the 12 months preceding their initial interview. Hair testing indicated a large proportion (38%) of the youths were marijuana users, and a smaller proportion cocaine users (22%). Comparison of their self-reports to their hair tests indicated that the youths were more willing to report the use of marijuana than cocaine.

Follow-Up Process

With the exception of official record analyses, the short-term data analyses involved the 278 of 315 eligible youths who provided a first follow-up interview that covered the 12 months following the youth's baseline interview. The long-term self-report data analyses referred to events up to 36 months following the youths' baseline interviews. We used the youth's last available follow-up interview as the best measure of long-term outcome. These short- and long-term analyses took into account group differences on a wide variety of demographic, offense history, abuse-neglect history, and baseline psychosocial variables. It is important to note that the FEI and ESI groups did not differ significantly on any of these variables, and neither did the youths who completed the FEI differ from those who did not complete it. Thus, differences in outcome cannot be attributed to baseline differences among the groups.

OFFICIAL RECORD ANALYSES OF POST-INTERVENTION CHARGES AND ARRESTS

The official record data analyses included 303 youths entering the project between September 1, 1994, and December 31, 1997. Short-term analyses focused on the number of new charges and new arrests in the 12 months following random assignment to the FEI or ESI group. The FEI and ESI youths did not differ significantly in their total numbers of new charges and new arrests during the first follow-up period. However, youths completing the FEI had significantly lower rates of new charges and new arrests than youths not completing the FEI (new charges: 1.05 vs. 1.81, new arrests: 0.71 vs. 1.34, respectively). Further study showed clearly that the intervention was successful only for those youths who completed it. ESI youths averaged fewer crimes than the FEI non-completers and more than FEI completers, but they were more similar to the FEI non-completers.

The long-term studies of official record data on the youths covered 12 to 48 months following their random assignment to the FEI or ESI group. The results indicated that youths completing the FEI had marginally significantly lower cumulative arrest charges and very close to statistically significant lower cumulative new arrests over the 48 month follow-up period, than youths not competing the FEI. These results supported the efficacy of the FEI, although at a more modest level than in the short-term analyses.

SELF-REPORTED DELINQUENCY, POST-INTERVENTION

Outcome analyses involving the youths' self-report data studied the number of new delinquent behaviors in five areas (general theft, crimes against persons, index crimes, drug sales, and total delinquency [self-reported involvement in 23 different delinquent behaviors]). The short-term analyses indicated that youths receiving the FEI reported a marginally significant lower rate of engaging in drug sales than ESI youths. Further analyses comparing youths completing the FEI and those not completing the FEI found FEI completers reported significantly less involvement in crimes against persons, drug sales, and total delinquency, and marginally significantly less involvement in theft and index crimes, than youths not completing the FEI. The long-term self-report data analyses found no significant FEI vs. ESI differences in reported delinquency during the period covered by the youths' last available follow-up interview. However, youths completing the FEI reported significantly less involvement in crimes against persons, drug sales, and total delinquency, than youths not completing the FEI.

ALCOHOL/OTHER DRUG USE

In addition to self-reported alcohol/other drug use, we used RIAH® hair tests to assess the recent use of marijuana, cocaine, amphetamines, opiates, and PCP. In our short-term study, separate analyses were performed on the reported frequency of getting very high or drunk on alcohol, the reported frequency of marijuana/hashish use, and recent use of marijuana and cocaine as indicated by the youths' hair test results. Youths receiving FEI services reported significantly fewer occasions of getting very high or drunk on alcohol, and a lower frequency of marijuana use, during the first follow-up period, than ESI youths. Youths receiving FEI services had a significantly lower rate of positive hair tests for marijuana than youths receiving ESI services. No FEI-ESI differences were found in predicting the youths' hair test results for cocaine, although a significant interaction effect was found: Compared to ESI services, FEI services were beneficial (i.e., a lower rate of positive hair tests for cocaine) among diversion (non-serious offender) cases, but among non-diversion cases the result was in the opposite direction. Once again, comparison of youths who did and did not complete the FEI showed clearly that its success was due to those youths who completed the intervention. Youths who did not complete the FEI did not differ from ESI youths. The long-term analyses did not find any FEI-ESI effect. However, FEI completers reported getting very high or drunk on alcohol significantly less often than FEI non-completers.

EMOTIONAL/PSYCHOLOGICAL FUNCTIONING

Emotional/psychological functioning was measured by the SCL-90-R (Derogatis, 1983). At baseline, youths reported significantly fewer emotional/psychological functioning problems than the normative sample, but other studies have found that delin-quents have more problems (Cocozza & Skowyra, 2000; Otto et al., 1992). This may suggest that these youths may under-report psychological problems, just as they under-reported cocaine use, because they are stigmatizing. No significant short-term FEI-ESI differences or long-term FEI-ESI or FEI completer-FEI non-completer differences in emotional/psychological functioning were found.

Another important area of emotional/psychological functioning is changes in the youths' satisfaction with their families and their communication with parents—a per-ceived improvement in the quality of family life. We used, with permission, the family satisfaction questions developed by Olson and Wilson (1982) to probe the youths' sat-isfaction with various aspects of their relationship with their families. Because some youths' living circumstances changed significantly over time, baseline interview and first follow-up interview information on satisfaction with family were compared for 248 youths. (The 248 youths tended to be younger and more often African-American than the 67 youths not included in this analysis.) Analysis of covariance compared the ESI youths, youths not completing the FEI, and youths completing the FEI on a summary measure of satisfaction with the family, controlling for their reported family satisfaction at their baseline interview. ESI youths claimed the lowest family satisfaction, youths not completing the FEI the next lowest satisfaction, and youths completing the FEI the high-est reported satisfaction with their family. When ESI youths were compared to all FEI youths, the difference was marginally statistically significant. (Since the three groups did not differ significantly on baseline demographic, psychosocial, offense history, and abuse-neglect history variables, it was not necessary to control for them.)

COST-SAVING BENEFITS OF FEI

We also estimated the direct cost savings to the juvenile justice system by providing FEI services to diversion-eligible youths in Hillsborough County, Florida. This analy-sis incorporated information on the costs of new arrests and incarceration of youths receiving ESI and FEI services during each 12-month period following random assign-ment. The results of this analysis suggest that the justice system can anticipate sub-stantial direct cost savings from use of this intervention.

A distinctive feature of the FEI was that the families were served by intervention workers, the FCs, who were not trained therapists—although they were trained by and performed their work under the direction of licensed clinicians. The choice of parapro-fessionals was based on a cost-effectiveness argument, supported by experimental research indicating that, at least for some treatments, paraprofessionals produce out-comes that are better than those under control conditions, and similar to those involving professional therapists (Christensen & Jacobson, 1994; Weisz et al., 1995). By requir-ing less previous therapy training, the FEI, if proven effective, would be highly attrac-tive to agencies providing services to juvenile offenders, which often operate with financial constraints.

In our cost-benefit analysis, we estimated the three-year cumulative direct cost sav-ings to the Hillsborough County juvenile justice system by providing FEI services to the 3,600 diversion-eligible youths who are processed in a year at the JAC. Diversion cases were chosen because they represented the least costly group of offenders to process and involve in service programs. Justice system processing costs were provided by the following agencies: Hillsborough County Sheriff's Office, State's Attorney's Office, Public Defender's Office, 13th Judicial Circuit Court Administrator's Office, and the Florida Department of Juvenile Justice. In addition, we developed cost figures for implementing the FEI: $1,154 per family (based on $24,000 yearly salary and 18% fringe benefits for each FC, cost of pager and mobile telephone, supervision and training costs, and travel expenses to the site of family meetings). The calculations of justice system costs were based on new arrest rates for FEI youths compared to ESI youths (both diversion and nondiversion cases) in each cumulative period. In regard to incarceration costs, from justice system records we determined the number of days ESI and FEI youths were incarcerated during each cumulative period following random assignment to the ESI or FEI group. Some youths were incarcerated in county jail, juvenile justice residential commitment programs, or Florida Department of Corrections prisons, each of which has different daily costs. However, all incarcerated youths spent time in juvenile detention facilities; for many youths, juvenile detention represented their only type of incarceration. Hence, for illustrative purposes, we used the daily cost for placement in a juvenile detention center ($95) to calculate the average incarceration cost per category of youth. Since the FEI is an overlay service, costs of providing additional FEI services are projected to exceed those of providing current diversion services by $2,266,898 in the first year. However, by the end of Year 2, due to lower incarceration rates for youths provided FEI services, providing FEI services are projected to save the juvenile justice system $934,139. By the end of Year 3, the projected cumulative cost savings to the justice system as a result of providing FEI services rises to $4.7 million.

CONCLUSIONS

The several documented short-term effects of the family empowerment intervention were expected. However, since the intervention was designed to be short-term, and no additional services were systematically provided following completion of the FEI, the long-term outcomes we found were particularly gratifying. Since FEI completers did not differ from FEI non-completers in baseline characteristics, the differences in outcome can be attributed to the effect of the intervention. The long-term recidivism and psychosocial outcome findings are particularly important in light of experience showing that the salutary effects of intervention programs for high-risk youths are, unfortunately, often short-lived. The University of Colorado Center for the Study and Prevention of Violence (1999) reports that the treatment or intervention gains of most programs are lost after participation in the intervention or soon thereafter. Further, substantial direct cost savings can be anticipated for the justice system from using this intervention.

About the Authors

Richard Dembo, Ph.D., is a professor in the Criminology Department at the University of South Florida, Tampa, Florida. James Schmeidler, Ph.D., is assistant clinical professor at the Mt. Sinai School of Medicine, New York, NY. Dr. Dembo may be reached by phone at (813) 931-3345.

References

Bateson, G. (1979). *Mind and body*. New York: E. P. Dutton.

Bateson, G., Jackson, D., Haley, J., & Weakland, J. (1956). Toward a theory of schizophrenia. *Behavioral Science 1*, 251-264.

Butts, J.A., & Harrell, A.V. (1998). *Delinquents or criminals: Policy options for young offenders*. Washington, DC: The Urban League.

Cervenka, K.A., Dembo, R., & Brown, C. H. (1996). A family empowerment intervention for families of juvenile offenders. *Aggression and Violent Behavior: A Review Journal, 1*, 205-216.

Christenson, A., & Jacobson, N.S. (1994). Who (or what) can do psychotherapy: The status and challenge of non-professional therapies. *Psychological Science, 5*, 8-14.

Cocozza, J.J., & Skowyra, C. (2000). Youth with mental health disorders in the juvenile justice system: Trends, issues and emerging responses. *Juvenile Justice, 7*, 3-13.

Dembo, R., & Schmeidler, J. (2002). *Family empowerment intervention: An innovative service for high-risk youths and their families*. Binghamton, N.Y.: Haworth.

Dembo, R., & Schmeidler, J. (2003). A classification of high-risk youths. *Crime and Delinquency, 49*, 201-230.

Dembo, R., Schmeidler, J., Chin Sue, C., Borden, P., Manning, D., & Rollie, M. (1998). Psychosocial, substance use, and delinquency differences among Anglo, Hispanic White, and African-American male youths entering a juvenile assessment center. *Substance Use & Misuse, 33*, 1481-1510.

Dembo, R., Turner, G., Schmeidler, J., Chin Sue, C., Borden, P., & Manning, D. (1996) Development and evaluation of a classification of high risk youths entering a juvenile assessment center. *International Journal of the Addictions, 31*, 303-322.

Dembo, R., Williams, L., & Schmeidler, J. (1998). A theory of drug use and delinquency among high-risk youths. In A.R. Roberts (Ed.), *Juvenile justice: Policies, programs and services,* 2nd ed. Chicago: Nelson-Hall.

Derogatis, L.D. (1983). *SCL-90-R administration, scoring and procedures manual*. Towson, MD: Clinical Psychometric Research.

Minuchin, S. (1974). *Families and family therapy*. Cambridge, MA: Harvard University Press.

Minuchin, S. (1981). *Family therapy techniques*. Cambridge, MA: Harvard University Press.

Minuchin, S. (1984). *Family kaleidoscope*. Cambridge, MA: Harvard University Press.

National Institute of Justice (1999). *1998 annual report on drug use among adult and juvenile arrestees*. Washington, DC: U.S. Department of Justice.

Office of National Drug Control Policy (1998). *The national drug control strategy, 1998*. Washington, DC: ONDCP.

Olson, D.H., & Wilson, M. (1982). *Family satisfaction*. Department of Family Social Services. St. Paul: University of Minnesota.

Otto, R. K., Greenstein, J. J., Johnson, M. K., & Friedman, F. M. (1992). Prevalence of mental disorders among youth in the juvenile justice system. In J.J. Cocozza (Ed.), *Responding to the mental health needs of youth in the juvenile justice system*. Seattle, WA: The National Coalition for the Mentally Ill in the Criminal Justice System.

Snyder, H., & Sickmund, M. (2000). *Juvenile offenders and victims: A national report*. Washington, DC: Office of Juvenile Justice and Delinquency Prevention.

University of Colorado Center for the Study and Prevention of Violence Model Program Selection Criteria. (1999). Available FTP: 128.138.129.25. File: *www.colorado.edu/cspu/blueprints/about/criteria.htm*.

Weisz, J.R, Weiss, B., Han, S.S., Granger, D.A., & Norton, P. (1995). Effects of psychotherapy with children and adolescents revisited: A meta-analysis of treatment outcome studies. *Psychological Bulletin, 117*, 450-468.

Winters, K. C. (1998, November). Substance abuse and juvenile offenders. University of Minnesota. Paper presented at the Physicians Leadership for National Drug Policy Conference-Washington, D.C.

Chapter 25

Inhalant Users: A Juvenile Justice Population of Special Risk

by Jane Carlisle Maxwell, Ph.D., and Richard Spence, Ph.D.

Juvenile Inhalant Use and Related Delinquency Patterns 25-1
Damage Caused by Inhalant Abuse 25-2
Findings of the 2000-2001 Texas Youth Commission Study 25-3
    Purpose and Methodology 25-3
    Usage Patterns Differ by Gender and Ethnicity 25-3
    Co-Occurring Risk Factors Found in Inhalant Users 25-5
    Relationship of Inhalant Use to Criminality 25-5
Implications for Treatment Planning 25-7

JUVENILE INHALANT USE AND RELATED DELINQUENCY PATTERNS

Inhalant use by youth appears to be an indicator of risk of delinquency and dropping out of school. Even within the juvenile justice system, inhalant usage appears to be a predictor of additional problems.

One of the most remarkable and consistent findings of the public school surveys of drug usage is the lifetime prevalence of reported inhalant usage that declines by age from the eighth grade through the twelfth grade. This pattern stands in sharp contrast to the reported increased use of all other substances with age. The leading interpretation of this pattern is that the students who drop out of school are more likely to be inhalant users than those who remain in school. In the most recent Texas school survey, 23% of eighth graders reported lifetime experience with inhalants compared to only 15% of seniors (Liu & Maxwell, 2001).

Inhalant abuse is highly prevalent among youth in the juvenile justice system (Jacobs & Ghodse, 1987). A study of male adolescent delinquents in West London found regular solvent abusers were more depressed, their age of first arrest was younger, and more had used heroin, amphetamines, hallucinogens, and alcohol

---

This chapter originally appeared in Offender Substance Abuse Report, *Vol. 2, No. 5, September/October 2002.*

(Jacobs & Ghodse, 1988). Analysis of a sample of over 13,000 Illinois students in grades 7-12 found inhalant users to be different from other drug users: they had more in common with general delinquents than with other drug users (Mackesy-Amiti & Fendrich, 1999). Inhalant-using youths from a city in the Southwest, when compared with other delinquents, had been arrested almost three times as often, were arrested more often for more serious crimes, and were younger at first arrest (Reed & May, 1984).

Among inhalant users in a Texas program, chronic inhalers had been arrested an average of nine times, 40 times more than non-drug users and twice as often as occasional inhalers (Stybel et al., 1976). A survey of youths in the Oklahoma juvenile justice system found 28% reported lifetime prevalence of inhalants (Oklahoma Department of Mental Health and Substance Abuse Services, 2001).

A study of predominantly middle class Anglos found inhalant users had more police problems and were more likely to be runaways (Crites & Schuckit, 1979). Among incarcerated adolescents, inhalants were used by more non-minority than minority youths and these non-minority inhalers were significantly more likely to have used drugs earlier, to have sold drugs, bought drugs from dealers, threatened to hurt people, and committed crimes while under the influence or to get money to buy drugs (McGarvey et al., 1996).

Youths entering the Texas Youth Commission's (TYC) reform schools have been surveyed on a periodic basis, beginning with interviews with 946 youths in 1989 (Fredlund et al., 1990; Wallisch, 1992), and interviews with 1,030 youths in 1994 (Fredlund et al., 1995). The 2000-2001 survey interviewed 1,026 youths (Wallisch & Kerber, 2001). The 1989 survey of TYC youths reported lifetime use of inhalants at 39%, the 1994 survey reported a slightly lower 33% lifetime use, and the 2000-2001 survey detailed later in this article reported lifetime use was 36%.

DAMAGE CAUSED BY INHALANT ABUSE

Chronic inhalant abuse can cause central nervous system damage resulting in dementia and cerebellar dysfunction. Typically there is a loss of cognitive and other higher functions, gait disturbance, and loss of coordination. Computerized tomography demonstrates a loss of brain mass (Fornazzari et al., 1983), and magnetic resonance imaging shows white matter degeneration (Filley et al., 1990).

Rosenberg (1990) reported that chronic toluene abuse can cause permanent central nervous system injury. Inhaling glue has been implicated in severe vasospastic phenomena resulting in a right cerebral artery stroke (Parker et al., 1984) and a coronary artery spasm resulting in an anterior myocardial infarction (Cunningham et al., 1987). Gasoline causes both peripheral and central nervous system toxicity resulting in seizures and EEG changes (Poklis & Burkett, 1977), ataxia, tremor, and myoclonus (McHugh, 1987).

Cognitive difficulties from inhalant use include lower scores on the Halstead-Reitan Neuropsychology Test Battery, danger to self and others, and chronic depression (Korman, 1977); antisocial personality disorders (Dinwiddie et al., 1987); and psychiatric illnesses (Malm & Lying-Tunell, 1980; Roberts et al., 1988).

FINDINGS OF THE 2000-2001 TEXAS YOUTH COMMISSION STUDY

Purpose and Methodology

This survey is part of an on-going series of juvenile justice studies that began with a survey of youths in the TYC in 1989 and again in 1994. In this most recent study, in-person interviews were conducted with youths who entered TYC intake facility at Marlin, Texas, between February 2000 and February 2001. TYC is the state juvenile corrections agency that provides custody, care, rehabilitation, and reestablishment for Texas's most violent or chronically delinquent youth offenders. Ninety percent of the youths committed to TYC have committed one or more felony-level offenses.

The interviews covered the youths' history of licit and illicit substance use, criminal history, past substance abuse treatment experiences and current motivation for treatment, family and peer relationships, gang involvement and gang activities, physical and mental health, gambling behaviors, experiences in school, and demographics. Youths were chosen randomly from a list of all entering offenders and asked to participate in the study; the response rate was 98%. The interviews averaged 45 minutes to complete and were conducted in private offices inside the facilities. Office doors were left ajar, but guards remained in the hallways and out of earshot.

Usage Patterns Differ by Gender and Ethnicity

Of the youths interviewed, 87% were male, 24% were Anglo, 30% were African American, 42% were Hispanic, and 5% were Other. Average age was 15.5 years. Forty percent came from families who received public assistance and 52% qualified for free lunches at school.

Ninety-one percent of TYC youth reported lifetime experience with illicit drugs and 31% reported lifetime usage of inhalants. By contrast, only 34% of public secondary school students in Texas reported lifetime illicit drug use and 19% had used inhalants. Table 25.1 shows the differences by gender for the prevalence of inhalant use from the *Substance Use and Delinquency Among Youths Entering Texas Youth Commission Facilities: 2000-2001* survey compared with the *Texas School Survey of Substance Use Among Students: Grades 7-12, 2000* (Liu & Maxwell, 2001).

Table 25.1: Prevalence of Use of Inhalants as Reported in the TYC and Texas Secondary School Surveys: 2000-2001

	TYC (2000-2001)		Secondary School Students (2000)	
	Girls	Boys	Girls	Boys
Ever Use (Lifetime)	35.7%	29.4%	17.8%	20.2%
Past Year (Not Past Month)	16.9%	14.6%	2.9%	3.3%

Table 25.2: TYC Youths and Texas Secondary School Students Who Had Ever Used Specific Inhalants: 2000-2001

	TYC Survey: 2000-2001	Secondary School Survey: 2000
Spray Paint	61%	8%
Gasoline	41%	6%
Freon	17%	2%
Octane Booster	14%	2%
Lacquer/Toluene	13%	4%
Other Aerosol Sprays	11%	4%
Airplane Glue	7%	5%
Correction Fluid	6%	8%
Nitrous Oxide	3%	6%
Poppers	4%	2%

Table 25.3: Characteristics of Entering TYC Youths by Number of Times Used Inhalants: 2000-2001

	None	1-10 Times	11-49 Times	50+ Times
Number of Subjects	709	193	63	59
Anglo	21%	34%	22%	30%
Hispanic	35%	54%	64%	64%
Black	39%	9%	8%	2%
Other	5%	2%	6%	5%
Total	100%	100%	100%	100%
Substance Dependence (DSM)	47%	75%	85%	89%
Gang Membership	32%	54%	62%	56%
Lived on the Street for a Month or More	7%	11%	14%	17%
Been in Substance Abuse Treatment	29%	42%	56%	65%
# Times Arrested	5.81	8.22	9.97	10.75
# Times in Jail or Detention	4.63	5.63	6.14	6.34
Used Alcohol Past Year	74%	87%	92%	95%
Used Marijuana Past Year	76%	89%	89%	90%
Used Powder Cocaine Past Year	30%	59%	78%	83%
Used Crack Cocaine Past Year	9%	21%	25%	46%
Used Heroin Past Year	5%	10%	16%	20%
Used Inhalants Past Year	0%	45%	62%	73%

Lifetime use was higher among Hispanic youths (42%) and Anglo youths (39%) than among African-American youths (8%). About 36% of the 315 TYC inhalant users had tried inhalants only once or twice, while 38% had used them more than 10 times in their lives. About 37% of lifetime users reported that they usually inhaled enough to stagger or pass out.

As Table 25.2 shows, TYC youths were more likely than Texas school students who were not in TYC to use particular toluene-based and other inhalants that may cause damage to the central nervous system.

As indicated in Table 25.3, Hispanic youths are at particular risk for heavy inhalant usage compared to other racial/ethnic groups, while African American youths are unlikely to use inhalants more than a few times. These data also suggest that a history of inhalant usage is related to a youth's meeting the DSM criteria for substance dependence and having been in treatment previously. Furthermore, the extent of past inhalant usage appears to be related to the extent of other problems, most notably gang membership, being homeless, number of arrests, and the usage of cocaine and heroin.

Co-Occurring Risk Factors Found in Inhalant Users

Inhalers are significantly more likely than non-inhalant users within TYC to have been abused as children; to be at risk of HIV/AIDS; and to be depressed, suicidal, or have other mental health problems (difference between inhalers and non-inhalers is significant at p <.0001). There was also the same level of significant difference in terms of ever having been in a gang, committed a drug-related crime in the past year, sold or stolen drugs, and driven while intoxicated.

Relationship of Inhalant Use to Criminality

As Table 25.4 shows, the intensity of inhalant use also appears to be related to criminality. This relationship between inhalants and crime is evident even within a popula-

Table 25.4: Percentage of TYC Youths Who Committed a Crime in the Past Year by Frequency of Use of Inhalants

	None	1-10 Times	11-49 Times	50+ Times
Any Property Crime	76%	81%	80%	90%
Any Drug-Related Crime	58%	71%	78%	86%
Any Violent Crime	70%	71%	83%	76%
Robbery	24%	29%	34%	40%
Assault	22%	24%	39%	33%
Threatened With Gun or Knife	24%	37%	43%	31%
Carried a Gun	24%	25%	34%	32%
Pimping or Prostitution	3%	8%	8%	8%

Table 25.5: Percentage of TYC Youths Who Sold Any Drugs in the Past Year by Number of Times of Lifetime Inhalant Use: 2000-2001

	None	1-10 times	11-49 Times	50+ Times
Sold Any Drug	48%	52%	61%	65%
Sold Crack	34%	26%	35%	31%
Sold Other Drugs	39%	47%	57%	63%

Table 25.6: Percentage of TYC Youths Who Committed a Drug-Related Crime in the Past Year, by Type of Crime Linkage: 2000

Model	All TYC Youths	Youths Who Used Inhalants More Than 10 Times
Economic-Compulsive	39%	68%
Pharmacological	29%	52%
Systemic	44%	62%

tion of offenders (100%) and drug users (91%). Property crime includes burglary, shoplifting, vandalism and property damage, car theft, buying stolen goods, auto parts theft, pick pocketing or purse snatching, forgery or fraud, and stealing from an employer. Any drug-related crime includes selling drugs, committing a property crime or threatening someone with a weapon to get drugs or money for drugs, stealing drugs for own use, having sex to get drugs, threatening or using violence while high on drugs or to protect a drug operation, or using alcohol or drugs to remove the fear of danger while committing the crime. Violent crime includes assault with or without a weapon, threatening someone with a weapon, robbery, serious injury or murder, and sexual assault.

TYC youth with a history of heavy inhalant use were not only likely to have used other drugs, but they were also more likely to have sold drugs, as Table 25.5 shows.

The relationship between inhalant use and crime has not been studied in depth. However, in the TYC study an analysis was performed using the conceptual framework of Goldstein (1985), which posits three models for the link between drugs and crime:

- *The economic-compulsive model* suggests that some drug users resort to criminal behavior to support their drug habits. Economic-compulsive crimes include committing property crimes to get money for drugs, threatening someone with a weapon to get money for drugs, stealing drugs for one's own use, selling drugs to support a habit, and having sex to get drugs or money for drugs.

- *The pharmacological model* suggests that some drug users engage in irrational or violent behavior as a result of the psychological or physiological effects of a drug. Such crimes would include using or threatening violence because one was on drugs and did not know what he or she was doing or using alcohol or drugs to remove the fear of danger in committing a crime.

- *The systematic model* holds that drug-related crime is related to drug trafficking and sales, with crimes such as selling drugs for a profit (but not to support personal drug use) or using or threatening violence to protect a drug operation.

As Table 25.6 shows, among youthful offenders, users of inhalants are more likely than other offenders to have engaged in all three types of drug-related crime.

IMPLICATIONS FOR TREATMENT PLANNING

Inhalant users are at risk for delinquency, dropping out of school, and ending up in the juvenile justice system. Even within the incarcerated youth population, heavy inhalant users seem to stand out as a priority sub-population of concern. Although over 90% of TYC youth have a history of illicit drug use, the heavy inhalant users are comparatively more prone to heavy criminality, gang membership, homelessness, and involvement with "hard drugs." Multiple categories of drug-crime linkage appear to be operational for inhalant users compared to other respondents.

Interventions planned for this high-risk group of youth should take into consideration particular cultural and social factors that are associated with inhalant usage as indicated in this analysis. While the Texas data showed a need for a services for Hispanic youth, other ethnic populations may be at particular high risk in other states. In all locales, there is a need to focus on living and family environments that provide replacements for gang membership. Cognitive impairment from long-term inhalant use should be assessed and considered in rehabilitative planning, which may call for long-term treatment and alternative cognitive learning strategies. Treatment needs assessments should be made for dependency on multiple drugs and case managers should be aware of the likelihood of multiple problems including health, social, and psychological and cognitive areas of concern. Inhalant-using youth should be considered highly likely to recidivate and to end up in the adult correctional system. Future research efforts should attempt to identify effective intervention methods and to establish the effect of treatment as a method of interrupting progression to an adult career of crime and incarceration.

About the Authors

Jane Carlisle Maxwell, Ph.D., and Richard T. Spence, Ph.D. are research scientists with the Gulf Coast Addiction Technology Transfer Center in the School of Social Work at the University of Texas at Austin. The authors may be contacted by email at jcmaxwell@mail.utexas.edu.

The authors wish to acknowledge the Texas Commission on Alcohol and Drug Abuse for making this dataset available. The survey was conducted under a contract funded by the Center for Substance Abuse Treatment, Substance Abuse and Mental Health Services Administration.

References

Crites, J., & Schuckit, M. (1979). Solvent misuse in adolescents at a community alcohol center. *Journal of Clinical Psychiatry, 40*, 39-43.

Cunningham, S., Dalzell, G., McGir, P., & Khan, M. (1987). Myocardial infarction and primary ventricular fibrillation after glue sniffing. *British Medical Journal, 294*, 739-740.

Dinwiddie, S., Zorumski, C., & Rubin, E. (1987). Psychiatric correlates of chronic solvent abuse. *Journal of Clinical Psychiatry, 48*, 334-337.

Filley, C., Heaton, R., & Rosenberg, N. (1990). White matter dementia in chronic toluene abuse. *Neurology, 40*, 532-534.

Fornazzari, L., Wilkinson, D., Kapur, B., & Carlen, P. (1983). Cerebellar cortical and functional impairment in toluene abusers. *Acta Neurologica Scandinavica, 67*, 319-329.

Fredlund, E., Farabee, D., Blair, L., & Wallisch, L. (1995). *Substance use and delinquency among youths entering Texas Youth Commission facilities: 1994.* Austin, TX: Texas Commission on Alcohol and Drug Abuse.

Fredlund, E., Spence, R., Maxwell, J., & Kavinsky, J. (1990). *Substance use among youth entering Texas Youth Commission facilities, 1989: First report.* Austin, TX: Texas Commission on Alcohol and Drug Abuse.

Goldstein, P. (1985). The drugs/violence nexus: A tripartite conceptual framework. *Journal of Drug Issues, 15*(4), 493-506.

Jacobs, A., & Ghodse, A. (1987). Depression in solvent abusers. *Social Science and Medicine, 24*, 863-866.

Jacobs, M., & Ghodse, A. (1988). Delinquency and regular solvent abuse: An unfavorable combination? *British Journal of Addiction, 83*, 965-968.

Korman, M. (1977). Clinical evaluation of psychological factors. In C. Sharp & M. Brehm, (Eds.), *Review of inhalants: Euphoria to dysfunction.* Rockville, MD: National Institute on Drug Abuse.

Liu, L., & Maxwell, J. (2001). *Texas school survey of substance use among students: Grades 7-12, 2000.* Austin, TX: Texas Commission on Alcohol and Drug Abuse.

McGarvey, E., Canterbury, R., & Waite, D. (1996). Delinquency and family problems in incarcerated adolescents with and without a history of inhalant use. *Addictive Behaviors, 21*(4), 537-542.

McHugh, M. (1987). The abuse of volatile substances. *Pediatric Clinics of North America, 34*, 333-340.

Mackesy-Amiti, M., & Fendrich, M. (1999). Inhalant use and delinquent behavior among adolescents: A comparison of inhalant users and other drug users. *Addiction, 94*(4), 555-564.

Malm, G., & Lying-Tunell, U. (1980). Cerebellar dysfunction related to toluene sniffing. *Acta Neurologica Scandinavica, 62*(3): 188-190.

Oklahoma Department of Mental Health and Substance Abuse Services, Oklahoma State Treatment Needs Assessment Program. (2001). *Face-to-face surveys of criminal justice populations.* Oklahoma City, OK: Oklahoma Department of Mental Health and Substance Abuse Services.

Parker, M., Tarlow, M., & Milne-Anderson, J. (1984). Glue sniffing and cerebral infarction. *Archives of Disease in Childhood, 59*, 675-677.

Poklis, A., & Burkett, C. (1977). Gasoline sniffing: A review. *Clinical Toxicology, 11*, 35-41.

Reed, B., & May, P. (1984). Inhalant abuse in juvenile delinquency: A control study in Albuquerque, New Mexico. *International Journal of Addictions, 19*(7), 789-804.

Roberts, F., Lucas, E., Marsden, C., & Trauer, T. (1988). Near-pure xylene causing reversible neuropsychiatric disturbance (letter). *Lancet 2*, 273.

Rosenberg, N. (1990). Neurotoxicity from solvent inhalant abuse and occupational exposure to solvents. Paper presented at the Inhalant Abuse Research symposium, Houston, TX, June, 1990.

Stybel, L., Lewis, F., & Allen, P. (1976). Deliberate hydrocarbon inhalation among low-socioeconomic adolescents not necessarily apprehended by the police. *International Journal of Addictions, 11*, 345-361.

Wallisch, L. (1992). *Substance use among youth entering Texas Youth Commission facilities, 1989: Second report; Substance use and crime.* Austin, TX: Texas Commission on Alcohol and Drug Abuse

Wallisch, L., & Kerber, L. (2001). *Substance use and delinquency among youths entering Texas Youth Commission facilities: 2000-2001.* Austin, TX: Texas Commission on Alcohol and Drug Abuse.

Part 5

Factors Impacting Treatment

The dynamics of substance abuse treatment for offenders—whether in correctional settings or via referral to community-based programs—are somewhat different from those found in treatment programs designed primarily to serve voluntary clients. This is not to say that all offenders enter treatment involuntarily, nor is it true that all "voluntary" clients enter treatment on their own accord (Farabee, Prendergast, & Anglin, 1998). But the criminal justice system is a unique source of external pressure that has the ability to mandate and monitor treatment compliance and drug use more effectively than friends, family, or even an employer. The unique individual- and system-level factors that substance-abusing offenders bring with them to treatment hold important implications for the treatment process. A number of these implications are explored in this section.

In Chapter 26, Julien Devereux points out that longer treatment retention (of at least 90 days) consistently predicts positive post-treatment outcomes. He then describes how economic forces and conflicting goals of funding sources have curtailed publicly funded treatment—both in the length and number of services offered. Although the author bases his observations on the Texas treatment system, the barriers he identifies are widespread. The chapter concludes with recommendations as to how treatment providers can balance the treatment needs of their clients against the exigencies of the political and economical climate.

Chapter 27, by D. Dwayne Simpson and Kevin Knight, provides an overview of the TCU Treatment Process Model as it applies to correctional settings. Their model represents a wide variety of pretreatment (e.g., motivation, client characteristics), during treatment (e.g., therapeutic relationship, ancillary services), and outcome variables (e.g., drug use, crime, social relations) and depicts their functional relationships. This proposed model is useful for both clinicians and researchers as we attempt to shed some light in the "black box" of treatment.

Chapters 28 (by Sandra Dees, Donald Dansereau, and D. Dwayne Simpson), and 29 (by Donald Dansereau, Selby Evans, Michael Czuchry, and Tiffiny Sia) address the critical issue of how to enhance motivation and readiness for treatment among substance-abusing offenders. The first of these two chapters describes a set of activities developed by the authors specifically for the purpose of enhancing treatment motivation among correctional clients. The second chapter offers a more conceptual overview of the key elements of change.

Chapter 30, by Michael Prendergast, David Farabee, and Jerome Cartier, focuses on the interaction between treatment and custody influences in a prison-based therapeutic community. Whereas most correctional treatment evaluations tend to limit their outcomes to post-release behaviors, Prendergast and colleagues report on the impact that a therapeutic community has on the prison environment itself, including disciplinary rates, correctional staff perceptions, and correctional staff absenteeism.

In the final chapter of this section, Chapter 31, David Farabee, Haikang Shen, Michael Prendergast, and Jerome Cartier explore the importance of motivation among clients in a mandated prison-based treatment program in California. Their study examined whether the generally positive findings regarding coerced treatment among community-based offenders could be replicated in a sample of incarcerated offenders. Unlike the community studies, inmates who were coerced into treatment had significantly higher recidivism rates than those who expressed a desire for—and received—treatment. Overall, the best outcomes were for inmates whose desire for treatment was concordant with whether or not they received it. Their findings call into question the assumption that the coerced treatment findings based on community offender samples can be generalized to offenders remanded to treatment while in prison.

References

Farabee, D., Prendergast, M. L., & Anglin, M. D. (1998). The effectiveness of coerced treatment for drug-abusing offenders. *Federal Probation*, 62, 3-10.

Chapter 26

Who Decides Length of Stay in Substance Abuse Treatment?

by Julien Devereux, LMSW-ACP, LCDC

Introduction 26-1
Research Supports Extended Stays 26-2
Why Not Long-Term Treatment for Everyone? 26-3
External Factors Impact How Much and What Kind of Treatment Is Provided . . . 26-3
Special Problems of the Dually Diagnosed 26-3
How Political Issues Influence Lengths of Stay in the Criminal Justice Arena . . 26-4
How Economic Issues Dictate Length of Stay 26-5
     Introduction of Managed Care 26-5
     Interplay of Politics With Economics 26-5
Ethical Issues 26-6
Bottom Line: What Treatment Providers Can Do 26-7

INTRODUCTION

As a predictor variable of long-term success in drug abuse treatment, length of stay or number of treatment contacts continues to be one of the best measures. As an administrator of several substance abuse programs over the last 13 years, I have engaged in formal and informal research in which this variable continues to hold up. But despite the large body of research indicating length of stay as a reliable predictor variable of long-term success, increased pressure from several sources continues to erode the length of stay in treatment programs. This chapter analyzes some of the research, clinical, political, economic, and ethical components of this issue—and draws some conclusions for providers and policy makers who must continue to provide quality services in a volatile and fluid treatment system environment. The length-of-treatment decision is often a battleground between treatment providers and funders. While this chapter focuses on some issues specific to some treatment pro-

This chapter originally appeared in Offender Substance Abuse Report, *Vol. 1, No. 1, January/February 2001.*

grams in Texas, readers should be able to make use of the conclusions in light of conflicts within their own states.

RESEARCH SUPPORTS EXTENDED STAYS

As noted above "length of stay" is a valid and reliable predictor of long-term success in recovery from addiction. My first experience with studying this variable was in graduate school. Post-treatment follow-up forms required by the Texas Commission on Alcohol and Drug Abuse (TCADA) referred to as CODAP (Client Oriented Data Acquisition Program) forms were compared (n = 129) using a multiple regression analysis that indicated that the number of days in treatment was significantly correlated with decreased arrests 60 days post-treatment and increased attendance at 12-step support groups 60 days post-treatment (Devereux, 1990). The post treatment follow-up questionnaires also showed a strong relationship with 11 DSM-IIIR (American Psychiatric Association, 1987) symptom criteria that indicated full remission from active addiction or abuse. Both of these findings were indicative of a client doing well after treatment.

Since 1993, researchers at the Texas Christian University (TCU) Institute of Behavioral Research conducted a follow-up evaluation at the Dallas County Judicial Treatment Center (DCJTC), operated by Cornell Companies, Inc., for the Dallas County Community Supervision and Corrections Department (CSCD). A thorough evaluation was done of two annual cohorts admitted to the DCJTC from 1993-94 and 1994-95. The results were similar to other studies of therapeutic community treatment. The primary indicator of significant success in these two groups was treatment completion as evidenced by the number of days in treatment. These graduates had re-arrest rates of 6% at six months, 11% at one year, and 27% at two years. This was significantly lower than or equal to other criminal justice treatment programs that were the same length or longer.

Other TCU Studies, such as the Drug Abuse Reporting Program (DARP; Simpson, 1981) and the Drug Abuse Treatment Outcome Studies (DATOS; Simpson, et al., 1997), also indicates that the more effective treatment a person receives, the more likely he or she is to be at a reduced risk to be rearrested or to relapse. I have seen no research that indicates that less treatment is more effective. I am also not aware of any studies that indicate that decreasing lengths of stay saves money over a long period of time.

All this research has actually boiled down to two salient points:

1. We have very few indicators that are as predictive of long-term success as length of stay in a treatment program.

2. The length of stay in treatment that is most significantly indicative of long-term success appears to be between three and six months. Most of these studies indicate that fewer than 90 days of treatment may not be effective at all, while there is a natural falling off of willingness to remain in treatment beyond six months, even when a longer time is mandated by the courts.

WHY NOT LONG-TERM TREATMENT FOR EVERYONE?

If treatment were designed solely on the basis of the client's individual need and the researched effectiveness of a particular model or treatment, long-term treatment for anyone with a serious, chronic problem might be the rule. One of the National Institute on Drug Abuse's 13 principles of effective substance abuse treatment is adequate length of stay. This is in line with the TCADA regulations, which state that treatment should be individualized based on the client's assessed needs. This principle also states that an individual usually reaches a significant improvement threshold at about three months in treatment and that programs should work to improve their ability to retain people in treatment.

EXTERNAL FACTORS IMPACT HOW MUCH AND WHAT KIND OF TREATMENT IS PROVIDED

In the real world, not all treatment decisions are based on the clinically assessed need of the client. The concerns that a clinician has on admission begin with whether, given the resources available, he or she ethically has anything to offer the client. An adequate assessment must be accomplished that is multi-dimensional and standardized and, in Texas, must fulfill the DSM-IV (American Psychiatric Association, 1994) criteria for dependence, abuse, or withdrawal. This assessment should be the basis for the initial match to a treatment model and for the recommended or proposed length of stay. The clinician has to assess the client based on the client's need for treatment and not the program's need for a client. The court-mandated criminal justice client with a pre-adolescent history of heavy drug and alcohol use, an eighth grade education, and no job history will definitely need more rehabilitation than someone who was sent to treatment by his wife or employer to dry out from drinking too much.

The severity of the addiction and the related affected systems can be assessed but these only imply that more services are needed in order to establish stable recovery. These services may or may not be provided by a substance abuse program but must be realistically coordinated with the substance abuse services in order to yield a positive outcome. There is very little research that evaluates the significance of coordinated wraparound services for substance abuse clients but any experienced counselor can cite examples where family support, vocational skills or rehabilitation, or education became the primary reason for a client's success or failure. One argument for an extended length of stay is to provide a comprehensive and intensive treatment intervention that includes these elements, as at the DCJTC (Barthwell, et al., 1995).

SPECIAL PROBLEMS OF THE DUALLY DIAGNOSED

There are additional circumstances that create pressure on the drug treatment system and the criminal justice system. Clients who are referred to drug treatment have a more complex history of substance abuse combined with mental and chronic medical illness. The mental health and mental retardation system in some areas continues to fail to meet the challenge of successfully addressing the mental illness problems when there is a concurrent substance abuse problem, especially when there is criminal justice involvement. Clients who have criminal justice involvement end up in a special needs category—but tend to receive very little in the way of special services. The criminal justice system is not designed typically to accommodate special needs and by its very nature must treat all inmates or clients essentially the same. To begin to single out clients for individual services is counter to the basic philosophy of corrections and can lead to allegations of abuse or favoritism from clients.

I am sure that this is not the system that we intended to develop but it is what exists currently in Texas. If someone is indigent and law abiding then there is very little treatment available and there may be a long waiting list for services. The severity of the impairment and the complexity of related physical and mental disorders and the indigence of the client are inversely proportionate to the availability of effective treatment. If the client is in the criminal justice system, he will receive some type of treatment but it will not necessarily match his needs in type, intensity, or length of stay. Clearly savings could be achieved by a well managed and funded mental health system that provides what is mandated to lessen these clients' involvement in the criminal justice system, which actually increases an expensive residential length of stay. Mental illness is not a crime.

HOW POLITICAL ISSUES INFLUENCE LENGTHS OF STAY IN THE CRIMINAL JUSTICE ARENA

At the DCJTC two funding sources collided in 2000 on the length of stay issue and these were both in conflict with the licensing regulations that insist that treatment be individualized. The grant from the Governor's Office requires that clients be treated in a residential treatment center for no less than 180 days. The Community Justice Assistance Division (CJAD) agency contract will not allow a client to remain in treatment for more than 180 days. This creates a conundrum that is out of sync with the TCADA regulations. TCADA regulations state that treatment centers should adopt the American Society of Addiction Medicine's Patient Placement Criteria 2 (ASAM PPC-2, 1996), which only allows for 90 days of residential treatment and says that treatment should be individualized to each client's need.

Each agency is trying to give a nod to the research on length of stay but they use different language, end up in conflict with each other, and dictate clinical decisions. The ASAM PPC-2 is not necessarily applicable to a population with more severe rehabilitation needs, but is based on the opinions of doctors with varied experience and operates completely from a medical/psychological perspective with little acknowledgement of social and rehabilitative needs. Until the length of stay decision is returned to clinical decision-makers who have full knowledge of and experience with their specific population, it will be used as a political football and the clients in treatment will be the primary losers. Not everyone needs the same size shoe.

Additionally, many services provided at the DCJTC are not specifically drug and alcohol counseling but are cognitive interventions for criminal thinking and behavior, social skill training. These require longer lengths of stay in order to provide a wraparound comprehensive service. Rehabilitative services such as vocational and educational services require daily classes and an unpredictable length of job search. These services are often critical for long-term recovery and coordinating these services as part of treatment makes clinical and economic sense.

HOW ECONOMIC ISSUES DICTATE LENGTH OF STAY

Introduction of Managed Care

In my previous positions working in hospital-based treatment, length of stay originally was dictated by the multidisciplinary team. As managed care was introduced, around 1988, this decision was handled by a Utilization Review person who became the gatekeeper for services. Finally this decision was relegated to someone within the Behavioral Health Organization. Hospital-based treatment for addiction quickly disappeared altogether, except for a three- to five-day detoxification as a medical necessity. Addiction treatment counseling programs were not considered medically necessary. Those programs that did not become more resilient and creative in the types of services they offered went out of business. This did help drive out inefficient providers, but some of those providers were effective with clients. In some ways this environment improved the product and reduced the cost from $1,000 per day to less than $500 for detox and even less for partial hospitalization and outpatient services. The downside for the consumer is that the diversity of types of services, location of providers, and number of quality providers decreased.

The current unfortunate state of drug treatment is that the primary determinant of length of stay is economic and not clinical. The influence of managed care in this area is significant. Clinicians tend to go along with the trend and not advocate too loudly for clients with managed care coverage or have stepped out of managed care completely and just work with clients who can pay. Of course the managed care system would not have developed to its current state if the profiteering of the early and mid 1980s had not occurred. Clinicians have considerable responsibility for creating an environment that needed regulation. This leaves the indigent client, the one most in need, with few or no options. These more severely impaired clients must rely on treatment provided by non-profit agencies that are dependent on federal, state, or community funds. In the past year in the Dallas area, these funds have been distributed by a managed care system that was designed to improve access but has yet to prove that it can do so.

Interplay of Politics With Economics

Allocating resources for a particular strategy for social change is always a political decision and drug treatment is no exception. There have been very few studies that develop strong arguments for the positive cost/benefit ratio of dollars spent on treatment against long-term savings in the criminal justice system due primarily to the difficulty in research designs that require long-term follow up in order to illustrate this savings. Also there is continued pressure on the criminal justice system to find cost saving alternatives to incarceration and to simply serve more clients with the same or fewer dollars. This translates often to a reduction in something. Either the type, frequency, duration or intensity of the treatment suffers due to cuts in funding.

The cycle of appropriately funding a program, developing it into a successful strategy, reducing funds due to economic or political pressure, then abandoning the program as ineffective continues to plague drug treatment programs. Strong models of treatment that have proven efficacy and long-term outcomes that are significantly higher than traditional criminal justice community-based programs should continue to be funded at levels that do not impact the program design. Performance measures that monitor process and contract requirements during the course of treatment should replace dictated lengths of stay. These performance measures are usually required in RFP's but are not well designed or easily monitored. Cost efficiencies should be part of any treatment program balanced against effectiveness. Additionally, programs that have developed over several years should be able to provide data that indicates both their effectiveness and efficiency to policy makers prior to funds being reduced. When inevitable cuts are necessary, the providers should be at the table to decide what to reduce.

ETHICAL ISSUES

What do you deliver to your client when you have no control over length of stay? The ethical dilemmas are numerous and have caused many quality providers to fold up their tents and leave the field to managed care or to return clients to voluntary self help groups when treatment can no longer be provided. I believe that practitioners can find a way to continue to serve their clients provided that they don't get too stuck in their favorite model.

The DCJTC has had to reconfigure at least three times over nine years in operation. The first time, due to cuts in funding, the number of beds was reduced without reducing the intensity, duration, type, or frequency of treatment. The next time there was a reconfiguration to serve more females, to solve problems of inequitable waiting time for treatment. This actually improved the entire process. The third reconfiguration reduced the length of stay, the intensity (or "amount") of treatment in later phases of the process, and increased the number served. This was the largest and most significant change and resulted in significant staff turnover and adjustments in program operation. New staff hired from managed care funded programs were impressed with the length of stay for clients compared to the programs they had just left. They had to learn the therapeutic community model of treatment as it is delivered at DCJTC. Much time was lost in the transition and treatment outcomes suffered from the transition. At each program contract interval, funding cuts and contract adjustments resulted in lost time and quality of treatment.

Is there an ethical concern if the clients are receiving the best treatment that a funding agency is willing to pay for even if there is better treatment available? Is releasing a client who is not really prepared to transition an ethical issue for a treatment program licensed by an agency that insists on individualized treatment? Are the policy makers who determine length of stay—whether non-profit agencies, managed care, or funding agencies—qualified and trained to determine the length of stay? Even determining length of stay for an unknown client is an ethical problem for a responsible clinician.

BOTTOM LINE: WHAT TREATMENT PROVIDERS CAN DO

How do we, as treatment providers, balance length of stay with the political, economic, and ethical issues that intervene in what is an ideal model? There are several critical points:

- *Be accountable for establishing a treatment model that is effective with your client population and is supported by outside evaluation.* This accountability should include the efficiencies required to keep treatment within an economically viable model by focusing on realistic treatment goals, effective case management, and midstream corrections of inefficient and ineffective processes.

- *Be involved in a continuous performance improvement process that informs what you do.* This is not a separate activity or task but should be built into the everyday performance and supervision of every clinician and every client treatment episode. It is this focus on self-evaluation that will allow clinicians to suggest or implement cost efficiencies before they are required by the political and economic pressures.

- *Advocate for funding to be allocated according to the two previous criteria, with some funds available for new or demonstration initiatives.* Ongoing performance measures should be built into the process and audited regularly for compliance. These should have economic consequences as well as the usual sanctions.

- *Base length-of-stay decisions on each client's need and no other mandated criteria.* Program design should include estimates of how long it should take to achieve certain clinical goals but there should always be some allowance for individuals who need more.

- *Focus research on long-term cost-benefit analysis to balance the short-term legislative budget mentality that currently controls resource allocation.* The best possible individualized service for an individual based on his or her need should be the primary criteria for length of stay. The funding should follow the client as the least restrictive level of care is offered.

- *Speak up to challenge dictates of length of stay by funding sources.* Help call attention to the arbitrary nature of these policy decisions and engage in problem solving with policy makers to develop a new method to control costs.

- *Policy makers should drive the process through a results oriented management of funds.* Established programs with proof of effectiveness should be continued with some set aside for new and innovative programs but with focused performance measures to insure accountability. Additional funding would be awarded based on trial period outcomes.

- *The criminal justice system should only support those programs that reduce cost and recidivism.* The mental health system should take responsibility for those clients who were abandoned to the criminal justice system and use their resources to prevent them from falling into the criminal justice system. To do otherwise is poor practice and should be identified as such. Accountability in the mental health system is the missing ingredient.

How long a person stays in a drug treatment program is a decision that cannot be made ethically by someone who has no knowledge of the individual case, and should not be made by policy makers. Only clinicians should make clinical decisions. The economic drivers need to be reformulated to put the burden of decision as to how best to spend the money on the treatment provider. Focused performance measures with targeted outcomes, both short- and long-term, will help funders identify the responsible and efficient providers that should be funded.

About the Author

Julien Devereux, LMSW-ACP, LCDC, is the Regional Director for Cornell Companies, Inc., supervising all the pre-release and juvenile programs in Texas. Trained as a social worker and chemical dependency counselor, his most recent years in the substance abuse field have been as a program director and regional oversight administrator. For six years he was the Director at the Dallas County Judicial Treatment Center, which was recognized in 1997 by the American Correctional Association as a "Best Practice" program.

References

American Psychiatric Association. (1987). *Diagnostic and statistical manual of mental disorders* (3rd ed., Revised). Washington, DC: Author.

American Psychiatric Association. (1994). *Diagnostic and statistical manual of mental disorders* (4th ed.). Washington, DC: Author.

ASAM PPC-2 (1996). American Society of Addiction Medicine, Patient Placement Criteria for the Treatment of Substance-Related Disorders (ASAM PPC-2). Chevy Chase, MD: American Society of Addiction Medicine.

Barthwell, A. G., Bokos, P., Bailey, J., Haser, N., Nisenbaum, M., Devereux, J., & Senay, E. C. (1995). Interventions/Wilmer: A continuum of care for substance abusers in the criminal justice system. *Journal of Psychoactive Drugs, 27*(1), 39-47.

Devereux, J. (1990). *Pre/Post treatment functioning of poly drug abusers.* Master Thesis for MSSW at UTA Graduate School of Social Work.

Simpson, D. D. (1981). Treatment for drug abuse: Follow-up outcomes and length of time spent. *Archives of General Psychiatry, 38*(8), 875-880.

Simpson, D. D., Joe, G. W., Broome, K. M., Hiller, M. L., Knight, K., & Rowan-Szal, G. A. (1997). Program diversity and treatment retention rates in the Drug Abuse Treatment Outcome Study (DATOS). *Psychology of Addictive Behaviors, 11*(4), 279-293.

Chapter 27

Correctional Treatment and the TCU Treatment Model

by D. Dwayne Simpson, Ph.D., and Kevin Knight, Ph.D.

Introduction 27-1
    Scope of Problem 27-1
    Positive Impact of Treatment Programs 27-2
    Not Enough Treatment Spots 27-2
Delivering and Managing Effective Treatment 27-3
The TCU Treatment Process Model 27-3
Special Interventions and Counseling Manuals 27-5
Process Evaluation Can Lead to Better Outcomes 27-6
Disseminating and Applying Research Findings 27-6

INTRODUCTION

Scope of Problem

According to the Bureau of Justice Statistics (BJS), the U.S. adult prison and jail inmate population has reached the two million mark, with drug-involved offenders comprising the majority of the incarcerated population (BJS Bulletin, 2000). In a 1997 BJS survey, approximately half of all state and federal inmates reported that they had used drugs in the month before their offense, and over three-quarters indicated that they had used drugs during their lifetime (BJS 1999). Almost one in three prisoners said they had committed their current offense while under the influence of drugs (not including alcohol), and about one in six had committed their offense to get money for drugs. In addition, a quarter of state and a sixth of federal prisoners had experienced problems consistent with a history of alcohol abuse or dependence. For example, 41% of state prisoners and 30% of federal prisoners reported having con-

Reprinted, with updates, with permission of the American Corrctional Association, Latham, Maryland, from the 2000 State of Corrections. *An earlier version of this chapter appeared in* Offender Substance Abuse Report, *Vol. 1, No. 4, July/August 2001, also with permission of the ACA.*

sumed as much as a fifth of liquor in a single day, and 40% of state and 29% of federal prisoners said they had a past alcohol-related domestic dispute.

Along with contributing to a record level for inmate capacity, offenders with serious drug problems are having a profoundly negative impact on our nation's public safety and financial health. For example, in a report by the National Center on Addiction and Substance Abuse (1998), 43% of those identified as "regular drug users" in state correctional systems were incarcerated for a violent offense, including murder, manslaughter, rape, robbery, kidnapping, and aggravated assault. Financially, the U.S. spends $246 billion annually in direct costs related to alcohol and drug abuse (Harwood et al., 1998), with an additional $30 billion spent each year to incarcerate offenders with drug problems (National Center on Addiction and Substance Abuse, 1998).

Positive Impact of Treatment Programs

By providing therapeutic intervention, however, criminal justice agencies have a unique opportunity to identify and rehabilitate (or habilitate) drug-involved offenders who are likely, if untreated, to return to a personally and socially destructive pattern of drug use and criminal activity following release from prison. Indeed, research has shown that focused rehabilitation-oriented treatment services can lead to favorable outcomes following incarceration (Andrews et al., 1990; Gendreau, 1996). Particularly within correctional settings, intensive long-term treatment programs (such as modified in-prison therapeutic communities) have been found to reduce post-incarceration relapse (i.e., return to drug use) and recidivism (i.e., arrests, reconviction, and reincarceration). For example, a Bureau of Prisons' outcome evaluation based on 1,866 inmates treated at 20 institutions showed they were 73% less likely than an untreated comparison group to be rearrested in the first six months after release from prison (Pelissier et al., 1998). Results of urinalysis tests also suggested that treatment was associated with a 44% reduction in use of drugs during those months. Likewise, recent evaluations of Delaware's Key-Crest, California's Amity, and Texas's Kyle New Vision prison-based therapeutic community (TC) treatment programs have shown that, compared to their untreated counterparts, drug-involved inmates who complete in-prison drug treatment are significantly less likely to return to a life of drug use and crime following release from prison (Knight et al., 1999; Martin et al., 1999; Wexler et al., 1999). Furthermore, these findings are even more pronounced among those who participate in aftercare treatment (Griffith et al., 1999; Hiller et al., 1999).

Not Enough Treatment Spots

Nevertheless, the majority of offenders with substance abuse problems continue to return to society untreated, and go back to a life of alcohol and drug use and criminal activity. Simply put, there are not enough treatment slots within the correctional system to meet the demand. In a 1997 survey of state departments of corrections, 70% to 85% of state prisoners were found to be in need of substance abuse treatment; yet only 13% were receiving treatment prior to release (National Center on Addiction and Substance Abuse, 1998). Even with the recent initiatives to expand the availability of treatment to criminal offenders, it is unlikely that the demand for treatment can be met fully.

DELIVERING AND MANAGING EFFECTIVE TREATMENT

Given the limited availability of treatment, therefore, it is critical that treatment institutions identify individuals who are the most appropriate candidates for their programs and determine which of their treatment components are the most likely to lead to positive behavioral changes. These goals can be realized, in part, by looking into the "black box" of treatment process; that is, by documenting and critically examining what occurs during treatment. Should treatment programs target only inmates who recognize they have a drug problem, who see the need for help, and have the desire to be treated? Or are the greatest gains to be achieved by targeting the less motivated, higher-risk inmates (perhaps the ones who also commit a disproportionately higher number of crimes) with programming specifically tailored to their needs? In addition, are inmate perceptions of self, peers, counselors, and/or custodial staff related to how well they participate in the treatment program and how successful they are at refraining from post-treatment drug use and criminal activity? Only through examination of the therapeutic process will there begin to be trustworthy answers to these questions.

At issue is a widely shared interest in improving the overall effectiveness and efficiency of correctional drug treatment in this country. Some call it "matching clients (or offenders) with treatment," but simply stated it means providing services that are appropriate to the needs of offenders. Studies of treatment process and its therapeutic components, including how individuals become engaged in treatment, are fundamental to reaching these goals. In order to disaggregate the ingredients underlying treatment retention effects, better assessment and dynamic process models are required. By conceptualizing treatment in discrete phases—e.g., outreach, induction, engagement, treatment, and aftercare—intervention and evaluation strategies come into sharper focus (Simpson, 1997).

Client sociodemographic and other pretreatment characteristics traditionally have not been strong predictors of outcomes. However, improved assessments of client functioning and analytic techniques in recent years are modifying this view. Addiction severity (particularly cocaine use), alcohol use, criminal history, social resources, and psychological dysfunction at treatment intake influence engagement and retention. Of particular importance are the client's motivation for treatment and readiness to change (Simpson & Joe, 1993).

THE TCU TREATMENT PROCESS MODEL

A major focus of drug abuse treatment research at the Institute of Behavioral Research (IBR) at Texas Christian University (TCU) has been to develop a model of "treatment process" (Simpson, 2001; see Figure 27.1). The TCU Treatment Process model is intended to identify key therapeutic components involved in the delivery of effective treatment, establish their functional linkages and sequential stages, and document how they are related empirically to client outcomes (Joe et al., 1994, Sells et al., 1977; Simpson, 1998). Improved assessments of these indicators and their systematic monitoring over time by treatment program staff therefore are very important, especially when examined in association with particular interventions and therapeutic stages.

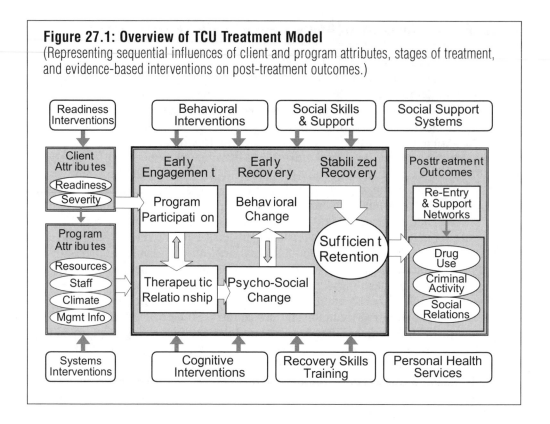

Figure 27.1: Overview of TCU Treatment Model
(Representing sequential influences of client and program attributes, stages of treatment, and evidence-based interventions on post-treatment outcomes.)

The foundation for the TCU Treatment Process Model began over three decades ago with the beginning of large-scale public funding for community-based drug abuse treatment in the United States. Over these years, basic and applied research in this arena has been carried out and reported at an unprecedented rate, based in part on the requirements of federal agencies to evaluate the effectiveness of our national drug abuse treatment system. Beginning in the early 1970s with the Drug Abuse Reporting Program (DARP), followed by the Treatment Outcome Prospective Study (TOPS) a decade later, and continuing through the 1990s with the Drug Abuse Treatment Outcome Studies (DATOS), national evaluations have examined over 65,000 admissions to 272 treatment programs using multimodality and multisite sampling plans that allow the study of treatment in natural settings. These national projects comprise only part of the large body of evidence accumulated over the past 30 years that supports the general effectiveness of drug treatment (Gerstein & Harwood, 1990; Hubbard et al., 1989; Simpson & Brown, 1999; Simpson & Curry, 1997; Simpson & Sells, 1982).

Key to effective treatment process, an individual's length of stay in drug abuse treatment has been found to be one of the most consistent findings across these evaluations. It has been one of the best predictors of follow-up outcomes, with the general relationship between treatment retention and outcomes being replicated across all major modalities in all three national evaluation studies funded by the National Institute on Drug Abuse (NIDA). Retention represents a convenient index of several client, therapeutic, and environmental factors that contribute to treatment effectiveness. Factors that influence a person to remain in treatment include interactions among individual needs, motivation factors, social pressures, and aspects of the treatment program itself such as policy and practices, counselor assignment, accessibility, and level of services offered. In general, these represent an "engagement" process that occurs in several sequential phases.

As illustrated in Figure 27.1, the TCU Treatment Process Model describes these phases, including several key ingredients in the so-called "black box of treatment." In general, there are sequential therapeutic elements that link together over time to help sustain treatment retention and thereby improve outcomes after discharge. More specifically, higher program participation as measured by counseling session attendance is associated with better therapeutic relationships (including rapport with counselor and confidence in treatment), and these factors promote positive behavioral changes and psychosocial functioning later in treatment. These indicators of early recovery, in turn, are related to longer retention. Understanding these dynamics is particularly important because clients who stay in methadone treatment for at least a year are *five times* more likely to have favorable follow-up outcomes on drug use and criminality measures (Simpson, Joe, & Rowan-Szal, 1997). Multivariate analytic models tested in a variety of community and correctional settings have helped to establish more clearly the directional relationships between client motivation, treatment process variables (i.e., therapeutic rapport, program participation, behavioral compliance, and psychosocial improvements), retention, and follow-up outcomes (Broome et al., 1997; Joe et al., 1999; Simpson, Joe, Dansereau, & Chatham, 1997; Simpson et al., 2000; Simpson, Joe, Rowan-Szal, & Greener, 1997).

SPECIAL INTERVENTIONS AND COUNSELING MANUALS

Because offenders enter correctional drug treatment programs with different levels of motivation and problem severity, it is not surprising that many can benefit from special "induction" efforts to clarify the needs and purpose of treatment during the initial planning stage (Blankenship et al., 1999).

Several interventions also have been applied successfully to impact treatment engagement and early recovery indicators for clients. For example, counseling based on a cognitive visual representation technique (called node-link mapping) improves client engagement, progress during treatment, and follow-up outcomes (Dansereau et al., 1995; Dansereau et al., 1993; Joe et al., 1997; Pitre et al., 1998).

"Contingency management" protocols that offer social recognition, small gifts, or treatment supportive items—e.g., bus tokens or cab fare—can increase counseling attendance and the rate of drug-free urine screens, thereby strengthening positive behaviors early in treatment (Rowan-Szal et al., 1994; Rowan-Szal et al., 1997).

Specialized group education materials—such as HIV/AIDS prevention, sexual health and communication skills training for women and men, and transition to aftercare training—were shown to improve knowledge and psychosocial functioning (Bartholomew et al., 2000; Bartholomew et al., 1994; Boatler et al., 1994; Hiller et al., 1996).

Each of these modules for special needs has counselor manuals that provide detailed guidelines on group discussions and procedures. Likewise, we have found that positive change in the family and social support networks of clients accompanies therapeutic engagement and early recovery (Knight & Simpson, 1996).

PROCESS EVALUATION CAN LEAD TO BETTER OUTCOMES

Improving drug abuse treatment effectiveness requires an understanding of the dynamic components of therapeutic process, including client strengths and deficits, program participation, therapeutic relationships, psychosocial functioning, and behavioral compliance. Our research has identified several measurable domains with direct connections to better treatment retention and outcomes:

- *Progress reports.* The findings suggest that *client-level reports* on needs and progress throughout treatment as well as *program-level reports* based on aggregated client records could improve clinical care and program management. More specifically, each offender's cognitive and behavioral responses to services can be used to evaluate progress through successive stages of engagement and recovery.

- *Program statistical reports.* At the agency level, efficient assessment systems that include routine monitoring of client retention (or drop-out) rates, services delivered, and therapeutic interactions are feasible for better accountability of program functioning. In the long run, this will facilitate efforts to match client needs with appropriate services and manage clinical care.

DISSEMINATING AND APPLYING RESEARCH FINDINGS

Comprehensive instruments for assessing clients throughout treatment, counselor and client interactions, delivery of services, and outcomes are available free-of-charge at the IBR website (*www.ibr.tcu.edu*). Also included are comprehensive lists of publications and instructions on how to obtain electronic versions (via free downloads from the website) or hard copies (at cost of printing) of the series of counseling manuals developed and being disseminated to the field. Collectively, these materials are intended to help improve treatment assessments and targeted interventions that can raise the overall quality of services for individuals with drug-related problems.

About the Authors

D. Dwayne Simpson, Ph.D., is Director and S. B. Sells Professor of Psychology at the Institute of Behavioral Research, Texas Christian University. Kevin Knight, Ph.D., is Research Scientist at the Institute, and is co-editor of OSA.

This project was supported by Grant No. 1999-RT-VX-K027 awarded by the National Institute of Justice, Office of Justice Programs, U. S. Department of Justice. Points of view in this document are those of the authors and do not necessarily represent the official position or policies of the U. S. Department of Justice. Correspondence should be addressed to Institute of Behavioral Research, Texas Christian University, TCU Box 298740, Fort Worth, TX 76129. More information (including data collection instruments that can be downloaded) is available on the Internet at www.ibr.tcu.edu and electronic mail can be sent to ibr@tcu.edu.

References

Andrews, D. A., Zinger, I., Hoge, R. D., Bonta, J., Gendreau, P., & Cullen, F. T. (1990). Does correctional treatment work? A clinically relevant and psychologically informed meta-analysis. *Criminology, 28,* 369-404.

Bartholomew, N. G., Hiller, M. L., Knight, K., Nucatola, D. C., & Simpson, D. D. (2000). Effectiveness of communication and relationship skills training for men in substance abuse treatment. *Journal of Substance Abuse Treatment, 18*(3), 217-225.

Bartholomew, N. G., Rowan-Szal, G. A., Chatham, L. R., & Simpson, D. D. (1994). Effectiveness of a specialized intervention for women in a methadone program. *Journal of Psychoactive Drugs, 26*(3), 249-255.

Blankenship, J., Dansereau, D. F., & Simpson, D. D. (1999). Cognitive enhancements of readiness for corrections-based treatment for drug abuse. *The Prison Journal, 79*(4), 431-445.

Boatler, J. F., Knight, K., & Simpson, D. D. (1994). Assessment of an AIDS intervention program during drug abuse treatment. *Journal of Substance Abuse Treatment, 11*(4), 367-372.

Broome, K. M., Knight, D. K., Knight, K., Hiller, M. L., & Simpson, D. D. (1997). Peer, family, and motivational influences on drug treatment process and recidivism for probationers. *Journal of Clinical Psychology, 53*(4), 387-397.

Bureau of Justice Statistics. (1999, January). *Substance abuse and treatment, state and federal prisoners, 1997.* NCJ-172871. Washington, DC: U.S. Department of Justice.

Bureau of Justice Statistics Bulletin. (2000, August). *Prisoners in 1999* (NCJ-183476). Washington, DC: U.S. Department of Justice.

Dansereau, D. F., Dees, S. M., Greener, J. M., & Simpson, D. D. (1995). Node-link mapping and the evaluation of drug abuse counseling sessions. *Psychology of Addictive Behaviors, 9*(3), 195-203.

Dansereau, D. F., Joe, G. W., & Simpson, D. D. (1993). Node-link mapping: A visual representation strategy for enhancing drug abuse counseling. *Journal of Counseling Psychology, 40*(4), 385-395.

Gendreau, P. (1996). Offender rehabilitation: What we know and what needs to be done. *Criminal Justice and Behavior, 23,* 144-161.

Gerstein, D. R., & Harwood, H. J. (Eds.). (1990). *Treating drug problems: Vol. 1. A study of the evolution, effectiveness, and financing of public and private drug treatment systems.* Washington, DC: National Academy Press.

Griffith, J. D., Hiller, M. L., Knight, K., & Simpson, D. D. (1999). A cost-effectiveness analysis of in-prison therapeutic community treatment and risk classification. *The Prison Journal, 79*(3), 352-368.

Harwood, H., Fountain, D., & Livermore, G. (1998). *The economic cost of alcohol and drug abuse in the United States, 1992.* Prepared by the Lewin Group, the National Institute on Drug and Alcohol Abuse (NIDA), and the National Institute on Alcohol Abuse and Alcoholism (NIAAA). Available online: *www.165.112.78.61/EconomicCosts/Intro.html.*

Hiller, M. L., Knight, K., & Simpson, D. D. (1999). Prison-based substance abuse treatment, residential aftercare and recidivism. *Addiction, 94*(6), 833-842.

Hiller, M. L., Rowan-Szal, G. A., Bartholomew, N. G., & Simpson, D. D. (1996). Effectiveness of a specialized women's intervention in a residential treatment program. *Substance Use & Misuse, 31*(6), 771-783.

Hubbard, R. L., Marsden, M. E., Rachal, J. V., Harwood, H. J., Cavanaugh, E. R., & Ginzburg, H. M. (1989). *Drug abuse treatment: A national study of effectiveness.* Chapel Hill: University of North Carolina Press.

Joe, G. W., Dansereau, D. F., Pitre, U., & Simpson, D. D. (1997). Effectiveness of node-link mapping enhanced counseling for opiate addicts: A 12-month posttreatment follow-up. *Journal of Nervous and Mental Disease, 185*(5), 306-313.

Joe, G. W., Simpson, D. D., & Broome, K. M. (1999). Retention and patient engagement models for different treatment modalities in DATOS. *Drug and Alcohol Dependence, 57,* 113-125.

Joe, G. W., Simpson, D. D., & Sells, S. B. (1994). Treatment process and relapse to opioid use during methadone maintenance. *American Journal of Drug and Alcohol Abuse, 20*(2), 173-197.

Knight, D. K., & Simpson, D. D. (1996). Influences of family and friends on client progress during drug abuse treatment. *Journal of Substance Abuse, 8*(4), 417-429.

Knight, K., Simpson, D. D., & Hiller, M. L. (1999). Three-year reincarceration outcomes for in-prison therapeutic community treatment in Texas. *The Prison Journal, 79*(3), 337-351.

Martin, S. S., Butzin, C. A., Saum, C. A., & Inciardi, J. A. (1999). Three-year outcomes of therapeutic community treatment for drug-involved offenders in Delaware. *The Prison Journal, 79*(3), 294-320.

National Center on Addiction and Substance Abuse. (1998, January). *Behind bars: Substance abuse and America's prison population.* New York: Author.

Pelissier, M. M., Gaes, G., Rhodes, W., Camp, S., O'Neil, J., Wallace, S., & Saylor, W. (1998, January). *TRIAD drug treatment evaluation project six month interim report.* Washington, DC: Federal Bureau of Prisons, Office of Research and Evaluation.

Pitre, U., Dansereau, D. F., Newbern, D., & Simpson, D. D. (1998). Residential drug abuse treatment for probationers: Use of node-link mapping to enhance participation and progress. *Journal of Substance Abuse Treatment, 15*(6), 535-543.

Rowan-Szal, G. A., Joe, G. W., Chatham, L. R., & Simpson, D. D. (1994). A simple reinforcement system for methadone clients in a community-based treatment program. *Journal of Substance Abuse Treatment, 11*(3), 217-223.

Rowan-Szal, G. A., Joe, G. W., Hiller, M. L., & Simpson, D. D. (1997). Increasing early engagement in methadone treatment. *Journal of Maintenance in the Addictions, 1*(1), 49-60.

Sells, S. B., Demaree, R. G., Simpson, D. D., Joe, G. W., & Gorsuch, R. L. (1977). Issues in the evaluation of drug abuse treatment. *Professional Psychology, 8*(4), 609-640.

Simpson, D. D. (1997). Effectiveness of drug abuse treatment: A review of research from field settings. In J. A. Egertson, D. M. Fox, & A. I. Leshner (Eds.), *Treating drug abusers effectively* (pp. 41-73). Cambridge, MA: Blackwell Publishers of North America.

Simpson, D. D. (1998). *TCU data collection forms for methadone outpatient treatment.* Available online: *www.ibr.tcu.edu.* Fort Worth: Texas Christian University, Institute of Behavioral Research.

Simpson, D. D. (2001). Modeling treatment process and outcomes. *Addiction, 96*(2), 207-211.

Simpson, D. D., & Brown, B. S. (Eds.). (December, 1999). Special issue: Treatment process and outcome studies from DATOS. *Drug and Alcohol Dependence, 57*(2).

Simpson, D. D., & Curry, S. J. (Eds.). (1997). Special issue: Drug Abuse Treatment Outcome Study (DATOS). *Psychology of Addictive Behaviors, 11*(4).

Simpson, D. D., & Joe, G. W. (1993). Motivation as a predictor of early dropout from drug abuse treatment. *Psychotherapy, 30*(2), 357-368.

Simpson, D. D., Joe, G. W., Dansereau, D. F., & Chatham, L. R. (1997). Strategies for improving methadone treatment process and outcomes. *Journal of Drug Issues, 27*(2), 239-260.

Simpson, D. D., Joe, G. W., Greener, J. M., & Rowan-Szal, G. A. (2000). Modeling year 1 outcomes with treatment process and posttreatment social influences. *Substance Use & Misuse, 35*(12-14), 1911-1930.

Simpson, D. D., Joe, G. W., & Rowan-Szal, G. A. (1997). Drug abuse treatment retention and process effects on follow-up outcomes. *Drug and Alcohol Dependence, 47*, 227-235.

Simpson, D. D., Joe, G. W., Rowan-Szal, G. A., & Greener, J. M. (1997). Drug abuse treatment process components that improve retention. *Journal of Substance Abuse Treatment, 14*(6), 565-572.

Simpson, D. D., & Sells, S. B. (1982). Effectiveness of treatment for drug abuse: An overview of the DARP research program. *Advances in Alcohol and Substance Abuse, 2*(1), 7-29.

Wexler, H. K., Melnick, G., Lowe, L., & Peters, J. (1999). Three-year reincarceration outcomes for Amity in-prison therapeutic community and aftercare in California. *The Prison Journal, 79*(3), 321-336.

Chapter 28

Implementing a Readiness Program for Mandated Substance Abuse Treatment

by Sandra M. Dees, Ph.D., Donald F. Dansereau, Ph.D., and D. Dwayne Simpson, Ph.D.

Introduction 28-2

Readiness for Treatment a Key to Success 28-2

    Methods Not Designed for Criminal Justice 28-2

    Special Issues for Corrections 28-3

Brief Description of the Treatment Program 28-3

Intent of the Readiness Series 28-4

Session 1: Activities to Enhance Mood and Self-Esteem 28-4

    Tower of Strengths 28-4

    Weekly Planner 28-5

Session 2: Activities to Develop a Need for Positive Change 28-5

    Downward Spiral 28-5

    Change Maps 28-6

Session 3: Activities to Develop a Positive View of the Program and
  Identify Important Personal Actions 28-6

    Believe It or Not 28-6

    Personal Action List 28-6

    Top 10 Reasons for "Working the Program" 28-7

Session 4: Activities Providing Strategies for Making the Most of This Time . . . 28-7

    Set Effects: Seal Act/Costume Ball 28-7

    Set: Sleep/Strength List 28-7

    Pegword Memory Technique 28-7

    Science of Imagery 28-8

Impact of the Readiness Activities: Research Findings 28-8

    Comparisons of During-Treatment Impact: Standard vs. Enhanced 28-8

An earlier version of this chapter appeared in Offender Substance Abuse Report, *Vol. 2, No. 2, March/April 2002.*

Reactions to the Series of Activities: A "Consumer
Satisfaction" Questionnaire 28-9
Designing a Readiness for Treatment Program: Conclusions and Caveats 28-10
Motivation to Change or to "Work the Program" 28-10
Implementation Issues 28-11
Final Comments 28-11

INTRODUCTION

This chapter describes a series of activities that were designed and implemented, in the context of a research study, to enhance the motivation of individuals (proba-tion violators) participating in a mandated, residential substance abuse treatment pro-gram. These activities were created for specific, but not exclusive, use in a criminal justice treatment setting and target the early stages of treatment—the period when voluntary clients frequently drop out and when mandated clients decide to either actively participate and become personally involved, or, conversely, just "do the time" but never fully engage in the process. The series has come from the second phase of the Cognitive Enhancements for the Treatment of Probationers (CETOP) research project, a collaborative study involving criminal justice and a Texas Christian University (TCU) research team. (For first-phase results, using node-link mapping, see Pitre et al., 1997). This chapter sets out the conceptual base underlying these activities, briefly describes the activities themselves, and summarizes research findings on the series.

READINESS FOR TREATMENT A KEY TO SUCCESS

A model of the treatment process, based on three decades of empirical research at the TCU Institute of Behavioral Research (IBR) reveals that client motivation for treatment, along with interventions that promote readiness and engagement, are key factors in determining treatment effectiveness (Simpson, 1997). Extensive research, both from the IBR and other sectors, identifies readiness, for either voluntary or mandated treatment, as a critical prerequisite to treatment success (e.g., Farabee et al., 1995). Motivation to make life changes and engage in treatment (Simpson & Joe, 1993), as well as confidence that treatment can be successful (DiClemente et al., 1995), are also identified factors that promote treatment readiness.

Methods Not Designed for Criminal Justice

To date, however, systematic efforts to develop and evaluate methods for enhanc-ing readiness by building motivation and confidence have been limited and highly focused. Examples of these efforts are the work on treatment role induction (e.g., Ravndal & Vaglum, 1992), attempts to enhance self-efficacy (e.g., DeJong, 1994), and research on enhancing motivation for treatment through initial interview tech-niques (e.g., Miller,1996). These techniques differ from traditional treatment strategies (which focus on defining problems, examining problem history and behavior, and looking for solutions) by placing heavy emphasis on the need to prepare clients for their roles in treatment and to uncover positive personal strengths that can provide a foundation for building self-confidence. Unfortunately, these approaches are well suited to individual or small group counseling but are not readily applicable to the larger group settings of the criminal justice system. This is an important consideration in view of the high cost of individual counseling and the pervasiveness of group-based treatment in criminal justice settings.

Special Issues for Corrections

In correctional settings, the lack of motivation and readiness for change are especially important barriers to effective intervention efforts (DeLeon et al., 2000). The most obvious threat to treatment effectiveness comes from individuals who are motivated to avoid additional jail time rather than to make serious changes in their lifestyles. In addition, since incarcerated individuals routinely exhibit greater cognitive deficits than the general population of drug abusers (Ross & Fabiano, 1985), some treatment concepts and planning activities will be lost on them unless they have the motivation to "stick"—i.e., to stay involved with a treatment thrust until it is clear how a particular concept or experience applies to their own lives. Criminal justice programs are frequently conducted in relatively large groups (18-30) and, consequently, count on individual motivation and responsibility for both individual and group progress. The "readiness series" described here incorporates what is not heavily emphasized in a traditional treatment program (e.g., preparing clients for their roles in treatment and uncovering positive personal strengths to build self-confidence) and provides treatment activities designed for use with large groups (18-35 participants).

BRIEF DESCRIPTION OF THE TREATMENT PROGRAM

Tarrant County judges sent probation violators with drug problems to this 16-week residential substance abuse treatment facility (SATF) program in Mansfield, Texas. Operated by the county Department of Community Supervision and Corrections, it provided modified therapeutic community treatment for approximately 420 probationers each year, with four "communities" of 30-40 probationers in residence at any given time.

During this 18-month second phase of CETOP, 615 offenders ("residents") were admitted to treatment; 500 completed treatment (excluding a community in which counselors were changed and a small percentage who refused to participate, were illiterate, absconded, or were transferred). A new community, designated by the project design as "standard" or "enhanced," was formed each month from a random (in order received) county list of mandated offenders. In all, residents of eight enhanced communities (n=253) received readiness activities; eight communities (n=247) received the standard program. These residents were 71% male; 54% Anglo, 34% African American, 9% Hispanic, and 3% Other, with 60% having a high school diploma/GED. Average age was 30.2 years. Alcohol was the most frequently used drug, followed by marijuana, and crack and/or cocaine. Only 7% reported weekly heroin use.

INTENT OF THE READINESS SERIES

The four-session series of activities was presented over an approximately nine-day span of time in the fourth and fifth weeks of the 16-week residential treatment program. Each session lasted two hours, was conducted by a TCU research staff psychologist and/ or an SATF counselor with the full community (30-40 participants) present, and followed the sequence indicated in the following descriptions.

Specifically, the TCU Readiness Series was intended to:

- Provide opportunities for boosting confidence in personal ability to do positive things;

- Indirectly show the need for treatment and provide evidence that treatment works;

- Allow participants to learn and use strategies (e.g., mnemonics, visualization) that can enhance treatment effects; and

- Require participants to identify personal actions needed to get the most from treatment.

Effort was made to diverge from traditional treatment techniques in a unique way, often attacking objectives indirectly but always requiring active participant involvement with activities that would address the issues of self-efficacy, motivation, and the client's role in treatment. Participants were given multiple opportunities to construct personal reasons for getting the most out of treatment, to make plans for treatment, and to have enough personal confidence and confidence in the program to move on those plans. The following sections briefly describe each readiness curriculum activity by session, in the order that they are implemented. (Specific details and scripts are documented in three manuals: Dees & Dansereau, 1997; Czuchry et al., 1998; Sia et al., 1998).

SESSION 1: ACTIVITIES TO ENHANCE MOOD AND SELF-ESTEEM

Tower of Strengths

This activity uses a very simple sorting task and a graphic "tower" to focus individuals into an hour of constructive and positive thinking about themselves. Given 60 cards containing "personal strength" descriptors (e.g., "caring," "strong," "hard working"), a participant chooses the 10 best self-descriptors plus the five descriptors that fall in the desired ("wish I could be like this") category. Self-descriptors are written into the base of the tower ("foundation") and the wish list is put at the top ("ideal"). On each card is a code letter indicating a personal category for this descriptor. The "Parts of You" code sheet briefly outlines six personal categories: social, thinking, health and performance, emotional, motivational, and life view. To make the strengths and this activity more memorable, participants record the number of strengths they've chosen for each code, then draw pictures or write a word or phrase to help them remember each strength. Scripted small group discussions follow the sorting activity. Each group follows a list of discussion topics (e.g., "Name one of your strengths. How many others named this strength? How have you used this strength in the past? Could it be used in your current situation?"). A counselor or other leader monitors the discussions and provides focus and thought-provoking questions as needed.

Weekly Planner

Following the "Tower" discussions, each participant receives a set of 80 quotations and a seven-day planner sheet with instructions to choose a favorite, motivating quote for each day and write it into the planner. The planner is to be put in a place where it can be seen and read each day. This provides a reminder of the entire session, with the potential of facilitating efforts to focus on positive, constructive thinking and a good feeling about both self and treatment.

SESSION 2: ACTIVITIES TO DEVELOP A NEED FOR POSITIVE CHANGE

Downward Spiral

This Monopoly-like board game is designed to show—in an experiential, role-playing mode—the need for positive change (see Figure 28.1). Five to six players

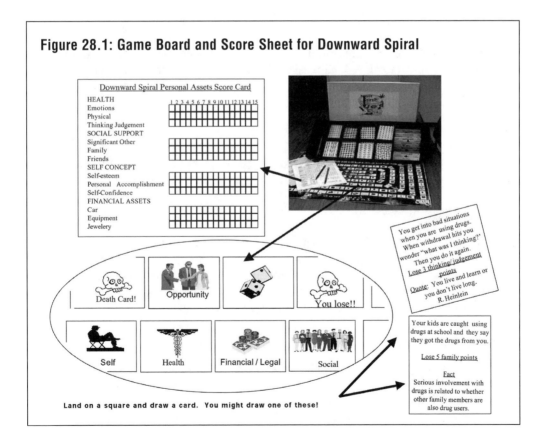

Figure 28.1: Game Board and Score Sheet for Downward Spiral

start from the premise that each is continuing to abuse alcohol and/or drugs; all start equally with personal asset points (45 each for "health," "social support," "self-concept") and a $7,000 value on "financial assets." They throw dice to see how far they can move around the "downward spiral" that snakes in a circle to the center of the board. A move forward on the board may cause a player to draw a card describing a drug episode and its consequences, with the player as central character. The episode is read aloud, along with an associated fact, a quote, and a statement of the loss ("lose 5 family-social support points"). Other cards send players directly to jail or to the hospital, remove a player from the game with the "death card," or provide a chance to actually earn points by remembering a fact or quote read by another player. When time is called, the "winner" is the last player left alive and/or the one who loses the least number of personal assets. All of the episode cards were created from feedback collected during focus group sessions with offenders receiving mandated treatment; they are blunt and realistic. Losses in the game are tied as accurately as possible to the impact of consequences. The group discussion which follows the game focuses on the reality of these encounters, the consequences, and the losses in players' lives, both in the past and the future. The message from this friendly game with a group of peers is never overtly stated but is quite clear: "If you continue with drugs and alcohol, you will probably lose most of what you value in life and, ultimately, you stand to lose life itself."

Change Maps

As a follow-up to the Downward Spiral game and to stimulate personal thinking about change, two "guide maps" (fill-in-the-blank graphics) are assigned as homework. One map guides an individual's thinking about successful changes in the past. The other, a "magical change" map, asks what would happen if that individual "could magically change things about myself" without worrying about factors that might work against these changes. The following session opens with a brief discussion of feelings and insights from these maps.

SESSION 3: ACTIVITIES TO DEVELOP A POSITIVE VIEW OF THE PROGRAM AND IDENTIFY IMPORTANT PERSONAL ACTIONS

Believe It or Not

Participants are asked to rate as true or false a series of statements about the treatment program (e.g., information about relapse rates, previous responses to the program by other offenders). They then receive the correct answers, all of which confirm the premise that the program works. This, and the next three activities are intended to help participants develop a positive view of the program.

Personal Action List

This activity instructs participants to think of the personal actions they need to take during treatment and select the six most important. Small group discussions (the Team Activity) then refine the personal action list (PAL) so that each action is specific and easy to evaluate as done or not done. "Script" cards are used to cue the discussions to insure appropriate evaluation of each activity and participation from each group member. This is the construction of a very specific personal treatment plan, critiqued by peers for its workability.

Top 10 Reasons for "Working the Program"

This is an off-beat David Letterman-type look at the program through the humor of previous program participants. The activity uses prison slang (no profanity) and was taken from actual attempts made by former residents to come up with humorous statements of (essentially true) reasons for "working the program."

SESSION 4: ACTIVITIES PROVIDING STRATEGIES FOR MAKING THE MOST OF THIS TIME

Set Effects: Seal Act/Costume Ball

Half of the participants receive written instructions that they will see, on a five-second view of an overhead projection, a picture of a "seal act." Instructions for the other half of the group indicate the picture will be of a "costume ball." Participants then briefly see an ambiguous picture and are asked to answer questions about it. Through group discussion, they find that what they have "seen" differs from what others in their group have experienced. They eventually discover the difference in instructions and then can discuss the effect of initial "set" and how different expectations have actually resulted in different visual experiences. The indirect lesson here, and in the next activity, is that expectations strongly influence behavior and the perception of reality. Expectations about treatment, and their importance to outcomes, are discussed. This and the next three activities present ideas and strategies that can be used for making the most of treatment time.

Set: Sleep/Strength List

Participants are exposed to a list of words related to the process of sleep but from which the word "sleep" has been intentionally omitted. Asked to recognize words from this list later, many individuals will include the word sleep even though it was not, in fact, on the list. This effect of "set" on memory is used to illustrate that even memories can be influenced by what we expect: items from the list were about sleep and therefore, the word "sleep" led to an erroneous expectation that it too would have been on the list. There is a brief discussion of personal recall or friends' memories of past treatment experiences and how these might affect an individual's current participation in treatment. Participants are then asked to recall their strengths from the Tower of Strengths activity and consider how expectations may have affected that recall.

Pegword Memory Technique

Participants are taught a visualization strategy for remembering a sequence of items and discover that it allows them to learn and recall at a later time even a list of 10 unrelated items with a high degree of accuracy. The strategy ties common objects into a rhymed sequence ("One is a bun... two is a shoe... 10 is a hen") which is learned via group recitation. Then, given a list of 10 items, participants are instructed to create bizarre visual associations between these items and the objects in the rhyme. Subsequent memory for this sequence of items, tested immediately, at the end of the session, and later in treatment is amazingly accurate. This performance comes as a pleasant surprise to those whose faculties have been slowed by drugs and alcohol.

Science of Imagery

The power of imagery—mental visualization and stimulation—is described and examples are given from actual studies of the use of visualization in sports. The uses of imagery in preparing to stay drug free are discussed. Participants receive home-work assignments to use imagery with their personal action lists.

IMPACT OF THE READINESS ACTIVITIES: RESEARCH FINDINGS

Comparisons of During-Treatment Impact: Standard vs. Enhanced

Three studies to date have reported on impact of the readiness series comparing enhanced treatment versus the standard program with no readiness enhancement. Czuchry and Dansereau (1999) found that participants who received these activities rated their communities as significantly more engaged in treatment and more helpful to them than those receiving the standard treatment. (A comprehensive data collection system designed to assess treatment impact for the duration of the grant project provided during-treatment process information both for individuals in enhanced and non-

---

Table 28.1: Means and Standard Deviations by Question Over All Activities on the "Consumer Satisfaction" Questionnaire *[Scale of 1 ("not at all") to 7 ("a lot")]*

Question	N	Mean	SD
1. "Did you get any new ideas from this activity?"	228	5.10	1.02
2. "Did this activity increase your motivation to 'work the program' (get the most out of treatment)?"	225	5.01	1 . 1 6
3. "Do you think this activity will help motivate other residents in your community to work the program?"	223	4.90	1 . 1 5
4. "Did this activity increase your motivation to make positive changes in your life?"	221	5.08	1 . 2 6
5. "Do you think future residents would benefit from this activity?"	219	5.16	1 . 2 5

Note: Means for questions 1,4, and 5 were significantly different from the means of questions 2 and 3 (p values < .02).

enhanced treatment communities (see Simpson et al., 1997). Sia et al. (2000) found that participants receiving the enhanced program rated themselves as more involved in treatment and gave higher ratings to the treatment program and personnel. Finally, a study by Blankenship, Dansereau, and Simpson (1999) showed positive effects specific to less-educated probationers: Those with less than eleventh grade education who participated in the readiness activities (approximately half of the enhanced sample population) showed greater motivation to participate in treatment and more confidence about what treatment could do for them than did their counterparts in standard treatment. This group also expressed greater motivation to resist drugs and alcohol in the future and more confidence in their ability to do so.

Reactions to the Series of Activities: A "Consumer Satisfaction" Questionnaire

For the enhanced-treatment communities only, a questionnaire was distributed after the last session covering all sessions of the eight-hour readiness set. Participants rated each activity on a 1-7 scale (with 1 as "not at all" and 7 as "a lot") for each of five questions (see Table 28.1). Mean ratings for each of these questions appear in Table 28.1. Data were analyzed using one-way repeated measures analyses of variance (a) to assess participants' direct perceptions of series impact via differences in

Table 28.2: Means and Standard Deviations for Each Session and Activity Over Five Questions on the "Consumer Satisfaction" Readiness Questionnaire

[Scale of 1 ("not at all") to 7 ("a lot") *]

Session/ Activity	N	Mean	SD
Session 1: Enhance mood, self-esteem.	227	5.15	1.17
Tower of Strengths		5.23	1.25
Weekly Planner	179**	4.97	1.27
Session 2: Develop a need for positive change.	225	5.21	.26
Downward Spiral		5.41	1.51
Change Maps		5.01	1.41
Session 3: See the program positively, plan.	228	4.86	1.19
Believe It or Not	179**	4.89	1.28
Personal Action List (PAL)		4.94	1.32
PAL Team Activity		4.73	1.44
Top 10 Reasons (for program)		4.92	1.54
Session 4: Thinking strategies that work.	227	5.15	1.19
Seal Act		5.06	1.36
Sleep List		5.17	1.37
Pegword		5.19	1.40
Science of Imagery	178**	5.29	1.38

*Means for sessions 1, 2, and 4 were significantly different from the mean of session 3 (p values of contrasts < .0001).

**These activities were inadvertently left off of the first two communities' rating forms, making the N lower.

responses to the five survey questions (collapsed across sessions) and (b) to assess differences in responses to the four separate sessions (with ratings collapsed across survey questions) as well as to the separate activities.

Analyses of data by questions indicated that "Did this activity increase your motivation to 'work the program'?" and "Do you think this activity will help motivate other residents in your community to work the program?" were given significantly lower ratings than the three questions related to new ideas, motivation to make positive changes, and benefit to future residents. See Table 28.1.

Session and activity analyses (Table 28.2) revealed that Session 3 was least appreciated and differed significantly from the other two sessions. Although responses were generally positive to all aspects of the readiness series, the activities that received the most positive responses were those that differed most from the traditional treatment program. Highest ratings were given for the Downward Spiral game, the Science of Imagery, the Tower of Strengths, the Sleep List, and the Pegword Memory Technique.

Although differences may appear small in Tables 28.1 and 28.2, they are significant from a qualitative and a quantitative standpoint. A majority of participants responded at the high ends of the scales, narrowing both the range of ratings and the range of differences.

DESIGNING A READINESS FOR TREATMENT PROGRAM: CONCLUSIONS AND CAVEATS

Overall reaction to these activities was quite good; responses to the questionnaire probes fell firmly in the positive areas of the rating scales, providing a straightforward answer to the question of whether or not a mandated treatment population would accept this program. In addition, the impact of the enhanced readiness program was clearly evident. Data collected at mid-term for both enhanced and non-enhanced communities showed that individuals who received these activities felt their communities were more involved in treatment and more helpful to them, and were themselves more involved in treatment and more positive about the program and staff. Those with less education who received the enhanced series showed more motivation to participate, more confidence in the program, and more motivation and confidence related to "staying clean" in the future.

Motivation to Change or to "Work the Program"

It is interesting that participants felt these enhancements worked more to increase their own options and motivation to change their lives (and would for future participants as well) than to increase motivation (either their own or that of their peers) to "work the program." One interpretation of this is that the series was identified as different, or at least separate, from the standard treatment activities. This is underscored by the fact that the sessions (and activities) that received the most positive responses were those that differed most from both didactic and confrontational approaches commonly used in treatment programs. Ratings (across all survey questions) were lowest for the Day 3 Session which focused primarily on planning for treatment individually and through group discussion, with a secondary intent of providing very hopeful facts about treatment outcomes, as well as some humor related to the treatment process. The irony here, of course, is that this group of offenders downgraded a link between the readiness series and treatment, but then went on to indicate greater treatment involvement and participation than offenders in communities that did not receive the series.

Implementation Issues

Counselor training and comprehension of why these techniques are being used is especially important with this program. Because these activities have a different look and feel to them as they are brought into a criminal justice setting, they may be discounted by some counselors. There must be an understanding that the differences are intentional and have a purpose. Offenders themselves may grumble initially about "kid stuff," but usually forget this line of commentary as they become more and more involved with the materials.

Final Comments

Does this program increase readiness for treatment? Our results suggest that it does, to the extent that it increases perceived participation in treatment, motivation during treatment, and confidence in one's ability to benefit from treatment. Although participants felt that it provided new ideas and motivated change, they also saw the series as less pertinent to the immediate and specific treatment program than to their own efforts to change. Nevertheless, the effect of the series appears to have been to increase motivation for treatment. Our intent was to provide activities that were for the most part different, both in format and content, from those in the standard treatment program. We hoped that this difference would ultimately stimulate greater involvement in treatment, and we feel that it did. While this program is not ideal, it has given us the basis for future fine-tuning of a conceptually-based readiness program that can be effectively presented to large groups to provide a "jumpstart" for substance abuse treatment.

About the Authors

Sandra M. Dees, Ph.D., Donald F. Dansereau, Ph.D., and D. Dwayne Simpson, Ph.D., are Research Scientist, Professor/Senior Research Scientist, and Director, respectively, at the Institute of Behavioral Research, Texas Christian University. Dr. Dees may be contacted by email at: s.dees@tcu.edu.

This work was supported by the National Institute on Drug Abuse (Grant No. R01DA08608). The interpretations and conclusions, however, do not represent the position of NIDA or the Department of Health and Human Services. The authors are deeply grateful to the Community Supervision and Corrections Department (CSCD) of Tarrant County and the CSCD Substance Abuse Treatment Program in Mansfield, Texas, for their assistance in conducting this research project.

References

Blankenship, J., Dansereau, D. F., & Simpson, D. D. (1999). Cognitive enhancements for treatment readiness among low-educated probationers. *The Prison Journal, 79(4),* 431-445.

Czuchry, M., & Dansereau, D. F. (1999). Drug abuse treatment in criminal justice settings: Enhancing community engagement and helpfulness. *American Journal of Drug and Alcohol Abuse, 26(4),* 537-552.

Czuchry, M., Sia, T. L., Dansereau, D. F., & Blankenship, J. (1998). *Downward Spiral: The game you really don't want to play.* Bloomington, IL: Lighthouse Institute Publishing.

Dees, S. M., & Dansereau, D. F. (Eds.). (1997). *A jumpstart for substance abuse treatment: Readiness activities, a TCU/CETOP manual for counselors.* Fort Worth, TX: Institute of Behavioral Research, Texas Christian University.

DeJong, W. (1994). Relapse prevention: An emerging technology for promoting long-term drug abstinence. *International Journal of the Addictions, 29(6),* 681-705.

DeLeon, G. Melnick, G., Thomas, G., Kressel, D., & Wexler, H. K. (2000). Motivation for treatment in a prison-based therapeutic community. *American Journal of Drug and Alcohol Abuse, 26(1):* 33-46.

DiClemente, C. C., Fairhurst, S. K., & Piotrowski, N. A. (1995). Self-efficacy and addictive behaviors. In J. E. Maddux (Ed.), *Self-efficacy, adaptation, and adjustment: Theory, research, and application.* New York: Plenum Press.

Farabee, D., Simpson, D. D., Dansereau, D. F., & Knight, K. (1995). Cognitive inductions into treatment among drug users on probation. *Journal of Drug issues, 25,* 669-682.

Miller, W. R. (1996). Motivational interviewing: Research, practice, and puzzles. *Addictive Behaviors, 21,* 835-842.

Pitre, U., Dees, S. M., Dansereau, D. F., & Simpson, D. D. (1997). Mapping techniques to improve substance abuse treatment in criminal justice settings. *Journal of Drug Issues, 27(2),* 431-444.

Ravndal, E., & Vaglum, P. (1992). Different intake procedures. *Journal of Substance Abuse Treatment, 9,* 53-58.

Ross, R., & Fabiano, E. (1985). *Time to think: A cognitive model of delinquency prevention and offender rehabilitation.* Johnson City, TN: Institute of Social Sciences and Arts.

Sia, T. L., Czuchry, M., Dansereau, D. F., & Blankenship, J. (1998). *Preparation for change: The Tower of Strengths and The Weekly Planner.* Fort Worth, TX: Institute of Behavioral Research, Texas Christian University.

Sia, T. L., Dansereau, D. F., & Czuchry, M. (2000). Treatment readiness training and probationers' evaluation of substance abuse treatment in a criminal justice setting. *Journal of Substance Abuse Treatment, 19,* 459-467.

Simpson, D. D. (1997). Effectiveness of drug abuse treatment: A review of research from field settings. In J. A. Egertson, D. M. Fox & A. I. Leshner (Eds.), *Treating drug abusers effectively* (pp. 41-73). Cambridge, MA: Blackwell Publishers of North America.

Simpson, D. D., & Joe, G. W. (1993). Motivation as a predictor of early dropout from drug abuse treatment. *Psychotherapy, 30,* 357-568.

Simpson, D. D., Joe, G. W., Dansereau, D. F., & Chatham, L. R. (1997). Strategies for improving methadone treatment process and outcomes. *Journal of Drug Issues, 27(2),* 239-260.

Chapter 29

Readiness and Mandated Treatment: Development and Application of a Functional Model

by Donald F. Dansereau, Ph.D., Selby H. Evans, Ph.D., Michael Czuchry, Ph.D., and Tiffiny L. Sia, Ph.D.

Introduction 29-2
Key Elements of a Treatment Readiness Model 29-2
    Focus on the Consequences of Change ("What if I Change?") 29-2
    Focus on the Treatment Process ("How Do I Change?") 29-4
A Road Map for Readiness 29-4
Practical Applications of the Model 29-6
"What if" Activities 29-7
    Knowledge of Change 29-7
    Acceptance/Attractiveness of Change 29-7
    Resources for Change 29-7
    Confidence in Resources for Dealing With Change 29-8
"How to" Activities 29-8
    Knowledge of Process 29-8
    Resources for Process 29-8
    Confidence in Process 29-9
    Acceptance/Attractiveness of Process 29-9
    Treatment Planning 29-9
Conclusions 29-9

This chapter originally appeared in Offender Substance Abuse Report, *Vol. 3, No. 1, January/February 2003.*

INTRODUCTION

A wealth of empirical evidence has shown that treatment readiness is a key predictor of success for individuals receiving substance abuse treatment both within (e.g., Broome et al., 1997) and outside of the criminal justice system (e.g., De Leon et al., 2001; Simpson & Joe, 1993). Treatment readiness refers to an individual's level of preparedness to actively engage in the behavioral and cognitive changes required in the treatment process. Global models of change and treatment process—e.g., Prochaska & Diclemente's Stages of Change (Prochaska et al., 1992; De Leon's (1996) Integrative Recovery Model; Simpson's (2002) Treatment Process Model—recognize readiness or preparedness as key components of the change process. But because they are global, a more detailed functional model is needed to help guide the development of new interventions as they relate to subcomponents of treatment readiness.

KEY ELEMENTS OF A TREATMENT READINESS MODEL

We have developed one such model, the elements of which are presented in Table 29.1. The first column of the table points out two factors a person needs to consider when seriously confronting a possible change for some undesirable behavior (in this case the undesirable behavior involves legal repercussions of continued substance abuse or other illegal behaviors). First, obviously, are the consequences of changing or not changing (what if?). Second, less obviously, is the process required to achieve the desired change (how to?). Thus, the model captures two primary decision processes that have been identified by others in the substance abuse treatment field (De Leon, 1996; Simpson, 2001; Simpson & Joe, 1993). The present model is designed to provide more detail on the subcomponents of readiness within these two general processes.

Focus on the Consequences of Change ("What if I Change?")

Consider, for illustration, male probationer "Ted" who has been mandated to treatment for a drug offense. Even though it should be clear by default that he has a problem (Ted is, after all, now part of the criminal justice system), he may be only vaguely aware of the full impact that continued substance use entails. For example, Ted also knows he gets into fights with his family and his girlfriend, and that he cannot keep a job, but he does not connect these problems to his drug use. He just feels unlucky to have been caught.

In terms of the model (see Table 29.1), Ted has not yet satisfactorily asked the question, "What will happen if I change?" Ted's limited awareness of the connection between problems in his life and his substance abuse is similar to the precontemplation stage of Prochaska and DiClemente's model (Prochaska et al, 1992), but it is important to note that in our model, this level of awareness—e.g., awareness of the consequences of changing or not changing, or "what if?"—represents a type of readiness that is distinct and separate from readiness for the *process* of change (or "how to?"). Our model is perhaps more similar, in this regard, to De Leon's Integrative Recovery Model (De Leon, 1996), in which he distinguishes between readiness for change and readiness for treatment, but our model provides somewhat greater functional detail.

In Ted's case, he is aware of problems in his life but this knowledge is inadequate and not concretely applied to him. He wants a better life, but in his mind this would not

Table 29.1: Descriptions of the Readiness Elements

FOCUS	ELEMENTS	DESCRIPTIONS	DESCRIPTIVE QUESTIONS
CONSEQUENCES OF CHANGING OR NOT CHANGING	**Knowledge**	Knowledge of how things will be if a change is made or not. Includes awareness of responsibilities, risks, costs, and benefits that would follow changing or not changing.	"What will my life be like after this change is made?" "What will my life be like if I don't make this change?"
	Attractiveness/ Acceptability	The *relative* attractiveness or acceptability of the consequences of changing compared to not changing.	"How attractive or acceptable will my life be following this change as compared to how it will be if I don't change?"
	Resources	Internal (e.g., personal strengths) and external (e.g., social support) resources for managing the consequences of change.	"What strengths do I have (or can I develop) to maintain the change?" "What outside support do I have (or can I develop) to maintain the change?"
PROCESS OF CHANGING "How do I change?"	**Confidence**	Confidence in the potency of internal and external resources for maintaining the change.	"Do I personally have what it takes to maintain the change?" "Do I have enough outside support to maintain the change?"
	Knowledge	Knowledge of what is involved in making the change. This includes awareness of responsibilities, risks, costs, and benefits associated with the process of changing.	"What will it take for me to make this change?"
	Attractiveness/ Acceptability	Attractiveness or acceptability of the process of changing.	"How attractive or acceptable will the process of change be?"
	Resources	Internal and external resources for making the change.	"What strengths do I have (or can I develop) to make the change? "What outside support do I have (or can I develop) to make the change?"
	Confidence	Confidence in the potency of internal and external resources for making the change.	"Do I personally have what it takes to make the change?" "Do I have enough help to make the change?"

involve giving up drugs, as he does not see them as a problem. We use the word "knowledge" rather than "information" to emphasize that verbally presented information is likely to be inadequate. What is needed is concrete knowledge that is meaningful to Ted. Given that Ted has yet to change, we can say, tautologically, that he lacks motivation or readiness. He does not yet see the consequences of not changing as sufficiently unattractive, and the consequences of changing as sufficiently attractive, to justify the effort.

Once Ted has more fully considered the attractiveness/unattractiveness of change, he will still need to examine his resources, both internal (e.g., ability to stick to an objective, problem-solving skills, social skills) and external (e.g., social support, substitute activities, mechanisms to remind him of his objectives) to manage the consequences of change. An assessment of his internal resources would contribute to Ted's sense of self-efficacy; an assessment of his external resources would establish a social support network that could serve as scaffolding to help him change.

In terms of the model, "confidence that he can change" reflects Ted's appraisal that his internal and external resources are sufficient to meet the demands change will require. Although the resources and his confidence in them may not be prominent in his thinking at this point, we would recognize that these elements must become important issues if he were to think seriously about changing.

Focus on the Treatment Process ("How Do I Change?")

Since Ted is not seriously thinking about changing, he has also not given much thought to the process of change—i.e., treatment. Because he has had no previous experience at such change, he may assume that there is no process beyond "Just Say No!" In fact, Ted would likely never have considered the treatment process (nor the consequences of changing) if he had not gotten into trouble with the law and been sent to treatment.

In order to increase his readiness, Ted would have to decide that treatment is to his advantage. He would need to develop confidence that the treatment resources are adequate to see him through the change. And finally, if he is actually going to make the change, he would have to decide to accept the costs (time, effort) required by the process of treatment. In reality, Ted (as many probationers) has been forced to consider the process of treatment prior to considering the consequences of personal change. In other treatment settings, especially those involving voluntary admission, there may be a greater tendency for individuals to enter treatment after having already considered the consequences and thus need for change. But Ted has examined neither "What if I change?" nor "How do I change?" and yet he finds himself in a treatment environment. We could say that Ted's cart (treatment) has come before his horse (motivation for change).

If we want to help him to get ready to change, we will need to assist him in further developing the elements he needs. In doing so, we must deal with the specific elements that are relevant to his *current* state. In his current state, for example, it would probably not be useful to concentrate on the treatment process exclusively. Ted knows he is in treatment. Attempting to get Ted to "buy into" the treatment process at this point may encourage treatment compliance, but not active engagement. Instead, we should work to focus his attention on the consequences of changing or not changing and get him to reevaluate the differences in outcome that would occur as a result of these two options.

A ROAD MAP FOR READINESS

Figure 29.1 presents a dynamic view of the model. It makes explicit that the model deals with two forms of readiness that combine to create treatment readiness. Each requires its own readiness "rhombus." Individuals may enter the model at different points or take different routes through it. As noted above, Ted entered, somewhat

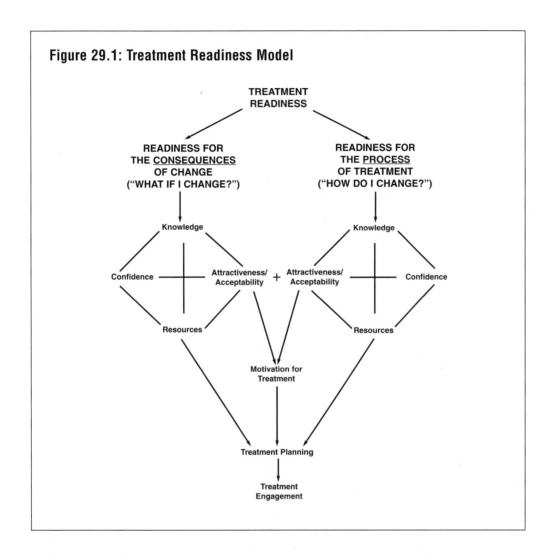

Figure 29.1: Treatment Readiness Model

unwillingly, the right side of the model labeled "Readiness for the *process* of treatment." As a result of not entering treatment voluntarily, it may be more beneficial if Ted were to focus on the consequences of change. In contrast, an individual who enters treatment voluntarily has likely graduated from the left side of the model and probably needs to focus on the process of treatment to increase readiness.

We begin our discussion on the left side of the map, focusing on the consequences of change. An adequate level of concrete knowledge about the consequences is required before anything else can happen. There must also be some assessment that the consequences of change are definitely attractive relative to the consequences of not changing. Otherwise there is not sufficient motivation to think seriously about the process of changing. We left Ted (and many mandated clients) with inadequate development in a number of these readiness elements and thus expected no change without some form of intervention. Ted is upset that he is in treatment and would be very reluctant to "buy into" a treatment process that he feels he does not need. Professional intervention at this point would be most effective if it dealt with knowledge about the consequences and the relative attractiveness of those consequences that would result from change.

If Ted becomes convinced that the balance favors consideration of change, he is ready to cross (at the plus sign in Figure 29.1) to the process rhombus. Of course, deciding to change takes time, and Ted will have already accumulated some knowledge about the treatment process. For example, he is aware of how much time it will take (or at least how long he must be in the system). He knows how pleasant or unpleasant it has been thus far. However, there may be additional considerations that will affect his confidence in the process: What is its rate of success? Supporting that confidence, of course, would be information about the resources that can be brought to bear. In addition to these difficulties Ted faces, a repeat offender may also have much to unlearn before he or she is able to reevaluate the treatment process favorably.

For purposes of our illustration, assume that as Ted accumulates more treatment experiences he makes repeated assessments of the attractiveness/acceptability of it. If the issue is not clear, he seeks more knowledge. As his knowledge, confidence, and self-efficacy develop, the issue becomes clearer and he decides to engage in the treatment process. Because Ted now perceives treatment to be beneficial, and because treatment readiness is a dynamic process, he returns to the consequences of change rhombus to evaluate the resources available for coping with change and to evaluate his confidence in those resources. Ted's overall level of readiness is thus determined by assessments from both sides of the model.

Ted is now motivated to change and be actively involved in treatment. He and his counselor can begin active treatment planning. They develop plans for how he will draw upon resources and how he will adjust his daily activities to accommodate to the requirements of treatment.

PRACTICAL APPLICATIONS OF THE MODEL

In the following sections, we present activities developed to influence specific readiness elements in the model. These activities were developed as part of a NIDA-sponsored project, Cognitive Enhancements for Treatment of Probationers (CETOP; see *www.ibr.tcu.edu* for further information). The activities described here were provided to eight communities of probationers (approximately 35 persons per community) while eight others received the standard approach used at the treatment facility. The results indicate that the probationers positively received the activities and that a number of indicators of treatment readiness were significantly enhanced by this curriculum in comparison to the standard approach (Czuchry & Dansereau, 2000; Sia et al., 2000). It should be noted that some of the activities illustrated in this section were expected to have benefits beyond the readiness elements targeted. Note: the activities described here are not exhaustive; practitioners can use the model to develop additional targeted interventions. The readiness elements presented in this section first focus on the consequences of change ("What if I change?"), followed by the process of treatment ("How do I change?").

"WHAT IF" ACTIVITIES

Knowledge of Change

A unit that targets this readiness element should encourage and assist the client in developing concrete knowledge of the long-term consequences of continued substance abuse and of a change to abstinence. Because mandated clients may not be motivated to pay attention to this aspect of readiness, it is important that the activities are engaging and encourage active participation.

For example, to target knowledge of change, as well as several other objectives, we developed a board game called "Downward Spiral" (Sia et al., 1996; see also Dees et al., Chapter 28, this volume). This is a sole survivor game, played in groups of five or six participants. Players move their pieces around a specially designed board and randomly receive cards that describe negative episodes they are likely to experience if they continue to use drugs. Each episode takes its toll on the player's social, physical, mental, and fiscal status. The winner is the one who has incurred the least amount of personal damage.

The game does not preach about the dangers of drugs but, instead, allows randomly selected, common drug episodes and consequences to guide peer discussion, thus reducing resistance that often occurs with more direct approaches (e.g., Bensley & Wu, 1991). Results of studies with Downward Spiral (Czuchry et al., 1999) indicate that it has a strong impact on the attitudes and behavioral intentions of participants. The episodes and associated facts and quotes about drug use promote lively discussions among the players. For example, clients have expressed the sense that someone (or even God) was trying to tell them something with the cards they received, or have tearfully shared events that have occurred in their own lives.

Acceptance/Attractiveness of Change

A unit that targets this readiness element should encourage and assist the client in assessing the long-term consequences of change/no-change in terms of their relative merits. The definition of substance abuse implies that a rational assessment of these consequences strongly favors change.

For example, in our work we stimulated general motivation for making changes by having participants map out what things they would like to magically change about themselves without worrying about barriers to these changes. Subsequent peer discussion focused on how the treatment program might help facilitate these changes. And, more indirectly, the Downward Spiral game described above encouraged the clients to recognize the unfavorable consequences of continued substance abuse.

Resources for Change

A unit that targets this readiness element should acquaint the client with external resources commonly available to support abstinence, what they offer, how to know when they are needed, and how they may be accessed. The unit should also encourage and assist the client in identifying and using internal resources. In our work, the Tower of Strengths activity (discussed below) was used to help clients identify internal resources. The treatment program itself addressed external resources and so no further intervention was necessary.

Confidence in Resources for Dealing With Change

A unit that targets this element of readiness should encourage and assist clients in building confidence that they could deal effectively with the problems of long-term maintenance. For example, our clients were given evidence that previous failures did not lower the prospects of future success.

"HOW TO" ACTIVITIES

Knowledge of Process

A unit that targets this readiness element should provide concrete knowledge about the treatment process, including the experiences and feelings clients might encounter. In our work, discussions of actual treatment scenarios were used to foster knowledge of the treatment process.

Resources for Process

A unit that targets this readiness element should provide concrete knowledge about the external and internal resources available in the treatment process. The client should learn what external resources are available and required (probation, aftercare, 12-step programs), what they offer, how to know when they are needed, and how to access them. In our work, external resources provided by treatment were emphasized by describing them and by promoting peer discussion about them.

Clients should also assess their own internal resources and recognize those that are adequate. The unit should also encourage and assist clients in further developing internal resources that are inadequate. In our work, existing internal resources were assessed in the Tower of Strengths activity. For this activity, each person sorted through 60 cards containing personal strengths and selected at least 10 that he or she possessed. The groups then discussed these strengths and how they could be used to help a person thrive in the treatment program. The clients also filled out worksheets on successful, positive, personal changes they had made in the past, and how the approaches they had used at that time might help them now. Our work with the Tower of Strengths has shown that it can be used to calibrate appropriate levels of mood and self-esteem (Sia et al., 1999).

In addition, to increase personal resources, participants were given training and practice on three critical processes in learning: (1) identifying important and useful ideas/actions that could help accomplish future goals, (2) remembering these ideas/actions, and (3) projecting them into appropriate future contexts via mental and actual simulation. Mnemonic and mental imagery techniques formed the basis of this training.

Confidence in Process

A unit that targets this readiness element should present evidence and reasons to show the clients that treatment offers a reasonable prospect of success. For example, in our work participants were asked to rate a Believe It or Not List (i.e., true or false statements) about the treatment program (e.g., information about relapse rates, consumer satisfaction). Subsequent discussions of the correct answers were designed to promote an awareness of the program and its impact on probationers.

Acceptance/Attractiveness of Process

A unit that targets this readiness element should encourage and assist clients in recognizing the benefits of the treatment program and in accepting the uncomfortable aspects as necessary for treatment.

For example, in our work a humorous list of top 10 reasons for working the program (i.e., seriously engaging in the program) was created by previous clients and used to stimulate motivation for fully participating in the treatment process.

Treatment Planning

A unit that targets this element of readiness should encourage and assist clients in developing plans for effective participation in the treatment program and in long-term maintenance. In our work, to plan for the program clients created a Personal Action List of the six most important actions they needed to take during treatment. Group discussion helped refine the actions based on concreteness, potency, and feasibility. This process was designed to give the participants experience in forming workable plans.

In addition, to plan for maintenance of change, participants identified five personal strengths they would like to eventually achieve and then used quotes selected from a large collection to create a weekly planner that would serve to remind them of their goals and ways to achieve them.

CONCLUSIONS

The model of readiness described here has been used to develop treatment readiness activities. Practitioners can use this model as a framework in the design of their own interventions or systematic assessments that might serve diagnostic, predictive, or evaluative purposes. In addition, this model provides an important framework for treatment that takes place within the criminal justice system. The separation of readiness into "What if I change?" and "How do I change?" is an important consideration, since the reality of mandated treatment is that many probationers enter treatment without having genuinely considered the consequences of change. As a result, treatment programs may only instill treatment compliance and not meaningful desire for change. The model also makes it clear that to encourage meaningful change, counselors and probationers need to address key readiness questions that are relevant to the client's current mental state.

About the Authors

Donald F. Dansereau, Ph.D., is a Professor/Senior Research Scientist at the Institute of Behavioral Research, Texas Christian University. Selby H. Evans, Ph.D., is a retired Professor at TCU. Michael Czuchry, Ph.D., and Tiffiny L. Sia, Ph.D., are Associate Research Scientists at the Institute of Behavioral Research at TCU.

This work was supported in part by the National Institute on Drug Abuse (Grant No. R01 DA08608). The interpretations and conclusions are the authors, and do not necessarily represent the position of NIDA or the Department of Health and Human Services.

References

Bensley, L.S., & Wu, R. (1991). The role of psychological reactance in drinking following alcohol prevention messages. *Journal of Applied Social Psychology, 21*(13), 1111-1124.

Broome, K.M., Knight, K., Hiller, M., & Simpson, D.D. (1997). Peer, family, and motivational influences on drug treatment process and recidivism for probationers. *Journal of Clinical Psychology, 53*, 387-397.

Czuchry, M., Sia, T.L., & Dansereau, D.F. (1999). Preventing alcohol abuse: An examination of the "Downward Spiral" game and educational videos. *Journal of Drug Education, 29*(4), 323-335.

Czuchry, M., & Dansereau, D.F. (2000). Drug abuse treatment in criminal justice settings: Enhancing community engagement and helpfulness. *The American Journal of Drug and Alcohol Abuse, 26*(4), 537-552.

DeLeon, G. (1996). Integrative recovery: A stage paradigm. *Substance Abuse, 17*(1), 51-63.

De Leon, G., Melnick, G., & Tims, F.M. (2001). The role of motivation and readiness in treatment and recovery. In F.M. Tims, C.G. Leukefeld & J.J. Platt (Eds.), *Relapse and recovery in addictions.* New Haven, CT: Yale University Press.

Prochaska, B.J., DiClemente, C.C., & Norcross, J.C. (1992). In search of how people change: Applications to addictive behaviors. *American Psychologist, 47*, 1102-1114.

Sia, T.L., Czuchry, M., & Dansereau, D.F. (1999). Considering personal strengths: The effect of three methods on mood, arousal, and self-esteem. *Journal of Applied Social Psychology, 29*(6), 1151-1171.

Sia, T.L., Czuchry, M., & Dansereau, D.F. (1996). *The Downward Spiral of Substance Abuse.* Instructional game. Fort Worth, TX: Institute of Behavioral Research, Texas Christian University.

Sia, T.L., Dansereau, D.F., & Czuchry, M.L. (2000). Treatment readiness training and probationers' evaluation of substance abuse treatment in a criminal justice setting. *Journal of Substance Abuse Treatment, 19*, 459-467.

Simpson, D.D., & Joe, G.W. (1993). Motivation as a predictor of early dropout from drug abuse treatment. *Psychotherapy, 30*, 357-568.

Simpson, D.D. (2001). Modeling treatment process and outcomes [editorial]. *Addiction, 96*(2), 207-211.

Chapter 30

Corrections-Based Substance Abuse Programs: Good for Inmates, Good for Prisons

by Michael Prendergast, Ph.D., David Farabee, Ph.D., and Jerome Cartier, M.A.

Introduction 30-1
Background: TC Philosophy 30-2
The Substance Abuse Treatment Facility at Corcoran State Prison 30-2
Impacts of the SATF TC Programs 30-3
    Substance Use Among SATF Participants 30-3
    Disciplinary Actions 30-3
    Staff Ratings of SATF 30-4
    Staff Absenteeism 30-4
Staff and Inmate Perceptions of SATF 30-5
Implications for Prison Management and Planners 30-6

INTRODUCTION

Federal and state prisons have witnessed an increase in substance abuse treatment programs over the past decade as the number of inmates with a history of drug abuse or incarcerated on drug-related charges has risen. Prison-based treatment programs, particularly those that follow the therapeutic community (TC) model, are becoming a popular alternative to traditional "lock 'em 'n leave them" forms of incarceration after findings from a number of evaluation studies revealed the effectiveness of these programs in successfully reducing substance abuse and recidivism among participating drug-abusing offenders (Inciardi et al., 1997; Knight et al., 1997; Pelissier et al., 1998; Prendergast et al., 1996; Simpson et al., 1999; Wexler et al., 1992). While the post-release benefits of prison-based treatment programs for offenders are well documented, the more immediate impact of such programs on the management of host prisons

This chapter originally appeared in Offender Substance Abuse Report, *Vol. 2, No. 6, November/ December 2002.*

is less clear. Research indicates that such programs may have positive effects on in-prison behavior and on the social environment of the prison (Wexler & Lipton. 1991), including fewer disciplinary actions and inmate appeals, reduced substance use and drug trafficking within the institution, and high staff morale.

BACKGROUND: TC PHILOSOPHY

The TC philosophy regards substance abuse as a disorder of the whole person. Rather than being regarded as a disease, substance abuse and addiction are perceived as a symptom of a larger disorder that encompasses the users' values, cognitions, social skills, and general behavior. A TC provides a total environment where change in the drug users' conduct, attitudes, and emotions are fostered, monitored, and mutually reinforced by the daily regimen (De Leon, 1995). The thrust of TC treatment is to change the inmate overall, not just the inmate's addictive behavior. The programs are organized and operated so that the TC culture pervades all aspects of the inmates' daily life, emphasizing respect and responsibility in a structured environment and promoting prosocial goals, attitudes, and behaviors.

THE SUBSTANCE ABUSE TREATMENT FACILITY AT CORCORAN STATE PRISON

The Substance Abuse Treatment Facility (SATF) reviewed here opened in September 1997 at the newly built state prison in Corcoran, California. The overall institution has a housing capacity of 6,013 beds. Two self-contained treatment units at the institution are specifically designed to provide housing and programming space for residential substance abuse treatment for 1,056 Level I and II offenders (1,478 with 140% overcrowding). Treatment participants are completely separated from the general inmate population—an arrangement seldom achieved in other prison-based treatment programs. The California Department of Corrections (CDC) is responsible for custodial operations at the facility; treatment services are provided by two California-based treatment organizations: Walden House and Phoenix House. Both providers offer treatment programming consistent with the TC model.

Admission to one of the SATF treatment programs requires a documented history of substance abuse (including alcohol), Level I or II classification, more than six months but less than 18 months remaining to serve at the time of program placement, no violence or weapons charges within the past year, non-involvement/membership in a prison gang, and no active or potential felony or U.S. Immigration and Naturalization Service (INS) holds. About 20% of the inmates who are admitted to one of the SATF treatment programs are discharged for various reasons, including refusal to adhere to program requirements and felony or INS holds discovered after admission.

Treatment programming is structured into three phases: orientation, primary treatment, and pre-release transitioning. The in-prison treatment lasts from six to 18 months (with an average stay of about eight months), followed by a community treatment aftercare phase. The in-prison programs are highly structured and include a minimum of 20 hours per week of substance abuse treatment and 10 or more hours of structured optional activities.

IMPACTS OF THE SATF TC PROGRAMS

In examining the impact of TC programs on prison management, we examined several elements of the prison environment: inmates' substance use, staff ratings of the program, disciplinary actions, and absenteeism among correctional staff. In addition, we conducted focus groups with correctional staff and program participants that included questions about perceptions of the impact of the treatment programs on institutional operations.

Substance Use Among SATF Participants

Random urine testing is a widely used objective measure of drug use and program impact. Urine specimens are tested for alcohol, THC, methamphetamine, morphine, codeine, heroin, barbiturates, PCP, and cocaine. Approximately 28 treatment participants in each program are randomly selected for testing each day, six days per week. Over a one-month period, this represents 40%-45% of the total monthly population of the programs. From February 1998 through June 1999, 9,769 weekly random urine tests were conducted among the SATF treatment participants, with only 23 positive results for non-prescribed substances, representing .003% of all tests. There is no comparison of positive rates between the treatment and non-treatment yards because random testing did not occur in the non-treatment facilities at Corcoran at the time of these tests. But across state and federal correctional agencies that conducted drug testing of inmates in 1997, the average rate of positive drug test results was 4.8% (Camp & Camp, 1998), in contrast to the SATF results of far less than one percent. A recent prevalence estimate of drug use at four California prisons using random testing of 20% of inmates at each institution found an overall positive rate of 8.9% (Prendergast et al., 2000).

Disciplinary Actions

The incidence of disciplinary actions for violations and infractions of rules serves as an indicator of inmate behavior. From April 1998 through March 1999, disciplinary actions at the SATF treatment yards were compared with those at two non-treatment yards of the same security level. Within the CDC, rule violations, or "115s," may be issued by both correctional and treatment staff. In response to the issuance of a 115, a hearing process ensues; on average, the hearing process rules guilty on about 90% of the 115 reports. During the 12-month period, 594 violations were reported for treatment facilities and 998 for the non-treatment facilities. Since the non-treatment facilities each house an average of 200 more inmates than do the treatment facilities, reported violations are shown in Figure 30.1 in rates per 100 inmates. In spite of having more staff (correctional plus treatment) on the treatment yards and thus a greater likelihood of detecting inmate infractions, the treatment yards had lower rates of disciplinary actions in most months.

Disciplinary actions can be categorized as either "serious" or "administrative." Examples of serious violations are acts of violence, disruption of facility operation, and possession of controlled substances. Administrative violations are those that do not involve violence or threats to facility security. Over the 12-months combined, the percentage of serious disciplinary actions in the SATF treatment population was somewhat lower than that in the non-treatment population (73.2% and 79.3%, respectively).

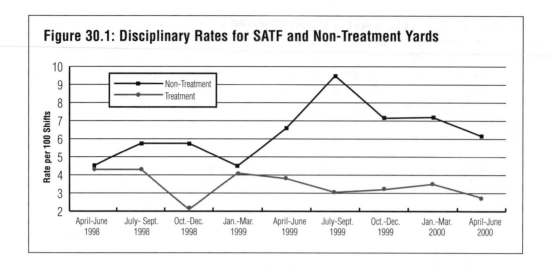

Figure 30.1: Disciplinary Rates for SATF and Non-Treatment Yards

Staff Ratings of SATF

Questionnaire-guided assessments by staff can provide valuable information on the level of success or problems within a facility or program. In April 1998, October 1998, and July 1999, 66% of the corrections staff assigned to the SATF treatment facilities completed the Correctional Institutions Environment Scale (CIES) instrument, which assesses the social climate of prison and jail settings (Moos, 1974). The short-form of the CIES consists of 36 true/false items and measures nine dimensions of the prison environment: Involvement, Support, Expressiveness, Autonomy, Practical Orientation, Personal Problem Orientation, Order and Organization, Clarity, and Self-Control. The staff responses to the CIES were compared with those from a national sample of correctional officers who rated their own institutions (see Figure 30.2). Higher scores on the subscales indicate more positive responses. Correctional officers who worked with the substance abuse programs at SATF generally had more favorable impressions of their facilities than did officers in other institutions. Exceptions to this trend were for "Involvement" and for "Order and Organization" when comparing the ratings of the national sample with those of the April 1998 SATF sample.

The first administration of the CIES occurred about six months after activation of the treatment programs at SATF, and the scores on these subscales probably reflect the "growing pains" of the new programs. Subsequent administrations of the CIES at SATF resulted in higher "Involvement" and "Order and Organization" scores than for the national sample, indicating the progressive improvement in SATF program operation as inmates and staff became familiar with what was expected of them.

Staff Absenteeism

Absenteeism may reflect poor morale and dissatisfaction among staff, which can be a proxy for poor conditions within an institution or poor program processes. Figure 30.3 indicates that for most of the months from July 1998 through March 1999, staff absenteeism, as measured by the number of sick days per 100 shifts, was lower among

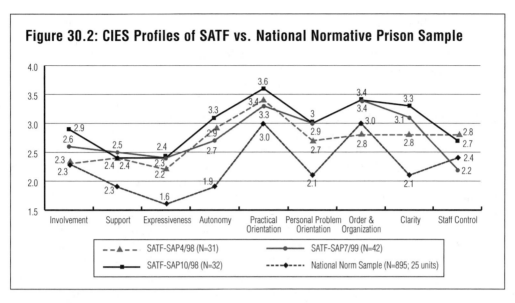

Figure 30.2: CIES Profiles of SATF vs. National Normative Prison Sample

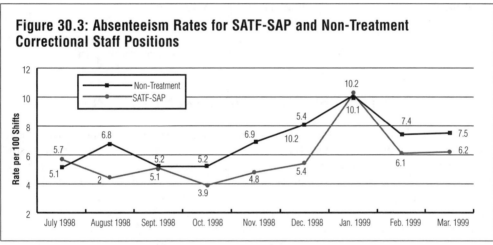

Figure 30.3: Absenteeism Rates for SATF-SAP and Non-Treatment Correctional Staff Positions

correctional officers in the SATF treatment facilities than among those in non-treatment facilities. The consistency of this trend over time suggests that these differences are not due to spurious deviations at specific points in time. The increase in absenteeism over November, December, and January is most likely attributable to people taking time off for the holidays. Overall, the average rate of absenteeism per 100 shifts between July 1998 and March 1999 was 6.9 for positions on the non-treatment yards and 5.8 for positions on the treatment SATF yards.

STAFF AND INMATE PERCEPTIONS OF SATF

Focus groups with corrections staff and treatment participants on several occasions provided a qualitative understanding of the impact of the treatment programs at SATF.

Of the correctional staff assigned to the treatment yards, all of the participants agreed that the programs were able to achieve racially integrated yards (although it should be noted that known members of prison gangs, which are ethnically based, are excluded from participation in the SATF treatment programs). Racial integration led to fewer instances of violence and gang-related disruptions. Racial integration also allowed the inmates to complete their remaining time in the facility with a significantly reduced level of tension. Inmates who participated in focus groups also commented favorably on the decrease in racial tension and violence in the treatment facilities.

Correctional officers on the treatment yards said that they looked forward to coming to work in the morning, largely because of the reduced level of tension and fewer acts of violence or gang activities. They reported that working conditions in the treatment facilities were better than in other areas of the prison or in other prisons where they had previously worked.

These findings receive support from a study conducted by researchers at the Pacific Southwest Addiction Technology Transfer Center, University of California, San Diego (Deitch et al., 2000). Surveys of custody personnel assigned to facilities where substance abuse TCs exist tended to have an overall better perception of their health, particularly their emotional condition and stress, as compared with other staff members working in traditional non-treatment custodial environments. They also had significantly fewer on-the-job injuries and illness-related absences. In short, the quality of well being and a safer, less problematic and more satisfying work environment were more likely seen in a treatment setting than a traditional corrections setting.

IMPLICATIONS FOR PRISON MANAGEMENT AND PLANNERS

Corrections-based substance abuse treatment is effective, and treatment has benefits for the drug-abusing inmate and for society. But a more immediate gain from prison-based substance abuse programs is improved conditions within the facility and better behavior among the participants in treatment. Consideration of these positive impacts of treatment programs on institutional operations provides additional advantages of including therapeutic community programs within prisons.

On the narrow measure of reduced substance abuse, the SATF is clearly a very successful facility. These programs also appear to have a positive impact on the racial tension that characterizes many prisons. The decrease in racial hostility at the SATF treatment facilities is partly explained by the exclusion of inmates with known gang affiliation and by the isolation of inmates participating in treatment from the influences of the general prison population. At other institutions with treatment programs, where participants are housed separately but still mix with the general population, racial hostility remains a problem, despite the influence of the TC programs.

Prison management can expect near-term and long-term advantages resulting from more effective approaches (such as TC programs) to inmates' substance abuse problems. Notably, fewer behavioral problems among inmates participating in the TC programs and better staff morale are two bonuses of these comprehensive substance abuse treatment efforts. Clearly, lower rates of staff absenteeism and turnover mean a more efficiently operated facility for management—and a more rehabilitative experience for inmates. Costs and consequences to society are reduced because of lessened recidivism, and near-term prison-specific costs are also reduced. For example, the positive effect of TCs is evident in reduced disciplinary actions among SATF participants and the resultant reduction in staff time devoted to processing disciplinary actions or investigating incidents. Because the TCs are able to reduce the number of disciplinary violations, particularly serious ones, cost savings also ensue by avoiding reclassification and assignment of inmates with multiple violations to a higher custody level with increased costs.

In conclusion, the investment in prison treatment programs is expected to yield benefits in terms of lower rates of reincarceration and reductions in other criminal justice and social costs (Griffith et al., 1999). But the more immediate effect is a positive impact on the social and operational environment of prisons that have TC programs, leading to likely reductions in prison management costs.

About the Authors

Michael Prendergast, Ph.D., is Research Historian, UCLA Integrated Substance Abuse Programs, Los Angeles, CA, and is a member of the Offender Substance Abuse (OSA) *Editorial Advisory Board. David Farabee, Ph.D., is Associate Research Psychologist, UCLA Integrated Substance Abuse Programs, and is co-editor of* OSA. *Jerome Cartier, M.A. is Project Director, UCLA Integrated Substance Abuse Programs. Dr. Prendergast may be reached by email at mlp@ucla.edu.*

Preparation of this paper was supported by California Department of Corrections Contract #97.243. The authors are grateful to CDC staff for providing some of the data used; the views and conclusions expressed here, however, are those of the authors and do not necessarily reflect the position of the CDC. The authors wish to thank Brian Perrochet and Thanh-Le Nguyen for editorial services and Sylvia Sanchez for preparing the tables and figures.

References

Camp, C.G., & Camp, G. M. (1998). *The corrections yearbook, 1998.* Middletown, CT: Criminal Justice Institute, Inc.

De Leon, G. (1995). Therapeutic communities for addictions: A theoretical framework. *International Journal of the Addictions, 30,* 1603-1645.

Deitch, D. A., Koutsenok, I., Burgener, M., Marsolais, K., & Cartier, J. (2000). In-custody therapeutic community substance abuse treatment: Does it have an impact on custody personnel? Unpublished manuscript. San Diego: Pacific Southwest Addiction Technology Transfer Center, Department of Psychiatry, University of California, San Diego.

Griffith, J. D., Hiller, M.L., Knight, K., & Simpson, D.D. (1999). A cost-effective analysis of in-prison therapeutic community treatment and risk classification. *Prison Journal, 79*(3), 352-368.

Inciardi, J.A., Martin, S.S., Butzin, C.A., Hooper, R.M., & Harrison, L.D. (1997). An effective model of prison-based treatment for drug-involved offenders. *Journal of Drug Issues, 27*(2), 261-278.

Knight, K., Simpson, D.D., Chatham, L.R., &. Camacho, L.M. (1997). An assessment of prison-based drug treatment: Texas' in-prison therapeutic community program. *Journal of Offender Rehabilitation, 24*(3/4), 75-100.

Moos, R.H. (1974). *Correctional Institutions Environment Scale.* Palo Alto, CA: Consulting Psychologists Press, Inc.

Pelissier, B.M., Gaes, G., Rhodes, W., Camp, S., O'Neil, J., Wallace, S., & Saylor, W. (1998). *TRIAD Drug Treatment Evaluation Project: Six-month interim report.* Washington, DC: Office of Research and Evaluation, Federal Bureau of Prisons.

Prendergast, M., Farabee, D., & Campos, M. (2000). *Drug reduction strategy evaluation: First annual report.* Submitted to the California Department of Corrections. Los Angeles: UCLA Drug Abuse Research Center.

Prendergast, M.L., Wellisch, J., & Wong, M.M. (1996). Residential treatment for women parolees following prison-based drug treatment: Treatment experiences, needs and services, outcomes. *Prison Journal, 76*(3), 253-274.

Simpson, D.D., Wexler, H.K., & Inciardi, J.A. (Eds.) (1999). Drug treatment outcomes for correctional settings (Special Issue, Parts 1 and 2). *Prison Journal, 79*(3, 4), 291-445.

Wexler, H.K., Falkin, G.P., Lipton, D.S., & Rosenblum, A.B. (1992). Outcome evaluation of a prison therapeutic community for substance abuse treatment. In C. G Leukefeld & F. M. Tims (Eds.), *Drug abuse treatment in prisons and jails (NIDA Research Monograph 118).* (pp.156-175). Rockville, MD: National Institute on Drug Abuse.

Wexler, H.K., & Lipton, D.S. (1991). Project REFORM: Developing a drug abuse treatment strategy for corrections. *Journal of Drug Issues, 21*, 469-490.

Chapter 31

The Effectiveness of Coerced Admission to Prison-Based Drug Treatment

by David Farabee, Ph.D., Haikang Shen, Ph.D., Michael Prendergast, Ph.D., and Jerome Cartier, M.A.

Introduction 31-1
The California Substance Abuse Treatment Facility 31-2
Study Design and Methods 31-3
    Sample Population 31-3
    Study Measures 31-4
        Substance Use Severity 31-4
        Motivation for Treatment 31-4
        Recidivism 31-5
Results 31-6
    SATF vs. Comparison Group 31-6
    Desire for Treatment 31-7
    Treatment-Desire Interaction 31-7
    Multivariate Models Predicting Six-Month Recidivism 31-8
Discussion 31-9
    Matching Treatment to Inmate's Motivation Is Critical 31-9
    Study Limitations 31-10
Conclusion 31-10

INTRODUCTION

Several evaluations have provided evidence that prison-based substance abuse treatment combined with aftercare is associated with reduced levels of recidivism (Inciardi et al., 1997; Knight et al., 1997; Pelissier et al., 2000; Prendergast et al., 1996; Simpson et al., 1999; Wexler et al., 1999). However, in all of these evaluations, the subjects were

This chapter originally appeared in Offender Substance Abuse Report, *Vol. 4, No. 4, July/August 2004.*

admitted to treatment voluntarily. That is, despite the coercive environment of the prison generally, inmates with substance abuse problems were informed of the availability of treatment and then decided whether to participate (as a client and as a research subject).

Thus, the existing literature regarding the effectiveness of prison-based substance abuse treatment has drawn from samples of inmates who were at least moderately amenable to receiving treatment. Moreover, the frequently cited studies that support the use of coerced treatment were based on samples of offenders who received treatment in the community (e.g., Anglin, 1988; Anglin et al., 1989; Collins & Allison, 1983; Simpson & Friend, 1988; see Farabee et al., 1998, for a review), where the incentives and consequences are much different than in prison. These latter studies have demonstrated that substance-abusing offenders under community supervision tend to perform at least as well as other clients.

A recent exception to the community focus of the extant coerced treatment literature was a study of inmates in a prison-based therapeutic community (TC) conducted by De Leon et al. (2000). Using a path analysis to examine the relationship between initial treatment motivation, treatment progress, and post-release outcomes, the authors found an indirect relationship between motivation and 12-month recidivism. Specifically, inmates with higher treatment motivation were more likely to enter and complete aftercare, which, in turn, was associated with a reduced likelihood of being returned to custody. Still, it should be noted that admission to this program was voluntary and that the mean motivation score of these inmates was 75% of the maximum possible score. As a result, the restricted range in motivation among this sample precludes a more thorough analysis of the impact of coerced treatment in prison.

Most of the incentives (e.g., expunged records, diversion from prison) and consequences (e.g., revocation of probation or parole) offered to offenders in the community are not available in prison settings. Being given the option to go to treatment *or* go to prison is clearly not the same as being required to go to treatment *and* stay in prison. Hence, it is possible that the apparent effectiveness of coercion demonstrated with community-based offender samples does not generalize to incarcerated offenders.

To examine whether coerced treatment findings based on community programs also apply to prison-based programs, the present study capitalized on a California Department of Corrections' policy in which inmates with substance abuse histories can be remanded to drug treatment while in prison, regardless of their motivation for treatment. The data for this study were collected as part of a larger process and outcome evaluation of the Substance Abuse Treatment Facility located in Corcoran, California.[1]

THE CALIFORNIA SUBSTANCE ABUSE TREATMENT FACILITY

The California Substance Abuse Treatment Facility (SATF) and State Prison at Corcoran, which opened in September 1997, has a total housing capacity of 6,013. The two self-contained substance abuse treatment units at the institution were specifically designed to provide housing and residential treatment for 1,056 minimum-security (Level I) and moderate-security (Level II) risk offenders (1,478 with 40% overcrowding). The California Department of Corrections (CDC) is responsible for custodial operations at the facility, and treatment services are provided under contract to two private treatment organizations.

The admission criteria for a classification assignment to treatment at SATF are as follows:

- A history of drug and/or alcohol abuse, which can be established through either self-report or review of documents such as probation reports, criminal history, or reports of in-custody behaviors;

- An offender classification score between 0 and 27 (Level I and II inmates within the California correctional system);

- No less than six months and no more than 18 months left to serve at the time of the classification committee review for placement at SATF;

- No placement in a secured housing unit (SHU) during the last year for violence or weapons charges;

- Not a validated member of a prison gang; and

- No active or potential felony or U.S. Immigration and Naturalization Service holds, which could possibly lengthen the inmate's sentence or result in his deportation.

Inmates can volunteer for treatment at SATF and will be admitted if they meet the eligibility criteria. Since the number of voluntary clients falls short of the number needed to maintain capacity, CDC screens inmates throughout the system and mandates those who meet the eligibility criteria to treatment at SATF.

The SATF treatment program involves a residential in-prison phase, followed by a voluntary community treatment phase. Aside from some minor differences, both programs adhere to the basic TC philosophy and structure (for a detailed discussion of the therapeutic philosophy and processes, see De Leon et al., 2000). Programs are highly structured and include a minimum of 20 hours per week of substance abuse treatment, as well as 10 or more hours per week of structured optional activities. The in-prison treatment lasts from six to 18 months. The inmate's length of time to serve at the time of the program admission classification hearing determines the actual length of time in treatment for any single inmate.

STUDY DESIGN AND METHODS

Sample Population

The present study was based on a sample of outcome study participants from the SATF (N = 404) and an untreated comparison group drawn from a comparable California prison in which treatment was not yet available (N = 403). Seven subjects were not included in these analyses because they had missing data concerning their treatment motivation, reducing the analysis sample to 800. Subjects for this study were recruited between June, 1999, and June, 2000. Random assignment to treatment and non-treatment conditions was not possible for this study. Therefore, to ensure that the subjects in the comparison group were in fact comparable to those in the SATF, a one-to-one matching procedure was employed. For each SATF inmate who agreed to participate in the outcome study, a list of similar (non-treatment) inmates from the comparison institution was generated, among those with less than one year left to serve. This list was based on downloads from the CDC Offender-Based Information System (OBIS) database. Specific matching criteria consisted of age, race/ethnicity, commitment offense, custody level, and prior history of sex offenses.

Once this list was generated, the research staff reviewed each prospective comparison subject's central file to determine whether or not there was evidence of prior substance abuse. This process is consistent with that used by correctional classification counselors to identify and refer inmates to institutional treatment programs. Of those who had evidence of a substance abuse history, three names were randomly selected as possible comparison subjects. To recruit these inmates for participation, the research staff would request an audience with small groups of potential subjects, explain the purpose of the study, and obtain consent from those who volunteered to participate. The baseline interview would either be conducted at this time or scheduled within the next few weeks. Ninety-three percent of the SATF inmates who were invited to participate in this study agreed to do so; the participation rate for the comparison institution was 76%. (According to the field research staff, the disparity in participation rates between the treatment and comparison sample was largely due to the fact that most of the inmates in the latter group had full-time job assignments. Consequently, a larger percentage of potential comparison subjects were reluctant to participate in the study since it would have resulted in lost work time. In contrast, because the treatment subjects were only employed part time, participating in the study did not necessarily conflict with their work schedules.) Background characteristics of the resulting SATF and comparison samples are shown in Table 31.1.

Study Measures

This study was part of a comprehensive process and outcome evaluation involving a large number of assessments. The descriptions below are limited to those measures that were pertinent to our examination of coerced treatment and recidivism.

Substance Use Severity. Indices of alcohol and illicit drug use severity were created based on an eight-item scale assessing the frequency of problems associated with each. Subjects were asked to rate how often their drug/alcohol use affected such areas as their physical health; relations with family and friends; ability to concentrate, find and keep a job, etc. Response options ranged from 0 = Never to 4 = Always. These overall scores were converted to quartile scores (ranging from 1-4) to normalize the distributions, with higher scores reflecting higher levels of severity.

Motivation for Treatment. The measure of the inmates' desire for treatment was collected as part of the baseline interview for all subjects in the outcome study. Reliance on this measure (rather than on voluntary status) was based on prior research indicating that perceived coercion and perceived treatment need are only modestly correlated. In fact, many offenders who indicate having no control over the referral process also acknowledge a high motivation for treatment (Farabee et al., 2002). The item read, "You believe you would like to receive drug/alcohol treatment while in prison," which is one of the marker items on the Desire for Treatment scale developed by Knight et al. (1994). The response options were as follows: 0 = Disagree Strongly (31.8%), 1 = Disagree Somewhat (2.8%), 2 = Not Sure (6.0%), 3 = Agree Somewhat (9.1%), or

Table 31.1: Demographic Characteristics of SATF and Comparison Subjects (N=807)*

Variable	COMPARISON		SATF	
	Low Motivation	High Motivation	Low Motivation	High Motivation
N	213	184	41	362
Demographics				
Age (SD)		36.0 (9.1)[a]	36.1 (8.2)[a]	31.7 (9.4)[b]
36.5 (9.7) a				
Race/Ethnicity				
African American (%)	46.5	36.4	31.7	41.2
Hispanic (%)	17.4	22.3	22.0	18.2
White-Non Hispanic (%)	33.3	39.1	36.6	37.3
Other (%)	2.8	2.2	9.8	3.3
High School Graduate/GED (%)	45.5	38.6	36.6	36.5
Employed Full-time (%)[1]	50.2[a]	45.1[a,c]	56.1[a]	39.0[c]
Co-Morbid Psych. Diagnosis (%)[2]	19.8	24.0	19.5	26.7
Substance Use				
Alcohol severity (SD)	1.9 (1.1)[a]	2.2 (1.2)[b]	2.0 (1.0)[a,b]	2.1 (1.2)[a,b]
Drug severity (SD)	2.1 (1.2)[a,d]	2.6 (1.2)[b]	1.8 (1.0)[a,d]	2.4 (1.1)[c]
Criminal History				
Number of prior arrests (SD)	16.7 (20.3)	17.2 (15.4)	20.7 (31.1)	20.4 (28.7)

[a, b, c, d] Values with the same superscript are not significantly different (p>.05).

[1] Based on six months prior to incarceration.

[2] Co-morbid psychiatric problems were based on determinations made by California Department of Corrections psychiatric staff. Specific diagnoses were not available; however, these diagnoses typically refer to Axis I disorders that require psychotropic medication.

4 = Agree Strongly (50.4%). Inmates responding to this statement with a 0 or 1 were coded as not wanting treatment (later referred to as the "no desire for treatment" group). Those responding with a 2 or above were coded as amenable to receiving treatment (later referred to as the "desire for treatment" group). This threshold resulted in a distribution where 31.8% were not motivated for treatment, and the remaining 68.2% were at least amenable to receiving treatment while in prison.

Recidivism. The present study is based on recidivism data obtained from the Offender Based Information System (OBIS). Recidivism was defined as a return to prison for either a new charge or for violation of the terms of parole within the first six months following release from prison. As a result, outcomes reported here are likely to be conservative, given that they exclude undetected offenses and offenses that resulted in a commitment to a local jail rather than prison.

RESULTS

The analyses in this section are presented in four subsections. In the first two, treatment condition (SATF vs. comparison group) and desire for treatment (high vs. low) are examined as single predictors of six-month return to custody. In the third subsection, we examine the treatment-desire interaction as a predictor of six-month returns. In the fourth subsection, we present a full exploratory logistic regression model and a reduced logistic model to assess the predictive efficacy of the treatment-motivation interaction after controlling for standard covariates of recidivism (i.e., alcohol use severity, drug use severity, number of prior arrests, age, education, and any psychiatric diagnosis).

SATF vs. Comparison Group

For this analysis, the two institutional treatment providers were combined to form a single treatment group and contrasted with the matched comparison group. This decision was based on analyses showing that the six-month recidivism outcomes from both of the SATF treatment programs were virtually identical.

Overall, 27% of the parolees had been returned to custody within six months of release. The likelihood of returning to custody during this period did not differ significantly by treatment condition, with approximately 28% of SATF parolees being returned compared to 26% of parolees from the comparison sample (statistical significance criterion for all comparisons is $p<.05$). As shown in Table 31.2, membership in the treatment condition was associated with a statistically non-significant odds ratio of 1.14 (95% CI: 0.83,1.56) of being returned to custody within the first six months following release.

Table 31.2: Predicting the Probability of Return-to-Custody (RTC) by Drug Treatment, Treatment Desire, and Treatment-Desire Match

Testing model	Effect tested	Odds Ratio	95% C.I.
Univariate model 1	Treatment	1.14	(0.83, 1.56)
Univariate model 2	Motivation for Treatment	1.30	(0.92, 1.84)
Univariate model 3	Treatment-Motivation Match	**0.69**	**(0.49, 0.97)**
Interaction model	Treatment	**2.31**	**(1.12, 4.74)**
	Motivation for Treatment	**1.72**	**(1.09, 2.72)**
	Interaction	**0.36**	**(0.16, 0.81)**
Modified interaction model	Treatment	1.38	(0.92, 2.08)
	Treatment Motivation	1.03	(0.68, 1.55)
	Treatment-Motivation Match	**0.60**	**(0.40, 0.90)**

Note: Bold figures denote significance at the .05 level

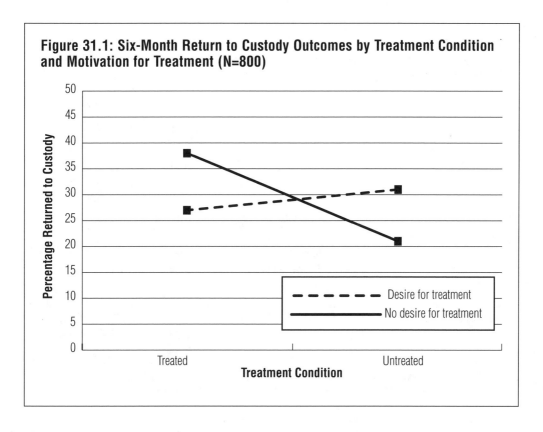

Figure 31.1: Six-Month Return to Custody Outcomes by Treatment Condition and Motivation for Treatment (N=800)

Desire for Treatment

Subjects who were amenable to receiving substance abuse treatment while in prison were slightly more likely to be returned to custody within six months than those who reported that they did not want treatment (28.4% vs. 23.3%, respectively). However, this difference was not statistically significant (Chi square [1, N=796]=2.2, p=n.s.). This result was confirmed using logistic regression, where having a desire for treatment as a single predictor in a logistic model was associated with a non-significant odds ratio of 1.30, or a 30% increase in the likelihood of being returned to custody within six months of release (95% CI: 0.92,1.84; see Table 31.2).

Treatment-Desire Interaction

To assess the impact of coercion (as defined by desire for treatment) on the effectiveness of the treatment program, return-to-custody outcomes were contrasted among inmates who (1) wanted treatment but did not receive it (N=168; 21.0%), (2) wanted treatment and did receive it (N=356; 44.5%), (3) did not want treatment and did not receive it (N=229; 28.6%), and (4) did not want treatment but did receive it (N=47; 6.0%).

As shown in Figure 31.1, the poorest outcomes occurred among those who were referred to the SATF despite not having a desire for treatment. In fact, this group was 81% more likely to have been returned to custody than the untreated subjects who

Table 31.3: Predicting the Probability of Six-Month Return-To-Custody (RTC) by Drug Treatment, Treatment Desire, Treatment-Desire Match, and Relevant Background Variables

Testing model	Effect tested	Odds Ratio	95% C.I.
Full exploratory model	Alcohol Use Severity	1.00	(0.98, 1.02)
	Drug Use Severity	1.01	(0.99, 1.02)
	Number of Prior Arrests	**1.01**	**(1.00, 1.02)**
	Age	**0.98**	**(0.96, 0.99)**
	High School Graduate	0.82	(0.59, 1.15)
	Mental Health Problems	0.94	(0.64, 1.39)
	Treatment	1.30	(0.86, 1.97)
	Treatment Motivation	1.04	(0.68, 1.60)
	Treatment-Motivation Match	**0.64**	**(0.42, 0.96)**
	Interaction	*0.40*	*(0.18, 0.93)**
Significance model	Number of Prior Arrests	**1.01**	**(1.00, 1.02)**
	Age	**0.98**	**(0.96, 0.99)**
	Treatment-Motivation Match	**0.69**	**(0.49, 0.97)**

*Indicating the size and significance of the treatment-Motivation interaction effect, when the effect of the treatment-Motivation match was replaced by the interaction term in the same exploratory model. Changes of the other effects in the model were minimal.

Note: Bold figures denote significance at the .05 level.

reported that they did not want to receive treatment (38% vs. 21%, respectively). Among those who reported that they did want to receive treatment, however, SATF participants performed slightly better than the untreated comparison group (27% vs. 31%, respectively), although this difference was not statistically significant. However, as shown in Table 31.2, the treatment-motivation interaction term (where 1 = matched, 0 = unmatched) was statistically significant, with a match being associated with an odds ratio of .69 (95% CI: 0.49, 0.97), or a 31% decrease in the likelihood of being returned to custody within six months of release.

It should be reiterated, however, that the matching procedures were designed for making treatment versus non-treatment comparisons. Thus, the derivations of motivational subgroups, discussed above, are likely to be confounded by other group differences. For example, as shown in Table 31.1, relative to subjects who reported a desire for treatment, participants who did not want treatment were more likely to report full-time employment during the six months prior to incarceration and to have lower drug use severity scores.

Multivariate Models Predicting Six-Month Recidivism

To verify that the differential effect described above could be attributed to a treatment-motivation interaction, we conducted two multivariate logistic regression models—full and reduced—to see if this variable remained a significant predictor of six-month recidivism even after controlling for baseline demographic differences and criminal background (i.e., alcohol use severity, drug use severity, number of prior arrests, age, education, and any psychiatric diagnosis). As shown in the full exploratory model (Table 31.3), the effect of the treatment-motivation interaction persisted even after controlling for these background differences in a multivariate model.

Specifically, the treatment-motivation interaction term in the full model indicates that those who wanted and received treatment were 60% less likely to return to custody than subjects in the other three categories combined (i.e., those wanting treatment/not receiving it, not wanting treatment/receiving it, and not wanting treatment/not receiving it) (OR = .40; 95% CI 0.18, 0.93). A modified interaction term was also created where those who did not want treatment and did not receive it or did want treatment and did receive it were coded as 1; and those who wanted treatment but did not receive it or did not want treatment but did receive it were coded as 0. The model with the modified interaction term indicates that subjects in the treatment-motivation matched group were 36% less likely to return to custody than the treatment-motivation unmatched group. Last, a reduced multivariate logistic model was conducted consisting only of the significant predictors identified in the full model (i.e., number of prior arrests, age, treatment-motivation match [reference group = unmatched]). Note: Two versions of the interaction term are reported here: (1) the conventional interaction term (denoted as "interaction") which compares those who wanted treatment and received it with all other subjects combined, and (2) the "modified" interaction term which compares the treatment-motivation-matched versus unmatched subjects. As shown in the bottom half of Table 31.3, the results of the reduced model indicate that the size and significance of the treatment-motivation match effect (with ORs of 0.64 and 0.69) and the interaction effect (with ORs of 0.36 and 0.40) are quite stable with or without controlling for the influence of the other predictors.

DISCUSSION

Matching Treatment to Inmate's Motivation Is Critical

The purpose of this study was to examine whether the generally positive findings regarding coerced treatment among community-based offenders could be replicated in a sample of incarcerated offenders. Verifying the applicability of the results derived from community offenders to incarcerated offenders is critical in light of the growing emphasis in many states on treating offenders while they are in prison.

In contrast to previous findings based on community offender samples, neither treatment condition nor motivation for treatment was significantly associated with the six-month recidivism outcomes. However, the interaction between these two variables was highly predictive, with SATF participants who did not want treatment being 41% more likely to have been returned to custody than those who did want treatment (38% vs. 27%, respectively), and 81% more likely to have been returned to custody than the inmates in the non-treatment group who did not want treatment (21%). Moreover, these trends persisted even after controlling for background differences between the four categories of offenders. In fact, all other things equal, inmates whose receipt of treatment was consistent with their preference for treatment were 36% less likely than unmatched inmates to have been returned to custody within six months of release.

Study Limitations

Proper interpretation of the following results requires that several methodological limitations of this analysis be noted. First, practical and ethical issues precluded the use of a true experimental design, in which eligible inmates would have been randomly assigned to either a treatment or non-treatment (control) condition. Instead, the comparison group was matched *post hoc* with the treatment group based on age, race/ethnicity, substance abuse history, commitment offense, sex offense history, and custody level. While this resulted in an extremely close match between groups, it is still possible that the two groups differ in other ways that were not measured.

Another limitation of this study relates to the timing of the evaluation of the SATF treatment program. Most programs require at least one year to stabilize and operate as they were designed. However, the size of the SATF program, the largely involuntary clientele, and difficulties in recruiting and retaining treatment staff resulted in a much slower development phase. As a result, it is possible that the outcomes of the present cohort (i.e., those admitted to SATF from June, 1999, through June, 2000) do not represent those of a mature program.

Last, the reliance of this outcome study on return to custody is at best an imprecise proxy of criminal behavior. In an analysis comparing self-reported criminal activity and number of arrests during the six months prior to incarceration, inmates reported one arrest for every 190 criminal acts committed (excluding drug use and traffic violations). Hence, according to these findings, official records reflect approximately one half of one percent of actual crimes reported. This is consistent with other reports that have shown that the majority of studies where discrepancies occurred in the frequency of arrests, the number of self-reported arrests were almost always higher than the number indicated in official records (Lagenbucher & Merrill, 2001).

CONCLUSION

In spite of these limitations, the present study offers compelling new evidence contradicting the popular belief that coerced clients in substance abuse treatment do as well or better than voluntary clients, at least in a prison setting. Although the unique findings presented here cannot be directly attributed to the differences in being coerced into a prison-based program relative to a community program, they do undermine the assumption that the coerced treatment findings based on offenders in the community can be generalized to incarcerated offenders.

Future research in this area could clarify these findings by using alternative measures of motivation or coercion and by assessing the treatment-motivation matching effect by directly contrasting community- and prison-based treatment samples. If this effect is demonstrated to be reliable across different measures and program types in prison, greater attention would need to be devoted to enhancing motivation among coerced treatment clients in prison. For now, state correctional systems with limited treatment capacity would be justified in using treatment motivation as a primary screening criterion for program admission.

About the Authors

David Farabee, Ph.D., is Associate Research Psychologist, UCLA Integrated Substance Abuse Programs, and is co-editor of Offender Substance Abuse Report *(OSA). Haikang Shen, Ph.D., is a Senior Statistician at the UCLA Integrated Substance Abuse Programs. Michael Prendergast, Ph. D., is Research Historian, UCLA Integrated Substance Abuse Programs, and is a member of the OSA Editorial Advisory Board. Jerome Cartier, M.A., is Project Director, UCLA Integrated Substance Abuse Programs. Dr. Farabee may be contacted by email at dfarabee@ucla.edu. Preparation of this paper was supported by California Department of Corrections (CDC) Contract #97.243. The views and conclusions expressed in the paper, however, are those of the authors and do not necessarily reflect the position of CDC.*

Endnote

[1] Study procedures were approved by the UCLA Institutional Review Board and by the California Department of Corrections. Although inmates may have been mandated to the treatment program, participation in the study was voluntary and required written informed consent.

References

Anglin, M. D. (1988). The efficacy of civil commitment in treating narcotics addiction. Special issue: a social policy analysis of compulsory treatment for opiate dependence. *Journal of Drug Issues, 18(4)*, 527-545.

Anglin, M.D., Brecht, M., & Maddahian, E. (1989). Pretreatment characteristics and treatment performance of legally coerced versus voluntary methadone maintenance admissions. *Criminology, 27(3)*, 537-557.

Collins, J.J., & Allison, M.A. (1983). Legal coercion and retention in drug abuse treatment. *Hospital and Community Psychiatry, 34(12)*, 1145-1149.

De Leon, G., Melnick, G., Thomas, G., Kressel, D., & Wexler, H.K. (2000). Motivation for treatment in a prison-based therapeutic community. *American Journal of Drug and Alcohol Abuse, 26(1)*, 33-46.

Farabee, D., Prendergast, M.L., & Anglin, M.D. (1998). The effectiveness of coerced treatment for drug-abusing offenders. *Federal Probation, 62(1)*, 3-10.

Farabee, D., Shen, H., & Sanchez, S. (2002). Perceived coercion and treatment need among mentally ill parolees. *Criminal Justice and Behavior, 29(1)*, 76-86.

Inciardi, J. A., Martin, S. S., Butzin, C.A., Hooper, R. M., & Harrison, L. D. (1997). An effective model of prison-based treatment for drug-involved offenders. *Journal of Drug Issues, 27(2)*, 261-278.

Knight, K., Holcom, M., & Simpson, D. D. (February, 1994). *TCU Psychosocial Functioning and Motivation Scales: Manual on psychometric properties*. Fort Worth: Texas Christian University, Institute of Behavioral Research.

Knight, K., Simpson, D. D., Chatham, L. R., & Camacho, L. M. (1997). An assessment of prison-based drug treatment: Texas' in-prison therapeutic community program. *Journal of Offender Rehabilitation, 24(3/4)*, 75-100.

Lagenbucher, J., & Merrill, J. (2001). The validity of self-reported cost events by substance abusers. *Evaluation Review, 25(2)*, 184-210.

Pelissier, B., Rhodes, W., Saylor, W., Gaes, G., Camp, S.D., Vanyur, S.D., Wallace, S. (2000). *TRIAD Drug Treatment Evaluation Project Final Report of Three-Year Outcomes: Part 1*. Washington, DC: Federal Bureau of Prisons.

Prendergast, M. L., Wellisch, J., & Wong, M. M. (1996). Residential treatment for women parolees following prison-based drug treatment: Treatment experiences, needs and services, outcomes. *Prison Journal, 76(3)*, 253-274.

Simpson, D.D., & Friend, H.J. (1988). Legal status and long-term outcomes for addicts in the DARP followup project. In C.G. Leukefeld and F.M. Tims (Eds.), *Compulsory treatment of drug abuse: Research and clinical practice*. NIDA Research Monograph 86, DHHS number (ADM) 89-1578, pp. 81-98.

Simpson, D. D., Wexler, H. K., & Inciardi, J. A. (Eds.). (1999). Drug treatment outcomes for correctional settings (Special Issue, Parts 1 and 2). *Prison Journal, 79(3, 4)*, 291-445.

Wexler, H.K., De Leon, G., Thomas, G., Kressel, D, & Peters, J. (1999). The Amity prison TC evaluation: Reincarceration outcomes. *Criminal Justice and Behavior, 26(2),* 147-167.

Part 6

Aftercare

A critical component in the continuum of opportunities to treat addicted offenders is aftercare. While primary treatment, such as long term in-prison therapeutic community treatment, helps offenders recover from drug addiction and a criminal lifestyle, aftercare helps offenders sustain their recovery and provides them with the assistance and skills needed in transitioning back into the community. Particularly for higher-risk offenders, the benefits of in-prison treatment are most apparent for those who go on to participate in an integrated aftercare component (Knight, Simpson, & Hiller, 1999).

Chapter 32, by Faye Taxman, discusses how reductions in recidivism can be achieved through a seamless system of care. The development of this type of system has been impeded, in part, because of problems associated with the integration of drug treatment into the criminal justice system. After describing how treatment can lead to improved public safety as well as public health, the author providers the reader with 12 principles for effective systems of care focusing on transitional policies and treatment retention.

In Chapter 33, Gary Field also points to the importance of continuity of offender treatment, particularly from the institution to the community. The Oregon demonstration project, begun in 1990, is described as an example of a statewide system of integrated treatment services. Particularly important in achieving this kind of model is the need to recognize and overcome potential obstacles to providing a continuity of offender treatment, such as the need for coordination between the criminal justice system and substance abuse treatment programs.

In Chapter 34, by Harry Wexler, the importance of addressing employment needs as part of an integrated approach to aftercare is discussed. The chapter emphasizes the importance of building on the success of prison-based treatment by developing viable integrated aftercare models that focus on employment. Ways to bridge the gap between aftercare treatment and employment services that often exist are provided, including the use of distance learning, the need to address employer's legal concerns, and the creation of a multi-value framework to guide the integrative process.

Chapter 35, by Faye Taxman, concludes this section by pointing to the fact that offenders participating in the continuum of treatment often are supervised by correctional agencies and, thus, there is a need to increase supervision's effectiveness. To this end, she provides an evidence-based model for supervision that focuses on the different stages of the supervision process, each of which has different goals that can ultimately lead to an offender achieving and sustaining behavioral change.

References

Knight, K., Simpson, D. D., & Hiller, M. L. (1999). Three-year reincarceration outcomes for in-prison therapeutic community treatment in Texas. *The Prison Journal*, 79(3), 337-351.

Chapter 32

Reducing Recidivism Through a Seamless System of Care: Components of Effective Treatment, Supervision, and Transition Services in the Community

by Faye S. Taxman, Ph.D.

Introduction 32-2
Barriers to—and Bonuses of—Providing Substance
  Abuse Treatment to Offenders 32-2
    Treatment Perceived as Opportunity, Not Punishment 32-3
    Offenders Often Unwanted in Community Treatment System 32-3
    Offenders Have Better Treatment Completion Rates 32-3
Longer Stay in Treatment and Continuum of Care Improve Outcomes 32-4
Recognizing Treatment as a Means of Crime Control Is Good Public Policy . . . 32-4
Twelve Principles for Effective Systems of Care Focusing on
  Transitional Policies and Treatment Retention 32-5
    #1: Make Recidivism Reduction the Goal 32-5
    #2: Treatment and Criminal Justice System
      Features Must Be Policy Driven 32-5
    #3: Treatment and Criminal Justice Professionals
      Must Function as a Team 32-5
    #4: Use Drug Testing to Manage Offenders 32-6
    #5: Target Offenders Whose Treatment Will Have Broad Impact 32-6
    #6: Use Treatment Matching Practices 32-7

This chapter originally appeared in Offender Substance Abuse Report, *Vol. 2, No. 3, May/June 2002.*

#7: Create a Treatment Process and Extend

    Length of Time in Treatment 32-7

#8: Use Behavioral Contracts 32-8

#9: Use Special Agents to Supervise Offenders in Treatment 32-8

#10: Sanction Non-Compliant Behavior 32-9

#11: Reward Positive Behavior 32-10

#12: Focus on Quality, Not Quantity 32-10

Summary.. 32-10

INTRODUCTION

A major challenge affecting the public health system is the overwhelming number of clients that are involved in the criminal justice system. Similarly, offenders in the criminal justice system have a great need for substance abuse treatment. The six million-plus Americans involved in the criminal justice system account for 50% to 60% of the cocaine and heroin consumed in the United States. Addressing the demand for drugs among this population is synonymous with addressing the drug problem in this country. By targeting the addiction problem of the majority of known consumers of drugs, we impact the various marketplaces for selling drugs, the associated crime and violence, and improve the quality of life for many communities.

The vast number of studies on drug treatment over the last 20 years have clearly demonstrated that drug treatment is a powerful tool in the "war on drugs" in *all* correctional settings. The effectiveness is enhanced when offenders are provided treatment in jail or prison, balanced by continued treatment in the community (Lipton, 1995; Taxman & Spinner, 1997; Simpson et al., 1999). In order to have an impact on the drug problem, drug treatment must be offered as a general practice instead of on an isolated basis. Research has identified the components of effective treatment programs that reduce drug use and criminal behavior. These research studies illustrate how treatment services, in conjunction with drug testing, supervision, and immediate consequences (sanctions), are critical components of an effective treatment delivery system.

This chapter presents a model for improving the delivery of substance abuse treatment, testing, and sanctions for offenders to improve client outcomes. Integration is a key concept to ensure that the criminal justice and treatment systems are focused on reducing recidivism; in other words, they agree to a common goal to achieve both public safety and public health needs.

BARRIERS TO—AND BONUSES OF—PROVIDING SUBSTANCE ABUSE TREATMENT TO OFFENDERS

The integration of drug treatment into the criminal justice system has been a struggle that underscores differing philosophies about criminal offenders, recovery, rehabilitation, and the value of leverage in changing the behavior of offenders/addicts. Both the treatment and the criminal justice systems have struggled with allowing each other to achieve their own independent goals. The conflicting priorities and practices of the criminal justice and treatment systems often adversely affect offenders' ability to access treatment programs or be placed in appropriate treatment programs, as well as providers' ability to use the leverage of the criminal justice system to retain the client in treatment. Many myths about the futility of treating offenders exist because of the failure of the treatment and criminal justice systems to develop systemic approaches to address common, but not insurmountable, issues.

Treatment Perceived as Opportunity, Not Punishment

While the criminal justice system has the goal of protecting society and reducing the risk from offenders, the public health system is primarily charged with the goal of providing services to improve health and social productivity. Harm reduction, in terms of criminal behavior, has never been a primary goal of treatment programs. It is only within recent years that the public health treatment system has realized that treatment can be part of the strategy to reduce the demand for drugs and reduce criminal behavior. While treatment is not considered punishment, the coerced treatment model allows treatment to be a tool of the criminal justice system to deter drug use and crime.

Offenders Often Unwanted in Community Treatment System

Slightly fewer than 15% of the offender population is actually engaged in treatment services. "Treatment services" as used here include self-help groups, educational groups, therapeutic communities, group therapy, individual counseling, etc. Most of the services provided to offenders can be categorized as self-help groups and educational groups. Thus, the actual percentage of offenders who participate in clinical interventions is much smaller than 15%.

One of the major stumbling blocks to getting more offenders into treatment is that some public health agencies do not want to treat the criminal justice client. The attitudes and values of the treatment system often preclude prioritizing different populations for services (Duffee & Carlson, 1996). Part of this attitude derives from community agencies having their own perspective of the ideal client/offender, while the other part derives from the criminal offender being perceived as a "difficult client."

With the exception of pregnant women and HIV-positive addicts, the first-come, first-served model of treatment services prevails in the public health system. Under this model, everyone is viewed as equally needy for care. Addicts appearing at the treatment program door are accepted based on program-specific criteria, which often do not include societal harm (e.g., criminal behavior) posed by the client. As noted by Schlesinger and Dorwart (1993), the first-come, first-served public health model allows treatment programs to select the clients they would like to serve and "avoid clients with the most difficult problems" (p. 224). There is no triage system in place to prioritize the type of addict that should receive care based on societal harm, matching of client to program, or any systematic process.

Offenders Have Better Treatment Completion Rates

A common myth is that "treatment volunteers" are more motivated, and thus more willing, to change their behavior than addicts coerced into treatment. This assumption has not been substantiated. Research has shown that criminal justice offenders in treatment are more likely to complete their treatment than volunteers (Simpson, 1981;

Hubbard, et al., 1989). Most addicts do not "volunteer" for treatment services without some precipitating factors, such as an employer, family or life partner, or some life crisis prompting the addict to seek treatment. These factors drive the client to seek treatment, as does the legal system. Recent research on motivation of addicts in treatment has shown that the treatment process can contribute to engaging the addict in treatment and motivating the client to change his or her behavior (Simpson, et al., 1997a).

Both treatment and supervision agencies experience problems with compliance with program requirements. A widely reported problem with public health treatment programs is that dropout rates are typically high and relapse to drugs and criminality among dropouts is a problem (Hubbard, et al., 1989; Simpson, Joe, & Brown, 1997b). Taxman and Byrne (1994) and Langan and Cunniff (1992) estimate that approximately 50% of offenders do not meet supervision requirements. Compliance problems create difficulties by reducing the integrity of the treatment and supervision programs.

With the oversight of the criminal justice system, criminal justice agencies have the leverage to motivate the offender to participate in treatment and complete the treatment regime. Studies have found that legal coercion is an important variable for the offender to stick with the treatment program (Anglin & Hser, 1990; CASA, 1998). Many new treatment initiatives for the criminal justice client feature graduated sanctions or immediate consequences for non-compliance.

LONGER STAY IN TREATMENT AND CONTINUUM OF CARE IMPROVE OUTCOMES

Length of stay in treatment has been found to be a critical variable in reducing recidivism and substance abuse (DeLeon et al., 1982; Condelli & Hubbard, 1994; Hubbard, et al., 1989; Simpson, 1998; Simpson & Sells, 1982). Managed care and cost containment efforts have led to shorter treatment programs, which result in reduced length of stay in treatment. A continuing trend in the field is minimizing services and reducing the length of time clients are in treatment (Etheridge, et al., 1997). The implications for the future of this trend are unknown. However, researchers have supported the proposition that offender populations, due to the societal harm of criminal behavior, should participate in a minimum of one year of treatment (Lipton, 1995). Providing for a continuum of care is one systemic process to increase the length of time in treatment by having offenders participate in different phases of treatment. The concept of a continuum extends the length of treatment while adjusting the intensity of the services based on the progress of the client. Several continuum models have been adopted: residential, jail, or prison treatment, followed by outpatient; intermediate care (28-day residential) with intensive outpatient and outpatient; intensive outpatient and outpatient; and outpatient and aftercare. The continuum of care model provides the client with longer stays in treatment (up to 12 months), while reducing the costs of delivering services.

RECOGNIZING TREATMENT AS A MEANS OF CRIME CONTROL IS GOOD PUBLIC POLICY

The coerced treatment model is a crime control approach focused on behaviors that contribute to the criminal activity. By focusing efforts on offenders under supervision (e.g., inmates or probationers and parolees), the behavior of these offenders can be monitored. Treatment is used to change the behavior of the offender by engaging him/her in services that address the substance abuse factors that trigger criminal behavior. Treatment becomes the cornerstone of the sentence by reinforcing the importance of behavioral change for the offender. Since the offender is under the control of the criminal justice system, oversight measures can be used to monitor his or her behavior. Compliance measures (graduated sanctions) become tools to monitor the progress of the client and assist the offender in maintaining his/her commitment to recovery.

TWELVE PRINCIPLES FOR EFFECTIVE SYSTEMS OF CARE FOCUSING ON TRANSITIONAL POLICIES AND TREATMENT RETENTION

To achieve the most gains from treatment for offenders, the principles of effective systems of care are designed to reduce recidivism and increase retention in treatment programs. These two goals are commingled to allow quality treatment to impact reductions in recidivism.

#1: Make Recidivism Reduction the Goal

Treatment and criminal justice systems typically have two differing goals, neither of which is directly focused on reducing recidivism. The emphasis on recidivism reduction brings the systems into alignment, requiring each to rethink operations and priorities for the agencies individually, jointly, and reallocating resources.

#2: Treatment and Criminal Justice System Features Must Be Policy Driven

Interagency system features—integrated screening, placement, testing, monitoring, and sanctions—do not typically exist. The recognition that these policies are critical to effective service delivery requires the systems to develop supporting policies. A policy-driven forum is needed to develop and implement targeted policies and practices. Various players of the system, including administrators of the treatment/health programs; probation and parole, jail, and law enforcement officials; and judges, court administrators, and other criminal justice or social agencies, must work together as a policy team. With a renewed focus on reaching certain goals, this is one way to address organizational or turf battles that are considered sacred cows (Woodward, 1993).

#3: Treatment and Criminal Justice Professionals Must Function as a Team

The work of the policy team is to define and develop policy as well as provide the needed resources. The next step is to carry policy into practice and operation. For example, a policy that states that drug test results will be shared between the criminal justice and treatment systems is designed to ensure that both agencies are informed of the client's progress. The policy directs the supervisors and staff to develop a mechanism for sharing drug test information on a timely basis. At the staff level, this removes the potential for individual staff members to make individual decisions about whether or not they wish to share drug test results. It also provides an agency process to share drug test results such as faxing positive results, using interagency automated systems, etc.

#4: Use Drug Testing to Manage Offenders

Urinalysis allows for immediate confirmation of an offender's use of drugs. While it is clearly a tool for both the treatment and criminal justice systems, drug testing results have not been integrated into practice in either system. Few systems have policies that use drug test results to screen offenders for treatment programs. Even fewer systems have policies in effect that provide guidelines on how to handle positive drug tests while the offender is in treatment or under supervision. Treatment placement and program compliance are two areas that require standards and practices. Working together as a team will allow the systems to use available drug test resources widely.

#5: Target Offenders Whose Treatment Will Have Broad Impact

Targeting is probably one of the most difficult issues in corrections and criminal justice policies. Boot camps, drug treatment programs, intensive supervision, and other correctional innovations have all experienced difficulties with the targeting problem (Austin, Jones, & Bolyard, 1993; Byrne & Pattavina, 1992; Andrews & Bonta, 1994; Taxman et al., 2003). The tendency is often to provide services to "low risk" offenders, which some contend reduces the societal impact of the treatment programs (Andrews & Bonta, 1994). To have an impact on recidivism and drug consumption, the focus of treatment should be on offenders who are both addicts and criminally active.

Both criminal justice and treatment issues must define the target definition for scarce treatment resources. From the criminal justice perspective, the offender with a prior arrest and conviction history is more likely to be causing harm to the community. That is, offenders' substance abuse habits drive their criminal behavior in such volume that the individual is likely to be committing many crimes. First, the criminal justice history may also dictate that the offender is likely to be incarcerated for long periods of time. Targeting these offenders is likely to have little impact on crime in the community. Next, the legal status is an important variable. Many pretrial offenders use participation in treatment to convince judges of their substance abuse problems, only to drop out of treatment after the criminal charge has been dismissed or the offender is placed on probation. The focus on the sentenced offender has several advantages, including the offender being more likely to continue with treatment as part of the requirement of supervision, the offender being less likely to drop out of treatment, and the offender being more likely to be motivated to change his/her behavior over the long period of supervision.

Three other treatment issues are the severity of drug use, type of drugs used, and prior treatment experience. Severity of drug use might be an indicator of need; with priority given to addicts who have daily habits compared to those with less frequent usage patterns (e.g., binge behavior, weekly use, etc.). Similarly, the type of drug abused might also be an important factor in determining priority for treatment given the knowledge that some addicts are more criminally active than others. Finally, prior treatment experience may be a useful variable to determine appropriateness of an offender for a particular type of program. Standardized instruments can ensure that treatment and criminal justice staff collect consistent information on clients, as well as make decisions based on agency priorities. Some agencies use instruments like the Addiction Severity Index as a guide to alcohol and drug problems, and use the composite to identify those most in need of treatment.

The integration of treatment and criminal justice information in targeting decisions is frequently discussed, but infrequently applied. The difficulty in administering the policy is that treatment and criminal justice agencies do not share information gathered in their respective disciplines. Often the treatment system does not have criminal justice information, other than self-reported criminal justice history. Conversely, criminal justice agencies often rely on the offender to report prior treatment experience and drug use patterns. The focus on recidivism-reduction policies will require triaging available treatment slots for offenders who create harm in the community by their drug use *and* their criminal behavior. Ultimately, criminal justice and treatment agencies will have to determine how to gather and use information from the different systems to make triage decisions.

#6: Use Treatment Matching Practices

The tendency of most systems is to place offenders in the first available treatment slots. Often the available "slot" is not suitable for the offender's needs, but merely reflects an opening. However, by using information gathered for targeting purposes, more informed decisions can be made about the type of offender who should be placed in residential, intensive outpatient, and outpatient programs. A mixture of treatment needs and criminal justice risk factors can assist in making this determination. For example, offenders with more involvement in the criminal justice system are likely to require more external controls (e.g., residential or intensive outpatient settings with more structure, etc.) on their behavior as compared to those with less prior criminal justice history. Since many jurisdictions have some services in the jail or prison, consideration should be given to the continuity of care (e.g., suitability of the treatment philosophy and approaches) from the jail/prison program to the community-based program. The American Society of Addiction Medicine has developed a protocol for treatment placement (ASAM, 1991). Although this protocol does not include criminal justice risk factors, policy teams can modify their approaches to incorporate treatment and criminal justice needs.

#7: Create a Treatment Process and Extend Length of Time in Treatment

Research continues to affirm the importance of the length of time in treatment for addicts, with better results usually occurring from longer participation in treatment programs. Many short-term residential and outpatient treatment programs are four months or less in duration (Etheridge, et al., 1997); few long-term residential programs (greater than six months) exist. The goal should be to engage the offender in treatment for longer periods of time, with the treatment process consisting of program phases (Simpson, 1998). The combination of intensive and less intensive services results in a less intrusive treatment environment, as well as being cost effective.

Since most treatment and correctional systems thrive on episodic treatment experiences, policies are required to create the continuum of care practices at the individual level. It is not sufficient to have an array of services without the supporting policies to move offenders through the continuum. These policies need to address the following:

- Establishing a reservation system to alert programs of the expected date of placement in their program;

- Creating a behavioral contract to inform the offender of the likely continuum;

- Establishing criteria for placing offenders in different treatment programs based on progress in the subsequent treatment program;

- Training criminal justice and treatment personnel on the use of a continuum; and, finally,

- Establishing treatment policies that step up or step down the level of care based on progress.

#8: Use Behavioral Contracts

A behavioral contract is a tool of the treatment and criminal justice systems to specify the expectations for the client as well as identify treatment and criminal justice services. Informing the offender of the programmatic components clarifies the treatment and criminal justice experiences. Core components of the contract are: (1) assignment of treatment programs and hours of therapy—e.g., each phase or treatment program should be specified, including jail-based treatment programs; (2) supervision schedule and location of supervision agent; (3) drug testing schedule; (4) graduated sanctions to identify set responses to common issues such as positive drug tests and missed appointments; (5) incentives; and (6) special conditions of treatment and/or supervision—e.g., community service hours, electronic monitoring, house arrest, self-help groups, etc. The behavioral contract should be signed by the offender, treatment provider, and criminal justice agent (and potentially the judge) to serve as a binding contract. The contractual component of the plan requires all parties to be equally committed to the different phases of the treatment and criminal justice protocol.

#9: Use Special Agents to Supervise Offenders in Treatment

To become a team with treatment, the probation and/or criminal justice staff must understand the treatment process and support treatment goals. This requires a close working relationship among the treatment and criminal justice staff. The team process in a seamless system relies on the staff to be considerate and supportive of the roles and needs of each discipline.

With a core staff, it is feasible to use the tools of corrections to control the behavior of the offender in the community and to increase compliance with treatment and criminal justice requirements. Probation involves a number of functions that can improve the integrity of the treatment process such as drug testing (to confirm abstinence), collateral contacts (to identify potential problems in the community, etc.), face-to-face contacts (to observe and discuss treatment progress and compliance with general court conditions), and community service (to help repay society for the crime and to fulfill sentence obligations). In addition, the probation officer can modify most conditions of the sentence (within a range) to intensify the structure should the offender have difficulties in the treatment/supervision or reduce supervision/structure through treatment services. The supervision services offer the potential to enable and facilitate all services by monitoring the offender's performance. Supervision provides the leverage of the criminal justice system to keep the offender in the appropriate treatment services (Visher, 1990; Collins & Allison, 1983).

#10: Sanction Non-Compliant Behavior

A cornerstone of recidivism reduction policies addresses the area of non-compliance, or the "what to do with" practices of how to address offenders who fail to fulfill treatment or supervision conditions. Contingency management, token economies, and behavior modification systems are systemic practices that are used in the treatment field to address compliance. Sanctions provide the tools to hold offenders accountable under their behavioral contract. The sanctions are essentially preventive measures to reduce revocations and recidivism, as demonstrated by the D.C. Drug Court (Harrell & Cavanagh, 1996).

Sanctions policies should have four components:

- *Infractions or violation behavior must be clearly identified.* By informing the offender of the negative behavior, the process clarifies expectations for the offender. Typical infraction behaviors are positive urine tests, missed appointments in treatment or supervision, and failure to abide by program conditions.

- *Sanctions must be swift, occurring shortly after the behavior presents itself.* As a rule, it is important to have the sanctions occur within 24 hours of the behavior, which reduces the denial of the behavior by the offender. Such a policy also requires that treatment and criminal justice systems respond appropriately to potential crime-producing behavior.

- *Sanctions must be clearly specified.* It is important that the offender knows the consequences for violating the treatment and supervision norms. Clearly specified responses include specified days in jail, hours of community service, or increased reporting requirements. These certain responses clarify for the offender that the lack of compliance will result in a negative response.

- *The sanction schedule must be progressive.* It is unlikely that the response for negative behavior will be the same each time the offender fails to comply. Instead, a sanctions schedule increases in severity as the offender continues to persist in violating treatment and supervision rules. For example, the first positive urine results in one day in jail, the second results in three days in jail, and the third results in five days in detoxification. This type of progressive schedule makes clear that the consequences become more severe as the offender continues to persist in his or her negative behavior.

Developing a set of polices that are agreed upon by the criminal justice system will require input from treatment providers, criminal justice actors, and the judiciary. The statutory authority of the probation and/or parole agents in a given jurisdiction may affect the use of sanctions. In some jurisdictions, probation and/or parole officers cannot incarcerate an offender without approval of the judiciary. In other jurisdictions, the agents have the authority. Since the probation department is generally responsible for executing court orders, the sanction schedules should be developed in coordination with the criminal justice system, particularly judges.

#11: Reward Positive Behavior

The criminal justice system infrequently acknowledges positive achievements made by offenders. An incentive system, similar to a sanctions schedule, provides an opportunity to formalize recognition for good behavior so that restraints on the offender are reduced as progress occurs. An incentive system should be swift, certain, and progressive in the same fashion as a sanctions system. The system provides the positive reinforcements often missing from the criminal justice and treatment systems. Positive incentives provide a rationale for the offender to comply with treatment and criminal justice conditions and reward the attainment of individual goals. In a seamless process, the good and the bad must be equally recognized.

#12: Focus on Quality, Not Quantity

The seamless system underscores the importance of policy-driven practices to reduce recidivism. A critical component of recidivism reduction practices is improving outcomes of offenders. Generally this involves ensuring that the treatment and criminal justice systems have the appropriate quality control measures in place to fulfill their obligations. This may require reallocating existing resources to commit to the desired outcomes. It also may result in some short time changes in the number of offenders that can be served through the process. Many agencies operate from a mindset of trying to serve the maximum number of clients possible. Although criminal justice agencies seldom have the opportunity to limit their "clientele," the seamless system process provides the forum to focus on outcomes.

An important component of quality is in the type of treatment services offered. The tendency of the criminal justice system is to offer less intensive, less expensive services. Self-help groups and educationally oriented services (although valuable service units) dominate the field (CASA, 1998). Yet, to achieve the gains from treatment, other clinical services are needed (e.g., therapeutic community, cognitive behavior skills, milieu therapy, etc.) (Lipton, 1995; Andrews & Bonta, 1994). The focus on outcomes helps systems redefine their service systems on quality or services that are more likely to change behavior. The emphasis on scientifically proven interventions will show gains in better outcomes.

SUMMARY

Effective treatment services are synonymous with effective criminal justice services. The seamless system protocol provides a systemic process to address some of the criticisms of the existing service offered by treatment and criminal justice agencies. It removes discretionary practices and institutionalizes operations to address the traditional barriers to treatment for offender populations. Many scholars, policy makers, and practitioners highlight how critical it is to provide good treatment services to ensure that the public has confidence in criminal justice polices. Through the seamless system approach, it is feasible to ensure that these policies become operational.

About the Author

Faye S. Taxman, Ph.D., is Director, University of Maryland, College Park Bureau of Governmental Research.

This paper was originally prepared for the Office of National Drug Control Policy's Treatment and Criminal Justice System Conference in March, 1998. This project is sponsored by the National Drug Control Policy, the National Institute of Justice, and the National Institute on Drug Abuse. All opinions are those of the author and do not reflect the opinion of the sponsoring agencies. All questions should be directed to Dr. Taxman at www.bgr.umd.edu.

References

American Society of Addiction Medicine (ASAM). (1991). *Patient placement criteria for the treatment of psychoactive substance abuse disorders.* Washington, DC: Author.

Andrews, D. A., & Bonta, J. (1994). *The psychology of criminal conduct.* Cincinnati, OH: Anderson Publishing.

Anglin, M. D., & Hser, Y. (1990). Treatment of drug abuse. In M. Tonry & J. Q. Wilson (Eds.), *Drugs and crime* (pp. 393-460). Chicago, IL: University of Chicago Press.

Austin, J., Jones, M., & Bolyard, M. (1993). The growing use of jail boot camps: The current state of the art. [Research in Brief.] Washington, DC: National Institute of Justice.

Byrne, J. M., & Pattavina, A. (1992). The effectiveness issue: Assessing what works in the adult community corrections system. In J. M. Byrne, A. J. Lurigio & J. Petersilia (Eds.), *Smart sentencing* (pp. 281-303). Newbury Park, CA: Sage Publications.

Center on Addiction and Substance Abuse at Columbia University (CASA). (1998). *Behind bars: Substance abuse and America's prison population.* New York, NY: National Center on Addiction and Substance Abuse at Columbia University.

Collins, J. J., & Allison, M. (1983). Legal coercion and retention in drug abuse treatment. *Hospital and Community Psychiatry, 34:*1145-1149.

Condelli, W. S., & Hubbard, R.L. (1994). Relationship between time spent in treatment and client outcomes from therapeutic communities. *Journal of Substance Abuse Treatment 11:*25-33.

DeLeon, G., Wexler, H. K., & Jainchill, N. (1982). The therapeutic community: Success and improvement rates 5 years after treatment. *International Journal of the Addictions, 17:*703-747.

Duffee, D., & Carlson, B. (1996). Competing value premises for the provision of drug treatment to probationers. *Crime and Delinquency, 42 (4):* 574-593.

Etheridge, R. M., Hubbard, R, L., Anderson, J., Craddock, S.G., & Flynn, P.M. (1997). Treatment structure and program services in the Drug Abuse Treatment Outcome Study (DATOS). *Psychology of Addictive Behaviors, 11:* 244-260.

Harrell, A., & Cavanagh, S. (1996). *Preliminary results from the evaluation of the DC Superior Court drug intervention program for drug felony defendants.* Washington, DC: National Institute of Justice.

Hubbard, R. L., Marsden, M. E., Rachal, J. V., Harwood, H. J., Cavanaugh, E. R., & Ginzburg, H. M. (1989). *Drug abuse treatment: A national study of effectiveness.* Chapel Hill, NC: University of North Carolina Press.

Langan, P., & Cunniff, M.A., (1992). Recidivism of felons on probation 1986-1989. *Criminology, 27(4):* 721-746.

Lipton, D. S. (1995). The effectiveness of treatment for drug abusers under criminal justice supervision. Presentation at the Conference on Criminal Justice Research and Evaluation. Washington, DC: National Institute of Justice.

Schlesinger, M., & Dorwart, R. A. (1993). Falling between the cracks: Failing national strategies for the treatment for substance abuse. *Daedalus, 121 (3):* 195-237.

Simpson, D. D., Wexler, H., & Inciardi, J. 1999. The introduction. *The Prison Journal, 79(4):* 381-383.

Simpson, D. D. (1998). DATOS first-wave findings released. *Research Roundup, 7(4):*1- 8. Institute of Behavioral Research at Texas Christian University.

Simpson, D. D., Joe, G.W., Broome, K. M., Hiller, M. L, Knight, K., & Rowan-Szal, G. A.. (1997a). Program diversity and treatment retention rates in the Drug Abuse Treatment Outcome Study (DATOS)." *Psychology of Addictive Behaviors, 11(4):* 279-293.

Simpson, D. D., Joe, G. W., & Brown, B.S. (1997b). Treatment retention and follow-up outcomes in the Drug Abuse Treatment Outcome Study (DATOS). *Psychology of Addictive Behaviors, 11(4):* 294-307.

Simpson, D. D., & Sells, S.B. (1982). Effectiveness of treatment for drug abuse: An overview of the DARP research program. *Advances in Alcohol and Substance Abuse Treatment, 2:*7-29.

Simpson, D. D. (1981). Treatment for drug abuse: Follow-up outcomes and length of time spent. *Archives General Psychiatry 38:*875-880.

Taxman, F., Byrne, J., & Young, D. (2003). *Targeting for reentry: Matching needs and services to maximize public safety.* Washington, DC: National Institute of Justice. Available online at http://www.bgr.umd.edu/pdf/May_2003_Target/pdf.

Taxman, F. 1998. Reducing recidivism through a seamless system of care: Components of effective treatment, supervision, and transition services in the community. Washington, DC: Office of National Drug Control Policy [available online: http:// www.whitehousedrugpolicy.gov/treat/consensus/consensus.html].

Taxman, F.S., & Spinner, D. (1997). *Jail Addiction Services (JAS) demonstration project in Montgomery County, MD: Jail and community based substance abuse treatment program model.* College Park, MD: University of Maryland.

Taxman, F.S., & Byrne, J. (1994). Locating absconders: Results from a randomized field experiment. *Federal Probation 58:* 13-23.

Visher, C. A. (1990). Incorporating drug treatment in criminal sanctions. *NIJ Reports, 221:*2-7.

Woodward, R., 1993. Establishing and maintaining the policy teams. In P. McGuarry & M. Carter (eds.) *Handbook for policy makers: Implementing intermediate sanctions.* Washington, DC: National Institute of Corrections.

Chapter 33

Continuity of Offender Treatment: From the Institution to the Community

by Gary Field, Ph.D.

Background: Effectiveness of Offender Treatment 33-2
How Continuity of Offender Treatment Improves Ultimate
   Treatment Success Rates 33-2
      Recent Outcome Studies Show Positive Effects 33-2
      The Oregon Demonstration Project 33-3
Theoretical Underpinnings of Programs 33-4
      Justice System Perspective 33-4
      Offender Perspective 33-5
Obstacles to Continuity of Offender Treatment 33-5
      Segmentation of the Criminal Justice System 33-5
      Lack of Coordination Between Justice System
        and Treatment Programs 33-6
      Loss of Post-Release Structure for Offenders 33-6
      Loss of Incentives and Sanctions at Release 33-6
      Lack of Services in the Community 33-6
      Lack of Treatment Provider Experience With Offenders 33-6
      Community Funding Challenges 33-7
Successful Program Models 33-7
      Outreach Programs 33-7
      Reach-In Programs 33-7
      Third-Party Continuity Program 33-7
      Mixed Model 33-8

This chapter originally appeared in Offender Substance Abuse Report, *Vol. 3, No. 2, March/April 2003.*

BACKGROUND: EFFECTIVENESS OF OFFENDER TREATMENT

The effectiveness of jail and prison substance abuse treatment is now well established (Lipton, 1995; Leshner, 1997). Among inmate treatment programs, pre-release therapeutic communities (TCs) have been the most studied. These programs have a well documented record of success (Wexler, et. al., 1988; Field, 1989; Simpson, et. al, 1999a; 1999b). For example, in the evaluation of the Stay 'N Out TC, Wexler and his colleagues examined the progress of more than 2,000 inmates over a 10-year period and found that the TC was successful with clients with extensive criminal records. Many of these pre-release TC programs have had active aftercare components (Field, 1989; Chaiken, 1989).

Studies have also shown that community-based offender drug treatment can be successful. National studies (Simpson, 1984; Hubbard, et. al., 1984; Simpson, et. al., 2002) have shown that a variety of substance abuse programs are effective with populations that include offenders. Anglin and McGloughlin (1984) present impressive long-term follow-up data on the California Civil Addict Program. Treatment Alternatives to Street Crimes (TASC) Programs had more than 40 independent evaluations between 1972 and 1982 demonstrating their effectiveness (Cook & Weinman, 1988). Studies of the TASC programs have particular significance because these programs have focused on transition of offenders from the institution to the community.

In summary, there are institution pre-release models that work (e.g., TCs), and there are community models that work (e.g., intensive supervision with treatment). However, too little attention has been given to the process of transition from institution to community. Both criminal justice and substance abuse treatment experts have observed that important gains made during incarceration are not being sustained when offenders returned to the community because continuity of care was either inadequate or non-existent (Peters, 1993). According to Peters:

> Many offenders report feeling overwhelmed by the transition from a highly structured correctional environment to a less structured environment following release. At this time of concentrated stress, an offender enters a culture where little or no support exists—no job, no money, weakened or broken family ties—with immediate needs to plan daily activities, to begin interacting constructively in non-adversarial relationships, and to manage personal or household finances and problems. (p. 15).

Authors in related fields of study have made similar observations. The juvenile justice field has been emphasizing the need for aftercare (Altschuler & Armstrong, 1996), and evaluations of boot camp and shock incarceration programs have emphasized the critical component of aftercare and coordination to aftercare in both theory and research (MacKenzie & Souryal, 1994; MacKenzie & Hebert, 1996).

HOW CONTINUITY OF OFFENDER TREATMENT IMPROVES ULTIMATE TREATMENT SUCCESS RATES

Recent Outcome Studies Show Positive Effects

More recently, researchers have examined the specific effects of continuity of offender treatment from institution to community on outcome success rates. Inciardi

(1996) found that drug-involved offenders who participated in a continuum of drug treatment (prison focused TC treatment followed by treatment in a work-release center) in the Delaware system had lower rates of drug use and recidivism than the offenders in the institutional program alone:

> The findings indicate that at 18 months after release, drug offenders who received 12-15 months of treatment in prison followed by an additional 6 months of drug treatment and job training were more than twice as likely to be drug-free than offenders who received prison-based treatment alone. Furthermore, offenders who received both forms of treatment were much more likely than offenders who received only prison-based treatment to be arrest-free 18 months after their release (71 percent compared to 48 percent). (p. 1)

Wexler (1996), in a similar study in California, found that drug-involved offenders who participated in both the Amity prison TC program and the Amity community-based TC program on release had substantially reduced rates of recidivism over those offenders who participated in the prison-based program alone. Simpson, Wexler, and Inciardi (1999a; 1999b) present a data comparison from Texas, California, and Delaware TC programs showing similar improved outcomes of prison treatment plus continuity into community treatment over prison treatment alone.

The Oregon Demonstration Project

Oregon has tried a somewhat different approach. While the prison-based TC programs in Oregon have always stressed continuity of treatment into the community (Field, 1989), program planners hypothesized that shorter and less intensive prison programs with intensive continuity of treatment into a substantial community program for inmates with lower levels of addiction and criminality would yield results similar to the more intensive TC programs that were targeted to more criminal and more highly addicted inmates.

In 1990 the Oregon Department of Corrections began a demonstration project to show the effects of a thorough transition program from institution to community treatment. Inmates began a three- to six-month pre-release day treatment program in an Oregon prison release facility, and then were followed intensively for six to nine months in community treatment and supervision. Key program elements were as follows:

- *Service providers "reach in" to the institution.* Parole and drug treatment services began while the individual was still incarcerated, usually several months before parole. Individual county inmates had their own group led by county drug treatment providers.

- *Joint institution/community release planning.* Release center staff developed the inmate's release plan cooperatively with the inmate, the parole officer, and drug treatment coordinator. Inmates were included in the planning process, and signed an agreement of program participation that included a listing of graduated program incentives and sanctions.

- *Intensive supervision.* Once the drug-involved offender was paroled, he or she was placed on an intensive supervision caseload in the community.

- *Continuity of treatment.* Group treatment continued into the community, usually with the same group leader and with many of the same members of the individual's institution group. Peer support for abstinence and recovery was an important theme of these groups.

- *Careful management of incentives and sanctions.* Throughout the process, offenders were provided with incentives for program participation and sanctions for noncompliance or relapse. In the release center, participating inmates were given desirable housing, could earn extra pass time, were provided with special job-skills counseling, and were given special consideration for release subsidy funding. They were monitored more closely, including urinalysis, and lost privileges according to a graduated schedule. In the community, program participants also were monitored more closely, experienced graduated sanctions, and were provided the incentives of housing, employment, and other specialized services.

Outcome studies of this program have shown that arrest rates of participating offenders dropped by 54%, and their conviction rates dropped by 65% during the year following treatment (Field & Karecki, 1992). In 1993, three more of these pre-release day treatment programs were begun. The three programs vary in design and population served (one is for women with young children; one is for male Hispanics who primarily speak Spanish; one is rural), but each emphasizes preparation for community supervision and treatment. A study by Finigan (1997) shows the effectiveness of these programs, including improvement in employment and community adjustment along with decreases in recidivism and community burden.

THEORETICAL UNDERPINNINGS OF PROGRAMS

Justice System Perspective

The reasons for the importance of continuity of treatment from institution to community can be examined from the perspectives of both the criminal justice system and the individual offender. From the criminal justice system perspective, the offender is confronted with and by a system that largely isn't a system in the usual sense. Little program coordination exists between arrest, diversion, conviction, probation, revocation, jail, prison, and parole or post-prison supervision. While there are examples of excellent coordination to be found between some of these points in the criminal justice system, they are exceptions to the more common phenomena of lack of coordination.

Were an average person to examine a criminal justice flow chart, and be asked where continuity would be the best, that person would probably identify the point of transfer from prison to community supervision. If the offender is under prison supervision and in a prison program, and being sent to community supervision and a community program, what possible excuse is there not to coordinate programs? Given that prison inmates include the most dangerous offenders in the criminal justice system; and given that heavy substance abusing offenders are among the highest risk inmates; and given that considerable societal resources are spent on prison supervision, prison treatment, community supervision, and community treatment; shouldn't the public expect efficient and effective coordination of programs from institution to community supervision? Offenders, particularly recidivistic offenders, frequently demonstrate antisocial characteristics. Part of antisocial character includes finding and exploiting any gap in supervision or monitoring. Therefore, the absence of continuity from institution to community programs can be expected to result in an undermining of treatment gains, which in turn wastes treatment resources while decreasing community safety.

Offender Perspective

From the individual offender's perspective, leaving prison, particularly after a lengthy incarceration, can be an intimidating experience. Most people become overly comfortable with highly structured environments, a process called "institutionalization." Individuals with psychological disorders appear to have relatively more difficulty readjusting to community living after living in highly structured environments. This phenomenon seems to occur across disorders such as mental illness or addiction, although it may be expressed differently depending on the person and the disorder. Partly because of the disorder itself and partly because of anxiety surrounding the disorder, institutionalized individuals have difficulty transferring learning from one situation to another. What they learn in the institution program does not easily transfer to the community. Institution programs start a recovery process in an environment whose structure helps the change process to begin, and that does not possess a risk to the community. But recovery and self-management skill learning begun in the institution program need reinforcement and some degree of re-learning in the community follow-up program. Without good coordination between the programs the offender's disorder, anxiety, or both are likely to weaken treatment gains and trigger a relapse. Parole officers have long observed the high-risk status of offenders newly released from prison. As has often been noted in the mental health treatment literature, rather than lament the institution to community transfer of learning problem exhibited by these individuals, we should program to account for it.

OBSTACLES TO CONTINUITY OF OFFENDER TREATMENT

If continuity of offender treatment is necessary and shown to be effective, why does it still only occur in exceptional programs, rather than in general practice? Several factors weigh against continuity practices. We need to clearly identify these impediments in order to overcome them and move forward.

Segmentation of the Criminal Justice System

The criminal justice system is not a discrete, well-coordinated system, but is actually a cluster of independent agencies and entities with separate justice responsibilities. These entities include jails, prisons, pretrial agencies, probation and parole agencies, the courts, law enforcement, and community organizations working with offenders. Successful transition of offenders into the community requires collaboration among all these entities. However, most of these agencies are under separate funding streams, with differing organizational missions, and they often have little understanding of the other components of the system. (National Task Force on Correctional Substance Abuse Strategies, 1991).

Lack of Coordination Between Justice System and Treatment Programs

Beyond the discontinuities within the criminal justice system, substance abuse programs most often develop within health or human resource systems that have traditions, values, and goals that are different than the criminal justice system. Bringing these different perspectives together into a common mission can be challenging. Discontinuity occurs more frequently between community treatment and community supervision than it does between institutional treatment and the institution, but the community discontinuity often makes coordination between the institutional treatment program and community treatment programs difficult.

Loss of Post-Release Structure for Offenders

Those who have been incarcerated for extended periods of time may lack many basic life skills and the ability to solve day-to-day problems. The decisions about these new obligations can lead to serious consequences, yet often no individual or system is responsible for helping offenders prioritize and balance the challenges of life in the community.

Loss of Incentives and Sanctions at Release

Formal incentives and sanctions to participate in treatment and to maintain prosocial behavior may not be as strong in the community as they are in the institution. Without these incentives to continue sobriety and a crime-free life style, offenders struggling with community adjustment may slip into old patterns of behavior. This is particularly true where community supervision has been eliminated, or is not strongly enforced.

Lack of Services in the Community

Offenders need a variety of services during their transition to life in the community. Many of these are considered "ancillary," although without them treatment success is unlikely. For example, an offender will not be able to participate in outpatient treatment if he or she doesn't have housing and transportation. A range of services is necessary for effective treatment.

Lack of Treatment Provider Experience With Offenders

In some areas community substance abuse treatment providers are inexperienced in adapting substance abuse treatment to people who also bring a history of a criminal lifestyle. Lack of appreciation for the additional problems of criminal thinking and the anxieties surrounding release from incarceration significantly weaken community-based treatment. Further, some community treatment programs fail to recognize the work that already has been done in the institutional treatment program, serving to further frustrate the offender and increase program dropout.

Community Funding Challenges

The criminal justice population comprises a major percentage of those in need of substance abuse treatment, yet within many community programs there is a lack of specialized staff and few services targeted to meet offenders' needs. This is in part due to the fact that substance abuse treatment agencies have not always identified offenders as a priority population, and agencies that provide community supervision do not always fund treatment services during probation or parole.

SUCCESSFUL PROGRAM MODELS

Strategies for offender treatment continuity from institution to community can be conceptually organized into four types: outreach, reach-in, third party, and mixed program models.

Outreach Programs

In outreach programs institution staff reach out to community supervision and treatment program providers to ensure continuity. This model is most effective when the case management resources are available within the institution, and when the community services are not sufficiently organized to begin service before the offender leaves prison. An example of an outreach program is The Key program in Delaware where program planners and researchers developed the companion Crest program in the community to meet offender continuity treatment needs (Inciardi, 1996).

Reach-In Programs

Reach-in programs are those where community supervision staff, treatment program staff, or both begin services before the offender leaves prison. This model requires an investment strategy approach by the community agency; seeing the advantage of getting out in front of problems rather than reacting to problems. Oregon prison TC and pre-release day treatment programs have employed a number of strategies to build on this continuity of treatment model including program design, interagency agreements, and funding that follows the inmate/offender (Finigan, 1997).

Third-Party Continuity Programs

Third-party continuity means that an agency separate from corrections or treatment takes primary responsibility for ensuring service continuity. The third-party continuity programs are best represented by TASC programs (Weinman, 1992), which are to be found in several jurisdictions. TASC programs serve as bridges between the separate systems of criminal justice and substance abuse treatment. According to the written mission and philosophy statement, TASC programs endeavor to address the justice system's concern for public safety while recognizing the need for community treatment to decrease substance abuse and thereby reduce criminal behavior. TASC participates in justice system processing as early as possible, identifying, assessing, and referring non-violent offenders to treatment as an alternative or supplement to justice system sanctions. TASC then monitors the offender's compliance with the expectations set for abstinence, employment, and social functioning.

Mixed Models

The three program models noted above can be combined in various combinations into mixed continuity models. For example, the Amity program at the Donovan facility in California began as a prison TC, then developed its own follow-up TC for prison program graduates (Wexler, 1996).

About the Author

Gary Field, Ph.D., is Administrator, Counseling and Treatment Services, Correctional Programs Division, Oregon Department of Corrections. He may be reached by email at gary.d.field@doc.state.or.us.

This article is an update of a paper originally written for the Office of National Drug Control Policy in 1998.

References

Altschuler, D., & Armstrong, T. (1996). Aftercare not afterthought: Testing the IAP model. *Juvenile Justice, 3*(1), 15-22.

Anglin, D., & McGlothlin, W. (1984) Outcome of narcotic addicted treatment in California. In F. M. Tims & J. P. Ludford (Eds.), *Drug abuse treatment evaluation: Strategies, progress, and prospects* (Research Monograph No. 51, pp. 105-128). Rockville, MD: National Institute on Drug Abuse.

Chaiken, M. (1989). Prison programs for drug-involved offenders. *Research in Action*. Washington, DC: National Institute of Justice.

Cook, L. F., & Weinman, B. (1988). Treatment alternatives to street crime. In C.G. Leukefeld & F. M. Tims (Eds.), *Compulsory treatment of drug abuse: Research and clinical practice* (Research monograph No. 86, pp. 99-105). Rockville, MD: National Institute on Drug Abuse.

Field, G. (1989). The effects of intensive treatment on reducing the criminal recidivism of addicted offenders, *Federal Probation, 53*, 51-56.

Field, G., & Karecki, M. (1992). *Outcome study of the parole transition release project.* Salem, OR: Oregon Department of Corrections.

Finigan, M. (1997). *Evaluation of three Oregon pre-release day treatment substance abuse programs for inmates.* Washington, DC: Center for Substance Abuse Treatment.

Hubbard, R. L., Rachal, J. V., Craddock, S. G., & Cavanaugh, E. R. (1984). Treatment outcome prospective study (TOPS): Client characteristics and behaviors, before, during and after treatment. In F. M. Tims & J. P. Ludford (Eds.), *Drug abuse treatment evaluation: Strategies, progress, and prospects* (Research Monograph No. 51, pp. 42-68). Rockville, MD: National Institute on Drug Abuse.

Inciardi, J. A. (1996). *A corrections-based continuum of effective drug abuse treatment.* Washington, DC: National Institute of Justice.

Leshner, A. (1997). Addiction is a brain disease, and it matters. *Science, 278*, 45-46.

Lipton, D. (1995). *The effectiveness of treatment of drug abusers under criminal justice supervision.* Washington, DC: National Institute of Justice.

MacKinzie, D., & Hebert, E. (1996). *Correctional boot camps: A tough intermediate sanction.* Washington, DC: National Institute of Justice.

MacKinzie, D., & Souryal, C. (1994). *Multisite evaluation of shock incarceration.* Washington, DC: National Institute of Justice.

National Task Force on Correctional Substance Abuse Strategies (1991). *Intervening with substance-abusing offenders: A framework for action.* Washington, DC: National Institute of Corrections.

Peters, R. H. (1993). Relapse prevention approaches in the criminal justice system. In Gorski, T. T., Kelley, J. M., Havens, L., & Peters, R. H. *Relapse prevention and the substance-abusing criminal offender.* Technical Assistance Publication (TAP) Series, Number 8 DHHS Pub. N (SMA) 95-3071. Rockville, MD: Center for Substance Abuse Treatment.

Simpson, D. D. (1984). National treatment system based on the drug abuse program (DARP) follow-up research. In F. M. Tims & J. P. Ludford (Eds.), *Drug abuse treatment evaluation: Strategies, progress, and prospects* (Research Monograph No. 51, pp 29-41). Rockville, MD: National Institute on Drug Abuse.

Simpson, D. D., Wexler, H. K., & Inciardi, J. A. (Eds.). (1999a). Special Issue: Drug treatment outcomes in correctional settings. Part 1. *The Prison Journal, 79*(3).

Simpson, D. D., Wexler, H. K., & Inciardi, J. A. (Eds.). (1999b). Special Issue: Drug treatment outcomes in correctional settings. Part 2. *The Prison Journal, 79*(4).

Simpson, D. D., Joe, G. W., & Broome, K. M. (2002). A national 5-year follow-up of treatment outcomes for cocaine dependence. *Archives of General Psychiatry, 59*, 538-544.

Weinman, B. A. (1992). Coordinated Approach for Drug-Abusing Offenders: TASC and Parole. *NIDA Research Monograph, 118*, 232-245.

Wexler, H. (1996). The Amity prison TC evaluation: Inmate profiles and reincarceration outcomes. Presentation for the California Department of Corrections, Sacramento, CA.

Wexler, H., Falkin, G., & Lipton, D. (1988). *A model prison rehabilitation program. An evaluation of the Stay 'N Out therapeutic community.* A final report to the National Institute of Drug Abuse by Narcotic and Drug Research, Inc.

Chapter 34

An Integrated Approach to Aftercare and Employment for Criminal Justice Clients

by Harry K. Wexler, Ph.D.

Offender Employment a Critical Incentive 34-1
Effectiveness of Aftercare in Reducing Recidivism 34-2
Case Management: The TASC Model 34-2
Synergy Between Aftercare Treatment and Employment Services 34-3
    Programmatic Difficulties to Overcome 34-3
    Provider Issues 34-4
Bridging Program-Provider Gaps 34-4
    Using Distance Learning 34-4
    Addressing Employers' Legal Concerns 34-4
    Creating a Multi-Value Framework 34-5
    New CREW Model 34-5
Conclusion 34-5

OFFENDER EMPLOYMENT A CRITICAL INCENTIVE

This chapter presents a proposal for rehabilitating drug-involved offenders and helping them move into the American mainstream through an approach that integrates recovery, education, and work. The widespread acceptance of prison-based treatment for substance abuse has focused attention on the importance of developing viable aftercare models to assist the growing numbers of treated inmates released to the community (Wexler, 1995). A consensus has emerged within the criminal justice and treatment systems that justice accountability is a powerful adjunct for treatment and that public health (effective treatment) and public safety are strongly interdependent. While cooperation between the criminal justice and treatment communities has succeeded in creating effective programs capable of reducing recidivism rates, however, there is a growing need for programs that focus primarily on meaningful employment. The inte-

This chapter originally appeared in Offender Substance Abuse Report, *Vol. 1, No. 2, March/April 2001.*

gration of services and the thoughtful use of incentives that benefit all participants—clients, agencies, and employers—are two core concepts that underlie the proposed approach. This incentive-based approach has the potential to recruit and maintain ex-offenders in a habilitative process that also benefits both the ex-offender and society, first, by reducing recidivism and relapse; second by transitioning individuals, who have been a costly societal burden, into productive tax-paying employees and contributors to society.

The reasonable expectation of well-paid employment, including the potential for advancement, is one of the primary realistic social incentives available to us. The proposed model includes a sequence of incentives and opportunities that ex-offenders can earn, beginning with treatment, education, and training leading to meaningful employment, and ending with eligibility for sealing of criminal records. The model is based on the understanding that maximally effective aftercare requires the full integration of recovery and education that results in meaningful employment.

EFFECTIVENESS OF AFTERCARE IN REDUCING RECIDIVISM

Prison-based treatment is widely accepted (Wexler, 1995; Wexler & Lipton, 1993). The rationale for therapeutic communities (TC) treatment in prisons—a main treatment modality that is used—is that the drug problems characteristic of most inmates require high-intensity treatment to restructure attitudes and thinking and to provide social and relapse prevention skills for adjustment in the community after release (Wexler, 1995). Acceptance of the correctional TC is based primarily on the positive outcomes of studies showing significantly lower recidivism rates for program completers (Lipton, 1995).

Aftercare's contribution to reducing recidivism has been reported by studies in Texas (Knight, et al., 1997) and Delaware (Inciardi, et al., 1997), and by the Bureau of Prisons (Pelissier, et. al., 1998). These studies all used follow-up periods of 12 to 24 months, but studies of longer duration of post release are needed to assess the stability of correctional treatment effects. More recent evaluation studies reported positive outcomes at three years after release to the community (Knight, et al., 1999; Martin, et al., 1999; Wexler, et al., 1999).

TC evaluations typically find significant positive treatment outcomes from a prospective follow-up, particularly among inmates who completed both in-prison TC and aftercare. One study that reported 36-month outcomes showed that positive treatment effects were maintained only for inmates who received both prison treatment and aftercare (27.4% of the inmates who completed both the prison TC and aftercare recidivated, vs. 75% for other groups; Id., 1999).

CASE MANAGEMENT: THE TASC MODEL

An essential ingredient of aftercare services is case management. Of the case management approaches to assisting recovering offenders' transition into the community, the most frequently used is Treatment Accountability for Safer Communities (TASC; formerly known as Treatment Alternatives to Street Crime). For almost three decades TASC has provided a framework for partnerships between justice and treatment delivery systems, including linkages between institution-based substance abuse treatment services, community-based supervision, and treatment and aftercare services. Currently there are over 200 TASC programs nationwide.

TASC focuses on managing offenders who are moving through complex levels of criminal processing, supervision, and sanctioning in conjunction with the application of multiple treatment interventions and modalities. The TASC service model provides assessment, treatment (or referral to treatment), case management, and monitoring and reporting services. This model can:

- Screen and identify large numbers of drug users (Toborg, et al., 1976);

- Increase treatment retention (Hubbard, et al., 1988); and

- Help reduce drug use, crime, and HIV risk behaviors (Anglin, et al., 1999).

Exploration of integrating the modified TC prison substance abuse treatment with aftercare models and the TASC approach is clearly warranted by the accumulating evaluation research.

SYNERGY BETWEEN AFTERCARE TREATMENT AND EMPLOYMENT SERVICES

There is a need to find jobs for people who have successfully completed prison rehabilitation programs and are being released into the community. Evaluation studies have consistently shown that employment is related to a decreased likelihood of relapse and recidivism. (See Platt, 1995, for an excellent review of studies of the relationship between vocational training and substance abuse treatment.) The integration of continuing community treatment (aftercare), education/training, and placement in meaningful jobs is a synergistic mix that maximizes the likelihood of success.

Programmatic Difficulties to Overcome

However, a number of "disconnects" need to be addressed so that a major advance in securing meaningful employment can be achieved:

- Good jobs are hard to find because criminal justice clients and substance abusers cannot meet educational, skill, and experience requirements.

- Training programs generally needed for better-paying jobs require high levels of commitment and take time to complete.

- Socially dysfunctional persons often come from poorer backgrounds, did poorly in school, became involved with drugs and criminal behaviors at a young age, and have had few opportunities for success.

- Substance abuse treatment programs often lack strong educational and training components. When training is available it is usually aimed at relatively low skill levels.

Provider Issues

The work of treatment, education, and business is conducted by groups that operate in different environments, face different challenges, have different training, often have different values and goals, and speak somewhat different "languages." In addition, the government often pays for and regulates treatment and training, while businesses depend on paying customers and the ability to operate efficiently in competitive markets.

The education and business communities have little experience with training and hiring recovering persons. The scope of programs conducted by educational institutions in prisons has been limited mostly to basic literacy, GED, and entry-level job training. Likewise, businesses have restricted their involvement with criminal justice populations because of perceived risk and limited profit potential. And public-sector program developers, concerned that business groups may be exploitative while placing low priority on the target population's treatment and training needs, rarely invite business organizations to participate in design and implementation.

BRIDGING PROGRAM-PROVIDER GAPS

A pressing need exists for an initiative dedicated to bridging these gaps, and for a culture that can facilitate the effective integration and coordination of the key rehabilitation components (recovery, education, and work). No federal groups and few state and local groups are dedicated to integrating systems and fostering innovations across systems. Although government agencies often discuss the need for partnering and system integration, these are rarely primary goals.

Using Distance Learning

The education and training of ex-offenders and recovering substance abusers can be advanced by Web-based "distance learning" approaches that allow unprecedented access to information. The possible benefits to incarcerated populations are great and could be an essential ingredient in developing the skills necessary for gainful employment. An obvious, but not insurmountable, obstacle is the perceived security risk of giving inmates access to the public through the Internet. Currently, a few correctional institutions are experimenting with Intranets that can be designed as closed systems that block access to the public Internet while providing wide arrays of information and training opportunities. Solving this problem will be a major step forward in prison rehabilitation.

Addressing Employers' Legal Concerns

Important legal issues need to be considered when developing employment programs for criminal justice clients. A potential obstacle is legitimate employer concern about liability. Some state laws forbid the complete barring of ex-offenders for employment, and others hold employers responsible for on-the-job criminal acts under certain conditions. Full awareness of legal considerations and expert legal consultation is necessary when offering job programs to assist ex-offenders if the jobs include increased responsibility.

Creating a Multi-Value Framework

The partnering of business, government, treatment providers, and educators requires a value framework capable of guiding the integrative process. This framework must take into account multiple perspectives including the public-service values of providing service and rehabilitation programs, the business value of "bottom line profits," and the principles of contribution and payback that underlie the self-help approach. The incentive-based suggestions presented below could facilitate the process:

- All participants contribute their resources to the work and receive benefits in proportion to the contribution or investment. (Clients have few resources in the beginning and are expected to work hard on their rehabilitation, sobriety, and education.)

- At successful completion of the program, clients are expected to pay back at least a substantial fraction of their "education" costs, somewhat like student loans. The amount must be reasonable and proportional to the client's financial success.

- Government can contribute tax incentives and special contractual relationships with businesses that work in the incentive employment program.

- Businesses can provide (1) design assistance to the education and skills training program components to ensure a state-of-the art curriculum that meets the needs of employers; (2) internship opportunities; and (3) a portion of profits for program support.

New CREW Model

The Coalition for Recovery, Education and Work (CREW) is a new coalition of individuals and organizations dedicated to improving the effectiveness of treatment and the integration of substance abusers and offenders into society. The coalition's goal is to develop integrated approaches for rehabilitation of substance abusing felons through treatment, education, and employment building on earlier successes such as TCs and TASC, and on new technologies such as distance learning that can provide the framework and technology for a powerful education component. Full participation by business is encouraged in order to provide leadership, specification of training requirements, and jobs. Strategic planning and operations groups are being formed to design and implement model programs in several states. A research and evaluation component to monitor program implementation and outcomes will be an integral part of the model programs.

CONCLUSION

It is important to build on the success of prison-based treatment by developing viable integrated aftercare models that focus on employment. The success of therapeutic communities and the TASC approach suggest that effective aftercare programs will have structure, encourage ex-offenders to take responsibility, and capitalize on cooperation by a network of agencies. The current labor market offers an opportunity to integrate employment into an aftercare model, and this opportunity will be enhanced by increased education and training programs for ex-offenders. A partnership of treatment providers, the criminal justice system, government, and business would be a particularly effective way to develop an aftercare program comprised of recovery, employment, and educational elements, because each of these communities has different strengths to offer.

About the Author

Harry K. Wexler, Ph.D., is a nationally recognized expert on research, technology transfer, and policy in the area of substance abuse treatment in prisons and the community. This article relies heavily on an earlier article (Wexler, 2000). For additional information, contact Dr. Wexler by email: hkwexler@aol.com.

References

Anglin, M.D., Longshore, D., & Turner, S. (1999). Treatment alternatives to street crime: An evaluation of five programs. *Criminal Justice and Behavior, 26*(2), 168-195.

Hubbard, R.L., Collins, J.J., Rachal, J.V., & Cavanaugh, E.R. (1988). The criminal justice client in substance abuse treatment. In C.G. Leukfield & F.M. Tims (Eds.), *Compulsory treatment of drug abuse: Research & clinical practice* (NIDA Research Monograph 86, pp. 57-80). Rockville, MD: National Institute on Drug Abuse.

Inciardi, J.A., Martin, S.S., Butzin, C.A., Hooper, R.M., & Harrison, L.D. (1997). An effective model of prison-based treatment for drug-involved offenders. *Journal of Drug Issues, 27,* 261-278.

Knight, K., Simpson, D.D., Chatham, L.R., & Camacho, L.M. (1997). An assessment of prison-based drug treatment: Texas' in-prison therapeutic community program. *Journal of Offender Rehabilitation, 24,* (3/4), 75-100.

Knight, K., Simpson, D. D., & Hiller, M. (1999) In-prison therapeutic community treatment in Texas: 3-year reincarceration outcomes. *The Prison Journal, 79*(3), 337-351. Special Issue.

Lipton, D.S. (1995). The effectiveness of treatment for drug abusers under criminal justice sanctions. *NIJ Research Report 157642.* Washington, DC: U.S. Government Printing Office.

Martin, S.S., Butzin, C.A., Saum, C.A., & Inciardi, J.A.. 1999. Three-year outcomes of therapeutic community treatment for drug-involved offenders in Delaware: From prison to work release to aftercare. *The Prison Journal, 79*(3), 294-320. Special Issue.

Pelissier, B., Rhodes, W., Gaes, G., Camp, S., O'Neil, J., Wallace, S., & Saylor, W. (1998). *Alternative solutions to the problem of selection bias in an analysis of federal residential drug treatment programs.* Washington, DC: Federal Bureau of Prisons.

Platt, J.J. (1995) Vocational rehabilitation of drug abusers. *Psychological Bulletin, 117*(3), 416-433.

Raspberry, W. (1999, November 15). Modest proposal for a second chance. *The Washington Post*, Page A23.

Toborg, M.A., Levin, D.R., Milkman, R.H., & Couter, L.J. (1976). Treatment alternatives to street crime (TASC) projects. *National Evaluation Program, Phase I Summary Report.* Washington, DC: Government Printing Office.

Wexler, H.K. (1995). The success of therapeutic communities for substance abusers in American prisons. *Journal of Psychoactive Drugs, 27,* 57-66.

Wexler, H.K., (2000). Criminal Justice Aftercare: An Integrated Approach. *The Counselor*, July/August, 30-34.

Wexler, H.K., & Lipton, D.S. (1993). From REFORM to RECOVERY: Advances in prison drug treatment. In J. Inciardi (Ed.), Drug treatment and criminal justice. *Sage Criminal Justice System Annuals*, Vol. 29.

Wexler, H., Melnick, G., Lowe, L., & Peters, J. (1999). Three-year reincarceration outcomes for amity in prison therapeutic community and aftercare in California. *The Prison Journal, 79*(3), 321-336.

Chapter 35

Increasing Supervision's Effectiveness: An Evidence-Based Model

by Faye S. Taxman, Ph.D.

Introduction 35-1
Questions About the Effectiveness of Supervision 35-2
Traditional Social Control Supervision Framework 35-2
    Contact Model 35-2
    Supervision Objectives 35-3
    Supervision as a Process of Engagement 35-3
Engagement in Pro-Social Values and Behaviors 35-4
Engagement Process 35-5
The Supervision Plan 35-5
    Informal Social Controls 35-5
    Formal Controls/Services 35-6
Making the Commitment to Change (Early Change) 35-6
    Ground Rules 35-8
    Agent Deportment 35-8
    Communication 35-9
Sustained Change for the Long Term 35-9
Conclusion 35-10

INTRODUCTION

Offenders in drug treatment are often supervised by probation and parole agencies, and many systems struggle with getting the treatment and supervision systems to work effectively to reduce recidivism and reduce drug use. Improving the supervision system, and how it reinforces the importance of treatment, has not been thoroughly addressed. This chapter discusses a model of supervision that is compatible with the treatment process, and uses the supervision contact to be more goal-oriented.

This chapter, which originally appeared in Offender Substance Abuse Report, *Vol. 2, No. 6, November/ December 2002, was adapted by the author from a longer version and is reprinted here with permission, "Supervision: Exploring the dimensions of effectiveness,"* Federal Probation, *66(2) 14-27 (September, 2002).*

QUESTIONS ABOUT THE EFFECTIVENESS OF SUPERVISION

With over 4.2 million adults under criminal supervision and over one-third of the new intakes to prison each year failures from community corrections supervision, the effectiveness of supervision is frequently questioned. More research has been conducted on intensive supervision than on supervision in general. The consensus appears to be that intensive supervision is ineffective (Mackenzie, 2000; Sherman, et al., 1997; Taxman, 2002). This leaves the question open about the effectiveness of general supervision, since it is generally presumed that general supervision is different than intensive supervision. More than 60% of offenders complete any supervision without a technical violation or new arrest (Bureau of Justice Statistics, 2001a; 2001b) and therefore supervision is viable. But few studies to date have assessed the varying frameworks for supervision that reflect different missions/goals, different theoretical frameworks, and different operational components. And these available studies, have not tried to measure the differential effects of various types of supervision.

The field of probation/parole supervision overall has had few rigorous assessments of the effectiveness of different interventions. The majority of studies addressed issues related to caseload size and intensive supervision. Little has been done on case management, risk assessment, or models testing different philosophies of supervision.

TRADITIONAL SOCIAL CONTROL SUPERVISION FRAMEWORK

Overall supervision is considered atheoretical in that it is the process of monitoring. It is typically not based on a theory other than one of social control. Monitoring is recognized as a form of external control by the provision of an authority figure to monitor an offender's adherence to certain restrictions (e.g., curfews, drug use, gun possession, etc.). Essentially the external control model presumes that the offender has the capacity and skills to internalize the required change as part of the compliance process. It also assumes that the external controls will be perceived as limiting in the eyes of the offender, which will ultimately improve offender compliance.

Contact Model

Supervision services are built on the framework that "contacts," or the relationship between the offender and the supervision agent, are the cornerstone to managing and/or changing offender behavior. (Even in the control model, the anticipated change is compliance with the rules of supervision, including being crime-free). Contacts provide the means to monitor the performance of offenders and to provide direction to the offender. As defined by most agencies, a supervision contact refers to the number of times that an offender meets the probation/parole officer (e.g., the exposure rate between a supervision agent and an offender). Contacts can also take the form of face-to-face interactions, telephone calls, collateral contacts (e.g., employer, family member, sponsor, etc.), and notification from service agencies (e.g., drug treatment, mental health, etc.). Generally contacts are categorized as direct (face-to-face) or collateral (with someone other than agent).

Contacts became accepted in the supervision field because they are easily quantifiable and can be measured in a workload formula. In the risk management literature, the assumption is that the number of contacts will increase as the offender is deemed to be more of a risk to recidivate (O'Leary & Clear, 1984). Contacts are generally considered an important component of the supervision process, with the general assumption that more contacts are needed for high-risk offenders to provide external controls on their behavior. The question is: how can we make contacts more meaningful, particularly toward guiding the offender to a crime-free or drug-free lifestyle?

Supervision Objectives

Supervision has been dominated by surveillance and control strategies, with some efforts toward brokering treatment and employment services. The approach has generally been to rely upon the treatment interventions that serve offender populations to incorporate the research principles instead of developing within supervision such evidenced-based practices. Yet, supervision, by its nature, is designed to work on "...the offender's attitudes, by strengthening the offender as a person, by reducing various external pressures and by increasing supports and opportunities, and by helping the offender become more satisfied and self-fulfilled within the context of society's values" (Palmer, 1995). Using procedural justice and behavioral interventions, a model of supervision can be achieved to garner greater compliance with the conditions of release, and therefore increase the specific deterrence impact. In essence, supervision is a means to engage the offender in a process of improving compliance with general societal norms including the conditions of release. Supervision has the following objectives that are the focus on offender compliance:

- To use the supervision period to engage the offender in a process of change;

- To assist the offender in understanding his or her behavior and becoming committed to behavioral change;

- To assist the offender in learning to manage his or her behavior and comply with societal norms.

Supervision as a Process of Engagement

A model of supervision is illustrated in Exhibit 35.1, which identifies how the supervision process works. That is, supervision must be perceived to be a process that involves a series of steps and progress measures in order to bring about changes in the offender's behavior. This model complements that proposed by Simpson and Knight (1999) for treatment programs. There are three key areas of the supervision process:

1. Engagement of the offender in the process of change through the assessment of criminogenic factors and development of a plan to address these factors;

2. Involvement in early behavioral changes through the use of targeted services (e.g., treatment, etc.) and controls; and

3. Sustained change through compliance management techniques.

The glue of the process is deportment or the manner of being between the offender and the supervision agent. The contact is the key because it is the means to focus the purpose of supervision and it allows the offender and agent to develop a rapport. As in

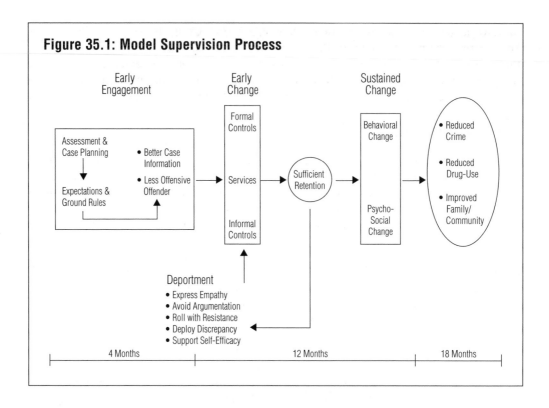

Figure 35.1: Model Supervision Process

the therapeutic setting, the degree of rapport between the offender and agent is an important component for the supervision process to achieve better outcomes. To make supervision the most successful, contacts must have a function that exceeds the mere exchange of information. The contact is more of an engagement process that is designed to achieve desired outcomes.

ENGAGEMENT IN PRO-SOCIAL VALUES AND BEHAVIORS

Initial impressions are usually very important, and in fact can define the agent-offender relationship. As part of the process of wedding the offender to behavior change, the first stage of the supervision process should be devoted to understanding the criminogenic risk and needs of the offender. Usually referred to as intake, the introduction to supervision is more than a mere formality. It provides the setting to diagnose factors contributing to criminal behavior, to outline the ground rules and expectations for supervision, and to engage the offender in assuming responsibility for his success on supervision. The engagement process requires the use of diagnostic processes to put together a case plan and/or behavioral contract that respond to the criminogenic factors. The six general areas that should be addressed are: anti-social personality, low self-control, deviant peers, substance abuse, antisocial values, and family issues. These are dynamic factors that change over time and are less likely to be static (i.e., less susceptible to change).

ENGAGEMENT PROCESS

The engagement process should be devoted to getting the offender ready to address these criminogenic factors by illustrating how the factors contribute to legal troubles. The "honeymoon" period is basically designed to engage offenders in the change process by preparing them to deal with issues that affect criminal behavior. This preparation is critically important because it addresses the two main factors that prevent people from making the commitment to change:

* *Defensiveness*—the walls that are put up around dealing with issues that affect criminality; and

* *Ambivalence*—the process of being non-committal.

It is hypothesized that by using different rapport and communications strategies the contact can be used to break down defensiveness and increase an offender's commitment to change. To break down the defensiveness and ambivalence of the offender requires skills focusing on moving the offender into recognizing that certain issues (e.g., family, employment, substance abuse, etc.) are problem behaviors and that there are means to address these behaviors. Similar to Prochaska and DiClemente's (1986) stages of change model, this is moving from precontemplation to contemplation.

The end goal of the engagement period is a case plan that moves the offender into an action plan to address criminogenic factors. The action plan should use controls and services to prepare the offender to begin to make psychosocial behavioral changes. The assessment should place the offender in one of the following boxes: high-risk/high-need; high-risk/low-need; low-risk/high-need; low-risk/low-need. The placement should determine the degree of services and controls that are needed to maximize public safety. The risk factors should also respond to the offender's special needs, based on his or her typology (drug-involved, alcohol-involved, mental health needs, sexually deviant behavior, disassociated/not connected to the community), and persistent offending.

THE SUPERVISION PLAN

The supervision plan should address criminogenic factors through the use of services and control of the offender's behavior. Based on research evidence, the plan should have three major components.

Informal Social Controls

Involving the community, a support group, and/or family in the supervision plan is part of the process to build the offender's sense of responsibility and sense of belonging to the community. The informal social controls will transcend the justice system to provide "natural" protectors when the justice system is no longer involved. Informal social controls can also be trained to understand the offender's deviant behavior (e.g., sex offenders) that can be instructive for the natural system that must work with the offender to minimize harm to the community. The supervision agent is then working with the offender and the natural system to develop controls that can transcend the justice system.

From the restorative justice perspective, this capacity building is advantageous for both the offender and the victim. Research studies on the importance of support systems in minimizing criminal behavior (Sampson & Laub, 1993) provide convincing support for developing these natural systems for the purpose of ensuring that offenders work toward the goal of being contributing members of the community during the supervision period.

A new mechanism used by some correctional agencies, particularly when an offender does not have a natural support system, is community advocates or guardians. These advocates are citizens who volunteer (or are paid) to be vehicles to communicate with offenders, and provide daily guidance in living in the community. The advocate is a community companion who is available to assist the offender in acquiring and maintaining employment and services (e.g., health, mental health, social, drug or alcohol treatment, etc.). The advocate's relationship to the offender is similar to that of a sponsor in a self-help group.

Formal Controls/Services

The supervision plan should also include a mixture of clinical and control services. Informational controls are needed as part of the service matching to ensure that offenders are maintaining the integrity of the case plan. Most of these formal controls can actually be considered as informational controls—that is, they provide feedback to the supervision agent on the progress of the offender. Drug testing, curfews, electronic monitoring, progress reports, etc., are needed to provide objective information about the degree to which the offender is internalizing the behavior change. The formal controls should complement the informal social controls and services.

Table 35.1 illustrates the integration of the different services and formal and informal social controls to control and change the behavior of the offender (Taxman, Young, & Byrne, 2002). The degree of social controls should depend on the severity of the criminogenic risk factors. More restrictions are warranted for more serious behavior and criminogenic risk factors. For example, technology can provide enhancements to monitor an offender's behavior and provide objective measures of behavior. The electronic monitoring device is one tool to limit the behavior of an offender when area restrictions or curfews are insufficient. That is, offenders who have more difficulty controlling their behavior may need the electronic monitor to provide the external controls. Drug testing is another tool to determine whether an offender is using illicit substances. Plethysmography is a technological tool to measure the arousal behavior of sex offenders, which has been successfully used by a number of community corrections officials in monitoring serious sex offenders. This technology can be used to reassess the performance of the offender in the community for the purpose of adjusting the supervision plan.

MAKING THE COMMITMENT TO CHANGE (EARLY CHANGE)

The second part of the model is the commitment to change. The case plan will detail the formal controls, services, and informal controls that are used to guide an offender in the change process. The commitment to change is illustrated by two variables: (1)

Table 35.1: Examples of Different Controls for Different Types of Offenders

Type of Offender	Clinical Services	Formal Social Controls	Informal Social Controls
All offenders	Educational/ Vocational	Area restrictions or curfews; Electronic monitors; Drug testing; Police-supervision contacts; Face-to-face contacts; Graduated sanctions	Guardian; Transitional housing
Drug-dependent or involved offenders	Substance abuse treatment; Curfew restrictions; Graduated sanctions	Drug testing; Treatment	Self-help groups; Guardian/Advocate; Transitional housing
Mentally ill offenders	Counseling; Psychotropic medication	Treatment/Counseling; Psychotropic medication	Self-help groups; Counseling; Advocate; Transitional housing
Sex offenders	Counseling/Therapy	Curfew and area restrictions; Plethysmography; Polygraph; Medications; Counseling; Victim awareness; Graduated sanctions	Family/Support; System monitor; Behavior; Area restrictions
Repeat offender	Therapy	Area restrictions or curfews; Electronic monitors; Drug testing; Alcohol monitoring; Victim awareness; Community service; Graduated sanctions	Advocates/Guardians; Transitional housing

compliance with the case plan; and (2) retention in the recommended services. The supervision agent can determine an offender's level of commitment to behavior change by assessing how well the offender is adhering to the case plan. Critical issues surround the retention in recommended therapeutic services and employment. In the drug treatment literature, treatment retention has repeatedly been found to be a determining factor of better outcomes (Simspon et al., 1997). The same is true for supervision—offenders in treatment services are more likely to do better in terms of outcomes from supervision (Petersila & Turner, 1993). They were less likely to be noncompliant with the conditions of release, in fact, since technical violations drive negative offender outcomes.

Ground Rules

During the period of early commitment, the tools of graduated responses should be used to address problems of noncompliance and ambivalence. Ground rules are needed to clarify the expectations during the supervision period and to identify the consequences of compliance and noncompliance. The presentation of ground rules is part of a procedural justice process whereby the rules are clearly articulated and implemented. The offender must be aware that the ground rules will be applied swiftly, with certainty, and with graduation in responses based on a pattern of consistent behavior. Graduated sanctions have been found to be critical in ensuring compliance in that they resemble contingency management and token economies where the offender is rewarded for positive behavior and sanctioned for negative behavior. The key to success is consistency in the application of the model, one of the tenets of procedural justice. The ground rules should be used to focus on retention and continued commitment to the case plan.

During this period of time, the focus should be on gauging where the offender is in the process of change, the degree of compliance, and modifications of the case plan to further engage the offender in the change process. This is a period where compliance management should drive the next steps, with the supervision agent using the informal social controls and services to maximize commitment to the change process. The role of the agent in this period is to facilitate the change. The key during this period is to continue the offender in the process of change. It is often during this period that offenders begin to test the system by beginning the process of noncompliance. Emphasis on the relationship between the offender and agent will maintain the commitment to the goals of supervision—behavioral change. Use of the ground rules is the most visible component, but equally important is the focus on deportment.

Agent Deportment

Deportment becomes a key component of the process: the stronger the offender-agent rapport, the greater the degree of compliance. During this time, the keys of effective communication are critical to improve rapport and address the issues that threaten retention. The goal of deportment is for the agent to build a trusting relationship with the offender. Deportment has four main components:

1. *Eye contact*, which is a standard protocol to give respect to the offender as well as to learn to assess the offender's body language during the different phases of supervision;

2. *Social graces* (shaking hands, being prompt for appointments, and other typical signs of mutual respect), used to signify to the offender that he or she is a member of the community;

3. *Candid review* of offender information, without ascribing blame, where the agent informs the offender of results from assessments, informational controls, and performance; and

4. *Empathy* or the use of active listening skills, which acknowledge the offender's perspective yet identify the ground rules.

The deportment process depends on communication skills of the agent to build the relationship that will work to move the offender from a point of ambivalence to action.

Communication

To facilitate the change process, the contacts between the offender and agent must enhance communication. Communication can be achieved in the following way:

- Express empathy for the offender's situation and the difficulty of achieving small gains (e.g., being crime-free, being drug-free, obtaining and retaining a job, etc.).

- Avoid arguing with the offender about any conditions or requirements of supervision. Argument is generally a threat to the agent's power and begins to erode the validity of the case plan. It is critical, as part of the process, that the agent review the case information and risk/need factors that support the agreed-upon case plan.

- Roll with resistance by recognizing that some negative attitudes and rigidity are part of the offender's defense mechanisms. The process of behavioral change is difficult for the offender and therefore some resistance is considered part of the ambivalence. Focus on the case plan and commitment to its components, and ignore the offender's negativity; this can enhance focus on measurable outcomes.

- Identify discrepancies that may occur, particularly those that affect compliance issues. In many ways, the offender reports information to divert the agent's attention to less important issues. Instead of examining the discrepancies, focus on the case plan and progress towards the goals and objectives.

- Support self-efficacy by providing the offender with some of the skills to review his or her behavior.

A critical part of this process is building the offender's self-efficacy skills. All of these are identified in effective practices using motivational interviewing techniques, where the goal is to utilize effective communication with the offender to retain commitment to the case plan and crime-free goals of supervision. Communication tools are part of the overall strategy of strengthening the contact, by making the contact a means to maintain commitment to the case plan. Then, the contact becomes more meaningful.

SUSTAINED CHANGE FOR THE LONG TERM

Underlying this approach is a belief that the engagement and early commitment to change will result in sustained change. The change process will require the use of different psychosocial processes, development of social networks, development of competencies in key areas (e.g., employment, family, etc.), and accountability. Sustained change will be shown by improvements in key areas such as employment, family, housing, and peer associations—all issues important to reducing recidivism. Improvements in these domains will improve offenders' family and community commitments while reducing offenders' criminal behavior and drug use. It is during this stage that a revised case plan is needed that focuses more on relapse prevention or maintenance goals—sustaining the change. The focus of the contacts is on rehearsing with the offender the skills gained to prevent problem behaviors.

CONCLUSION

While it is generally assumed that supervision contacts are for the purpose of monitoring an offender's progress with required conditions, the purpose and intent of the contact varies based on the time under supervision and the compliance with required conditions. The evidence-based model for supervision presented here focuses on the different stages of the supervision process, each of which has different goals that can ultimately lead to an offender's achieving sustaining behavioral change. The challenge to supervision and community corrections is to incorporate this model into operational practices.

About the Author

Faye S. Taxman, Ph.D., is Director, University of Maryland, College Park Bureau of Governmental Research. For more information about this model and implementation, she may be contacted by email at ftaxman @bgr.umd.edu or by phone at (301) 403 4403. Additional information is also available on the internet at www.bgr.umd.edu.

References

Bureau of Justice Statistics. (2001a). Special Report. Trends in state parole, 1990-2000 [NCJ 184735]. Washington, DC: U.S. Department of Justice.

Bureau of Justice Statistics. (2001b). U.S. correctional population, 1999 [NCJ 183508]. Washington, DC: U.S. Department of Justice.

MacKenzie, D.L. (2000). Evidenced-based corrections: Identifying what works. *Crime and Delinquency, 46,* 457-471.

O'Leary, V., & Clear, T. (1984). *Managing the offender in the community.* Washington, DC: National Institute of Corrections.

Palmer, T. (1995). Programmatic and nonprogrammatic aspects of successful intervention: New directions for research. *Crime and Delinquency, 41(1),* 100-131.

Petersilia, J., & Turner, S. (1993). Evaluating intensive supervision probation/parole: Results of a nationwide experiment. *Research in Brief.* Washington, DC: National Institute of Justice.

Prochaska, J.O., & DiClemente, C.C. (1986). Toward a comprehensive model of change." In W.R. Miller & N. Heather (Eds.), *Treating addictive behaviors: Processes of change.* New York: Plenum Press.

Sampson, R.J., & Laub, J. H. (1993). *Crime in the making: Pathways and turning points through life.* Cambridge, MA: Howard University Press.

Sherman, L.W., Gottfredson, D., MacKenzie, D., Eck, J., Reuter, P., & Bushway, S. (1997). *Preventing crime: What works, what doesn't, what's promising.* Washington, DC: Office of Justice Programs.

Simpson, D. D., &. Knight, K. (1999). *TCU model of treatment process and outcomes in correctional settings.* Washington, DC: U.S. Department of Justice, National Institute of Justice.

Simpson, D.D., Joe, G.W., Broome, K.M., Hiller, M.L., Knight, K., & Rowan-Szal, G.A. (1997). Program diversity and treatment retention rates in the drug abuse treatment outcome study (DATOS). *Psychology of Addictive Behaviors 11(4),* 279-293.

Taxman, F.S., (2002). Supervision: Exploring the dimensions of effectiveness, *Federal Probation,* 66(2): 14-27.

Taxman, F.S., Young, D., & Byrne, J.M. (2002). *Targeting for reentry: Matching needs and services to maximize public safety.* Washington, DC: National Institute of Justice, forthcoming.

Part 7

Research to Practice

Providing an effective continuum of opportunities to treat addicted offenders is contingent on the delivery of evidence-based services. Unfortunately, correctional agencies continue to provide programming or services that are not evidence-based. For example, even though research has demonstrated that "boot camps" are ineffective at reducing recidivism (U.S. Department of Justice, 2003), the use of boot camps continues as a means for dealing with addicted offenders, particularly adolescent offenders, in many states. This section focuses on the clinical applications of research and how strong science leads to strong practice.

In Chapter 36, Richard Hayton and Mary Beth Johnson describe how the Addiction Technology Transfer Centers (ATTCs) play an important role in creating effective interventions that bridge the gap between research and practice. Particular emphasis is placed on getting new knowledge into the field, creating meaningful partnerships, and applying effective change strategies within systems so practitioners can use the new interventions and change their practice behavior.

Chapter 37, by Mark Gornik, points to the "what works" literature to illustrate how proven practices can be used to change criminal behavior. Included in the chapter is a description of the elements of effective programs, including successful cognitive programs, and a discussion on applying theoretical principles to practice. As the author states, the ultimate challenge is to translate the various roles of an integrated system into role-specific language so that they can be valued, used, and passed on.

As pointed out by Igor Koutsenok, David Deitch, Karin Marsolais, and Michael Franc in Chapter 38, a key to successful "research to practice" is effective training, especially training of substance abuse treatment practitioners for work in a correctional environment. Of particular importance is the need for skill enhancement, including organizational skills and case management skills. The chapter provides very practical information on training, including eight basic training concepts and a description of six successful training methods.

Chapter 39, by Wayne Welsh and Gary Zajac, illustrates how Pennsylvania's ongoing review has improved treatment programming for offenders. Through a collaborative relationship with the Pennsylvania Department of Corrections (DOC), Temple University's Center for Public Policy was able to establish an ongoing working relationship to facilitate the production of useful knowledge for the department. Through the use of a survey, Temple researchers were able to document for the DOC considerable variation in program duration and intensity, consistency in treatment approach, consistency in program topic coverage, variation in program types, and variation in admission criteria. This chapter also illustrates how research findings can have an impact on the management of treatment programs.

This section concludes with Chapter 40, by Laura Winterfield, Dan Mears, and Gretchen Moore, which shows how research can be linked to correctional drug treatment at the national level. Researchers from the Urban Institute developed key recommendations for the National Institute on Drug Abuse (NIDA) in order to identify activities

NIDA might undertake to address the unique challenges posed when integrating treatment services with a public health orientation into correctional environments. Their summary includes a list of principles of effective prison-based drug treatment, strategies to encourage science-based drug treatment in prisons, and research gaps on drug treatment in the adult prison system.

References

U.S. Department of Justice. (2003). *Correctional boot camps: Lessons from a decade of research*. Washington, DC: Department of Justice.

Chapter 36

From Research to Practice: How the Addiction Technology Transfer Centers Bridge the Corrections Gap

by Richard Hayton, M.A., and Mary Beth Johnson, M.S.W.

Responding to the Connection Between Substance Abuse and Crime 36-2
What Technology Transfer Is 36-2
The ATTC Network's Role in Creating Effective Interventions
  That Bridge the Gap 36-3
      Federal and State Ties Enhance Effectiveness 36-3
      Implementing Change 36-3
Cross-Training Curricula 36-4
      Criminal Justice and Substance Abuse Partnerships 36-4
      California-Specific Training 36-5
      TC Training 36-5
      Substance Abuse and Mental Disorders 36-5
      Female Offenders 36-6
Creating Meaningful Partnerships in Both Systems 36-6
Applying Change Strategies 36-6
      Need to Work With "Big Picture" 36-7
      Program Examples 36-7
Summary 36-8

An earlier version of this chapter appeared in Offender Substance Abuse Report, *Vol. 1, No. 2, March/April 2001.*

RESPONDING TO THE CONNECTION BETWEEN SUBSTANCE ABUSE AND CRIME

Corrections research findings over the past decade clearly show there is a strong nexus between criminal behavior and substance abuse. We consistently document high involvement of drug abuse among criminal justice clients: from 50%-75% of adults and 40%-70% of juveniles test positive for drugs at time of arrest (Travis, 1999; Lipton, 1997; CASA, 1998). This documented connection continues to reinforce the efficacy of providing substance abuse treatment to individuals in correctional settings.

Given the strong connection between substance abuse and crime, and the rapid pace of new knowledge development in both fields, we face three major challenges:

1. We must create effective interventions that bridge the gap between new knowledge and its application in both fields.

2. We need to create meaningful partnerships between substance abuse treatment and corrections systems.

3. We need to apply effective change strategies within both systems so practitioners use the new interventions and change their practice behavior.

This chapter discusses the important role of the Addiction Technology Transfer Center (ATTC) Network in responding to these challenges.

The Substance Abuse and Mental Health Services Agency (SAMHSA) first funded the ATTC Network in 1993. Today 14 ATTC Regional Centers work locally to cultivate systems change, prepare the workforce, and harness technologies for application in the field, while the National Office initiates and supports national projects. In short, the mission of the ATTC is to facilitate the movement of knowledge from research to practice. Since its inception the ATTC has focused on creating inroads for transferring the technology of substance abuse treatment to practitioners within the corrections system.

WHAT TECHNOLOGY TRANSFER IS

The notion of technology transfer is frequently not well understood outside of academic circles. Simply put, technology transfer is moving research-based knowledge and skills into standard professional practice. Technology transfer involves creating a mechanism by which a desired change is accepted, incorporated, and reinforced at all levels of an organization or system (The Change Book, 2000).

Transferring substance abuse treatment technologies to practitioners in correctional settings and vice versa is complicated by a number of issues. One is the difference in the cultures of the two practice systems—e.g., public safety vs. individual recovery. In addition, each system must deal with a number of similar pressures. Substance abuse treatment as a profession and a body of knowledge is dynamic and rapidly changing as a result of major discoveries in biochemistry, human behavior, and pharmacology. The field is also strongly influenced by national and local political policies as well as health care movements like managed care. At the same time new technologies such as motivational interviewing and pharmacological therapies continue to emerge. Rapid change and quickly evolving methods are also characteristics of the field of corrections, as evidenced by an increasing emphasis on community corrections, restorative justice, privatization of inmate services, and increasingly conservative public attitudes towards offenders.

THE ATTC NETWORK'S ROLE IN CREATING EFFECTIVE INTERVENTIONS THAT BRIDGE THE GAP

This complex and dynamic arena is where the ATTC Network facilitates the technology transfer process both within and between the corrections system and the substance abuse treatment system to help professionals realize their unique roles as change agents in the lives of offenders with substance use disorders. The ATTC network employs an impressive array of strategies and engages in many learning activities to bridge the gap between new knowledge and its application in both fields.

Federal and State Ties Enhance Effectiveness

The ATTC is in a unique position because of its relationship with federal research agencies such as the National Institute on Alcohol Abuse and Alcoholism and the National Institute on Drug Abuse, federal service agencies such as the Center for Substance Abuse Treatment and the Office of Justice Programs, and federal policy agencies such as the Office of National Drug Control Policy. At the same time, the ATTC Regional Centers serving their respective states have close ties to the substance abuse Single State Agencies and the state departments of corrections. This central position allows the ATTC to engage in finding solutions and leading exploration of emerging issues for both state and federal systems while serving as the link between federal and local interests.

Implementing Change

Technology transfer is the work of the ATTC Network. The principles, steps, strategies, and activities of technology transfer are clearly explained in the June 2000, ATTC publication entitled, "The Change Book: A Blue Print for Technology Transfer." This landmark document provides tools and guidance for implementing technology transfer initiatives in local and regional settings. Furthermore, it includes a clear step-by-step workbook for local agencies to use in building their own change initiative.

The change model employed in the Change Book is built around 10 steps for creating sustainable change, as follows:

1. Identify the problem.

2. Organize a team for addressing the problem.

3. Identify the desired outcome.

4. Assess the organization or agency.

5. Assess the specific audience(s) to be targeted.

6. Identify the approach most likely to achieve the desired outcome.

7. Design action and maintenance plans for your change initiative.

8. Implement the action and maintenance plans for your change initiative.

9. Evaluate the progress of your change initiative.

10. Revise your action and maintenance plans based on evaluation results.

In addition to the implementation steps, it is critical that any change initiative that focuses on improved treatment in correctional settings adhere to the seven principles of successful technology transfer. For example, if practitioners know that research supports treating individuals in the criminal justice system because it reduces recidivism, they are more likely to find training on substance abuse treatment important to them. Before adopting the new knowledge or skill, the practitioner must be convinced that it is relevant. That is the first principle. In addition to relevant, a successful change initiative must be timely, clear, credible, multifaceted, continuous, and bi-directional (The Change Book, 2000). From its inception, the ATTC network was constructed to transfer technology based on these principles.

The ATTC Network has made major inroads for transferring the technology of substance abuse treatment to practitioners within the corrections system using multiple technology transfer and organizational change activities. Some typical technology transfer activities include developing strategic plans, mentoring and providing technical assistance, providing clinical supervision, conducting needs assessments, teaching college courses and workshops, developing web sites, and circulating fact sheets and journal articles.

The ATTC has developed over 500 technology transfer products since 1993. These range from brief in-service training outlines, to weeklong intensive experiential training curricula, to on-line academic courses, to full bachelor and masters degree programs. Many of these products are specific to the issues faced by practitioners who provide substance abuse treatment in correctional settings.

CROSS-TRAINING CURRICULA

Criminal Justice and Substance Abuse Partnerships

One of the first ATTC Network offerings to help both systems achieve bi-directional communication in working with substance using offenders was the development of the cross training curriculum entitled "Criminal Justice/Substance Abuse Cross Training: Working Together for Change." The Mid-Atlantic ATTC was the lead center for this national effort. This training curriculum includes experiential exercises to assist substance abuse treatment and corrections professionals in communicating their unique roles as change agents in the lives of clients. In addition the curriculum addresses special needs of the clients such as co-occurring disorders and women's issues. Many trainers who have presented this curriculum have reported that during this training experience they witnessed local substance abuse treatment and criminal justice staff having meaningful, productive discussions about shared clients for the first time. These conversations often lead to the development of strategic partnerships between the two systems. The Mid-America ATTC revised this curriculum in 2001 with assistance from the Gulf Coast ATTC to incorporate new research findings and to expand the process based on the collective ATTC Network training experience.

California-Specific Training

In 2000 Pacific Southwest ATTC developed an intensive week long cross training curriculum particular to the needs of the California Department of Corrections and the regional treatment system. In addition to the cross training efforts, the Pacific Southwest ATTC was heavily invested in the training agenda of the California Department of Corrections. The Pacific Southwest ATTC provided core curricula through 2001 on the basics of substance abuse and addictive behavior for corrections staff, and training for treatment practitioners in custody settings on the therapeutic community model of treatment. This training is continued by the Addiction Training Center established in 2001 at the University of California-San Diego.

TC Training

In response to an increasing need for training on the therapeutic community (TC) model of treatment in prison, Mid-America ATTC developed an intensive five-day experiential training curriculum for practitioners in that setting. Because research findings document reduced reincarceration rates for therapeutic community graduates who complete aftercare (CASA, 1998), many jurisdictions are bringing up TC programs in their institutions. Demand for trained staff outdistanced supply, resulting in a critical shortage of trained TC practitioners. With the contributions of David Deitch, Ph.D., former director of the Pacific Southwest ATTC, George DeLeon, Ph.D., and others, a research-based training curriculum for staff and a training of trainers was developed and disseminated nationally and internationally, resulting in an increased number of trained TC practitioners.

Substance Abuse and Mental Disorders

The Gulf Coast ATTC collaborated with both the Texas Department of Criminal Justice and the Texas Department of Corrections to provide monthly TC for their staff. The training provided information on the dynamics of substance abuse and its effects on behavior in custody settings. They also provided quarterly immersion training, which is an experiential training for criminal justice personnel to assist them in understanding the experiences of an inmate undergoing substance abuse treatment.

Addressing the need in the field for knowledgeable personnel who are competent to work with offenders who have both mental health and substance abuse disorders, the Mid-America ATTC took the lead in developing and implementing a major cross training product. This product brings together mental health, substance abuse treatment, and criminal justice practitioners. The development of this cross training curriculum included contributions from multiple ATTC Regional Centers in partnership with the National GAINS Center.

Female Offenders

The Iowa Department of Corrections requested help from the Prairielands ATTC to develop a curriculum focusing on female offenders. Prairielands produced the learning materials that were piloted in April 2000. This intervention is used to train the counseling and security staff working in both community and institutional settings to respond more therapeutically to the gender specific needs of the women.

CREATING MEANINGFUL PARTNERSHIPS IN BOTH SYSTEMS

The Great Lakes ATTC has developed partnerships with substance abuse treatment agencies, Illinois TASC (Treatment Alternatives for Safe Communities), the Department of Criminal Justice at Loyola University in Chicago, academic institutions and criminal justice systems and institutions in Illinois, Ohio, and Wisconsin. One product developed by in this region in collaboration with Governors State University is a localized cross-training package for criminal justice and substance abuse treatment providers. This curriculum also includes a videotape-training program for the Illinois Department of Corrections.

An example of how partnerships can increase the capacity of both partners is evident in the relationship between the Missouri Department of Corrections, the Missouri substance abuse treatment providers, and the Mid-America ATTC. This partnership focuses on improving the level of substance abuse training and staff development in corrections using internal resources where possible. To do this, the venture depends on needs assessment and joint planning, developing training capacity within the Missouri DOC, and increasing coordination and collaboration among the state's substance abuse treatment resources. The Missouri DOC funded Mid-America ATTC to custom design seven curricula and train staff to deliver the material. By July, 2002, more than 1,000 employees were trained in substance use disorders and nearly 40 Missouri DOC staff had been developed as trainers within the system.

On the West Coast, the Pacific Southwest ATTC was able to create a partnership that included state policy makers and budgeting agencies along with corrections and treatment. This partnership resulted from a series of problem solving symposia addressing significant and problematic issues relevant to substance abuse treatment in corrections such as screening and assessment, sex offenders, and pre-release assessment and planning.

Another example of an effective and productive partnership is the ATTC of New England's joint initiative with the Massachusetts Supreme Judicial Court to increase awareness and use of the court's Standards on Substance Abuse. This project was designed to help the court respond to substance abuse issues of those appearing before the court. The goal of the project was to increase public safety, reduce crime and expedite courtroom proceedings.

APPLYING CHANGE STRATEGIES

Use of new interventions and changes in practice behavior are the true tests of technology transfer. Nationwide, criminal justice systems are struggling with such issues as increasingly violent, aggressive inmates serving longer sentences; tighter budgets and conservative management; increasingly conservative public attitudes toward offenders; greater involvement of elected officials in prison management; and privatization and contracting with the private sector. All these trends have made it important for criminal justice professionals to examine traditional ways of doing things, and to adopt changes throughout the system. These changes take the form of increased emphasis on community corrections, restorative justice and restitution programs, and an increased demand for treatment services that result in behavior modification and behavior management. Because of these changes and the inextricable link between substance abuse and crime, agencies of change and technology transfer like the ATTC Network of necessity have a vital role to play in defining the preferred future of both systems.

Need to Work With "Big Picture"

In forming the mission of the ATTC Network around technology transfer and organizational change, the Center for Substance Abuse Treatment ensured that the many facets and contexts of substance abuse treatment and rehabilitation would be addressed. The substance abuse system brings together a complex network of researchers, institutional care providers, corrections and criminal justice professionals, community-based services, private sector treatment services, policy makers at all levels, academics, trainers, educators, and technical assistance and consultation service providers. Addressing the needs of one facet of the system has a ripple effect on all other dimensions of the system that is continuous and multi-directional. By working with the "big picture" and connecting all facets of the system, the ATTC is able to facilitate change and find common ground both within and across systems.

Program Examples

Because of these connections and partnerships, systems change occurs throughout the country as a result of new interventions and partnerships that the ATTC helped to create in criminal justice and treatment programs. In Virginia, for instance, the Mid-Atlantic ATTC implemented an extensive course of study to give juvenile probation officers the coursework to meet requirements for substance abuse counselor certification in Virginia. This resulted in a change in how the system provides services to juvenile offenders using existing staff. Mid-Atlantic continues to work with this group of trainees to provide continuing education in the areas of motivational interviewing, strength-based practice, and screening and assessment.

In Wisconsin, the Great Lakes ATTC has recently completed a technical assistance review of the entire treatment milieu in the corrections department, from arrest to post-release treatment. The review will lead to a model design for a new, more innovative statewide corrections-based treatment system incorporating research-based interventions and collaborative partnerships between key stakeholders.

The Great Lakes ATTC's Center for Excellence in Criminal Justice at TASC is another example of how creating effective partnerships promote systems change. In creating the Center, the ATTC brought together diverse groups such as judges, court services, TASC programs, and academic institutions to address major systems-wide issues and institute changes that would improve both safety and treatment. The Center's major outcomes included creation of gender-specific services for females in the Cook County Department of Corrections and a system change initiative in that same department to restructure substance abuse services, including changes in how custody officers learn about and deal with substance abuse issues.

System change is also occurring in the State of California, where the Addiction Training Center at UCSD (formerly Pacific Southwest ATTC) manages the Work Force Development Training Project for treatment practitioners in custody settings. In addition, a Continuous Quality Improvement (CQI) Program has been developed to provide an avenue for sharing the best practices and to sustain the system changes that have occurred.

SUMMARY

The ATTC Network has proven to be an effective vehicle for facilitating knowledge from research to practice by using tested principles and strategies for transferring technology. The Network plays an important role in creating interventions that that bridge the gap between new knowledge and its application in the field. The Network also plays an important role in creating partnerships among corrections and treatment systems at state and local levels as well as links to federal and national products and resources. By integrating product development and delivery, and organizational development and change, the ATTC Network has become an important conduit to the field for essential knowledge and skills that will ultimately transform the lives of people served by both systems.

About the Authors

Richard Hayton, M.A., is currently a criminal justice training consultant for Mid-America Addiction Technology Transfer Center; he has 30 years experience in substance abuse treatment as a halfway house manager, counselor, and state programs administrator for the Missouri Division of Alcohol and Drug Abuse. Mary Beth Johnson, M.S.W., is Director of the Addiction Technology Transfer Centers National Office, Kansas City, MO.

References

Carlson, P. (1996, August). Corrections trends for the twenty-first century, *Corrections Compendium, XXI* (8), 1-4.

Lipton, D. S. (1997). *The effectiveness of treatment for drug abusers under criminal justice supervision.* National Institute of Justice Research Report.

National Center on Addiction and Substance Abuse at Columbia University (1998, January). *Behind bars: Substance abuse and America's prison population.* New York: Columbia University.

National Office, Addiction Technology Transfer Centers. (2000). *The change book.* Kansas City, MO: ATTC.

Travis, J. (1999, December). *Drugs, alcohol abuse, and crime: A research and policy perspective.* Presentation at the National Assembly on Drugs, Alcohol Abuse, and the Criminal Offender, Washington, DC.

Chapter 37

Moving From Correctional Program to Correctional Strategy: Using Proven Practices to Change Criminal Behavior

by Mark Gornik, M.S.

Introduction 37-2
Attributes Associated With Criminal Behavior and Recidivism 37-2
Elements of Effective Programs 37-2
Applying Theoretical Principles to Practice 37-3
    The Criminogenic Risk Principle 37-3
    The Criminogenic Need Principle 37-4
    The Responsivity Principle 37-4
    Interplay of Principles 37-4
Cognitive Behavioral Intervention 37-4
    Criminal Thinking—Understanding the Logic and Rewards 37-4
    Targeting Offender Behavior—Social Learning and
      Behavioral Intervention 37-5
Models of Social Learning 37-6
    Community Model of Resocialization for Offenders 37-6
    Types of Community Models 37-6
Elements of Successful Cognitive Programs 37-6
    Basic Program Essentials 37-6
    Cognitive Approaches 37-7
    Incorporating the Principle of Responsivity 37-7
Taking an Integrated Approach 37-8
    Relapse Prevention Strategies 37-8
    Sanctions and Treatment: Accountability and Change 37-8

This chapter originally appeared in Offender Substance Abuse Report, *Vol. 1, No. 4, July/August 2001.*

Evidence-Based Program Structure 37-9
        The Cognitive Community 37-9
        Staff as Community Members and Agents of Change 37-10
Maximizing Results 37-11

INTRODUCTION

A considerable amount of research in the corrections arena has now established that cognitive behavioral and social learning approaches have answered the question "What works?" to change undesirable offender behavior. "What works" is a term used nationally by correctional agencies in reference to research principles and practices common to effective public safety and offender programming. "What works" research also has identified "criminogenic risks and needs" that successful correctional programs must target (Gendreau & Andrews, 1990). Although the principles and practices discussed in this chapter are approached as general strategies to change offender behavior, they have been found to be effective especially in the area of substance abuse treatment.

ATTRIBUTES ASSOCIATED WITH CRIMINAL BEHAVIOR AND RECIDIVISM

First, research with offenders (Gendreau & Andrews, 1990), including substance abusers, has shown clearly that attributes associated with criminal behaviors and recidivism include:

- Anti-social attitudes, values, and beliefs (criminal thinking);

- Pro-criminal associates and isolation from pro-social associates;

- Particular temperament and behavioral characteristics (e.g., egocentrism);

- Weak problem-solving and social skills;

- Criminal history;

- Negative family factors (i.e., abuse, unstructured or undisciplined environment, criminality in the family, substance abuse in the family);

- Low levels of vocational and educational skills; and

- Substance abuse.

ELEMENTS OF EFFECTIVE PROGRAMS

Meta-analysis (Gendreau & Andrews, 1990) also has identified common characteristics that must exist in programs if they are to be successful. These include:

- Support by community and policymaker partnerships;

- Support by qualified and involved leadership who understand program objectives;

- Being designed and implemented around proven theoretical models, beginning with assessment and continuing through aftercare;

- Use of standardized and objective assessments of risk and need factors to make appropriate program assignments for offenders;

- Targeting crime-producing attributes and using proven treatment models to prepare offenders for return into the community;

- Delivery of services in a manner consistent with the ability and learning style of the individuals being treated;

- Implementation by well-trained staff who deliver proven programs as designed; and

- Regular evaluation to ensure quality.

Although most correctional agencies have come to accept and are attempting to implement these practices, many jurisdictions are frustrated in their ability to combine these "best practices" in a complementary continuum of services. Understanding the various elements of effective offender intervention and integrating them into substance abuse treatment is the challenge before us.

To accomplish this goal, effective substance abuse treatment should be guided by the principles that are known to maximize their effectiveness. Programs should:

- Target the criminogenic risk and need (discussed below) emphasizing a clear understanding of criminal logic;

- Incorporate the principle of responsivity (also discussed below);

- Be cognitive behavioral in nature and incorporate social-learning practices;

- Incorporate a balanced integrated approach to sanctions and interventions and, when appropriate, relapse prevention strategies; and

- Have therapeutic integrity.

APPLYING THEORETICAL PRINCIPLES TO PRACTICE

The Criminogenic Risk Principle

The risk principle embodies the assumption that criminal behavior can be predicted for individual offenders on the basis of certain factors. Some factors, such as criminal history, are static and unchangeable. Others, such as substance abuse, antisocial attitudes, and antisocial associates, are dynamic and changeable. With proper assessment of these factors, practitioners have demonstrated that it is possible to classify offenders according to their relative likelihood of committing new offenses with as much as 80% accuracy

Application of the risk principle requires matching levels or intensity of treatment with the risk levels of offenders. High-risk offenders require intensive interventions to reduce recidivism, while low-risk offenders benefit most from low-intensity interventions or no intervention at all (Gendreau & Andrews, 1990).

The Criminogenic Need Principle

Most offenders have many needs. However, certain needs are directly linked to crime. Criminogenic needs constitute dynamic risk factors or attributes of offenders that, when changed, influence the probability of recidivism—e.g., in the case of substance abusers, peer associations related to drug using behavior. Noncriminogenic needs such as interpersonal anxiety may also be dynamic and changeable, but they are not directly associated with new offense behavior (Gendreau & Andrews, 1990).

The Responsivity Principle

The responsivity principle refers to the delivery of treatment programs in a manner that is consistent with the ability and learning style of an offender. Substance abuse treatment effectiveness (as measured by recidivism) is influenced by the interaction between offender characteristics (relative empathy, cognitive ability, maturity, etc.) and service characteristics (location, structure, skill and interest of providers, etc.). Characteristics such as the gender and ethnicity of an offender also influence responsivity to treatment.

Interplay of Principles

Application of the risk principle helps identify *who should receive treatment*. The criminogenic need principle focuses on *what should be treated*. The responsivity principle underscores the importance of *how treatment should be delivered* (Gendreau & Andrews, 1990).

COGNITIVE BEHAVIORAL INTERVENTION

Criminal Thinking—Understanding the Logic and Rewards

When surveyed, most correctional practitioners admit that dealing effectively with antisocial logic is the single most important part of public safety and offender change. While they admit it is important, staff also report lacking the necessary understanding and skill to deal with criminal thinking (Gornik, et al., 1999).

Antisocial thinking is very seldom simply a matter of imagining crimes or plotting assaults. With most offenders, there is almost always a subtler network of attitudes, beliefs and thinking patterns that create an entitlement and righteousness about selfish and harmful acts. Antisocial thinking provides a self-validating and rewarding escape from responsibility and social norms. Many offenders are accustomed to feeling unfairly treated and have learned a defiant, hostile attitude as part of their basic orientation toward life and other people. Hostile responses and victim-stance thinking are learned cognitive behaviors. For the offender, feeling like a victim creates a sense of outrage, power, and self-gratification. These powerful emotional experiences create cognitive reinforcement. Conversely to admit a mistake would be a sign of weakness and vulnerability.

Relationships with other people are adversarial and dominated by a struggle for power. Cooperation is seldom more than a passing convenience. A win-lose (us vs. them) orientation dominates offenders' personal relationships. In their minds, winning is defined as forcing someone else to lose. The gratification that comes with this kind of winning is, for some offenders, the only real satisfaction and gratification they have ever learned. This need to win is exaggerated in the offenders' interactions with security staff. Whether they win or lose, the underlying cognitive structure is reinforced. This self-serving logic creates a vicious cycle (Bush & Bilodeau, 1994). As offenders progress through treatment, respect for custody staff is an important measure of change

Targeting Offender Behavior—Social Learning and Behavioral Intervention

Offender change and re-socialization provide direct instructional methods, modeling and observation of the individuals in the environment. Behavioral psychologists such as Albert Bandura have shown us the value that social learning plays in teaching and modeling socially acceptable behavior.

Many, if not most, offenders have significant deficits in understanding what to do and how to act in a socially responsible manner. In fact, most offenders see little value in socially responsible behavior, either because it is not supported within their peer culture or it doesn't provide the immediate gratification and excitement of crime. Often, offender thinking patterns are so entrenched that they cannot break free without a considerable period of de-conditioning followed by re-conditioning. Old patterns of behavior are extinguished and new behaviors reinforced by the process of appropriate application of punishment and rewards. Ultimately, offenders learn to practice self-regulation and self-management skills.

The elements that support the environment in which social learning can take place are *structure* and *accountability*. Structure organizes the behavior of members toward a common goal of "right living." Staff, operating as a rational authority, provides an organized structure of values, rules, roles, and responsibilities. The necessary information is provided to increase awareness and knowledge of behavioral, attitudinal, and/or emotional consequences. Accountability teaches respect for structure and moves the offender from an observer stance (strong denial and resistance), to a participant stance (willing to comply, but attitudinally still in criminal thinking mode), to a member stance (a willing participant who shares the new values of right living). The environment provides the opportunity for practice and success. This process continually reinforces gains and builds self-efficacy.

MODELS OF SOCIAL LEARNING

Community Model of Resocialization for Offenders

The community model is an environment within a correctional institution that both supports and provides offenders with the experience in living a pro-social lifestyle as a strategy to combat the traditional "convict code" and lifestyle found in traditional prison populations. Community models incorporate the evidence-based principles and practices of social learning and behavioral programs such as social learning principles and practices that include: empathy; encouragement of self-efficacy; non-authoritarian, non-blaming, effective modeling; effective reinforcement; effective disapproval; self-regulation and self-management skills; relapse-prevention strategies; advocacy; brokerage; planned practice; extinction; concrete verbal suggestions; token economy; resource provision; and effective use of punishers (Bush & LaBarbera, 1995).

Types of Community Models

Community models can take many shapes and designs. The most familiar interpretation of the community model is the therapeutic community or TC. The TC has shown success with the most severely drug-abusing and criminogenic offenders. TCs have also been used in modified forms to help develop pro-social behavior among other special needs populations, such as sex offenders, mentally ill offenders, and dually diagnosed offenders. The TC has shown success with these populations. There is some evidence that offenders who are more pro-socially oriented (low-risk offenders) do not require the highly structured, long-term, and expensive therapeutic community modality. Although modified TC models are sometimes employed with low-risk offender populations, successful correctional programs treat low- and high-risk offenders separately.

ELEMENTS OF SUCCESSFUL COGNITIVE PROGRAMS

Basic Program Essentials

Cognitive programs operate with the following assumptions:

- *Cognitive behavior is the key to social behavior.* Problem behavior is almost always rooted in modes of thinking that promote and support that behavior. Permanent change in problem behavior demands change at a cognitive level, i.e., change in the underlying beliefs, attitudes, and ways of thinking.

- *Authority and control that increases resentment and antisocial attitudes is counterproductive.* Punitive methods of controlling behavior all too often reinforce modes of thinking that were responsible for the initial antisocial behavior. The alternative to punitive measures is not permissiveness but, rather, a rational strategy of authority and control combined with programs of cognitive change.

- *Authority and control can achieve both compliance and cooperation.* Authority can define rules and enforce consequences while reminding and encouraging offenders to make their own decisions. As offenders learn to make conscious and deliberate decisions they accept responsibility for their behavior.

• *Pro-social thinking can be taught.* Programs of cognitive change can teach pro-social ways of thinking, even to severely criminogenic and violent offenders. The effectiveness of cognitive programs in changing antisocial behavior has been demonstrated by practical application over time.

• *The values of cognitive strategies extend well beyond the correctional environment.* Cognitive principles can be applied to victim restitution, educational settings, personal development, and as an overall approach to public safety and offender change.

Cognitive Approaches

There are two main types of cognitive programs: cognitive skills and cognitive restructuring. Cognitive skill training is based on the premise that offenders have never learned the "thinking skills" required to function productively and responsibly in society. This skill deficit is remedied by systematic training in skills such as problem solving, negotiation, assertiveness, anger control, and social skills focused on specific social situations like making a complaint or asking for help.

Cognitive restructuring is based on the premise that offenders have learned destructive attitudes and thinking habits that point them to criminal behavior. Cognitive restructuring consists of identifying the specific attitudes and ways of thinking that point to criminality and systematically replacing them with new attitudes and ways of thinking.

Cognitive restructuring and cognitive skills approaches are complementary and can be combined in a single program. When practiced in a community model, resocialization can be enhanced and accelerated. Both cognitive strategies take an objective and systematic approach to change. Change is not coerced; offenders are taught how to think for themselves and to make their own decisions.

Cognitive corrections programs regard offenders as fully responsible for their behavior. Thinking is viewed as a type of learned behavior. Dishonesty and irresponsibility are the primary targets for change. Limit-setting and accountability for behavior do not conflict with the cognitive approach to offender change, they support it. These programs are particularly useful for substance abusers because acceptance of limit setting is a primary need associated with early recovery.

Incorporating the Principle of Responsivity

Responsivity addresses the importance of delivering treatment services in a manner that facilitates the learning of new pro-social skills by the offender and creates appropriate competencies in staff. Thus, successful programs (1) match the treatment approach with the learning style and personality of the offender; (2) match the characteristics of the offender with those of the treatment provider; and (3) match the skills of the treatment provider with the type of program.

One aspect of responsivity often overlooked in correctional programs is appropriate communication. Communication is the primary means of getting and using information needed to treat and manage offenders effectively. Cognitive/behavioral communication strategies provide both custody and treatment staff with the competencies necessary to make use of what we know about antisocial logic. In order for staff to communicate in a manner that has an effect on the offender's view of the world, the communication must intrude on, disrupt, or confront the offender's normal thought process. A critical correctional communication competency is to know when to use behavioral confrontation and when to use cognitive confrontation. Behavioral confrontation describes the behavior and is followed by appropriate disapproval/approval. On the other hand, cognitive confrontation must come through personal self-disclosure, awareness, and the connection between thoughts, behavior, and consequences. Competent communication also requires combining confrontation with the appropriate application of positive and negative reinforcers. Understanding antisocial logic and the effective use of these techniques can mean the difference between failure and success in offender programs.

Effective communication defines the interpersonal relationship between staff and offenders as one of accountability and support. For maximum treatment outcome custody, treatment, and administration staff must all become competent in the use of the various correctional communication skills. Some of the more promising techniques include cognitive reflective communication, motivational interviewing, and a social learning application of behavioral confrontation.

TAKING AN INTEGRATED APPROACH

Relapse Prevention Strategies

Essential to any integrated approach is the inclusion of relapse prevention strategies that typically incorporate the following elements:

- Development of an individualized plan and rehearsal of alternative pro-social responses that are specific to the behaviors or circumstances that increase the risk of re-offending for the offender in question;

- Development of self-monitoring skills and the ability to anticipate problem situations; and

- Training of significant others such as family, friends, and employers to reinforce pro-social behavior and to recognize triggers and risk situations regardless of the risk factors.

In addition, it is often important to provide booster sessions to offenders after they leave formal treatment or are released into the community.

Sanctions and Treatment: Accountability and Change

Currently, sanctions are seldom used intentionally as companions to offender treatment or strategies to modify behavior. These include such things as intensive supervision, home confinement, frequent drug testing, restitution, shock incarceration, electronic monitoring, and mandated 12-Step programs.

The primary intent of most sanctions is for purposes other than their impact on re-offense behavior. For example, drug testing and intensive supervision are often employed to monitor compliance (or detect noncompliance) with conditions of probation or parole. Restitution is a component of restorative justice rather than an attempt at crime control. Similarly, interventions such as home confinement, electronic monitoring, and short periods of shock incarceration are sometimes imposed because they are less expensive forms of punishment. None of these strategies have shown any significant results. Further, sanctions—*if not accompanied by appropriate treatment*—have shown or little or no evidence of reducing recidivism.

The key idea is simply this: Effective correctional intervention must produce a change in the offenders' fundamental worldview, especially their perception of authority, rules, and accountability. This marks an essential difference between prosocial and antisocial attitudes and behaviors. Addressing this aspect of antisocial logic is a vital part of effective program strategy.

This part of a correctional strategy should be conceived as three messages with one voice:

1. Our society's determination to enforce social limits and the law;

2. Extension of a genuine opportunity to change; and

3. Respect for offenders' capacity to make their own choices.

In this message, security (in the broad sense of the term, including law enforcement and accountability) and treatment are complementary. Neither is an isolated component, able to stand alone. Each derives its meaning by its relation to the other. The same applies to the condition of respect. Society must not impose an insurmountable barrier between itself and the guilty offender. This is not a matter of altruism, but rather a matter of effective strategy and social learning theory applied. Each of the three messages qualifies and defines the others. Consequently, the message provides closer monitoring, better supervision, and has positive effects on recidivism. With a clear understanding of these principles even punishment and retribution can be combined appropriately with interventions to produce enhanced outcomes (Bush & Bilodeau, 1994).

EVIDENCE-BASED PROGRAM STRUCTURE

The Cognitive Community

Treatment models that maximize outcomes as part of correctional strategy incorporate an in-depth understanding of antisocial logic, social learning, cognitive/behavioral programs, and appropriate communication. Such a program could be referred to as a "cognitive community." Programs producing maximum results have developed competence in the concept skills and attitudes of these program elements. Competence includes appropriate situational and interchangeable application of these methods. One example of application is knowing when and how to confront crime-producing attitudes and beliefs thinking (cognitive restructuring and cognitive skill-building) and when to use the behavioral confrontation tools of the therapeutic community. In a cognitive community, cognitive behavioral programs are not simply a type of group to be placed into a therapeutic environment as a learning experience or a group activity and social learning must not become rote compliance or peer coercion. The treatment model employed must be flexible enough to encompass self-actualization, but structured enough to create a climate for peer accountability and consequences (Gornik, et al., 1999).

The cognitive community is especially useful for substance abusers because both substance abuse and criminogenic risk factors must be addressed simultaneously for optimum treatment outcomes.

In the cognitive community, thinking and behavior are both exposed to the larger community. The community then becomes the baseline and milieu in which new learning and change can take place. Once implemented, the cognitive community is as much like real life as possible. All staff, including custody staff, participates in the cognitive community practices. Thoughts and behaviors that typically lead to relapse are discovered more quickly. Staff's ability to recognize the internalization of offender change is more efficient. The cognitive community operates 24 hours a day, seven days a week, and 365 days a year. Social learning and cognitive change operates as the oxygen and lifeblood of the community and fosters a "no place to hide" philosophy. Cognitive/behavioral practices form the lifestyle in which all other operations and activities exist including work both on and off the living unit, educational programming, drug treatment and counseling, specialized programs and groups, visitation, family re-unification, and transition planning.

Staff and offender growth is measured in stages, and competency is measured in three domains (knowledge, skills, and attitude). Competency measured in this way insures the full range of abilities necessary for internalized and lasting change. This type of competency measurement can track offender progress more effectively through the process from compliance to endorsement. Initially, staff will be primarily responsible for modeling and enforcing pro-social values and behaviors. However, as the community matures, the community itself becomes the primary agent of change. This is the core of social learning.

Staff as Community Members and Agents of Change

In healthy communities, the involvement and support of every member is important. Within correctional treatment communities it is essential. Correctional officers, probation and parole officers, teachers, counselors, and volunteers all make excellent members of the treatment team and are considered part of the community. The authority represented by correctional staff, including uniformed officers, is a positive enhancement—not a detriment—to the credibility and effectiveness of cognitive behavioral social-learning programs. People with good interpersonal skills, but no clinical training, can be trained to deliver and benefit by cognitive social learning programs. The crucial element is consistent modeling by a staff that practices and believes in the principle they are espousing. As staff participate in the principles and practices of the correctional programs, staffers are less likely to burn out, lose job satisfaction, or use authority inappropriately. Multidisciplinary involvement is one more critical element of integrated correctional strategy and becomes a one voice-one message philosophy.

MAXIMIZING RESULTS

After some 30 years of involvement with the criminal justice system, from personal incarceration to state program administrator, I have come to some conclusions about offender treatment. Over time, these opinions have been validated by research and experience in my various roles: addict, offender, counselor, program manager, administrator, and justice-treatment consultant.

Effective programs require an understanding of self-centeredness and oppositional behavior, not only in offenders but also in staff and the organization as a whole. Successful programs utilize competent, well-trained, and well-supervised staffs which possess good communication skills. However, program failure is more often due to an attitudinal problem than a lack of skill or knowledge. Everyone in the organization and its community partners must believe in and practice the values given to offenders in the change process. Social learning principles practiced at the organizational level provide a safe atmosphere for staff to disclose, seek help, and correct personal and program problems. Staff health goes hand in hand with good offender treatment

A balanced integrated approach to security and treatment must go beyond practices targeted at offender change and management. Accountability and change must become a system norm supported and practiced by leadership. Implementing a seamless continuum of service between prison programs and the community means participation by leadership and involvement by the community. Proper assessment of need and appropriate ongoing care should be seen as a universal practice good for all people in the system

Practices used to promote public safety and offender change should be understood and continuously evaluated by all stakeholders from policymakers to offenders. Informed decision-making demands responsible examination of one's own attitudes and, beliefs prior to evaluating others. The combination of these best practices provides therapeutic integrity. The challenge before us is to translate the various roles of an integrated system into role specific language so that can be valued, used, and passed on.

About the Author

Mark Gornik, M.S., is Bureau Chief, Offender Programs, Idaho Department of Correction (IDOC), where he coordinates and trains statewide offender programs including; substance abuse, sex offender, cognitive/behavioral, volunteer services, and other treatment related programs. He also serves as a consultant to the National Institute of Corrections Academy in Longmont, Colorado and the Department of Justice, Office of Justice Programs in Washington, D.C., and is an adjunct faculty member of Boise State University.

References

Bush, J., & Bilodeau, B. (1994). *Cognitive self-change. Cognitive approaches to changing offender behavior.* Longmont, CO: National Institute of Corrections Seminar.

Bush, D., & LaBarbera, M. (1995). *Design and implementation issues for drug treatment in the correctional setting.* Washington, DC: Bureau of Justice Assistance.

Gendreau, P., & Andrews, D.A. (1990). Tertiary prevention: What the meta-analysis of the offender treatment literature tells us about "what works." *Canadian Journal of Criminology, 32,* 173-184.

Gornik, M., Bush, D., & LaBarbera, M. (1999). *Strategies for application of the cognitive behavioral/social learning model to offender programs. Technical Assistance Proposal.* Washington, DC: National Institute of Corrections.

Chapter 38

Enhancing Substance Abuse Treatment Skills in Correctional Settings

by Igor Koutsenok, M.D., David A. Deitch, Ph.D., Karin Marsolais, and Michael Franc, Psy.D.

Preconceptions a Barrier to New Understanding of Addiction 38-1
The Gap Between Science and Clinical Practices 38-2
      Practitioners Want Specific Answers From Science 38-2
      Researchers Need to Consider Under-Studied Treatment Strategies 38-3
      Challenges in Transferring Clinical Success to Treatment Programs 38-3
How Bias Affects Treatment and Training 38-3
Continuity of Care 38-4
Training Adult Learners 38-5
Basic Concepts of Training 38-5
Skill Enhancement 38-6
      Organizational Skills 38-6
      Case Management Skills 38-7
Successful Training Methods 38-8
Conclusion 38-8

PRECONCEPTIONS A BARRIER TO NEW UNDERSTANDING OF ADDICTION

Dramatic advances over the past two decades in neuroscience, brain imaging, molecular neurobiology, and behavioral science have revolutionized our understanding of drug abuse and addiction. Unfortunately, the wide gap between scientific facts and their implementation in clinical reality has become even wider. One of the major barriers is that clinical personnel who come to be trained in the subject of substance abuse most likely arrive with a preconceived set of biases based on personal experience, varied expectations, previous training experiences, professional orientation, and beliefs about addiction itself. In addition, many drug abuse workers are in recovery themselves, having had success with

An earlier version of this chapter appeared in Offender Substance Abuse Report, *Vol. 3, No. 4, July/August 2003.*

one particular model. They therefore zealously defend that single approach, even in the face of contradictory scientific evidence. They may feel very strongly that their "way" is the only way and may carry this belief into their staff roles. Some believe that addiction is a medical symptom, episodic in nature, and that the way to deal with it is through detoxification. Others believe that denial is the largest stumbling block to recovery and that once denial is conquered, recovery is sure to follow. Those schooled in therapeutic-community (TC) and 12-step models may find it difficult to open themselves to new ideas based on different paradigms. In addition, nonmedical health professionals may very well be grappling with some aversion to the drug-abusing population. This aversion can take the form of hopelessness, helplessness, dislike, disgust, discomfort, and affective distancing (Minkoff, 1987). All of these attitudes are further exacerbated in substance abuse treatment professionals working in correctional environments. In the correctional setting the situation is unique for the clients because they are often in a particular institution only for a short amount of time before they transfer to another institution or they parole or are discharged and undergo treatment in the community. It is only too common for them to violate their parole or commit new offenses and get placed in jails and subsequently in other prisons. One problem is a notorious lack of communication between the various programs dealing with these clients. Furthermore, the ideas about the proper model of treatment vary greatly among the various agencies so there is no continuity of care to speak of.

Because of the strong convictions that both medical and nonmedical personnel bring to the arena, training in this field needs to be particularly sensitive.

THE GAP BETWEEN SCIENCE AND CLINICAL PRACTICES

Researchers perceive that many science-developed innovations have improved the treatment of drug abuse. For example, methadone maintenance treatment began as a research effort (Ball & Ross, 1991), relapse-prevention techniques were honed by research investigations (Marlatt & Gordon, 1985), the stages and processes of behavioral change were studied in depth (Prochaska & DiClemente, 1986), and motivational enhancement techniques have been shown to improve retention in treatment (Miller & Rollnick, 1991). Although significant advances have been made in the behavioral treatment of drug abusers (Stitzer & Higgins, 1995), however, and studies have found that treatment intensity and systematic follow-up improve treatment outcomes (Simpson et al., 1997), few of these findings have been incorporated into standard treatment settings.

Practitioners Want Specific Answers From Science

The treatment practitioners are on the other side of the gap. Faced with the challenges of providing services on a daily basis, they are frustrated by what they see as the failure of research to provide them with specific answers to their important day-to-day questions. Many of their questions about how to use the information are related to policy and fiscal areas that, at least until recently, have been under-researched. They perceive that current policy, including funding policy, provides little opportunity or incentive for treatment programs to implement new scientific findings. The barriers between science and practice are multiple, but the insufficient training in evidence-based practices is one of the most prominent and disturbing.

Researchers Need to Consider Under-Studied Treatment Strategies

Just as research findings have been underutilized by the treatment community, there are treatment approaches that have been under-studied by the research community. For example, only a few researchers are studying TCs, and the research that has been done tends to focus on assessing their overall effectiveness, rather than investigating how they work, why they work, or for whom they work (Chasnoff et al, 1996). There is a strong body of evidence, however, of positive outcomes in prison-based therapeutic communities, particularly if followed by continuing care.

Challenges in Transferring Clinical Success to Treatment Programs

Even when studies document that a treatment can be successfully implemented in a clinical setting, the challenges in the final stage of transfer to treatment programs are the provision of additional training for staff in delivering the new treatment, changing the attitudes of the providers, and providing evidence that the new treatment is effective within the unique cultural or local clinical environment. Each of these training components poses problems for the treatment programs. Training must be planned, systematic, and protective of the fidelity of the treatment. Researchers who establish treatment effectiveness in tightly controlled settings are often not able to translate the intervention into standard practice through training for daily activities. With the right skills and resources, researchers can provide the requisite training, anticipate the difficulties, and assist in the process of changing provider attitudes. Further, shared technology transfer can encourage providers to "own" the research. If this transfer of knowledge does not happen, the prospects are poor for sustaining the intervention once the researchers are no longer involved (Altman, 1995).

HOW BIAS AFFECTS TREATMENT AND TRAINING

As noted above, those who come to drug abuse training programs often do so with strong biases. These biases result from prior professional or lay education, as well as personal experience, and they have a significant impact on the way in which people approach training. Preconceived beliefs about substance abuse and what constitutes an appropriate response to substance abuse often create a tunnel through which only some addicts can pass (American Psychiatric Association, 1996). If people are convinced that their treatment ideas are the "only" correct ideas, they tend to herd people through a rigid set of interventions that simply are not flexible enough to bend to individual needs. Cultural beliefs (be they national, regional, neighborhood, or association) further complicate these practitioner biases. Strongly held cultural views may dictate that only certain kinds of treatment are valid, meaningful, or useful. An unfortunate number of professionals involved in the treatment of addicts still view addiction as a choice and think of it in terms of right and wrong or good and bad. Some of the biases in basic thinking about substance abuse are as follows:

1. Drug abuse and drug dependence are phases of a disease process;

2. Working with a client who is actively using drugs is "enabling";

3. If clients do not think of drug abuse as an out-of-control disease, they are in denial;

4. If a client does admit to having a "disease," a 12-step program is the only concrete, long-lasting solution;

5. Psychotherapy is ineffective;

6. Psychotherapy is requisite to produce long-term recovery;

7. Medical intervention in the form of medication is destructive or impedes recovery;

8. The only real, cost-effective help lies in a medicopharmacological response;

9. Drug-dependent people most likely have substance-dependent parents;

10. The TC approach is the only long-lasting rehabilitation that is drug free;

11. TC approaches work with only a small segment of the drug-using population; and

12. Regardless of original drug use patterns, all "recovering" people must abstain from any drug use (e.g., alcohol, medications) for the rest of their lives.

Obviously, these divergent convictions can create a chaos of misunderstanding in both treatment and training programs. No one approach is right. No one approach can be right, given the cultural, economic, experiential, and personality differences of substance abusers. The goal of training should be to create an atmosphere in which people are actually able to listen openly to new ideas and to offer a range of care options broad enough to encompass many kinds of addicts, at many stages of addiction.

CONTINUITY OF CARE

As states become more concerned over their budgets, the problem of recidivism of the prison population is increasingly coming under scrutiny. Individual entities involved with services to correctional populations are frustrated with the lack of communication among them. The absence of continuity of treatment and services to addicted or dually diagnosed offenders, parolees, and ex-offenders is becoming apparent. Lack of data-sharing among treatment providers is often detrimental to the success of inmates after release. Where residential treatment is warranted, the parolees or ex-offenders often end up homeless instead. Granted, much of this is due to budgetary restraints. However, the situation could be greatly improved in many cases if:

1. There were a clear communication among treatment specialists involved regarding previous successes and failures in a treatment of each particular client, as clients often migrate from one treatment method in one setting to another method in another setting to no treatment at all; and

2. There was better education among treatment providers about various forms of intervention and treatment.

Treatment method often espouses a whole philosophy and accompanying rhetoric, which a client becomes a part of and believer in. The clients structure the narratives of their life stories around these philosophies and rhetorics. The often-mentioned comparison of Alcoholics Anonymous (AA) and religion is a great example. When clinicians adopt new clients without knowing what previous treatments the clients experienced; or, due to lack of objective training disregard previous treatments as faulty philosophies, it is the clients who pay the price by failing, by returning to custody, or worse.

TRAINING ADULT LEARNERS

Adults are a special group of learners, requiring appropriate adult education concepts to maximize learning. They perceive of themselves as responsible, self-directing, independent persons, and they demand that the instructor accept them as such. Resistance to learning solidifies under conditions that are not in keeping with this concept of self-direction. The best approach to teaching adults is to view training as a planned, sequential process designed to provide the self-awareness, skills, knowledge, and attitudes needed to perform particular tasks.

This is not to say that instructors will not make some decisions for trainees. However, whenever possible, trainees should be responsible for suggestions regarding training content and design. This increases their feelings of "ownership" and fosters personal engagement with the training. The most effective training for adults is designed with the following points in mind:

- A climate of mutual respect must exist between trainer and trainees;

- An open, friendly, and casual atmosphere facilitates the exchange of differing viewpoints and ideas;

- Trainees should be aided in diagnosing their own skills and growth needs, as well as in analyzing the specific training elements needed by their agency;

- Adult learners learn best that which is relevant and useful to them. "Here and now" challenges should be the focus of training. Whenever possible, training ideas should be applied to current work situations. The emphasis should always be on illustrating new concepts as they relate to the life and work experiences of the trainees (Kolb, 1984).

BASIC CONCEPTS OF TRAINING

Successful training in drug abuse treatment is predicated on certain fundamental ideas. These basic ideas permeate all parts of the curriculum and serve the dual purpose of being immediately applicable to both the training setting and the workplace. They include:

- *Personal responsibility:* Methods that help mobilize the individual impulse toward health, despite personal and environmental obstacles;

- *Self-help:* Technology whereby both individuals and groups can become effective in coping and problem solving on an ongoing basis;

- *Social systems perspective:* Information that stresses practitioners' awareness of the interdependence of individuals and their social environment and provides for richer assessments and increased alternatives for intervention;

- *Social support:* Methods for creating and/or using helping networks that can enhance the functioning of individuals and help maintain change;

- *Transdisciplinary practice:* Skills and attitudes that prepare the different disciplines to collaborate toward "whole person" responses in planning, goal setting, and problem solving;

- *Systematic problem solving:* A goal-oriented perspective that recognizes a common systemic and empirical process of stages and strategies that can be applied in assessing and treating problems at the individual, family, community, and societal levels;

- *Interorganizational relations:* Concepts and perspectives relevant to understanding the forces that shape service-delivery systems; and

- *Cooperative learning:* Concepts and techniques to enhance self-esteem, acquisition of knowledge, and prevention of drug use (Deitch, 1989).

SKILL ENHANCEMENT

Although the inclusion of general information about the context of drug abuse treatment and models is essential to training, it must be accompanied by skill development—pragmatic techniques that help practitioners perform their jobs better. For those people fighting daily in the trenches of drug abuse treatment programs, skill development is of the utmost importance. The job can be so challenging and difficult that many practitioners yearn for magical solutions—theories or step-by-step directions—that can make their job less trying and more effective. More often than not, clients act out, regress, misbehave, deny problems, try to run away from treatment, have dysfunctional families, and act irresponsibly. Those who work with them often look for formulaic answers to reassure themselves and diminish their understandable anxiety, as they work in a climate riddled with the demands of funding agencies for bureaucratic compliance.

Organizational Skills

Because the demands on practitioners are complex, skill enhancement for drug treatment personnel can be divided into two categories. The first category concerns skills demanded by the funding and oversight agencies, which require evermore accurate and specific reporting mechanisms and management systems. Practitioners who are overwhelmed by paperwork simply cannot perform effectively with clients. In light of this, many training candidates need specific organizational information, such as how to keep clinical records and how to track client and management activities. Mastery of these skills can be a great relief to those in daily contact with drug addicts.

Case Management Skills

The second category of skills needed by treatment personnel in the field includes the art of specific case management, including treatment planning, case note making, and assessment skills. These skills are all part of the practitioner's main concern: How do I improve my ability to do the required paperwork while successfully treating this client? Some of the ground that needs to be covered in this area of clinical skill enhancement includes answers to the following questions:

- How do I engage the client on a personal level?

- How do I interview a client?

- What are the varying levels of client resistance and how do I get through them?

- How do I motivate the correctional client to accept mandated treatment?

- How do I determine the severity of my client's symptoms and indications?

- How do I assess my client's criminal background, social background, family background, psychological background, and academic background?

- How do I assess my client's unique and special family, job, living, or environmental resources?

- How do I interview the client's parent(s)?

- What model of treatment should I pursue with the client in a residential program, day care, outpatient care, hospitalization, etc.?

- How do I enable the client to change his or her behavior?

- How do I assist the family in understanding the client's problem?

- How do I help the family change in ways that support the client's new behavior?

- How do I get the client invested in his or her treatment and outcome?

- How do the client and I set the orientation for treatment?

- How do I confront the client, particularly in a prison context?

- What specific skills do I need to function in an induction group, in a behavior change group, in a therapy group, in individual counseling?

- How do I help my client identify short-term, achievable goals, while maintaining a long-term plan for recovery?

- How can my client and I create enduring and meaningful behaviors that promote change?

- How can I motivate the in-custody client to pursue aftercare?

SUCCESSFUL TRAINING METHODS

It is important for training sessions to include a mix of methods. This counters boredom and acknowledges that people learn in different ways. Six methods used in successful training are described below. Critical to each of these training methods are written and/or oral commitments to action on the part of the trainees:

1. *Didactic presentations:* The history of drug abuse and treatment approaches may be best presented in lecture format, as is theoretical and organizational material about groups, counseling principles, program planning, etc.;

2. *Small groups:* The small group as a learning tool has as its theoretical underpinning the assumption that individuals learn best in a group structure that demands interdependence. This interdependence heightens self-awareness and awareness of others;

3. *Large groups:* Large groups are the most appropriate setting for brainstorming, process observations, daily training program evaluation, action planning, homework, reading, and practice;

4. *Simulation and role playing:* Theatrical techniques bring problems to life and vividly demonstrate how trainees can effectively respond in new and useful ways. They can be a dramatic means of revealing other people's points of view and of uncovering one's own misconceptions and misjudgments;

5. *Task groups:* The task group has as its purpose the completion of clearly defined work. The work at hand should be based on real tasks from the trainees' work sites. Some possible task group work may be identifying problems, solving problems, and collecting data; and

6. *Videotapes:* Videotape is an effective learning tool for isolating and identifying behaviors that trainees may be unaware of, both in individuals and in group dynamics.

CONCLUSION

As with many endeavors in education and professional training, substance abuse treatment and training originally began as apprenticeship training—learning by doing. Gradually, more formal training emerged—first, by treatment agencies themselves; next, by government agencies with hopes of expanding resources; then, by groups or agencies with similar operating philosophies; next, by groups allied with certain agencies that offer certification (these tended to validate a particular approach); and finally, by colleges or universities granting credit for specific courses.

These various approaches to formal training have led to debate and controversy over which type of certification should carry weight. Should certificates be granted only by those programs approved by public funders, license agencies, or insurance payers? Schools themselves argue about which department should implement or credit such training. Certainly, all professional human service schools should offer compulsory exposure to substance abuse and addictive behavior issues. At the very least, this information should foster an awareness of the symptoms and psychosocial implications of substance abuse. Perhaps the mandatory curriculum should go so far as to include engagement or referral strategies.

There are many future psychologists in graduate schools today who believe that they should not treat addicted clients until they are "cured" of their addiction and would refer them to, for example, a 12-step program. There are, however, also many who believe they should deal with their client's addiction in their own practice but feel they are ill equipped to do so.

When it comes to specific techniques of treatment or prevention, however, more extensive and specialized training is required. Such exposure aimed at drug abuse practitioners faces many challenges. Certainly, the interplay of client needs, available funds, community-agency operating philosophies and goals, as well as diverse trainee beliefs and assumptions can, and often do, conflict. In this light, training should be viewed as a growth process that occurs within the context of a facilitative relationship and information exchange.

About the Authors

Igor Koutsenok, M.D., is assistant adjunct professor of psychiatry, and David A. Deitch, Ph.D., is professor of clinical psychiatry in the Department of Psychiatry at the University of California, San Diego, School of Medicine. Karin Marsolais is associate director of the School of Medicine's Addiction Training Center. Michael Franc, Psy.D., works at UCSD as a program mananger of the Transitional Case Management Program for the California Department of Corrections and is also on the faculty at Chapman University. Igor Koutsenok can be reached at ikoutzenok@ucsd.edu; David Deitch can be reached at ddeitch@ucsd.edu; and Karin Marsolais can be reached at kmarsolais@ucsd.edu.

References

Altman, D.G. (1995). Sustaining interventions in community systems: On the relationship between researchers and communities. *Health Psychology, 14*, 526–536.

American Psychiatric Association. (1996). Position statement on training needs in addiction psychiatry. *American Journal of Psychiatry, 153*, 852.

Ball, J.C., & Ross, A. (1991). *The effectiveness of methadone maintenance treatment.* New York: Springer-Verlag.

Chasnoff. I.J., Marques, P.R., Strantz, I.H., Farrow, J., & Davis, S. (1996). Building bridges: Treatment research partnership in the community. *NIDA Research Monographs, 166*, 6–21.

Deitch, D. (1989). Training material. Berkeley, CA: Daytop International Associates Training Institutes.

Kolb, D.A., (1984). *Experiential learning: Experience as the source of learning and development.* Englewood Cliffs, NJ: Prentice-Hall.

Marlatt, G.A., & Gordon, J.R. (1985). *Relapse prevention: Maintenance strategies in the treatment of addictive disorders.* New York: Guilford.

Miller, W.R., & Rollnick, S. (1991). *Motivational interviewing. Preparing people to change addictive behavior.* New York: Guilford.

Minkoff, K. (1987) Resistance of mental health professionals to working with the chronic mentally ill. In A.T. Meyerson (Ed.). *Barriers to treating the chronic mentally ill.* San Francisco, CA: Jossey-Bass, pp. 31–33.

Prochaska, J.O., & DiClemente, C.C. (1986). Toward a comprehensive model of change. In W.R. Miller & N. Heather (Eds.). *Treating addictive behaviors: Processes of change* (pp. 110–131). New York: Plenum.

Simpson, D.W., Joe, G.W., Brown, B.S. (1997). Treatment retention and follow-up outcomes in the Drug Abuse Treatment Outcomes Study (DATOS). *Psychology of Addictive Behaviors, 11(4)*, 294–307.

Stitzer, M.L., & Higgins, S.T. (1995). Behavioral treatment of drug and alcohol abuse. In F.E. Bloom & D.J. Kupfer (Eds.). *Psychopharmacology: The fourth generation of progress* (pp. 1807–1819). New York: Raven.

Chapter 39

Assessing Prison-Based Drug and Alcohol Treatment: Pennsylvania's Ongoing Review Has Improved Programming

by Wayne N. Welsh, Ph.D., and Gary Zajac, Ph.D.

The National Picture 39-2
    Need Outpaces Program Services 39-2
    Open Question: Which Drug Abuse Programs Work 39-2
Pennsylvania Partnership Purpose and Goals 39-4
    Demonstration Project 39-4
    DOC Goals 39-4
    DOC's Alcohol or Other Drug Programs 39-4
Survey of Drug and Alcohol Programs in Pennsylvania Prisons 39-5
    Survey Findings 39-5
        Point #1: Considerable Variation in Program
          Duration and Intensity 39-5
        Point #2: Consistency in Treatment Approach 39-6
        Point #3: Consistency in Program Topic Coverage 39-6
        Point #4: Great Variation in Program Types 39-6
        Point #5: Great Variation in Administrative Criteria 39-6
    Practical Implications of Findings 39-7
        Program Variability Inhibits Effective Management 39-7
        We Need to Know More About Process Effect on Outcome . . . 39-7
        Better Tracking Required 39-8
Outcome Evaluation of Pennsylvania's Prison-Based Drug Treatment 39-8
Translating Research to Practice 39-9
    The Department as a Learning Organization 39-9

An earlier version of this chapter appeared in Offender Substance Abuse Report, *Vol. 1, No. 6, November/December 2001.*

Evaluation Recommendations Implemented or
    Under Current Review 39-10
        New Screening Tools 39-10
        Program Standardization 39-10
        Improved Documentation 39-10
        Future Projects 39-10
Conclusion 39-11

THE NATIONAL PICTURE

Need Outpaces Program Services

Nearly two million inmates were incarcerated in U.S. jails and prisons at midyear 2000, a rate of 702 per 100,000 adults (up from 458 in 1990) (Beck & Karberg, 2001). Although estimates of alcohol or other drug dependence among inmate populations vary widely, depending upon the type of assessment procedure used, most professionals accept estimates based upon the DSM-IV Structured Clinical Interview (SCID-IV) as among the most reliable (Peters et al., 1998). Administering this instrument to a sample of 400 state prison inmates, Peters and his colleagues estimated lifetime prevalence rates of substance abuse or dependence disorders among 74% of the inmate population. Over half were diagnosed as exhibiting substance abuse or dependence disorders for the 30 days prior to their current incarceration.

About two out of three inmates admit drug histories, but less than 15% receive any systematic treatment while in prison (Mumola, 1999). In 1997, 9.7% of state prison inmates (101,729) and 9.2% of federal prison inmates (8,070) reported participation in drug treatment (i.e., residential treatment, professional counseling, detoxification, or use of a maintenance drug) since their admission (Mumola, 1999)). Participation in much less intensive drug abuse programs (e.g., self-help, peer group, or drug education classes) was more common: 20% of state and 9% of federal prison inmates reported participation in such programs. According to a recent report by the Substance Abuse and Mental Health Services Administration (SAMHSA; 2000), 40% of all correctional facilities nationwide (federal and state prisons, local jails, and juvenile facilities) provided some sort of on-site substance abuse treatment (i.e., detoxification, group or individual counseling, rehabilitation, and methadone or other pharmaceutical treatment) to inmates in 1997. However, only about 11% of inmates in these institutions received any treatment, most frequently in a general facility population program. Few of these inmates were treated in specialized treatment units (28%) or hospital or psychiatric inpatient units (2%). Given available estimates of treatment need and availability, it is unlikely that even a majority of inmates with serious substance abuse problems receive intensive treatment (Lipton, 1995).

Open Question: Which Drug Abuse Programs Work

While estimates of inmate need for treatment, program availability, and participation in treatment are useful, surprisingly little information is available about the *variety* (e.g., intensity, duration, and quality) of prison-based drug abuse programs. For example, say that Inmate A receives six weeks of group counseling consisting of two one-hour sessions per week for a total treatment exposure of 12 hours, while Inmate B completes a one-year residential drug treatment program consisting of 30 hours of individual and group counseling per week for a total treatment exposure of 1,560 hours. Estimates of inmate participation in treatment and program availability do not adequately distinguish between different programs (and inmates), and program evaluations only rarely account for such critical variations in programming.

Although in-prison therapeutic community (TC) programs in several states have been evaluated and found to be effective (e.g., Knight et al., 1999, Martin et al., 1999, Pearson & Lipton, 1999; Wexler et al., 1999), most prison-based drug abuse programs remain unevaluated and relationships between inmate characteristics, treatment process, and outcomes remain only poorly understood (Lipton & Pearson, 1998; NIDA, 1981, 1999). For example:

- How are drug and alcohol needs assessments conducted, and to what degree does adequate assessment and program placement moderate treatment effects?

- Are inmates with different levels and types of needs matched with the appropriate treatment (e.g., Andrews et al., 1990)?

- Which inmates are best suited for which programs, and which variables affect retention (Hiller et al., 1999; Lipton & Pearson, 1998; Pearson & Lipton, 1999)?

- Do intensive treatment programs accept inmates with higher levels of need?

- Do factors other than assessed need influence program placement decisions (e.g., security concerns, inmate work schedules, severe mental health or medical problems, minimum length of sentence remaining, inmate refusal to participate, biases in the referral process, etc.)?

- How do demands of other agencies (e.g., parole) influence the type of programming provided to specific inmates? How do variations in program content and structure affect treatment outcomes?

- To what extent do observed treatment effects depend upon variations in treatment programming, inmate characteristics (e.g., drug and alcohol needs assessments, psychological functioning), or research design (e.g., adequacy of matching procedures)?

- How is quality of program implementation related to treatment outcomes?

This chapter describes how a successful research partnership between a correctional agency and a public university was developed in Pennsylvania, and how it facilitated progress in prison-based drug treatment program development, implementation, and evaluation. We address: (1) the goals and implementation of the research partnership, (2) results from a statewide survey and on-site process evaluations of drug and alcohol programs, (3) design of an outcome evaluation, and (4) how this partnership has affected department policy and goals.

PENNSYLVANIA PARTNERSHIP PURPOSE AND GOALS

Demonstration Project

The purpose of this project, funded by the National Institute of Justice (NIJ), was to develop a collaborative research partnership between the Pennsylvania Department of Corrections and Temple University's Center for Public Policy. A demonstration research project included three main elements: (1) a descriptive assessment of alcohol or other drug (AOD) programming (through surveys and a one-day symposium with treatment staff); (2) an intensive on-site process evaluation of AOD programs at two institutions; and (3) design of an outcome evaluation.

An essential part of NIJ's overall evaluation strategy has been the development of greater research and evaluation capacity within state and local criminal justice systems in order to increase data-driven decision making and policy development. Recognizing that most agencies do not have substantial in-house research and evaluation expertise and resources, NIJ encouraged partnerships between correctional agencies and research institutions that could provide such expertise specifically tailored to meet state and local needs (Welsh, 2000a). The stated purpose of these NIJ-supported partnerships was to stimulate collaborative efforts that would develop into lasting, productive relationships.

DOC Goals

The Pennsylvania Department of Corrections (DOC) identified several specific goals for this project, including development of an ongoing working relationship with a major Pennsylvania research university to facilitate the production of useful knowledge for the department, demonstration of the DOC's ability to utilize external research expertise and to secure funding for needed studies, and production of information that is responsive to legislative and other demands for reporting on DOC program performance.

DOC's Alcohol or Other Drug Programs

The Department's approach to AOD programs is informed by a holistic health model that treats substance abuse as a complex problem with physiological, psychological, emotional, behavioral, spiritual, environmental, and sociopolitical dimensions (Pennsylvania Department of Corrections, 2001). Long-term goals are to reduce recidivism, drug dealing, and drug use, and increase the prospects for successful reintegration into society.

The Department's AOD programming is grouped into four major categories:

1. *Drug and Alcohol Education Programs*, offered by the Department to inmates identified as having any level of drug and alcohol involvement;

2. *Outpatient Treatment Programs*, offered to inmates who are in need of intermediate levels of intervention including individual and group counseling sessions;

3. *Therapeutic Communities (TCs)*, offered to inmates identified as needing intensive (approximately one year), residential substance abuse intervention; and

4. *Ancillary Groups*, such as self-help, peer counseling, and relapse prevention, offered to inmates as a supplement to other treatment, or when slots are not available in the more intensive treatment modalities.

TC drug treatment programs are of particular interest (DeLeon, 2000; Inciardi, 1995; Inciardi et al., 1997; Lipton, 1995; Lipton et al., 1992; ONDCP, 1996, 1999). The aim of the TC is total life-style change, including abstinence from drugs, elimination of antisocial behavior, and development of prosocial attitudes and values. Individual and group counseling, encounter groups, peer pressure, role models, and a system of incentives and sanctions form the core of these programs. Inmate residents of the TC live together, participate in self-help groups, and take responsibility for their own recovery. All TCs have a highly defined structure and daily activities to reinforce the mission of the TC (Welsh, 2000a, 2000b).

SURVEY OF DRUG AND ALCOHOL PROGRAMS IN PENNSYLVANIA PRISONS

This was a survey of AOD programming. Surveys collected three types of descriptive information: program content—e.g., what type, duration; program staff—e.g., duties, staffing ratios; and inmates—e.g., eligibility, intake procedures. We also conducted on-site process evaluations—e.g., structured observations, inmate and staff interviews, and review of case files and program documents—at two institutions. We examined similarities and variations in programming, and discussed the implications of results for program planning and evaluation. Prior to implementing a formal outcome evaluation research design (i.e., collecting outcome data for program participants and comparison groups), researchers sought programs with clearly specified treatment activities, well-articulated, measurable objectives, and useful information systems (e.g., inmate intake and monitoring data) (Welsh & Harris, 1999).

Survey respondents were DOC staff responsible for directing AOD programs at each state institution. One survey was completed for each program. We received 118 completed surveys from 24 institutions. Programs included 44 Education programs, 58 Outpatient Treatment programs, 10 Drug Abuse Treatment Units (DATUs), living units that generally house inmates participating in various AOD education and outpatient programs, and six TCs. Surveys collected three types of descriptive information: (1) program content and structure (e.g., type, duration), (2) target population (e.g., eligibility, intake procedures), and (3) program staff (e.g., duties, responsibilities).

Survey Findings

Our survey brought out five major points about AOD program structure, content, and target populations:

Point #1: Considerable Variation in Program Duration and Intensity. Except for TCs, there was considerable variation in program duration and intensity (Figures 39.1 and 39.2). TCs last longer (mean=46 weeks) and provide more total hours of programming per week (mean=29.5) than other AOD program types. DATUs last from eight to 52 weeks (mean=22 weeks), and provide anywhere from two to 20 hours of programming per week (mean=8 hr/wk). Outpatient Programs last from four to 36 weeks (mean=13 weeks), and provide anywhere from one to 28 hours of programming per week (mean=3 hr/wk). AOD Education Programs last from four to 32 weeks (mean=12 weeks), and provide anywhere from one to 14 hours of programming per week (mean=3 hr/wk).

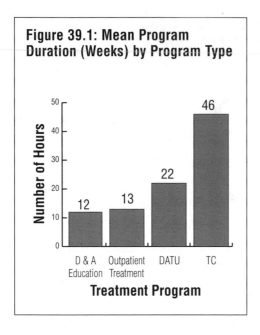

Figure 39.1: Mean Program Duration (Weeks) by Program Type

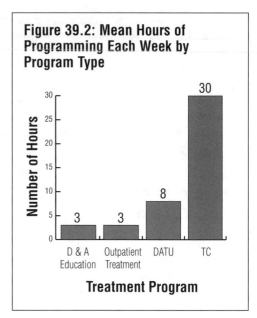

Figure 39.2: Mean Hours of Programming Each Week by Program Type

Point #2: Consistency in Treatment Approach. Programs displayed greater consistency in treatment approach. Across all program types, reality therapy (44%), cognitive therapy (49%), and cognitive-behavioral therapy (53%) were the techniques most frequently reported as a "primary approach." Less likely to be used as primary approaches were rational emotive therapy (38%), behavior modification (20%), milieu therapy (16%), psychotherapy (13%), dual diagnosis (9%), or transactional analysis (1%). (TCs were more likely to report psychotherapy (50%) and milieu therapy (50%) as a "primary approach.")

Point #3: Consistency in Program Topic Coverage. Some specific types of program content were used very consistently across the four program types. One survey question asked about specific types of program content covered in the different AOD programs. This is a particularly important question, given a current AOD program standardization initiative within the DOC. When we combined responses by those programs reporting that they spent "a great deal" or a "moderate" amount of time on each topic, program content was generally consistent (see Table 39.1), with a few exceptions.

Point #4: Great Variation in Program Types. However, the use of several specific types of program content varied enormously across programs. One example illustrates this variability. Twenty-seven percent of Education programs spent a great deal of time on problem solving skills; 36% spent a moderate amount of time; 34% spent very little time; and 2% of programs spent no time at all on this topic. Similar variability was found for Outpatient programs.

Point #5: Great Variation in Administrative Criteria. Use of different admission criteria varied considerably across programs. For example, level of drug involvement was

Table 39.1: Percentage of Programs Reporting They Spend "a Great Deal" or "Moderate" Amount of Time on Each Topic

Impacts of Drug Use	96%	Social/Communication Skills	79%
Thinking Errors	95%	Lifeskills	78%
Obstacles to Treatment	90%	Self Esteem	78%
Antisocial Peer Associations	89%	Anger/Temper Control	75%
Family Issues	89%	Focus on Harm Done to Victim	73%
Criminality/Antisocial Attitudes	88%	Stress Management	71%
Relapse Prevention	86%	Models of Addiction	66%
Working Steps Toward Recovery	85%	Job Issues	65%
Problem Solving Skills	84%	Assertiveness Training	65%
Addiction and Spirituality	83%	Pharmacology	52%
Interpersonal Relationships	82%	AIDS/Infectious Diseases	38%

rated as a "very important" admission criterion for all TCs (100%); but only 63% of Education programs, 54% of Outpatient programs, and 50% of DATUs. Level of motivation was rated as "very important" in 83% of TC programs, but only in 23% of Education programs, 44% of Outpatient programs, and 30% of DATUs.

Research by Andrews et. al. (1990) and Gendreau (1996) suggests that screening and assessment of inmate needs is crucial for adequate program placement (i.e., matching inmate needs to appropriate treatment). It is important to ask exactly who is the target population: how are eligible targets actually recruited, selected, and admitted (Welsh & Harris, 1999)? Prior to designing outcome evaluations (e.g., forming valid comparison groups), it is necessary to determine the degree to which the targets intended for specific programs are the ones actually being treated. Otherwise, potential selection bias may subvert evaluation efforts.

Practical Implications of Findings

Program Variability Inhibits Effective Management. Three major recommendations emerged from these findings. First, there was considerable variation in AOD program structure, content, and target populations (e.g., inmate eligibility, assessment, and placement procedures). Such variation inhibits effective program monitoring, management, and evaluation. Although DOC has been quite proactive in identifying and addressing program variability, such variation is not at all unique to Pennsylvania (e.g., Inciardi et al., 1992; ONDCP, 1999). Specific strategies to address program variability are described later.

We Need to Know More About Process Effect on Outcome. Second, we need current, reliable, basic information about AOD Programs to better understand how program process (e.g., program duration, treatment approach) influences outcome.

Otherwise, AOD programming is a "black box" that defies easy description (Hiller et al., 1999; Inciardi et al., 1992). In order to demonstrate that any specific program (X) changes specific inmates (Y) to produce specific outcomes (Z), we must be able to specify what "X" and "Y" were in the first place (Welsh, 1998).

Better Tracking Required. Finally, inmate exposure to different levels and types of treatment should be better recorded and factored into evaluation studies. Evaluation capacity would be enhanced by the development of computerized, offender-based treatment databases (see U.S. Department of Justice, 1998). At a minimum, such a database would include an inmate's name and number; date of each AOD program admission and discharge; name, location, and type of program; and reason for discharge (e.g., successful vs. unsuccessful).

OUTCOME EVALUATION OF PENNSYLVANIA'S PRISON-BASED DRUG TREATMENT

Based upon the foundation provided by the research partnership and the demonstration research project, NIJ funded a second grant evaluating drug treatment outcomes. The purpose of this 18-month study was to evaluate TCs at five different institutions. A quasi-experimental design with matched comparison groups was used. The experimental group consisted of all inmates entering TC programs at five institutions. Comparison groups were formed from similar inmates participating in much lower-intensity AOD programs (AOD Education and Outpatient) at the same institutions, using a matching design to control for differences in drug involvement (i.e., assessed AOD need) and overall risk (e.g., current offense and criminal history).

All inmates entering TC, education, or outpatient treatment programs between January 1, 2000, and November 30, 2000, were approached and asked to participate in the study. Those who agreed to participate signed a Subject Consent Form and completed the TCU Drug Screen (Simpson, 1994; Simpson & Knight, 1998). TC inmates were also asked to complete the TCU Resident Evaluation of Self and Treatment (REST) form, and TC staff were asked to complete the TCU Counselor Rating of Client (CRC) form for each current TC inmate. We examined in-treatment measures and multiple post-release outcomes for 2,809 inmates who participated in TC drug treatment programs (n = 749) or comparison groups (n = 2,060) at five state prisons. Matched comparison groups made up of TC-eligible inmates participating in less intensive forms of treatment (e.g., short-term drug education and outpatient treatment groups) at the same five institutions were constructed based upon known predictors such as drug dependency, need for treatment and criminal history. Process and outcome measures incorporated a range of institutional, intermediate (e.g., attitudinal and behavioral change, participation in treatment) and post-release measures (e.g., drug relapse, rearrest and reincarceration, employment, levels of parole supervision). Follow-up data are currently being collected on this sample (Welsh, 2002).

This project has gradually led to development of a comprehensive data set describing prison-based drug and alcohol programming, inmate characteristics (e.g., motivation for treatment, psychological functioning), and responses to treatment. Because we closely track admissions and discharges from each program, we are able to control for important process variables potentially related to outcome, including level of exposure to drug treatment (e.g., one month vs. one year) and whether or not an inmate successfully *graduates* from a specific program. We are also able to control for differences in program structure and content (e.g., number of hours, primary treatment approach, etc.). This rich database will allow researchers to closely examine relationships between program process, inmate characteristics, and treatment outcomes.

TRANSLATING RESEARCH TO PRACTICE

The Department as a Learning Organization

These research findings have already had an impact on the Pennsylvania DOC's management of treatment programs. The DOC Steering Committee established to oversee this project is committed to using the evaluation findings to inform the design and refinement of drug and alcohol treatment programs throughout the department. The context in which this evaluation has taken place is that of *organizational learning*, where the department, in cooperation with the researchers, actively and openly seeks out information about the operations of its programs. This information feeds inquiry and analysis of the strengths, weaknesses, and overall effectiveness of these programs. This inquiry and analysis informs plans to address program deficits and build upon program successes. Evaluation of these changes will continue, producing an ongoing cycle of organizational inquiry, learning, and change. The ultimate utility of the evaluation exercise will itself be evaluated by the extent to which it has empowered the department to become its own agent of positive change (Zajac & Comfort, 1997).

Research has taken place within an atmosphere of participation and ownership. The Steering Committee includes stakeholders directly involved in providing and managing drug treatment services to inmates, most critically drug treatment staff from the field. Extensive efforts have been made to communicate evaluation findings widely throughout the department, and to solicit feedback from interested parties. All evaluation activities have been reviewed and approved by the committee, with all members invited to critique research plans. During the data collection phase at the institutions, the committee and the researchers on-site have attended to the concerns of field staff. To the extent possible, evaluation activities have been integrated into the daily operations of treatment programs. The goal is to have evaluation seen not as something foreign, arcane, or threatening, but rather as an open and participatory process.

Toward this end, the Partnership Steering Committee organized and hosted a one-day symposium in May 1999 that was attended by 48 Drug & Alcohol Treatment Specialists (DATS) nominated by Superintendents of the 24 state correctional institutions (two from each institution). Three primary goals included presenting survey results regarding similarities and differences in AOD programming across institutions, discussing implications of results for AOD programming, and discussing future plans for evaluation. Treatment staff raised four key concerns in small group sessions: (1) a perceived need for more diverse programming that matches the needs of a diverse population of inmates, (2) the dilemma of balancing program quality against institutional demands to provide many programs for large numbers of inmates, (3) high inmate-to-staff ratios, and (4) institutional and departmental policies that impact curriculum selection, counseling techniques, and record keeping. Further discussion is provided elsewhere (Welsh, 2000a).

The partnership and evaluation has enhanced the capacity of the department to identify evaluation needs and to develop plans for meeting those needs. The partnership has served as a model for subsequent collaborations with other researchers to evaluate parenting, educational/vocational, and other treatment programs. The DOC has been able to undertake these projects in cooperation with outside experts and utilizing third-party funding, while maintaining control over the direction and utilization of the research. Thus, the capacity of the department to initiate and manage evaluation activities has been enhanced.

Evaluation Recommendations Implemented or Under Current Review

This partnership produced a comprehensive database of DOC AOD treatment programs, and informed the design of a rigorous outcome evaluation that is currently underway. Perhaps more important, the department made some changes to its drug treatment programs as a result of the evaluation findings.

New Screening Tools. First, DOC reviewed its tools for screening and assessing inmates' substance abuse problems and needs, as well as its procedures for placing inmates into programs. The process evaluation pointed out the importance of placing the right inmates into the right program(s) for the right reasons, and recommended a more structured approach to assessment. DOC has reviewed the drug and alcohol screening instrument (the PACSI) that was developed and validated in-house and used within the department during the 1990s, concluding that the Drug Screen produced by Texas Christian University (TCU), which was used in the evaluation, would better suit DOC needs. The department replaced the PACSI with the TCU Drug Screen in January of 2001. Other TCU instruments have also been adopted, and a more comprehensive review of assessment options is presently under way. The objective is to ensure that inmates enter programs that best meet their needs, level of risk, and readiness for change.

Program Standardization. Second, this project contributed to an overall program standardization effort that has been underway in the department for the past several years. The finding of great variation and fragmentation in the implementation and operation of drug treatment programs reinforces the need for standardized procedures for providing all types of treatment to inmates across all institutions. Standardization will promote consistent delivery of services and will facilitate the development of a true "treatment system" within the department. The committee overseeing the standardization effort has reviewed the process evaluation report and has utilized its conclusions and recommendations in its own planning efforts.

Improved Documentation. Third, the evaluation activity so far has identified gaps in automated treatment information available to the department. While participation and progress in treatment programs is documented in individual inmate files, there is no comprehensive, centralized treatment database for the department. This has hampered evaluation efforts. The department is presently working with a contractor to build a treatment database into an existing inmate management information system.

Future Projects. Finally, researchers presented recommendations regarding other issues, such as space resources available to drug treatment programs, staffing patterns, aftercare options, and procedures for managing inmate interactions within the TCs. The department is reviewing these recommendations and attempting to use this information to inform our future program plans. For example, recommendations regarding aftercare for inmates completing treatment programs are under review, and new program offerings are being developed.

CONCLUSION

Careful description of prison-based drug and alcohol treatment is an essential precursor to valid program evaluation. Through program surveys and process evaluations, we have focused on providing detailed descriptive assessments of treatment programming, assessing strengths and weaknesses, and making recommendations for program planning, implementation, and evaluation. It is unlikely that the strengths and weaknesses in prison-based drug and alcohol programming reported here are unique to Pennsylvania. Process evaluations of prison-based drug and alcohol treatment in other states have reported numerous implementation problems including inadequate numbers of trained and experienced counseling staff and lack of standardized screening, assessment, and selection processes (e.g., Inciardi, Martin, Lockwood, Hooper & Wald, 1992; Martin, Butzin & Inciardi, 1995). Few studies have attempted the scope and detail described here, however, and we hope that that other states and localities may learn from the research methods, data, and conclusions presented here. Until critical variations in different types of programs are better accounted for, the true impact, generalizability, and potential of prison-based drug treatment will remain largely unknown.

About the Authors

Wayne N. Welsh, Ph.D., is Associate Professor, Department of Criminal Justice, Temple University, Philadelphia, PA. Gary Zajac, Ph.D., is Research and Evaluation Manager, Pennsylvania Department of Corrections, Camp Hill, PA.

The research reported here was supported by Grant # 98-CE-VX-0016 from the U.S. Department of Justice, National Institute of Justice (NIJ). Opinions expressed here are those of the authors and not necessarily of the U.S. Department of Justice. Any errors or omissions, of course, are the responsibility of the authors alone. We wish to acknowledge the valuable contributions of Graduate Research Associates Kelley Klick, Joseph Michaels, Patrick McGrain, and Judith Rushall. We also express gratitude to all Department of Corrections personnel on our Steering Committee.

References

Andrews, D., Zinger, I., Hoge, R.D., Bonta, J., Gendreau, P., & Cullen, F.T. (1990). Does correctional treatment work? A clinically relevant and psychologically informed meta-analysis. *Criminology, 28,* 369-404.

Beck, A. J., & Karberg, J.C. (2001, March). *Prison and jail inmates at midyear 2000.* Bureau of Justice Statistics Bulletin (NCJ-185989). Washington, DC: U.S. Department of Justice, Office of Justice Programs.

De Leon, G. (2000). *The therapeutic community: Theory, model and method.* New York: Springer-Verlag.

Gendreau, P. (1996). The principles of effective intervention with offenders. In A. T. Harland (Ed.), *Choosing cor-*

rectional options that work: Defining the demand and evaluating the supply. Thousand Oaks, CA: Sage.

Hiller, M.L., Knight, K., & Simpson, D.D. (1999). Risk factors that predict dropout from corrections-based treatment for drug abuse. *The Prison Journal, 79,* 411-430.

Inciardi, J.A. (1995). The therapeutic community: An effective model for corrections-based drug abuse treatment. In K.C. Haas & G.P. Alpert (Eds.), *The dilemmas of punishment* (pp. 406-417). Prospect Heights, IL: Waveland Press.

Inciardi, J. A., Martin, S.S., Butzin, C.A., Hooper, R., & Harrison, L.D. (1997). An effective model of prison-based treatment for drug-involved offenders. *Journal of Drug Issues, 27,* 261-278.

Inciardi, J. A., Martin, S.S., Lockwood, D., Hooper, R.M., & Wald, B.M. (1992). Obstacles to the implementation and evaluation of drug treatment programs in correctional settings: Reviewing the Delaware KEY experience. In C.G. Leukefeld & F.M. Tims (Eds.), *Drug abuse treatment in prisons and jails* (pp. 176-191). Washington, DC: U.S. GPO.

Knight, K., Simpson, D., & Hiller, M. (1999). Three-year reincarceration outcomes in-prison therapeutic community treatment in Texas. *The Prison Journal, 79,* 321-33.

Lipton, D.S. (1995). *The effectiveness of treatment for drug abusers under criminal justice supervision* (NCJ 157642). Washington, DC: U.S. Department of Justice, Office of Justice Programs, National Institute of Justice.

Lipton, D.S., & Pearson, F.S. (1998, November 10). The effectiveness of correctional treatment revisited: Preliminary meta-analytic findings from the CDATE Study. Paper presented at the Physician Leadership on National Drug Policy (PLNDP) Meeting, Washington, DC.

Lipton, D.S., Falkin, G.P., & Wexler, H.K. (1992). Correctional drug abuse treatment in the United States: An overview. In C.G. Leukefeld & F.M. Tims (Eds.), *Drug abuse treatment in prisons and jails* (pp. 8-30). NIDA Monograph No. 118. HHS. Rockville, MD: USGPO.

Martin, S., Butzin, C., Saum, C., & Inciardi, J. (1999). Three-year outcomes of therapeutic community treatment for drug-involved offenders in Delaware: From prison to work release to aftercare. *The Prison Journal, 79,* 294-320.

Martin, S.S., Butzin, C.A., & Inciardi, J. (1995). Assessment of a multistage therapeutic community for drug-involved offenders. *Journal of Psychoactive Drugs, 27,* 109-116.

Mumola, C. J. (1999, January). *Substance abuse and treatment, state and federal prisoners, 1997.* Bureau of Justice Statistics Special Report (NCJ-172871). Washington, DC: U.S. Department of Justice, Office of Justice Programs.

National Institute on Drug Abuse (NIDA). (1981). *Drug abuse treatment in prisons.* Treatment Research Report Series. Washington, DC: National Institute on Drug Abuse, U.S. GPO.

National Institute on Drug Abuse (NIDA). (1999). *Principles of drug addiction treatment: A research-based guide.* (NIH-99-4180). Washington, DC: National Institute of Health, National Institute on Drug Abuse.

Office of National Drug Control Policy (ONDCP). (1999). *Therapeutic communities in correctional settings: The prison based TC standards development project. Final report of Phase II.* (NCJ-179365). Washington, DC: Executive Office of the President, Office of National Drug Control Policy.

Office of National Drug Control Policy (ONDCP). (1996). *Treatment protocol effectiveness study.* Washington, DC: Executive Office of the President, Office of National Drug Control Policy.

Pearson, F.S., & Lipton, D.S. (1999). A meta-analytic review of the effectiveness of corrections-based treatments for drug abuse. *The Prison Journal, 79,* 384-410.

Pennsylvania Department of Corrections. (2001, February). *Philosophy and framework: Alcohol and other drug treatment.* Camp Hill, PA: Pennsylvania Department of Corrections, Bureau of Inmate Services.

Peters, R.H., Greenbaum, P.E., &. Edens, J.F. (1998). Prevalence of DSM-IV substance abuse and dependence disorders among prison inmates. *American Journal of Drug and Alcohol Abuse, 24,* 573-587.

Simpson, D. D. (1994). *TCU/PTA forms manual: Texas prison-based treatment assessment (PTA Project).* Fort Worth: Texas Christian University, Institute of Behavioral Research.

Simpson, D.D., & Knight, K. (1998). *TCU data collection forms for correctional residential treatment.* Fort Worth: Texas Christian University, Institute of Behavioral Research. Available online at *www.ibr.tcu.edu.*

Substance Abuse and Mental Health Services Administration (SAMHSA). (2000). *Substance abuse treatment in adult and juvenile correctional facilities: Findings from the uniform facility data set, 1997 survey of correctional facilities.* Available online at http://www.samhsa.gov/OAS/UFDS/CorrectionalFacilities97/Correctional Facilities 97.pdf.

U.S. Department of Justice. (1998). *State and federal corrections information systems: An inventory of data elements and an assessment of reporting capabilities.* A joint project: Association of State Correctional Administrators; Corrections Program Office, Office of Justice Programs; Bureau of Justice Statistics; and National Institute of Justice (NCJ 171686). Washington, DC: U.S. Department of Justice, Office of Justice Programs, Bureau of Justice Statistics.

Welsh, W.N. (1998, November). An X-Y-Z Model for understanding recidivism. Panel on Measuring Recidivism. Pennsylvania Commission on Crime and Delinquency, 1998 Criminal Justice Research Symposium, Harrisburg, PA.

Welsh, W.N. (2000a). *Building an effective research collaboration between the Pennsylvania Department of Corrections and the Center for Public Policy at Temple University. Volume 1: Development of the research partnership and results from a survey of drug and alcohol programs.* Final Report to the National Institute of Justice (Grant #98-CE-VX-0016). Philadelphia: Center for Public Policy, Temple University.

Welsh, W.N. (2000b). *Building an effective research collaboration between the Pennsylvania Department of Corrections and the Center for Public Policy at Temple University. Volume 2: Evaluability assessment and process evaluation of prison-based drug and alcohol programs: Findings and recommendations.* Final Report to the National Institute of Justice (Grant #98-CE-VX-0016). Philadelphia: Center for Public Policy, Temple University.

Welsh, W.N. (2002). *Evaluation of prison based drug treatment in Pennsylvania: A research collaboration between the Pennsylvania Department of Corrections and the Center for Public Policy at Temple University.* Final Report to the National Institute of Justice, Grant #99-CE-VX-0009. Philadelphia: Temple University, Center for Public Policy.

Welsh, W.N., & Harris, P.W. (1999). *Criminal justice policy and planning.* Cincinnati, OH: Anderson Publishing Co.

Wexler, H., Melnick, G., Lowe, L., & Peters, J. (1999). Three-year reincarceration outcomes for Amity in-prison therapeutic community and aftercare in California. *The Prison Journal, 79,* 321-33.

Zajac, G., & Comfort, L.K. (1997). The spirit of watchfulness: Public ethics as organizational learning. *Journal of Public Administration Research and Theory, 7(4),* 541-570.

Chapter 40

Strong Science for Strong Practice: Linking Research to Correctional Drug Treatment

by Laura Winterfield, Ph.D., Dan Mears, Ph.D., and Gretchen Moore, M.S.

Introduction 40-2
Some Principles of Effective Prison-Based Drug Treatment 40-2
Strategies to Encourage Science-Based Drug Treatment in Prisons 40-4
    Create Manual of Correctional Drug Treatment Principles 40-5
    Educate the Public, Policymakers, Legislators, and Prison Officials . . . 40-5
    Promote Boundary-Spanning Efforts to Provide Drug
        Treatment in the Criminal Justice System 40-5
    Isolate a Range of Proven, Available, Feasible In-Prison
        Treatment Options 40-6
Research Gaps on Drug Treatment in Corrections 40-6
    Determine Nature and Extent of Current Drug
        Treatment Need and Practice 40-6
    Develop Validated Screening and Assessment Instruments
        for Various Decision Points 40-6
    Determine the Balance of Incentives and Sanctions Available 40-7
    Better Understand Role of Motivation and Coercion in Treatment 40-7
    Examine Treatment Delivery in Context of
        Different Stages of a Prison Term 40-7
    Examine How Effectiveness of Drug Treatment
        Might Be Affected Based on Prison Security Levels 40-7
    Explore How Transitioning Into and Out of Prison Influences
        Effectiveness of Treatment 40-8
    Assess Cost-Effectiveness 40-8

This chapter originally appeared in Offender Substance Abuse Report, *Vol. 3, No. 2, March/April 2003.*

Learn What Factors Determine Available Treatments—
    and Which Are Appropriate 40-8
Learn How Correctional Staff and Systems-Level
    Factors Impact Treatment 40-8
Conclusion 40-9

INTRODUCTION

In response to concerns about the lack of science-based drug treatment in correctional settings, the National Institute on Drug Abuse (NIDA) asked the Urban Institute to undertake a project, *Strong Science for Strong Practice*, in order to identify activities NIDA might undertake to address the unique challenges posed when integrating treatment services with a public health orientation into correctional environments.

To help achieve this goal, the project included several tasks: (1) performing a literature review of what is and is not known about corrections-based drug treatment along six dimensions—prevalence of drug abuse needs, screening and assessment, treatment programs and approaches, treatment effectiveness, linkages with post-release supervision, and barriers to implementation of drug treatment; (2) conducting interviews with practitioners—e.g., directors of state correctional agencies or programming divisions—to determine their perceptions of barriers to using research-based knowledge concerning drug treatment; and (3) hosting a meeting of researchers and practitioners to discuss issues raised by the literature review and interviews. This chapter sets out what was learned, highlighting principles of effective drug treatment in correctional settings, strategies for increasing science-based correctional drug treatment practices, and potential research gaps. These principles, strategies, and research gaps are summarized in Table 40.1.

SOME PRINCIPLES OF EFFECTIVE PRISON-BASED DRUG TREATMENT

We identified a range of broad-based principles of effective prison-based drug treatment, set out below, drawing from our literature review and interviews. These principles are statements about how drug treatment in correctional settings should be designed and implemented if it is to be effective; they are supported by both existing research and the experiences and insights of researchers and practitioners who have had long-standing involvement with studying or implementing drug treatment in correctional settings:

- *Provide treatment.* A passive approach to drug treatment—i.e., ignoring drug treatment needs—can undermine crime control approaches and is largely ineffective. A more effective approach to crime control, as well as to reducing drug abuse, addiction, and related problems, is to employ a range of drug treatment interventions.

- *Distinguish between screening and assessment.* Screening and assessment serve different purposes—e.g., identifying potential drug treatment needs, confirming these needs, developing a complete inventory of needs, identifying

Table 40.1: Summary of Key Recommendations

Some Principles of Effective Prison-Based Drug Treatment

- Provide treatment—the failure to provide treatment is ineffective.
- Distinguish between screening and assessment.
- Assess prisoner needs and tailor treatment to need and level of risk.
- Ensure that services are available for assessed needs.
- Address each inmate's diverse and co-occurring needs.
- Implement drug treatment interventions and strategies that address the unique needs of different populations.
- Ensure that drug treatment is of sufficient duration.
- Develop sustained, broad-based support throughout prisons for drug treatment.
- Link aftercare services in community-based drug treatment to prison-based drug treatment.
- Employ a comprehensive and integrated approach to drug treatment.

Strategies to Encourage Science-Based Drug Treatment in Prisons

- Create a manual of correctional drug treatment principles.
- Educate the public, policymakers, and prison officials that drug treatment
  - can be an effective crime control measure, and
  - can be a cost-effective approach to maintaining prison control and reducing drug use.
- Encourage prison systems to view drug treatment as part of a comprehensive approach to prison control and reductions in recidivism.
- Disseminate information about drug treatment interventions and effectiveness through diverse media.
- Identify specific strategies for promoting boundary-spanning efforts to provide drug treatment in prisons.
- Identify a range of proven, available, and feasible treatment options.

Research Gaps on Drug Treatment in the Adult Prison System

- Define more precisely and consistently what is meant by "drug treatment need" and practice.
- Develop validated screening and assessment instruments for various decision points within prisons and throughout the criminal justice system.
- Determine the balance of incentives and sanctions that are needed to be most effective with prison inmates and that are available in prison settings.
- Understand the role of motivation and coercion in treatment better.
- Identify effective treatments for different stages of a prison term.
- Examine how the effectiveness of drug treatment varies depending on the security levels of prisons.
- Explore how the transition into prisons and the reentry process into society influence the effectiveness of drug treatment.
- Assess the cost-effectiveness of different drug treatment interventions.
- Conduct research on drug treatment within prison systems, not just specific drug treatment interventions
- Conduct research on the relevance of general treatment principles to drug treatment in correctional settings
- Evaluate how treatment orientations or philosophies in prisons affect drug treatment implementation.
- Conduct systems-level research on correctional drug treatment, not just on the effectiveness of specific drug treatment interventions.
- Examine boundary-spanning and its impact on drug treatment in prisons.

appropriate treatment modalities. For either function to be effectively performed, the purposes must be clearly identified, and appropriate instruments developed and administered.

- *Assess prisoner risk and need; tailor treatment appropriately.* Prisoner risk and needs should be identified and then matched with appropriate services. Treatment effectiveness increases when an intervention addresses an inmate's level of treatment need and risk.

- *Ensure services are available for assessed needs.* For assessments to be viewed as valuable and for staff to be motivated to ensure that assessments are well done, there must be a complete range of services available for prisoners with specific needs.

- *Address each inmate's diverse and co-occurring needs.* Drug treatment tends to be more effective with prisoners when co-occurring needs—e.g., psychological, medical, and social—are also addressed.

- *Address unique needs of different prison groups.* Different prisoner populations—including specific racial/ethnic, age, and gender groups—may have unique needs that must be addressed for drug treatment to be effective. Implement drug treatment interventions and strategies that target these needs.

- *Ensure treatment is of sufficient duration.* Drug treatment is more likely to be effective when it is implemented for a sufficient period of time, generally six months or more, but the duration may vary according to the extent of need and the type of treatment.

- *Develop sustained, broad-based support throughout prisons for drug treatment.* The best-designed instruments and programs will produce minimal results if they are poorly implemented. To be effective, any drug treatment-related activity must have the ongoing support of prison officials, staff, and providers.

- *Provide aftercare.* Link aftercare services in community-based drug treatment to prison-based drug treatment. Drug treatment in a prison-based setting is much more likely to result in a sustained decline in drug use if it is linked to drug-treatment after release from prison.

- *Use a comprehensive, integrated approach.* Drug treatment is most likely to be effective when it is comprehensive and systematically integrated across all stages of the criminal justice system, such as pretrial, sentencing, and incarceration (Mercer & Woody, 1999; see also Gaes et al., 1999; Cullen & Gendreau, 2000). Additionally, an offender's particular risk and needs should be re-evaluated so that changes in treatment delivery are made at each stage as necessary.

STRATEGIES TO ENCOURAGE SCIENCE-BASED DRUG TREATMENT IN PRISONS

We recommend that federal agencies such as NIDA consider strategies like those set out below, in concert with corrections or other state partners, to increase and improve appropriate, science-based correctional treatment of offenders with drug problems.

Create Manual of Correctional Drug Treatment Principles

Create a manual outlining principles of effective drug treatment in correctional settings, including (1) well-established findings about drug treatment in the criminal justice system and (2) how drug treatment should be implemented to achieve the best results. This manual should be similar to NIDA's (1999) earlier publication, *Principles of Drug Addiction and Treatment: A Research-Based Guide,* containing principles tailored to the context of correctional settings. For example, this manual could discuss how repeated screening and assessment might be operationalized within an institutional system, or address the role of medication, typically frowned upon in corrections.

Educate the Public, Policymakers, Legislators, and Prison Officials

Key stakeholders need to know that drug treatment can be not only an effective crime control measure but also a cost-effective approach to improving and maintaining prison control and reducing drug use. In general, political and correctional support is easier to obtain for crime control objectives than for treatment objectives. For this reason, the crime control aspects of effective drug treatment should be emphasized.

In addition to reducing recidivism, drug treatment can be cost-effective in reducing prison control problems and drug use. Educating the public, policymakers, and prison officials about these potential benefits may result in increased support for prison-based drug treatment services and programs.

To make sure your message gets out, use diverse media to raise awareness among the public, policy-makers, and practitioners about leading developments and progress in the area of corrections-based drug treatment. All information should use consistent definitions of key terms (e.g., "risk," "dependency") and use language accessible to practitioners. Use reports, brief fact sheets or research summaries, videos, and televised conferences that present information about drug treatment in a manner accessible to diverse sets of practitioners. Examples of these types of approaches include the publications produced by the Institute of Behavioral Research at Texas Christian University (2000; 2001) and the Schneider Institute for Health Policy (2001). In our project, practitioners expressed considerable interest in "one-stop shop" sources of information, such as the two special issues of *The Prison Journal* (1999) on drug treatment outcomes in correctional settings. An additional strategy could be to present scientific findings at annual or semiannual meetings of legislators, practitioners, and policymakers.

Promote Boundary-Spanning Efforts to Provide Drug Treatment in the Criminal Justice System

Provide criminal justice officials with concrete, science-based advice concerning ways they can develop collaborative, boundary-spanning initiatives with social service, welfare, and community-based agencies to increase and improve drug treatment services for prisoners and offenders throughout the criminal justice system.

Isolate a Range of Proven, Available, Feasible In-Prison Treatment Options

Organize existing research in an easily accessible manner so that prison officials can determine what evidence-based treatment interventions or strategies are most appropriate to their prison system. As more research is conducted on drug treatment effectiveness in correctional settings, modifications to the list of options should be made accordingly.

RESEARCH GAPS ON DRUG TREATMENT IN CORRECTIONS

Although implementing the principles and strategies discussed above would provide a link between research and correctional drug treatment, important areas for further research remain. In this section, we present some of the most salient research gaps— gaps representing areas in which research is needed in order to improve the effectiveness and the implementation of drug treatment interventions and strategies in correctional settings. In each instance, we focus on gaps that are policy relevant and that may be feasible.

Determine Nature and Extent of Current Drug Treatment Need and Practice

Currently, relatively little consistent or accurate information exists concerning the state of prison-based drug treatment need or practice, including drug treatment-related activities such as screening, assessment, and reentry planning. Basic descriptive research is required about the extent of need and state of practice, with both being consistently defined.

Develop Validated Screening and Assessment Instruments for Various Decision Points

This is needed both within prisons and throughout the criminal justice system. There is a need for simple, short, and accurate screening and assessment instruments that have been empirically validated. These instruments should serve clear and distinct purposes:

- *Screening instruments* should allow for the accurate identification of prisoners with potential drug treatment needs.

- *Assessment instruments* should allow for accurate identification of the full range of prisoner needs and the most appropriate type and level of treatment, while taking into account security considerations.

All instruments developed need to be empirically validated. Screening instruments should generate results that are moderately correlated with those of other standard screening instruments, while assessment instruments should be predictive of particular outcomes (e.g., drug treatment need, mental or physical disorder, aggressive behavior, recidivism). It is important that these assessment instruments be validated for decisions being made at specific points throughout the criminal justice system because the goals of assessment may vary at each decision point—for example, the in-out decision contemplated at pretrial or pre-sentencing hearings is different from the security classification and treatment assignment decision that occurs in prison.

Determine the Balance of Incentives and Sanctions Available

What incentives and sanctions are available in prison settings that would be effective with substance-abusing prisoners? Research should consider the unique set of incentives and sanctions available in a prison setting to identify the balance necessary to achieve the largest and most sustained reductions in drug use and criminal behavior among prison inmates. This research should also consider how these could best be applied on a case-by-case basis.

Better Understand Role of Motivation and Coercion in Treatment

Although research suggests that coerced drug treatment can be effective, motivation, including readiness for change, is nonetheless important. Many researchers and practitioners believe motivation is one of the most critical issues to ensuring successful participation in and long-term benefits from prison-based drug treatment (Reuter, 2001). It can, for example, play a significant role in whether a prisoner stays in treatment and how treatment is both perceived and experienced. To date, however, relatively little research addresses this issue specifically within correctional settings, and there needs to be an examination of how motivation interacts with coerced treatment. Additionally, more research is needed on the types of coercion that work and how perceptions of coercion play a role in reducing or increasing treatment effectiveness.

Examine Treatment Delivery in Context of Different Stages of a Prison Term

Research is needed on the degree to which sequencing different kinds of treatment in relationship to incarceration length might enhance treatment effectiveness. That is, what kinds of treatment work best for prisoners at the beginning of incarceration as opposed to those nearing the end; at what specific times during incarceration is treatment most effective (e.g., throughout incarceration, at the beginning of a term of incarceration, or just prior to release); and what combinations of treatment work best to reduce drug use and crime?

Examine How Effectiveness of Drug Treatment Might Be Affected Based on Prison Security Levels

Relatively little is known about whether, how, or why drug treatment interventions vary in their effectiveness across minimum, medium, maximum, and super-maximum security prisons. For example, does the security level of prisons affect specific treatment modalities, and, if so, what is the impact on treatment effectiveness?

Explore How Transitioning Into and Out of Prison Influences Effectiveness of Treatment

Each transition—both into prison and then the reentry process into society—presents a range of challenges, any one of which might reduce treatment effectiveness and requires targeted programming as well as collaborative efforts (e.g., within the criminal justice system and between the justice system and social service and community agencies).

Assess Cost-Effectiveness

Because prisons operate with limited budgets, they require information about the most cost-effective approaches to increasing prison control and reducing longer-term drug use and crime. Few studies of the cost-effectiveness of different drug treatment interventions exist, however. In addition, research is needed on identifying the levels of drug treatment funding or programming in prisons that is most cost-effective for achieving these diverse goals.

Learn What Factors Determine Available Treatments—and Which Are Appropriate

We need to conduct research on the factors, both internal and external to corrections, which determine the menu of treatment options available to offenders. Research also should focus on identifying factors that drive decision-making about levels and types of drug treatment programming that were provided in correctional settings.

We also need research on the relevance of general treatment principles to drug treatment in correctional settings. Considerable research attests to the importance of many principles of effective treatment, but the value and appropriateness of many of these principles have not been systematically evaluated in the context of correctional environments (Gaes et al., 1999; see also Cullen & Gendreau, 2000).

Learn How Correctional Staff and Systems-Level Factors Impact Treatment

We need to evaluate how correctional staff attitudes about or philosophy toward drug treatment affect implementation. Diverse sources suggest that treatment orientations or philosophies of prison officials, staff, and providers can affect drug treatment delivery and, ultimately, effectiveness. How and to what extent does prison staff and the training received affect awareness about drug treatment needs? In addition, how does prison staff affect drug treatment implementation and, ultimately, treatment effectiveness? Research is needed on precisely how a supportive treatment orientation can be fostered and sustained, especially among corrections officers, as well as how this support affects treatment implementation and, ultimately, treatment effectiveness.

We also need to conduct systems-level research on correctional drug treatment, not just on the effectiveness of specific drug treatment interventions. Research is needed on system-level factors that may influence the quality and effectiveness of all drug treatment interventions, not just specific interventions. To date, most research has focused on specific interventions while largely ignoring the larger institutional context affecting all drug treatment interventions.

Last, we need to conduct research on how boundary-spanning across different systems—e.g., justice, social service, welfare—can enhance the levels and kinds of drug treatment services provided in prisons and throughout the criminal justice system.

CONCLUSION

The results of the Urban Institute's three-pronged project suggest one overarching lesson: There are many opportunities to advance both practice and research in correctional settings. Although much is known, much remains unknown. In the meantime, the need for drug treatment services of various kinds remains widespread throughout the criminal justice system, though the precise magnitude and nature of this need require greater clarification.

Many researchers and practitioners believe that there currently is a unique opportunity for a sustained and comprehensive research agenda on corrections-based drug treatment. They point to the exponential growth in the number of prisoners returning to society—numbers likely to grow as more states use early release to solve current and foreseeable budget shortfalls—and the accompanying drug treatment needs. They also point to the increasing interest among correctional administrators, legislators, and the public at large for reliance on evidence-based strategies to reduce crime and improve the lives of offenders and their victims, families, and the communities in which they reside. These observations support a general conclusion: There is a considerable demand for strong science that supports strong drug treatment practice in the criminal justice system.

About the Authors

Laura Winterfield, Ph.D., and Daniel Mears, Ph.D., are Senior Research Associates at the Urban Institute. Gretchen Moore, M.S., is a Research Associate. This project was funded by the National Institute of Health, National Institute on Drug Abuse, contract #N01DA-1-1104. The opinions expressed are the views of the authors, and do not necessarily reflect the views of the funding agency, or the Urban Institute, its Board of Trustees, or its sponsors.

References

Cullen, F.T., & Gendreau, P. (2000). Assessing correctional rehabilitation: Policy, practice, and prospects. In J. Horney (Ed.), *Criminal justice 2000: Policies, processes, and decisions of the criminal justice system*, vol. 3, (pp. 109–176). Washington, DC: National Institute of Justice.

Gaes, G.G., Flanagan, T.S., Motiuk, L.L., & Stewart, L. (1999). Adult correctional treatment. In M.H. Tonry & J. Petersilia (Eds.), *Prisons* (pp. 361–426). Chicago: University of Chicago Press.

Institute of Behavioral Research. (1999, December). *Research summary: Focus on drug treatment in correctional settings.* Fort Worth, TX: Author [Available online at: www.ibr.tcu.edu].

Institute of Behavioral Research. (2000, April). *Research summary: Focus on treatment processes and outcomes.* Fort Worth, TX: Author [Available online at: www.ibr.tcu.edu].

Institute of Behavioral Research. (2000–2001, Winter). *Research summary: Treatment outcome studies in criminal justice.* Fort Worth, TX: Author [Available online at: www.ibr.tcu.edu].

Mercer, D.E., & Woody, G.E. (1999). *Therapy manuals for drug addiction*. Manual 3. Washington, DC: National Institute on Drug Abuse.

National Institute on Drug Abuse. (1999). *Principles of drug addiction treatment: A research-based guide*. Washington, DC: Author.

Reuter, P. (2001). Why does research have so little impact on American drug policy? *Addiction, 96*, 373–376.

Schneider Institute for Health Policy. (2001). *Substance abuse: The nation's number one health problem*. Waltham, MA: Brandeis University, Schneider Institute for Health Policy.

The Prison Journal (September 1999). Special Issue: Drug treatment outcomes in correctional settings, Vol. 79(3).

The Prison Journal (December 1999). Special Issue: Drug treatment outcomes in correctional settings, Vol. 79(4).

Afterword

Treating the Addicted Offender: What We Know and Don't Know

by David Farabee, Ph.D., and Kevin Knight, Ph.D.

We are grateful to the scholars who have contributed to this book (and to the Offender Substance Abuse Report, from which many of these chapters were selected). The information provided by this exceptional group truly represents the latest thinking in the field of offender substance abuse treatment.

The chapters comprising this book were organized into seven domains representing what the editors conceive to be a continuum of opportunities to intervene with substance-abusing offenders, ranging from initial screening and referral to post-prison aftercare. In this final commentary, we step back from these categories and attempt to distill from this collective body of work some promising implications for clinical practice and correctional supervision.

WHAT WE KNOW

To advance the field of offender treatment we are obliged to identify gaps in our existing knowledge that merit further attention; but advancement also requires that we take the time to periodically inventory the findings that have proven reliable enough over time to serve as our foundation. Based on the chapters appearing in this book, and the broader literature that they reflect, we propose three general areas we believe have made the transition from truisms to truths: (1) the need for standardized testing, screening, and referral, (2) the clear benefits of "matching" the level or intensity of treatment services to the severity of client problems, and (3) the importance of enhanced communication between researchers and practitioners. Admittedly, this is a short list of accomplishments, but they hold many important implications that we have only begun to put into practice.

Standardized Screening and Referral

In 1954, psychologist Paul E. Meehl published *Clinical Versus Statistical Prediction: A Theoretical Analysis and a Review of the Evidence* (Meehl, 1954/1996), in which he reported the results of approximately 20 published studies comparing the predictive efficacy of informal clinical judgments with that of standardized actuarial assessments. In every one of these comparisons, the actuarial approaches performed as well as or better than the subjective approaches. Nevertheless—and in spite of a later meta-analysis by Grove and Meehl (1996) of 136 studies which produced similar results—many clinical psychologists remain reluctant to supplant their clinical impressions with mechanical algorithms.

With regard to screening and assessment for substance use disorders among prison inmates, we find a similar pattern. Many state correctional systems continue to determine treatment need based on a loose set of criteria including criminal histories involving drug use (as well as sales, manufacturing, or possession), inmate requests for treatment, or simply the need to fill existing treatment beds (see Farabee et al., 1999). Such approaches rely neither on clinical nor actuarial information and can result in the dilution of the treatment milieu as well as the displacement of substance abusers who might have derived benefit from treatment had they been correctly identified. Indeed, several studies have demonstrated that providing an intensive level of treatment to offenders with low substance use and criminal severity is an ineffective use of resources (Knight et al., 1999; Wexler, Melnick, & Cao, 2004; see also Chapter 6). This intuitive, yet widely ignored, pattern also has been referred to as the "Risk Principle," which states that the most intensive treatments should be reserved for offenders with the most serious problems (Andrews, Bonta, & Hoge, 1990). But putting such a straightforward finding into practice requires the use of standardized screening procedures in place of subjective or convenient (i.e., whatever it takes to keep the beds filled) approaches.

A number of screening instruments for substance abuse currently exist (see Peters et al., 2000 for a review of screening instruments used with prisoners). In Chapter 1, Knight points out that the practical requirements for brief, low-cost, and self-administered measures in prison need not be a hindrance to gathering useful data that can guide initial screening and placement decisions. Beyond this, we would do well to combine the sources of data used to determine treatment need. Bonta (2002) describes the four most common methods as (1) paper and pencil, (2) interview-based, (3) behavioral, and (4) file extraction procedures. Each of these techniques has known weaknesses, but combining multiple approaches, and determining how their contributions should be weighted, seems an appropriate direction for future research.

Client-Treatment "Matching"

The sheer size of federal, state, and even many local correctional populations necessitates the use of a staged screening and assessment process. As discussed above, and in the first section of this book, screening procedures in this context should serve the rather modest goal of identifying offenders who have a moderate or severe substance use problem. Once this occurs, an offender is referred ideally for further assessment. Unfortunately, this assessment often takes place in the program to which he or she was assigned and the treatment plan is based on what the program offers rather than what the offender needs.

This one-size-fits-all approach has long been criticized, but only recently have researchers produced enough information to provide meaningful guidance. We have already mentioned the importance of substance use severity as a basic consideration in determining treatment length and intensity, but the preceding pages go well beyond this to offer a number of newly observed client factors that also interact with treatment. We have seen, for example, that in a prison setting inmates mandated to enter treatment in spite of their wishes have worse outcomes than mandated treatment clients who acknowledged a need for help (Chapter 30). Correspondingly, we have seen examples of pro-gramming that have proven effective at enhancing motivation among coerced treatment clients (Chapters 27 and 28). We have also seen certain co-occurring psychiatric diag-noses that affect treatment amenability and how certain legal and clinical enhancements can be employed to overcome these challenges (Chapters 10, 16, 20, 21, and 22).

In short, the field of offender substance abuse treatment has begun to make significant progress from making vague declarations regarding client-treatment matching to offering specific and practical recommendations as to who should be matched with what.

Enhanced Communication Between Researchers and Practitioners

Part 7 of this book is devoted to clinical applications of research. There is likely nothing controversial in our including the need for enhanced communication between researchers and practitioners as a widely accepted truth in the field of offender treat-ment. Research findings, whether from local program evaluations or more traditional academic research, must be routinely shared with those who are actually providing the services as well as those who make the policies that govern them. But agreement over the importance of moving research to practice does not mean that we have been suc-cessful in carrying it out. Nor does it acknowledge that the direction of this communi-cation, when it does occur, is too often unidirectional.

There are, of course, many organizations that specialize in transferring research knowledge into practice, perhaps most notably the Addiction Technology Transfer Centers (ATTCs) funded by the Substance Abuse and Mental Health Services Agency. The issue we raise here is not that there are insufficient conduits to pass the informa-tion along, but that much of the information generated by researchers fails to address the needs of providers.

In Chapter 40, Laura Winterfield and colleagues vividly illustrate this point in their list of research gaps, generated primarily by practitioners, which include the need to clarify the role of motivation and coercion, identify effective treatment for different stages of a prison term, examine how the effectiveness of drug treatment varies depending on the level of security of the prisons, and assess the relevance of general treatment principles to programs operating in correctional settings. These are critical questions, and the fact that researchers have yet to respond adequately suggests that the communication between researchers and practitioners has been one-sided historically. Accordingly, we must ensure that the fundamental questions regarding offender sub-stance abuse treatment are not bypassed in the pursuit of more esoteric research goals. One way to accomplish this is to encourage private and federal funding agencies to routinely canvass practitioners before determining how their research priorities (and funding) will be weighted.

WHAT WE DON'T KNOW

In keeping with the research to practice issue described above, we pose some of our own research questions that we believe represent a reasonable balance of academic and practical interests. This is not to say that these questions have not been addressed in the past, only that we as a field may have been premature in declaring them resolved. In this section we have selected four such questions: (1) How effective is correctional treatment without aftercare? (2) What do we know about non-therapeutic community alternatives? (3) How long is long enough? (4) Can we really make people change if they're not ready?

How Effective Is Correctional Treatment Without Aftercare?

Virtually all of the prominent evaluations of prison-based therapeutic communities (TCs) report positive outcomes for those who completed prison treatment and also attended community-based aftercare. Over time, the apparent combined impact of these two phases of treatment has been simplified and offered as support for prison-based treatment generally. But the majority of these studies show that, without contin-ued care, in-prison substance abuse treatment appears to have little or no durational effect after release from prison (see Wexler, Prendergast, & Melnick, 2004).

Does this suggest that the second phase of treatment builds upon and complements the first? Or should we gather from this that we should abandon (or at least shorten) prison treatment and shift more resources to aftercare programs? Even more heretical, since most offenders self-select into aftercare, how do we know that even the aftercare effect is not the sole product of selection bias? In Chapter 15, Weinman et al. address some of these potential confounds in their research on programs operated by the Federal Bureau of Prisons, but the field of correctional treatment research in general has yet to provide convincing answers to these questions—all of which are directly testable. At the most basic level, more research is needed contrasting prison treatment only with aftercare only, using an experimental design.

What Do We Know About Non-TC Alternatives?

The majority of the published literature on prison-based substance abuse treatment has centered on the TC model, or variations of this approach. The TC's emphasis on personal responsibility and the adoption of prosocial attitudes and behaviors certainly lends to its intuitive appeal. But TCs are designed to be long-term interventions—rang-ing from six months to more than a year. Are there briefer, less costly alternatives that might be at least as effective as the traditional TC approach?

In a large meta-analysis of correctional treatment, researchers from National Development and Research, Incorporated (NDRI) reported that the seven cognitive skills programs in their review reduced recidivism, on average, from 57.4% successes in the experimental groups compared to 42.7% successes in the comparison groups (Pearson et al., 2002). In Chapter 16, Glenn Walters outlines the elements of another cognitive behavioral program for substance-abusing offenders. How does such a program compare to a TC? Are TCs more appropriate for more serious offenders, and cognitive behavioral programs better suited for those early in their drug use careers? The research literature cannot yet provide the answers to these questions, but it is clear that doing so will require that we resist the temptation to prematurely commit ourselves to a single approach.

How Long Is Long Enough?

One of the most reliable findings in the substance abuse treatment literature is that longer stays in treatment are associated with better outcomes (Gossop et al., 1999;

Simpson et al., 1997). In Chapter 26, Julien Devereux makes the important point that the length of time a client stays in treatment is too often determined by funding rather than clinical need. Most would agree that this decision should be based on what is best for the client, but what is best for the client? The correlational research that has provided guidance in this area thus far is a good start, but the nature of these studies does not allow us to disentangle whether the improved outcomes of long-term clients can be attributed to the impact of the program or certain client characteristic(s) that cause these clients to remain in treatment while others drop out.

This is an exceedingly practical issue that is far from being resolved. But it is also complex. Even by randomly assigning clients to varying treatment lengths we cannot guard against the confounds of dropout or administrative discharge for non-compliance. Likewise, since not all treatments are the same, comparisons would have to be nested by program type and certain client factors (e.g., drug use severity, psychiatric comorbidity, etc.). Far from perfect, a move to conduct more randomized studies of treatment length is the appropriate next step in building on the large foundation of quasi-experimental studies on which our dose-response assumptions are currently based.

Can We Really Make People Change If They Are Not Ready?

Because the majority of studies on coerced treatment were conducted in community treatment settings, little information is available regarding the effect of coercion on clients treated in prison or of the peripheral impact that coerced clients may have on voluntary clients in the same program. As we have seen in Chapter 31, inmates who enter treatment involuntarily are significantly more likely to recidivate than those who enter treatment with a desire for treatment.

Indeed, even the community-based coercion studies make it difficult to draw firm conclusions regarding the effectiveness of coercing substance abusers into treatment. In a review of 170 English-language articles (published since 1988) concerning compulsory substance abuse treatment, Wild, Roberts, and Cooper (2002) identified only 18 "effectiveness" studies. Of these, the most popular outcome measured was treatment retention, accounting for 56% of the studies; only one-third of the studies examined criminal behaviors between coerced and non-coerced subjects. The authors reported mixed findings—often varying by the type of outcome measured. For example—55% of the studies showed compulsory treatment was superior with regard to retention; 33% of the studies showed lower recidivism for coerced clients (half of the studies showed no difference); and 25% of the studies examining drug use showed superior results for compulsory clients, while 75% showed no difference. In other words, most of the studies emphasizing treatment retention showed positive effects of compulsory treatment, while most of the studies focusing on drug use and criminal behavior showed no differences. Thus, the commonly cited belief that coerced clients do as well or better than non-coerced clients may be true, but better only refers to retention. Furthermore, compulsory, coerced, mandated, and involuntary (to name a few) are not always synonymous.

Gaining a better understanding of the effectiveness of coerced treatment will depend on how precisely these two variables are measured in the future. From a more applied perspective, assessing the impact of motivational enhancements (such as those described in Chapters 27 and 28) as they relate to post-treatment drug use and crime—

rather than just retention—should be a priority for correctional treatment researchers, as it already is for practitioners (Chapter 40).

SUMMARY

The French anthropologist Claude Levi-Strauss (1964) once remarked "the scientific mind does not so much provide the right answers as ask the right questions." We hope that this volume has at least modestly succeeded in doing both. The research and observations offered by our distinguished contributors represent the culmination of many decades of empirical and clinical work. They describe a broad array of opportunities to effectively intervene with addicted offenders across the corrections continuum and, even where the findings are more suggestive than conclusive, they move us further along our own continuum toward improving lives and protecting public safety.

References

Andrews, D.A., Bonta, J., & Hoge, R.D. (1990). Classification for effective rehabilitation: Rediscovering psychology. *Criminal Justice and Behavior, 17*, 19-52.

Bonta, J. (2002). Offender risk assessment: Guidelines for selection and use. *Criminal Justice and Behavior*, 29(4), 355-379.

Farabee, D., Prendergast, M.L., Cartier, J., Wexler, W., Knight., K., & Anglin, M.D. (1999). Barriers to implementing effective correctional treatment programs. *The Prison Journal, 79*(2), 150-162.

Gossop, M., Marsden, J., Stewart, D., & Rolfe, A. (1999). Treatment retention and one year outcomes for residential programmes in England. *Drug and Alcohol Dependence, 57*(2), 89-98.

Grove, W.M., & Meehl, P.E. (1996). Comparative efficiency of informal (subjective, impressionistic) and formal (mechanical, algorithmic) prediction procedures: The clinical-statistical controversy. *Psychology, Public Policy, & Law, 2*(2), 293-323.

Knight, K., Simpson, D.D., & Hiller, M.L. (1999). Three-year reincarceration outcomes for in-prison therapeutic community treatment in Texas. *The Prison Journal, 79*(3), 337-351.

Levi-Strauss, C. (1964). *The raw and the crooked*. Chicago: Chicago University Press.

Meehl, P.E. (1996). *Clinical versus statistical prediction: A theoretical analysis and a review of the evidence*. Northvale, NJ: Jason Aronson (Originally published in 1954).

Pearson, F.S., Lipton, D.S., Cleland, C.M., & Yee, D.S. (2002). The effects of behavioral/cognitive-behavioral programs on recidivism. *Crime & Delinquency, 48*, 476-496.

Appendix

Legal Issues

by Margaret R. Moreland, J.D., M.S.L.S.

Sentencing Issues App.-1
Treatment Programs and Program Requirements App.-8
Drug Testing of Offenders App.-14
Standards of Care App.-17
Drug Addiction as a Disability Under the ADA App.-21
The Religious Nature of AA and Similar Programs App.-23
Substance Use and Visitor Privileges App.-28

[*Editors' note: This appendix contains commentary on selected legal cases involving substance using offenders and related substance abuse programming, drawn from columns by the author that appeared in* Offender Substance Abuse Report *between January 2001 and January 2004. This material is reprinted here to give our readers a general sense of some of the legal issues that may arise in this field, but any decision reported here must be checked to see if it has been superceded by later cases, statutes, or regulations. Further, readers with specific legal questions or problems are advised to consult a professional with expertise in their particular jurisdictions.*]

SENTENCING ISSUES

Limits on "Eligibility" Impediments for Drug Treatment Leading to Sentence Reduction

The Violent Crime Control and Law Enforcement Act's Requirements. The Violent Crime Control and Law Enforcement Act of 1994, 18 U.S.C. 3621 (b), provides that the Bureau of Prisons (BOP) "shall make available" residential drug treatment programs for eligible prisoners. The motivation behind this provision is easily linked to issues of public safety, given the "abundance" of statistics that find a link between substance abuse and crime. Some crimes are committed while under the influence of alcohol or drugs, others in order to obtain money for drugs, and still others in connection with drug trafficking (Edwards, 2000, p. 304). However, current psychological thinking recognizes that compulsory addition treatment can be ineffective (Edwards, 2000, p. 338 *et seq.*). Congress's enactment of the drug treatment provisions conformed with this thinking. "Eligible" prisoners were defined as those who the BOP identified with a substance abuse problem and who were "willing to participate" in a drug treatment program. To encourage participation, Congress also allowed for a sentence reduction of up to one year for prisoners who successfully completed such programs *if* they had been "convicted of a nonviolent offense." This is the phrase that has generated most of the litigation surrounding the availability of drug treatment programs for federal prisoners.

Tenth Circuit Says BOP Must Base Eligibility Criteria on Conviction, Not Sentence. Congress's clear intent was that the BOP would establish additional criteria for eligibility. Consequently, in 1994 the BOP promulgated a regulation providing that any prisoner whose "current offense" was a "crime of violence" as defined by 18 U.S.C. 924 (c)(3) would not be eligible for sentence reduction. 28 C.F.R. 550.58. Then, in 1995, the BOP issued Program Statement No. 5162.02, which further stated that any offense would be considered a "crime of violence" whenever a sentencing court had enhanced the basic term because of the possession of a dangerous weapon during the commission of the offense.

This Program Statement was often challenged, and found to contradict the plain language of the statute. A list of these cases can be found in *Ward v. Booker*, 202 F.3d 1249, 1252 (10th Cir. 2000). As a result, the BOP issued a revised regulation and a new Program Statement. The current regulation does not link ineligibility to sentence enhancement resulting from possession of a dangerous weapon during the commission of the current offense. Instead, it specifically states that inmates are not eligible for early release if their "current offense is a felony ... [t]hat involved the carrying, possession, or use of a firearm or other dangerous weapon ...." 28 C.F.R. 550.58(a)(1)(vi)(B). The related Program Statement stated that inmates would be precluded from receiving certain benefits, such as sentence reduction, if their current offense was a felony that "involved the carrying, possession, or use of a firearm or other dangerous weapon ...." It also included a specific example of how this provision would operate: "an inmate who was convicted of manufacturing drugs ... and received a two-level enhancement for possession of a firearm has been convicted of an offense that will preclude him from receiving certain Bureau program benefits." It was not very long before the new BOP regulation and Program Statement were challenged as well.

In *Ward v. Booker* the Tenth Circuit Court of Appeals was asked to determine whether the BOP's new "methodology" was, in fact, "meaningful and significant." 202 F.3d at 1253. It found that it was not. The court referred to its decisions in previous cases where it had discussed the clear language of the statute. It previously held that eligibility for sentence reduction had to be based upon convictions and that "*any* use of sentence enhancements to turn a conviction of a nonviolent offense into a violent offense ... was impermissible, simply because it ran afoul of the statute's clear language." 202 F.3d at 1256. The court noted that there had been no change in the language of the statute regarding eligibility for sentence reduction since those cases were decided. Therefore, the focus remained on conviction, not sentencing. The BOP's new regulation and Program Statement, like the previous ones, were an attempt by the agency to contravene the intent of Congress by changing the eligibility standard. "Couching it as an exercise of discretion does not make it any less contrary to the statute." 202 F.3d at 1256.

COMMENT: The Tenth Circuit noted that it had no intent to undermine the discretion granted to the BOP by Congress. It referred to a Seventh Circuit case where it was stated: "Eligibility is not entitlement." The agency still had "broad discretion to determine who among eligible prisoners may receive a sentence reduction following participation in a substance abuse treatment program." 202 F.3d at 1257.

A Contrary Decision in the Eighth Circuit. *Bellis v. Davis*, 186 F.3d 1092 (8th Cir. 1999), cert. granted 2000 U.S. LEXIS 2842 (April 24, 2000), is a case that began with petitions for habeas corpus by 10 federal prisoners who either had completed or were about to complete BOP-administered residential substance abuse treatment. In spite of successful completion, each would be denied a sentence reduction. The basis for denial was either that they had been convicted of being a felon in possession of a firearm, or that their sentences had been enhanced due to the fact that they were in possession of a dangerous weapon while committing a federal drug offense.

The court here first noted that the language of 18 U.S.C. 3621(e)(2)(B) is discretionary. In other words, the BOP is not required to grant a sentence reduction to every prisoner who successfully completes a drug treatment program, or even to everyone in a particular class of prisoners. Neither is the BOP required to make individual assessments of the eligibility of each prisoner convicted of a nonviolent offense. In fact, the Court viewed the BOP's identification of ineligible groups as "manifestly permissible," given that the "underlying conduct" of some prisoners "indicates that they pose a serious risk to public safety." 186 F.3d at 1095.

This decision was contrasted with an earlier one in which the Eighth Circuit had disallowed any consideration of sentencing factors in determining whether or not a prisoner was eligible for sentence reduction. In a fine distinction, the court explained that the earlier case had examined a regulation that "attempted to interpret the statutory term 'nonviolent offense,'" while this case turned on a regulation that merely "look[ed] to sentencing factors in deciding which individuals among statutorily eligible inmates are appropriate candidates for early release." 186 F.3d at 1095.

COMMENT: It would seem that this case should fall under the Tenth Circuit's parameter of "a distinction without a difference." However, at least in the Eighth Circuit, the BOP seems to have been successful in its attempt to narrow the definition of a "nonviolent offense." Congress enacted the sentence reduction provision in order to encourage more inmates to take part in substance abuse programs. If fewer are eligible, and fewer participate in the programs, what has been gained by this decision?

*[**Editor's note:** The Supreme Court ultimately decided this dispute between the circuits, holding that an inmate convicted of committing a felony while carrying, possessing, or using a firearm will be denied early release eligibility whether or not the felony was a violent crime. See discussion of* Lopez v. Davis, *121 S.Ct. 714 (2001) later in this Appendix.]*

"Successful" Completion of Substance Abuse Programs Also Required. Haywood Alexander is a federal prisoner who was serving a sentence under a conviction for conspiracy to distribute narcotics and money laundering. While incarcerated he had participated in a BOP-administered residential drug treatment program, and claimed that his completion of the program entitled him to a reduction of his sentence. However, because there was a state detainer against Alexander that was still outstanding, he was unable to participate in the community-based treatment phase of the program. In a brief decision, *Alexander v. Flowers*, 2000 U.S. App. LEXIS 2767 (10th Cir. February 24, 2000), the Court of Appeals in the Tenth Circuit held that the BOP was acting within its statutory discretion when it denied the sentence reduction because Alexander had not successfully completed the program.

COMMENT: Whether or not a prisoner voluntarily withdraws from a program before completion is not an issue. Successful completion of a BOP residential drug treatment program is a per se prerequisite for sentence reduction.

Courts Have Leeway to Impose Rehabilitation-Related Treatment Conditions

Making a transition out of the prison environment and back into the community can be extremely difficult for many inmates. An example of this is the case of Juan Jose Lopez, an offender with a criminal history that had lasted for over 25 years. A Presentence Report noted that his ongoing criminal activity had made him "an outright danger to the community" during this period. It also stated that his behavior in prison had been "menacing," and that his record of adjustment to parole and probation was poor. In addition, his sister had expressed the fear that, after years of incarceration, Lopez had become "institutionalized." His most recent conviction had been for bank robbery and, after serving 64 months in a federal prison, Lopez was transferred to the Pacific Furlough Facility for the final three months of his sentence. He had objected to the transfer, seemingly because of his fear of the freedom and fast pace of life in a half-way house. Initially, Lopez did well at his job, and he looked to the older prisoners for advice on "making it." However, after just a month at the half-way house he tested positive for morphine, and walked away from the facility rather than face the associate director. He was apprehended and re-arrested 10 days later. After pleading guilty to one count of escape, Lopez was sentenced to 21 months of incarceration and three years of supervised release. *U.S. v. Lopez*, 258 F.3d 1053 (9th Cir. 2001).

The sentencing court is empowered by law to establish the conditions of an offender's supervised release. In this case, the court set up a number of conditions, including the not unusual condition that Lopez participate in a drug or alcohol rehabilitation program. In addition, the court decided that he must take part in a mental health treatment program, and that he must consent to having the reports detailing his treatment and status made to the court and to his probation officer. Lopez objected to these last two conditions, basing his appeal upon separate theories. First, he alleged that requiring mental health treatment was an unusual, upward departure from the statutory guidelines governing supervised release. As such, a defendant is entitled to receive reasonable notice that such a condition is going to be imposed, along with an opportunity to comment on the reasonableness of the condition. Second, he claimed that it was an abuse of discretion for the court to impose these conditions without any evidence that he actually had a mental illness.

The Ninth Circuit held that, rather than being a departure from statutory guidelines, the requirement that the appellant participate in a mental health treatment program is specifically described in U.S. Sentencing Guidelines 5D1.3(d)(5). The court cited the section with the recommendation: "If the court has reason to believe that the defendant is in need of psychological or psychiatric treatment—a condition requiring that the defendant participate in a mental health program approved by the United States Probation Office." Since this condition—although "special"—was not a departure from the guidelines, no special notice was required to be given.

The appellate court also held that, even without definitive evidence that Lopez was mentally ill, it was not an abuse of discretion for the sentencing court to require that he participate in a mental health treatment program. Quoting previous Ninth Circuit cases, the court stated that the issue was whether or not the disputed condition for supervised release was "primarily designed to affect the rehabilitation of the probationer or insure the protection of the public." It acknowledged that the conditions placed on an offender during the term of his supervised release might involve some curtailment of his liberties. However, the law permits these deprivations as long as they are "reasonably necessary 'to afford adequate deterrence to criminal conduct; to protect the public from further crimes of the defendant; to provide the defendant with needed educational or vocational training, medical care, or other correctional treatment in the most effective manner'" (citing 18 U.S.C. 3553(a)(2)(B)-(D)). The court stated that the lower court record, as well as the defendant's own words regarding his inability to "adjust to a non-custodial lifestyle," sufficiently demonstrated his need for counseling. Lopez's further objection to the disclosure of his mental health treatment records to the court and his probation officer was also rejected. The appellate court noted that he had a record of non-compliance with conditions of supervised release, making such disclosure necessary in order to adequately supervise "his reintegration into society."

COMMENT: The fact that the U.S. Sentencing Guidelines specifically provide for the possibility of requiring that a parolee participate in a mental health treatment program is an acknowledgement that there is a relationship between the substance abuse and mental health issues of prison and jail inmates. There is evidence that an estimated 16% of prison and jail inmates are mentally ill (Ditton, 1999). More important, in the context of this discussion of the Lopez case, is the fact that almost 60% of mentally ill inmates have reported that they were under the influence of either alcohol or drugs when they committed their most recent offense. A slightly higher number have reported using drugs during the month prior to committing that offense. Utilizing a diagnostic instrument, Ditton states that it has also been determined that 34% of mentally ill state prison inmates, 24% of mentally ill federal prison inmates, and 38% of mentally ill jail inmates had a history of alcohol dependence.

Rehabilitation Needs Can Be Considered in Determining Consequences of Condition Violations

The Appellate courts have upheld the imposition of a lengthy prison term as a consequence of a violation of supervised release conditions, where the term promotes rehabilitation of the offender. Two recent cases are described below.

James Rodriguez alleged, on appeal, that he would not have received the maximum sentence for violating the conditions of his supervised release if he had the financial means that would allow him to participate in a private drug rehabilitation program. In its memorandum opinion, the Ninth Circuit rejected this "equal protection" argument. It noted that Rodriguez had participated in inpatient treatment programs on two occasions during the term of his supervised release. He failed at both. The lower court judge apparently was skeptical of his chances for success in another, similar program. He asserted his belief that Rodriguez's only chance for future success was the kind of "intense treatment" that he could receive while confined prison. On this record, the appellate court found no evidence that the lower court would have given Rodriguez a shorter sentence if he had the means to enroll in a private drug rehabilitation program. *U.S. v. Rodriguez*, 2001 U.S. App. LEXIS 24131 (9th Cir. October 31, 2001)

In another case, the District Court for the Eastern District of North Carolina imposed a sentence of 24 months on Carson Norwood Sutton after several violations of the conditions of his parole, because this was the minimum time necessary for "intensive drug counseling." Sutton repeatedly tested positive for drug use while on parole, and was also arrested for driving while intoxicated, in spite of his required participation in drug treatment programs. After re-sentencing, he appealed the length of the term imposed asserting that the lower court had abused its discretion. He alleged that it had been improper to take his need for drug rehabilitation into consideration. In *U.S. v. Sutton*, 2001 U.S. App. LEXIS 20535 (4th Cir. September 17, 2001), the Fourth Circuit stated that, to the contrary, "the statute governing the imposition and revocation of supervised release expressly permits consideration of a defendant's need for rehabilitation." The statutory authority cited by the court is 18 U.S.C.A. 3583 and 3553(a).

COMMENT: Some of the arguments of those who violate the conditions of their supervised release are reminiscent of the story of the imaginary child who killed his parents and then asked for mercy from the court because he had become an orphan. Appellate courts must sometimes look at the arguments made upon appeal with a similar incredulity.

Downward Departures From the Sentencing Guidelines

In *U.S. v. Sandra Rhodes*, No. 03-20008, 2003 U.S. Dist. LEXIS 18839 (C.D. Ill. October 21, 2003), the court was presented with defendant's argument for a substantial reduction in the sentence established under the U.S. Sentencing Guidelines. Sandra Rhodes, the defendant, a middle-aged white female with a college education, had pled guilty to two Class C felonies—the possession of between 50 and 150 grams of methamphetamine with the intent to distribute and money laundering.

Although this was Rhodes's first conviction, during the course of her association with law enforcement, it became known that she had a history of significant drug activity. In fact, she had handled more than 24 pounds of methamphetamine, as well as cannabis, and had laundered between $85,000 and $100,000. The federal Sentencing Guidelines provide that her conviction on these two Class C felonies should result in 210 to 262 months of incarceration, at least three years of supervised release, and fines between $20,000 and $1,500,000.

However, because Rhodes offered significant assistance to the authorities, assisting in the arrest and conviction of a number of drug dealers, the government recommended a 30% reduction in the prescribed minimum sentence. The case was presented to U.S. District Judge Harold A. Baker for a final hearing and entry of the final disposition. Both sides had accepted the contents of the pre-sentencing report without objection, but defendant Rhodes argued that the downward departure in the sentence should be more substantial based on both her physical condition and the significant assistance she had given to the government. In the written opinion, the court expressed its wholehearted agreement with her position.

Mitigating Circumstances. Section 5K2 of the U.S. Sentencing Guidelines allows for a departure in sentencing when "there exists an aggravating or mitigating circumstance of a kind, or to a degree, not adequately taken into consideration by the Sentencing Commission in formulating the guidelines. . . ." In order to do so, the U.S. Circuit Court of Appeals for the Seventh Circuit has held that a departure must be based on "particularized findings." *U.S. v. Sherman*, 53 F.3d 782 (7th Cir. 1995). Therefore, District Judge Baker begins with a lengthy description of the defendant's medical condition and resulting needs, based on both the pre-sentencing report and the testimony of several expert witnesses.

As a result of a vicious attack in her home, Rhodes was blinded in both eyes and she sustained serious injuries to her head and brain. At the time of this final hearing, she was able to live independently only with the support of a rehabilitation counselor, an independent living specialist, and two personal assistants. Guided by the rehabilitation counselor's plan, she had been able to make significant progress in adapting to her blindness and in becoming more independent.

Rhodes has two ocular prostheses that must be treated with topical antibiotics to prevent infection. The injury to her brain during the attack has resulted in epileptic seizures, which must be controlled by medication, and the damage to her face and sinus cavities has exacerbated her pre-existing asthma. The trauma and resulting blindness caused posttraumatic stress disorder and depression for which she takes medication, but these conditions are improving as she regains her self-confidence and independence. Rhodes also suffers from Graves disease, treated with a synthetic thyroid medication; adult-onset diabetes, requiring medication and daily monitoring of her blood sugar; sleep apnea, necessitating the use of a CPAP machine at night; and the continuing effects of bariatric and other abdominal surgeries.

Dr. Ballom, the clinical director of the correctional facility where Rhodes would be incarcerated, testified that he had no experience treating a blind prisoner with special medical needs, and that there was no separation of the general population from the medical prisoners. The facility's administrator hospital testified the cost of Rhodes' care would be between $75,000 and $100,000 annually, that she would be dependent upon her cellmate to guide her, and that he did not know how they would deal with a request for Braille instruction or training a blind person for employment.

By contrast, Rhodes' rehabilitation counselor testified that the current cost of care ($10,000 annually) would be ending in about a year after she had gained additional independence, although vocational training costs would then rise for a finite period of time.

The court came to the conclusion that if Rhodes was incarcerated, "she will loose the self-sufficiency and independence of movement that she has gained [and] be dependent upon another inmate assigned to her as a guide and personal assistant [and] lose the impetus to gain vocation independence. . . ." It also expressed serious concerns about her physical safety based upon her disability and the likelihood of retribution for her assistance to law enforcement. District Judge Baker stated: "The court is not so naïve or inexperienced about prison life not to recognize that a blind person, especially a 'snitch,' is vulnerable to abuse and mistreatment by other inmates."

Purpose Served by Incarceration. The opinion next addressed what purpose would be served by Rhodes' incarceration. While recognizing that rehabilitation is no longer "the primary end of the criminal law" and that it is now, in fact, "a distinct last," Baker insists that the question of rehabilitation is still a significant consideration in determining a sentence. Given that she has "an extraordinary physical impairment" as mentioned in the Section 5H1.4 of the Sentencing Guidelines, would home detention be preferable to detention in an institution. A prison could not provide the programs now available to her, her progress toward independence would be ended, and the costs would be higher.

Looking at the question of punishment, the court expresses its belief that "punishment by incarceration . . . pales compared to the punishment she has already received from her fellow criminals and the prison to which they have consigned her." The aim of deterrence has already been accomplished because "her blindness and remorse . . . make recidivism most unlikely," and because her work with young people may deter others from following her path.

Assistance Given Government. The defendant's additional argument—that a 30% departure was inadequate given the nature of her assistance to the government—also found favor with the court. Rhodes' assistance was crucial in convicting the Los Angeles police officer who was her drug supplier, two other drug dealers, and the three men who attacked and blinded her. That assistance, coupled with the risks the defendant will continue to face because of her physical disability and her cooperation with the authorities, "calls for a sentence of home confinement following minimum incarceration. . . ." The court entered a sentence of one day of imprisonment and five months and 29 days of home detention, followed by three years of supervised release. It stated that this sentence will be less costly to the state, while efficiently carrying out the purposes of criminal justice.

District Judge Baker added that he had been "genuinely puzzled" by the prosecution's position. He noted that the case was not even brought until six months before the statute of limitations was due to expire, and that it was "truly questionable how the ends of the criminal law are served by incarcerating this woman for eleven years." He stated his support of Attorney General Ashcroft's directive to seek maximum penalties in order to put away violent and dangerous criminals such as "drug kingpins," but observed that "Sandra Rhodes is none of the criminals he mentioned as targets."

COMMENT: This opinion was an excellent review of the issues of cost of incarceration, rehabilitation, and the valuable contribution of those who render assistance to law enforcement officials. The decision seems an eminently practical one, considering the high cost of incarceration as well as the ends of justice. However, as this book went to press the prosecution had already objected once to the sentence, resulting in an amended final disposition order that included one day of incarceration, and they may be heard from again.

TREATMENT PROGRAMS AND PROGRAM REQUIREMENTS

Pennsylvania Looks at Minimum Program Requirements

The Commonwealth Court of Pennsylvania has held that the licensing standards of the Pennsylvania Public Welfare Code need not be met by the substance abuse treatment programs conducted in the state's prisons. Gilbert McGill, a state inmate, was denied parole by the Pennsylvania Board of Probation and Parole. He was then informed that at future parole hearings the Board would consider whether he had participated in the Department of Corrections' Therapeutic Community (TC) Program that had been recommended by his counselor. McGill objected to the program because of its alleged failure to comply with Pennsylvania law. Specific allegations were that (1) the program had not been licensed by the state Department of Health (DOH), (2) its clinical supervisors and counselors did not have the requisite qualifications, and (3) the prisoner-counselor ratio exceeded the amount required for licensing. In deciding whether or not to dismiss the plaintiff's petition, the court had to accept the facts as pled by McGill. However, it still was able to dismiss the case because it found that, under its definition of "facility," the state's Public Welfare Code specifically excluded drug and alcohol treatment facilities operated by either the state or the federal government. *McGill v. Pennsylvania Department of Health, Office of Drug & Alcohol Programs*, 2000 Pa. Commw. LEXIS 477 (August 18, 2000).

Judge Friedman, in a strong dissent, presented his arguments against the dismissal of plaintiff's petition. This program was funded by a block grant from the federal government. Independent peer review of all funded programs is required each year to see if they are meeting "accepted standards." This judge noted that, since licensing itself is not sufficient to show that a program meets those standards, and it is seen as a possibility that licensed facilities might not meet the standards, "it is highly unlikely, if not impossible, that an unlicensed program would meet 'accepted standards.'" Nevertheless, the judge recognized that the plaintiff's petition should fail with regard to the federal requirements because he had an alternative remedy. "McGill need only notify federal authorities that the Commonwealth is not in compliance with its funding agreement, and the federal government will investigate the matter." On the other hand, Judge Friedman felt that the inmate's petition should stand up under state law. He noted that, although the Public Welfare Code excluded treatment facilities operated by the state or federal government from its licensing requirements, that exclusion does not apply to the DOH's statutory authority under the Drug Abuse Act to establish standards for inmate programs. Since the Department of Health had been exercising its authority by using the licensing standards of the Public Welfare Code, those requirements should also have been applied to the TC program.

COMMENT: Without commenting on the efficacy of Pennsylvania's TC program, it must be noted that correctional substance abuse treatment programs must at least be required to meet minimum standards. If substandard programs are allowed to operate in correctional facilities they will no doubt fail to provide efficacious treatment and, consequently, will be a waste of federal and state monies.

Is "Brainwashing" in Drug Treatment Programs Unconstitutional?

In *Kerr v. Puckett*, 138 F.3d 321 (7th Cir. 1998), a former inmate filed suit after his release charging that prison programs designed to reduce drug and alcohol dependence had tried to "brainwash" him in violation of his constitutional rights. He alleged: "All of the prison drug rehabilitation programs ... contain 'criminal thinking' portions. The purpose of the 'criminal thinking' portions of the programs Mr. KERR was assigned to was to change the participant's 'attitudes, values, beliefs and thinking patterns.'" He then proceeded to list the tactics used in the programs in which he participated. The Seventh Circuit Court of Appeals noted that no court had ever supported this position. It stated: "Perhaps it is unrealistic to suppose that prisoners' 'criminal thinking' rather than other elements of their background or opportunities influence the recidivism rate [and] perhaps prison officials overstate the extent to which these programs affect the likelihood of "criminal thinking" [but] states are free to approach matters otherwise, and to seek rehabilitation even if that entails programs that prisoners find unpleasant." After contrasting lawful hard labor to the "few uncomfortable hours" that can result in the shortening of a prisoner's sentence, the appellate court had no trouble in affirming the dismissal of plaintiff's complaint.

COMMENT: This seems to have been a far-fetched complaint. Prisons and jails are the very places where society should be making an attempt to change "criminal thinking."

Duty to Ensure Prisoner Has Maximum Opportunity to Shorten Sentence

Delay in Program Entry Delays Inmate's Release. The Treatment Provision of the Violent Crime Control and Law Enforcement Act of 1994 provides that substance abuse treatment shall be provided for prisoners who meet the eligibility requirements "with priority for such treatment accorded based on an eligible prisoner's proximity to release date." 18 U.S.C. 3621(e)(1).

Inmate Maurello had been convicted of fraud and had begun serving his 36-month sentence at the Federal Prison Camp at Allenwood when he applied for admission to the facility's residential substance abuse treatment program. Successful participation in such programs may result in as much as a one-year reduction in a prisoner's sentence. Allenwood had a nine-month program, with each class limited to 24 inmates. Those eligible for admission to the program were placed on a waiting list in order of their scheduled release dates. Because Maurello's record showed no evidence of a substance abuse problem, he was required to submit documentation from an outside source. Dr. Findlay, the program's director, received that documentation on June 20, 1995. Maurello's Residential Treatment Eligibility Interview was completed on July 3, and on July 7 he received a progress report indicating that he had been accepted into the class beginning on July 18. However, Dr. Findlay asserted that an inmate was not eligible to be placed on the waiting list until after he had reviewed and approved the inmate's record, and Maurello's eligibility was not so determined until July 14, 1995.

In the meantime the list of inmates who were to participate in the July 18 program had already been finalized and they had been moved into program housing. A decision was made not to move any inmates out again, although four of those in the July 18 class had later release dates than Maurello. Maurello was admitted to the following class, completed the program more than satisfactorily, and was ultimately released on December 17, 1996. However, if he had been admitted to the earlier program he would have been released on October 31, 1996, 51 days sooner. After his release, Maurello filed a claim under the Federal Tort Claims Act for compensatory and punitive damages in the amount of $1,051,000.

Summary Judgment Against Plaintiff. In *Maurello v. United States*, 2000 U.S. Dist. LEXIS 10180 (D.N.J. June 30, 2000), the government's motion for summary judgment was granted on jurisdictional grounds. The court found that Maurello's claim was essentially one for false imprisonment, and sovereign immunity was not waived for such an action under the Federal Tort Claims Act. Nevertheless, the court chose also to discuss the substantive validity of plaintiff's claims. The court found no precedent for the existence of an intentional tort based upon "the intentional violation of a federal statute depriving someone of the benefit of a government program." Similarly, it could not accept the plaintiff's contention that there was negligence as a matter of law. The court stated: "the Treatment Provision was designed to assist prisoners with their substance abuse problem and to benefit society as a whole by the expected reduction in substance-abuse-related crimes committed by prisoners following their release from prison, not to provide early release to prisoners."

COMMENT: Although it did not need to explore this territory, since plaintiff's claim had already been defeated, the District Court was determined to make it clear that this incentive was not an entitlement.

Lawful Change in Policy Cannot Be Applied Retroactively to Detriment of Those Who Already Relied on Previous Policy

The BOP is unwavering in its belief that those who carry a weapon during the commission of a crime should not benefit from early release. When the Treatment Provision of the Violent Crime Control and Law Enforcement Act of 1994 was enacted to provide substance abuse treatment for prisoners, eligibility was limited to those who had not committed a crime of violence. As noted above, participation may lead to sentence reduction. At first the BOP interpreted "crime of violence" so that anyone who had been in possession of a firearm while committing a crime would be excluded. However, a series of court cases found that mere possession was not sufficient for exclusion. In response, the BOP has exercised its perceived discretion and amended the qualifications for early release in its Drug Abuse Manual. The October 9, 1997, amendment specifically states that "inmates whose current offense is a felony ... that involved the carrying, possession, or use of a firearm or other dangerous weapon or explosives ..." are not eligible for early release. In the wake of these changes, a number of prisoners who no longer meet the eligibility requirements applied for habeas corpus relief. They all had been convicted of non-violent crimes but lost their eligibility because they were in possession of a firearm when arrested. One group of prisoners had already been admitted provisionally to a substance abuse treatment program, and the other had not yet been admitted. *Bowen v. Hood*, 202 F.3d 1211 (9th Cir. 1999), *cert. denied* 121 S.Ct. 854 (2001).

Ninth Circuit Says BOP Within Allowable Discretion, But Amended Regs Cannot Be Applied Retroactively. In a split decision, the Ninth Circuit Court of Appeals ruled that the BOP was within its allowable discretion when it amended the eligibility rules. It found that the clear intent of Congress was for the Bureau to establish the criteria for early release and to apply the criteria uniformly. Thus it joined two other circuits that had previously made similar rulings. *Lasora v. Menfee*, 10 F. Supp. 2d 316 (S.D.N.Y. 1998), *aff'd* 182 F.3d 900 (2d Cir. 1999) and *Bellis v. Davis*, 186 F.3d 1092 (8th Cir. 1999) *(see below for the subsequent Supreme Court decision in this case)*. The Ninth Circuit also stated that it saw "nothing unreasonable in the Bureau's making the common-sense decision that there is a significant potential for violence from criminals who carry, possess or use firearms while engaged in their felonious employment, even if they have wound up committing a nonviolent offense this time." Therefore, the court concluded that the new regulations could be applied to those inmates who had not yet been admitted to a substance abuse treatment program.

The court relied heavily upon the reasoning of it earlier decision in *Cort v. Crabtree*, 113 F.3d 1081 (9th Cir. 1997), where it held that prisoners who had already been accepted into *and actually entered* a substance abuse treatment program could not then be denied their eligibility for early release. It noted that "retroactivity is not favored in the law" and found no indication in the new regulations that the intent was to apply them retroactively. The argument based on the language of the acceptance ("this eligibility is provisional and may change") was rejected as well, since BOP's own definitions stated that "provisional" merely referred to the fact that eligibility for early release could be withdrawn if the substance abuse treatment program was not successfully completed. The court emphasized the importance of honoring the commitments made to prisoners: "this is not a game of Lucy and the football from the world of Charles Schultz."

Circuit Judge Fernandez disagreed with the majority opinion with regard to the retroactive application of the new regulation. His view was that the group of prisoners who had not yet begun the program should have had no "settled expectation" of early release, even though they had been notified of their acceptance into the program. He based his view on a standard dictionary definition of the word "provisional" and on the fact that they had not actually started a substance abuse treatment program.

The dissent of Circuit Judge Thomas has broader implications, since it is not limited to the small group of prisoners who were notified of eligibility before the new regulations took effect. That situation will not repeat itself. Rather, Thomas looked at whether or not the new regulations were permissible at all, and found them to be in direct contravention of the intent of Congress and the judicial opinions interpreting that intent. He noted that Congress's clear intent, based upon evidence that recidivism is greatly reduced by participation in substance abuse treatment programs, was to provide an incentive so that more inmates would participate in such programs. Although there is no doubt that the BOP does have a degree of discretion in this regard, Thomas stated that "a discretionary decision that conflicts with the plain and unambiguous language of the statute merits no deference." In his interpretation, he joined the Tenth and Eleventh Circuits (*Ward v. Booker*, 202 F.3d 1249 (10th Cir. 2000) and *Kilpatrick v. Houston*, 197 F. 3d 1134 (11th Cir. 1999)), concluding that the Bureau of Prisons may not avoid the intent of Congress or the instructions of the courts "under the guise" of its discretionary power.

U.S. Supreme Court Rules on Issue. The Eighth Circuit case that was followed by the Ninth Circuit majority ultimately reached the Supreme Court, re-named *Lopez v. Davis*, 121 S.Ct. 714 (2001). Justice Ginsberg wrote the majority opinion that affirmed the lower court's decision. This case also involved an inmate who would have qualified for early release after participating in a substance abuse treatment program, save for the fact that he was categorically excluded from early release because he possessed a firearm at the time he committed the offense for which he was incarcerated. The Supreme Court noted the discretionary language of the statute, using "may" rather than "shall," and observed that this is a "familiar situation, where Congress has enacted a law that does not answer 'the precise question at issue,' [and where] all we must decide is whether the Bureau, the agency empowered to administer the early release program, has filled the statutory gap 'in a way that is reasonable in light of the legislature's revealed design.'" [citations omitted] Justice Ginsberg, was joined by Justices O'Connor, Scalia, Souter, Thomas, and Breyer, in the conclusion that the Bureau's action in excluding this group from eligibility for early release had been reasonable. "[A]n inmate's prior involvement with firearms, in connection with the commission of a felony, suggests his readiness to resort to life-endangering violence...."

The Supreme Court's decision was not unanimous. Justice Stevens wrote a dissent, joined by Chief Justice Rehnquist and Justice Kennedy. They looked back at the history of the legislation, to the congressional debate on the question of which groups of prisoners should be categorically excluded from receiving the benefit of early release. In the original drafts of the bill no prisoners were categorically excluded but, in the end, Congress decided to exclude those who had been convicted of "violent offenses." Therefore, the dissent felt that "the precise question at issue" had already been answered by the legislature. It stated: "By moving this line [between violent and non-violent offenses], the BOP exceeded its authority and sought to exercise its discretion on an issue with regard to which it had none." With reference to the words "may" and "shall" in the statute, the dissent concluded that this pertained to no more than the case-by-case analysis that already takes place after an inmate has completed a substance abuse treatment program. Sentence reduction is not guaranteed for anyone. All the statute ensures is that prisoners be considered for early release. The dissent noted that their view would not preclude the BOP from establishing a uniform set of criteria to be used for those considerations—with "dispositive weight" for certain post-conviction factors and "near-dispositive weight" for pre-conviction factors—as long as the criteria did not "contravene policy decisions explicitly made by the statute's drafters."

COMMENT: Although this was a 6-3 split decision, and the dissent set forth some compelling arguments, the Supreme Court has now spoken on the issue and it seems clear that these regulations will stand. An inmate convicted of committing a felony while carrying, possessing, or using a firearm will categorically be denied eligibility for early release, whether or not the felony was a "crime of violence."

Methadone Treatment Allowed to Continue in Vermont Jails

Catch-22 in Drug Treatment Policy. Vermont law permits methadone to be dispensed for the treatment of drug addiction only within "treatment programs" located within hospitals or medical school facilities, and only when the facilities have agreed to provide those treatment services. This restriction resulted in a Catch-22 predicament for Keith Griggs, a Vermont state inmate on furlough. At the time of his furlough, there was no methadone clinic in Vermont, and anyone needing such treatment had to travel to a neighboring state. As a condition of his furlough on a forgery conviction, Griggs had been participating in a program for nonviolent offenders with substance abuse problems and, for over two years, had been receiving methadone from a Massachusetts clinic. When he was sentenced to 15 days in a correctional facility after he failed to complete an assignment for the program, he brought his prescribed doses of methadone with him to the facility and asked that he be allowed to continue receiving treatment while in jail. Officials from the Vermont Department of Corrections, however, denied his request because they decided that providing methadone to incarcerated heroin addicts would violate existing state law and a DOC policy against opiates of any kind in correctional facilities. Griggs brought suit against DOC officials. After eight days, he was suffering from intense withdrawal symptoms. Although the county court found in his favor, and despite a possible $1,000 a day penalty, the DOC refused to comply with that court's order and appealed.

Court Overrules DOC. Vermont's highest court upheld the lower court decision requiring the DOC to administer prescribed methadone to Griggs. *Griggs v. Gorczyk*, 172 Vt. 641, 782 A.2d 86 (2001). Although the decision is unpublished, newspaper accounts relate that Justice Skoglund stated that providing this treatment would not turn the correctional facility into a health-care facility and would not contravene Vermont law on treatment programs. She made note of the fact that one condition of Griggs's participation in the DOC's program for nonviolent offenders was that he continue with his methadone treatment unless it was discontinued by his doctor. Other judges have also required methadone treatment as a condition of release, in spite of the fact that it must be sought outside of Vermont. Therefore, Justice Skoglund stated that the DOC "should have anticipated the possibility that, should Mr. Griggs violate his furlough and be admitted to a correctional facility, his methadone addiction would need to be addressed in a medically sound and humane manner and that the Massachusetts doctor would have the authority to determine 'the manner in which defendant's methadone is discontinued.'" Faced with this decision by the Vermont Supreme Court, rendered at 9 p.m. on a Saturday night, the DOC decided to release Griggs that night—five days before the end of the sentence.

A Different Decision in Another Case. Six weeks later, there was a different decision when the issue arose again. Vermont's Prisoners' Rights Office petitioned a Superior Court to order that gradually decreasing doses of methadone be administered to Gibson, a heroin-addicted inmate, on the grounds that such treatment was medically necessary. Gibson was being held without bail while awaiting a hearing on a probation violation that could result in several years of incarceration. In this instance, the same judge who initially heard the Griggs case (and ruled in his favor) held that Gibson was receiving adequate treatment for withdrawal symptoms in accordance with DOC policy and that, because he could not receive any other kind of treatment within the state of Vermont, he was being treated no differently than any other state resident. "The state has a method of dealing with drug addiction that does meet the community standard." There was a different result because, unlike the *Griggs* case, methadone treatment was never a condition of Gibson's probation.

State DOC Amends Treatment Policy. At the end of 2001, the Vermont Department of Corrections amended its policy with regard to methadone treatment. Pending the opening of an in-state methadone clinic that would administer treatments within the facilities, the DOC would allow inmates to receive methadone in jail if they had short sentences and were successfully participating in a methadone program before being incarcerated. It was expected that the first methadone clinic in Vermont would open within a few months. An attorney from the Vermont Prisoners' Rights Office speculated that the change was made because, once methadone treatment became available within the state, it could no longer be argued that inmates were receiving the same level of medical care for narcotic addiction as other Vermont residents.

COMMENT: *Methadone treatment is more costly than treatments that are usually provided by correctional systems. However, there is nothing in the record indicating that the DOCs' original decision was based on anything but its desire to comply with Vermont law. Further information on these cases and the issue of methadone treatment for inmates can be found in: Emily Stone, "Prisons to Allow Treatment," The Burlington Free Press B1 (November 28, 2001); Leslie Wright, "Judge Denies Inmate's Methadone," The Burlington Free Press A1 (August 11, 2001); Leslie Wright, "Methadone Issue Back in Court," The Burlington Free Press B1 (August 8, 2001); Tom Zolper, "Lawmakers Critical of Corrections' Decision," The Burlington Free Press A1 (July 3, 2001); Adam Silverman, "Addicted Inmate Released," The Burlington Free Press A1 (July 1, 2001); Leslie Wright, "Addicted Prisoner Denied Methadone," The Burlington Free Press A1 (June 29, 2001)*

DRUG TESTING OF OFFENDERS

Cases Confirming Legality of Random Drug Testing in Prison

For over 30 years it has been settled in the law that the reasonableness of conduct by prison officials will be determined by "balancing the significant and legitimate security interests of the institution against the privacy interests of the inmates." *Bell v. Wolfish*, 441 U.S. 520, 560 (1979). This is the standard that is applied to evaluate the reasonableness of urinalysis tests that are administered to prison inmates. In *McElhiney v. Booker*, 2000 U.S. App. LEXIS 7767 (10th Cir. April 25, 2000), the Tenth Circuit stated clearly: "Plain and simple, federal inmates are subject to urinalysis." The interest that prison officials have in preventing substance abuse among prisoners is both legitimate and substantial. The fact that there was a pending criminal prosecution against this particular inmate had no effect on the outcome since the testing was conducted randomly.

In another case, the Seventh Circuit reiterated the position that urinalysis is a search and, therefore, under the Fourth Amendment must be conducted in a reasonable manner. However, absent any proof from the plaintiff that the urinalysis testing policy was used for purposes of harassing inmates, the court upheld the reasonableness of the random testing. *Bridges v. Parke*, 1999 U.S. App. LEXIS 17914 (7th Cir. June 23, 1999).

Keep in mind that department regulations may provide for informing inmates of the consequences in the event they refuse urinalysis. In *Webb v. Goord*, 691 N.Y.S.2d 226 (A.D. 1999), the appellate court annulled the lower court finding against the petitioning inmate. It based its decision on the fact that it had not been established that the inmate had been advised of his rights upon refusal. This was required by the regulations of the New York Department of Corrections. In New York refusal can result in the same penalty as a positive test result.

Procedural Requirements

Chain of Custody. Webb v. Anderson, 224 F.3d 649 (7th Cir. 1999), is a reminder that the basic rules of evidentiary procedure must be followed in cases involving testing for inmate drug use. The result of a positive drug test is often the loss of an inmate's good time credits. It has been well-settled since *Wolff v. McDonnell*, 418 U.S. 539 (1974), that under those circumstances the inmate must have received the benefit of "those minimum procedures appropriate under the circumstances and required by the Due Process Clause [of the Bill of Rights]...." *Wolff* at 557.

In this case the plaintiff alleged that the chain of custody had been broken twice. First, the evidence did not confirm that the inmate's urine sample had been received by the laboratory technician in a sealed condition. Second, the name of the technician who performed the urinalysis was omitted from the report. Some lapses in the chain of custody, of course, will be tolerated. Here it was shown that the sample was received by the hospital in a sealed condition and the court found no reason to suspect that it had been tampered with in the 24-hour period before it was actually tested. Similarly, although the technician was anonymous, there was no reason to suspect that the sample had not been tested by the laboratory that issued the toxicology report. The Seventh Circuit Court of Appeals did view these omissions as "significant," but it did not see them as sufficiently material to the outcome of the case. Therefore, the appellate court did not disallow the reliance on the toxicology report as evidence of Webb's drug use.

COMMENT: When procedures become routine, often the attention to detail is lost. Although the evidence in this case was not disallowed, prison officials should see this decision as a reminder of how carefully courts look at the chain of custody.

Inmates' Requests for Drug Testing. An inmate's request for a retest of pipe residue was denied in the Fifth Circuit. *Henson v. United States Bureau of Prisons*, 213 F.3d

897 (5th Cir. 2000). In this case there was no doubt that correctional officers had found a pipe in Henson's possession. A field test of the residue in the pipe then showed it to be positive for marijuana. A subsequent test of his urine, as requested by the inmate, had a negative result. Henson's request for a re-test of the pipe residue, at his expense, was denied by prison officials. Disciplinary proceedings for possession then resulted in the loss of 14 days of good time credit and 30 days of visiting time, commissary time, and telephone privileges; in addition, he was placed in administrative segregation for 15 days. Henson's appeal was limited to the loss of the good time credit because he had a "statutorily-created liberty interest" in such credit.

The court noted: "When a prisoner has a liberty interest in good time credit, revocation of such credit must comply with minimal procedural requirements." It cited *Superintendent, Massachusetts Correctional Inst. v. Hill*, 472 U.S. 445 (1985), which listed the procedural requirements that usually must be observed in such cases:

- Notice;

- The opportunity to present evidence;

- "Some evidence" to support the decision; and

- Written findings that explain the basis of the decision.

On the other hand, courts recognize that the requirement of procedural safeguards must be carefully balanced against "legitimate penological interests." The Supreme Court also stated that these legitimate interests will include "assuring the safety of inmates and prisoners, avoiding burdensome administrative requirements that might be susceptible to manipulation, and preserving the disciplinary process as a means of rehabilitation." *Hill* at 455.

The evidence in *Henson* showed that the retest of the pipe residue was denied because the inmate did not allege any problems with the reliability or administration of the first test. Also, it was not clear whether there was even sufficient residue remaining to conduct a second test. The court noted further that a negative retest would not necessarily have resulted in a different outcome of the disciplinary proceeding, since the first test would remain as "some evidence" that he was guilty of possession. Finally, the court referred to several cases in other jurisdictions (Eighth and Ninth Circuits; Iowa) where retests were denied under similar circumstances.

COMMENT: The "legitimate penological interests" of prison administrators weigh heavily when balanced against Fourth Amendment safeguards.

Drug Testing Procedures Considered "Prison Condition"

Giano v. Goord, 250 F.3d (2nd Cir. 2001), dealt with the question of whether or not a complaint about drug testing procedures was "in respect to prison conditions." Julio F. Giano, a New York state inmate at the Wende Correctional Facility, brought an action against various defendants based on allegations that his drug tests had been contaminated. He believed that several corrections officers had taken these actions against him because of the role he had played in a prison protest. Specifically, he alleged that his urine samples were purposely contaminated with marijuana on two occasions—resulting in time in "keeplock," the loss of privileges, and other punishment.

Apparently, the urine samples gathered for purposes of drug testing were not kept in tamper-proof bottles or placed in a secure room. A lower court dismissed this claim because Giano had failed to exhaust his administrative remedies as required by the Prison Litigation Reform Act for complaints regarding "prison conditions."

The appellate court referred to previous case law within the circuit in which it defined "prison conditions" as "those aspects of prison life affecting the entire prison population" and, therefore, it reversed the lower court's ruling. Since Giano had alleged that the specific retaliatory actions were directed only against him, the statute did not require him to exhaust his administrative remedies before bringing this action. On the other hand, the court held that his other complaints were properly dismissed by the lower court since they related to the security of the prison's drug testing procedures in general. Drug testing procedures would be considered a condition that affects the entire prison population. (Although not requiring by law, the appellate court also expressed its feeling that the plaintiff should have received notice before that part of his claim was dismissed because "it is bad practice for a district court to dismiss without affording a plaintiff the opportunity to be heard in opposition"). The Second Circuit did not make any comment about the merits of plaintiff's action, but merely remanded the case for further proceedings.

In still another drug testing case, *Moore v. Atherton*, 2001 U.S. App. LEXIS 24457 (10th Cir. November 14, 2001), the plaintiff asserted that his constitutional rights had been violated by prison officials when they changed the established drug testing procedures without any notice to the inmates. Drug testing had previously been done with urine samples that were taken from the inmates, while the new procedure consisted of a drug "patch" test. The Tenth Circuit Court of Appeals had no trouble at all in affirming the district court's dismissal of this claim. It stated curtly that "[e]ven liberally construed, it is not clear from Mr. Moore's complaint what constitutional right he alleges was violated."

COMMENT: Since actions based on drug testing procedures seem to be brought by those who have failed such tests, success on the merits may turn out to be unlikely. Nevertheless, it remains important that the procedures are—and are perceived to be—both secure and fair.

STANDARDS OF CARE

Inmates With Symptoms of Intoxication/Withdrawal

Tenth Circuit Holds Jail's Policy and Manual Sufficient to Preclude Liability for Suicide of Inmate With DTs. Van Curen v. McClain County Board of County Commissioners, 2001 U.S. App. LEXIS 952 (10th Cir. January 23, 2001), without published opinion at 242 F.3d 392, arose as a result of the suicide of a county jail inmate who was suffering from delirium tremens. His condition was quite obvious, with symptoms that included paranoia, agitation, disorientation, and hallucinations, and therefore he was placed in a padded cell with instructions that he be checked on a regular basis. The inmate's abnormal behavior continued over the course of two days. The last time he was checked he had his jumpsuit on his head, but he responded to a command that he put his clothes back on. Although he had generally been checked every 20 to 30 minutes, this last time 90 minutes passed before he was checked again. It was then discovered that he was dead, with the probable cause being "complications of alcoholism (probable delirium tremens)."

As tragic as this incident was, the Tenth Circuit held that the plaintiff in this case, the inmate's mother, had not alleged any facts that would prove that there had been "inadequate supervision and training of jail personnel, rising to the level of a policy of indifference." The jail's policy and procedure manual provided for 24-hour emergency medical services, and set out the procedures for dealing with inmates who were withdrawing from alcohol. Because these procedures, which the jailers were required to become familiar with, were designed to protect the inmates' health and well-being, it could not be said that their training and supervision were inadequate.

Fifth Circuit Holds Even Where Jail Policy Is Sufficient, Individual Officer Can Be Liable for Delay of Treatment.

Thompson v. Upshur County, Texas, 245 F.3d 447 (5th Cir. 2001), was complicated by the admitted fact that this inmate, who was also suffering from delirium tremens, had persisted in his refusal to be transported to a hospital for treatment and had signed a refusal-of-medical-treatment form. Therefore, instead of being transferred to a hospital, the inmate was transferred from the Marion County jail back to the Upshur County jail. That facility had a detoxification cell where it was thought that the inmate could be more easily observed and treated.

One of the defendants, Sgt. Whorton, was the officer on duty as the inmate's condition worsened. Whorton placed him in a straight jacket, cleaned the wound on the back of his head (received from a fall), and placed additional mattresses on the floor of the cell, but she did not fit him with the helmet that was used to protect inmates in this condition. When Whorton's shift ended, she allegedly made a number of statements to the jailers coming on duty, including that: (1) there was nothing that could be done for the inmate and that he should be left alone unless he was bleeding to death, (2) he would soon be transferred and would no longer be their problem, (3) inmates were not taken to the hospital unless they were dying, and (4) help should not be summoned without calling Whorton at home, but that she should not be called unless the inmate was dying. One of the other jailers stated that they would have called an ambulance but that they did not want to go over Whorton's head. Furthermore, in light of her instructions, they were reluctant to call her at home. Early the following morning the inmate seemed to have a seizure, he stopped breathing, and he was declared dead upon arrival when he reached the hospital. The parents of the deceased inmate brought this suit against Whorton and others.

The appellate court held, as a matter of law, that the sheriffs in charge of the county jails were not guilty of deliberate indifference to this inmate's serious medical needs. The court did note that delirium tremens had been recognized as a serious medical condition in the Fifth Circuit as least as early as 1979. However, with regard to the sheriff of the Marion County jail, it found that his actions were not unreasonable because at the time when this incident occurred there was no established duty to "force a conscious, incompetent, but clearly refusing inmate to undergo medical treatment or seek a surrogate decision-maker for the same." Similarly, the Upshur County sheriff was found to be not liable. The court held that it had not been presented with any evidence to show that there was an Upshur County jail policy that would have prevented the inmate from receiving the care he needed.

However, the court did find that sufficient issues of fact were raised with regard to Sgt. Whorton's conduct to require a trial on these issues. The court stated that it was well settled in the law that the delay or denial of treatment for delirium tremens would be an unconstitutional violation of a prisoner's rights under the Eighth Amendment. It observed that the facts, as alleged by the plaintiff, would establish that it would be unreasonable to fail to summon medical aid before the inmate reached the point of death, and it would be unreasonable to instruct subordinates as Whorton did with regard to calling an ambulance or calling her at home. The judges stated further: "We do not believe that [the inmate's] refusal of medical care in Marion County could be reasonably understood to absolve Whorton of her constitutional duty to summon professional medical assistance several hours later or justifies her imposition of the verge of death standard for the provision of professional medical assistance."

COMMENT: As in all cases where summary judgment in favor of one party is reversed, the court looked at the alleged facts in a light most favorable to opposing party. Reversing summary judgment merely means that the truth of the alleged facts must still be established at trial. In this case it meant that "[t]he issue of Whorton's state of mind is for the trier of fact...."

Fourth Circuit Says Appropriate Response to Drug Withdrawal Risks Precludes Liability Even if Harm Not Averted. In *Brown v. Harris*, 340 F.3d 383 (4th Cir. 2001), the inmate in question committed suicide after he had been imprisoned for a probation violation as a result of an action by his probation officer. The inmate had failed a random urinalysis and he had admitted using drugs and attempting suicide. The probation officer informed the processing supervisor at the Virginia Beach General Jail of these facts, although she placed most of her emphasis on the fact that he now might become "volatile" since he had a history of attacking a staff member while withdrawing from drugs. The inmate was put on "medical watch" and housed in one of the 28 cells that could be under continuous observation on small video screens. Three days after his re-arrest the inmate hanged himself using his own shoelaces. His action was not observed by the officer in charge of monitoring the video screens; the "code" was called by someone else. At trial it was shown that the inmate was deprived of oxygen for four minutes before being discovered and treated. He was hospitalized and put on a ventilator, but he died after seven days.

The Fourth Circuit Court of Appeals ruled in favor of the defendants as a matter of law. Citing the landmark case of *Farmer v. Brennan*, 511 U.S. 825 (1994), the appellate court held that "an official 'who actually [knows] of a substantial risk to inmate health or safety may be found free from liability if [he] responded reasonably to the risk, even if the harm was not ultimately averted.' " The risk of an attempt at suicide is certainly the type of "serious harm" that has been contemplated by the courts in the past. Furthermore, in this case it seemed that the defendants all acted reasonably in light of that risk. The probation officer did inform the jail officials that there was a risk of a suicide attempt, even if he put more emphasis on the risk that this inmate might pose to jail personnel. In turn, jail officials did immediately place him on "medical watch." Indeed, even if there were some additional precautions that could have been taken by those in charge—and perhaps should have been taken—the court stated that it would be evidence of negligence rather than "deliberate indifference."

COMMENT: The courts may question the absence of procedures for dealing with drug withdrawal, or for dealing with inmates undergoing alcohol detoxification. However, it seems that if procedures are in place, and are substantially followed, corrections personnel will not be seen as liable for the consequences—however tragic.

Offender's Right to Adequate Medical Treatment

Arrestee Denies Problem; Declines Treatment. Whenever law enforcement officers or corrections officials become aware that there is a serious risk to the health of an individual over whom they have control, they are charged with responsibility for ensuring that the individual will receive adequate medical treatment to abate that risk. But what are the parameters of that responsibility?

Ralph L. Watkins, Jr., was arrested after a search of his apartment for drugs, pursuant to a search warrant. The arresting officers found a torn plastic bag, some loose crack cocaine, and other evidence that aroused a suspicion that Watkins had just swallowed some drugs. However, in spite of assurances that he would not face any additional charges if that were the case, and warnings about the possibility of dying from the effect of the swallowed drugs, Watkins denied swallowing anything. He also declined medical treatment. Apparently assured by his statements, the police officers did not communicate their suspicions to anyone else.

After being transported to county jail, Watkins began to complain of an upset stomach, and also behaved as if he were drunk or high. This time it was the jail employees who asked him if he had ingested any drugs or alcohol, and assured him again that admission of that fact would not result in additional charges. Again Watkins denied that he had swallowed drugs, and he gave reasonable explanations for his behavior. He was not required to undergo any medical evaluation and, shortly thereafter, he was placed in an observation cell.

No doubt because he was still complaining of feeling ill, Watkins was apparently observed by one deputy or another at about 15-minute intervals. At these times he was sitting, standing, or walking about the cell. In spite of these precautions, not long after, during a routine head count, he was found behind the privacy wall in his cell. He was not breathing and had no pulse. CPR was administered, but Watkins could not be revived. Thereafter, Lily V. Watkins, as the representative of Watkins' estate, brought an action based on alleged violations of Watkins' constitutional rights.

Did the Officers Do Enough? The District Court for the Western District of Michigan granted summary judgment for the defendants, and the Court of Appeals for the Ninth Circuit voted two to one to affirm. *Watkins v. City of Battle Creek*, 273 F. 3d 682 (6th Cir. 2001).

It has been consistently held that, even though pretrial detainees may be not protected by the Eighth Amendment, the due process guarantees of the Fourteenth Amendment function to provide analogous rights—including the right to adequate medical treatment. Under both of these amendments, it is necessary to establish that there was deliberate indifference to a serious medical need. Here, although the medical need was serious, it was not proven that the defendants had been deliberately indifferent to the decedent's condition. Arguments might be raised as to whether or not the defendants, the police officers in particular, had enough knowledge and experience to recognize that Watkins was experiencing a drug overdose—but that is not the standard to which they are held. No police officer saw Watkins swallow the drugs and, despite repeated questioning and the offer of medical assistance, he repeatedly denied that accusation and countered suspicions with reasonable explanations. The jail officers, despite the fact that no red flags had been raised, reacted as soon as Watkins complained of feeling sick. He was questioned about his symptoms and kept under observation, and may have received still more attention had he not refused medical treatment and denied—again—ingesting drugs. Furthermore, in light of the fact that the evidence failed to prove that there were violations of Watkins' rights under the Eighth Amendment, plaintiff's allegations that the officers and deputy sheriffs were improperly trained must also fail.

With regard to the plaintiff's Fifth Amendment claim, the court held that there was "absolutely no evidence that could lead a reasonable jury to find that any of the defendants intended to punish Watkins."

The dissenting judge raised the issue of whether any defendants were aware of facts that would be sufficient to cause a reasonable person to draw the inference that there was a serious risk to Watkins' health, and whether they responded in a reasonable way to that risk. A jury can reach the conclusion that an inference should have been drawn based upon direct evidence or circumstantial evidence, or when the risk is obvious. Judge Moore argued that, according to the facts as alleged, it seemed as if the police officers did have sufficient information to raise a suspicion that Watkins had swallowed drugs. She viewed the decision rendered by the other two judges to affirm summary judgment in favor of defendants as an indication that, even after the defendants realized that there could be a serious risk to his health, "Watkins' lies insulate the defendants from liability...." However, she noted that the plaintiff had alleged that it was obvious that Watkins' statements were lies and therefore medical treatment should have been provided. In the final analysis, Judge Moore regarded the dispute about whether or not it was reasonable to believe Watkins' statements to be a material question of fact and, as such, believed that it would have been better to leave this question for a jury.

COMMENT: The differing opinions underscore the uncertainty in the record regarding what the defendants really believed, and assessment of credibility is a function of the trier of facts. Based on an observation that the police and corrections officers do not usually seem to be so willing to rely on the word of suspects and inmates, it seems clear that defendants' assertion that their suspicions had been allayed by Watkins' statements should have been subject to jury scrutiny.

DRUG ADDICTION AS A DISABILITY UNDER THE ADA

Ninth Circuit Says Addiction Is a Disability

On a critical issue of first impression in the Ninth Circuit, the Court of Appeals examined whether state inmates who are recovering from addiction to drugs should be considered "disabled" under the Americans with Disabilities Act (ADA). *Thompson v. Davis*, 282 F.3d 780 (9th Cir. 2002), arose because the plaintiffs, Thompson and Bogovich, were denied parole by the California Board of Prison Terms. Both men had been imprisoned for second-degree murder, sentenced to terms of 15 years to life; both had become eligible for parole in 1993. When they were initially incarcerated, the plaintiffs were both addicted to drugs. However, while in prison, they both participated in drug abuse treatment with the result that Bogovich had been drug-free since 1984 and Thompson since 1990. At the time the suit was filed neither inmate had yet been granted parole, and they alleged that they had been wrongfully denied parole based on the Board of Prison Term's unwritten policy that parole should automatically be denied for prisoners with a history of drug abuse. Because of this alleged policy, the plaintiffs believed that they had both been denied individual assessments on the question of whether they would pose a threat to the community if they were granted parole. They based their claim on the protections granted under the ADA. The lower court dismissed their action, holding that the ADA does not apply in a criminal context. The plaintiffs subsequently appealed.

Necessary Elements for ADA-Based Discrimination Claim. The appellate court examined the plaintiffs' allegations to see if they had stated a claim for discrimination on the basis of a disability. To do so, the plaintiffs had to have alleged four elements:

1. That they were individuals with disabilities;

2. That they were otherwise qualified to participate in, or receive the benefit of some service, program, or activity provided by a public entity;

3. That they were excluded, or denied benefits, or otherwise discriminated against by the public entity; and

4. That their treatment was a result of their disability.

The court held that drug addiction is, in fact, a disability as defined by the ADA, because it "substantially limits one or more of the major life activities"—the ability to learn, to reason, to make rational judgments, and to work. It emphasized that, unlike the plaintiffs, individuals who were currently using illegal drugs would not be considered "qualified." However, those who were no longer using drugs and who were also participating in a drug rehabilitation program, as well as those who had successfully completed such programs—like the plaintiffs—did fit the definition of "qualified" individuals. Also qualified would be those who were erroneously believed to be drug addicts.

ADA Applies in Corrections and Criminal Law. The Ninth Circuit had previously decided that parole proceedings (*Armstrong v. Wilson*, 124 F.3d 1019 (9th Cir. 1997); *Armstrong v. Davis*, 275 F.3d 849 (9th Cir. 2001)), as well as prison disciplinary hearings (*Duffy v. Riveland*, 98 F.3d 447 (9th Cir 1996); *Boner v. Lewis*, 857 F.2d 559 (9th Cir. 1988)), were subject to the ADA in terms of access, and the plaintiffs' statutory eligibility for parole established that, save for the fact of the discrimination, they would have been considered for parole.

Defendants' argument that the ADA does not apply in a criminal context was summarily rejected by the appellate court. It referred to *Pennsylvania Department of Corrections v. Yeskey*, 524 U.S. 206 (1998), in which the Supreme Court had already established that the ADA is to apply in prisons, stating that parole boards also fit the definition of a public entity: "Any department, agency ... or other instrumentality of a State ... or local government." Furthermore, the appellate court pointed out that in *Gohier v. Enright*, 186 F.3d 1216 (10th Cir. 1999), the Tenth Circuit had held that the ADA also applies to arrests. Although this issue had not yet been adjudicated in the Ninth Circuit, the court decided that "the weight of authority on the applicability of the ADA to arrests suggests that a state's substantive decision-making processes in the criminal law context are not immune from the anti-discrimination guarantees of federal statutory law." The unsigned, *per curiam* opinion also referred to the legislative history of the ADA and drew an analogy between racial discrimination—which, of course, is impermissible in making parole decisions—and discrimination on the basis of a disability. The statutory prohibitions against both types of discrimination find their roots in the Constitution's equal protection guarantees. The Ninth Circuit firmly stated: "The fact that considering a prisoner for parole is a substantive, criminal law decision does not license the decision-maker to discriminate on impermissible grounds." The plaintiffs' case was remanded for further proceedings.

COMMENT: The plaintiffs' claim had been dismissed before trial, so the truth of their allegations had not yet been established. The appellate court, therefore, did not comment on the merits of the claim. The decision was limited to a holding against the lower court's broad ruling that parole proceedings do not fall within the scope of the ADA. That, clearly, "is not the law."

Amended Opinion Issued on the Issue of Drug Addiction as a Disability under the ADA

In *Thompson v. Davis*, 282 F.3d 180 (9th Cir. 2002), reviewed above, the Ninth Circuit Court of Appeals held that state inmates recovering from an addiction to drugs should be considered "disabled" under the Americans with Disabilities Act (ADA) and, therefore, that it would be impermissible discrimination to consider their disability when considering whether or not to grant parole to such prisoners.

In referring to the legislative history of the ADA, the court drew an analogy to racial discrimination, which also has its roots in guarantees of equal protection under the Constitution. The purpose of the amended opinion seems to be to clarify that comparison, and highlight where the two types of discrimination might be dissimilar. In particular, the court adds a footnote that states: "Of course the practical operation of consideration of race and disability in the parole context will be different." Although racial discrimination can never be considered in the making of parole decisions because "that factor cannot be relevant to the assessment of a person's future dangerousness," the same cannot be said of a disability such as drug addiction. A history of drug addiction might, in fact, be relevant to a parole decision if it might lead "to a propensity to commit crime...." The court does not back away from its original holding that prison officials may not "categorically exclud[e] from consideration for parole all people with substance abuse histories." It is merely emphasizing that there must be "an individualized assessment of the threat they pose to the community ...." *Thompson v. Davis*, 295 F. 3d 890 (9th Cir. 2002).

THE RELIGIOUS NATURE OF AA AND SIMILAR PROGRAMS

Must Religion Go Hand-in-Hand With Addiction Treatment?

Alcoholics Anonymous (AA), and its 12-step progeny, are the primary treatment tools in the criminal justice system. Forty-four states use AA, Narcotics Anonymous (NA), or Cocaine Anonymous (CA) for drug treatment in their prisons and jails (Edwards, 2000, p. 310). However, a major component of these programs is the acceptance of a relationship with a "higher power" (Edwards, 2000, p. 312). This was the basis of several constitutional challenges.

Seventh Circuit Finds Violation of Establishment Clause. In *Kerr v. Farrey*, 95 F.3d 472 (7th Cir. 1996), the plaintiff challenged a prison requirement that all inmates with chemical dependence problems had to attend NA meetings. He was told that failure to attend would result in a higher security risk rating and less likelihood of being granted parole. The warden of the facility countered that inmates were only required to "observe" the meetings and, at any rate, "the higher being" concept could range from a religious concept of God to the non-religious concept of individual willpower." 95 F.3d. 475. There is no doubt that the Establishment Clause of the U.S. Constitution precludes the creation of a state religion or forcing anyone to practice a particular faith. In applying those principles to the facts of this case, the Court had no trouble in deciding that the State of Wisconsin had acted in a manner designed to coerce the plaintiff into attending NA meetings. It also found that NA's 12 steps were "based on the monotheistic idea of a single God or Supreme Being" and, therefore, that the state's action "favor[ed] religion in general over non-religion." 95 F.3d at 480.

Second Circuit Reasons Similarly. The Second Circuit came to a similar conclusion in *Warner v. Orange County Dep't of Probation*, 173 F.3d 120 (2nd Cir. 1999), cert. denied, 1999 U.S. LEXIS 7525. In this case the plaintiff, after pleading guilty to drunk driving and driving without a license, had been granted a term of probation with conditions. One of the conditions was that he attend AA meetings. (This was his third offense and he had voluntarily begun to attend AA meetings before sentencing, hoping to receive probation rather than jail time.) As an atheist, he objected to the religious content of the meetings but his probation officer encouraged him to continue attending meetings. After doing so for almost two years, he filed a complaint challenging this condition of probation. Thereafter, the Orange County Department of Probation offered alternative therapy. At trial, the district court found that plaintiff's rights had indeed been violated. However, because it found that plaintiff had incurred no substantial damages, it only awarded damages in the amount of one dollar.

The case was remanded to address the question of "whether, at the time he was sentenced, Warner was sufficiently aware of the nature and extent of A.A.'s religious component that his failure to object to, or appeal from, his sentence should be deemed a consent, waiver, or forfeiture." 173 F.3d at 121. The District Court found that he was not. The Circuit Court affirmed, allowing the decision in plaintiff's favor to stand. It noted that the plaintiff's early doubts were dispelled after assurances that the program was "spiritual" rather than religious. Nevertheless, the court felt compelled to "reiterate our unhappiness with imposing damages on a governmental entity whose officials were seeking not to impose obligatory religion but to require an alcoholic to deal with his addiction." 173 F.3d at 122. In noting that it was constrained to accept the lower court's decision, the appellate court also managed to express its opinion that "the district court's decision to set damages at the symbolic level of one dollar was just about right." 173 F.3d at 122.

COMMENT: No matter how altruistic the motive, it seems that requiring individuals to attend AA or other 12-step meetings will not be allowed due to the religious content of such programs. However, if 12-step programs with a religious basis are merely offered as one treatment option and there is a non-religious alternative, it is believed that the constitutionality of these requirements will be upheld.

Inmate Gets Only Token Damages for Constitutional Violation. In *Alexander v. Schenk*, 118 F.Supp. 2d 298 (N.D. N.Y. 2000), a federal district court in New York joined a number of other courts in recognizing that the religious nature of 12-step recovery programs runs afoul of the freedom of religion protections in the Establishment Clause. *Alexander* involved a plaintiff who had been placed in an alcohol and substance abuse treatment program at the facility where he was incarcerated in spite of the fact that he did not consent to the placement and repeatedly asked to leave the program. Although he claimed that he had been excused from participating in some activities because of a conflict with his own religious beliefs, the inmate was disciplined for sleeping during at least three group sessions and ordered to participate in all future group sessions.

In his subsequent action against facility officials the District Court agreed with his contention that he had been placed in the program against his will and that this violated his constitutional rights. There is no doubt that the program had a religious component, and governmental entities are prohibited from coercing participation in the exercise of religion. It also emphasized that the sincerity of the plaintiff's religious beliefs was not properly an issue because "[t]he Establishment Clause was not drafted to protect individuals with sincerely held beliefs." However, the court also made note of the fact that the purpose of the program was not to promote religion but to help participants to overcome their addictions by means of a well-proven structure. Although there had been a constitutional violation, the benevolent motives of the facility and the doubts about the plaintiff's beliefs led this court to the conclusion that there had not been any meaningful injury. Therefore, the court awarded the plaintiff damages in the amount of $1.00.

Inmate's Right to Raise Religious Freedom Issues

Another case, *Rauser v. Horn*, 241 F.3d 330 (2001), illustrates the principle that a prisoner may not be retaliated against for raising constitutional issues such as freedom of religion. Rauser, a state prison inmate eligible for parole, was told that he had to complete a number of behavioral programs including AA and NA, before he would be recommended for release. Although he objected to AA and NA for religious reasons, he was offered no alternatives. He filed an action against the prison officials and, thereafter, he was transferred to a prison much farther from his home and family, his job classification was reduced from the highest to the lowest, and his pay was reduced from $.41/ hour to $.18. The appellate court noted that a claim of retaliation requires proof of three elements:

- The action leading to the retaliation must be constitutionally protected;

- The alleged retaliation must be adverse to the inmate's interests; and

- There must be a causal connection between the constitutionally protected action and the retaliation.

Corrections cases are somewhat different than those where the alleged retaliation took place outside of the prison context since legitimate penological concerns must be considered. The court stated: "This means that, once a prisoner demonstrates that his exercise of a constitutional right was a substantial or motivating factor in the challenged decision, the prison officials may still prevail by proving that they would have made the same decision absent the protected conduct for reasons reasonably related to a legitimate penological interest." However, in this case the court found that enough evidence was presented by the plaintiff, including the timing of the retaliatory acts, so that "a reasonable jury could conclude that the prison officials penalized him because he insisted on exercising his First Amendment rights."

[**Editor's Note:** *It seems to be well-accepted that a dominant theme of 12-step recovery programs is the belief in a "Supreme Being." It is also well-accepted that these programs have been effective in helping addicts to recover. This leaves prison officials in a quandary if an inmate bases his objections to such treatment on religious grounds. It seems that it is still permissible to encourage participation, but that any attempt at coercion or retaliation will not be tolerated. An interesting case that was ultimately settled in the Second Circuit occurred when a taxpayer (the mayor of Middletown, New York) objected to the use of state revenues to fund private alcohol treatment, including AA, as a violation of the Establishment Clause of the U.S. Constitution. The lower court dismissed the claim on the merits, holding that the inclusion of AA in funded programs was permissible as long as participation was not coerced. DeStefano v. Miller, 67 F.Supp.2d 274 (S.D.N.Y. Sep 10, 1999) (NO. 96 CIV. 9124 CM). However, the appellate court vacated that judgment and remanded the case for further action based on its holding: "We must decline to distinguish A.A. from other religions for Establishment Clause purposes, ... we must be content to observe the rough boundary that the cases have established between that which is and that which is not 'religion' for these purposes [and] A.A., our cases teach, is on the religious side of the line." DeStefano v. Emergency Housing Group, Inc., 247 F.3d 397 (2nd Cir. 2001). Can this really mean that state funding will be terminated for all programs like AA? The court's belief, "That must, for us, be the end of the matter," is highly questionable. Even in the state where this decision was rendered there will be more heard on the matter. The latter case has nothing left to tell us, however, as just before a new trial was to start, the matter was settled when the New York State Office of Alcoholism and Substance Abuse Services and Mayor DeStefano came to an agreement over the way these types of programs are presented to parolees.*]

Alcoholics Anonymous and Confidential Communications

As discussed above, series of cases seem to support the conclusion that AA is a religious organization because it invokes spiritual values and emphasizes a "Higher Power." The Second Circuit has previously held that a county Department of Probation violated the Establishment Clause of the First Amendment by making attendance at AA meetings a condition of probation. The basis of its decision was the Constitutional guarantee that our government will not coerce anyone into supporting or participating in any religion. *Warner v. Orange County Department of Probation*, 115 F.3d 397 (2d Cir. 1997), reaff'd after remand, 173 F.3d 120 (2d Cir. 1998), cert. denied, 528 U.S. 1003 (1999). Through the summer of 2002, the Second Circuit was not aware of any decisions to the contrary in cases where an Establishment Clause issue was raised with regard to AA and similar 12-step programs.

Cleric-Congregant Privilege Claimed. In *Cox v. Miller*, 296 F.3d 89 (2d Cir. 2002), the defendant (an AA member) raised the issue of whether the lower court had acted in a discriminatory manner and had improperly exercised its discretion when it refused to apply the cleric-congregant privilege to confidential communications made to other members of AA. This privilege originated with the Roman Catholic sacrament of penance and was later adopted into English common law. The common law rule has evolved and been codified by all 50 states, and federal evidentiary rules provide that such privileges "shall be governed by the principles of the common law ... in light of reason and experience." New York State's law reads: "Unless the person confessing or confiding waives the privilege, a clergyman, or other minister of any religion or duly accredited Christian Science practitioner, shall not be allowed [to] disclose a confession or confidence made to him in his professional character as spiritual advisor." N.Y. Civ. Prac. Laws & Rules § 4505. During the early morning hours of New Year's Eve 1988, while extremely intoxicated, Paul Cox broke into the house where he had lived as a child and killed the occupants, Dr. Lakshman Rao Chervu and Dr. Shanta Chervu, with a knife he took from their kitchen. Cox contended that he heard a report of the murder a few days later but, because of an alcohol-induced blackout, was unaware that he had killed the occupants of his childhood home. The killing was unsolved for more than four years. In 1990, after more binge drinking and another blackout, Cox began to attend AA meetings. He stopped drinking, joined AA, and remained sober. However, his dreams and flash-backs eventually made him realize that he had murdered the two doctors. AA's tenets include making a moral inventory of oneself and admitting "to God, to ourselves, and to another human being the exact nature of our wrongs." Cox began to confide in other members of AA, sometimes in great detail, and continued to do so during the following two years. Eventually, one of them, on the advice of a psychiatrist, went to the police. When questioned by the police, others also repeated Cox's statements. After arresting Cox, police found that his palm print matched one found at the house where the murders took place. Defense's pretrial motion regarding confidentiality was denied and again, at trial, the court denied a motion to exclude the palm print evidence despite the argument that Cox would not even have been a suspect without the disclosure of confidential statements.

Non-Spiritual Guidance Not Protected. On appeal, the Second Circuit held that defendant's statements were not protected by New York's cleric-congregant privilege because there was no evidence that they were made for the purpose of obtaining spiritual guidance. New York law and previous cases have made it clear that four questions are critical in determining whether the privilege can be applied:

1. Is the recipient "a clergyman, or other minister of any religion";

2. What is the scope of the statute;

3. Who "owns" the privilege; and

4. What is the effect of granting the privilege?

However, the court felt that it was only necessary to address the scope of the communications protected by the statute. New York's highest court has held that privileged statements must have been made "in confidence and for the purpose of obtaining spiritual guidance." *People v. Carmona*, 627 N.E.2d 959 (1993). Although the Second Circuit expressed uncertainty over "whether we would treat A.A. the same as we treat traditional religions in this context," it did not find it necessary to reach that question in order to find that Cox's statements were not protected. There was no evidence that Cox spoke with his fellow members in order to obtain spiritual guidance. To the contrary, the court found that his statements concerning the murders were made "primarily to unburden himself, to seek empathy and emotional support, and perhaps in some instances to seek practical guidance (e.g., legal advice)." It acknowledged that Cox's conviction generated a great deal of controversy because the prosecutors used statements made to fellow members of AA, and that confidentiality may indeed be critical to the recovery of its members. In response, the Second Circuit concluded its lengthy opinion by explaining the political realities and constraints under which it rendered its decision. "Our role is not to decide the policy issues that underlie the State of New York's legislative or judicial choice to adopt or reject such an evidentiary privilege whether the confidentiality of A.A., and the social values it may promote, outweigh the State's interests in enforcing its criminal law and promoting the public's right to every person's evidence."

COMMENT: The appellate court referred to several articles that discussed the policy issues. Was it calling for New York State's legislators to read these articles as well? Judith G. Weiner, "'And the Wisdom to Know the Difference': Confidentiality vs. Privilege in the Self-Help Setting," 144 U. Pa. L. Rev. 243 (1995); Jan Hoffman, "Faith in Confidentiality of Therapy is Shaken," The New York Times, p. A2 (June 15, 1994); Jimmy Breslin, "Without a Shield, AA May Not Survive," Newsday (June 14, 1994).

SUBSTANCE USE AND VISITOR PRIVILEGES

Prisoner's Substance Use Doesn't Warrant Ban on Visitors

Some Limits Allowed. It is a settled principle of constitutional law that "[a] prison inmate retains those First Amendment rights that are not inconsistent with his status as a prisoner or with the legitimate penological objectives of the correctional system." *Pell v. Procunier*, 417 U.S. 817, 822 (1974). Recently the Sixth Circuit had to address the question of how much the First Amendment right to freedom of association could be limited in pursuit of legitimate penological objectives. In 1995 the Michigan Department of Corrections issued a number of new regulations governing visitation. The stated objective was to make it easier to supervise visits, which were increasing in tandem with an increasing prison population, and to reduce the smuggling of drugs and weapons into prisons. The U.S. Supreme Court had already ruled that prisoners do not have a constitutional right to contact visits—those that allow physical contact and that must be supervised by a corrections officer. *Kentucky Department of Corrections v. Thompson*, 490 U.S. 454 (1989). In its opinion, however, the Court emphasized that nothing therein should be taken as an indication that they would be inclined to rule the same way with regard to "a prison regulation permanently forbidding all visits to some or all prisoners" without the protections of due process.

In 1995, when Michigan's new regulations were first challenged, the Sixth Circuit followed the precedent set by the Supreme Court. At the time, it was led to believe that the regulations were only being applied to prisoners' contact visits. The Sixth Circuit came to recognize that this was not the case at all: "it turned out that the department seriously misled us and was applying the regulations to all visits, contact and non-contact." As a result, the same plaintiffs filed a new suit with regard to the restrictions that were placed on non-contact visits. The decision was significantly different. *Bazzetta v. McGinnis*, 286 F.3d 311 (6th Cir. 2002).

Corrections officials are required to present evidence to support their assertion that there is a connection between a challenged regulation and "legitimate penological objectives" but, once they have done so, the courts generally will not substitute their own judgment for the conclusions of those with more penological expertise. Here, there were both restrictions and a permanent ban to consider. The restrictions on minor brothers, sisters, nieces, and nephews, on natural children when a prisoner's parental rights have been terminated, and on minor children unless accompanied by an immediate family member or legal guardian all seemed to be related only to the desire to reduce the number of prison visitors. The appellate court supported the lower court's view that this was "an exaggerated response to perceived problems in prison visitation" that would place a strain on family relationships. In the case of a prisoner's own children, it is even a "cruel policy." Similarly, the restriction on non-contact visits by former prisoners, justified as a way to prevent disruptive activity, is also an "exaggerated response" that might cause significant negative consequences. The court noted that an alternative to this type of "blanket ban" was already in place, and urged the corrections department to improve the screening procedures for visitors.

Two-Strikes Visitor Ban Knocked Down. The Sixth Circuit also found that the permanent "two-strikes" ban on visitors violated the First, Eighth, and Fourteenth Amendments of the Constitution. The new regulations provided that two major misconduct violations related to substance abuse could result in the termination of all visitation privileges, with the exception of visits with attorneys and the clergy. These major misconduct violations are failure to submit to a drug test or possession of narcotics, alcohol, unauthorized prescription drugs, or drug paraphernalia. After a hearing, violations can result in the imposition of administrative punishments. Under the disputed regulations, no separate hearing is required before a permanent ban on visitation may be imposed and, although both the warden and the department director must approve, no explanation is required from the officials. The ban may be lifted after two years, upon request of the prisoner, but the regulations provide no criteria for evaluating such requests.

The appellate court emphasized that these regulations were unconstitutional both on their face and in practice. Bans were imposed "capriciously and according to no reviewable standards." In some instances they were "not imposed until well after a prisoner incurred the violations; an average of seven months … and in a few cases three years…." Sometimes the bans were "imposed for what is effectively a single drug infraction." The practices followed in lifting, or not lifting, the ban on visitation after two years also troubled the court. Removal of the ban was a matter of total discretion, and "the department has turned 'permanent restrictions for substance abuse … into a tool for general behavior management, where restrictions are routinely continued on the basis of behavior for which policy does not authorize a visiting restriction in the first place'" [Quoting from the lower court decision]. There was no evidence that imposition of a permanent ban on visitors had any effect on the deterrence of drug abuse in prisons, a legitimate penological goal. The ban did, however, have a severe effect on the prisoners' First Amendment right of association.

Cruel and Unusual Punishment. The ban on visitation also violated the Eighth Amendment's prohibition against cruel and unusual punishment. The appellate court stated that "depriving an inmate of all visitors for a period stretching indefinitely into the future is an extremely harsh measure, removing [what is, in the view of the district court] the 'single most important factor in stabilizing a prisoner's mental health, encouraging a positive adjustment to . . . incarceration, and supporting a prisoner's successful return to society." In *Farmer v. Brennan*, 511 U.S. 825 (1994), the Supreme Court established a test for judging cruel and unusual punishment: deprivation of one of the "minimal civilized measures of life's necessities" and wanton disregard of the consequential risk to a prisoner's health or safety. Is visitation one of life's necessities? The district court stated that it "goes to the essence of what it means to be human; it destroys the social, emotional, and physical bonds of parent and child, husband and wife, body and soul. Nothing could be more fundamental." A knowledge and disregard of the risk to prisoners' health and safety can be inferred in this instance since it "should be clear to any prison official minimally concerned with prisoners' welfare." Finally, the Fourteenth Amendment required due process in the implementation of these regulations since "a complete ban on all visitors is such a grievous loss that it infringes on a liberty interest protected by substantive due process." The Sixth Circuit Court of Appeals confirmed judgment in favor of the plaintiffs and through its decision it upheld the contemporary belief that, if we are a civilized society, our prisoners must be treated with a minimum standard of decency. In support of this view, it quotes Winston Churchill: "'[a] calm and dispassionate recognition of the rights ... even of convicted criminals against the state, a constant heart-searching by all those charged with the duty of punishment ... these are the symbols in which the treatment of crime and criminals mark and measure the stored-up strength of a nation."

COMMENT: Apparently, Herbert L. Drayton based his challenge of the Michigan regulations on the wrong theory. This prisoner also challenged the permanent ban on visitation after "two or more violations of the major misconduct charge of substance abuse." However, in his suit, he argued that the ban had been imposed for retaliatory reasons because he had previously filed administrative grievances. To establish a claim of retaliation, a prisoner must prove: (1) that his conduct was protected, (2) that the treatment received would prevent a reasonable person from engaging in that conduct in the future, and (3) that the conduct was at least partly the reason for the adverse treatment. Drayton could prove the first and second elements, but could not establish that there was a connection between the two. Contrary to the holding in Bazzetta, *in this case the appellate court found no problem with a three-year delay in imposing the ban because "several prisoners besides Drayton were subjected to permanent visitation restrictions several years after their misconduct convictions occurred." The delay seems to have been caused by a change in the regulations. In 1995 the matter of referral to the Department of Corrections was left to the discretion of the warden, but a 1998 amendment made that referral mandatory. It also specifically made subject to the new policy all "tickets" that had been received by prisoners after August 25, 1995, for major misconduct relating to substance abuse—at least a two and a half year difference. Interestingly, none of the members of this three-judge panel were the same as the three who heard the* Bazzetta *appeal.*

Conditions of Visitation While on Probation

In an earlier case, the Tenth Circuit has held that a prohibition on family visitation for a six-month period, in conjunction with a court ordered drug rehabilitation program, does not constitute cruel and unusual punishment under the Eighth Amendment. Angela Romero was convicted of six counts of residential burglary but, in lieu of an 18-year sentence, she was placed on probation for a period of four years and ordered to participate in a drug rehabilitation program. When Romero violated that probation, rather than re-instating the original sentence, the court imposed the additional condition that she complete a specified long-term residential rehabilitation program. However, Romero did not even enter the required program. At the time she had five minor children, and one was a 13-year-old who had recently run away and with whom she was trying to re-establish contact. In appealing the re-instatement of the original 18-year sentence, Romero alleged that she had fled only after she learned that the program would not permit any contact with the members of her family during the first six months of rehabilitation. Citing the first *Bazzetta* case, among others, the Tenth Circuit appellate court stated: "Visitation with family members may be restricted when necessary to meet penological objectives such a rehabilitation of prisoners ...." In this case the plaintiff was unable to demonstrate that the six-month ban on visits with her family members was unrelated to the legitimate goal of rehabilitation. *Romero v. Lucero,* 1998 U.S. App. LEXIS 16371 (10th Cir. July 17, 1998) [unpublished opinion].

About the Author

Margaret R. Moreland, J.D., M.S.L.S., is Librarian for Research Services at Pace University School of Law Library.

References

Ditton, Paula M. (1999). *Mental health and treatment of inmates and probationers.* (Bureau of Justice Statistics Special Report, NCJ-174463). Washington, DC: U.S. Department of Justice.

Edwards, Timothy *The Theory and Practice of Compulsory Drug Treatment in the Criminal Justice System,* 2000 Wisconsin L. Rev. 284, 304 (2000).

Index

[References are to page numbers.]

A

ACA. *See* American Correctional Association (ACA)

ADA. *See* Americans with Disabilities Act (ADA), drug addiction as disability under

ADAM program. *See* Arrestee Drug Abuse Monitoring (ADAM) program

Addiction
barriers to understanding, 38-1–38-2

Addiction Severity Index (ASI), 1-4

Addiction Technology Transfer Center (ATTC) Network
California-specific training curriculum, 36-5
change strategies, application of
"big picture" need to work with, 36-7
examples of programs, 36-7–36-8
issues, 36-6–36-7
Criminal Justice/Substance Abuse Cross Training curriculum, 36-4–36-5
cross training curricula
California-specific training curriculum, 36-5
Criminal Justice/Substance Abuse Cross Training curriculum, 36-4–36-5
female offenders, 36-6
mental disorders, substance abuse and criminal justice practitioners, 36-5
therapeutic community (TC) training, 36-5
examples of programs, 36-7–36-8
female offenders cross training curriculum, 36-6
funding of, 36-2
Great Lakes ATTC
Center for Excellence in Criminal Justice at TASC, 36-7–36-8
partnerships with substance abuse agencies by, development of, 36-6
technical assistance review, 36-7
Gulf Coast ATTC; cross training for mental disorders, substance abuse and criminal justice practitioners, 36-5
interventions to bridge gap, role in creating
"Change Book," 36-3–36-4
federal and state relationships, enhancement of, 36-3
implementation steps, 36-3–36-4
transfer activities and products, 36-4
mental disorders, substance abuse and criminal justice practitioners, cross training curriculum for, 36-5
Mid-America ATTC
partnerships with substance abuse agencies by, development of, 36-6
therapeutic community (TC) cross training curriculum, 36-5
Mid-Atlantic ATTC
Criminal Justice/Substance Abuse Cross Training curriculum, 36-4–36-5
juvenile probation officers, course of study for, 36-7
mission of, 36-2

New England ATTC, development of partnerships with substance abuse agencies by, 36-6
Pacific Southwest ATTC
California-specific cross training curriculum, 36-5
Continuous Quality Improvement (CQI) Program, 36-8
partnerships with substance abuse agencies by, development of, 36-6
Work Force Development Training Project, 36-8
partnerships with substance abuse agencies by, development of, 36-6
Prairielands ATTC; female offenders cross training curriculum, 36-6
role of, xii
Substance Abuse and Mental Health Services Agency (SAMHSA) funding of, 36-2
therapeutic community (TC) training
cross training curricula, 36-5

Adolescents
adolescence-limited offenders, 3-2
co-occurring mental health and substance abuse disorders in, rates of, 2-2

Adoption and Safe Families Act (AFSA)
engine of reform, as, 10-3
New York Family Drug Treatment Courts (FTCs) obligation to implement, 10-3–10-4
parents, demands on, 10-1

Adult learners
training, 38-5

Adult programs
drug court, 9-3

Affective disorders, 2-7–2-8

AFSA. *See* Adoption and Safe Families Act (AFSA)

Aftercare services
Amity Therapeutic Community at Richard J. Donovan Correctional Facility (RJDCF) development of, 13-7–13-8, 33-8
case management, 34-2–34-3
continuity-of-care model. See Continuity-of-care model
drug court, 9-6
employment. See Employment
sex offenders, for substance abusing, 17-8
supervision in, xi
Treatment Accountability for Safer Communities (TASC) program case management, 34-2–34-3
treatment without, efficacy of, A-4
twelve principles of effective systems to reduce recidivism and increase retention in treatment programs. *See* Twelve principles of effective systems to reduce recidivism and increase retention in treatment programs

Age
psychopathy and, 22-5

Agents of change
staff as, 37-10

Alcoholics Anonymous
   religious issues. *See* Religious issues

Alcoholism
   sex offenders, relationship between, 17-4

Alexander v. Flowers, App.-3

Alexander v. Schenk, App.-24–App.-25

Alumni activities
   drug court, 9-6

American Correctional Association (ACA)
   therapeutic community draft standards, 14-5

Americans with Disabilities Act (ADA), drug addiction as disability under
   amended opinion by Ninth Circuit, issuance of, App.-23
   corrections and criminal law, application of ADA to, App.-22–App.-23
   discrimination claim, elements necessary for, App.-22
   Ninth Circuit ruling on
      amended opinion, issuance of, App.-23
      case law, App.-21–App.-22
      corrections and criminal law, application of ADA to, App.-22–App.-23
      discrimination claim, elements necessary for, App.-22

American University Drug Court Clearinghouse and Technical Assistance Project (DCCTAP)
   research findings, P2-1–P2-2, 8-4, 9-3

Amity Therapeutic Community at Richard J. Donovan Correctional Facility (RJDCF)
   aftercare component, development of, 13-7–13-8, 33-8
   bottom line savings, 13-10
   coordination between program and staff, 13-4–13-5
   cross training, 13-10
   curriculum, 13-9–13-10
   effectiveness of program, 13-10–13-11, 20-2
   eligibility parameters, expansion of, 13-6–13-7
   general prison life, integration into, 13-6
   impetus for, 13-3–13-4
   implementation of
      aftercare component, 13-7–13-8
      coordination between program and staff, 13-4–13-5
      eligibility parameters, expansion of, 13-6–13-7
      inmate population, working with, 13-5
      integration into general prison life, 13-6
      life sentence prisoners as peer mentors, 13-6–13-7
      screening of inmates, 13-5
   inmate population, working with, 13-5
   integration into general prison life, 13-6
   Little Hoover Commission report, 13-2–13-3
   mixed model of continuity-of-care, as, 33-8
   outcome findings
      days on parole prior to first return to custody, 13-7
      percent returned to custody, 13-7
      regarding adverse behaviors, 13-11
   peer mentors, life sentence prisoners as, 13-6–13-7
   Project Recovery, 13-3
   results of surprise urine test, 13-12
   savings, bottom line, 13-10
   screening of inmates, 13-5
   staffing, 13-8–13-9
   structure and duration, 13-8

   training, 13-9
   warden, recruitment of, 13-4

Anti-Drug Abuse Acts
   Federal Bureau of Prisons (BOP) drug abuse treatment programs, effect on, 15-3

Antisocial personality disorder (ASPD)
   "garbage category," as, 22-3
   intimate partner violence (IPV), as characteristic of, 23-3–23-4
   psychopathy, distinguished from, 22-2–22-3
   sex offenders, as barrier to treating substance abusing, 17-7

Anxiety disorders
   See also specific disorder
   types of, 2-8
   women and, 2-8

Arizona
   Community Outreach Project on AIDS in Southern Arizona (COPASA for Women). *See* Community Outreach Project on AIDS in Southern Arizona (COPASA for Women)

Armstrong v. Davis, App.-22

Armstrong v. Wilson, App.-22

Arrestee Drug Abuse Monitoring (ADAM) program
   drawbacks of, 4-2–4-3
   findings, 20-1–20-2, P1-1–P1-2
   Houston data
      analysis and findings, 4-4–4-5
      descriptives, 4-4
      disaggregation of, benefits of, 4-7
      drug prevalence, 4-4–4-6
      limitations, 4-4
      methodological limitations, 4-6–4-7
      research caveats, 4-6–4-7
      sample, 4-3, 4-4
      self-report data, 4-3
      urine screen, 4-4

ASI. *See* Addiction Severity Index (ASI)

ASPD. *See* Antisocial personality disorder (ASPD)

Association of State Correctional Administrators (ASCA)
   national survey on therapeutic communities (TCs), 14-2, 14-4

Atherton, Moore v., App.-17

ATTC Network. *See* Addiction Technology Transfer Center (ATTC) Network

B

Bazzetta v. McGinnis, App.-28

Behavioral contracts
   use of, 32-8

Bellis v. Davis, App.-2, App.-11

Bell v. Wolfish, App.-15

Bench warrants
   drug courts, issued by, 9-10

Biopsychosocial model of treatment
   Federal Bureau of Prisons (BOP), 15-3–15-4

Black box of treatment
   Correctional Program Assessment Inventory (CPAI), insight provided by, 7-4

TCU Model of Treatment Processes and Outcomes, length of stay as critical component in, 27-4

Boner v. Lewis, App.-22

Booker, McElhiney v., App.-15

Booker, Ward v., App.-2, App.-12

BOP. *See* Federal Bureau of Prisons (BOP) drug abuse treatment programs

Bowen v. Hood, App.-11

Brennan, Farmer v., App.-19, App.-30

Bridges v. Parke, App.-15

Brown v. Harris, App.-19

C

Cadre Program
Kyle New Vision Program, 12-4

California
Addiction Technology Transfer Center (ATTC) Network cross training curriculum, 36-5
Amity Therapeutic Community at Richard J. Donovan Correctional Facility (RJDCF). *See* Amity Therapeutic Community at Richard J. Donovan Correctional Facility (RJDCF)
Corcoran State Prison Substance Abuse Treatment Facility (SATF). *See* Substance Abuse Treatment Facility (SATF) at Corcoran State Prison
drug courts, 9-3
expansion of prison therapeutic communities (TCs) in, 13-2, 17-2
female inmates
California Department of Corrections (CDC) treatment expansion initiative for, 18-6
Forever Free program, 18-4–18-5
Forever Free program, 18-4–18-5
mandatory prison-based treatment programs, 17-3
Proposition 36, P2-1
Richard J. Donovan Correctional Facility (RJDCF). *See* Amity Therapeutic Community at Richard J. Donovan Correctional Facility (RJDCF)
Substance Abuse Treatment Facility (SATF) at Corcoran State Prison. *See* Substance Abuse Treatment Facility (SATF) at Corcoran State Prison
therapeutic communities (TCs) programs
Amity Therapeutic Community at Richard J. Donovan Correctional Facility (RJDCF). *See* Amity Therapeutic Community at Richard J. Donovan Correctional Facility (RJDCF)
California Department of Corrections (CDC) treatment expansion initiative for female inmates, 18-6
expansion of, 13-2, 17-3
female inmates, 18-4–18-5, 18-6
Forever Free program for female inmates, 18-4–18-5
California Department of Corrections (CDC)
Amity Therapeutic Community at Richard J. Donovan Correctional Facility (RJDCF). *See* Amity Therapeutic Community at Richard J. Donovan Correctional Facility (RJDCF)
Corcoran State Prison Substance Abuse Treatment Facility (SATF). *See* Substance Abuse Treatment Facility (SATF) at Corcoran State Prison

Drug Reduction Strategy (DRS) project. *See* California Department of Corrections (CDOC) Drug Reduction Strategy (DRS) project
female inmates, treatment expansion initiative for, 18-6
Office of Substance Abuse Programs (OSAP), 13-3
Project Recovery, 13-3
Richard J. Donovan Correctional Facility (RJDCF). *See* Amity Therapeutic Community at Richard J. Donovan Correctional Facility (RJDCF)
sex offenders, treatment for substance abusing. *See* Sex offenders
substance abuse problems, 13-3
Substance Abuse Treatment Facility (SATF) at Corcoran State Prison. *See* Substance Abuse Treatment Facility (SATF) at Corcoran State Prison
task force studying substance abuse problems, 13-3–13-4
therapeutic community (TC). *See* Amity Therapeutic Community at Richard J. Donovan Correctional Facility (RJDCF)
treatment expansion initiative for female inmates, 18-6
California Department of Corrections (CDOC) Drug Reduction Strategy (DRS) project
additional drug detection measures
implementation of, 5-4
results, 5-5
conclusions, 5-6
drug-detection equipment, 5-6
drug interdiction efforts
drug-detection equipment, 5-6
K-9 teams, 5-5–5-6
implementation of
additional drug detection measures, 5-4
phase II (random urinalysis), 5-4
phase I (weekly urinalysis), 5-3–5-4
K-9 teams, 5-4, 5-5–5-6
program design
phases, 5-2–5-3
sites/prisons, 5-2
random urinalysis testing
implementation of, 5-4
results, 5-4–5-5
results
additional drug detection measures, 5-5
random urinalysis testing, 5-4–5-5
urine testing, P1-2, 5-3–5-4
Violent Offender Incarceration and Truth-in-Sentencing (VOI/TIS) Incentive Program, 5-1

Cannabis users, prediction of violent behavior in adolescent
Cannabis Youth Treatment (CYT) Study, 3-2, 3-3
Global Appraisal of Individual Needs-Crime and Violence Index (GAIN-CVI). *See* Global Appraisal of Individual Needs-Crime and Violence Index (GAIN-CVI)

Cannabis Youth Treatment (CYT) Study
methodology, 3-3
predictions, 3-2

Carmona, People v., App.-27

Case law
Alexander v. Flowers, App.-3
Armstrong v. Davis, App.-22
Armstrong v. Wilson, App.-22

Case law, *continued*
    Bazzetta v. McGinnis, App.-28
    Bellis v. Davis, App.-2, App.-11
    Bell v. Wolfish, App.-15
    Boner v. Lewis, App.-22
    Bowen v. Hood, App.-11
    Bridges v. Parke, App.-15
    Brown v. Harris, App.-19
    Cort v. Crabtree, App.-11
    Cox v. Miller, App.-26
    Duffy v. Riveland, App.-22
    Farmer v. Brennan, App.-19, App.-30
    Giano v. Goord, App.-16
    Gohier v. Enright, App.-22
    Henson v. United States Bureau of Prisons,
        App.-15–App.-16
    Kentucky Department of Corrections v. Thompson,
        App.-28
    Kerr v. Farrey, App.-23
    Kerr v. Puckett, App.-9
    Lasora v. Menfee, App.-11
    Lopez v. Davis, App.-3, App.-12
    Maurello v. United States, App.-10
    McElhiney v. Booker, App.-15
    Moore v. Atherton, App.-17
    Pell v. Procunier, App.-28
    Pennsylvania Department of Corrections v. Yeskey,
        App.-22
    People v. Carmona, App.-27
    Rauser v. Horn, App.-25
    Romero v. Lucero, App.-31
    Superintendent, Massachusetts Correctional Inst. v. Hill,
        App.-16
    Thompson v. Davis, App.-21, App.-23
    Thompson v. Upshur County, Texas, App.-18
    U.S. v. Lopez, App.-4–App.-5
    U.S. v. Rodriguez, App.-5
    U.S. v. Sandra Rhodes, App.-6
    U.S. v. Sherman, App.-6
    U.S. v. Sutton, App.-6
    *Van Curen v. McClain County Board of County
        Commissioners*, App.-17
    Ward v. Booker, App.-2, App.-12
    Warner v. Orange County Dep't. of Probation, App.-24
    Watkins v. City of Battle Creek, App.-20
CDC. *See* California Department of Corrections (CDC)
Center for Substance Abuse Treatment (CSAT)
    Cannabis Youth Treatment (CYT) Study, 3-2, 3-3
    Persistent Effects of Treatment Study of Adolescents
        (PETS-A), 3-3
Central Placement Unit (CPU). *See* New York City
    Department of Probation (DOP) drug treatment initiative
CETOP. *See* Cognitive Enhancements for the Treatment of
    Probationers (CETOP)
Child endangerment
    systems addressing, 10-2–10-3
CIDI–SF. *See* Composite International Diagnostic
    Interview–Short Form (CIDI–SF)
CIES. *See* Correctional Institutions Environment Scale
    (CIES)
City of Battle Creek, Watkins v., App.-20

Client Oriented Data Acquisition Program (CODAP) forms
    Texas Commission on Alcohol and Drug Abuse
        (TCADA), 26-2
Coalition for Recovery, Education and Work (CREW)
    model
    employment program-provider gaps, as bridge for, 34-5
CODAP forms. *See* Client Oriented Data Acquisition
    Program (CODAP) forms
Coerced admission to substance abuse treatment control
    program
    means of crime control, as, 32-4–32-5
Coerced admission to Substance Abuse Treatment Facility
    (SATF) at Corcoran State Prison, study of
    desire for treatment
        interaction between, 31-7–31-8
        results, 31-7
    incentives, 31-2
    limitations of study, 31-10
    matching treatment to inmate's motivation, 31-9
    multivariate models predicting six-month recidivism,
        31-8–31-9
    results
        desire for treatment, 31-7
        multivariate models predicting six-month
            recidivism, 31-8–31-9
        SATF vs. comparison group, 31-6
        treatment-desire interaction, 31-7–31-8
    return-to-custody (RTC)
        predicting probability of, 31-6
        six-month outcomes, 31-7, 31-8
    sample population, 31-3–31-4
    SATF vs. comparison group, results of, 31-6
    study design and methods
        demographic characteristics, 31-5
        motivation for treatment, measure of, 31-4–31-5
        recidivism rates, 31-5
        sample population, 31-3–31-4
        study measures, 31-4–31-5
        substance use severity, measure of, 31-4
Coercion
    effect of, A-5–A-6
    understanding role of motivation and coercion in
        treatment, 40-7
    Urban Institute project linking research to correctional
        drug treatment research, 40-7
Cognitive behavioral intervention
    criminal thinking–understanding logic and rewards,
        37-4–37-5
    targeting offender behavior–social learning and
        behavioral intervention, 37-5
Cognitive community
    criminal behavior, changing, 37-9–37-10
Cognitive Enhancements for the Treatment of Probationers
    (CETOP)
    believe it or not activity, 28-6
    change maps, 28-6
    corrections, special issues for, 28-3
    criminal justice system, applicability of research
        methods to, 28-2–28-3
    Downward Spiral game, 28-5–28-6, 29-7
    mood and self-esteem, activities to enhance

self-descriptors, selection of, 28-4
towers of strength activity, 28-4–28-5
weekly planner, 28-5
need for positive change, activities to develop
change maps, 28-6
Downward Spiral game, 28-5–28-6, 29-7
offenders in study, statistics of, 28-3
personal action list (PAL), 28-6–28-7
positive view of program and identification of important
personal actions, activities to develop
believe it or not activity, 28-6
personal action list (PAL), 28-6–28-7
top 10 reasons for "working the program," 28-7
research findings on TCU Readiness Series
"Consumer Satisfaction" questionnaire,
28-9–28-10
during-treatment impact, comparisons of,
28-8–28-9
enhanced treatment impact, comparison of
standard treatment to, 28-8–28-9
final comments, 28-11
strategies for making the most of the time, activities
providing
imagery, use of, 28-8
pegword memory technique, 28-7–28-8
seal act/costume ball, 28-7
sleep/strength list, 28-7
TCU Readiness Series
intent of, 28-4
mood and self-esteem, activities to enhance.
See subhead: mood and self-esteem,
activities to enhance
need for positive change, activities to develop.
See subhead: need for positive change,
activities to develop
positive view of program and identification of
important personal actions, activities to
develop. See subhead: positive view of
program and identification of important
personal actions, activities to develop
research findings. See subhead: research findings
on TCU Readiness Series
session 1. See subhead: mood and self-esteem,
activities to enhance
session 2. See subhead: need for positive change,
activities to develop
session 3. See subhead: positive view of program
and identification of important personal
actions, activities to develop
session 4. See subhead: strategies for making the
most of the time, activities providing
strategies for making the most of the time,
activities providing. See subhead:
strategies for making the most of the
time, activities providing
top 10 reasons for "working the program," 28-7
towers of strength activity, 28-4–28-5
treatment program, description of, 28-3
treatment readiness
corrections, special issues for, 28-3
criminal justice system, applicability of research
methods to, 28-2–28-3
key to success, as, 28-2

treatment readiness model activities. See Treatment
readiness model
Cognitive programs for changing criminal behavior
approaches, 37-7
assumptions, 37-6–37-7
essentials of, 37-6–37-7
responsivity, incorporation of, 37-7–37-8
Cognitive restructuring
basis of, 37-7
Cognitive skill training
basis of, 37-7
Communication
researchers and practitioners, enhancement between, A-3
supervision in aftercare, facilitating, 35-9
Community-based offender drug treatment
criminal justice system to, transition from. See
Continuity-of-care model
effectiveness of, 33-2
Community-based RSAT
assessment of, 7-4–7-6
Community models
resocialization for offenders, elements of, 37-6
therapeutic communities (TCs), 37-6
types of, 37-6
Community Outreach Project on AIDS in Southern Arizona
(COPASA for Women)
civil law difficulties, 19-4
criminal charges, 19-4–19-6
findings
drug use, association of legal problems to, 19-8
fear and avoidance of legal system, 19-8–19-9
implications for professionals, 19-9–19-10
study limitations, 19-9
goals of, 19-3
lack of faith in legal system, 19-6–19-7
legal component and instrumentation of study,
19-3–19-4
legal issues participants want help with, 19-7–19-8
legal problems reported, 19-4-19-5
legal system
fear and avoidance of, 19-8–19-9
issues participants want help with, 19-7–19-8
lack of faith in, 19-6–19-7
reasons for not utilizing, 19-6–19-7
reasons for not utilizing legal system, 19-6–19-7
statistics of participants, 19-4
study limitations, 19-9
Composite International Diagnostic Interview–Short Form
(CIDI–SF)
psychiatric screening instrument, 21-6
Computer-generated mapping programs
Arrestee Drug Abuse Monitoring (ADAM) program.
See Arrestee Drug Abuse Monitoring (ADAM)
program
drawbacks of, 4-2–4-3
drug-use data collection efforts, federal, 4-2
examples of, 4-1
purpose of, 4-1–4-2
Conduct disorders
substance abuse and, 2-7
symptoms, 2-10

Conflict Tactics Scale (CTS)
    domestic violence screening, 23-4
Contextualized questioning
    intimate partner violence (IPV), as screening and
        assessment strategy for substance abuse treatment
        providers with co-occurring, 23-4–23-5
Contingency management protocols
    positive behavior in early treatment, 27-5
Continuity-of-care model
    community funding as obstacle to, 33-7
    justice system perspective, 33-4–33-5
    lack of coordination between criminal justice system
        and treatment programs as obstacle to, 33-6
    lack of services in community as obstacle to, 33-6
    lack of treatment provider experience with offenders as
        obstacle to, 33-6
    loss of incentives and sanctions upon release as obstacle
        to, 33-6
    loss of post-release structure for offenders as obstacle to,
        33-6
    mixing models/programs, 33-8
    obstacles to
        community funding, 33-7
        lack of coordination between criminal justice
            system and treatment programs, 33-6
        lack of services in community, 33-6
        lack of treatment provider experience with
            offenders, 33-6
        loss of incentives and sanctions upon release, 33-6
        loss of post-release structure for offenders, 33-6
        segmentation of criminal justice system, 33-5
    offender perspective, 33-5
    Oregon demonstration project, 33-3–33-4
    outcome studies, results from, 33-2–33-3
    outreach programs, 33-7
    perspectives of
        justice system perspective, 33-4–33-5
        offender perspective, 33-5
    programs, theoretical underpinnings of, 33-4–33-5
    reach-in programs, 33-7
    segmentation of criminal justice system as obstacle to,
        33-5
    successful models, strategies for, 33-7–33-8
    third-party continuity programs, 33-7–33-8
    treatment practitioners, ideas for, 38-4–38-5
Continuum of care
    length of stay in treatment, effect of, 32-4
Co-occurring mental health and substance abuse disorders in
    adolescents, rates of
    characteristics of optimal instrument for, 2-3
    Diagnostic Interview Schedule for Children (DISC), 2-2
    Practical Adolescent Dual Diagnostic Interview
        (PADDI). See Practical Adolescent Dual
        Diagnostic Interview (PADDI)
COPASA for Women. See Community Outreach Project on
    AIDS in Southern Arizona (COPASA for Women)
Cornerstone Program
    effectiveness of, 20-2
Correctional Institutions Environment Scale (CIES)
    staff rating of SATF, 30-4, 30-5

Correctional Program Assessment Inventory (CPAI)
    advantages of, 7-4
    limitations of, 7-3–7-4
    problems with, P2-1
    residential substance abuse treatment (RSAT) programs,
        assessment of program integrity of. See
        Residential substance abuse treatment (RSAT)
        programs, subhead: assessments of
    scoring, 7-3
    sections of, 7-3
Cort v. Crabtree, App.-11
Cox v. Miller, App.-26
CPAI. See Correctional Program Assessment Inventory
    (CPAI)
CPU. See Central Placement Unit (CPU)
Crabtree, Cort v. Crabtree, App.-11
CREW. See Coalition for Recovery, Education and Work
    (CREW) model
Crime and Violence Index (CVI). See Global Appraisal of
    Individual Needs-Crime and Violence Index (GAIN-CVI)
Crime control
    treatment as means of, 32-4–32-5
Criminal and drug lifestyles. See Lifestyles, drug and
    criminal
Criminal behavior, changing
    accountability and change, integration of, 37-8–37-9
    agents of change, staff as, 37-10
    attributes attributed to criminal behavior and recidivism,
        37-2
    cognitive behavioral intervention
        criminal thinking—understanding logic and
            rewards, 37-4–37-5
        targeting offender behavior–social learning and
            behavioral intervention, 37-5
    cognitive community, 37-9–37-10
    cognitive programs. See Cognitive programs for
        changing criminal behavior
    criminogenic need principle, 37-4
    criminogenic risk principle, 37-3–37-4
    effective programs, elements of, 37-2–37-3, 37-11
    integrated approach to
        accountability and change, 37-8–37-9
        relapse prevention strategies, 37-8
        sanctions and treatment, 37-8–37-9
    members of treatment team, staff as community, 37-10
    principles, interplay of, 37-4
    relapse prevention strategies, 37-8
    responsivity principle, 37-4
    sanctions and treatment, integration of, 37-8–37-9
    social learning. See Social learning
Criminal justice system
    drug courts. See Drug courts
    drugs on, impact of, 8-1
    percentage of drug users in, 8-2
    transition to community from. See Continuity-of-care
        model
Criminogenic need principle
    criminal behavior, changing, 37-4
Criminogenic risk principle
    criminal behavior, changing, 37-3–37-4

Cross training
    Amity Therapeutic Community at Richard J. Donovan
        Correctional Facility (RJDCF), 13-10
Cross training curricula
    Addiction Technology Transfer Center (ATTC)
        Network. *See* Addiction Technology Transfer
        Center (ATTC) Network
CSAT. *See* Center for Substance Abuse Treatment (CSAT)
CTS. *See* Conflict Tactics Scale (CTS)
CYT study. *See* Cannabis Youth Treatment (CYT) Study

D

Dallas County Judicial Treatment Center (DCJTC)
    funding sources, influence of politics on, 26-4–26-5
    reconfigurations, 26-6
    Texas Christian University (TCU) Institute of Behavioral
        Research evaluation of, 26-2
DAP units. *See* Drug Abusers Program (DAP) units
DARP study. *See* Drug Abuse Reporting Program (DARP)
    study
DAST. *See* Drug Abuse Screening Test (DAST), findings of
DATOS-A. *See* Drug Abuse Treatment Outcome Study for
    Adolescents (DATOS-A)
DATOS study. *See* Drug Abuse Treatment Outcome Studies
    (DATOS) study
Davis, Armstrong v., App.-22
Davis, Bellis v., App.-2, App.-11
Davis, Lopez v., App.-3, App.-12
Davis, Thompson v., App.-21, App.-23
DAWN. *See* Drug Abuse Warning Network (DAWN)
DCCTAP. *See* American University Drug Court
    Clearinghouse and Technical Assistance Project
    (DCCTAP)
DCJTC. *See* Dallas County Judicial Treatment Center
    (DCJTC)
Delaware Key/Crest Program
    effectiveness of, 20-2
    outreach program, as example of, 33-7
Depression
    intimate partner violence (IPV), as characteristic of, 23-4
Diagnostic and Statistical Manual of Mental Disorders
    (DSM)
    screening instrument, as, 1-4
Diagnostic and Statistical Manual of Mental Disorders-IV
    (DSM-IV), 2-8, 3-3
    antisocial personality disorder (ASPD), 17-7, 22-2–22-3
    paraphiliac, defined, 17-3
    psychiatric disorders, assessment strategies and screening
        instruments for, 21-6
Diagnostic Interview Schedule for Children (DISC)
    co-occurring conditions, evaluation of, 2-2
DISC. *See* Diagnostic Interview Schedule for Children
    (DISC)
DLSI. *See* Drug Lifestyle Screening Interview (DLSI)
Downward Spiral game
    Cognitive Enhancements for the Treatment of
        Probationers (CETOP), 28-5–28-6, 29-7

DRS project. *See* California Department of Corrections
    (CDOC) Drug Reduction Strategy (DRS) project
Drug abuse
    See also Substance abuse
    self-report screen focus on, 1-4
Drug Abuse Reporting Program (DARP) study
    Texas Christian University (TCU), 26-2
Drug Abusers Program (DAP) units
    implementation of, 15-3
Drug Abuse Screening Test (DAST), findings of
    sex offenders, 17-4
Drug Abuse Treatment Outcome Studies (DATOS) study
    Texas Christian University (TCU), 26-2
Drug Abuse Treatment Outcome Study for Adolescents
    (DATOS-A)
    co-occurring conditions, evaluation of, 2-2
Drug Abuse Warning Network (DAWN)
    national probability survey, 4-2
Drug and criminal lifestyles. *See* Lifestyles, drug and
    criminal
Drug Court Clearinghouse and Technical Assistance Project
    (DCCTAP). *See* American University Drug Court
    Clearinghouse and Technical Assistance Project
    (DCCTAP)
Drug courts
    additional funding, need for, 9-8
    adult programs, 9-3
    aftercare services, 9-6
    alumni activities, 9-6
    American University Drug Court Clearinghouse and
        Technical Assistance Project (DCCTAP) research
        findings. *See* American University Drug Court
        Clearinghouse and Technical Assistance Project
        (DCCTAP)
    arrest and entry to program, time between, 9-9
    assessment process, 9-4–9-5
    assignment of cases to judge(s), 9-6
    bench time for judges, 9-8
    bench warrants issued by, 9-10
    California, 9-3
    community relationships, 9-7
    completion and graduation, successful, 9-10
    cross-training of personnel, 9-7
    defendants, requirements for, 11-2
    development of, 8-2
    effective treatment processes, identification and
        improvement of, 8-6–8-8
    eligibility criteria, 9-4
    employment services, lack of. See Employment services
    entry to program, time between arrest and, 9-9
    existing criminal case process, changes to, 9-9
    family/abuse and neglect programs, 9-3
    Family Drug Treatment Courts (FTCs), New York. *See*
        Family Drug Treatment Courts (FTCs), New York
    Florida, 9-2, 9-3
    goals of, 9-3
    graduation, 9-10
    "Healing to Wellness Court," 9-3
    income from participant fees, 9-8–9-9

Drug courts, *continued*
    judges
        assignment of cases to, 9-6
        bench time for, 9-8
    judicial process, locus of program in, 9-4
    judicial status hearings. *See* Judicial status hearings in
            drug courts
    juvenile programs, 9-3
    Kentucky
        number of programs in, 9-3
        vocational assistance, gender differences in. *See*
                Kentucky
    key components of, 11-2
    knowledge gaps regarding processes and outcomes,
            addressing, 8-8
    law enforcement, collaboration with, 9-7–9-8
    Missouri, 9-3
    multidisciplinary nature of, 9-7
    national expansion of, 9-2–9-3
    New York
        Family Drug Treatment Courts (FTCs). *See*
                Family Drug Treatment Courts (FTCs),
                New York
        New York City Department of Probation (DOP)
                drug treatment initiative. *See* New York
                City Department of Probation (DOP)
                drug treatment initiative
        number of programs in, 9-3
    noncompliance with, results of, 11-2
    offenses targeted, 9-4
    Ohio, 9-3
    organization and operation of
        assignment of cases to judge(s), 9-6
        community relationships, 9-7
        law enforcement, collaboration with, 9-7–9-8
        program phases, 9-5
        program policies and procedures, 9-7
        treatment services, provision of, 9-5–9-6
    oversight/advisory committees, 9-7
    participant fees, income from, 9-8–9-9
    participants
        benefits to, 8-3–8-4
        contacts with, 9-11
        eligibility criteria for, 9-4
        termination of unsuccessful, 9-10
    permutations of, 9-2–9-3
    persons involved with, 8-3
    phased treatment structure of, 8-7
    phases, program, 9-5
    policies and procedures, program, 9-7
    positive trends in, 8-8–8-9
    process, program
        contacts with participants, 9-11
        existing criminal case process, changes to, 9-9
        graduation, 9-10
        progress or rearrest, court response to, 9-9–9-10
        successful completion and graduation, 9-10
        time between arrest and entry to program, 9-9
        unsuccessful participants, termination of, 9-10
    program basics, 8-2–8-3
    program phases, 9-5
    progress or rearrest, court response to, 9-9–9-10
    public health benefits, facilitation of, 8-5–8-6

public health services, 9-6
purpose of, 11-1–11-2
questions, research and policy, 9-3
rearrest, court response to, 9-9–9-10
recidivism outcomes, 8-4
referral process, 9-4
research and policy challenges
    effective treatment processes, identification and
            improvement of, 8-6–8-8
    knowledge gaps regarding processes and
            outcomes, 8-8
    public health benefits, facilitation of, 8-5–8-6
    staff training, identification and improvement of,
            8-6
    target population, identification and reaching, 8-6
    treatment retention, improving, 8-5
research findings
    American University Drug Court Clearinghouse
            and Technical Assistance Project (DCC-
            TAP). *See* American University Drug
            Court Clearinghouse and Technical
            Assistance Project (DCCTAP)
    participants, benefits to, 8-3–8-4
    recidivism outcomes, 8-4
    taxpayer savings, potential, 8-4–8-5
resources, program
    additional funding, 9-8
    bench time for judges, 9-8
    income from participant fees, 9-8–9-9
screening process, 9-4–9-5
services provided, 8-3, 9-5
special populations, services for, 9-6
staff training, identification and improvement of, 8-6
successful completion and graduation, 9-10
target population, identification and reaching, 8-6
taxpayer savings, potential, 8-4–8-5
time between arrest and entry to program, 9-9
treatment initiatives
    program basics, 8-2-8-3
    use of, 8-2
    treatment retention, need for improving, 8-5
treatment services, provision of, 9-5–9-6
tribal programs, 9-3
unsuccessful participants, termination of, 9-10

Drug dependence
    self-report screen focus on, 1-4

Drug-involved women
    Community Outreach Project on AIDS in Southern
            Arizona (COPASA for Women). *See* Community
            Outreach Project on AIDS in Southern Arizona
            (COPASA for Women)
    health consequences of, 19-2
    HIV infection
        Community Outreach Project on AIDS in
                Southern Arizona (COPASA for
                Women). *See* Community Outreach
                Project on AIDS in Southern Arizona
                (COPASA for Women)
        increased risk of, 19-2
        National Institute on Drug Abuse (NIDA) studies,
                19-2–19-3
    incarceration rates, 19-2
    National Institute on Drug Abuse (NIDA) studies on

HIV infection. *See* Community Outreach Project on AIDS in Southern Arizona (COPASA for Women)
negative health impact of, 19-2

Drug Lifestyle Screening Interview (DLSI)
purpose of, 16-3

Drugs
criminal justice system
impact on, 8-1

percentage of drug users in, 8-2
Drug testing of offenders
legality of random testing in prison, cases confirming, App.-14–App.-15
"prison condition," consideration of testing procedures as, App.-16–App.-17
procedural requirements
chain of custody, App.-15
inmates' requests for drug testing, App.-15–App.-16
random testing in prison, cases confirming legality of, App.-14–App.-15
urine testing. *See* Urine testing

Drug-use data collection efforts
federal, 4-2

Drug Use Forecasting (DUF) Program. *See* Arrestee Drug Abuse Monitoring (ADAM) program

Drug use testing, screening and referral. *See* Testing, screening and referral

DSM. *See* Diagnostic and Statistical Manual of Mental Disorders (DSM)

Duffy v. Riveland, App.-22

DUF Program. *See* Drug Use Forecasting (DUF) Program

Duluth model of treatment
intimate partner violence (IPV), 23-7

E

ECA study. See Epidemiological Catchment Area (ECA) study

Effective functioning
defined, 12-4

"Eligibility" impediments for drug treatment leading to sentence reduction. *See* Sentencing issues

EMIT. *See* Enzyme Multiplied Immunoassay Test (EMIT)

Employment
Coalition for Recovery, Education and Work (CREW) model as bridge for program-provider gaps, 34-5
distance learning to bridge program-provider gaps, use of, 34-4
employers' legal concerns, 34-4
female inmates, employment/educational issues of, 18-7
incentive in aftercare phase, critical, 34-1–34-2
Kentucky Drug Court programs employment interventions. *See* Kentucky Drug Court programs
multi-value framework to bridge program-provider gaps, creation of, 34-5
offenders, as critical incentive for, 34-1–34-2
program-provider gaps, bridging
Coalition for Recovery, Education and Work (CREW) model, 34-5
dedication to, 34-4

distance learning, use of, 34-4
employers' legal concerns, 34-4
multi-value framework, creation of, 34-5
recidivism rates, effect on, 34-1

Employment services
aftercare treatment and, synergy between
programmatic difficulties, 34-3
provider issues, 34-4
study results, 34-3
gender differences in, 20-2–20-3
Kentucky Drug Court program. *See* Kentucky
lack of, 20-2

Enright, Gohier v., App.-22

Enzyme Multiplied Immunoassay Test (EMIT)
drugs screened for, 4-4
judicial status hearings in drug courts study, 11-4

Epidemiological Catchment Area (ECA) study
psychiatric screening instrument, 21-7

ESI. *See* Extended Services Intervention (ESI)

Establishment Clause
violations of, App.-23–App.-25

Ethical considerations
length of stay in treatment programs, 26-6

Ethnicity
psychopathy and, 22-5
Texas Youth Commission (TYC) reform schools study on juvenile inhalant users, differences in, 25-4–25-5

Extended Services Intervention (ESI)
Family Empowerment Intervention (FEI), comparison with. *See* Family Empowerment Intervention (FEI)

F

Family/abuse and neglect programs
drug court, 9-3

Family Drug Treatment Courts (FTCs), New York
admissions of guilt in, 10-4
Adoption and Safe Families Act (AFSA), obligation to implement, 10-3–10-4
challenges for, 10-5–10-6
community/capacity as challenge for, 10-5
evaluation of, 10-4–10-5
incentives, 10-3–10-4
leadership as challenge for, 10-5
partnership possibilities, 10-6
proliferation of
as challenge, 10-5
factors in, 10-1
research on, 10-4–10-5
support offered by, 10-3–10-4

Family Empowerment Intervention (FEI)
alcohol/drug use post-intervention, 24-6
charges and arrests post-intervention, official record analyses of, 24-5–24-6
clinical trial, implementation and evaluation of, 24-4–24-5
consultation phase, 24-3
cost saving benefits of, 24-7–24-8
demographic characteristics of participants, 24-5

Family Empowerment Intervention (FEI), *continued*
  emotional/psychological functioning post-intervention, 24-6–24-7
  enrollment process, 24-4
  family work phase, 24-4
  field consultant (FC), 24-3
  follow-up interviews, 24-5
  goals of program, 24-3
  graduation phase, 24-4
  introduction phase, 24-3
  outcomes, 24-8
  phases of intervention, 24-3–24-4
  post-intervention
    alcohol/drug use, 24-6
    charges and arrests, official record analyses of, 24-5–24-6
    emotional/psychological functioning, 24-6–24-7
    self-reported delinquency, 24-6
  psychoeducational approach, 24-3
  psychosocial characteristics of participants, 24-5
  self-reported delinquency post-intervention, 24-6
  structural approach, 24-2–24-3
  systematic approach, 24-2
  theoretical foundations of, 24-2–24-3
  transgenerational approach, 24-3

Farmer v. Brennan, App.-19, App.-30

Farrey, Kerr v., App.-23

Federal Bureau of Prisons (BOP) drug abuse treatment programs
  Anti-Drug Abuse Acts, effect of, 15-3
  biopsychosocial model of treatment, 15-3–15-4
  challenges and issues in
    comorbidity, 15-8–15-9
    curriculum content, 15-8
    dual disorders, 15-8–15-9
    inmate recruitment, 15-7–15-8
    organizational culture and climate, 15-6–15-7
    program implementation and staffing, rapid pace of, 15-6
  comorbidity issue, 15-8–15-9
  current practices, 15-3–15-4
  curriculum content, challenges in establishing, 15-8
  Drug Abusers Program (DAP) units, 15-3
  drug treatment and corrections professionals, recommendations of, 15-3
  dual disorders issues, 15-8–15-9
  "eligibility" requirements for prisoners
    conviction, eligibility based on, App.-2–App.-3
    successful completion of programs, requirement for, App.-3
    Violent Crime Control and Law Enforcement Act, under, App.-1–App.-2
  female inmates, for, 18-5
  future directions, 15-8–15-9
  historical overview, 15-2–15-3
  inmate misconduct, effect on, 15-5–15-6
  inmate recruitment issues, 15-7–15-8
  in-prison functioning, effect on, 15-5–15-6
  issues in. *See* subhead: challenges and issues in
  Narcotic Addict Rehabilitation Act (NARA), effect of, 15-2
  "narcotics farms," 15-2

  National Institute of Drug Abuse (NIDA) funding for outcome evaluation process, 15-5
  nine-month residential program, phases of treatment in, 15-4
  organizational culture and climate issues, 15-6–15-7
  outcome evaluation results, 15-4–15-6
  principles for, recommended, 15-9–15-10
  program implementation and staffing, rapid pace of, 15-6
  Program Statement, App.-2
  recidivism, effect on, 15-5
  sentence reduction
    conviction, eligibility based on, App.-2–App.-3
    "eligibility" requirements for prisoners, App.-1–App.-2
    successful completion of programs, requirement for, App.-3
  staffing issues, 15-6
  successful completion of programs, requirement for, App.-3
  treatment approach, shift in, 15-3
  Violent Crime Control and Law Enforcement Act (VCCLEA)
    "eligibility" requirements under, App.-1–App.-2
    inmate recruitment, effect on, 15-7–15-8

FEI. *See* Family Empowerment Intervention (FEI)

Female inmates, therapeutic community (TC) treatment for
  California Department of Corrections (CDC) treatment expansion initiative, 18-6
  California Forever Free program, 18-4–18-5
  drug use and criminal involvement issues, 18-6–18-7
  employment/educational issues, 18-7
  federal Bureau of Prisons (BOP) programs, 18-5
  Forever Free program, 18-4–18-5
  medical issues, 18-7
  mothers, for, 18-7–18-8
  New York Stay'n Out program, 18-3–18-4
  parenting issues, 18-7–18-8
  patterns of drug abuse, 18-2
  physical abuse issues, 18-8
  post-treatment outcome studies
    California Department of Corrections (CDC) treatment expansion initiative, 18-6
    comparison of, 18-3–18-4
    federal Bureau of Prisons (BOP) programs, 18-5
    Forever Free program, 18-4–18-5
    selection bias, 18-6
    Stay'n Out program, 18-3–18-4
  psychological issues, 18-9
  relationship issues, 18-8
  research, need for additional, 18-9–18-10
  selection bias in post-treatment outcome studies, 18-6
  sexual issues, 18-8
  statistics of incarcerated women, 18-2
  Stay'n Out program, 18-3–18-4
  treatment needs
    drug use and criminal involvement issues, 18-6–18-7
    employment/educational issues, 18-7
    medical issues, 18-7
    mothers, for, 18-7–18-8
    parenting issues, 18-7–18-8

physical abuse issues, 18-8
psychological issues, 18-9
relationship issues, 18-8
sexual issues, 18-8

Florida
drug court movement. See Drug courts

Flowers, Alexander v., App.-3

Forever Free program
female therapeutic community (TC), 18-4–18-5

FTCs. *See* Family Drug Treatment Courts (FTCs), New York

G

GAIN-CVI. *See* Global Appraisal of Individual Needs-Crime and Violence Index (GAIN-CVI)

Gender
psychopathy and, 22-5
Texas Youth Commission (TYC) reform schools study on juvenile inhalant users, differences in, 25-3–25-5

Giano v. Goord, App.-16

Global Appraisal of Individual Needs-Crime and Violence Index (GAIN-CVI)
administration time, 2-2–2-3
Cannabis Youth Treatment (CYT) Study, 3-3
drug use changes, limitations of failure to isolate, 3-5–3-6
dynamic explanation of criminal careers, 3-6–3-7
illegal activity, changes in social environment related to changes in, 3-5
items measured by, 3-3
life-course persistent offenders, hope for, 3-6
limitations of, 3-5–3-6
Moffitt Theory of Criminal/Violent Behavior. *See* Moffitt Theory of Criminal/Violent Behavior
predicting future crime/violence, 3-6
results of, 3-5–3-6
scope of treatment evaluation, need to expand, 3-6
self-report data, limitations of, 3-5–3-6
usefulness of, P1-1

Gohier v. Enright, App.-22

Goord, Giano v., App.-16

Goord, Webb v., App.-15

Gorczyk, Griggs v., App.-13–App.-14

Griggs v. Gorczyk, App.-13–App.-14

H

Harris, Brown v., App.-19

"Healing to Wellness Court"
planning of, 9-3

Henson v. United States Bureau of Prisons, App.-15–App.-16

Hill, Superintendent, Massachusetts Correctional Inst. v., App.-16

HIV infection
women, in. *See* Drug-involved women

Hood, Bowen v., App.-11

Horn, Rauser v., App.-25

Houston Arrestee Drug Abuse Monitoring (ADAM) program data. *See* Arrestee Drug Abuse Monitoring (ADAM) program

I

Incarceration
alternatives to, x

Inhalant abuse
damage caused by, 25-2
juvenile inhalant users. *See* Juvenile inhalant users

In-prison treatment control programs
coerced treatment. *See* Coerced admission in substance abuse treatment control program
Kyle New Vision Program. *See* Kyle New Vision Program
New Vision In-Prison Therapeutic Community (IPTC) and Substance Abuse Felony Punishment (SAFP) Drug Treatment Program. *See* Kyle New Vision Program
Richard J. Donovan Amity TC programs. *See* Richard J. Donovan Amity TC programs
Substance Abuse Treatment Facility (SATF) at Corcoran State Prison. *See* Substance Abuse Treatment Facility (SATF) at Corcoran State Prison
therapeutic communities (TCs). *See* Therapeutic communities (TCs)

Institutional program treatment options
self-report screens to, matching, 1-5–1-6

Interventions
Addiction Technology Transfer Center (ATTC) Network role in creating. *See* Addiction Technology Transfer Center (ATTC) Network
application of, 27-5
cognitive behavioral intervention
criminal thinking–understanding logic and rewards, 37-4–37-5
targeting offender behavior–social learning and behavioral intervention, 37-5
Extended Services Intervention (ESI). *See* Family Empowerment Intervention (FEI)
Family Empowerment Intervention (FEI). *See* Family Empowerment Intervention (FEI)
intimate partner violence (IPV), 23-8
Kentucky Drug Court employment interventions. *See* Kentucky Drug Court programs
New York City Department of Probation (DOP) drug treatment initiative, appropriate interventions in, 6-2
principles of effective, 7-2–7-3
social learning and behavioral intervention, 37-5

Interviews
as part of self-report screens, 1-4–1-5
Diagnostic Interview Schedule for Children (DISC), 2-2
Practical Adolescent Dual Diagnostic Interview (PADDI). *See* Practical Adolescent Dual Diagnostic Interview (PADDI)

Intimate partner violence (IPV)
antisocial personality disorder (ASPD) as characteristic of, 23-3–23-4
classifications of offender types, 23-3–23-3
clinical characteristics of
depression, 23-4

Intimate partner violence (IPV), *continued*
        personality disorders, 23-3–23-4
        post-traumatic stress syndrome (PTSD), 23-4
   clinicians, training and supervision of, 23-9
   community providers of, 23-8
   contextualized questioning as screening and assessment
      strategy for substance abuse treatment providers,
      23-4–23-5
   depression as characteristic of, 23-4
   Duluth model of treatment, 23-7
   future trends, 23-9
   integrated treatment, 23-7, 23-8
   interventions, planning, 23-8
   linkages to referral options, 23-8–23-9
   mixed-gender group treatment, 23-8
   offender typologies, 23-3–23-3
   personality disorders as characteristic of, 23-3–23-4
   post-traumatic stress syndrome (PTSD), as characteristic
      of, 23-4
   referral approach to treatment, 23-8
   risk assessment as strategy for substance abuse treatment
      providers, 23-5–23-6
   safety planning throughout treatment, 23-6
   structured treatment, 23-7
   substance abuse, co-occurrence of
      rate of, 23-1–23-2
      screening for, 23-2
      special treatment planning, 23-2
   substance abuse treatment providers, screening and
      assessment strategies for
      contextualized questioning, 23-4–23-5
      risk assessment, factors considered in, 23-5–23-6
      treatment. *See* subhead: treatment
      victim input, 23-5
   treatment
      decision of what to treat first, 23-7
      Duluth model, 23-7
      integrated approaches, 23-7, 23-8
      interventions, 23-8
      mixed-gender groups, 23-8
      referral approach to, 23-8
      safety planning, 23-6
      structured, 23-7
   victim input as screening and assessment strategy for
      substance abuse treatment providers, 23-5
IPV. *See* Intimate partner violence (IPV)

J

Judges, drug court
   assignment of cases to, 9-6
   bench time for, 9-8
Judicial status hearings in drug courts
   bi-weekly or as needed, study of
      first study of outcomes. *See* subhead: first study of
        outcomes, study of effect on
      follow-up study results. *See* subhead: follow-up
        study results
   case manager, monthly meetings with, 11-4
   conclusions from studies of, 11-7–11-8
   first study of outcomes, study of effect on
      case manager, monthly meetings with, 11-4
      counseling and attendance, effect on, 11-2

      high-risk and low-risk offenders, effects for, 11-3
      length of programs, 11-3–11-4
      limitations of, 11-3–11-4
   follow-up study results
      bi-weekly condition for participants, superiority of
        interaction effects on, 11-6–11-7
      distribution across study conditions, confirmation
        of, 11-4–11-5
      general estimating equation (GEE), use of, 11-5
      participants, characteristics of, 11-4
      risk/benefit ratio, end of recruitment in response to
        shift in, 11-7
      study conditions, confirmation of distribution
        across, 11-4–11-5
      study conditions, differences between, 11-5
      study recruitment stopped in response to shift in
        risk/benefit ratio, 11-7
   outcomes, study of effect on
      first study. *See* subhead: first study of
      follow-up study results. *See* subhead: follow-up
        study results
Juvenile Assessment Center, Hillsborough County. *See*
   Family Empowerment Intervention (FEI)
Juvenile inhalant users
   damage caused by inhalants, 25-2
   delinquency patterns related to, 25-1–25-2
   Texas Youth Commission (TYC) reform schools study
      co-occurring risk factors, 25-5
      criminality, relationship of inhalant use to,
        25-5–25-7
      gender and ethnicity, difference in usage patterns
        by, 25-3–25-5
      purpose and methodology, 25-3
      statistics, 25-2
      treatment planning, implications for, 25-7
   treatment planning, implications of Texas Youth
      Commission (TYC) reform schools study on, 25-7
Juvenile justice system
   Family Empowerment Intervention (FEI), cost saving
      benefits of, 24-7–24-8
   need for substance abuse programs in, 24-1–24-2
Juvenile programs
   drug court, 9-3
Juvenile RSAT program
   assessment of, 7-7–7-8

K

K6/K10 scales
   psychiatric screening instrument, 21-7–21-8
Kentucky Department of Corrections v. Thompson, App.-28
Kentucky Drug Court programs
   criminal involvement, gender differences in, 20-7
   employment history by gender, 20-5
   employment interventions
      data collection method, 20-4
      developmental phases of, 20-3–20-4
      findings, 20-7–20-8
      focus group findings, 20-3
      motivational interviewing, 20-3
      participants, effect on, 20-3–20-4
      site selection, 20-4

structured story telling, 20-3
thought-mapping, 20-3
employment problems, gender differences and
    employment history by gender, 20-5
    findings, 20-7–20-8
    statistics, 20-5
gender differences
    criminal involvement, 20-7
    employment history. *See* subhead: employment
        problems, gender differences and
    substance use. *See* subhead: substance use, gender
        differences in
number of programs, 9-3
substance use, gender differences in
    findings, 20-7–20-8
    statistics, 20-6, 20–7
Kerr v. Farrey, App.-23
Kerr v. Puckett, App.-9
Key/Crest Program
    effectiveness of, 20-2
    outreach program, as example of, 33-7
Kyle New Vision Program
    academic education, 12-7
    accreditation of, 12-8
    Cadre Program, 12-4
    chemical dependency education, 12-5
    community-based TTCs, 12-3
    community-clinical management, 12-6
    community enhancement activities, 12-5
    components, critical program. *See* subhead: program
        components
    counseling groups, 12-5–12-6
    effective functioning, defined, 12-4–12-5
    enhancements, program, 12-7–12-8
    Family Education Program, 12-7
    future plans, innovative, 12-8
    graduates of, 12-2
    hierarchical structures, 12-5
    high-risk substance abusing offenders, intensive treat-
        ment for, 12-2
    incentives and privileges, 12-6
    Main Treatment Phase, 12-3
    Orientation Phase, 12-3
    personal studies, 12-9–12-10
    phases of, 12-3–12-4
    program components
        academic education, 12-7
        chemical dependency education, 12-5
        community-clinical management, 12-6
        community enhancement activities, 12-5
        counseling groups, 12-5–12-6
        enhancements, 12-7–12-8
        Family Education Program, 12-7
        incentives and privileges, 12-6
        sanction system, 12-6
        Twelve-Step Fellowships, 12-6
        volunteer programs, 12-7
    program enhancements, 12-7–12-8
    pull-up sanction system, 12-6
    recidivism rates, 12-2
    Re-Entry Phase, 12-3
    Relapse Prevention Group, 12-8
    residents of, 12-2

sanction system, 12-6
success stories, 12-9–12-10
Texas Christian University (TCU) study on recidivism
    rates of graduates from, 12-2
therapeutic community (TC) approach
    effective functioning, defined, 12-4
    elements of, 12-4
    hierarchical structures, 12-5
    primary goals of, 12-4–12-5
    utilization of, 12-4–12-5
transition celebration, 12-8
Twelve-Step Fellowships, 12-6
volunteer programs, 12-7

L

Lasora v. Menfee, App.-11
Law enforcement
    drug courts, collaboration of, 9-7–9-8
LCSF. *See* Lifestyle Criminality Screening Form (LCSF)
Legal issues
    Americans with Disabilities Act (ADA), drug addiction
        as disability under. *See* Americans with Disabilities
        Act (ADA), drug addiction as disability under
    drug testing of offenders. *See* Drug testing of offenders
    religious issues. *See* Religious issues
    sentencing issues. *See* Sentencing issues
    standards of care. *See* Standards of care
Length of stay in treatment programs
    assessment
        client's needs, 26-3
        treatment type, 26-3
    Client Oriented Data Acquisition Program (CODAP)
        forms, 26-2
    client's needs, based on assessment of, 26-3
    continuum of care, effect of, 32-4
    Dallas County Judicial Treatment Center (DCJTC). *See*
        Dallas County Judicial Treatment Center (DCJTC)
    Drug Abuse Reporting Program (DARP) study, Texas
        Christian University (TCU), 26-2
    Drug Abuse Treatmen Outcome Studies (DATOS) study,
        Texas Christian University (TCU), 26-2
    dually diagnosed clients, problems associated with,
        26-3–26-4
    economic issues, determination based upon, 26-5–26-6,
        A-4–A-5
    economics/resources influencing political decisions,
        26-5–26-6
    ethical considerations, 26-6
    extended stays, research supporting, 26-2
    factors affecting, 26-5–26-6, A-4–A-5
    judicial status hearings in drug courts, 11-3–11-4
    long-term success, as predictor of, 26-2
    managed care, influence of, 26-5
    mentally ill clients, problems associated with, 26-3–26-4
    political decisions, economics/resources influencing,
        26-5–26-6
    political issues, influence of, 26-4–26-5
    predictor of success, as, 26-1, 26-2
    principles of effective systems to reduce recidivism and
        increase retention in treatment programs, as,
        32-7–32-8
    role of treatment providers, 26-7–26-8

Length of stay in treatment programs, *continued*
    special needs clients, problems associated with, 26-3–26-4
    TCU Model of Treatment Processes and Outcomes, 27-4
    Texas Christian University (TCU) studies, 26-2
    Texas Commission on Alcohol and Drug Abuse (TCADA), post-treatment follow-up forms required by, 26-2
    treatment providers, role of, 26-7–26-8
    treatment type, assessment of, 26-3

Lewis, Boner v., App.-22

Life-course persistent offenders
    hope for, 3-6
    Moffitt Theory of Criminal/Violent Behavior, 3-2

Lifestyle Criminality Screening Form (LCSF)
    purpose of, 16-3

Lifestyles, drug and criminal
    addressing and changing belief systems, core elements for
        community. *See* subhead: community as core element for addressing and changing belief systems
        confidence. *See* subhead: confidence as core element for addressing and changing belief systems
        listing of, 16-3–16-4
        meaning. *See* subhead: meaning as core element for addressing and changing belief systems
        responsibility. *See* subhead: responsibility as core element for addressing and changing belief systems
    behavior modification, use of life lessons to encourage, 16-4
    belief systems
        addressing and changing. *See* subhead: addressing and changing belief systems, core elements for
        rigid, 16-3
        supporting, 16-2–16-3
    case example, 16-3
    cognitive simplicity, challenging, 16-7
    commonalities of, 16-2–16-3
    community as core element for addressing and changing belief systems
        case example, 16-8
        sense of connection, encouragement of client's, 16-8
        social support, ensuring, 16-7–16-8
    confidence, lack of, 16-3
    confidence as core element for addressing and changing belief systems
        case example, 16-6
        self-confidence, promotion of, 16-5–16-6
        self-efficacy, methods of enhancement of, 16-5
    connection between drugs and crime, 16-2
    criminal lifestyle, interactive patterns of irresponsibility in, 16-2
    drug lifestyle, interactive patterns of irresponsibility in, 16-2
    Drug Lifestyle Screening Interview (DLSI), 16-3
    enabling behaviors, discouragement of, 16-4

    labeling, avoidance of, 16-6–16-7
    lifestyle concept, defined, 16-2
    Lifestyle Criminality Screening Form (LCSF), 16-3
    meaning as core element for addressing and changing belief systems
        case example, 16-7
        cognitive simplicity, challenging, 16-7
        labeling, avoidance of, 16-6–16-7
    non-accountability, sense of, 16-2
    reductionism, 16-7
    responsibility as core element for addressing and changing belief systems
        behavior modification, use of life lessons to encourage, 16-4
        case example, 16-5
        enabling behaviors, discouragement of, 16-4
    rigid belief systems, 16-3
    self-confidence, promotion of, 16-5–16-6
    self-efficacy, methods of enhancement of, 16-5
    sense of connection, encouragement of client's, 16-8
    social support, ensuring, 16-7–16-8
    weak social cohesion/community, presumption of, 16-3

Little Hoover Commission
    Amity Therapeutic Community at Richard J. Donovan Correctional Facility (RJDCF), report on, 13-2–13-3

Lopez, U.S. v., App.-4–App.-5

Lopez v. Davis, App.-3, App.-12

Lucero, Romero v., App.-31

M

Marijuana users, prediction of violent behavior in adolescent
    Cannabis Youth Treatment (CYT) Study, 3-2, 3-3
    Global Appraisal of Individual Needs-Crime and Violence Index (GAIN-CVI). *See* Global Appraisal of Individual Needs-Crime and Violence Index (GAIN-CVI)

MAST. *See* Michigan Alcoholism Screening Test (MAST)

Matching
    clients with treatment, 27-3, A-2–A-3
    psychiatric disorders, treatment-matching strategy for, 21-10
    treatment to inmate's motivation, 31-9

Maurello v. United States, App.-10

McClain County Board of County Commissioners, Van Curen v., App.-17

McElhiney v. Booker, App.-15

McGill v. Pennsylvania Department of Health, Office of Drug & Alcohol Programs, App.-8

McGinnis, Bazzetta v., App.-28

Medical treatment
    offender's right to. *See* Standards of care

Menfee, Lasora v., App.-11

Mental health and substance abuse disorders in adolescents
    rates of co-occurring, 2-2

Mental illness
    See also Psychiatric disorders
    severe mental illnesses (SMI)
        co-occurring substance abuse and, epidemiological study of, 21-4

treatment difficulties with, 21-3

Michigan Alcoholism Screening Test (MAST)
    sex offenders, 17-4–17-5

Miller, Cox v., App.-26

Mini-Neuropsychiatric Interview (MINI)
    psychiatric screening instrument, 21-6

Missouri
    drug courts, 9-3

"Modified" therapeutic communities (TCs)
    characteristics of, 14-5

Moffitt Theory of Criminal/Violent Behavior
    adolescence-limited offenders, 3-2
    life-course persistent offenders, 3-2
    social environment, role of, P1-1
    taxonomy, 3-2
    testing, 3-3–3-5

Monitoring the Future (MTF) project
    purpose of, 4-2

Moore v. Atherton, App.-17

Motivation for treatment among clients, enhancing. *See*
    Cognitive Enhancements for the Treatment of
    Probationers (CETOP)

MTF project. *See* Monitoring the Future (MTF) project

N

NADCP. *See* National Association of Drug Court
    Professionals (NADCP)

NARA. *See* Narcotic Addict Rehabilitation Act (NARA)

Narcotic Addict Rehabilitation Act (NARA)
    Federal Bureau of Prisons (BOP), effect on, 15-2

"Narcotics farms"
    Federal Bureau of Prisons (BOP), 15-2

National Association of Drug Court Professionals (NADCP)
    drug courts, key components of, 11-2

National Comorbidity Survey (NCS)
    psychiatric screening instrument, 21-7

National Development and Research, Incorporated (NDRI)
    non-TC programs, study of, A-4

National Household Survey on Drug abuse (NHSDA)
    purpose of, 4-2

National Institute of Drug Abuse (NIDA)
    funding for BOP outcome evaluation process, 15-5
    length of stay in drug abuse treatment program, studies
        on, 27-4–27-5
    research to correctional drug treatment, Urban Institute.
        See Urban Institute project linking research to
        correctional drug treatment
    Urban Institute project to identify challenges posed by
        integrating treatment services. *See* Urban Institute
        project linking research to correctional drug
        treatment
    Youth Support Project (YSP). *See* Family Empowerment
        Intervention (FEI)

National Institute of Justice (NIJ)
    funding of research partnership for prison-based drug
        treatment program. *See* Pennsylvania, subhead:
        research partnership for prison-based drug
        treatment program

New Vision In-Prison Therapeutic Community (IPTC) and
    Substance Abuse Felony Punishment (SAFP) Drug
    Treatment Program. *See* Kyle New Vision Program

New York
    drug courts, 9-3
    Family Drug Treatment Courts (FTCs). *See* Family
        Drug Treatment Courts (FTCs), New York
    New York City Department of Probation (DOP) drug
        treatment initiative. *See* New York City
        Department of Probation (DOP) drug treatment
        initiative
    Stay'n Out program, 18-3–18-4, 20-2

New York City Department of Probation (DOP) drug
    treatment initiative
    appropriate interventions, 6-2
    Central Placement Unit (CPU)
        creation of, 6-2
        importance of, 6-3
        population served, 6-3
        role of, 6-2
        systematic approach of, 6-3
        treatment options. *See* subhead: treatment options
        treatment participation, statistics on, 6-3
    client participation in outpatient drug treatment, statistics
        on, 6-4
    effectiveness of, 6-2
    Offender Profile Index (OPI), 6-6
    out-patient treatment, appropriateness of, 6-6, 6-7–6-8
    policy implications and recommendations, 6-8
    population served, 6-3
    probationer's drug treatment needs, systematic approach
        to meeting, 6-2–6-3
    recidivism rates, 6-4–6-6
    systematic approach to meeting probationer's drug treat-
        ment needs, 6-2–6-3
    treatment options
        out-patient treatment, appropriateness of, 6-6,
            6-7–6-8
        urine monitoring of probationers, 6-6
    treatment participation, statistics on, 6-3
    urine monitoring of probationers, 6-6

NHSDA. *See* National Household Survey on Drug abuse
    (NHSDA)

NIDA. *See* National Institute of Drug Abuse (NIDA)

NIJ. *See* National Institute of Justice (NIJ)

Node-link mapping
    client engagement, improvement of, 27-5

O

Offender Profile Index (OPI)
    New York City Department of Probation (DOP) drug
        treatment initiative, 6-6

Offenders
    adolescence-limited, 3-2
    aftercare services. *See* Aftercare services
    Cognitive Enhancements for the Treatment of
        Probationers (CETOP) study, statistics of offenders
        in, 28-3

Offenders, *continued*
    community-based offender drug treatment
        criminal justice system to, transition from. *See*
            Continuity-of-care model
        effectiveness of, 33-2
    community model of resocialization for offenders, 37-6
    continuity-of-care model. *See* Continuity-of-care model
    cross training curricula for female, 36-6
    drug testing of. *See* Drug testing of offenders
    employment as critical incentive for, 34-1–34-2
    female offenders cross training curriculum, 36-6
    intimate partner violence (IPV), offender typologies in,
        23-3–23-3
    judicial status hearings in drug courts, effects for high-
        risk and low-risk offenders of, 11-3
    Kyle New Vision Program, intensive treatment for high-
        risk substance abusing offenders in, 12-2
    life-course persistent offenders
        hope for, 3-6
        Moffitt Theory of Criminal/Violent Behavior, 3-2
    medical treatment, right to. See Standards of care
    New York City Department of Probation (DOP) drug
        treatment initiative Offender Profile Index (OPI),
        6-6
    Offender Profile Index (OPI), 6-6
    psychopaths, distinguished from, 22-5
    resocialization for, elements of community model for,
        37-6
    sex offenders. *See* Sex offenders
    treatment completion rates, 32-3–32-4
    treatment services, percentage of offender population in,
        32-3
    twelve principles of effective systems to reduce
        recidivism and increase retention in treatment
        programs. *See* Twelve principles of effective
        systems to reduce recidivism and increase
        retention in treatment programs
    urine testing to manage, 32-6
    youthful offenders, drug use among, 24-2
Office for Justice Programs Drug Court Clearinghouse and
    Technical Assistance Project at American University.
    See American University Drug Court Clearinghouse and
    Technical Assistance Project (DCCTAP)
Ohio
    drug courts, 9-3
OPI. *See* Offender Profile Index (OPI)
Orange County Dep't. of Probation, Warner v., App.-24
Oregon
    Cornerstone Program, 20-2
Oregon demonstration project
    elements of, 33-3–33-4
    outcome studies of, 33-4
Out-patient treatment
    New York City Department of Probation (DOP) drug
        treatment initiative, 6-6, 6-7–6-8
Outreach programs
    continuity-of-care, ensuring, 33-7
Oversight/advisory committees
    drug court, 9-7

P
PADDI. *See* Practical Adolescent Dual Diagnostic Interview
    (PADDI)
Paraphiliac
    defined, 17-3
Parke, Bridges v., App.-15
Parole. *See* Supervision in aftercare
PCL-R. *See* Hare Psychopathy Checklist-Revised (PCL-R)
PCL:SV. *See* Psychopathy Checklist Screening Version
    (PCL:SV)
Pell v. Procunier, App.-28
Pennsylvania
    alcohol and other drug (AOD) programs
        categories, 39-4–39-5
        demonstration project, as element of, 39-4
        survey of. *See* subhead: survey of alcohol and
            other drug (AOD) programs
    Department of Corrections (DOC) collaboration with
        Temple University Center for Public Policy on
        research partnership for prison-based drug treat-
        ment program. *See* subhead: research partnership
        for prison-based drug treatment program
    *McGill v. Pennsylvania Department of Health, Office of
        Drug & Alcohol Programs*, App.-8
    minimum treatment control program requirements,
        App.-8–App.-9
    National Institute of Justice (NIJ) funding of research
        partnership for prison-based drug treatment pro-
        gram. *See* subhead: research partnership for
        prison-based drug treatment program
    research partnership for prison-based drug treatment
        program
        alcohol and other drug (AOD) programs. *See*
            subhead: alcohol and other drug (AOD)
            programs
        benefits of, 39-9–39-10
        database formed by, 39-10
        demonstration project, 39-4
        documentation, improvement of, 39-10
        elements of demonstration project, 39-4
        evaluation recommendations, implementation of,
            39-10-30-11
        future projects planned, 39-10–39-11
        impact of, 39-9–39-10
        learning organization, department as, 39-9–39-10
        new screening tools, use of, 39-10
        outcome evaluation of, 39-8–39-9
        program standardization, 39-10
        purpose and goals of, 39-4–39-5
    survey of alcohol and other drug (AOD) programs
        findings, 39-5–39-7
        information collected, 39-5
        methodology, 39-5
        practical implications of findings, 39-7–39-8
    treatment control program
        minimum requirements, App.-8–App.-9
        research partnership for prison-based. *See*
            subhead: research partnership for prison-
            based drug treatment program
Pennsylvania Department of Corrections v. Yeskey, App.-22
Pennsylvania Department of Health, Office of Drug &

Alcohol Programs, McGill v., App.-8

People v. Carmona, App.-27

Persistent Effects of Treatment Study of Adolescents (PETS-A)
    Cannabis Youth Treatment (CYT) Study, follow-up on, 3-3

PETS-A. *See* Persistent Effects of Treatment Study of Adolescents (PETS-A)

Police
    drug courts, collaboration of, 9-7–9-8

Post-traumatic stress syndrome (PTSD)
    intimate partner violence (IPV), as characteristic of, 23-4

Practical Adolescent Dual Diagnostic Interview (PADDI)
    analysis, limitations of, 2-10
    clinical diagnoses, standardization of, 2-3
    co-occurring mental health and substance abuse disorders in adolescents, rates of, 2-2
    diagnostic findings, 2-7-2-8
    findings
        diagnostic, 2-7–2-8
        positive diagnoses, percentage of, 2-8
        problem prevalence by gender, 2-6
        victims of abuse, 2-6-2-7
    individuals, categorization of, 2-5
    interview administration
        findings, professional interpretation of, 2-3–2-4
        questions, 2-4
        training needed for, 2-3
    issues, relevant, 2-10
    limitations of analysis, 2-10
    positive diagnoses, percentage of, 2-8
    purpose of, 2-3
    research settings, design of assessment instruments for, 2-2–2-3
    responses, analysis of, 2-5
    sample, study procedures and. *See* subhead: study procedures and sample
    severity of conditions, extent and pattern of symptoms as indication of, 2-8–2-10
    study procedures and sample
        age, sex, and ethnicity of sample, 2-4
        educational achievement of sample, 2-4
        medication experience of sample, 2-5
        offenses committed by sample, 2-5
    symptom profiles for selected conditions, 2-9
    symptoms as indication of severity of conditions, extent and pattern of, 2-8–2-10
    victims of abuse, 2-6-2-7

Pregnancy
    drug use and, 10-2

Prison-based RSAT
    assessment of, 7-6–7-7

Prison populations
    statistics, 27-1
    substance use, 27-1–27-2

Probation
    See also Supervision in aftercare
    Central Placement Unit (CPU). *See* New York City Department of Probation (DOP) drug treatment initiative

Cognitive Enhancements for the Treatment of Probationers (CETOP). *See* Cognitive Enhancements for the Treatment of Probationers (CETOP)
New York City Department of Probation (DOP) drug treatment initiative. *See* New York City Department of Probation (DOP) drug treatment initiative
    visitation while on, conditions of, App.-30–App.-31

Procunier, Pell v., App.-28

Program integrity
    assessment of. *See* Correctional Program Assessment Inventory (CPAI)
    Correctional Program Assessment Inventory (CPAI). *See* Correctional Program Assessment Inventory (CPAI)
    measurement of, 7-1–7-2

Program-provider gaps, bridging. *See* Employment

Program quality
    measurement of, 7-2
    residential substance abuse treatment (RSAT) programs. *See* Residential substance abuse treatment (RSAT) programs

Program statistical reports
    treatment control programs, 27-6

Progress reports
    treatment control programs, 27-6

Project Recovery
    California Department of Corrections (CDC) participation in, 13-3

Psychiatric disorders
    assessment of, 21-2–21-3
    assessment strategies and instruments
        screening for comorbid mental illness, need for, 21-5
        screening instrument attributes, characteristics of optimal, 21-5–21-6
    BJS study findings, 21-4–21-5
    comorbidity rates for, 21-2
    co-occurring substance abuse and severe mental illness (SMI), epidemiological study of, 21-4
    diagnostic approach to screening, 21-6–21-7
    difficulty in treating comorbid, 21-2
    drug abuse and, 21-2
    eligible disorders for consideration, 21-3
    epidemiological studies
        BJS findings, 21-4–21-5
        co-occurring substance abuse and severe mental illness (SMI), 21-4
        psychiatric disorders in jail detainees, 21-3
    importance in treating comorbid, 21-10–21-11
    lack of attention to, 21-2–21-3
    psychiatric disorders in jail detainees, epidemiological study of, 21-3
    screening for comorbid mental illness, need for, 21-5
    screening instruments
        characteristics of optimal attributes in, 21-5–21-6
        diagnostic approach, 21-6–21-7
        symptom severity approach, 21-7–21-8

Psychiatric disorders, *continued*
    severe mental illnesses (SMI)
        co-occurring substance abuse and, epidemiological
            study of, 21-4
        treatment difficulties with, 21-3
    symptom severity approach to screening, 21-7–21-8
    treatment
        ancillary problem, as, 21-8–21-9
        specialized programming, 21-9–21-10
        treatment-matching strategy, 21-10
Psychological issues
    female inmates, therapeutic community (TC) treatment
        for, 18-9
Psychopaths
    behavioral characteristics of, 22-5
    other offenders, distinguished from, 22-5
    traits of, 22-2
    treatment planning, programming and individualized,
        22-8–22-10
Psychopathy
    age and, 22-5
    antisocial personality disorder (APD), distinguished
        from, 22-2–22-3
    clinical and research construct, as, 22-2
    ethnicity and, 22-6
    gender and, 22-6
    intelligence and, 22-2
    misconceptions and myths about, 22-2
    personality disorders and, distinguishing between,
        22-2–22-3
    Psychopathy Checklist-Revised (PCL-R). *See*
        Psychopathy Checklist-Revised (PCL-R)
    Psychopathy Checklist Screening Version (PCL:SV),
        22-2
    social learning model, integration of treatment into,
        22-6–22-7
    staff members into team treating, inclusion of, 22-6
    substance abuse treatment, integration of assessment
        into
        social learning model, integration into, 22-6–22-7
        staff members into team, inclusion of, 22-6
        testing, 22-7–22-8
    use in theory-building models, 22-1
Psychopathy Checklist-Revised (PCL-R)
    clinical rating items, 22-3, 22-4
    factor scores, 22-3
    interpretation of factors, 22-4
    psychopathy, measurement of, 22-2
    record review for, 22-7
    scoring, 22-3
Psychopathy Checklist Screening Version (PCL:SV)
    psychopathy, measurement of, 22-2
    record review for, 22-7
Psychoses, 2-7
Public domain screening instruments
    cost savings of, 1-3
Puckett, Kerr v., App.-9
Pull-up sanction system
    Kyle New Vision Program, 12-6

R

Rauser v. Horn, App.-25
RDS. *See* Referral Descision Scale (RDS)
Reach-in programs
    continuity-of-care, ensuring, 33-7
Readiness for treatment program
    Cognitive Enhancements for the Treatment of
        Probationers (CETOP). *See* Cognitive
        Enhancements for the Treatment of Probationers
        (CETOP)
    implementation of, 28-11
    "work the program," motivation to change or work,
        28-10–28-11
Recidivism
    aftercare on, effect of, 34-2
    attributes attributed to, 37-2
    Coerced admission to Substance Abuse Treatment
        Facility (SATF) at Corcoran State Prison, study of,
        31-5
    drug courts on, effect of, 8-4
    employment on, effect of, 34-1
    Federal Bureau of Prisons (BOP) drug abuse treatment
        programs effect on, 15-5
    Kyle New Vision Program, 12-2
    length of stay in treatment, effect of, 32-4
    New York City Department of Probation (DOP) drug
        treatment initiative, under, 6-4–6-6
    sex offenders, studies of, 17-4–17-5
    treatment programs, effect of, 7-1
    twelve principles of effective systems to reduce
        recidivism. *See* Twelve principles of effective
        systems to reduce recidivism and increase
        retention in treatment programs
Reductionism
    lifestyles, drug and criminal, 16-7
Re-entry. *See* Aftercare services
Referral, drug use. *See* Testing, screening and referral
Referral Descision Scale (RDS)
    psychiatric screening instrument, 21-6
Relapse prevention strategies
    elements of, 37-8
Religious issues
    addiction treatment programs, religion as component of
        damages for constitutional violation, inmate,
            App.-24–App.-25
        Establishment Clause, violation of,
            App.-23–App.-25
        Second Circuit ruling on, App.-24
        Seventh Circuit ruling on, App.-23–App.-24
    Alcoholics Anonymous and confidential communications
        cleric-congregant privilege, claiming of,
            App.-26–App.-28
        non-spiritual guidance, protection of,
            App.-27–App.-28
    cleric-congregant privilege, claiming of,
        App.-26–App.-28
    Establishment Clause, violation of, App.-23–App.-25
    inmate's right to raise religious freedom issues,
        App.-25–App.-26
    non-spiritual guidance, protection of, App.-27–App.-28

Residential substance abuse treatment (RSAT) programs, 7-8–7-9
  administrators, lessons for, 7-8–7-9
  assessments of
    community-based RSAT, 7-4–7-6
    juvenile RSAT program, 7-7–7-8
    prison-based RSAT, 7-6–7-7
    programs studied, 7-4
  community-based RSAT, assessment of, 7-4–7-6
  Correctional Program Assessment Inventory (CPAI), assessment of integrity by. *See* subhead: assessments of
  juvenile RSAT program, assessment of, 7-7–7-8
  lessons for administrators, 7-8–7-9
  prison-based RSAT, assessment of, 7-6–7-7
  upside of reviews, 7-9
Responsivity principle
  cognitive programs for changing criminal behavior, incorporation into, 37-7–37-8
  criminal behavior, changing, 37-4
Richard J. Donovan Correctional Facility (RJDCF)
  Amity Therapeutic Community. *See* Amity Therapeutic Community at Richard J. Donovan Correctional Facility (RJDCF)
Riveland, Duffy v., App.-22
RJDCF. *See* Richard J. Donovan Correctional Facility (RJDCF)
Rodriguez, U.S. v., App.-5
Romero v. Lucero, App.-31
RSAT programs. *See* Residential substance abuse treatment (RSAT) programs

S

SAMHSA. *See* Substance Abuse and Mental Health Services Administration (SAMHSA)
Sanctions
  changing criminal behavior, 37-8–37-9
  Continuity-of-care model, loss of incentives and sanctions upon release as obstacle to, 33-6
  Kyle New Vision Program system of, 12-6
  non-compliant behavior, sanctioning of, 32-9
  pull-up sanction system, 12-6
Sandra Rhodes, U.S. v., App.-6
SASSI. *See* Substance Abuse Subtle Screening Inventory (SASSI)
SATF. *See* Substance Abuse Treatment Facility (SATF) at Corcoran State Prison
Schenk, Alexander v., App.-24–App.-25
Science and clinical practices
  gap between. *See* Treatment
Screening, drug use. *See* Testing, screening and referral
Screening instruments
  Composite International Diagnostic Interview–Short Form (CIDI–SF) psychiatric screening instrument, 21-6
  Conflict Tactics Scale (CTS) domestic violence screening instrument, 23-4
  Diagnostic and Statistical Manual of Mental Disorders (DSM) as, 1-4

Diagnostic and Statistical Manual of Mental Disorders-IV (DSM-IV) for psychiatric disorders, 21-6
Drug Abuse Screening Test (DAST), 17-4
Drug Lifestyle Screening Interview (DLSI), 16-3
Enzyme Multiplied Immunoassay Test (EMIT), 4-4
Epidemiological Catchment Area (ECA) study, psychiatric screening by, 21-7
K6/K10 scales, psychiatric screening by, 21-7–21-8
Lifestyle Criminality Screening Form (LCSF), 16-3
Michigan Alcoholism Screening Test (MAST), 17-4–17-5
Mini-Neuropsychiatric Interview (MINI), psychiatric screening by, 21-6
National Comorbidity Survey (NCS), psychiatric screening by, 21-7
psychiatric disorders. *See* Psychiatric disorders
Psychopathy Checklist Screening Version (PCL:SV)
  measurements, 22-2
  record review for, 22-7
public domain, cost savings of, 1-3
Referral Descision Scale (RDS), psychiatric screening by, 21-6
self-report screens, selection and use of. *See* Self-report screens
Substance Abuse Subtle Screening Inventory (SASSI), 1-3
TCU Drug Screen. *See* TCU Drug Screen
Seamless system of care
  twelve principles of effective systems to reduce recidivism and increase retention in treatment programs. *See* Twelve principles of effective systems to reduce recidivism and increase retention in treatment programs
Self-administered self-report screens, 1-4–1-5
Self-report screens
  abuse, focus on, 1-4
  accuracy of, 1-2, 1-3
  Addiction Severity Index (ASI), 1-4
  administration of, 1-5
  administrative constraints
    cost, 1-3–1-4
    screening time, 1-3
    staff training, 1-3
  Arrestee Drug Abuse Monitoring (ADAM) project. *See* Arrestee Drug Abuse Monitoring (ADAM) program
  cost as constraint, 1-3–1-4
  decision process, statistical guidelines informing
    accuracy, 1-2, 1-3
    negative predictive value of, 1-3
    positive predictive value, 1-2–1-3
    sensitivity, 1-2
    specificity, 1-2
  delivery methods, 1-4–1-5
  dependence, focus on, 1-4
  Diagnostic and Statistical Manual of Mental Disorders (DSM), 1-4
  diagnostic criteria for abuse, 1-4
  factors in treatment, 1-5–1-6
  focus of, 1-4
  institutional program treatment options, matching screen to, 1-5–1-6

Self-report screens, *continued*
    interview as part of, 1-4–1-5
    negative predictive value of, 1-3
    positive predictive value of, 1-2–1-3
    public domain screening instruments, 1-3
    screening time as constraint, 1-3
    self-administered, 1-4–1-5
    sensitivity of, 1-2
    specificity of, 1-2
    staff training as constraint, 1-3
    treatment services, decisions related to, 1-1–1-2
    truthful responses, obtaining, 1-5
    window of detection, 1-4
Sentencing issues
    consequences of condition violation, rehabilitation needs
        considered in determining, App.-5–App.-6
    "eligibility" impediments for drug treatment leading to
        sentence reduction
    Federal Bureau of Prisons (BOP) eligibility criteria
        Eighth Circuit ruling on, App.-2–App.-3
        Tenth Circuit ruling on, App.-2
        Violent Crime Control and Law Enforcement Act
            requirements, App.-1–App.-2
    opportunity to shorten sentence, duty to ensure prisoner
        maximum
        delay in program entry, effect of, App.-10
        summary judgment against plaintiff, App.-10
    rehabilitation-related treatment conditions, leeway of
        courts to impose, App.-4–App.-5
    sentencing guidelines, downward departures from
        assistance to government, App.-8
        incarceration, purpose served by, App.-7
        mitigating circumstances, App.-6–App.-7
Severe mental illnesses (SMI)
    co-occurring substance abuse and, epidemiological
        study of, 21-4
    treatment difficulties with, 21-3
Sex offenders
    aftercare services, 17-8
    alcohol abuse, relationship with, 17-4
    antisocial personality disorder (ASPD), as barrier to
        treating substance abusing, 17-7
    barriers to treating substance abusing
        antisocial personality disorder (ASPD), co-occur-
            ring, 17-7
        clinical sex offender, identification of, 17-7
        denial, 17-6
        institutional policies against disclosure, 17-6
        "legal" and "clinical" sex offenders, importance of
            differentiating between, 17-7–17-8
        overcoming, differentiating between "legal" and
            "clinical" sex offenders as way of,
            17-7–17-8
        stigmatism, 17-6
        treatment staff, untrained/inexperienced, 17-6
    defined, 17-3
    denial as barrier to treating substance abusing, 17-6
    Drug Abuse Screening Test (DAST), findings of, 17-4
    identification and treatment of substance abusing
        aftercare services, 17-8
        differentiating between "legal" and "clinical" sex
            offenders, 17-7
        process for, 17-7–17-8

    treatment modality, identification of appropriate,
        17-8
    identification of clinical sex offender as barrier to treating
        substance abusing, 17-7
    institutional policies against disclosure as barrier to
        treating substance abusing, 17-6
    "legal" vs. "clinical" sex offenders, importance of
        distinction between, 17-3–17-4, 17-7
    Michigan Alcoholism Screening Test (MAST), findings
        of, 17-4–17-5
    paraphiliac, defined, 17-3
    recidivism studies of, 17-4–17-5
    statistics, 17-2
    stigmatism as barrier to treating substance abusing, 17-6
    studies of, 17-4–17-5
    substance abuse
        as trigger of sex offending behavior, 17-5
        barriers to treating. *See* subhead: barriers to treating
            substance abusing
        co-morbidity with, 17-4–17-5
        identifying and treating. *See* subhead: identification
            and treatment of substance abusing
        treatment of, reasons for, 17-5
    treatment modality, identification of appropriate, 17-8
    treatment of substance abuse, reasons for, 17-5
    treatment options, 17-3–17-4
    treatment staff, untrained/inexperienced as barrier to
        treating substance abusing, 17-6
Sherman , U.S. v., App.-6
SMI. *See* Severe mental illnesses (SMI)
Social learning
    behavioral intervention, and, 37-5
    community model of resocialization for offenders, 37-6
    models of, 37-6
    types of community models, 37-6
Specialized group education materials
    benefits of, 27-5
Specialized populations
    drug court services for, 9-6
    mentally ill offenders. *See* Mental illness
    women. *See* Women as specialized population
    youthful offenders. *See* Youthful offenders
Standards of care
    inmates with symptoms or intoxication/withdrawal
        appropriate response to drug withdrawal risks even
            if harm not averted, preclusion of liability
            for, App.-19
        delay of treatment, liability of officer for,
            App.-18–App.-19
        officer, liability for delay of treatment by,
            App.-18–App.-19
        suicide of inmate with DTs, preclusion of liability
            for, App.-17–App.-18
    medical treatment, offender's right to
        declining treatment, arrestee, App.-20
        denial of problem, arrestee, App.-20
        role of officers, App.-20–App.-21
State statutes
    Alexander v. Schenk, App.-24–App.-25
    Griggs v. Gorczyk, App.-13–App.-14
    *Pennsylvania Department of Health, Office of Drug &
        Alcohol Programs, McGill v.*, App.-8

Webb v. Goord, App.-15

Stay'n Out program
    female therapeutic community (TC), 18-3–18-4, 20-2

Substance abuse
    crime and, response to connection between. *See*
        Addiction Technology Transfer Center (ATTC)
        Network
    effective treatment programs, elements of, 37-3
    prison population, 27-1–27-2
    sex offenders and. See Sex offenders
    statistics, 20-1–20-2, 27-1–27-2
    two-strikes visitor ban, App.-29
    visitation rights while probation, App.-30–App.-31
    visitor bans and
        cruel and unusual punishment, as,
            App.-29–App.-30
        limits allowed, App.-28–App.-29
        two-strikes visitor ban, App.-29

Substance Abuse and Mental Health Services Agency
    (SAMHSA)
    Addiction Technology Transfer Center (ATTC)
        Network, funding of, 36-2
    drug use data collection, 4-2

Substance Abuse Subtle Screening Inventory (SASSI)
    cost considerations, 1-3

Substance Abuse Treatment Facility (SATF) at Corcoran
    State Prison
    absenteeism, staff, 30-4–30-5
    administrative violations requiring disciplinary actions,
        30-3
    admission to, 30-2, 31-3
    aftercare treatment, 30-2
    coerced admission to, study of. *See* Coerced admission
        to Substance Abuse Treatment Facility (SATF) at
        Corcoran State Prison, study of
    community treatment, 30-2
    comparison of coerced admission to program to. *See*
        Coerced admission to Substance Abuse Treatment
        Facility (SATF) at Corcoran State Prison, study of
    Correctional Institutions Environment Scale (CIES),
        staff ratings using, 30-4, 30-5
    disciplinary actions, 30-3–30-4
    impacts of, 30-3–30-5
    implications for prison management and planners,
        30-6–30-7
    in-prison treatment, 30-2, 31-3
    organizations providing services, 30-2
    overview, 30-2
    participants
        admission criteria, 30-2, 31-3
        perceptions of program by, 30-5–30-6
        statistics, 30-2, 31-2
        substance use among, 30-3
        urine testing of, 30-3
    perceptions of program by staff and participants,
        30-5–30-6
    phases of treatment program, 30-2, 31-3
    Phoenix House, 30-2
    prison management and planners, implications for,
        30-6–30-7
    ratings of, staff, 30-4, 30-5
    serious violations requiring disciplinary actions, 30-3

    staff
        absenteeism, 30-4–30-5
        perceptions of program by, 30-5–30-6
        ratings by, 30-4, 30-5
    substance use among participants, 30-3
    treatment programming phases, 30-2
    urine testing of participants, 30-3
    Walden House, 30-2

Suicidal ideation, 2-7

Superintendent, Massachusetts Correctional Inst. v. Hill,
    App.-16

Supervision in aftercare
    commitment to change
        early change. *See* subhead: early change
        factors preventing, 35-5
        sustained change for long term, 35-9
    community advocates, 35-6
    contact model framework, 35-2–35-3
    early change
        communication, facilitating, 35-9
        deportment process, components of, 35-8
        ground rules, 35-8
        variables illustrating, 35-6–35-7
    effectiveness of, questions about, 35-2
    engagement
        process of, 35-5
        pro-social value and behaviors, in, 35-4
        supervision as process of, 35-3–35-4
    formal controls/services as supervision plan component,
        35-6, 35-7
    guardians, 35-6
    improvement of, need for, 35-1
    informal social controls as supervision plan component,
        35-5–35-6
    social control framework
        contact model, 35-2–35-3
        supervision as process of engagement, 35-3–35-4
        supervision objectives, 35-3
    supervision as process of engagement, 35-3–35-4
    supervision objectives, 35-3
    supervision plan components
        formal controls/services, 35-6, 35-7
        informal social controls, 35-5–35-6
    sustained change for long term, 35-9

Sutton, U.S. v., App.-6

T

TASC programs. *See* Treatment Alternative to Street Crime
    (TASC) programs

TCA. *See* Therapeutic Communities of America (TCA)

TCADA. *See* Texas Commission on Alcohol and Drug
    Abuse (TCADA)

TCs. *See* Therapeutic communities (TCs)

TCU. *See* Texas Christian University (TCU)

TCU Drug Screen
    as self-administered drug screen, 1-4
    cost of, 1-3
    Pennsylvania research partnership for prison-based drug
        treatment program, 39-8

TCU Model of Treatment Processes and Outcomes
    black box of treatment
        components of, 27-4
        length of stay, 27-4
    critical components in black box of treatment. See
        subhead: black box of treatment
    foundation for, 27-4
    goal of, 27-3
    length of stay as key to treatment process, 27-4
    overview, 27-4
    phases, 27-4–27-5
TCU Readiness Series. See Cognitive Enhancements for the
    Treatment of Probationers (CETOP)
TCU Treatment Process Model. See TCU Model of
    Treatment Processes and Outcomes
Technology transfer, xii
    Addiction Technology Transfer Center (ATTC)
        Network. See Addiction Technology Transfer
        Center (ATTC) Network
    purpose of, 36-2–36-3
Testing, screening and referral
    Arrestee Drug Abuse Monitoring (ADAM) project. See
        Arrestee Drug Abuse Monitoring (ADAM) project
    California Department of Corrections. See California
        Department of Corrections drug reduction strategy
        project
    Global Appraisal of Individual Needs-Crime and
        Violence Index (GAIN-CVI). See Global
        Appraisal of Individual Needs-Crime and Violence
        Index (GAIN-CVI)
    methods of, A-2
    Moffitt Theory of Criminal/Violent Behavior. See
        Moffitt Theory of Criminal/Violent Behavior
    Practical Adolescent Dual Diagnostic Interview
        (PADDI). See Practical Adolescent Dual
        Diagnostic Interview (PADDI)
    psychiatric disorders, screening instruments for. See
        Psychiatric disorders
    self-report screens, selection and use of. See Self-report
        screens
    standardized, need for, A-1–A-2
    urine testing, California Department of Corrections.
        See California Department of Corrections drug
        reduction strategy project
Texas
    Arrestee Drug Abuse Monitoring (ADAM) program,
        Houston. See Arrestee Drug Abuse Monitoring
        (ADAM) program
    Cognitive Enhancements for the Treatment of
        Probationers (CETOP). See Cognitive
        Enhancements for the Treatment of Probationers
        (CETOP)
    Houston Arrestee Drug Abuse Monitoring (ADAM)
        program. See Arrestee Drug Abuse Monitoring
        (ADAM) program
    juvenile inhalant users. See Juvenile inhalant users
    Kyle New Vision Program. See Kyle New Vision
        Program
    New Vision In-Prison Therapeutic Community (IPTC)
        and Substance Abuse Felony Punishment (SAFP)
        Drug Treatment Program. See Kyle New Vision
        Program

Texas Youth Commission (TYC) reform schools study.
        See Juvenile inhalant users
Texas Christian University (TCU)
    Cognitive Enhancements for the Treatment of
        Probationers (CETOP) research project. See
        Cognitive Enhancements for the Treatment of
        Probationers (CETOP)
    Dallas County Judicial Treatment Center (DCJTC),
        Institute of Behavioral Research evaluation of,
        26-2
    Drug Abuse Reporting Program (DARP) study, 26-2
    Drug Abuse Treatment Outcome Studies (DATOS)
        study, 26-2
    Drug Screen. See TCU Drug Screen
    Institute of Behavioral Research evaluation of Dallas
        County Judicial Treatment Center (DCJTC), 26-2
    Kyle New Vision Program, study of recidivism rates for
        graduates of, 12-2
    TCU Model of Treatment Processes and Outcomes. See
        TCU Model of Treatment Processes and
        Outcomes
Texas Commission on Alcohol and Drug Abuse (TCADA)
    Client Oriented Data Acquisition Program (CODAP)
        forms, 26-2
Therapeutic Communities of America (TCA)
    draft standards, 14-5
Therapeutic communities (TCs)
    accreditation process, 14-5
    Addiction Technology Transfer Center (ATTC) Network
        cross training curricula, 36-5
    Amity Therapeutic Community at Richard J. Donovan
        Correctional Facility (RJDCF). See Amity
        Therapeutic Community at Richard J. Donovan
        Correctional Facility (RJDCF)
    Association of State Correctional Administrators
        (ASCA) national survey on, 14-2, 14-4
    as type community model, 37-6
    benefits of prison-based, 30-1–30-2
    California
        Amity Therapeutic Community at Richard J.
            Donovan Correctional Facility (RJDCF).
            See Amity Therapeutic Community at
            Richard J. Donovan Correctional
            Facility (RJDCF)
        programs, 13-2, 17-3
    challenges presented by rapid expansion of, 14-10
    critical factors for
        monitoring, 14-8
        quality assurance, 14-8
        staffing, 14-7–14-8
        structured programming, 14-8
        treatment model, selection of, 14-8–14-9
    critical standards and observable key indicators for,
        14-5, 14-6
    draft standards, 14-5
    employment services, lack of. See Employment services
    female inmates, treatment of. See Female inmates, thera-
        peutic community (TC) treatment for
    field review observations, 14-5
    inmates served by, ASCA findings on, 14-2, 14-4
    Kyle New Vision Program approach. See See Kyle New
        Vision Program

"modified" TC, characteristics of, 14-5
monitoring as critical factor, 14-8
National Development and Research, Incorporated
    (NDRI) study of non-TC programs, A-4
national survey on, ASCA findings from, 14-2, 14-4
new program start-ups, ASCA findings on extent of,
    14-2, 14-4
philosophy, 30-2
prison-based, benefits of, 30-1–30-2
prisons offering, 14-3
programming, ASCA findings on extent of, 14-2
psychopaths in, 22-5
quality assurance as critical factor, 14-8
questions remaining to be answered about effectiveness
    of, 39-3
rapid expansion of, challenges presented by, 14-10
"real" TC, characteristics of, 14-4–14-5
Richard J. Donovan Correctional Facility (RJDCF). See
    Amity Therapeutic Community at Richard J.
    Donovan Correctional Facility (RJDCF)
staffing
    ASCA findings on, 14-4
    critical factor, as, 14-7–14-8
structured programming as critical factor, 14-8
Substance Abuse Treatment Facility (SATF) at Corcoran
    State Prison. See Substance Abuse Treatment
    Facility (SATF) at Corcoran State Prison
Therapeutic Communities of America (TCA) draft
    standards, 14-5
treatment model, selection of, 14-8–14-9
Third-party continuity programs
    continuity-of-care, ensuring, 33-7–33-8
    Treatment Alternative to Street Crime (TASC)
        programs. See Treatment Alternative to Street
        Crime (TASC) programs
Thompson, Kentucky Department of Corrections v., App.-28
Thompson v. Davis, App.-21, App.-23
Thompson v. Upshur County, Texas, App.-18
Transition to community from criminal justice system. See
    Continuity-of-care model
Treatment
    as discrete event, ix
    as means of crime control, 32-4–32-5
    barriers to, 32-2–32-3
    bonuses of, 32-2–32-4
    completion rates of offenders, 32-3–32-4
    contingency management protocols, 27-5
    criminal behavior, changing. See Criminal behavior,
        changing
    effective, delivering and managing, 27-3
    goals of, 27-3
    length of stay in, 32-4. See Length of stay in treatment
        programs
    matching clients with treatment, 27-3, A-2–A-3
    motivation among clients, enhancing. See Cognitive
        Enhancements for the Treatment of Probationers
        (CETOP)
    node-link mapping, 27-5
    opportunity, as, 32-3
    outcomes, predictors of, 27-3
    predictors of outcomes, 27-3

psychiatric disorders, of. See Psychiatric disorders
readiness program. See Readiness for treatment program
science and clinical practices, gap between
    clinical success to treatment programs, challenges
        transferring, 38-3
    practitioners needs, 38-2
    researchers needs, 38-3
    under-studied treatment strategies, researchers
        consideration of, 38-3
specialized group education materials, 27-5
without aftercare, A-4
Treatment Accountability for Safer Communities (TASC)
    programs
    case management, 34-2–34-3
    services provided by, 34-3
Treatment Alternative to Street Crime (TASC) programs
    See also Treatment Accountability for Safer
        Communities (TASC) programs
    effectiveness of, 33-2
    need for, 8-2
    third-party continuity program, as example of, 33-7–33-8
Treatment control programs
    availability, needs outpacing, 39-2
    brainwashing in, constitutionality of, App.-9
    clinical success to, challenges of transferring, 38-3
    criminal behavior, changing. See Criminal behavior,
        changing
    effective, elements of, 37-3
    inadequate number of, 27-2
    induction efforts, 27-5
    in-prison. See In-prison treatment control programs
    interventions
        principles of effective, 7-2–7-3
        types of, 27-5
    methadone treatment in Vermont jails. See Vermont
    opportunity to shorten sentence, duty to ensure prisoner
        maximum
        delay in program entry, effect of, App.-10
        summary judgment against plaintiff, App.-10
    outcomes, process evaluations improving, 27-6
    Pennsylvania. See Pennsylvania
    policy changes, retroactive application of
        eligibility for early release, App.-11
        Ninth Circuit ruling on, App.-11–App.-12
        U.S. Supreme Court ruling on, App.-12–App.-13
    positive impact of, 27-2
    process evaluations, outcome improvement through, 27-6
    program integrity. See Program integrity
    program quality, measurement of
        importance of, 7-2
        residential substance abuse treatment (RSAT)
            programs. See Residential substance
            abuse treatment (RSAT) programs
    program statistical reports, 27-6
    progress reports, 27-6
    questions remaining to be answered about effectiveness
        of, 39-3
    readiness program. See Readiness for treatment program
    services, needs outpacing, 39-2

Treatment control programs, *continued*
    twelve principles of effective systems to reduce
        recidivism and increase retention in treatment
        programs. *See* Twelve principles of effective
        systems to reduce recidivism and increase
        retention in treatment programs
    types of, 39-2–39-3. *See also* specific treatment
        program
    Urban Institute project linking research to correctional
        drug treatment. *See* Urban Institute project linking
        research to correctional drug treatment
    variety of, 39-2–39-3
    Vermont. *See* Vermont

Treatment practitioners, substance abuse
    adult learners, training, 38-5
    barriers to understanding addiction, 38-1–38-2
    basic concepts of training, 38-5–38-6
    biases as barrier to understanding addiction
        effect of, 38-3–38-4
        preconceived, 38-1
    case management skills, enhancement of, 38-7–38-8
    communication between researchers and, enhancement
        of, 38-5
    continuity of care, ideas for improving, 38-4–38-5
    enhancement of communication between researchers
        and, 38-5
    organizational skills, enhancement of, 38-6–38-7
    preconceived biases as barrier to understanding
        addiction, 38-1
    researchers and, enhancement of communication
        between, 38-5
    skill enhancement
        case management skills, 38-7–38-8
        challenges of, 38-6
        organizational skills, 38-6–38-7
    trainees, commitments of, 38-8
    training
        adult learners, 38-5
        basic concepts of, 38-5–38-6
        growth process, as, 38-9
        ideas to improve, 38-9
    training methods, 38-8

Treatment readiness
    key predictor of success, as, 29-2

Treatment readiness model
    consequences of change, focus on. *See* subhead: "what
        if" activities
    elements of, 29-3
    "how to" activities
        acceptance/attractiveness of process, 29-9
        confidence in process, 29-9
        elements of, 29-3
        illustrated example, 29-4
        knowledge of process, 29-8
        resources for process, 29-8
        treatment planning, 29-9
    practical applications of, 29-6
    roadmap for, 29-4–29-6
    treatment process, focus on. *See* subhead: "how to"
        activities
    "what if" activities
        acceptance/attractiveness of change, 29-7

confidence in resources for dealing with change,
        29-8
Downward Spiral game, 29-7
elements of, 29-3
illustrated example, 29-2–29-4
knowledge of change, 29-7
resources for change, 29-7–29-8

Treatment services
    defined, 32-3
    first-come first-served model of, 32-3
    percentage of offender population in, 32-3

Treatment volunteers
    completion rates of, 32-3–32-4

Tribal programs
    drug court, 9-3

Twelve principles of effective systems to reduce recidivism
    and increase retention in treatment programs
    behavioral contracts, use of, 32-8
    drug testing to manage offenders, use of, 32-6
    focus on quality, 32-10
    length of time in treatment, extension of, 32-7–32-8
    non-compliant behavior, sanctioning of, 32-9
    positive behavior, rewarding, 32-10
    quality, focus on, 32-10
    recidivism reduction as goal, 32-5
    rewarding positive behavior, 32-10
    sanctioning of non-compliant behavior, 32-9
    special agents to supervise offenders, use of, 32-8–32-9
    supervision of offenders, use of special agents in,
        32-8–32-9
    targeting of offenders, 32-6–32-7
    treatment and criminal justice professionals, teamwork
        between, 32-5–32-6
    treatment and criminal justice system features, policy-
        driven, 32-5
    treatment matching practices, use of, 32-7
    treatment process, creation of, 32-7–32-8

U

United States, Maurello v., App.-10

United States Bureau of Prisons, Henson v., App.-15–App.-16

Upshur County, Texas, Thompson v., App.-18

Urban Institute project linking research to correctional drug
    treatment
    goal of, 40-2
    key recommendations, summary of, 40-3
    principles of effective prison-based treatment, 40-2–40-4
    research gaps on drug treatment in prisons
        balance of incentives and sanctions available,
            determination of, 40-7
        correctional staff and systems level factors impact
            on treatment, assessment of, 40-8–40-9
        cost-effectiveness, assessment of, 40-8
        effectiveness of drug treatment in varying prison
            security levels, examination of, 40-7
        factors determining available and appropriate
            treatments, assessing, 40-8
        nature and extent of current drug treatment and
            practice, determination of, 40-6
        summary of key recommendations, 40-3

transition into and out of prison influences effectiveness of treatment, exploration of, 40-8

treatment delivery in context of different stages of prison term, examination of, 40-7

understanding role of motivation and coercion in treatment, 40-7

validated screening and assessment instruments for various decision points, development of, 40-6–40-7

results of, 40-9

science-based drug treatment in prisons, strategies to encourage. *See* subhead: strategies to encourage science-based drug treatment in prisons

strategies to encourage science-based drug treatment in prisons

boundary-spanning efforts to provide drug treatment in criminal justice system, promotion of, 40-5

education of public, policymakers, legislators, and prison officials, 40-5

isolate proven, available, and feasible treatment options, 40-6

manual of correctional drug treatment principles, creation of, 40-5

summary of key recommendations, 40-3

tasks of, 40-2

Urine testing

Amity Therapeutic Community at Richard J. Donovan Correctional Facility (RJDCF), results of surprise test at, 13-12

Arrestee Drug Abuse Monitoring (ADAM) program, Houston, 4-4

California Department of Corrections. *See* California Department of Corrections drug reduction strategy project

California Department of Corrections (CDOC) Drug Reduction Strategy (DRS) project, 5-3–5-4

drug courts, issued by, 9-10

judicial status hearings in drug courts, 11-4

legality of, App.-15

New York City Department of Probation (DOP) drug treatment initiative, 6-6

prison, 5-2

Substance Abuse Treatment Facility (SATF) at Corcoran State Prison participants, 30-3

to manage offenders, use of, 32-6

U.S. v. Lopez, App.-4–App.-5

U.S. v. Rodriguez, App.-5

U.S. v. Sandra Rhodes, App.-6

U.S. v. Sherman, App.-6

U.S. v. Sutton, App.-6

V

Van Curen v. McClain County Board of County Commissioners, App.-17

VCCLEA. See Violent Crime Control and Law Enforcement Act (VCCLEA)

Vermont

Department of Corrections (DOC)

court decision on methadone treatment in jails, App.-13–App.-14

methadone treatment in jails. *See* subhead: methadone treatment in jails of

methadone treatment in jails of

court decisions on, App.-13–App.-14

policy, amendment of, App.-14

restrictions on, App.-13

Violent Crime Control and Law Enforcement Act (VCCLEA)

"eligibility" impediments for drug treatment leading to sentence reduction, requirements for, App.-1–App.-2

requirements of, 15-7–15-8

Treatment Provision of, App.-11

Violent Offender Incarceration and Truth-in-Sentencing (VOI/TIS) Incentive Program, 5-1

Visitation rights. *See* Substance abuse

VOI/TIS. *See* Violent Offender Incarceration and Truth-in-Sentencing (VOI/TIS) Incentive Program

W

Ward v. Booker, App.-2, App.-12

Warner v. Orange County Dep't. of Probation, App.-24

Watkins v. City of Battle Creek, App.-20

Webb v. Goord, App.-15

"What works." See Criminal behavior, changing

Wilson, Armstrong v., App.-22

Window of detection as consideration in self-report screens, 1-4

Wolfish, Bell v., App.-15

Women as specialized population

anxiety disorders, 2-8

drug-involved women. *See* Drug-involved women

female inmates, therapeutic community (TC) treatment for. *See* Female inmates, therapeutic community (TC) treatment for

Y

Yeskey, Pennsylvania Department of Corrections v., App.-22

Youthful offenders

Cannabis Youth Treatment (CYT) Study, 3-2, 3-3

drug use among, 24-2

Family Empowerment Intervention (FEI). *See* Family Empowerment Intervention (FEI)

juvenile inhalant users. *See* Juvenile inhalant users

National Institute of Drug Abuse (NIDA) Youth Support Project (YSP). See Family Empowerment Intervention (FEI)

Youth Support Project (YSP). *See* Family Empowerment Intervention (FEI)

YSP. *See* Youth Support Project (YSP)